D.H. LAWRENCE
A Guide to Research

Thomas Jackson Rice

GARLAND PUBLISHING, INC. • NEW YORK & LONDON
1983

Library of Congress Cataloging in Publication Data

Rice, Thomas Jackson.
    D.H. Lawrence : a guide to research.

    (Garland reference library of the humanities ; v. 412)
    Includes bibliographical references and indexes.
    1. Lawrence, D. H. (David Herbert), 1885–1930—
Bibliography. I. Title. II. Title: D. H. Lawrence
III. Series.
Z8490.5.R5   1983 [PR6023.A93] 016.823′912 82-49260
ISBN 0-8240-9127-2

Cover design by Laurence Walczak

Printed on acid-free, 250-year-life paper
Manufactured in the United States of America

TO
JENNIFER KELLY RICE

"She [was] his first little girl.
He had set his heart on her."

(*The Rainbow*, "The Child")

CONTENTS

Preface

It takes courage, or foolishness, to publish a bibliography on D.H. Lawrence. If the complexity of the publishing history of his works and the quantity of publications on him are not sufficiently discouraging, there is always the realization that Lawrence himself disdained bibliography: "What do I care for first or last editions?" ("The Bad Side of Books," *Phoenix*, p. 232), and distrusted even his best critics: "Never [do] I feel so baffled, confronting myself in my worst moments, as I feel when I read [an] 'elucidation' of myself" ("Accumulated Mail," *Phoenix*, p. 801). Lawrence's essentially reasonable objections to bibliography and criticism are that they tend to supersede the much more important business of reading and understanding, that, in their worst forms, they become kinds of intellectual parasitism as the bibliographer or critic, classifying or carping, saps the vitality of the work of art by imposing deadening formulas for organization or "elucidation": "You do me no favour by reading me . . . do you feel you acquire divine rights over [my] mind and soul . . . ? If you do, it's like your impudence. Therefore get it out of your heads that you are throned aloft like the gods, called upon to utter divine judgment" ("Accumulated Mail," p. 802).

Too often critics have ignored Lawrence's admonitions and so enthroned themselves, as a review of the secondary sections of this bibliography will show. But notice that Lawrence is not disputing the need for judgment in criticism or questioning the value of criticism (he was an impressive critic of art and literature himself); rather, he is attacking the divorce of judgment from respect or of opinion from sympathy and understanding. His best critics, in turn, seem to have learned from Lawrence to balance judgment and sympathy, to avoid the excesses of formulaic (often "formalist") rejection or uncritical adulation, and to follow Lawrence's own example, in his best critical essays, of matching intellectual objectivity with personal involvement.

In this research guide I hope to maintain a balance of discrimination and sympathy in my survey of Lawrence's publishing career and critical reputation, to encourage both a greater understanding of his works and a greater appreciation of his art. To be a discriminating guide, this volume must necessarily be selective. I have, however, included all English and foreign-language books, essay collections, monographs, pamphlets, and special periodical issues concerned with Lawrence and his works. These titles I have entered, *regardless of merit*, because they are conspicuous and I have always felt that one purpose of a research guide is, frankly, to tell its user that some peculiarly rhapsodic admirations or apoplectic condemnations of Lawrence are devoid of judgment or sympathy. I have been more selective with articles and chapters appearing in periodicals or in studies not exclusively concerned with Lawrence, since, while they are great in number, they tend toward considerable duplication and, at best, modest refinement of the same ideas. I have selected articles and chapters which offer original information and points of view, or which best represent certain repeated themes in Lawrence criticism. I have also included a number of discussions of Lawrence from standard surveys of fiction or of the modern period (again, because they are conspicuous), since a reader with limited access to a major research library will need to rely heavily or exclusively on these titles. If I have erred in this matter of selection, I believe I have been perhaps too generous rather than too restrictive.

In my annotations, throughout this guide, I have sought a balance between description and, in many cases, evaluation of a publication, feeling that a lengthy précis of a study without a judgment of its value guides the user as little as a brief and insipid evaluation which omits any mention of what the title is about. I have generally avoided an extended abstract of a book's thesis in the annotations, feeling that such condensations are comprehensible, if at all, only to someone who already knows the work and most users of this volume will know only a few of the titles included here well enough to profit from such abstracts. In the annotations throughout I have indicated various patterns among the critical responses to Lawrence's works, and the numerous relations of his critics to each other, to critical theory, or to their time. My final intention for the annotations, then, is that the user who "reads through" this guide should be able to trace the historical development of Lawrence's critical reception and recognize the chief tendencies, concerns, and needs of contemporary Lawrence criticism.

No work such as this can be completed without incurring numerous debts. For their help in translating I thank Steve Ackerman, David Danow, Masako Dorrill, and Marianne Wachter. For their advice and loans of materials I thank Christopher Brown, James T. Boulton, Donald Gutierrez, Janice H. Harris, Charles A. Huttar, A. Walton Litz, Joel A. Myerson, Yoshihiro Nakanishi, Bibhu Padhi, Hans Schwarze, William Thesing, and Carol F. Treacy; for providing detailed information on the ongoing *Cambridge Edition of D.H. Lawrence,* I thank, again, its general editor James T. Boulton and the editorial staff of the Cambridge University Press; and, for his prompt and expert response to numerous questions about Lawrence studies, I thank my friend and former colleague Keith Cushman. For their comments and suggestions concerning this bibliography, in its various permutations over the last ten years, I thank my editors Ralph Carlson, Duane DeVries, and Theodore Grieder. For assembling the author and title indexes and preparing the final typescript, I thank Dawn Bailey and Carol Cutsinger. For their encouragement and interest, I thank my wife, Diane, and my children. And for a special kind of inspiration, I thank my daughter Jennifer, to whom this book is dedicated.

Introduction

D. H. Lawrence: A Guide to Research is a selective annotated bibliography of works by and about D. H. Lawrence. It consists of three parts: (1) the primary bibliography which contains separate bibliographies of Lawrence's major publications, of collections and editions of his works, of his letters, and of concordances to his writings; (2) the secondary bibliography—which contains bibliographies of bibliographical, biographical, and critical publications concerning Lawrence generally or his individual works; and (3) Appendixes and Indexes—which include an extensive checklist of major foreign-language publications concerning Lawrence and a useful, topical and thematic subject index for the guide. The balance of this introduction will explain more fully the principles of selection, arrangement, and annotation for each of these sections of the volume.

The Primary Bibliography (Sections A through D)

Section A of the primary bibliography is a nine-part listing of all Lawrence's major works, arranged according to kind, or literary genre (e.g., novels, stories and novellas, paintings, plays, poetry, prose, etc.). Original publication data are provided for all titles, with brief factual annotations and contents for collections. Section B is a selective listing of the principal anthologies, collections, and selections of Lawrence's works, and a complete listing of scholarly editions of his writings, with descriptive and evaluative annotations. Section C lists all substantial publications of Lawrence's correspondence and section D lists concordances to his poetry and short fiction, with annotations. Cross-reference numbers in the annotations, in this primary section of the bibliography, generally send the user to important textual commentaries on and introductions to a title, which are themselves entered and annotated elsewhere in the guide.

Sectional headnotes likewise contain numerous cross references to titles of related interest which are to be found in other sections of the volume (e.g., the headnote to section C, the letters, provides cross-references for other published correspondence or for commentaries on Lawrence's correspondence).

The Secondary Bibliography (Sections E through Z)

By far the largest part of this volume, the secondary bibliography consists of twenty sections. Section E (bibliographies), is a broad but selective listing of previous primary and secondary bibliographies concerning Lawrence, as well as exhibition catalogues, descriptions of Lawrence collections, and essay-surveys of Lawrence's critical reputation. Annotations describe the nature of the bibliographies and evaluate their accuracy and usefulness. Section F (biographies, memoirs, reminiscences, and interviews) is a generous, but again selective listing of major biographical sources, published as books, articles, chapters, special journal issues, or essay collections. The annotations in this section describe and often evaluate the title and, when appropriate, provide some comment on the nature and duration of a memoirist's relationship with Lawrence. For the most part, this section omits brief notes and incidental mentions in published writings or in letters, as well as essays, articles, or notes since assimilated into larger studies.

Section G (book-length critical studies and essay collections) is a comprehensive bibliography of critical books, essay collections, monographs, and pamphlets concerned with Lawrence and his works generally, or with more than *two* of his works or genres. Studies limited to two of Lawrence's works or genres are entered in each of the two appropriate sections on the individual works and genres (sections J through Z—see below). Annotations are more detailed in this section, giving the general drift of the title's thesis, surveying its chief points, and evaluating both its contribution to Lawrence's critical reputation and its practical usefulness to the student of Lawrence. Dissertations are not considered published books for the purposes of this bibliography and are not included here, or elsewhere in the guide, unless subsequently published. (For recent listings of dissertations, theses, and honors theses on Lawrence, see Crump [E11] and Garmon, et al. [E23]).

Section H (general critical articles, or chapters) is a generous selection of critical essays and discussions of Lawrence generally, or, again, of more than *two* of his works or genres, published in periodicals, special issues of journals, essay collections, or general studies of English and World literatures, of modern writers, of the novel, and so on. For the most part, this listing excludes both brief notes and essays, articles, or notes later assimilated into larger studies which are entered and annotated elsewhere. It does, however, include a selection of pedestrian surveys, obviously not because they are meritorious, but because they are readily found in most general library collections and can be helpful, if the user realizes their superficial or derivative nature and has no access to a larger research library. A handful of other entries are, frankly, misguided, wrong-headed, or perverse, but they are included, with warning annotations, to show the diversity of Lawrence's reputation (and to provide occasional light relief). Most of the entries, however, survived the selection process by merit and their inclusion should indicate implicitly their value. Thus the majority of annotations in this section are brief, factual, and descriptive rather than evaluative.

Sections J through Z are extensive, annotated checklists of studies of Lawrence's novels (sections J through U), novellas and short stories (section V), paintings (section W), plays (section X), poetry (section Y), and miscellaneous writings (section Z). Sections J through Y generally consist of two subsections: "Books and Essay Collections" on the given work(s) and "Critical Articles or Chapters" on the work(s). The sections for the shorter fiction (V), plays (X), and poetry (Y), contain a third subsection devoted to "Studies of Individual Works." The organization of section Z, on the miscellaneous writings, is more elaborate, containing an initial listing of books on Lawrence's prose works followed by five checklists of commentaries on his essays and introductions, letters, history, translations, and travel writings, respectively.

Each of these sixteen sections on Lawrence's individual works opens with a lengthy introductory headnote, referring the user to textual, bibliographical, biographical, or critical commentaries, entered and annotated in other sections of this bibliography, which comment significantly on the given work(s). Those sections containing additional subsections devoted to individual titles also contain numerous additional headnotes, referring the user to significant commentaries on individual stories, novellas, story collections, plays, poems, etc., to be found elsewhere in the bibliography. All of this information, of course, can be found in the subject index and these repeated lists of cross references take considerable space, but this multiplication of the opportunities to locate pertinent publications should simplify the task of research, which, after all, is the basic purpose of this research guide.

As with sections G and H, the principles for selection and annotation vary within the subsections on Lawrence's individual works. The listings of book-length studies, essay collections, monographs, and pamphlets are comprehensive, and those of articles and chapters are generous, yet selective. Dissertations, again, are not considered published books, or entered in the bibliographies. Study guides or student "cribs" on the individual works are likewise excluded, though technically they are book-length studies as defined above. (Appendix B provides a checklist of these study guides.) Annotations for books are detailed and evaluative; for articles they are concise and generally descriptive.

Appendixes and Indexes

This bibliography also includes three appendixes: Foreign-Language Studies (Appendix A), Study Guides (Appendix B), and Unverified Titles (Appendix C). The most important of these, Appendix A, is an extensive, slightly annotated checklist of books and essay collections, chapters and essays, and periodical articles concerning Lawrence, originally published in languages other than English. Most of the books and a great many of the chapters and articles have also been entered in the secondary bibliography proper and annotated, either from their original publication or from their subsequent whole or partial publication in English translation. In all such cases of double-entry, a cross-reference number in this part of the bibliography sends the user to the prior entry and annotation. Likewise, titles appearing in sections A through Z, which were originally published in a foreign language, have been given a reference number to this portion of the bibliography so that the user may locate original foreign-language publication information. While most of the significant foreign-language studies of Lawrence have been annotated and included in the main sections of this bibliography, this separate checklist is included here both to encourage further study of Lawrence's international critical reputation (often he was received earlier and understood better outside of England and America) and to accommodate several titles which may be significant but will remain inaccessible to the majority of this guide's users (e.g., the numerous Japanese studies). The listing of foreign-language books and essay collections in Appendix A, consistent with the principles for the bibliography as a whole, is as complete as possible. The checklists of chapters and articles, however, are generous but selective. For additional foreign-language articles, then, the user should consult the several available checklists of international Lawrence studies, published in the *D. H. Lawrence Review* (see section E of this guide, passim).

This volume concludes with three indexes: authors, titles, and subjects. This last index should be a particularly useful means for tracing specific figures (literary and historical), ideas, places, themes, and titles in Lawrence criticism. In a way, it suggests a number of alternative topical arrangements that might have been used for organizing this bibliography and should give the user further options for research within the bibliography.

Cross-References

Cross-reference numbers are used throughout in entries to send the user to a main entry for a work or collection from which a particular title is extracted, in headnotes to refer the user to other titles which discuss a particular work or topic, and in the indexes. Cross-reference numbers found in the annotations for collections indicate the titles included in the collection which are entered and annotated elsewhere. Cross-reference numbers in the annotations throughout will also direct the user to a prior annotation for the same entry, refer the user to a title described in or relevant to the annotation, or send the user to Appendix A for original foreign-language publication information.

Abbreviations and Reference Terms

Abbreviations are used throughout this bibliography for D. H. Lawrence's name (DHL) and for his five major works of fiction:

SL = SONS AND LOVERS
R = THE RAINBOW
WL = WOMEN IN LOVE
PS = THE PLUMED SERPENT
LCL = LADY CHATTERLEY'S LOVER

Abbreviations are not used, however, in the titles, for the adjectival form of Lawrence's name (i.e., Lawrencean, not DHL'ean), in quotations, or whenever there appears to be a possibility for confusion. For journal abbreviations, see the list that follows.

The most frequently used, and perhaps unfamiliar reference terms are "passim" ("throughout the work" or "here and there") and "cf." (within parentheses—indicates a comparison made by the author of the book or article annotated). Quotations within the annotations are from the work annotated unless otherwise attributed.

Dates of Coverage and Item Count

The terminal date of this bibliography was 1 January 1983. A few last-minute notes on titles appearing early in 1983 were included, if practicable, in the last stages of the volume's preparation. As is often the case with bibliographies, essays and notes which have yet to appear will, when they appear, predate the 1983 deadline because of delays in periodical publication. This problem is especially significant for a D. H. Lawrence bibliography because the primary forum for Lawrence studies, the *D. H. Lawrence Review*, is nearly two years behind in its publication schedule. The most recent entries from the *D. H. Lawrence Review*, then, are from the Spring 1981 issue.

The total number of entries is 2,123.

Periodical Abbreviations

The following periodical abbreviations are used consistently throughout this guide, except when the periodical itself is the main entry. That is, special issues are classified as "essay collections" and entered alphabetically, by the name of the periodical.

AI	*American Imago*
AR	*Antioch Review*
ArQ	*Arizona Quarterly*
ASch	*American Scholar*
AUMLA	*Journal of the Australasian Universities Language and Literature Association*
AusQ	*Australian Quarterly*
BC	*Book Collector*
BuR	*Bucknell Review*
C&L	*Christianity and Literature*
CathW	*Catholic World*
CCC	*College Composition and Communication*
CE	*College English*
ChiR	*Chicago Review*
CL	*Comparative Literature*
CLAJ	*College Language Association Journal*
CLS	*Comparative Literature Studies*
ConL	*Contemporary Literature*
ConnR	*Connecticut Review*
ContempR	*Contemporary Review*
CR	*Critical Review*
CritQ	*Critical Quarterly*
DHLR	*D. H. Lawrence Review*
DR	*Dalhousie Review*
EA	*Études Anglaises*
EDH	*Essays by Divers Hands*
EIC	*Essays in Criticism*
ELH	*Journal of English Literary History*
ELN	*English Language Notes*

ELT	*English Literature in Transition (1880–1920)*
EM	*English Miscellany*
ES	*English Studies*
ESA	*English Studies in Africa*
GaR	*Georgia Review*
HudR	*Hudson Review*
HUSL	*Hebrew University Studies in Literature*
JAAC	*Journal of Aesthetics and Art Criticism*
JML	*Journal of Modern Literature*
JNT	*Journal of Narrative Technique*
KR	*Kenyon Review*
L&P	*Literature and Psychology*
LCrit	*Literary Criterion*
LCUT	*Library Chronicle of the University of Texas*
LFQ	*Literature/Film Quarterly*
LHY	*Literary Half-Yearly*
MD	*Modern Drama*
MFS	*Modern Fiction Studies*
MLN	*Modern Language Notes*
MLQ	*Modern Language Quarterly*
MLR	*Modern Language Review*
ModA	*Modern Age*
MP	*Modern Philology*
MR	*Massachusetts Review*
NCF	*Nineteenth-Century Fiction*
NS	*Die Neueren Sprachen*
NYTBR	*New York Times Book Review*
PBSA	*Papers of the Bibliographical Society of America*
PLL	*Papers on Language and Literature*
PMLA	*Publications of the Modern Language Association of America*
PQ	*Philological Quarterly*
PR	*Partisan Review*
PsyR	*Psychoanalytic Review*
QQ	*Queen's Quarterly*
REL	*Review of English Literature*
RES	*Review of English Studies*
RLV	*Revue Des Langues Vivantes*
RMS	*Renaissance and Modern Studies*
RS	*Research Studies*
SAB	*South Atlantic Bulletin*
SAQ	*South Atlantic Quarterly*
SatR	*Saturday Review (New York)*

SB	*Studies in Bibliography*
SHR	*Southern Humanities Review*
SNNTS	*Studies in the Novel*
SoR	*Southern Review*
SR	*Sewanee Review*
SSF	*Studies in Short Fiction*
SWR	*Southwest Review*
TCL	*Twentieth Century Literature*
TLS	*[London] Times Literary Supplement*
TQ	*Texas Quarterly*
TSLL	*Texas Studies in Literature and Language*
UKCR	*University of Kansas City Review*
UR	*University Review*
UTQ	*University of Toronto Quarterly*
VQR	*Virginia Quarterly Review*
VS	*Victorian Studies*
WHR	*Western Humanities Review*
WR	*Western Review: A Journal of the Humanities*
WSCL	*Wisconsin Studies in Contemporary Literature*
YES	*Yearbook of English Studies*
YR	*Yale Review*
YULG	*Yale University Library Gazette*

Part 1
Primary Bibliography

A. MAJOR WORKS

This slightly-annotated, chronological checklist provides basic initial publication information for DHL's principal works. It includes first English and American editions, foreign editions (only if first editions), and subsequent corrected, unexpurgated, or textual editions. The annotations provide contents for collections (*complete* for story collections, *selective* for essay collections, and *very selective* for poetry collections), original separate publication dates for collected writings, cross-reference information for whole or partial reprintings, and other important publication information (including cross-references to textual commentaries and publishing histories). For subsequently published anthologies, collections, editions, and selections of DHL's works, including the important PHOENIX and PHOENIX II volumes (B16 and B18), see section B below. For full bibliographical data on all of DHL's publications, including translations of his works, see Roberts's A BIBLIOGRAPHY OF D.H. LAWRENCE (E39; rev. ed., 1982). For manuscript locations also see E22, E48, E49, and E50.

The following section is subdivided into nine parts, paralleling the organization of sections J through Z of the secondary bibliography of this guide:

A, i.   Novels (A1-A14)
A, ii.   Stories and Novellas (A15-A37)
A, iii.   Paintings (A38)
A, iv.   Plays (A39-A47)
A, v.   Poetry (A48-A59)
A, vi.   Miscellaneous Prose--Essays (A60-A78)
A, vii.   Miscellaneous Prose--History (A79)
A, viii.   Miscellaneous Prose--Translations (A80-A86)
A, ix.   Miscellaneous Prose--Travel Writings (A87-A90)

Note: For a full list of works by DHL mentioned in this bibliography, see Lawrence, D.H., in the subject index.

A, i. Novels

Note: "Mr. Noon," an unfinished comic novel DHL based on the
rakish life of his boyhood friend George H. Neville (see
F124), was published as a fragment in A31. The remaining
two-thirds of the fragment, nearly 300 additional pages in
DHL's hand, has since come to light. The entire manuscript
is scheduled for publication *as a novel* in THE CAMBRIDGE EDI-
TION (vol. 7; see B1).

A1 THE WHITE PEACOCK. New York: Duffield; London: Heinemann,
    1911. Textual edition: Ed. Harry T. Moore and Matthew J.
    Bruccoli. Carbondale: Southern Illinois Univ. Press, 1966.

A2 THE TRESPASSER. London: Duckworth; New York: Kennerley,
    1912. Textual edition: Ed. Elizabeth Mansfield. Cam-
    bridge and New York: Cambridge Univ. Press, 1981.
        For textual commentary see K6 and K9.

A3 SONS AND LOVERS. London: Duckworth; New York: Kennerley,
    1913.
        Also see the facsimile edition of the SL manu-
        scripts (A14).

A4 THE RAINBOW. London: Methuen, 1915. Expurgated text:
    New York: Huebsch, 1915.
        For textual commentary and composition history
        see E39 and M6.

A5 WOMEN IN LOVE. New York: Privately printed [Seltzer],
    1920. London: Secker, 1921.
        For textual commentaries see M6, N15, N24, N31,
        N32, N103, and N104. Also see A35 and A36.

A6 THE LOST GIRL. London: Secker, 1920. New York: Seltzer,
    1921. Textual edition: Ed. John Worthen. Cambridge and
    New York: Cambridge Univ. Press, 1981.
        For textual commentary see P9.

A7 AARON'S ROD. New York: Seltzer; London: Secker, 1922.

A8 KANGAROO. London: Secker; New York: Seltzer, 1923.
        For textual commentary see R13 and R17.

A9 THE BOY IN THE BUSH (with Mollie L. Skinner). London:
    Secker; New York: Seltzer, 1924.

A10   THE PLUMED SERPENT (QUETZALCOATL). London: Secker; New
      York: Knopf, 1926.
          For textual commentary see T8.

A11   LADY CHATTERLEY'S LOVER. Florence: Privately printed
      [Orioli], 1928. First expurgated editions: London:
      Secker; New York: Knopf, 1932. First unexpurgated edi-
      tions [Orioli text]: New York: Grove Press, 1959. Har-
      mondsworth, Engl.: Penguin, 1960.
          For two subsequently-published, earlier ver-
      sions of LCL, see A12 and A13 below. For a
      full bibliographical summary of the various
      editions, forgeries, parodies, sequels, and
      translations of LCL, see Warren Roberts, A
      BIBLIOGRAPHY OF D.H. LAWRENCE, pp. 91-101,
      367-69, and passim (E39). For textual com-
      mentaries see U21, U66, U68, and U71. Also
      see U11 and U59.

A12   THE FIRST LADY CHATTERLEY. New York: Dial Press, 1944.
      London: Heinemann, 1972.
          Earliest and least "shocking" version of the
      novel.

A13   JOHN THOMAS AND LADY JANE. New York: Viking; London:
      Heinemann, 1972.
          First English-language publication of the sec-
      ond version of LCL, a longer and considerably
      different story. Includes a slight "Introduc-
      tion" by Roland Gant (pp. v-ix). Note: an
      Italian translation of this version was pub-
      lished, with the first and final versions, in
      LE TRE "LADY CHATTERLEY" (Milan: Mondadori,
      1954), pp. 247-627. See B29.

A14   *SONS AND LOVERS* BY D.H. LAWRENCE: A FACSIMILE OF A MANU-
      SCRIPT. Ed. Mark Schorer. Berkeley: Univ. of California
      Press, 1977.
          Photographic reproduction of six holograph frag-
      ments of "Paul Morel," the precursor of SL (55
      pp.), and of the holograph manuscript of SL
      (540 pp.). Includes a list of substantive var-
      iants between the manuscript and the first Eng-
      lish edition, and Schorer's introductory de-
      scription of the novel's composition and the
      subsequent history of the manuscript (pp. 1-9).

A, ii.   Stories and Novellas

Included here are all uncollected stories and story collections (first collected publication), including posthumous
publications.   Dates for previous separate publication of
individual stories in the collections are provided in the
annotations.   For fuller publication data, see Roberts (E39).
For subsequent anthologies, collections, editions, and selections of DHL's shorter fiction, see section B below.   Also
see P9 and headnote to section A, i above.

A15   "A Prelude." NOTTINGHAMSHIRE GUARDIAN, 7 Dec. 1907, n.
      pag.
            DHL's uncollected, first published story. Re-
            printed in an expensive limited edition (Thames
            Ditton, Engl.: Merle Press, 1949) and in B14
            and B18. Also see V117a.

A16   "The Fly in the Ointment." NEW STATESMAN, 1 (16 Aug.
      1913), 595-97.
            Uncollected story. Reprinted in F85 and in
            B18. Also reprinted, in a later version, in
            B14.

A17   THE PRUSSIAN OFFICER, AND OTHER STORIES. London: Duck-
      worth, 1914. New York: Huebsch, 1916.
            Contents:
                "The Prussian Officer" (1914)
                "The Thorn in the Flesh" (1914)
                "Daughters of the Vicar"
                "A Fragment of Stained Glass" (1911)
                "The Shades of Spring" (1913)
                "Second Best" (1912)
                "The Shadow in the Rose Garden" (1914)
                "Goose Fair" (1910)
                "The White Stocking" (1914)
                "A Sick Collier" (1913)
                "The Christening"
                "Odour of Chrysanthemums" (1911)
            All stories reprinted in A30 and B4. Selected
            stories reprinted in B19 and B28. Original
            title for collection (and title story): "Honour
            and Arms." Also see earlier versions of "Daugh-
            ters of the Vicar" (A29) and "Odour of Chrysan-
            themums" (A37). For textual commentaries on the
            volume see V124 and V126, and for textual com-
            mentaries on individual stories see V44, V115,
            and V164.

A18   "The Thimble." SEVEN ARTS, 1 (Mar. 1917), 435-48.
      Uncollected early version of "The Ladybird"
      (A21), reprinted in B14 and B18.

A19   "The Mortal Coil." SEVEN ARTS, 2 (July 1917), 280-305.
      Uncollected story, an early version of "The
      Captain's Doll" (A21), reprinted in B14 and
      B18. For textual commentary see V43.

A20   ENGLAND, MY ENGLAND, AND OTHER STORIES. New York:
      Seltzer, 1922. London: Secker, 1924.
      Contents:
          "England, My England" (1915)
          "Tickets, Please" (1919)
          "The Blind Man" (1920)
          "Monkey Nuts" (1922)
          "Wintry Peacock" (1921)
          "You Touched Me" (1920)
          "Samson and Delilah" (1917)
          "The Primrose Path"
          "The Horse Dealer's Daughter" (1922)
          "Fanny and Annie" (1921)
      All stories reprinted in A30 and B4. Selected
      stories reprinted in B19 and B28.

A21   THE LADYBIRD, THE FOX, THE CAPTAIN'S DOLL. London:
      Secker, 1923. Published as THE CAPTAIN'S DOLL: THREE
      NOVELETTES. New York: Seltzer, 1923.
      For earlier versions of "The Captain's Doll"
      and "The Ladybird," see A19 and A18. A fac-
      simile of an early version (c. 1919) of "The
      Fox" (1922), has also been published (A34).
      Missing passages of "The Ladybird" are pub-
      lished in V83. All three novellas collected
      in A30, B12, and B27. "The Fox" also reprinted
      in B19 and B28. For additional textual com-
      mentaries on the novellas see V43, V64, V69,
      and V70.

A22   ST. MAWR, TOGETHER WITH THE PRINCESS. London: Secker,
      1925. Published as ST. MAWR. New York: Knopf, 1925.
      Novella and story (1925). For the first book
      publication of "The Princess" in America, see
      THE PORTABLE D.H. LAWRENCE (B19). "St. Mawr"
      reprinted in A30, B8, B13, B21, and B27. "The
      Princess" reprinted in A30, B4, B8, B19, and
      B20. Extracts of both tales reprinted in B9.

A23   SUN.   Paris: Black Sun Press, 1928.
            First unexpurgated publication of DHL's story,
            also published earlier in abridged form (Lon-
            don: Archer, 1926). A pirated edition of the
            unexpurgated text was privately published in
            America, in 1929. Expurgated edition collected
            in THE WOMAN WHO RODE AWAY, AND OTHER STORIES
            (below); the unexpurgated edition is reprinted
            in B20. For textual commentary see V166.

A24   THE WOMAN WHO RODE AWAY, AND OTHER STORIES.   London:
      Secker; New York: Knopf, 1928.
            Contents:
                "Two Blue Birds" (1927)
                "Sun" (see above)
                "The Woman Who Rode Away" (1925)
                "Smile" (1926)
                "The Border Line" (1924)
                "Jimmy and the Desperate Woman" (1924)
                "The Last Laugh" (1925)
                "In Love" (1927)
                "Glad Ghosts" (1926; also separately pub-
                           lished, 1926)
                "None of That"
                "The Man Who Loved Islands" (1927; American
                           edition only)
            All stories reprinted in A30 and B4. Selected
            stories reprinted in B13, B19, and B28. Ex-
            tract of "The Woman Who Rode Away" reprinted
            in B9.

A25   THE ESCAPED COCK. Paris: Black Sun Press, 1929. Pub-
      lished as THE MAN WHO DIED. London: Secker; New York:
      Knopf, 1931. Textual edition: THE ESCAPED COCK. Ed.
      Gerald M. Lacy. Los Angeles: Black Sparrow Press, 1973.
            For information on the textual edition, see B11
            and V99. Reprinted under the more familiar,
            second title in A30, B5, B13, B21, and B27.

A26   THE VIRGIN AND THE GIPSY. Florence: Orioli; London:
      Secker; New York: Knopf, 1930.
            Novella, completed but not fully revised for
            publication at the time of DHL's death. Re-
            printed in A30. Collected in B27.

A27   LOVE AMONG THE HAYSTACKS, AND OTHER PIECES. London:
      Nonesuch, 1930.   New York: Viking Press, 1933.
            Previously unpublished title story (w. 1908,
            1911-13), and three sketches: "A Chapel Among

the Mountains," "A Hay Hut Among the Mountains,"
and "Once" (w. 1912), with a prefatory memoir
by David Garnett (pp. v-xiii). American edition also includes the previously published
travel sketch, "Christs in the Tirol" (1913;
reprinted in A87, B16, and B19). Novella reprinted in B12 and B27. First three sketches
reprinted in B14 and B18.

A28 THE LOVELY LADY. London: Secker; New York: Viking, 1933.
Contents:
"The Lovely Lady" (1927)
"Rawdon's Roof" (also separately published,
1928)
"The Rocking-Horse Winner" (1926)
"Mother and Daughter" (1929)
"The Blue Moccasins" (1929)
"Things" (1928)
"The Overtone"
"The Man Who Loved Islands" (1927)
"The Man Who Loved Islands" was previously col-
lected in the American edition of THE WOMAN WHO
RODE AWAY (A24). All stories reprinted in B4
and, minus "The Overtone," in A30. Selected
stories reprinted in B8, B19, B20, and B28.
For textual commentary on the title story see
V90.

A29 "Two Marriages." TIME AND TIDE, 24 Mar. 1934 (supplement).
First publication of an early (c. 1911), uncol-
lected version of "Daughters of the Vicar" (see
A17).

A30 THE TALES OF D.H. LAWRENCE. London: Secker, 1934.
Collects all story collections and novellas
publihed through 1933 (i.e., A17, A20, A21,
A22, A24, A26, and A28 above), with the exception of "Love Among the Haystacks" (in A27)
and "The Overtone" (in THE LOVELY LADY, A28).
Contains forty stories and six novellas.

A31 A MODERN LOVER. London: Secker; New York: Viking, 1934.
Contents:
"A Modern Lover" (1933)
"The Old Adam"
"Her Turn" (1913)
"Strike Pay" (1913)
"The Witch à la Mode" (1934)

"New Eve and Old Adam"
"Mr. Noon"
Previously uncollected early stories, the first
six writeen 1909-13. The first six stories reprinted in B4. "Mr. Noon" (w. 1920-21), reprinted in B18 (also see headnote to section
A, i above). Four stories reprinted in B14.

A32   "Delilah and Mr. Bircumshaw." VQR, 16 (1940), 257-66.
      First publication of DHL's uncollected early
      story (c. 1912-13). Reprinted in B14 and B18.

A33   "'The Man Who Was Through with the World': An Unfinished
      Story by D.H. Lawrence." Ed. John R. Elliott. EIC, 9
      (1959), 213-21.
      First publication of an unfinished story (1927),
      with the editor's introduction (pp. 213-17).
      Story reprinted in B20.

A34   "The Fox." In A D.H. LAWRENCE MISCELLANY. Ed. Harry T.
      Moore. Carbondale: Southern Illinois Univ. Press, 1959.
      Pp. 28-48, and n. pag. [pp. 282c-282x]. See G81.
      First version of the story (c. 1919), with a
      facsimile reproduction of the manuscript (22
      pp.). See A21.

A35   "Prologue to WOMEN IN LOVE." Ed. George H. Ford. TQ,
      6, No. 1 (1963), 98-111.
      DHL's cancelled opening chapter for his novel
      (1916). Reprinted in B5, B18, and M2. See N32.

A36   "'The Wedding' Chapter of D.H. Lawrence's WOMEN IN LOVE."
      Ed. George H. Ford. TSLL, 6 (1964), 137-47.
      Early version of "Sisters," the opening chapter
      of WL. Slight annotation. Includes introduc-
      tory commentary by Ford (pp. 134-36).

A37   "D.H. Lawrence's 'Odour of Chrysanthemums': An Early
      Version." Ed. James T. Boulton. RMS, 13 (1969), 12-48.
      Scrupulously edited and annotated text of the
      extensively revised proof sheets of the story
      (1910), with a brief introductory essay by
      Boulton (pp. 5-11). See A17.

A, iii. Paintings

A38 THE PAINTINGS OF D.H. LAWRENCE. London: Mandrake Press,
     1929.
         Includes DHL's introduction (see A71), and re-
         productions of sixteen oil paintings and ten
         watercolors. Selected works reproduced in B26,
         F85, F93, F123, F162, H27, and W4, and all re-
         collected in B15. Also see F93.

A, iv. Plays

A39 THE WIDOWING OF MRS. HOLROYD: A DRAMA IN THREE ACTS. New
     York: Kennerley; London: Duckworth, 1914.
         Collected in A42 and B2.

A40 TOUCH AND GO: A PLAY IN THREE ACTS. London: Daniel; New
     York: Seltzer, 1920.
         Collected in A42 and B2. DHL's "Preface," pp.
         5-12, reprinted in B18.

A41 DAVID: A PLAY. London: Secker; New York: Knopf, 1926.
         Collected in A42 and B2.

A42 THE PLAYS OF D.H. LAWRENCE. London: Secker, 1933.
         Collects DHL's three previously published plays
         (above).

A43 "Keeping Barbara." ARGOSY, 14 (Dec. 1933), 68-90.
         Early play (w. 1912), titled THE FIGHT FOR
         BARBARA in THE COMPLETE PLAYS (see B2).

A44 A COLLIER'S FRIDAY NIGHT. London: Secker, 1934.
         Collected in B2. Also see X9.

A45 "Altitude." LAUGHING HORSE, No. 20 (1938), pp. 12-35.
         Play fragment (w. 1924). Collected in B2.

A46 "The Married Man." VQR, 16 (1940), 523-47.
         Play (w. 1912). Collected in B2.

A47 "The Merry-Go-Round." VQR, 16 (Winter 1941), Christmas
     supplement.
         Play (w. 1910). Collected in B2.

A, v. Poetry

For textual commentaries on and samples of DHL's poems, in
earlier versions, see Y42, Y61, Y73-Y75 and Y128.

A48 LOVE POEMS AND OTHERS. London: Duckworth; New York: Ken-
     nerley, 1913.
          Thirty-two lyrics, all but one reprinted (with
          revisions) in A55. All reprinted in B3. In-
          cludes "Cherry Robbers," "Lightning," and "Love
          on the Farm" (as "Cruelty and Love"). For
          composition history see E21.

A49 AMORES. London: Duckworth; New York: Huebsch, 1916.
          Sixty lyrics, all but two reprinted (with re-
          visions) in A55. All reprinted in B3. In-
          cludes "Dreams Old," "Dreams Nascent," "Last
          Words to Miriam," "Sorrow," and "The Virgin
          Mother." For composition history see E21.

A50 LOOK! WE HAVE COME THROUGH! London: Chatto and Windus,
     1917. New York: Heubsch, 1918.
          Sixty-one poems, reprinted with four additional
          poems and one omission in A55, and with six ad-
          ditional poems in an edition illustrated by
          Michael Adam (Marazion, Engl.: Ark Press, 1958).
          All poems reprinted in B3. First edition in-
          cludes "Elegy," "Hymn to Priapus," and "Song
          of a Man Who Has Come Through." For composi-
          tion history see E21.

A51 NEW POEMS. London: Secker, 1918. New York: Huebsch,
     1920.
          Contains DHL's "Preface" (American edition
          only; reprinted as "Poetry of the Present"
          in B3, B16, and B23), and forty-two poems,
          including "Piano." The poems are reprinted
          in A55 and B3. For textual commentary see
          Y42 and for composition history see E21.

A52 BAY: A BOOK OF POEMS. London: Beaumont Press, 1919.
          Twenty war poems, reprinted in A55 and B3.

A53 TORTOISES. New York: Seltzer, 1921. In BIRDS, BEASTS
     AND FLOWERS. London: Secker, 1923.
          Six poems, reprinted in A55 and B3. Also see
          below.

A54   BIRDS, BEASTS AND FLOWERS. New York: Seltzer; London:
      Secker, 1923.
            Forty-two poems. The English edition adds the
            six TORTOISE poems (above). All poems reprinted
            in A55 and B3. Includes "Bat," "Figs," "Fish,"
            "Medlars and Sorb-Apples," and "Snake." DHL
            added a series of brief prefaces for the sub-
            sections of the volume, in 1930 (London: Cres-
            set Press), which are reprinted in B3 and B16.

A55   THE COLLECTED POEMS OF D.H. LAWRENCE. Vol. 1. RHYMING
      POEMS. Vol. 2. UNRHYMING POEMS. London: Secker, 1928.
      New York: Seltzer, 1929.
            First volume contains DHL's introductory "Note"
            (pp. 5-7) and collects, with some omissions and
            substantial revision, the poems in LOVE POEMS,
            AMORES, NEW POEMS, and BAY. Second volume col-
            lects LOOK! WE HAVE COME THROUGH! (slight re-
            vision and addition of "Song of a Man Who is
            Loved"), TORTOISES, and BIRDS, BEASTS AND FLOW-
            ERS. DHL's original introduction was first
            published in PHOENIX (B16), and is reprinted
            in L3 and, with all other contents of THE COL-
            LECTED POEMS, in B3.

A56   PANSIES: POEMS. London: Secker; New York: Knopf, 1929.
            Contains DHL's brief "Foreword" (pp. 5-6), and
            218 poems, including "How Beastly the Bourgeois
            Is." A later edition, containing fourteen ad-
            ditional poems and a different introduction (re-
            printed in B16, B23, and B26; also see Y106),
            was privately printed for DHL (London: 1929).
            All poems and both introductions reprinted in
            B3.

A57   NETTLES. London: Faber, 1930.
            Twenty-five poems. Reprinted, with two addi-
            tional poems, in B3.

A58   LAST POEMS. Ed. Richard Aldington and Giuseppe Orioli.
      Florence: Orioli, 1932. New York: Viking; London: Secker,
      1933.
            Two-part collection, containing Aldington's
            "Introduction" (see Y89), sixty-four "Last
            Poems," including "Bavarian Gentians" and
            "The Ship of Death," and 201 "More Pansies."
            Also includes five variant versions of the
            poems, in an appendix. All poems and variants
            reedited and reprinted with the "Introduction,"
            in B3.

A59   FIRE AND OTHER POEMS. San Francisco: Grabhorn Press,
       1940.
       Collects nine poems, seven of them published
       for the first time, for the "Book Club of
       California." Includes a brief "Foreword" by
       Robinson Jeffers (pp. iii-viii) and an intro-
       ductory "Note on the Poems" by Frieda (pp.
       ix-xii). All poems recollected in B3.

A59a   "D.H. Lawrence: Seven Hitherto Unpublished Poems." Ed.
       Thomas A. Smailes. DHLR, 3 (1970), 42-46.
       Publishes texts of seven poems (c. 1928), omit-
       ted from THE COMPLETE POEMS (B3).

A, vi. Miscellaneous Prose--Essays

The following is a selective listing of DHL's major essays.
For DHL's "Study of Thomas Hardy," which had not previously
been published, see PHOENIX (B16). PHOENIX and PHOENIX II
(B18) are excellent, extensive collections of DHL's essays.
For information on uncollected essays, notes, and marginalia
see E39, H372, Z13, and Z53.

A60   "The Crown." SIGNATURE, Nos. 1-3 (Oct.-Nov. 1915), pp.
       3-4, 1-10, 1-10.
       Collected in REFLECTIONS ON THE DEATH OF A
       PORCUPINE (A69) and reprinted in B18.

A61   "The Reality of Peace." ENGLISH REVIEW, 24 (1917), 415-
       22, 516-23, 25 (1917), 24-29, 125-32.
       Collected in B16.

A62   PSYCHOANALYSIS AND THE UNCONSCIOUS. New York: Seltzer,
       1921. London: Secker, 1923.
       Reprinted in Z66.

A63   FANTASIA OF THE UNCONSCIOUS. New York: Seltzer, 1922.
       London: Secker, 1923.
       Reprinted in Z66.

A64   "Surgery for the Novel, or a Bomb." LITERARY DIGEST
       INTERNATIONAL BOOK REVIEW, April 1923, n. pag.
       Criticism of Joyce, Proust, and Dorothy Rich-
       ardson, collected in B16. Reprinted in B23.

A65 STUDIES IN CLASSIC AMERICAN LITERATURE. New York: Seltzer, 1923. London: Secker, 1924.
> Critical essays, including "The Spirit of Place" and studies of Franklin, Crèvecoeur, Cooper, Poe, Hawthorne, Dana, Melville, and Whitman. Extracts reprinted in B5, B19, B22, B23, and B28. Also see the subsequently published early versions of these essays (A77).

A66 "Introduction." In MEMOIRS OF THE FOREIGN LEGION, by M[aurice] M[agnus]. London: Secker, 1924. Pp. 11-94.
> Reprinted in B18. Also see Norman Douglas's attack on DHL for this "Introduction" (Z2a), and subsequent commentaries on Douglas and DHL: F50, F158, G73, and Z30.

A67 "Art and Morality." CALENDAR OF MODERN LETTERS, 2 (Nov. 1925), 171-77.
> On Cézanne. Collected in B16.

A68 "Morality and the Novel." CALENDAR OF MODERN LETTERS, 2 (Dec. 1925), 269-74.
> Criticism, collected in B16. Reprinted in B23.

A69 REFLECTIONS ON THE DEATH OF A PORCUPINE, AND OTHER ESSAYS. Philadelphia: Centaur Press, 1925. London: Secker, 1934.
> Seven essays, including the title essay (reprinted in B13 and B22; extract reprinted in B9), "The Crown" (A60), and "The Novel" (reprinted in B5, B13, and B26). All essays reprinted in B18.

A70 "John Galsworthy." In SCRUTINIES. Comp. Edgell Rickword. London: Wishart, 1928. Pp. 51-72.
> Criticism, reprinted in B16, B22, and B23.

A71 "Introduction to These Paintings." In THE PAINTINGS OF D.H. LAWRENCE. London: Mandrake Press, 1929. Pp. 7-38.
> Collected in B16. Reprinted in B22, B23 (extract), B26, and Z20. Also see A38.

A72 MY SKIRMISH WITH JOLLY ROGER. New York: Random House, 1929. Rev. ed. published as A PROPOS OF *LADY CHATTERLEY'S LOVER:* BEING AN ESSAY EXTENDED FROM "MY SKIRMISH WITH JOLLY ROGER." London: Mandrake Press, 1930.
> First published in LADY CHATTERLEY'S LOVER (Paris: Privately printed, 1929,), pp. i-viii. Revised version reprinted in B18, B26, and U20.

A73   PORNOGRAPHY AND OBSCENITY. London: Faber, 1929. New
      York: Knopf, 1930.
            Reprinted in B16, B19, B23, and B26.

A74   "Nottingham and the Mining Countryside." NEW ADELPHI,
      3 (June-Aug. 1930), 255-63, 276-85, 286-97.
            Collected in B16. Reprinted in B10, B19, B22,
            and L3.

A75   ASSORTED ARTICLES. London: Secker; New York: Knopf, 1930.
            Twenty-three essays, including "Autobiograph-
            ical Sketch" (reprinted in B5, B10, B13, B23,
            and G48), "Cocksure Women and Hensure Men" (re-
            printed in B5, B22, and B26), "Hymns in a Man's
            Life" (reprinted in B5, B10, B13, and B23),
            "Making Pictures" (reprinted in B13, B15, B22,
            and W2), "Men Must Work and Women as Well" (re-
            printed in B10 and B19), "The Risen Lord" (re-
            printed in B13), and "Sex Versus Loveliness"
            (also separately published as SEX LOCKED OUT
            [London: Privately published, 1929]; reprinted
            in B22 and B26). All essays reprinted in B18.

A76   APOCALYPSE. Florence: Orioli; New York: Viking, 1931.
      London: Secker, 1932. Textual edition: D.H. LAWRENCE:
      APOCALYPSE AND THE WRITINGS ON REVELATION. Ed. Mara
      Kalnins. Cambridge: Cambridge Univ. Press, 1980.
            For information on the textual edition, see B6.
            Extract reprinted in B5. Also see F27, Z9, and
            Z42.

A77   THE SYMBOLIC MEANING: THE UNCOLLECTED VERSIONS OF *STUDIES
      IN CLASSIC AMERICAN LITERATURE*. Ed. Armin Arnold. Font-
      well, Engl.: Centaur Press, 1962. New York: Viking, 1964.
            Collects thirteen essays from the first and
            second versions of STUDIES IN CLASSIC AMERICAN
            LITERATURE (1917-18; 1920), which differ con-
            siderably from the final version (see A65).
            Selection reprinted in B18. Also see Z11 and
            Z84.

A78   "The First Edition of Lawrence's 'FOREWORD TO *WOMEN IN
      LOVE*.'" Ed. Seamus Cooney. LCUT, N.S., No. 7 (1974),
      pp. 71-79.
            Facsimile reproduction (pp. 76-79), with commen-
            tary, of DHL's scarce leaflet, issued at the time
            of WL's first publication (1920), with a table
            of variants for its three issues (1920, 1920,
            and 1936). The 1936 version is reprinted in
            B18 and M2.

A, vii. Miscellaneous Prose--History

A79 MOVEMENTS IN EUROPEAN HISTORY. London: Oxford Univ. Press,
       1921. New York: Oxford Univ. Press, 1971.
              First edition published under the pseudonym
              "Lawrence H. Davison," and DHL identified as
              author for the 1925 reissue. The 1971 reissue
              contains a previously unpublished "Epilogue"
              and James T. Boulton's introduction (see Z101).

A, viii. Miscellaneous Prose--Translations

A80 ALL THINGS ARE POSSIBLE, BY LEO SHESTOV. AUTHORIZED
       TRANSLATION (with S.S. Koteliansky). London: Secker,
       1920.
              DHL's "Foreword" (pp. 7-12) reprinted in B16
              and B23.

A81 "The Gentleman from San Francisco." In THE GENTLEMAN
       FROM SAN FRANCISCO, AND OTHER STORIES, BY I.A. BUNIN.
       Trans. S.S. Koteliansky and Leonard Woolf. Richmond,
       Engl.: Hogarth, 1922. Pp. 1-40.
              DHL's collaboration with Koteliansky in trans-
              lating the title story accidentally unacknow-
              ledged on the title page. Story reprinted in
              B18.

A82 MASTRO-DON GESUALDO, BY GIOVANNI VERGA. New York: Seltzer,
       1923. London: Cape, 1925.
              DHL's cancelled introduction is published in
              B16 (reprinted in B23). A substantially dif-
              ferent introduction (contained in a 1928 re-
              issue, by Cape), is reprinted in B18.

A83 LITTLE NOVELS OF SICILY, BY GIOVANNI VERGA. New York:
       Seltzer; Oxford: Blackwell, 1925.
              DHL's introductory "Note on Giovanni Verga"
              (pp. vii-x), is reprinted in B18.

A84 CAVALLERIA RUSTICANA, AND OTHER STORIES, BY GIOVANNI VERGA.
       London: Cape; New York: Dial Press, 1928.
              DHL's "Translator's Preface" (pp. 7-28), is
              reprinted in B16 and B23.

A85 THE STORY OF DOCTOR MANENTE, BEING THE TENTH AND LAST
     STORY FROM THE SUPPERS OF A.F. GRAZZINI CALLED IL LASCA.
     Florence: Orioli, 1929. London: Grey, 1930.
          DHL's "Foreword" (pp. ix-xxiv), is reprinted
          in B16.

A86 THE GRAND INQUISITOR, BY F.M. DOSTOEVSKY. Trans. S.S.
     Koteliansky. London: Mathews and Marrot, 1930.
          DHL probably collaborated in this translation,
          in addition to contributing an "Introduction"
          (pp. iii-xvi; reprinted in B16 and B23).

A, ix. Miscellaneous Prose--Travel Writings

A87 TWILIGHT IN ITALY. London: Duckworth; New York: Huebsch,
     1916.
          Extracts reprinted in A27, B19, B22, and B28.
          For textual commentary, see Z132. Also see Z114.

A88 SEA AND SARDINIA. New York: Seltzer, 1921. London: Sec-
     ker, 1923.
          Extract reprinted in B19. Also see Z114.

A89 MORNINGS IN MEXICO. London: Secker; New York: Knopf, 1927.
          Extracts reprinted in B9, B13, B19, B22, B28,
          and G66.

A90 ETRUSCAN PLACES. London: Secker; New York: Viking, 1932.
          Extract reprinted in B5. Also see Z114.

B. ANTHOLOGIES, COLLECTIONS, EDITIONS, AND SELECTIONS

The following is a selective listing of the most important
anthologies, collections, and selections, and the principal
editions of DHL's works. In England and more recently in America his writings have been generally available in Penguin
paperback texts. While originally conceived as a "complete"
edition of DHL's works (as was the Viking "Compass" edition
[25 vols., 1950-72], replaced by the American Penguin texts),
the over fifty titles released by Penguin since 1950, with
considerable duplication, have long since dropped the "Com-
memoration Edition" label. For additional significant selections of DHL's writings, see F11, F35, F85, G32, H113, L3,
L5, V23, and V28.

B1 THE CAMBRIDGE EDITION OF THE COMPLETE WORKS OF D.H. LAW-
    RENCE. Cambridge and New York: Cambridge Univ. Press,
    1979.
         Much-needed definitive textual editions of DHL's
         writings, including his letters (see C11). Gen-
         eral editor: James T. Boulton. Texts of the
         major works, omitting apparatus, will be pub-
         lished as reading editions by Viking-Penguin
         (U.S.) and Granada (England). For information
         on the volumes appearing through 1982, see A2,
         A6, B6, B8, and C11. Also see H43, R17, U66,
         and the headnotes to sections J through Z, below.

B2 THE COMPLETE PLAYS OF D.H. LAWRENCE. London: Heinemann;
    New York: Viking, 1965.
         Collects DHL's eight plays and two play-frag-
         ments. Contents:
             THE WIDOWING OF MRS. HOLROYD (A39)
             TOUCH AND GO (A40)
             DAVID (A41)
             THE FIGHT FOR BARBARA (A43)
             A COLLIER'S FRIDAY NIGHT (A44)
             ALTITUDE (A45)
             THE MARRIED MAN (A46)
             THE MERRY-GO-ROUND (A47)
             NOAH'S FLOOD (in B16)
             THE DAUGHTER-IN-LAW (previously unpublished)

Though never before published, THE DAUGHTER-IN-
LAW was performed, in 1936, in an adapted ver-
sion by Walter Greenwood, entitled "My Son's My
Son" (see X13). Also see X5.

B3   THE COMPLETE POEMS OF D.H. LAWRENCE. Ed. Vivian de Sola
     Pinto and Warren Roberts. 1964. 3rd ed. 2 vols. London:
     Heinemann, 1972.
          Excellent "attempt to provide a reliable text
          of the whole of Lawrence's extant writings in
          verse." Assimilates THE COLLECTED POEMS (A55),
          PANSIES (A56), NETTLES (A57), LAST POEMS (A58),
          FIRE (A59), and hitherto uncollected poems,
          published and unpublished. Also includes DHL's
          forewords and introductions, the poems in PS,
          Richard Aldington's "Introduction" to LAST POEMS
          (see Y89), a collection of juvenilia (supple-
          mented in 2nd and 3rd editions), variants and
          early drafts of several poems, and superb notes
          on the poems. See Y43. Also see A59a, D1, Y10,
          Y20, Y30, Y34, Y51, and Y96.

B4   THE COMPLETE SHORT STORIES. 3 vols. London: Heinemann,
     1955. New York: Viking, 1961. Published as THE COLLECTED
     SHORT STORIES. 3 vols. London: Heinemann, 1974.
          Forty-seven tales. Combines the contents of
          THE PRUSSIAN OFFICER (A17), ENGLAND, MY ENGLAND
          (A20), THE WOMAN WHO RODE AWAY (A24), THE LOVE-
          LY LADY (A28), and A MODERN LOVER (A31), omit-
          ting "Mr. Noon" (in A MODERN LOVER; reprinted
          in B18) and adding "The Princess" (from A22).
          The revised title, 1974, is more appropriate
          since several stories remain uncollected (see
          B14, B18, and B20).

B5   D.H. LAWRENCE. Ed. Mark Schorer. New York: Dell, 1968.
          A fine short biography (see F146) and anthology,
          including "England, My England" and "The Horse
          Dealer's Daughter" (both from A20), "The Man Who
          Died" (A25), the "Prologue" to WL (A35), extracts
          from R and LCL, several poems, "The Novel" (from
          A69), "Autobiographical Sketch," "Cocksure Women
          and Hensure Men," and "Hymns in a Man's Life"
          (from A75), "Adolf" (from B16), and extracts from
          STUDIES IN CLASSIC AMERICAN LITERATURE (A65),
          ETRUSCAN PLACES (A90), and APOCALYPSE (A76).

B6   D.H. LAWRENCE: *APOCALYPSE* AND THE WRITINGS OF REVELATION.
      Ed. Mara Kalnins. Cambridge and New York: Cambridge Univ.
      Press, 1981.
            Contains Kalnin's "Introduction" (see Z42),
            a corrected text of APOCALYPSE, and two re-
            lated essays by DHL: "Review of THE BOOK OF
            REVELATION by Dr. J. Oman" (1924; also re-
            printed in B18) and "Introduction to THE
            DRAGON OF THE APOCALYPSE by Frederick Carter"
            (1930; reprinted in B16). Also includes
            three substantial manuscript fragments, use-
            ful explanatory notes (pp. 203-40), and text-
            ual apparatus.

B7   D.H. LAWRENCE: A SELECTION. Ed. Roger H. Poole and P.J.
      Shepherd. London: Heinemann, 1970.
            Highly fragmented anthology of mostly brief
            extracts from DHL's letters, travel writings,
            essays, long and short fiction, and poetry.
            133 selections in all. See H293.

B8   D.H. LAWRENCE: ST. MAWR AND OTHER STORIES. Ed. Brian H.
      Finney. Cambridge and New York: Cambridge Univ. Press,
      1982.
            Contains the title novella (see A22), "The
            Overtone" (from A28), "The Princess" (A22),
            "The Wilful Woman" (from B20), and "The Fly-
            ing Fish" (from B16), with the editor's intro-
            duction, textual apparatus, and notes. Not
            seen.

B9   D.H. LAWRENCE AND NEW MEXICO. Comp. Keith Sagar.   Layton,
      Utah: Peregrine Smith, 1982.
            Contains eight poems, five essays (four re-
            printed from B16), excerpts from several let-
            ters, and extracts from "St. Mawr" and "The
            Princess" (A22), "The Woman Who Rode Away"
            (from A24), "Reflections on the Death of a
            Porcupine" (from A69), and MORNINGS IN MEXICO
            (A89). Includes a brief "Introduction" by
            Sagar (pp. vii-xi).

B10   D.H. LAWRENCE ON EDUCATION. Ed. Joy Williams and Raymond
      Williams. Harmondsworth, Engl.: Penguin, 1973.
            Selection of DHL's writings on education and
            related educational scenes or sketches from
            his fiction. Includes "Autobiographical Sketch"
            (from A75), "Lessford's Rabbits" and "A Lesson
            on a Tortoise" (from B18), extracts from R and

WL, "Education of the People" (from B16), "Hymns
in a Man's Life" and "Men Must Work and Women
as Well" (from A75), "Nottingham and the Mining
Countryside" (A74), and other works. See Z87.

B11   THE ESCAPED COCK.   Ed. Gerald M. Lacy.   Los Angeles:
Black Sparrow Press, 1973.
Restores "numerous passages" of DHL's "text
extant in the manuscripts but omitted in previous printings," arriving at a definitive
text through a complete study of all known
manuscripts and early printings. Includes
letters concerning "The Escaped Cock," a reprint of the original short story version
(1928), and an extended critical and textual
commentary (see V99). Also see A25.

B12   FOUR SHORT NOVELS BY D.H. LAWRENCE.   New York: Viking,
1965.
Includes "The Captain's Doll," "The Fox," and
"The Ladybird" (from A21), and "Love Among the
Haystacks" (from A27). See B27.

B13   THE LATER D.H. LAWRENCE.   Ed. William York Tindall.   New
York: Knopf, 1952.
Anthology of DHL's later writings. Contains
"St. Mawr" (A22), "The Woman Who Rode Away"
and "Sun" (from A24), "The Man Who Died" (A25),
six extracts from MORNINGS IN MEXICO (A89),
and nine essays, including "Reflections on the
Death of a Porcupine" and "The Novel" (from
A69), and "Autobiographical Sketch," "Making
Pictures," "Hymns in a Man's Life," and "The
Risen Lord" (from A75). See H379.

B14   THE MORTAL COIL, AND OTHER STORIES.   Ed. Keith Sagar.
Harmondsworth, Engl.: Penguin, 1971.
Seventeen early tales and sketches, gathered
from a variety of previously published collec-
tions, but never grouped together as a story
anthology. Supplements B4. Includes a brief,
general "Introduction" by Sagar (pp. 7-9), "A
Prelude" (A15), "The Fly in the Ointment" (A16),
"The Thimble" (A18), "The Mortal Coil" (A19),
"A Chapel Among the Mountains," "A Hay Hut Among
the Mountains," and "Once" (from A27), "The Old
Adam," "Her Turn," "The Witch à la Mode," and

"New Eve and Old Adam" (from A31), "Delilah
and Mr. Bircumshaw" (A32), "Adolf," "Rex,"
and "The Miner at Home" (from B16), and "Lessford's Rabbits" and "A Lesson on a Tortoise"
(from B18). Also see B20.

B15   THE PAINTINGS OF D.H. LAWRENCE. Ed. Mervyn Levy.   London:
Cory, Adams, and MacKay; New York: Viking, 1964.
Essays on DHL as artist (see W2) and by DHL
("Making Pictures," from A75), together with
sixteen color and thirty-one black and white
reproductions. Also see A38.

B16   PHOENIX: THE POSTHUMOUS PAPERS OF D.H. LAWRENCE. Ed.
Edward D. McDonald. New York: Viking; London: Heinemann,
1936.
Excellent compilation of ninety-six previously
uncollected essays on nature, travel, love and
sexuality, literature, art, education, ethics,
psychology, philosophy, and "personalia." In-
cludes the previously unpublished articles:
"[Autobiographical Fragment]" (reprinted in
B20), "The Flying Fish" (reprinted in B8 and
B20), "Education of the People" (reprinted in
B10), and "Study of Thomas Hardy" (reprinted
in B23 [extracts] and Z20). Also collects:
"Adolf" (1920; reprinted in B5, B14, B28, and
F85), "Art and Morality" (A67), "Introduction
to these Paintings" (A71), "John Galsworthy"
(A70), "Morality and the Novel" (A68), "Nottingham and the Mining Countryside" (A74),
"Pornography and Obscenity" (A73), "The Re-
ality of Peace" (A61), "Rex" (1921; reprinted
in B14), "Surgery for the Novel" (A64), and
"We Need One Another" (1930). Also includes
extracts from A27, A51, A54, A55, A56, A80,
A82, A84, A85, A86, and E31. McDonald's "Appendix" provides original publication information for the sixty-nine previously published
essays. For McDonald's "Introduction," see
Z52. For a thematic index to this collection,
see E41. Also see B9, B14, B18, B20, B22, B23,
G66, Z48, Z51, and Z77.

B17   THE PHOENIX EDITION OF D.H. LAWRENCE. 26 vols. London:
Heinemann, 1954-72.
Uniform edition. Several titles with brief
introductions by Richard Aldington. Will prob-
ably remain the standard reading edition, pending completion of THE CAMBRIDGE EDITION (B1).

B18   PHOENIX II: UNCOLLECTED, UNPUBLISHED, AND OTHER PROSE
      WORKS BY D.H. LAWRENCE. Ed. Warren Roberts and Harry
      T. Moore. London: Heinemann; New York: Viking, 1968.
           Valuable supplement to PHOENIX (B16). Roberts
           and Moore collect twelve stories and sketches,
           including "A Prelude" (A15), "The Fly in the
           Ointment" (A16), "The Thimble" (A18), "The
           Mortal Coil" (A19), "Delilah and Mr. Bircum-
           shaw" (A32), "Prologue to WOMEN IN LOVE" (A35),
           "Mr. Noon" (in A31), the previously unpublished,
           semi-fictional "Lessford's Rabbits" and "A Les-
           son on a Tortoise" (both reprinted in B10 and
           B14), and DHL's translation of Bunin's "The
           Gentleman from San Francisco" (A81). Of the
           nonfiction, they reprint "The Two Principles"
           (from A77), "Foreword to WOMEN IN LOVE" (see
           A78), "Introduction to MEMOIRS OF THE FOREIGN
           LEGION" (A66), and DHL's A PROPOS OF *LADY CHAT-
           TERLEY'S LOVER* (A72), REFLECTIONS ON THE DEATH
           OF A PORCUPINE (A69), and ASSORTED ARTICLES
           (A75), complete. Prominent among the essays
           in these last two reprinted collections are
           "The Crown," "The Novel," "Cocksure Women and
           Hensure Men," "Men Must Work and Women as Well,"
           "Autobiographical Sketch," "Hymns in a Man's
           Life," and "Making Pictures." Also included
           are extracts from A27, A40, A82, A83, and F123
           (the "Burns novel"). The editors provide orig-
           inal publication information for the sixty-two
           (of sixty-seven) previously published works.
           For the editors' "Introduction" see Z68. For
           a thematic index to this collection, see E41.
           Also see Z1, Z23, and Z31.

B19   THE PORTABLE D.H. LAWRENCE. Ed. Diana Trilling. New
      York: Viking, 1947.
           Collects an assortment of DHL's stories, poems,
           letters, and essays, together with extracts
           from R and WL. Compiled almost defensively,
           when DHL's reputation was at its lowest point,
           this anthology desperately needs revision.
           Contains, among other selections, "The Prus-
           sian Officer" (from A17), "Tickets, Please"
           and "The Blind Man" (from A20), "Two Blue
           Birds" (from A24), "The Lovely Lady" and "The
           Rocking-Horse Winner" (from A28), "The Prin-
           cess" (from A22), "The Fox" (from A21), the

novel extracts, twelve poems, extracts from
TWILIGHT IN ITALY (A87), SEA AND SARDINIA
(A88), MORNINGS IN MEXICO (A89), twenty-three
letters, four reviews of American novelists
(from B16), "Christs in the Tirol" (from A27),
"Nottingham and the Mining Countryside" (A74),
"Men Must Work and Women as Well" (from A75),
"Pornography and Obscenity" (A73), and "Edgar
Allan Poe" (from A65). See H385. Also see
H19.

B20   THE PRINCESS, AND OTHER STORIES. Ed. Keith Sagar. Harmondsworth, Engl.: Penguin, 1971.
Twelve late stories and sketches, including
the previously unpublished first chapter of
an unfinished novel ("The Wilful Woman"; reprinted in B8), and the original, unexpurgated
version of "Sun" (A23). Supplements B4. Also
includes a brief, general "Introduction" by
Sagar (pp. 7-12), "The Princess" (A22), "Mother
and Daughter," "The Blue Moccasins," "Things,"
and "The Overtone" (from A28), "The Man Who Was
Through With the World" (A33), "A Dream of Life"
(i.e. ["Autobiographical Fragment"]), "The Flying Fish," "Mercury," and "The Undying Man"
(from B16). Also see B14.

B21   ST. MAWR AND THE MAN WHO DIED. New York: Knopf, 1959.
Only accessible American publication of the
two novellas (A22 and A25).

B22   SELECTED ESSAYS. Ed. Richard Aldington. Harmondsworth,
Engl.: Penguin, 1950.
Thirty-six essays, representing DHL's chief
preoccupations: "love and life," travel, writ-
ing, and painting. Includes a slight "Intro-
duction" by the editor (pp. 7-10), "Cocksure
Women and Hensure Men," "Making Pictures," and
"Sex Versus Loveliness" (from A75), "Reflec-
tions on the Death of a Porcupine" (from A69),
"Introduction to These Paintings" (A71), "John
Galsworthy" (A70), "Nottingham and the Mining
Countryside" (A74), and several extracts from
STUDIES IN CLASSIC AMERICAN LITERATURE (A65),
TWILIGHT IN ITALY (A87), MORNINGS IN MEXICO
(A89), and PHOENIX (B16).

B23   SELECTED LITERARY CRITICISM. Ed. Anthony Beal. London:
       Heinemann, 1955. New York: Viking, 1956.
             Reprints all or part of forty-one literary art-
             icles, interspersed with extracts from sixty-
             three letters. Includes a slight "Introduction"
             by Beal (pp. ix-xii), "Surgery for the Novel"
             (A64), "Morality and the Novel" (A68), "John
             Galsworthy" (A70), "Pornography and Obscenity"
             (A73), "Autobiographical Sketch" and "Hymns in
             a Man's Life" (from A75), and extracts from NEW
             POEMS (A51), PANSIES (A56), STUDIES IN CLASSIC
             AMERICAN LITERATURE (A65), "Introduction to
             These Paintings" (A71), ALL THINGS ARE POSSIBLE
             (A80), MASTRO-DON GESUALDO (A82), CAVALLERIA
             RUSTICANA (A84), THE GRAND INQUISITOR (A86),
             "Study of Thomas Hardy" (in B16), and PHOENIX
             (B16). See H151 and Z47.

B24   SELECTED POEMS. Ed. Keith Sagar. Harmondsworth, Engl.:
       Penguin, 1972.
             The best recent selection. 150 poems (1906-29),
             with Sagar's brief and general "Introduction"
             (pp. 11-17). See Y10.

B25   SELECTED POEMS. Ed. Kenneth Rexroth. New York: New Di-
       rections, 1947.
             Ninety-seven poems. Good representative selec-
             tion. See Y50. Also see Y13.

B26   SEX, LITERATURE, AND CENSORSHIP. Ed. Harry T. Moore.
       New York: Twayne, 1953. London: Heinemann, 1955. Rev.
       ed. New York: Viking, 1959.
             American edition collects eight essays, and a
             painting, including "Cocksure Women and Hensure
             Men" and "Sex Versus Loveliness" (from A75),
             "Introduction to PANSIES" (from A56), "Pornog-
             raphy and Obscenity" (A73), and "A Propos of
             LADY CHATTERLEY'S LOVER" (A72); English edition
             adds three essays, including "Introduction to
             these Paintings" (A71) and "The Novel" (from
             A69), and reproductions of three paintings.
             Revised edition reprints the U.S. District
             Court decision on LCL (see U11). Also see
             F110 and Z70.

B27   THE SHORT NOVELS. 2 vols. London: Heinemann, 1956.
             Collects seven novellas, for the PHOENIX EDI-
             TION (see B17). Volume one includes: "The

Captain's Doll," "The Fox," "The Ladybird,"
"Love Among the Haystacks" (see similar Amer.
ed., B12). Volume two includes: "The Man Who
Died" (A25), "St. Mawr" (A22), and "The Virgin and the Gipsy" (A26).

B28 STORIES, ESSAYS, AND POEMS: D.H. LAWRENCE. Ed. Desmond
Hawkins. London: Dent, 1939.
Collects "Odour of Chrysanthemums" and "The
White Stocking" (from A17), "England, My Eng-
land" (from A20), "The Fox" (from A21), "The
Woman Who Rode Away" (from A24), "Things" and
"The Lovely Lady" (from A28), extracts from
TWILIGHT IN ITALY (A87) and MORNINGS IN MEX-
ICO (A89), three essays from PHOENIX (B16):
"Adolf," "Flowery Tuscany," and "Man is a
Hunter," DHL's critical essay on "Edgar Allan
Poe" (from A65), and thirty-four poems. Long-
est-lived anthology of DHL's works. See H170.

B29 TUTTE LE OPERE DI DAVID HERBERT LAWRENCE. 14 vols. Milan:
Mondadori, 1947-75.
The first-proposed collected edition, containing Piero Nardi's biography of DHL (vol. 1;
see F122), the poems (vol. 2), the novels
(vols. 3-7, including THE BOY IN THE BUSH and
all three versions of LADY CHATTERLEY'S LOVER
[see A13]), the novellas, short stories, and
fiction fragments (vols. 8-9), the travel
works, plays, history, philosophical and critical essays, and miscellaneous prose (vols.
10-13), and the letters (vol. 14). General
editor: Piero Nardi. Translations by Nardi
and several others. For full publication details on individual volumes, see Roberts (E39).
[In Italian.] Also see F122 and H273.

C. LETTERS

For additional publications of letters to, by, or concerning
DHL, and comments on DHL's correspondence, see B7, B9, B11,
B19, B23, and B29 above, and E4, E27, E40, E45, F4, F14, F18,
F20, F23, F28, F35, F38, F42, F46, F48, F54, F58, F59, F60,
F85, F87, F95, F96, F99, F100, F103, F112, F113, F123, F126,
F133, F142, F145, F149, F161, F164, F165, F167, F168, G20,
G42, G74, G123, H191, H254, H310, H387, L1, L3, L5, L7, M2,
Y42, Y61, Y128, Z103, Z111, AA159, and AA236, below. Section
Z, iii (items Z89 through Z100) lists "Critical Articles and
Chapters on Lawrence's Letters." The Cambridge Edition of
THE LETTERS OF D.H. LAWRENCE (C11 below) provides manuscript
locations for all letters published. For additional manu-
script locations, pending completion of the Cambridge Edition,
see C5, E4, E9, E45, E47, E48, and E50.

C1 THE CENTAUR LETTERS. Ed. Edward D. McDonald. Austin:
    Humanities Research Center, Univ. of Texas, 1970.
        Thirty letters from DHL to McDonald and Harold
    Mason, his American bibliographer and his publisher,
    coproprietors of the Centaur Bookshop. See C11.

C2 THE COLLECTED LETTERS OF D.H. LAWRENCE. 2 vols. Ed. Harry
    T. Moore. New York: Viking; London: Heinemann, 1962.
        To be superseded by the Cambridge edition (see
    C11). Assimilates much of the correspondence
    published to 1962 (e.g., in C10, F20, F87, F95,
    and F123), including Moore's edition of the
    LETTERS TO BERTRAND RUSSELL (1948), and pub-
    lishes considerable new correspondence, but
    neither claims nor is intended to be a complete
    edition. Includes over 1000 letters (1903-30),
    a reprint of Huxley's introduction to his edi-
    tion of THE LETTERS (see H191), two useful in-
    dexes, an excellent biographical "Who's Who"
    for the letters (pp. xxix-lvi), and Moore's
    general "Introduction" (pp. ix-xxvii). See
    F126, H254, and Z97.

C3   "D.H. Lawrence: Letters to Gordon and Beatrice Campbell."
     Ed. Peter L. Irvine and Anne Kiley. DHLR, 6 (1973), 1-20.
            Publishes, with commentary, fourteen letters
            (1915-30) from DHL to Lord and Lady Glenavy.
            See C11.

C4   "D.H. Lawrence and Frieda Lawrence: Letters to Dorothy
     Brett." Ed. Peter L. Irvine and Anne Kiley. DHLR, 9
     (1976), 1-116.
            146 letters (1924-30), to the painter and fel-
            low member of the Lawrences' Taos circle. In-
            cludes an editorial discussion of the Lawrence-
            Brett friendship (pp. 3-31) and notes. 121
            letters by DHL, to be assimilated into C11.
            See F48.

C5   "D.H. Lawrence's Letters to Catherine Carswell." YULG, 49
     (1975), 253-60.
            Announces Yale's acquisition of "almost two
            hundred letters and post cards" from DHL to
            Carswell and publishes, with commentary, seven
            items (1915-28). No editor identified. See
            C11.

C6   LAWRENCE IN LOVE: LETTERS TO LOUIE BURROWS. Ed. James T.
     Boulton. Nottingham: Univ. of Nottingham Press, 1968.
            168 letters by DHL, documenting his relation-
            ship with Burrows, one major prototype for
            Ursula Brangwen (in R and WL). Annotated and
            indexed. Extracts reprinted in L1. See C11
            and F18. Also see F46, F103, and F164.

C7   "Lawrence's Night-Letter on Censorship and Obscenity."
     Ed. Raymond M. Beirne. DHLR, 7 (1974), 321-22.
            Publishes, with commentary, DHL's "extremely
            concise" response to an attempt at censoring
            WL (published in THE NEW YORK TIMES, 11 Feb.
            1923). See C11.

C8   LETTERS. Ed. Richard Aldington. Harmondsworth, Engl.:
     Penguin, 1950.
            Selects 100 letters (1910-30), to a variety of
            correspondents, from Huxley's edition of the
            LETTERS (see C10). Reprints Huxley's "Intro-
            duction" as well (see H191).

C9   LETTERS FROM D.H. LAWRENCE TO MARTIN SECKER, 1911-1930.
     Ed. Martin Secker. Buckingham, Engl.: Secker, 1970.
            196 letters (1911-30), to DHL's English pub-
            lisher. Slight notes. See C11.

C10   THE LETTERS OF D.H. LAWRENCE. Ed. Aldous Huxley. London:
      Heinemann; New York: Viking, 1932.
           Collects 793 letters (1909-30), to various cor-
           respondents. Despite editorial flaws, an in-
           fluential early document in the restoration of
           DHL's reputation and in the recognition of his
           distinction as a letter-writer. See H191 and
           below. Also see F14, H387, Z94, Z95, and Z98.

C11   THE LETTERS OF D.H. LAWRENCE. Vol. 1, 1901-1913. Ed.
      James T. Boulton; Vol. 2, 1913-1916. Ed. George J. Zyta-
      ruk and James T. Boulton. Cambridge and New York: Cam-
      bridge Univ. Press, 1979; 1981.
           First two volumes of the impressive eight-
           volume, edition-in-progress of DHL's complete
           correspondence, for the CAMBRIDGE EDITION OF
           THE COMPLETE WORKS OF D.H. LAWRENCE (see B1).
           Both volumes contain biographical and histor-
           ical "Introductions" by their editors (pp. 1-
           20 and pp. 1-18 respectively), DHL chronolo-
           gies for the years of their coverage, and num-
           erous "Maps showing places visited by Lawrence"
           1885-1913 and 1913-1916. Volume one publishes
           an extensive Lawrence family genealogical chart
           (1786-1976), and 579 excellently annotated let-
           ters (annotations include manuscript locations).
           Volume two brings the total letter-count to
           1301 (through 31 Oct. 1916). Volumes three
           through seven will cover the intervals 1916-21
           (ed. Boulton and Andrew Robertson), 1921-24
           (ed. Warren Roberts and Elizabeth Mansfield),
           1924-27 (ed. David Farmer), 1927-28 (ed. Gerald
           M. Lacy), and 1928-30 (ed. Boulton and Keith
           Sagar). An eighth, "Index" volume will pre-
           sumably contain several indexes and any addenda
           and corrigenda. The entire edition will assim-
           ilate all letters published within the other
           entries listed in this section (over 5,000
           cards and letters) and, judging from the first
           two volumes, will be a model of scholarly edit-
           ing. For further information on this edition,
           see Z90, Z93, Z96, Z100.

C12   LETTERS TO THOMAS AND ADELE SELTZER. Ed. Gerald M. Lacy.
      Santa Barbara, Calif.: Black Sparrow Press, 1976.
           135 letters (1919-28), to DHL's chief American
           publisher (1920-25) and his wife. Includes a
           biographical essay (see F92) and a collection
           of letters concerning DHL by the Seltzers.
           Also see above.

C13 THE QUEST FOR RANANIM: D.H. LAWRENCE'S LETTERS TO S.S. KOTELIANSKY, 1914 TO 1930. Ed. George J. Zytaruk. Montreal: McGill-Queen's Univ. Press, 1970.
346 letters to "Kot," DHL's lasting friend and part-time collaborator in translation. Annotations, appendixes, and index. Beautiful edition. See C11 and F165.

C14 THE SELECTED LETTERS OF D.H. LAWRENCE. Ed. Diana Trilling. New York: Farrar, Strauss, and Cudahy, 1958.
181 previously published letters, drawn chiefly from Huxley's edition (see C10). See C11 and H383.

D. CONCORDANCES

Note: For glossaries of Nottinghamshire dialect words in DHL's works, see E41, H130, M85, and X11.

D1   Garcia, Reloy, and James Karabatsos, eds. A CONCORDANCE
     TO THE POETRY OF D.H. LAWRENCE. Lincoln: Univ. of Nebraska
     Press, 1970.
          Concordance to the first edition of THE COMPLETE
          POEMS (1964--see B3). Gives full line context
          and includes listings of special terms (e.g.,
          nature images). Omits numerous common words.

D2   -----. A CONCORDANCE TO THE SHORT FICTION OF D.H. LAWRENCE.
     Lincoln: Univ. of Nebraska Press, 1972.
          Word index to the incomplete and severely flawed
          American paperback texts of the stories and novel-
          las (Viking, 1961; see B4). Omits numerous com-
          mon words.

Part 2
Secondary Bibliography

For information on the scope and arrangement of this bibliography see the introduction.

Note: There are a number of journals which publish bibliographical, biographical, and critical materials chiefly concerned with DHL. The most important such author-centered periodical is the D.H. LAWRENCE REVIEW (1968--; abbreviated "DHLR"). Also of interest are THE PHOENIX (1938-40), an effusive, "cultist" magazine dedicated to preserving the Lawrencean "gospel" (and recently revived, though no longer concerned with Lawrence studies), the short-lived D.H. LAWRENCE NEWS AND NOTES (1959-61), and THE NEWSLETTER OF THE D.H. LAWRENCE SOCIETY OF NORTH AMERICA (1977--; initially published as THE D.H. LAWRENCE SOCIETY NEWSLETTER within DHLR). The "Japanese Study Circle of D.H. Lawrence" (Kyôto) publishes an annual, THE D.H. LAWRENCE STUDIES (1975--), which is usually devoted to one work or one aspect of DHL's writing. The English "D.H. Lawrence Society" also publishes a JOURNAL (1976--; not seen).

The vast majority of the articles appearing in DHLR have been entered and annotated in this bibliography. Furthermore, several special issues of DHLR have been listed here and treated in the same fashion as special numbers of other journals (i.e., as essay collections), with their contents summarized and with cross references provided for essays individually entered and annotated in the bibliography. However, a few short notes and letters appearing in DHLR and most of the contents of the remaining journals described above, have not been included here.

E. BIBLIOGRAPHIES

Also see Jackson (F77), Meyers (F109), Arnold (G7), Marnat (G73), Schwartz (H332), Stewart (H361), Widmer (H408), Ignjacević (AA164), and Kreemers (AA192).

E1 Allendorf, Otmar, comp. "Criticism of D.H. Lawrence in German: 1923-1970, A Bibliography." DHLR, 4 (1971), 210-20.
    Lists 101 German books, theses (published and unpublished), and articles on DHL.

E2 Altenberg, Bengt, comp. "A Checklist of D.H. Lawrence Scholarship in Scandinavia, 1934-1968." DHLR, 2 (1969), 275-77.
    Lists twenty Scandinavian books and essays on DHL.

E3 Arnold, Armin. "Appendix: A History of Lawrence's Reputation in America and Europe." In his D.H. LAWRENCE AND AMERICA. Pp. 163-223. See G7.
    Comments usefully on all major DHL criticism, through 1958, in a year-by-year chronicle of his reputation.

E4 Barez, Reva R. "The H. Bacon Collamore Collection of D.H. Lawrence." YULG, 34 (1959), 16-23.
    Describes the chief contents of the Yale DHL collection of manuscripts and first editions. Supplemented by a brief note, by Harry T. Moore, on DHL's correspondence with Henry Savage (ten letters, 1913-14, six at Yale) and the texts of three of the letters (pp. 24-33).

E5 Beards, Richard D., et al., comps. "D.H. Lawrence: Ten Years of Criticism, 1959-1968, A Checklist." DHLR, 1 (1968), 245-85.
    Supplements Beebe and Tommasi (E7). Also see below.

E6   -----, et al., comps. "The Checklist of D.H. Lawrence:
      Criticism and Scholarship." DHLR, 3 (1970), and contin-
      uing.
            Annual supplements to the checklists by Beebe
            and Tommasi (below) and above.

E7   Beebe, Maurice, and Anthony Tommasi, comps. "Criticism
      of D.H. Lawrence: A Selected Checklist with an Index to
      Studies of Separate Works." MFS, 5 (1959), 83-98.
            Excellent selected bibliography of DHL studies
            through 1958. See Beards' supplements (E5 and
            E6 above). Also see G78.

E8   Burwell, Rose Marie, ed. "A Catalogue of D.H. Lawrence's
      Reading, from Early Childhood." DHLR, 3 (1970), 193-330;
      6 (1973), 86-99.
            Catalogs "every book play, poem, essay, and
            manuscript" Burwell "can establish that Law-
            rence read," to 1909 (232 titles), and annually
            between 1910 and 1930 (922 titles). Her ad-
            denda lists sixty-five more titles, 1910-29.
            Both lists reprinted in E41.

E9   Cooke, Sheila M., comp. D.H. LAWRENCE: A FINDING LIST.
      1968. 2nd ed. Nottingham: Nottinghamshire County Council
      Leisure Services Department, 1980.
            Extensively revised and enlarged version of
            Edwards' listing (see E18). Catalogs the hold-
            ings of the Nottingham County and University
            DHL collections, including bibliographies (44
            titles), writings by DHL (252 titles, with mul-
            tiple editions of many titles), stage, tele-
            vision, radio, and cinema adaptations of DHL's
            works (46 titles), and 197 books, 411 chapters
            from books, 686 periodical articles, seven
            theses, and forty miscellaneous items concern-
            ing DHL, through 1979.

E10   Cowan, James C., ed. D.H. LAWRENCE: AN ANNOTATED BIBLI-
      OGRAPHY OF WRITINGS ABOUT HIM. Vol. 1. 1909-1960. De-
      kalb: Northern Illinois Univ. Press, [1982].
            Announced for 1982 publication, but not seen
            and publication unconfirmed. Cowan's bibli-
            ography, containing 2,061 entries, will include
            dissertations and foreign-language publications,
            and, if uniform with the Northern Illinois "An-
            notated Secondary Bibliography" series, will
            list all titles for each year alphabetically

by author, providing full abstracts for each
publication. Although Cowan's bibliography
will approach comprehensive coverage of journal and periodical publications, unlike this
book, its chronological rather than topical
format will make it less useful as a guide
to research.

E11   Crump, G.B., comp. "Doctoral Dissertations on D.H. Lawrence, 1931-1969: A Bibliography." DHLR, 3 (1970), 80-86.
        Lists 104 English-language and European dis-
        sertations. Supplements compiled by Gerald
        M. Garmon (DHLR, 5 [1972], 170-73), Dennis
        Jackson (DHLR, 8 [1975], 236-41), and Fleda
        B. Jackson (DHLR, 10 [1977], 299-304), list
        185 additional dissertations.

E12   Cushman, Keith. "A Profile of John E. Baker, Jr., and
His Lawrence Collection." DHLR, 7 (1974), 83-88.
        Profiles Baker and notes the major items in
        his impressive DHL collection ("among the
        finest in private hands in the United States").
        See E14.

E13   -----. "A Profile of John Martin and His Lawrence Collection." DHLR, 7 (1974), 199-205.
        Profiles Martin, owner of the Black Sparrow
        Press (Los Angeles), and describes his col-
        lection of DHL editions and manuscripts (since
        acquired by Univ. of Tulsa).

E14   -----, comp. AN EXHIBITION OF FIRST EDITIONS AND MANU-
SCRIPTS FROM THE D.H. LAWRENCE COLLECTION OF JOHN E.
BAKER, JR. Chicago: Univ. of Chicago, 1973.
        Exhibition catalogue and brief introductory
        note. See E12.

E15   DeFilippis, Simonetta, comp. "A Checklist of D.H. Lawrence Criticism and Scholarship in Italy, 1924-1976."
DHLR, 10 (1977), 286-98.
        Lists 155 Italian books, articles, and reviews
        concerning DHL.

E16   Draper, Ronald P. "A Short Guide to D.H. Lawrence Studies." CRITICAL SURVEY, 2 (1966), 222-26.
        Useful brief survey of standard critical works.

E17   -----. "Introduction." In D.H. LAWRENCE: THE CRITICAL
      HERITAGE. Ed. Draper. Pp. 1-29. See G34.
         A good summary of DHL's reputation during his
         lifetime.

E18   Edwards, Lucy I., comp. D.H. LAWRENCE: A FINDING LIST.
      HOLDINGS IN THE CITY, COUNTY, AND UNIVERSITY LIBRARIES
      OF NOTTINGHAM. Nottingham: Nottinghamshire County Coun-
      cil, 1968.
         Specialized, and now obsolete. See E9.

E19   Edwards, Lucy I., and David Phillips, comps. YOUNG BERT:
      AN EXHIBITION OF THE EARLY YEARS OF D.H. LAWRENCE. Not-
      tingham Museum and Art Gallery, 1972.
         Copiously illustrated catalogue of the 1972
         (July-Aug.) Nottingham DHL exhibition of 293
         paintings, photographs, and documents concern-
         ing DHL's backgrounds, life, and works (to
         1919). A number of illustrations here are
         also reproduced in H27. Includes Carl E.
         Baron's essay on DHL's paintings (see W3).
         Also see H27.

E20   Fabes, Gilbert H., ed. D.H. LAWRENCE: HIS FIRST EDITIONS:
      POINTS AND VALUES. London: Foyle, 1933.
         Buyer's guide to and brief bibliographical
         description of first editions of works by DHL,
         and of books concerned with DHL.

E21   Ferrier, Carole, ed. "D.H. Lawrence's Pre-1920 Poetry:
      A Descriptive Bibliography of Manuscripts, Typescripts,
      and Proofs." DHLR, 6 (1973), 333-59.
         Lists and locates forty-eight manuscripts and
         proofs and, in a second section, provides fur-
         ther details (titles, drafts, chronology) on
         thirty-two of the entries. Thirty-three more
         manuscripts (1920-28), with further details on
         twenty-seven, are listed in a supplementary
         bibliography by Ferrier, in DHLR, 12 (1979),
         289-304. Also see Y64.

E22   Finney, Brian. "A Profile of Mr. George Lazarus and His
      Lawrence Collection of Manuscripts and First Editions."
      DHLR, 6 (1973), 309-12.
         Describes Lazarus's extensive collection (be-
         queathed to the Univ. of Nottingham Library).

E23 Garmon, Gerald, Patsy C. Howard, and Edmund A. Bojarski,
comps. "Theses on D.H. Lawrence: 1931-1972: A Bibliography with Addenda of Senior Theses and Works in Progress."
DHLR, 6 (1973), 217-30.
> Lists 168 master's theses, nineteen senior and
> honors theses, and two works in progress. Pre-
> dominantly American and British coverage. Sup-
> plements compiled by Dennis Jackson (DHLR, 8
> [1975], 106-12) and Fleda B. Jackson (DHLR, 10
> [1977], 304-08) list 124 additional masters
> theses and twenty honors theses. Toshitaka
> Shirai (DHLR, 8 [1975], 233-35) lists thirty-
> nine Japanese master's theses.

E24 Gouirand, Jacqueline, comp. "D.H. Lawrence Translations,
Criticism, and Scholarship Published in France, 1927-
1976: A Bibliography." DHLR, 10 (1977), 70-81.
> Lists forty-five translations of DHL's works,
> and ninety-nine books, chapters, and reviews
> concerning DHL. Many omissions.

E25 Hepburn, James G., ed. "D.H. Lawrence's Plays: An Annotated Bibliography." BC, 14 (1965), 78-81.
> Corrects and supplements Roberts's listing of
> the plays (lists eight plays and two fragments
> and comments on two possibly lost plays). See E39.

E26 Hoffman, Frederick J., and Harry T. Moore. "D.H. Lawrence
and His Critics: An Introduction." In THE ACHIEVEMENT OF
D.H. LAWRENCE. Ed. Hoffman and Moore. Pp. 3-45. See G53.
> Excellent summary of DHL's reputation, divided
> into sections on the contemporary reception of
> his works, on the memoirs and biographies, and
> on the critical studies. Remains valuable de-
> spite its relatively early date (1953).

E27 Hoffmann, Lois, comp. "A Catalogue of the Frieda Lawrence Manuscripts in German at the University of Texas."
LCUT, N.S. No. 6 (1973), pp. 87-105.
> Catalogues the Texas collection of 133 German
> letters (1907-49), to and from Frieda and her
> family (correspondents include her parents and
> Otto Gross).

E28 Jackson, Dennis. "D.H. Lawrence in the 1970s: No More
the Great Unread." BRITISH BOOK NEWS (Apr. 1980), 198-202.
> Describes, with brief comments, an impressive
> number of the biographical and critical stud-
> ies of DHL, and textual editions of his work,
> published in the 1970s.

E29   Kai, Sadanobu, Yasuichirô Ôhashi, Taiji Okada, and Tôru
      Okumura, comps. "A Checklist of D.H. Lawrence Articles
      in Japan, 1951-1968." DHLR, 2 (1969), 172-91.
            Lists and arranges by subject (general studies,
            studies of individual works), 239 articles pub-
            lished in Japan (most in Japanese). The same
            compilers have published a supplement, for the
            years 1968-75, listing 172 additional articles
            (DHLR, 10 [1977], 193-208).

E30   Losa, Margarida, and John Remsbury, comps. "D.H. Law-
      rence: A Secondary Bibliography for Portugal." DHLR, 4
      (1971), 314-17.
            Lists seventeen translations of DHL into Portu-
            gese (1937-70) and thirteen studies of DHL pub-
            lished in Portugal (1933-71).

E31   McDonald, Edward D., ed. A BIBLIOGRAPHY OF THE WRITINGS
      OF D.H. LAWRENCE. Philadelphia: Centaur Press, 1925.
            A full descriptive bibliography of DHL's first
            editions (through Aug. 1924), translations,
            contributions to books and periodicals, poetry,
            and of studies and reviews concerning DHL.
            Supplemented by McDonald's later volume (be-
            low). Includes DHL's "The Bad Side of Books"
            (pp. 9-14), reprinted in B16.

E32   -----. THE WRITINGS OF D.H. LAWRENCE, 1925-1930: A BIB-
      LIOGRAPHICAL SUPPLEMENT. Philadelphia: Centaur Book Shop,
      1931.
            Reliable supplement to his above bibliography
            of DHL's works through 1924, though both are
            superseded by Roberts (see E39). McDonald's
            commentaries on individual items remain infor-
            mative.

E33   Miletić, Sonja, and Miroslav Beker, comps. "Criticism
      of D.H. Lawrence in Yugoslavia: 1926-1976: A Bibliography."
      DHLR, 11 (1978), 73-76.
            Lists fifty Yugoslavian articles and chapters
            on DHL.

E34   Parry, Albert. "D.H. Lawrence Through a Marxist Mirror."
      WR, 19 (1955), 85-100.
            Summarizes early Russian critical approval of
            DHL (1917), the paucity of comment on DHL in
            the 1920s, and the "full-blown" Marxist attacks
            on DHL, within Russia and without (1932-45).
            Partial bibliographical data for several arti-
            cles.

E35 Peterson, Richard F., and Alan M. Cohn. D.H. LAWRENCE:
AN EXHIBIT. Carbondale: Morris Library, Southern Illi-
nois Univ., 1979.
Not seen. (Pamphlet--40 pp.)

E36 Phillips, Jill M., ed. D.H. LAWRENCE: A REVIEW OF THE
BIOGRAPHIES AND LITERARY CRITICISM (A CRITICALLY ANNO-
TATED BIBLIOGRAPHY). New York: Gordon Press, 1978.
Annotates fifty biographies, critical studies,
and essay collections concerning DHL, and anthologies or editions of his work. Eccentric
selection, amateurish comments, and questionable purpose.

E37 Pinto, Vivian de Sola, ed. D.H. LAWRENCE AFTER THIRTY
YEARS, 1930-1960. Nottingham: Curwen Press, 1960.
Anniversary exhibition catalogue. [Not seen.]

E38 Powell, Lawrence Clark, ed. THE MANUSCRIPTS OF D.H. LAW-
RENCE: A DESCRIPTIVE CATALOGUE. Los Angeles: Los Angeles
Public Library, 1937.
Assimilated into Tedlock's bibliography of the
Frieda Lawrence collection (see E48). For re-
cent manuscript locations see E49 and E50.

E39 Roberts, Warren, ed. A BIBLIOGRAPHY OF D.H. LAWRENCE.
London: Hart-Davis, 1963.
Impressive and immensely useful primary bibliography, containing collations of and commentaries upon 102 "Books and Pamphlets" and sixty-
four "Contributions to Books." Roberts also
provides checklists of periodical contributions
by DHL (240 items), translations of his works
into over twenty languages (266 items), manuscript locations (447 items), and a list of
books about DHL (88 items). Includes appendixes on parodies, forgeries, and spurious
works. Indexed. For a supplementary listing
of books by DHL see below. For a revision and
expansion of the manuscript locations see E49
and E50, and for more complete information on
the dates of composition see below. A revised
edition of this bibliography has been announced
for publication, late in 1982, by Cambridge
Univ. Press.

E40   Sagar, Keith.   D.H. LAWRENCE: A CALENDAR OF HIS WORKS:
      WITH A CHECKLIST OF THE MANUSCRIPTS.   Manchester, Engl.:
      Manchester Univ. Press, 1979.
            Traces "month by month--often day by day"--
            the evidence for the time and order of compo-
            sition, revision, and publication of DHL's
            works, based chiefly on exhaustive research
            in the letters.   Supporting documents quoted
            throughout.   Excellently done and extremely
            useful.   Includes a supplementary listing of
            works published since Roberts's bibliography
            (pp. 271-72; see above), locations of DHL's
            major paintings (p. 267), and a checklist of
            his manuscripts (see E49).

E41   -----, ed.   A D.H. LAWRENCE HANDBOOK.   New York: Barnes
      and Noble, 1982.
            Useful reference work, containing a selective
            secondary bibliography (comp. Dennis Jackson),
            a checklist of DHL's reading (comp. Rose Marie
            Burwell; revision of E8), a social and eco-
            nomic history of Eastwood and the Nottingham-
            shire mining country (by A.R. and C.P. Grif-
            fin), a glossary of Nottinghamshire dialect
            and mining terms (comp. David E. Gerard; re-
            vision of H130), chronologies of DHL's life
            ("in the context of world events") and works
            (by Gerald M. Lacy and Keith Sagar), a DHL
            travel calendar (also by Sagar), identifica-
            tion of locations in DHL's fiction and travel
            writings (by Bridget Pugh; see F135), a list-
            ing of major productions of DHL's plays (comp.
            Sagar and Sylvia Sklar), a thematic index to
            PHOENIX and PHOENIX II (comp. Damian Grant;
            see B16 and B18), and a list of film and sound
            recordings relating to DHL (comp. David E. Ger-
            ard).   Received too late for these contribu-
            tions to be individually entered and annotated
            in this bibliography.

E42   Snyder, Harold Jay, comp.   CATALOGUE OF ENGLISH AND AMER-
      ICAN FIRST EDITIONS, 1911-1932, OF D.H. LAWRENCE.   New
      York: Privately printed, 1932.
            Bookseller's catalogue.   (Pamphlet--20 pp.)

E43   Spilka, Mark.   "Lawrence."   In THE ENGLISH NOVEL: SELECT
      BIBLIOGRAPHICAL GUIDES.   Ed. A.E. Dyson.   London: Oxford
      Univ. Press, 1974.   Pp. 334-48.
            Bibliographical essay and highly selective
            primary and secondary checklist.

E44 Stoll, John E., ed. D.H. LAWRENCE: A BIBLIOGRAPHY, 1911-
     1975. Troy, N.Y.: Whitston, 1978.
          Extended checklists of "easily accessible"
          titles by DHL, and of bibliographical sources
          (43), general studies (197), biographical
          works (101), books (135), articles (1543),
          and reviews (490), concerning DHL. Usable,
          though incomplete, inaccurate, and carelessly
          edited. Slight annotation. Author index
          only.

E45 Tannenbaum, Earl, ed. D.H. LAWRENCE: AN EXHIBITION OF
     FIRST EDITIONS, MANUSCRIPTS, PAINTINGS, LETTERS, AND
     MISCELLANY, AT SOUTHERN ILLINOIS LIBRARY, APRIL 1958.
     Carbondale: Southern Illinois Univ. Library, 1958.
          Annotated exhibition catalogue of books by
          and about DHL, and related materials. 212
          items.

E46 Tanselle, G. Thomas.   "The Thomas Seltzer Imprint." PBSA,
     58 (1964), 380-448.
          Summarizes the impressive but brief history
          of Seltzer's firm (1920-26) and provides pub-
          lication data for 219 titles issued by Seltzer
          (seventeen by DHL). Indexed.

E47 Tarr, Roger L., and Robert Sokan, eds. A BIBLIOGRAPHY
     OF THE D.H. LAWRENCE COLLECTION AT ILLINOIS STATE UNI-
     VERSITY. Bloomington, Ill.: Scarlet Ibis Press, 1979.
          Descriptive primary bibliography of DHL's works
          and checklist of studies of DHL in the Milner
          Library's DHL collection.

E48 Tedlock, Ernest W., ed. THE FRIEDA LAWRENCE COLLECTION
     OF MANUSCRIPTS: A DESCRIPTIVE BIBLIOGRAPHY. Alberquerque:
     Univ. of New Mexico Press, 1948.
          Description and dating of 202 manuscripts,
          with brief historical and textual commentar-
          ies. Tedlock also provides an introduction
          and an appendix on the three versions of LADY
          CHATTERLEY'S LOVER (see U71). For a more re-
          cent listing of manuscripts see below. Ex-
          tracts reprinted in F123.

E49 Vasey, Lindeth, ed. "A Checklist of the Manuscripts of
     D.H. Lawrence." In D.H. LAWRENCE: A CALENDAR OF HIS WORKS.
     Ed. Keith Sagar. Pp. 191-266. See E40.
          A revision and expansion of Roberts's listing
          (see E39), observing his numbering sequence

and entry format, and updating the location
information. New information presumably to
be assimilated into Roberts's revised edition
of his bibliography (1982; also see E39).

E50 Welch, M.A., comp. D.H. LAWRENCE COLLECTION CATALOGUE.
Nottingham: Univ. of Nottingham Manuscripts Department,
1979.
Complete listing of the extensive Nottingham
collections of letters, manuscripts, newspaper
cuttings, paintings, scripts, and other material by or relating to DHL. Includes the collections donated to Nottingham by Louie Burrows and Prof. J.D. Chambers (see C6 and F30).

E51 White, William, comp. D.H. LAWRENCE: A CHECKLIST. WRIT-
INGS ABOUT D.H. LAWRENCE, 1931-1950. Detroit: Wayne State
Univ. Press, 1950.
Arranged chronologically. Beebe's and Tom-
masi's checklist is more accessible (see E7),
as are Beards' annual supplements (see E5 and
E6).

E52 Wiley, Paul L., comp. "D.H. Lawrence (1885-1930)." In
THE BRITISH NOVEL: CONRAD TO THE PRESENT. Northbrook,
Ill.: AHM, 1973. Pp. 71-77.
Brief primary and secondary checklist.

F. BIOGRAPHIES, MEMOIRS, REMINISCENCES, INTERVIEWS

Also see, in Appendix A, Irie (AA17), Kitazawa (AA22), Wulfsberg (AA49), and Sorani (AA270).

F1 Aldington, Richard. D.H. LAWRENCE: PORTRAIT OF A GENIUS,
    BUT.... New York: Duell, Sloan, and Pearce, 1950.
            A balanced, judicious biography, as is indicated
            by the subtitle. Little critical comment and
            few new facts are offered. Superseded by bet-
            ter biographies, but remains interesting read-
            ing. Extracts reprinted in F123. Also see H218.

F2 -----. "Foreword." In D.H. LAWRENCE: A COMPOSITE BIOGRA-
    PHY. Ed. Edward Nehls. III, ix-xvii. See F123.
            Nehls's technique a stroke of genius appropriate
            for the biography of a genius. Reprinted in G81.

F3 -----. LIFE FOR LIFE'S SAKE: A BOOK OF REMINISCENCES. New
    York: Viking, 1941. Pp. 228-34, 301-09, 329-34, and passim.
            Memories of the Lawrences through the late teens
            and twenties. Extracts reprinted in F123 and
            F127.

F4 Allott, Kenneth, and Miriam Allott. "D.H. Lawrence and
    Blanche Jennings." REL, 1, No. 3 (1960), 57-76.
            Summarizes and quotes from DHL's important cor-
            respondence (20 letters, 1908-10) with Jennings,
            an Eastwood acquaintance and "enthusiast for
            socialism and Women's Suffrage."

F5 Alpers, Antony. THE LIFE OF KATHERINE MANSFIELD. 1953.
    2nd ed. New York: Viking, 1980. Passim.
            Numerous comments on the Lawrences and their re-
            lations with Mansfield and her husband, John Mid-
            dleton Murry.

F6 Armitage, Merle. TAOS QUARTET IN THREE MOVEMENTS. New
    York: Privately printed, 1950.
            Brief comments on the Lawrences and several barbed
            remarks about Mabel Luhan's "destructive" and "dan-
            gerous" influence on them. (Pamphlet--21pp.)

F7   Armytage, W.H.G. HEAVENS BELOW: UTOPIAN EXPERIMENTS IN
      ENGLAND, 1560-1960. London: Routledge, 1961. Pp. 385-97.
            History of the rise and fall of DHL's plan for
            an ideal community ("Rananim").

F8   Arnold, Armin. "D.H. Lawrence in Ascona?" In D.H. LAW-
      RENCE: THE MAN WHO LIVED. Ed. Robert B. Partlow and Harry
      T. Moore. Pp. 195-98. See G92.
            Speculation on DHL's feelings of jealousy (re:
            Otto Gross) and guilt (re: Ernest Weekley), dur-
            ing his solo travels in Switzerland (1913).

F9   Asquith, Cynthia M.E. "D.H. Lawrence." In REMEMBER AND
      BE GLAD. London: Barrie, 1952. Pp. 133-50.
            Memories of first meeting DHL, in 1913, his
            misery and despair during the war years, and
            his predominantly cheerful personality never-
            theless. Reprinted in F123 and F127.

F10   Asquith, Herbert H. "A Poet in Revolt." In MOMENTS OF
      MEMORY: RECOLLECTIONS AND IMPRESSIONS. London: Hutchin-
      son, 1937. Pp. 182-92.
            Memories of DHL (1913 and during the war), and
            appreciation of the poetic intensity of his
            prose.

F11   Barnes, T.R. "Introduction." In Lawrence's SELECTED
      POETRY AND PROSE. Ed. Barnes. London: Heinemann, 1957.
      Pp. vii-xv.
            Brief biographical summary, introducing a
            slender school-text anthology of DHL's works.

F12   Barr, Barbara Weekley. "I Look Back." TWENTIETH CENTURY,
      165 (1959), 254-61.
            Touching memoir of Frieda, by her daughter, and
            defense of her elopement with DHL: "I believe
            she was right to act as she did."

F13   -----. "Memoir of D.H. Lawrence." In D.H. LAWRENCE. Ed.
      Stephen Spender. Pp. 8-10, 19-36. See G113.
            Reminiscence by Frieda's youngest daughter, con-
            centrating on DHL's last years, death and funer-
            al. Extracts reprinted in G127.

F14   Bedford, Sybille. ALDOUS HUXLEY: A BIOGRAPHY. New York:
      Knopf, 1974. Pp. 209-13, 222-28, and passim.
            Covers DHL's relations with Aldous and Maria
            Huxley, DHL's death, and Huxley's editing of
            DHL's letters (see C10).

F15 Bell, Quentin. BLOOMSBURY. New York: Basic Books, 1968.
     Pp. 70-78.
          Reasonable account of DHL's antagonism toward
          members of the Bloomsbury circle.

F16 Bennett, Michael. A VISITOR'S GUIDE TO EASTWOOD AND THE
     COUNTRYSIDE OF D.H. LAWRENCE. Nottingham: Nottinghamshire
     County Library, 1972.
          Travel guide, similar to Pugh (F135). Pamphlet
          (22 pp.) Also see F151.

F17 Bobbitt, Joan. "Lawrence and Bloomsbury: The Myth of a
     Relationship." ESSAYS IN LITERATURE, 1, No. 3 (1973),
     31-42.
          DHL's response to individuals in the Bloomsbury
          circle mixed, contrary to the myth of his in-
          tense dislike perpetuated by Bloomsbury.

F18 Boulton, James T. "Introduction." In LAWRENCE IN LOVE.
     Ed. Boulton. Pp. ix-xxviii. See C6.
          DHL's love affair with Louie Burrows (1909-12).

F19 Brett, Dorothy. LAWRENCE AND BRETT: A FRIENDSHIP. Phila-
     delphia: Lippincott, 1933.
          First-person memoir addressed to DHL by the
          painter and neighbor of the Lawrences in Taos.
          Brett's portrait is sympathetic, but not adul-
          atory toward DHL, prejudiced against Frieda.
          Extracts reprinted in F123 and F127.

F20 Brewster, Earl, and Achsah Brewster. D.H. LAWRENCE: REM-
     INISCENCES AND CORRESPONDENCE. London: Secker, 1934.
          Collection of letters from DHL (1921-30), with
          commentary, and a brief, sympathetic memoir by
          Achsah Brewster. The Brewsters met and became
          friends with the Lawrences on the continent and
          in Ceylon. Extracts reprinted in F123 and F127.

F21 Brooks, Emily Potter. "D.H. Lawrence: A Day in the Coun-
     try and a Poem in Autograph." DHLR, 9 (1976), 278-82.
          Memory of DHL, in 1909, and text of "an early
          version of 'Cherry Robbers'" given to Brooks
          by DHL.

F22 Bynner, Witter. JOURNEY WITH GENIUS: RECOLLECTIONS AND
     REFLECTIONS CONCERNING THE D.H. LAWRENCES. New York: Day,
     1951.
          Memoir of DHL in New Mexico and Mexico by a
          neighbor and traveling companion. Unflatteringly

emphasizes DHL's unstable temperament and admires the "long-suffering" Frieda. Extracts
reprinted in F123 and F127.

F23   -----. THE WORKS OF WITTER BYNNER: SELECTED LETTERS. Ed.
James Kraft. New York: Farrar, Straus and Giroux, 1981.
Passim.
Numerous letters to and about DHL.

F24   -----. WITTER BYNNER'S PHOTOGRAPHS OF D.H. LAWRENCE. Santa
Fe, N.M.: Great Southwest Books, 1981.
Expensive, limited edition of twenty-five photo-
graphs of DHL and companions, in New Mexico and
Mexico (1922-23). [Not seen.]

F25   Callow, Philip. SON AND LOVER: THE YOUNG LAWRENCE. New
York: Stein and Day, 1975.
The story of DHL's life "reads like a novel."
So does this biography (through 1918). A more
useful and more objective account than many,
but still no competition for Moore (F112),
Nehls (F123), and Sagar (F143).

F26   Carswell, Catherine. THE SAVAGE PILGRIMAGE: A NARRATIVE
OF D.H. LAWRENCE. New York: Harcourt, 1932.
Sympathetic and well-balanced memoir, except
for some intrusive controversy with Murry (see
F121), by the novelist and London friend of
DHL. Its title has been widely adopted as an
apt metaphor for DHL's career. Extracts reprinted in F123, F127, G5, and G20. A recent
reprinting of THE SAVAGE PILGRIMAGE, by Cambridge Univ. Press (1982), includes a memoir
of Catherine Carswell by John Carswell, her
son. Also see F109.

F27   Carter, Frederick. D.H. LAWRENCE AND THE BODY MYSTICAL.
London: Archer, 1932.
Memoir of DHL and commentary on their shared
mystical ideas, by the author of DRAGON OF REV-
ELATION (1932), the book for which DHL's APO-
CALYPSE (A76) was originally intended as an
introduction.

F28   Chambers, Jessie. "The Collected Letters of Jessie Chambers." Ed. George J. Zytaruk. DHLR, 12 (1979), 1-237.
101 letters to various correspondents (1908-
43), by DHL's adolescent sweetheart and confi-
dante. Most letters concern DHL, though no

letters to DHL are included. Zytaruk provides
an "Introduction," generally concerned with
Jessie and the correspondents (pp. ix-xxxiii),
and extensive editorial notes.

F29 -----. [E.T.]. D.H. LAWRENCE: A PERSONAL RECORD BY E.T.
1935. 2nd ed. Ed. Jonathan D. Chambers. New York: Barnes
and Noble, 1965.
Recollections of early friendship with DHL, by
the original of Miriam in SONS AND LOVERS, con-
stituting one of the most valuable memoirs.
Jessie helps to indicate the importance of DHL's
early environment and family life for his work,
although part of her purpose, to correct the
fictional portrait in SONS AND LOVERS with fact,
is irrelevant. The second edition includes
brief pieces by J.D. Chambers, Helen Corke, May
Holbrook, and J.A. Bramley on the Lawrence-Jes-
sie relationship. Several portions published
previously in EUROPEAN QUARTERLY, 1 (1934), 36-
45; 106-14, 159-68. Extracts reprinted in F123,
F127, G20, L3, L5, and L7. Also see below,
F36, and F57.

F30 Chambers, Jonathan D. "Memories of D.H. Lawrence." RMS,
16 (1972), 5-17.
Reminiscences of DHL's relationship with his
sister, Jesse, the model for Miriam (in SL).
Also see above.

F31 Chambers, Maria Cristina. "Afternoons in Italy with D.H.
Lawrence." TQ, 7, No. 4 (1964), 114-20.
Memories of a stay with the Lawrences, in 1929,
by a Mexican-American acquaintance (no relation
to Jessie Chambers, above).

F32 Chapman, Robert T. "Lawrence, Lewis, and the Comedy of
Literary Reputations." STC, No. 6 (1970), pp. 85-95.
The falls and rises of DHL's and Wyndham Lewis's
reputations affected by public relations in the
publishing industry.

F33 Clark, Ronald W. THE LIFE OF BERTRAND RUSSELL. London:
Cape and Weidenfeld and Nicolson, 1975. Pp. 259-66 and
passim.
Describes DHL's and Russell's stormy association, during the war years. Also see F139, F140,
and V36.

F34   Cobau, William W. "A View from Eastwood: Conversations
       with Mrs. O.L. Hopkin." DHLR, 9 (1976), 126-36.
           Memories of DHL in Eastwood, provided by the
           second wife of one of DHL's "closest friends,"
           Willie Hopkin. See Émile Delavenay's response
           and corrections in DHLR, 9 (1976), 409-17.
           Also see F48 and F133.

F35   Cooke, Sheila M., comp. D.H. LAWRENCE AND NOTTINGHAMSHIRE,
       1885-1910. Nottingham: Nottinghamshire County Council Lei-
       sure Services Department, 1980.
           Packet of essays, stories, photographs, and let-
           ters, by or concerning DHL, illustrating his
           Nottinghamshire background.

F36   Corke, Helen. D.H. LAWRENCE: THE CROYDON YEARS. Austin:
       Univ. of Texas Press, 1965.
           Collects previously published memoirs of DHL
           (LAWRENCE AND APOCALYPSE [1933] and two later
           essays [1959, 1962]) and of Jessie Chambers
           (D.H. LAWRENCE'S "PRINCESS" [1951]), by the
           original of Helena in THE TRESPASSER, a teach-
           ing colleague at Croydon and early reader of
           his manuscripts. The memoir of DHL reconstructs
           their conversations, in an attempt to capture
           his thought. Extracts reprinted in F123. Also
           see F118.

F37   -----. "D.H. Lawrence: The Early Stage." DHLR, 4 (1971),
       111-21.
           Memories of DHL during "perhaps the most unhappy
           and sterile" period of his life (1909-12). More
           fully developed in her IN OUR INFANCY (below).

F38   -----. IN OUR INFANCY: AN AUTOBIOGRAPHY. PART I: 1882-
       1912. Cambridge: Cambridge Univ. Press, 1975. Pp. 160,
       166-67, 174-221.
           Account of her friendship with DHL (1908-12),
           with backgrounds to THE TRESPASSER (based on
           Corke's tragic love affair). Also includes
           her "Freshwater Diary," 1909-10 (pp. 222-35;
           reprinted in K6), which DHL used as a primary
           source in writing THE TRESPASSER, and several
           letters from DHL. Extracts reprinted in F127.
           Also see above, F118, and K1.

F39 Crotch, Martha Gordon. MEMORIES OF FRIEDA LAWRENCE. Edin-
burgh: Tragara Press, 1975.
> Memories of Frieda in Southern France and Flor-
> ence in the early thirties, of her developing
> liaison with Angelo Ravagli, and of her attempts
> to settle DHL's estate, extracted from a still
> unpublished memoir. (Pamphlet--39 pp.) Also
> see F113.

F40 Davies, Rhys. "The Bandol Phoenix." 1940. In PRINT OF
A HARE'S FOOT: AN AUTOBIOGRAPHICAL BEGINNING. London:
Heinemann, 1969. Pp. 136-48.
> The Welsh novelist's memories of DHL's "extra-
> ordinary attraction as a person," as well as
> his "irascibility and irritation," and account
> of their friendship during DHL's last years
> (1928-30). Reprinted in F123 and F127 (ex-
> tracts).

F41 Delany, Paul. D.H. LAWRENCE'S NIGHTMARE: THE WRITER AND
HIS CIRCLE IN THE YEARS OF THE GREAT WAR. New York: Basic
Books, 1978.
> Specialized biographical study of the Lawrences'
> four "critical" years in England during the war,
> 1914-18, which challenged DHL's "romantic and
> self-creating impulses." Delany shows the trans-
> formations in DHL's perceptions of man and so-
> ciety, reflected in his contemporary writings,
> and argues that any possibility for DHL achiev-
> ing "reconciliation" with the "English estab-
> lishment" was destroyed by his disastrous rela-
> tions with the London literati (Ottoline Mor-
> rell, Bertrand Russell, and the Bloomsbury
> group). Judicious biographical criticism in-
> terspersed throughout.

F42 -----, ed. "Halliday's Progress: Letters of Philip Heseltine, 1915-21." DHLR, 13 (1980), 119-33.
> Publishes, with commentary, four letters from
> Heseltine to various correspondents (1915-21),
> contributing background to DHL's portrait of
> him (as Halliday) and his mistress ("Minette")
> in WL.

F43 Delavenay, Émile. D.H. LAWRENCE: THE MAN AND HIS WORK:
THE FORMATIVE YEARS, 1885-1919. Trans. Katherine M.
Delavenay. Carbondale: Southern Illinois Univ. Press,
1972.
> English translation, slightly revised, of the
> 1969 French biography which, in turn, was largely

written in the mid-thirties and shows no recognition of more recent scholarship. Delavenay
attempts to reconstruct DHL's "psychological
and intellectual" formation as he notes the
influence of Edward Carpenter (style), John
Noyes (social idealism), Otto Weininger (androgyny) and Stewart Chamberlain (fascism). Some
useful ideological backgrounds and interesting
speculations on the real reasons for the sup-
pression of THE RAINBOW, but most of the biographical material is outdated and the suggestions of *Einfluss* tenuous. See F52 and AA7.

F44   -----. D.H. LAWRENCE AND EDWARD CARPENTER: A STUDY IN
EDWARDIAN TRANSITION. New York: Taplinger, 1971.
Despite the absolute lack of evidence to support
DHL's knowledge of Carpenter or his work, this
speculative *Einfluss* study traces stylistic and
ideological similarities between the two authors.
Delavenay sees THE RAINBOW and WOMEN IN LOVE
particularly indebted to Carpenter, especially
in the treatment of Birkin's homosexuality.
See H48.

F45   -----. "D.H. Lawrence and Jessie Chambers: The Traumatic
Experiment." DHLR, 12 (1979), 305-25.
Examines the sexual tensions between DHL and
Jessie leading to the eventual break-up of
their relationship.

F46   -----. "D.H. Lawrence entre six femmes et entre deux
cultures." EA, 22 (1969), 152-58.
DHL's letters to Louie Burrows best seen in
the context of his general relations with several women, between 1910 and 1912. Review of
Boulton's edition (see C6). [In French].

F47   D.H. LAWRENCE REVIEW. 2 (1969), iv-vi, 1-92. "John Middleton Murry Number."
Collects seven essays on Murry, chiefly concerned with his literary, political, and social
views. Includes Dorothy Brett's pencil sketch
of Murry, and two essays on his relationship
with DHL: F71 and F89.

F48   D.H. LAWRENCE REVIEW. 9 (1976), 1-156. "Correspondence
and Conversations."
Special issue containing the Lawrences' letters
to Dorothy Brett (see C4) and three biographical
articles. Includes F34, F126, and F141.

F49   D.H. LAWRENCE REVIEW. 14 (1981), 1-113. "D.H. Lawrence:
       Friendship and Reputation."
              Collects two important essays on DHL's literary
              reputation in the thirties, an article on his
              relationship with Mabel Luhan, a story by Eliz-
              abeth Von Vogt culminating at DHL's Taos ranch,
              and a set of poems by Alamgir Hashmi inspired
              by the ranch. Includes F77, F109, and F138.

F50   Douglas, Norman. "Mr. D.H. Lawrence." In LOOKING BACK:
       AN AUTOBIOGRAPHICAL EXCURSION. New York: Harcourt, 1933.
       Pp. 282-91.
              Negative view of DHL's diffuse and formless art,
              and his resentful personality. Reprinted in
              F123 and F127 (extract).

F51   Ehrenzweig, Robert [Robert Lucas]. FRIEDA LAWRENCE: THE
       STORY OF FRIEDA VON RICHTHOFEN AND D.H. LAWRENCE. 1972.
       Tr. Geoffrey Skelton. New York: Viking, 1973.
              Popular biography dealing at length with Frieda's
              and DHL's relationship, but offering no start-
              ling revelations. See AA63.

F52   Fabre-Luce, Alfred. LA VIE DE D.H. LAWRENCE. Paris: Ber-
       nard Grasset, 1935.
              Early, moderately successful attempt at an ob-
              jective, yet sympathetic biography, an accomp-
              lishment perhaps possible only from outside the
              arena of American and English controversy among
              DHL's disciples and despisers. The standard
              French biography, until superseded by Delavenay
              (see F43). [In French.]

F53   Fabricant, Noah D. "The Lingering Cough of D.H. Lawrence."
       In THIRTEEN FAMOUS PATIENTS. Philadelphia: Chilton, 1960.
       Pp. 116-27.
              Medical account of DHL's tuberculosis.

F54   Fay, Eliot Gilbert. LORENZO IN SEARCH OF THE SUN: D.H.
       LAWRENCE IN ITALY, MEXICO, AND THE AMERICAN SOUTHWEST.
       New York: Bookman Associates, 1953.
              Worshipful account of DHL's life, 1920-30,
              based on letters and published memoirs. Slight
              and outdated.

F55   Firchow, Peter E. "Rico and Julia: The Hilda Doolittle--
       D.H. Lawrence Affair Reconsidered." JML, 8 (1980), 51-76.
              The quadrangular relations among DHL, Aldington,
              H.D., and Arabella Yorke, in 1917, survive in sev-
              eral works of fiction (including AARON'S ROD).

F56 Ford, Ford Madox. "D.H. Lawrence." In PORTRAITS FROM
     LIFE. Boston: Houghton Mifflin, 1937. Pp. 70-89.
          Untrustworthy reminiscences of Ford's first
          meeting with DHL in his office at the ENGLISH
          REVIEW, in 1909. Also see F66. Reprinted in
          F123 and F127 (extract).

F57 Ford, George H. "Jessie Chambers' Last Tape on D.H. Law-
     rence." MOSAIC, 6, No. 3 (1973), 1-12.
          On Jesse's records of her relationship with DHL
          (see F29).

F58 Forster, E.M., T.S. Eliot, and Clive Bell. "Letter[s] to
     the NATION AND ATHENAEUM." 1930. In D.H. LAWRENCE: A
     CRITICAL ANTHOLOGY. Ed. Harry Coombes. Pp. 218-20. See
     G20.
          Convenient reprint of five important letters:
          Forster's protesting the scurrilous obituaries
          of DHL ("he was the greatest imaginative novel-
          ist of our generation"), Eliot's objection to
          his protest, and three responses to Eliot.

F59 Foster, Joseph O'Kane. D.H. LAWRENCE IN TAOS. Alburquer-
     que: Univ. of New Mexico Press, 1972.
          Semi-fictional memoir by one of the Taos circle,
          frequently paraphrasing the letters and other
          memoirs.

F60 Fraser, Grace Lovat. IN THE DAYS OF MY YOUTH. London:
     Cassell, 1970. Pp. 133-52.
          Memory of a year's friendship (1909-10) with a
          shy, insecure, yet affectionate DHL in London
          (among Pound, Ford, and others). Publishes
          eleven letters (1909-11) and a poem by DHL.

F61 Furbank, P.N. "D.H. Lawrence and Forster." In E.M. FOR-
     STER: A LIFE. London: Secker and Warburg, 1977-78. II,
     6-13 and passim.
          Forster's meeting, friendship, and quarrel with
          DHL, and his admiration for DHL's writings. See
          F58, H120, and Z28.

F62 Garnett, David. "D.H. Lawrence and Frieda." In GREAT
     FRIENDS. London: Macmillan, 1979. Pp. 74-93.
          "Bunny" Garnett's memories of the Lawrences
          (1912-18), drawn from his previously published
          three-volume autobiography THE GOLDEN ECHO

(1954-62), extracts of which have also been reprinted in F123 and F127. Earlier version originally published in G113.

F63 Gerhardie, William A. "D.H. Lawrence is Dim about Shaw."
     In MEMOIRS OF A POLYGLOT. 1931. Rev. ed. London: Mac-
     Donald, 1973. Pp. 278-84.
          Humorous and generally unsympathetic memoir of
          meeting DHL, in London, in 1925. Reprinted in
          F123 and F127 (extract).

F64 Ghiselin, Brewster. "D.H. Lawrence in Bandol: A Memoir."
     WHR, 12 (1958), 293-305.
          Valuable memoir of a fortnight's visit and con-
          versations with DHL, in January 1929, recalling
          his amusement with "human absurdity," his vivid
          speech, his composition of PANSIES, his self-
          detachment, and his uncertainty about his future.
          Reprinted in F123 and F127.

F65 Gillès, Daniel. D.H. LAWRENCE, OU, LE PURITAIN SCANDALEUX.
     Paris: René Julliard, 1964.
          Competent biography of DHL, contributing little
          new information about his life and avoiding crit-
          ical commentary on his works. [In French.]

F66 Goldring, Douglas. "D.H. Lawrence." In LIFE INTERESTS.
     London: MacDonald, 1948. Pp. 83-108.
          Memories of DHL, "the greatest figure among my
          contemporaries," from his first appearance at
          the ENGLISH REVIEW offices (1909), to his last
          years (also see F56). Includes reprint of Gold-
          ring's critical article on DHL (see H142), pp.
          100-08. Extracts reprinted in F123 and F127.

F67 Gray, Cecil. MUSICAL CHAIRS, OR BETWEEN TWO STOOLS. Lon-
     don: Home and Van Thal, 1948. Pp. 126-42.
          Recounts his friendship with DHL, in Cornwall
          and London (1917), describes the authorities'
          war-time persecution of DHL as an alleged spy,
          and remarks on the difficulty of remaining DHL's
          friend. Speculates that, because of his back-
          ground, personal magnetism, and psychological
          make-up, DHL, had he lived and not been an art-
          ist, might have become a British Hitler. Re-
          printed in F123.

F68   -----. "The War and D.H. Lawrence." In PETER WARLOCK: A
MEMOIR OF PHILIP HESELTINE. London: Cape, 1934. Pp. 93-
122.
>   The insurmountable demands DHL placed on his
>   friends, observed in an account of the rise
>   and fall of his friendship with Heseltine (1915-
>   16), whom he caricatures as Julius Halliday in
>   WL. Extracts reprinted in F123 and F127. Also
>   see F93 and N107.

F69   Green, Martin. "THE COMPOSITE BIOGRAPHY as Composition
Text." In A D.H. LAWRENCE MISCELLANY. Ed. Harry T. Moore.
Pp. 154-67. See G81.
>   Variety of styles and strategies of presenta-
>   tion in the biography (see F123).

F70   -----. THE VON RICHTHOFEN SISTERS: THE TRIUMPHANT AND THE
TRAGIC MODES OF LOVE. ELSE AND FRIEDA VON RICHTHOFEN, OTTO
GROSS, MAX WEBER, AND D.H. LAWRENCE IN THE YEARS 1870-1970.
New York: Basic Books, 1974.
>   Excellent backgrounds on Frieda's German adole-
>   scence, noting DHL's indirect connections with
>   the intelligentsia of Bavaria and, later, the
>   Weimar Republic.

F71   Griffin, Ernest G. "The Circular and the Linear: The Middleton Murry--D.H. Lawrence Affair." DHLR, 2 (1969), 76-
92.
>   The brief, "tangential" relationship of the dis-
>   similar personalities, Murry and DHL, their am-
>   bivalence toward each other, and Murry's life-
>   long attempt to "reconcile" his differences with
>   DHL (see F122). Reprinted, with revisions, in
>   his JOHN MIDDLETON MURRY (New York: Twayne,
>   1969), pp. 121-40. Also see F47.

F72   Hahn, Emily. LORENZO: D.H. LAWRENCE AND THE WOMEN WHO
LOVED HIM. New York: Lippincott, 1975.
>   Largely unnecessary, gossipy, and inaccurate
>   account of DHL's relationship with women (e.g.,
>   his mother, Jessie Chambers, Helen Corke,
>   Frieda, "H.D.," Mabel Luhan, Dorothy Brett,
>   and others).

F73   Heilbrun, Carolyn G. THE GARNETT FAMILY. New York: Macmillan, 1961. Pp. 142-62.
>   DHL's relationship with Edward Garnett, his lit-
>   erary mentor, with passing references to his
>   son, David Garnett, and the Lawrences.

F74 Holmes, Colin. "A Study of D.H. Lawrence's Social Origins."
     LITERATURE AND HISTORY, 6 (1980), 82-93, 42.
              DHL's social backgrounds less modest than most
              biographers realize. He was certainly not from
              the typical "working class" of his place and
              time.

F75 Holroyd, Michael. "Sex, Censorship, and D.H. Lawrence."
     In LYTTON STRACHEY: A CRITICAL BIOGRAPHY. New York: Holt,
     Rinehart, and Winston, 1968. II, 158-64.
              DHL's and Strachey's "mutual aversion" and
              Strachey's alarm at the "belligerent zealotry"
              of the authorities in their suppression of R,
              in 1915.

F76 Huxley, Juliette. "Ottoline." ADAM INTERNATIONAL REVIEW,
     Nos. 370-75 (1973), pp. 92-93.
              Reminiscence of the production of *tableaux viv-
              antes* at Garsington (Lady Ottoline Morrell's),
              Christmas 1916, an event incorporated by DHL
              into WL.

F77 Jackson, Dennis. "'The Stormy Petrel of Literature Is
     Dead': The World Press Reports D.H. Lawrence's Death."
     DHLR, 14 (1981), 33-72.
              Important correction to the received "history"
              of DHL's reputation. Jackson's survey of over
              200 English-language newspapers reveals that,
              contrary to the popular myth, DHL's death was
              reported prominently and with "considerably
              more praise and sympathy than condemnation."
              Summarizes and comments on several obituaries
              and provides an international bibliography of
              120 newspaper, journal, and other articles on
              his death. See F49.

F78 James, Clive. "D.H. Lawrence in Transit." In D.H. LAW-
     RENCE. Ed. Stephen Spender. Pp. 159-69. See G113.
              Summarizes DHL's travels, with slight comment
              on their influence on his fiction and on the
              travel books.

F79 Jarrett, James L. "D.H. Lawrence and Bertrand Russell."
     In A D.H. LAWRENCE MISCELLANY. Ed. Harry T. Moore. Pp.
     168-87. See G81.
              Study of DHL's and Russell's "brief friendship
              and long quarrel," concentrating on their ideo-
              logical differences.

F80   Juta, Jan. "Portrait in Shadow: D.H. Lawrence." COLUMBIA
      LIBRARY COLUMNS, 18, No. 3 (1969), 3-16.
              Memoir of DHL in Italy, by his portraitist
              (1920). Reprinted, with revisions, from F123.

F81   Keith, W.J. "Spirit of Place and *Genius Loci*: D.H. Law-
      rence and Rolf Gardiner." DHLR, 7 (1974), 127-38.
              Examines the acquaintance of DHL and Gardiner
              (English youth leader and agriculturist, 1902-
              71), in the 1920s, and their influences on one
              another. See subsequent comment by Émile Dela-
              venay and reply by Keith: DHLR, 7 (1974), 291-
              94.

F82   Keynes, John Maynard. "My Early Beliefs." In TWO MEMOIRS:
      DR. MELCHIOR: A DEFEATED ENEMY, AND MY EARLY BELIEFS. Lon-
      don: Hart-Davis, 1949. Pp. 78-103.
              First publication of Keynes's memoir (1938) of
              meeting DHL, in 1914, and summary of his per-
              sonal beliefs that DHL had summarily rejected.
              Extracts reprinted in F123 and F127.

F83   King, R.W. MR. DAVID HERBERT LAWRENCE: AN INFORMAL NOTE.
      Croydon: Education Committee, 1957.
              Not seen. (Pamphlet.)

F84   Land, Myrick. "As a Would-be Messiah, Mr. D.H. Lawrence
      Endures His Sad Lot Among a Host of Friends." In THE FINE
      ART OF LITERARY MAYHEM: A LIVELY ACCOUNT OF FAMOUS
      WRITERS AND THEIR FEUDS. New York: Holt, 1962. Pp. 136-60.
              Principally concerns John Middleton Murry's var-
              ious betrayals of DHL. See F121.

F85   Lawrence, Ada, and G. Stuart Gelder. YOUNG LORENZO: THE
      EARLY LIFE OF D.H. LAWRENCE: CONTAINING HITHERTO UNPUB-
      LISHED LETTERS, ARTICLES AND REPRODUCTIONS OF PICTURES.
      Florence: Orioli, 1931.
              Valuable and interesting account of DHL's youth,
              written, with assistance, by his sister. Much
              useful background to SONS AND LOVERS. Also in-
              cludes selected letters (1911-30), two poems,
              two essays, a story ("The Fly in the Ointment,"
              A16), and nine reproductions of DHL's paintings.
              The English edition (London: Secker, 1932) drops
              an essay and the paintings and adds a poem and
              the sketch "Adolph" (1920; see B16). Extracts
              reprinted in F127 and L3. Also see Z94.

F86   Lawrence, Frieda. "NOT I, BUT THE WIND..." New York:
      Viking, 1934.
              Well-written and interesting memoir of Frieda's
              and DHL's life together, from their meeting and
              elopement to 1930. Includes a moving account of
              DHL's death. Extracts reprinted in F123, F127,
              G20, and L3.

F87   -----. THE MEMOIRS AND CORRESPONDENCE. Ed. Ernest W.
      Tedlock. 1961. Rev. ed. New York: Knopf, 1964.
              A second memoir by Frieda, reconstructed from
              the fragmentary manuscript she left at her
              death. Tedlock has also collected many of
              her occasional papers and a large but not com-
              plete correspondence. Extracts reprinted in
              G1, G20, G48, L1, and L7. Also see F160.

F88   Lea, Frank A. "Murry and Marriage." DHLR, 2 (1969), 1-21.
              Murry gradually accepted the validity of DHL's
              attacks on his search for "exclusiveness" and
              "spirituality" in marriage. See F47.

F89   -----. THE LIFE OF JOHN MIDDLETON MURRY. London: Methuen,
      1959. Pp. 39-47 and passim.
              Valuable account of the Lawrence-Murry relation-
              ship.

F90   Leavis, F.R. "Romantic and Heretic?" SPECTATOR, 202
      (1959), 196-97.
              Acclaims Nehls's biography (F123) as a "clas-
              sical work...[that] gives us an incomparable
              insight into the nature of creative genius."
              Review essay. Reprinted in G20.

F91   Lesemann, Maurice. "D.H. Lawrence in New Mexico." BOOKMAN
      (New York), 59 (1924), 29-32.
              Memory of meetings and conversations with DHL
              shortly after his arrival in America in 1922.
              Reprinted in F123 and F127.

F92   Levin, Alexandra L., and Lawrence L. Levin. "The Seltzers
      & D.H. Lawrence: A Biographical Narrative." In Lawrence's
      LETTERS TO THOMAS AND ADELE SELTZER. Ed. Gerald M. Lacy.
      Pp. 171-201. See C12.
              Story of the Seltzers' publishing firm and their
              relations with DHL (c. 1920-25).

F93   Lindsay, Jack. FANFROLICO AND AFTER. London: Lane, 1962.
      Pp. 88-90, 149-52, and passim.
            Lindsay's objective account of Philip Hesel-
            tine's break with DHL (see F68) and memory of
            his role in the establishment of the· Mandrake
            Press, publisher of DHL's paintings (see A38).

F94   Lowenfels, Walter. ELEGY IN THE MANNER OF A REQUIEM IN
      MEMORY OF D.H. LAWRENCE. Paris: Carrefour, 1932.
            Bombastic and ecstatic elegy (506 lines). (Pamph-
            let--33 pp.)

F95   Luhan, Mabel Dodge. LORENZO IN TAOS. New York: Knopf,
      1932.
            Notoriously unreliable and often unintentionally
            comic memoir of DHL's stay in New Mexico, by an
            'unbalanced' worshipper. Luhan is jealous of
            all rivals to DHL's attention, particularly
            Frieda. Extracts reprinted in F123 and F127.

F96   Lunn, H.K. [Hugh Kingsmill]. THE LIFE OF D.H. LAWRENCE.
      New York: Dodge, 1938.
            Full biography of DHL, a pastiche of previously
            available materials from memoirs and letters.
            The book has no critical value, is unsympathetic
            to DHL, and has been superseded by better works.
            Extracts reprinted in F123 and F127.

F97   McDonald, Marguerite B. "An Evening with the Lawrences."
      DHLR, 5 (1972), 63-66.
            The wife of DHL's first bibliographer (see E31)
            recalls meeting the Lawrences in New York, in
            1925, and conversation concerning Mansfield and
            Murry, among other matters.

F98   MacKenzie, Compton. "Memories of D.H. Lawrence." In ON
      MORAL COURAGE. London: Collins, 1962. Pp. 104-19.
            Memoir of DHL (1914 and after), and suggestion
            that LCL was written in competition with ULYSSES
            (1922):"'This ULYSSES muck is more disgusting
            than Casanova,' he proclaimed. 'I *must* show
            that it can be done without muck.'" Also see
            U45.

F99   -----. MY LIFE AND TIMES: OCTAVE FIVE, 1915-1923. London:
      Chatto and Windus, 1966. Pp. 164-73, 176-79, 183-85, 190-
      93, and passim.
            Assorted memories of and correspondence from
            DHL (1919-20). MacKenzie's "fictionalized"

memories of DHL (1915, 1920) were also published in his FOUR WINDS OF LOVE tetralogy,
where DHL appears as Daniel Rayner in both
THE SOUTH WIND OF LOVE (1937) and THE WEST
WIND OF LOVE (1940). "Apart from names and
places most of it is factually and conversa-
tionally exact" (quoted by Nehls, II, 455,
n. 53; see F123). Also see extracts from
the novels reprinted in F123.

F100 Mansfield, Katherine. "A Letter about the Lawrences."
In A D.H. LAWRENCE MISCELLANY. Ed. Harry T. Moore. Pp.
131-33. See G81.
       Account of a Lawrence-Frieda quarrel (1916).

F101 -----. JOURNAL OF KATHERINE MANSFIELD. Ed. John Middleton Murry. 1927. Rev. ed. London: Constable, 1954.
Passim.
       Numerous references to the Lawrences as friends,
       neighbors, antagonists, and admirers. Extracts
       reprinted in F123.

F102 Marcel, Gabriel. "In Memoriam--D.H. Lawrence." NOUVELLE
REVUE FRANÇAISE, 34 (1930), 570-72.
       Obituary memoir, recalling (from a 1929 con-
       versation) DHL's great love of France and dis-
       appointment with human frailties and absurdi-
       ties. [In French.]

F103 Mason, H.A. "Lawrence in Love." CAMBRIDGE QUARTERLY, 4
(1969), 181-200.
       DHL's views and attitudes, c. 1906-12, based
       on a survey of his letters to Louie Burrows
       (Boulton's edition is also reviewed herein;
       see C6).

F104 Mayer, Elizabeth. "An Afternoon with D.H. Lawrence." In
A D.H. LAWRENCE MISCELLANY. Ed. Harry T. Moore. Pp. 141-
43. See G81.
       Records some of DHL's views on literary trans-
       lation, expressed during a conversation in 1927.

F105 Meckier, Jerome. "Huxley's Lawrencian Interlude: The
'Latin Compromise' that Failed." In ALDOUS HUXLEY: SAT-
IRE AND STRUCTURE. London: Chatto and Windus, 1969. Pp.
78-123.
       On Huxley's and DHL's personal and literary
       relationship, clarifying Huxley's equivocal
       attitude toward DHL when alive and his later
       rejection of DHL's "Latin compromise."

F106   Merrild, Knud. A POET AND TWO PAINTERS: A MEMOIR OF
       D.H. LAWRENCE. London: Routledge, 1938. Reprinted as
       WITH D.H. LAWRENCE IN NEW MEXICO: A MEMOIR OF D.H. LAW-
       RENCE. New York: Barnes and Noble, 1965.
              Memoir by a Danish painter and brief member
              of the Taos circle, including "imagined" con-
              versations reconstructed from DHL's writings.
              Although Merrild had some direct contact with
              DHL, it was considerably less than his book
              would suggest.

F107   Meyers, Jeffrey. "D.H. and Frieda Lawrence: A Genius For
       Living." In MARRIED TO GENIUS. New York: Barnes and
       Noble, 1977. Pp. 145-73.
              Frieda's and DHL's struggle between "emotional
              and artistic commitment" and between submis-
              sion and dominance in their stormy but "basic-
              ally content" marriage.

F108   -----. "Friendship with D.H. Lawrence, 1913-1923." In
       KATHERINE MANSFIELD: A BIOGRAPHY. London: Hamilton, 1978.
       Pp. 78-104.
              Summarizes the writers' relationship, oscil-
              lating "between profound attachment and ex-
              treme hostility," Mansfield's criticisms of
              DHL's "male ignorance," and DHL's incorpora-
              tion of Mansfield and Murry into his works.

F109   -----. "Memoirs of D.H. Lawrence: A Genre of the Thir-
       ties." DHLR, 14 (1981), 1-32.
              Comparative study and evaluation of eleven ma-
              jor memoirs of DHL (ten published between 1931
              and 1935), commenting on the Murry-Carswell
              controversy, and attributing the eclipse of
              DHL's reputation until the mid-1950s largely
              to Murry's "perverse books." See F49. Also
              see F26 and F121.

F110   Moore, Harry T. "Introduction: D.H. Lawrence and the
       'Censor-Morons.'" 1953. In SEX, LITERATURE, AND CEN-
       SORSHIP. Ed. Moore. Pp. 9-30. See B26.
              Surveys DHL's battles with the censors, from
              R to LCL.

F111   -----. POSTE RESTANTE: A LAWRENCE TRAVEL CALENDAR. Berk-
       eley: Univ. of California Press, 1956.
              A useful adjunct to Moore's biography (below),
              a calendar of where DHL was and when he was

there, from birth to death. Particularly
helpful for any biographical or historical
research on DHL between 1912 and 1930, the
years for which it is most accurate. Includes H329. Also see Sagar's similar "calendar" of DHL's works (E40).

F112   -----.   THE PRIEST OF LOVE: A LIFE OF D.H. LAWRENCE. 1954.
New York: Farrar, Straus and Giroux, 1974.
A nice complement to the anecdote-memoir
"Composite Biography" by Nehls (F123). Originally entitled THE INTELLIGENT HEART, Moore's
straight-forward, yet scholarly account of
DHL's life, refreshingly free of special bi-
ases, is based upon thorough research among
the numerous surviving letters, papers, memoirs, and documents. Moore avoids critical
discussion of the works (see his critical
study, G80). Both Moore and Sagar (see F143)
are highly-recommended, authoritative lives.
Extracts of original edition reprinted in
F123 and F127. (Note: A feature-length film
of DHL's life, based on Moore's biography,
was released in 1981.) Also see V47.

F113   Moore, Harry T., and Dale B. Montague, eds.   FRIEDA LAW-
RENCE AND HER CIRCLE: LETTERS FROM, TO AND ABOUT FRIEDA
LAWRENCE. Hamden, Conn.: Archon, 1981.
Gathers five groups of correspondence, between
Frieda and Edward W. Titus, publisher of LCL,
Frieda and Caresse Crosby, who with her hus-
band Harry published "The Man Who Died," among
Frieda, Ada Lawrence, and Martha Gordon Crotch
(see F39), between Frieda's third husband Ang-
elo Ravagli and Crotch, and between Frieda and
Richard Aldington. Provides considerable back-
ground on Frieda's protection and management
of DHL's estate and reputation. Includes 130
letters (1929-56). Indexed.

F114   Moore, Harry T., and Warren Roberts.   D.H. LAWRENCE AND
HIS WORLD. New York: Viking, 1966.
Pictorial biography. Pleasurable light read-
ing and a useful introduction to DHL.

F115   Mori, Haruhide, ed.   A CONVERSATION ON D.H. LAWRENCE. Los
Angeles: Friends of the UCLA Library, 1974.
Transcription of a tape-recorded discussion
of DHL among Frieda, Aldous Huxley, Dorothy

                G. Mitchell, and Lawrence Clark Powell (1952).
                (Pamphlet--46 pp.)

F116 Morrell, Ottoline. OTTOLINE: THE EARLY MEMORIES OF LADY
      OTTOLINE MORRELL; OTTOLINE AT GARSINGTON: MEMOIRS OF LADY
      OTTOLINE MORRELL, 1915-1918. Ed. Robert Gathorne-Hardy.
      London: Faber, 1963, 1974. Pp. 272-80 and passim; Pp.
      35-40, 69-70, 77-79, and passim.
           DHL and Frieda among Bertrand Russell, Mans-
           field and Murry, and Michael Arlen, at the
           Morrells' estate, Garsington, and in London
           in 1915. (Ottoline was the model for Hermione
           and her home for Breadalby, in WL.) Extracts
           reprinted in F127.

F117 Morrill, Claire. A TAOS MOSAIC: PORTRAIT OF A NEW MEXICO
      VILLAGE. Albuquerque: Univ. of New Mexico Press, 1973.
      Pp. 106-28.
           Portraits of three women associated with DHL
           and Taos (Brett, Frieda, and Luhan), and note
           on DHL's responses to life in New Mexico.

F118 Muggeridge, Malcolm, and Helen Corke. "The Dreaming Wo-
      man--Helen Corke, in Conversation with Malcolm Muggeridge,
      tells of her relationship with D.H. Lawrence." LISTENER,
      80 (1968), 104-07.
           Corke comments on the backgrounds to THE TRES-
           PASSER and on Jessie Chambers (both more fully
           discussed by her in F36 and F38). Extract re-
           printed in F127.

F119 Murry, John Middleton. BETWEEN TWO WORLDS: AN AUTOBIOG-
      RAPHY. London: Cape, 1935. Pp. 261-429 and passim.
           Much self-serving discussion of Murry's rela-
           tions with the Lawrences, interspersed with
           other matters. Extracts reprinted in F123.

F120 -----. REMINISCENCES OF D.H. LAWRENCE. London: Cape,
      1933.
           Essays on DHL (originally published in ADELPHI
           [1930-31]), with disparaging remarks on Cars-
           well's memoir (see F26) and collected reviews
           of DHL's novels (including WL, THE LOST GIRL,
           AARON'S ROD, and LCL). Murry's attempts to
           understand his friendship with DHL, and its
           failure, make this volume more interesting as
           a biographical document. Extracts reprinted
           in F123 and F127. Review of LCL (see U53)
           earlier published in G84. Reviews reprinted
           in G5 (AARON'S ROD, WL), G20 (WL), G34 (all
           four), and M2 (WL). Also see G38 and G61.

F121   -----.   SON OF WOMAN: THE STORY OF D.H. LAWRENCE.   New
       York: Cape and Smith, 1931.
            Provocative, controversial, and ultimately
            very damaging study of the Oedipal conflict
            in DHL, seeing him exclusively in terms of
            the sexual and social frustrations caused
            by his mother's death. DHL's failures with
            women made him a misogynist; the failure of
            mankind to reciprocate his love made him a
            misanthrope. All the works are read strictly
            within this autobiographical programme. See
            F26. Extracts reprinted in F127, G20, L5,
            L7, and M2. Also for additional comment on
            this biography and on Murry's relations with
            DHL, see F26, F47, F71, F84, F88, F97, F108,
            F109, F116, G22, G38, G61, and H107.

F122   Nardi, Piero. LA VITA DI D.H. LAWRENCE. Milan: Monda-
       dori, 1947.
            The first full-scale, scholarly biography of
            DHL. Nardi divides DHL's life into six phases
            ("Miriam," "Frieda," "New Heaven and New
            Earth," "Mabel," "Dorothy," and "The Finish")
            and documents extensively the story of DHL's
            travels, relations, and works. Published as
            volume one of the first-collected edition of
            DHL's writings (see B29). Nardi's biography
            testifies to the consistently high critical
            estimate of DHL in Italy, at the same time as
            he was being chiefly ignored or ridiculed in
            the English-speaking world. See H273.

F123   Nehls, Edward, ed. D.H. LAWRENCE: A COMPOSITE BIOGRAPHY.
       3 vols. Madison: Univ. of Wisconsin Press, 1957-59.
            An indispensable compilation (over 1500 pp.
            text) of autobiography, essays, letters, mem-
            oirs (published and unpublished), and inter-
            views. Nehls creates a composite portrait
            of DHL by himself and by those who knew him.
            There is no running editorial commentary, yet
            the selections are so skillfully arranged
            that such apparatus is unnecessary. A living,
            if not entirely coherent, picture of DHL
            emerges from the multiple perspectives. Nehls
            publishes much new or relatively inaccessible
            material (e.g., fragments of DHL's projected
            novel on Robert Burns [reprinted in B18], six
            reproductions of DHL's paintings [from A38],

and the Chambers papers [see F166]), and his
"notes and sources," his biographical glossary
of "The Lawrence Circle," and his table of
major first editions are excellent research
aids. Extracts reprinted in B18, F80, F127,
G20, and L3. Includes F2, F9, F40, F56, F63,
F64, F67, F91, F125, F130, F136, F139, H142,
and extracts from E48, F1, F3, F19, F20, F22,
F26, F29, F36, F50, F62, F66, F68, F82, F86,
F95, F96, F99, F101, F112, F119, F120, F148,
F159, G2, H87, H331, S6, and Y29. Also see
F69, F90, F166, H151, H198, and H254.

F124 Neville, George Henry. A MEMOIR OF D.H. LAWRENCE (THE
BETRAYAL). Ed. Carl E. Baron. Cambridge: Cambridge
Univ. Press, 1981.
        Previously unpublished memoir of DHL, through
        1911, by the closest friend of his adolescence
        and early adulthood. Neville reviews the cir-
        cumstances of DHL's early life (assimilates
        article below), corrects the distortions of
        DHL's own "descriptions" of his family life
        and parents, describes the sexually liberat-
        ing effect of the Chambers's farm on DHL as a
        sensitive, prim adolescent, reviews several
        events of DHL's maturation later figuring in
        his fiction (e.g., the death of his brother
        Ernest), disputes Murry's uninformed portrait
        in SON OF WOMAN (F121, "the betrayal"), and
        comments on DHL's matured views and character
        on the eve of his career. Baron contributes
        notes, appendixes, and an extended introduc-
        tion (pp. 1-31) summarizing Neville's life
        (1886-1959), his friendship with DHL and writ-
        ing of the memoir in the early 1930s, and
        DHL's views of Neville and use of him in his
        writings (e.g., in THE WHITE PEACOCK, THE
        MARRIED MAN, and "Mr. Noon"). Both Neville
        and Baron stress the importance of DHL's "re-
        tarded" adolescent sexual development for his
        preoccupation with human sexuality in his art.

F125 -----. "The Early Days of D.H. Lawrence." LONDON MER-
CURY, 23 (1931), 477-80.
        A friend of DHL's youth describes their child-
        hood and later association as "Pagans" (student
        social group), as well as DHL's relationship
        with Jessie Chambers. Reprinted in F123 and
        F127, and assimilated into memoir above.

F126   Owen, Frederick I. "D.H. Lawrence and Max Mohr: A Late
        Friendship and Correspondence." DHLR, 9 (1976), 137-56.
                DHL's friendship and correspondence with the
                dramatist Mohr (1927-30). Lists, "with selec-
                tive summaries," thirty-one letters, cards,
                and notes between DHL and Mohr not published
                in C2. Fourteen of the letters previously
                published in NEUE RUNDSCHAU, 44, pt. 1 (1933),
                527-40. Also see F48.

F127   Page, Norman. D.H. LAWRENCE: INTERVIEWS AND RECOLLEC-
        TIONS. 2 vols. New York: Barnes and Noble, 1980.
                "Brings together the testimonies of more than
                seventy of those who knew Lawrence, thus con-
                stituting a more or less continuous narrative
                of his life." Duplicates in conception, and
                often in contents, the work of Nehls (see
                F123). Includes F64, F125, and extracts from
                F3, F9, F13, F19, F20, F22, F26, F29, F38,
                F40, F50, F56, F62, F63, F66, F68, F82, F85,
                F86, F91, F95, F96, F112, F116, F118, F120,
                F121, F123, F131, F136, F140, F148, F159,
                H120, and H191.

F128   Palmer, Paul R. "D.H. Lawrence and the 'Q.B.' in Sardin-
        ia." COLUMBIA LIBRARY COLUMNS, 18, No. 1 (1968), 3-9.
                Describes the Lawrences' trip to Sardinia,
                1921-22. "Q.B.," or "Queen Bee," in the ti-
                tle was DHL's nickname for Frieda.

F129   Panichas, George A. "The End of the Lamplight." ModA,
        14 (1970), 65-74.
                DHL in Lady Cynthia Asquith's diaries. See F9.

F130   Patmore, Brigit. "A Memoir of Frieda Lawrence." In A
        D.H. LAWRENCE MISCELLANY. Ed. Harry T. Moore. Pp. 137-
        40. See G81.
                Sympathetic and insightful analysis of the
                Lawrence-Frieda relationship. Reprinted from
                F123.

F131   -----. "Conversations with Lawrence." LONDON MAGAZINE,
        4, No. 6 (1957), 31-45.
                Memories of numerous meetings with DHL and
                Frieda, before and during the war, and in the
                late 1920s, in London and southern France.
                Extracts reprinted in F127.

F132   Patmore, Derek. "A Child's Memories of D.H. Lawrence."
       In A D.H. LAWRENCE MISCELLANY. Ed. Harry T. Moore. Pp.
       134-36. See G81.
              DHL in London, among the Imagists (c. 1914).

F133   Pollak, Paulina S. "The Letters of D.H. Lawrence to Sal-
       lie and Willie Hopkin." JML, 3 (1973), 24-34.
              Summary of DHL's relationship with the Hop-
              kins, finding his letters to these Eastwood
              friends (1910-29) a small but significant
              portion of his correspondence. (Most of the
              thirty-seven letters discussed have already
              been published--none are printed here.) Also
              see F34.

F134   Pollinger, Gerald. "The Lawrence Estate." In D.H. LAW-
       RENCE: THE MAN WHO LIVED. Ed. Robert B. Partlow and Har-
       ry T. Moore. Pp. 13-23. See G92.
              DHL's literary executor summarizes his duties
              and publishes the chief documents relating to
              DHL's estate (e.g., DHL's and Frieda's wills).

F135   Pugh, Bridget. THE COUNTRY OF MY HEART: A LOCAL GUIDE
       TO D.H. LAWRENCE. Nottingham: Nottingham Local History
       Council, 1972.
              An attractive guide to the Lawrence country.
              Pugh comments on DHL's use of local sites in
              his works (long and short fiction, drama and
              poetry), and includes maps of several possi-
              ble tours. See F16 and F151. Also see E41.

F136   Rhys, Ernest. EVERYMAN REMEMBERS. New York: Cosmopoli-
       tan, 1931. Pp. 243-49.
              Memory of DHL's awkward reading of his poems
              at one of Rhys's "gatherings of young poets"
              (in 1909). Reprinted in F123 and F127 (ex-
              tract).

F137   Rouse, A.L. "Nottingham: A Midlands Capital"; "D.H. Law-
       rence at Eastwood." In THE ENGLISH PAST: EVOCATIONS OF
       PERSONS AND PLACES. London: Macmillan, 1951. Pp. 196-
       216; 217-37.
              Impressions of Nottingham, past and present
              (with specific reference to DHL, pp. 212-15),
              and visits to Eastwood and DHL's surviving
              acquaintances. Reprinted, with revisions, in
              Rouse's TIMES, PERSONS, PLACES (London: Mac-
              millan, 1965), pp. 22-39, 1-21.

F138 Rudnick, Lois P. "D.H. Lawrence's New World Heroine:
      Mabel Dodge Luhan." DHLR, 14 (1981), 85-111.
            Examines DHL's relationship with Luhan and
            her influence on his portraits of women in
            his fiction of the mid and late 1920s. See
            F49.

F139 Russell, Bertrand. "D.H. Lawrence." In PORTRAITS FROM
      MEMORY, AND OTHER ESSAYS. New York: Simon and Schuster,
      1956. Pp. 104-08.
            Memoir. DHL a "positive force for evil" and
            his followers a "cult of insanity" between
            the wars (cf. Nazism). Reprinted in F123 and
            G20. Also see F33.

F140 -----. THE AUTOBIOGRAPHY OF BERTRAND RUSSELL. Vol. 2:
      1914-1944. Boston: Little, Brown, 1968. Pp. 10-16, 59-65.
            Interesting account of their "brief and hec-
            tic" acquaintance. Russell reiterates his belief
            that DHL was a protofascist (see below). Ex-
            tract reprinted in F127. See F33.

F141 Sagar, Keith. "Lawrence and Frieda: The Alternative
      Story." DHLR, 9 (1976), 117-25.
            Describes a possibly unreliable, alternate
            version of DHL's and Frieda's first acquain-
            tance, antedating Frieda's account by several
            years. See F48.

F142 -----. "Lawrence and the Wilkinsons." REL, 3, No. 4
      (1962), 62-75.
            Describes the Lawrences' acquaintance with
            the Wilkinsons, "a family of artists," in
            Italy (1926-28), quoting several extracts
            from the Wilkinson diaries and DHL's letters.

F143 -----. THE LIFE OF D.H. LAWRENCE: AN ILLUSTRATED BIOG-
      RAPHY. New York: Pantheon, 1980.
            Fine, accurate, and readable biography, very
            generously illustrated (165 photographs and
            documents).

F144 Schoenberner, Franz. "More About My Collaborators: D.H.
      Lawrence is Shocked." In CONFESSIONS OF A EUROPEAN INTEL-
      LECTUAL. New York: Macmillan, 1946. Pp. 282-92.
            Bavarian literary editor's memory of meeting
            DHL, in 1927, and comment on the Nazi's "eager"
            exploitation of a "much cheaper edition" of
            Lawrencean anti-rationalism. Also see AA262.

F145   Schorer, Mark. LAWRENCE IN THE WAR YEARS. Stanford:
       Stanford Univ. Libraries, 1968.
              Brief lecture for an exhibition of DHL's cor-
              respondence at Stanford. (Pamphlet--15 pp.)

F146   -----. "The Life of D.H. Lawrence." In D.H. LAWRENCE.
       Ed. Schorer. Pp. 3-106. See B5.
              Excellent brief biography, placing the works,
              with critical insight, in the context of the
              life.

F147   Sitwell, Edith. "A Man With Red Hair." In TAKEN CARE
       OF: THE AUTOBIOGRAPHY OF EDITH SITWELL. New York: Athe-
       neum, 1965. Pp. 122-27.
              Memory of tea with the Lawrences, in Tuscany
              in 1927, mixed with some prudish criticism of
              LCL.

F148   Sitwell, Osbert. "Portrait of Lawrence." In PENNY FOOL-
       ISH: A BOOK OF TIRADES AND PANEGYRICS. New York: Macmil-
       lan, 1935. Pp. 293-97.
              Memoir of a brief meeting with DHL (1927),
              and genial, general comments on his works.
              Extracts reprinted in F123 and F127.

F149   Skinner, Mollie L. THE FIFTH SPARROW: AN AUTOBIOGRAPHY.
       Sidney: Sidney Univ. Press, 1972. Pp. 109-18, 121-33,
       136-53, 158-61, 165-70.
              Memories of DHL in Australia, their subsequent
              correspondence and collaboration (THE BOY IN
              THE BUSH). Quotes several letters from DHL.
              Assimilates S6. Also see S2.

F150   Smith, Anne. "A New Adam and a New Eve--Lawrence and
       Women: A Biographical Overview." In LAWRENCE AND WOMEN.
       Ed. Smith. Pp. 9-48. See G112.
              Summarizes the biographical evidence for DHL's
              feminine personality traits, his male insecur-
              ity and homosexual phase in the war years, and
              his evident attitudes toward the women he knew.

F151   Spencer, Roy. D.H. LAWRENCE COUNTRY: A PORTRAIT OF HIS
       EARLY LIFE AND BACKGROUND WITH ILLUSTRATIONS, MAPS, AND
       GUIDES. London: Woolf, 1980.
              Commentary on DHL's early life and environ-
              ment, accounts of his parents, and visitor's
              guide for the Lawrence country. See F16 and
              F135.

F152   Temple, Frédéric J.   "Au Nouveau-Mexique sur les pas de
        D.H. Lawrence." NOUVELLE REVUE FRANÇAISE, N.S. 10 (1962),
        562-67.
                Visits to Taos and to DHL's surviving acquain-
                tances (Bynner, Brett, "Spud" Johnson). [In
                French.]

F153   Thurber, James. "My Memories of D.H. Lawrence." 1937.
        In THE ACHIEVEMENT OF D.H. LAWRENCE. Ed. Frederick Hoff-
        man and Harry T. Moore. Pp. 88-90. See G53.
                A delightful parody of the DHL memoir vogue,
                by a man who never met him.

F154   Trease, Geoffrey. THE PHOENIX AND THE FLAME: D.H. LAW-
        RENCE: A BIOGRAPHY. New York: Viking, 1973.
                Superficial biography, "novelized" through
                the questionable method of reconstructed scene
                and dialogue. Far inferior to Moore (F112),
                Nehls (F123), and Sagar (F143).

F155   Vitoux, Pierre. "Aldous Huxley and D.H. Lawrence: An At-
        tempt at Intellectual Sympathy." MLR, 69 (1974), 501-22.
                Huxley's interest in the dissociated person-
                ality and his successive responses, in his
                work, to the "balanced" personality of DHL.

F156   Wade, John Stevens. "D.H. Lawrence in Cornwall: An Inter-
        view with Stanley Hocking." DHLR, 6 (1973), 237-83.
                Hocking's extensive memories of DHL, Frieda,
                Cecil Gray, and others, when the Lawrences
                were tenants on his family's Tregerthen farm,
                in Cornwall (1916-17).

F157   Waterfield, Lina. "The Fortress of Aulla and D.H. Law-
        rence." In CASTLE IN ITALY: AN AUTOBIOGRAPHY. London:
        Murray, 1961. Pp. 119-43.
                Memories of the Lawrences in Italy, 1913-14
                (chiefly pp. 134-43).

F158   Weintraub, Stanley. REGGIE: A PORTRAIT OF REGINALD TURNER.
        New York: Braziller, 1965. Pp. 193-205.
                DHL in Florence, with Turner, Norman Douglas,
                and Maurice Magnus (1919), and his later lam-
                pooning of this group in AARON'S ROD and KANG-
                AROO.

F159   West, Rebecca. D.H. LAWRENCE. London: Secker, 1950.
                A sympathetic obituary-memoir, surveying Lon-
                don's reaction to DHL's death. West considers

his life and work "a spiritual victory." Reprinted as "Elegy" in her ENDING IN EARNEST (1931). Extracts reprinted in F123 and F127.

F160   White, Victor. "Frieda and the Lawrence Legend." SWR, 50 (1965), 388-97.

Frieda's MEMOIRS AND CORRESPONDENCE (see F87) clarify her "singlemindedness" in creating and sustaining the "legend" of DHL and his "credo."

F161   Wilding, Michael. "D.H. Lawrence in Australia: Some Recently Published Letters." AUSTRALIAN LITERARY STUDIES, 9 (1980), 373-77.

Gathers additional DHL references to Australia found in diverse, recently published letters.

F162   Williams, Tennessee. I RISE IN FLAME, CRIED THE PHOENIX: ACTING EDITION. A PLAY IN ONE ACT ABOUT D.H. LAWRENCE. 1941. New York: Dramatist Play Service, 1951.

DHL's death rendered as an heroic drama. Williams's most emphatic testimonial to DHL's influence on his own work (also see G37, H322, and V182). Reprinted, with illustrations from DHL's paintings, in RAMPARTS, 6 (Jan. 1968), 14-19.

F163   Woodeson, John. MARK GERTLER: BIOGRAPHY OF A PAINTER, 1891-1939. London: Sidgwick and Jackson, 1972. Passim.

Numerous references throughout to DHL's association with and admiration of Gertler.

F164   Worthen, John. "D.H. Lawrence and Louie Burrows." DHLR, 4 (1971), 253-62.

Summarizes DHL's relationship with Louie Burrows (see C6), noting that he "left more of himself out to Louie" in his correspondence with her, than he did with Jessie Chambers.

F165   Zytaruk, George J. "Introduction." In THE QUEST FOR RANANIM. Ed. Zytaruk. Pp. xi-xxxvi. See C13.

Backgrounds to DHL's association with S.S. Koteliansky, among the war-time London literati.

F166   -----. "The Chambers Memoirs of D.H. Lawrence--Which Chambers?" RMS, 17 (1973), 5-37.

Argues the May Chambers Holbrook papers published by Nehls (see F123) are actually part of a projected novel by Jessie Chambers ("Miriam").

F167   -----, ed. "Dorothy Brett's Letters to S.S. Koteliansky."
       DHLR, 7 (1974), 240-74.
              Introduces and publishes twenty-four letters
              from Brett, to her "kind of father confessor"
              Koteliansky (1921-30), documenting some of
              the emotional entanglements among Brett, the
              Lawrences, and the Murrys. (Some "painful"
              passages suppressed, at Brett's request.)
              Includes several photographs.

F168   -----, ed. "The Last Days of D.H. Lawrence: Hitherto
       Unpublished Letters of Dr. Andrew Morland." DHLR, 1
       (1968), 44-50.
              Comments on DHL by the physician who attended
              him, in his last illness (four letters).

G. BOOK-LENGTH CRITICAL STUDIES AND ESSAY COLLECTIONS

Also see the numerous books, essay collections, monographs, and pamphlets on DHL's individual novels, novellas, and stories, and on his paintings, plays, poetry, and miscellaneous writings listed in sections J through Z below. A number of additional, foreign-language titles, unavailable for annotation and not entered in this section, are listed in Appendix A: see Beck (AA2a), Couaillac (AA6), Haya (AA14), Itô (AA18), Kitazawa (AA22), Kuramochi (AA24, AA25), LES LANGUES MODERNES (AA26), Mori (AA29), Nishimura (AA33, AA34), Sasaki (AA38), Shibata (AA41), IL VERRI (AA44), Wada (AA45), and Yamakawa (AA50). Also see Gilbert's study guide in Appendix B (AB4) and the following unverified titles in Appendix C: Beutmann (AC1), Kéry (AC2), Kim (AC3-AC5), Pollak (AC7), and Vallese (AC8).

This section includes studies, collections, monographs, and pamphlets concerned with DHL generally or with more than *two* of his individual *works* or principal *genres*. Thus, studies of DHL's nonfiction, poetry, or stories, for example, are entered in the appropriate generic sections though they obviously deal with more than two works and are, one could argue, general in significance. Studies of two works or genres (e.g., R and WL, or the poetry and essays), are entered and annotated (with cross references), in the *two* appropriate sections on individual works below.

G1 Adam, Michael. D.H. LAWRENCE & THE WAY OF THE DANDELION. Penzance, Engl.: Ark Press, 1975.
> DHL's exhortation to man to live for the moment. Also includes extract from F87. (Pamphlet--32 pp.)

G2 Aldington, Richard. D.H. LAWRENCE: AN APPRECIATION. 1927. Harmondsworth, Engl.: Penguin, 1950.
> Fourth revised and expanded version of the same essay, published originally as D.H. LAWRENCE: AN INDISCRETION (1927), and under variations of the present title in 1930 and 1935. A laudatory

study of the character, ideas, and work of England's "Heretic," by an early disciple. Extracts reprinted in F123.

G3 Alldritt, Keith. THE VISUAL IMAGINATION OF D.H. LAWRENCE.
Evanston, Ill.: Northwestern Univ. Press, 1971.
Study of the visual qualities of DHL's fiction.
Alldritt argues that DHL's mind was "marked by
the peculiarly visual sensibility of the Victorian period," as seen in the early fiction, and
that he abandoned his visual method and deter-
iorated as a novelist in the later novels because World War I and modernism in art (self-
conscious experimentation) combined to under-
mine his "characteristic mode of seeing." PS
and LCL, however, represent a partial recovery
of vision. In technique and meaning R depicts
through three generations the arch-Victorian,
"Ruskinite attitudes to architecture, culture
and society," while WL creates a masterful, delicate and doomed synthesis of modern and traditional visual art (cf. Cézanne). A unique approach to the novels and a perceptive analysis
of DHL's aesthetic development, as well as an
intriguing explanation for the "failures" of
his post-war fiction.

G4 Allendorf, Otmar. DIE BEDEUTUNG THOMAS HARDYS FÜR DAS
FRÜHWERK VON D.H. LAWRENCE [THE INFLUENCE OF THOMAS HARDY
ON THE EARLY WORK OF D.H. LAWRENCE]. Marburg: Lahn, 1969.
Extended, narrowly selective and unremarkable
comparison of Hardy and DHL. Allendorf argues
that DHL, who recognized his affinities with
the Georgian poets, looked upon Hardy as the
model for anti-Victorian reaction in the themes
and techniques of his early poetry, as did the
Georgians, well before his study of Hardy's
novels (c. 1914). Hardy's influence on DHL's
fiction he studies in a lengthy comparison of
JUDE THE OBSCURE (1895) and SL (structure, setting, characterization, influence of Sue Bride-
head, etc.). Allendorf concludes with a summary of DHL's "Study of Thomas Hardy" (in B16)
as the point of his departure both from his
early fictional methods and from the Hardy influence. [In German.]

G5   Andrews, Wyndham Thomas, ed. CRITICS ON D.H. LAWRENCE.
       Coral Gables, Fla.: Univ. of Miami Press, 1971.
            A curious collection of early reviews, extracts
            of memoirs, and articles, all previously pub-
            lished, intended to emphasize current British
            and Commonwealth critical activity. Contains
            brief extracts from early criticism, and re-
            prints of more recent essays. Includes H97,
            L64, L69, M30, N59, R5, U29, and extracts from
            F26, F120, G24, G44, G91, H20, H191, and Z8.

G6   Arnold, Armin. D.H. LAWRENCE. Berlin: Colloquium, 1972.
            Competent introductory monograph on DHL's life
            and works, for secondary-school and undergradu-
            ate students (86 pp.). Arnold summarizes DHL's
            activities and writings, chiefly the fiction
            and the poetry, with superficial critical com-
            mentary. Occasional observations on DHL's re-
            lations with Germany and German literature.
            [In German.]

G7   ------. D.H. LAWRENCE AND AMERICA. London: Linden Press,
       1958.
            Examination of DHL's personal, critical and
            literary relations with America. Although in-
            dividual sections have been superseded by more
            specialized studies, Arnold's extended compar-
            ative analysis of the three versions of STUDIES
            IN CLASSIC AMERICAN LITERATURE, the core of the
            book, remains required reading for students of
            DHL's critical and philosophic development.
            Also includes a lengthy international bibliog-
            raphy on DHL and a commentary on DHL's critical
            reputation, to 1958 (see E3). Also see A77.

G8   Arrow, John. J.C. SQUIRE v. D.H. LAWRENCE. London: Lahr,
       1930.
            Defense of DHL against the posthumous attack
            on his reputation by the editor of THE LONDON
            MERCURY (see H356). (Pamphlet--11 pp.)

G9   Beal, Anthony. D.H. LAWRENCE. New York: Grove Press, 1961
            Slight introductory survey of DHL's works and
            ideas. Beal devotes full chapters to R, WL,
            and LCL, and groups the remaining fiction under
            two headings: "The Early Novels" (especially SL)
            and "The Novels of Travel." Two other chapters
            cursorily review the shorter fiction, prose,
            and poetry, and sketch DHL's critical reputa-
            tion to 1960. Extract reprinted in G48.

G10   Becker, George J. D.H. LAWRENCE. New York: Ungar, 1980.
        Selective introduction to DHL's work, dismis-
        sing the poetry ("generally unrewarding"),
        drama ("best forgotten"), travel-works ("pot-
        boilers"), criticism ("doctrinal"), painting,
        and a large amount of the fiction (which is
        briefly treated), for concentrated discussion
        of SL, R, WL, and LCL (not a "major novel,"
        but historically significant). Becker's com-
        mentaries offer little for the experienced
        reader of DHL and his emphasis on DHL's rage
        against the "crushing materialist determinism
        of the modern age," as the source of his "perm-
        anence," reduces his art to sociological phe-
        nomena.

G11   Ben-Ephraim, Gavriel. THE MOON'S DOMINION: NARRATIVE DI-
        CHOTOMY AND FEMALE DOMINANCE IN LAWRENCE'S EARLIER NOVELS.
        East Brunswick, N.J.: Associated Univ. Presses, 1981.
        Study of the "revealing aesthetic pattern...
        of tension, harmony, and the reappearance of
        discord" as it develops through DHL's first
        five novels. Ben-Ephraim finds THE WHITE PEA-
        COCK and THE TRESPASSER divided between DHL's
        major preoccupation with female dominance and
        the simplification of the theme by his narra-
        tors (e.g., the superimposed, naive pastoral
        myth in the first novel). In SL, the "inter-
        fering teller" plays a "smaller role" as DHL
        more directly presents male-female relations
        as the subject of his tale. The tale of R re-
        solves the conflict with the teller, as it ac-
        cepts and explores "the imbalance between the
        sexes," while the discord reappears in WL as
        the teller "plays an increasing role," now as
        an "apologist for male superiority" (the rising
        preoccupation of the subsequent fiction). In-
        teresting thesis, yet pursues the pattern ex-
        clusively in terms of the five novels, to the
        exclusion of DHL's contemporaneous writings,
        and offers little new insight on DHL's dual-
        istic vision or narrative techniques.

G12   Boadella, David. THE SPIRAL FLAME: A STUDY IN THE MEANING
        OF D.H. LAWRENCE. Nottingham: Ritter Press, 1956.
        Eccentric criticism. Boadella, an enthusiastic
        believer in Wilhelm Reich's "orgone" theory,
        relates DHL's vitalism to Reich's eccentric

pseudo-physiological glorification of the radi-
ant energies of orgasm. Boadella forces an
entertaining but hardly informative comparison
between the miraculous cancer cures attributed
to Reich's orgone boxes and DHL's metaphors of
psychic or sexual energy. Nevertheless, we
may share his regret that DHL died ten years
too early to have been cured by orgone therapy.
Reprinted in PAUNCH, Nos. 50-51 (1977), pp. 5-
144.

G13 Bredsdorff, Elias. D.H. LAWRENCE: ET FORSØG PAA EN POLI-
TISK ANALYSE [D.H. LAWRENCE: AN ATTEMPT AT A POLITICAL
ANALYSIS]. Copenhagen: Levin and Munksgaard, 1937.
Useful summary of DHL's political ideas and attitudes, well-illustrated from the fiction and
essays. Bredsdorff nicely distinguishes DHL
from the superficially similar Nazi and fascist
idealogues, notes DHL's longing for a communal,
political connection with his world, and describes the chief features of his political
views: his reaction against the present, his
mysticism, his revolt against reason, his attitudes toward democracy, the sexes, and race,
his revolutionary, anarchist, and individualist
tendencies, his class consciousness, and his
religion. Presumably written to defend DHL
against charges of Nazi tendencies. Bredsdorff's book successfully argues that DHL's essential views emerged from a philosophic and
ideological tradition from which fascism is a
debased and eccentric offshoot. [In Danish.]

G14 Brunsdale, Mitzi M. THE GERMAN EFFECT ON D.H. LAWRENCE
AND HIS WORKS, 1885-1912. Berne: Lang, 1978.
Dissertation-study of the Germanophile DHL's
assimilation of German literature and philosophy (generally from "inadequate" translations),
and his reflections of the German effect on his
writings to 1912, the date of his meeting Frieda. Traces, often superficially, the impact of
Goethe, Novalis, Heine, Hoffmanstahl, Mann,
Rilke, Wagner, Schopenhauer, and Nietzsche in
a number of early essays, poems, stories, THE
WHITE PEACOCK, THE TRESPASSER, and "Paul Morel"
(early version of SL).

G15 Burns, Aidan. NATURE AND CULTURE IN D.H. LAWRENCE. New
     York: Barnes and Noble, 1980.
          Careful critical "analysis of Lawrence's text
          with a sustained philosophical perspective,"
          correlating DHL's views of "the nature of man
          and his situation in the modern world" with
          the perceptions of Nietzsche, Sarte, and Witt-
          genstein. Burns finds in STUDIES IN CLASSIC
          AMERICAN LITERATURE the "theoretical framework"
          of DHL's metaphysics and proceeds to examine
          his developing views of religion and language
          in THE WHITE PEACOCK and SL ("The Rejection of
          Idealism"), R ("The Self and Society"), WL
          ("Culture, Art and Language"), and LCL ("The
          Tyranny of the Phallic Consciousness"). Finds
          DHL a significant modern thinker, though too
          emphatically holds DHL to his own claim that
          "art is utterly dependent on philosophy."

G16 Cavitch, David. D.H. LAWRENCE AND THE NEW WORLD. New
     York: Oxford Univ. Press, 1969.
          Important, well-written study of the psychic,
          sexual, and geographic implications of DHL's
          quest for a "new world." Maintaining that DHL
          conceived of his art as a form of therapy for
          his spiritual and sensual isolation, as "an
          exploration of his own soul," Cavitch views
          each successive work as a renewed attempt to
          understand and thus to liberate the self. He
          portrays DHL as a questing, Romantic writer,
          rather than a modern, chiefly concerned with
          his subjective responses to experience rather
          than with the depersonalization of his art.
          DHL's bad art stems from self-deception, his
          great art from psychic breakthroughs. Rad-
          ically original analyses of R, WL, PS, STUDIES
          IN CLASSIC AMERICAN LITERATURE, the travel
          works, the poetry and the American stories.
          Extract reprinted in G48. Also see H226 and
          T29.

G17 Clark, L.D. THE MINOAN DISTANCE: THE SYMBOLISM OF TRAVEL
     IN D.H. LAWRENCE. Tucson: Univ. of Arizona Press, 1980.
          Having himself retraced DHL's extensive travels
          in Europe and America, Clark assesses DHL's
          evocation of "the spirit of place" in his writ-
          ings and suggests the pattern of DHL's develop-
          ing "geographical symbolism" (e.g., the Alps vs.
          the south; east vs. west) throughout his writ-
          ings. Includes thirty-five photographs.

G18   Clarke, Colin. RIVER OF DISSOLUTION: D.H. LAWRENCE AND
      ENGLISH ROMANTICISM. New York: Barnes and Noble, 1969.
            Study based on the assumption that DHL's atti-
            tude toward corruption and degradation was
            equivocal, that he viewed dissolution as a pos-
            sible alternative source of renewal. Clarke
            attacks those who have found a consistently
            positive moral emphasis in DHL's work (e.g.,
            Leavis), as well as those who, by systematizing
            his thought, have glossed over the ambiguities
            in what he actually says (e.g., DHL's implied
            anal-eroticism). He interestingly relates
            DHL's attitudes to the English Romantic tradi-
            tion ("half in love with easeful Death"), con-
            centrating his analysis on R and WL, the most
            appropriate works, although he does discuss
            PS, LCL, and the shorter fiction. Extracts re-
            printed in G48 and M2. See H351 and U64.

G19   Colin, Saul C. NATURALISME ET MYSTICISME CHEZ D.H. LAW-
      RENCE. Paris: Librairie Lipschutz, 1932.
            Study of DHL's ideas, his conceptions of life
            and human destiny, and his visions of the world
            and his fellow men. Colin reviews DHL's in-
            creasingly mystical searches into the "mystery
            of life" in his treatment of nature ("natural-
            isme"), marriage (R and WL), animals ("The Fox"
            and Mino in WL), godhood (chiefly PS), sexu-
            ality ("St. Mawr" and LCL), and love (AARON'S
            ROD, PANSIES, PS). Colin's concluding chapters
            suggest philosophic and personal sources for
            DHL's mysticism and trace his search for a new
            god and a new world. [In French.]

G20   Coombes, Harry, ed. D.H. LAWRENCE: A CRITICAL ANTHOLOGY.
      Harmondsworth, Engl.: Penguin, 1973.
            Collects 261 brief extracts from letters, re-
            views, and critical essays, illustrating DHL's
            intentions for and "the contemporaneous criti-
            cism" of his work (inferior to Draper's collec-
            tion of reviews, see G34), the "campaigning" to
            restore DHL's reputation, 1930-50, and the later
            criticism, 1951-71. Includes Coombes's general
            and sectional introductions, extracts from 159
            letters by DHL, and full or partial reprints
            from the following: F26, F29, F58, F86, F87,
            F90, F120, F121, F123, F139, G67, G68, G108,
            H107, H127, H142, H191, H315, H316, L38, P8,
            U41, U77, V47, Y20, Y77, Y99, Y104, Y105, Z48,
            and Z121.

G21 Corsani, Mary. D.H. LAWRENCE E L'ITALIA. Milan: Mursia,
1965.
>Well done, useful, yet limited study of DHL's
views of Italy and Italian life and culture,
concentrating on his Italian travel books, fiction (chiefly AARON'S ROD and several stories),
poems, translations (of Verga), and criticism
of Italian authors. In isolating DHL's ideas
of ancient and contemporary Italy, Corsani
misses DHL's foremost purpose, his frequently
implied contrast between Anglo-Saxon, Germanic
culture and the south, underestimating the
symbolic necessity of DHL's glorification of
the Etruscans, for example. Yet her book remains valuable as an Italian response to DHL's
responses to Italy. [In Italian.] Also see
Z108.

G22 Cowan, James C. D.H. LAWRENCE'S AMERICAN JOURNEY: A STUDY
IN LITERATURE AND MYTH. Cleveland, Ohio: Press of Case
Western Reserve Univ., 1970.
>DHL's American journey interpreted as a quest
for "symbols and myths whereby what he regarded
as the waste land of modern western civilization
might be revived." Cowan explores the backgrounds to this quest (DHL's belief in civilization's decline, his psychological and critical
theories) and the mythic dimensions of the works
that resulted from DHL's American experience.
While he devotes considerable attention to STUD-
IES IN CLASSIC AMERICAN LITERATURE, "The Princess," "The Woman Who Rode Away," "St. Mawr,"
and PS, as expected, Cowan's discussions of
DHL's theory of history, his psychoanalytic
essays, his four "anti-Murry" stories, and his
unfinished "The Flying Fish" are both surpris-
ingly pertinent and useful. Incorporates several previously published essays. See T29.

G23 Daiches, David. D.H. LAWRENCE. Brighton, Engl.: Privately
printed, 1963.
>DHL's "only permanent message is that men should
be men and women women." Broadcast talk. (Pamph-
let--24 pp.)

G24 Daleski, H.M. THE FORKED FLAME: A STUDY OF D.H. LAWRENCE.
Evanston, Ill.: Northwestern Univ. Press, 1965.
>Sees the development of DHL's fiction in light
of his theory of the dualistic nature of man,

as presented in the "Study of Thomas Hardy"
(in B16). Daleski divides DHL's career into
four "periods": the early works, especially
SL, explore the male and female principles;
R and WL attempt to reconcile sexual polariza-
tion, from the female (Ursula) and the male
(Birkin) viewpoints; the three aggressively
masculine studies of power respond to the un-
satisfactory reconciliation in WL; LCL, in
DHL's final phase, represents "an implicit
vindication of the female principle." Unor-
iginal thesis, but sensitive and illuminating
readings. Extract originally published in
G78. Extracts reprinted in G5, L5, M2, and
M4. Also see M72.

G25 D.H. LAWRENCE REVIEW. 5 (1972), iii, 187-323. "Phoenix
Number."
"Symposium of papers" on "the history of the
phoenix image in western literature...[and on]
the function of the phoenix image in various
pictorial media from the ancient world" to the
modern period. Includes articles by the issue
editor, James C. Cowan (see H79), and by Jessie
Poesch ("The Phoenix Portrayed"), Douglas J.
McMillan ("The Phoenix in the Western World
from Herodotus to Shakespeare"), and Lyna Lee
Montgomery ("The Phoenix: Its Use as a Literary
Device in English from the Seventeenth Century
to the Twentieth Century"). Numerous illustrations.

G26 D.H. LAWRENCE REVIEW. 8 (1975), 255-370. "D.H. Lawrence
and Women."
Four approaches to the perennially controversial questions of DHL's attitudes toward and
portraits of women. Includes H154, H319, M37,
and M43.

G27 D.H. LAWRENCE REVIEW. 13 (1980), 1-93. "D.H. Lawrence:
Myth and Occult."
Contains five articles on the mythic and occult
backgrounds to DHL's major fiction. Includes
H423, N93, T5, U18, and V61.

G28 D.H. LAWRENCE REVIEW. 13 (1980), 193-259. "D.H. Lawrence
Psychoanalysis and Existence."
Contains four examples of psychoanalytic and
existentialist criticism of DHL's works. Includes H4, H84, L42, and P6.

G29 Dix, Carol. D.H. LAWRENCE AND WOMEN. Totowa, N.J.: Rowman and Littlefield, 1980.
>   A journalist's survey of DHL's attitudes toward
>   women, drawing from the major fiction and es-
>   says. Dix examines, in turn, the status of
>   women at the turn of the century, DHL's handling
>   of the "feminine point of view," and various
>   topics concerning his treatment of women (e.g.,
>   duality, relationships, sexuality, homosexual-
>   ity, misogyny). On the whole far more sympa-
>   thetic to DHL, yet no more scholarly than Mil-
>   lett (see H255).

G30 Donnerstag, Jürgen. DIE STILENTWICKLUNG IM WERK VON D.H.
LAWRENCE [STYLISTIC DEVELOPMENT IN THE WORK OF D.H. LAW-
RENCE]. Cologne: Univ. of Cologne, 1969.
>   Intensive study of DHL's poetic and prose styles,
>   and their interrelationship, through the "three
>   phases" of his career. Donnerstag examines the
>   diction, imagery, language and syntax, and ton-
>   ality of the RHYMING POEMS (see A55) and THE
>   WHITE PEACOCK, of LOOK! WE HAVE COME THROUGH!
>   and R, and of BIRDS, BEASTS AND FLOWERS, LAST
>   POEMS, PANSIES, PS, and "The Man Who Died,"
>   tracing DHL's development from imitative and
>   conventional styles appropriate to his forms,
>   to a single, lyrically intense, mythic style
>   for both his poetry and his fiction (DHL's
>   "Gesamtstil"). Donnerstag comments usefully
>   on DHL's relations with his literary precursors
>   (e.g., Hardy, the Pre-Raphaelites), and contemp-
>   oraries (e.g., Yeats, Pound, and Eliot), yet
>   his overly-rigid, systematic thesis and limited
>   coverage weaken his study. [In German.]

G31 Drain, Richard L. TRADITION AND D.H. LAWRENCE. Groningen,
Neth.: Wolters, 1960.
>   Stresses DHL's proximity to the Victorian moral
>   tradition in literature against which he sup-
>   posedly rebelled. (Pamphlet--12 pp.)

G32 Draper, Ronald P. D.H. LAWRENCE. New York: Humanities
Press, 1969.
>   Brief introduction to DHL, with critical com-
>   mentary on a number of extracts from his prose
>   illustrating his style, characterization, sym-
>   bolism, and basic themes. Slight value.

G33   -----. D.H. LAWRENCE. New York: Twayne, 1964.
      One of the few introductions to DHL that avoids
      a restrictive, biographical approach. The first
      chapter covers the early life and some basic
      themes, while the body of the study discusses
      the novels, tales, and poetry. Includes a good
      final chapter on DHL's critical reputation and
      literary influence.

G34   -----, ed. D.H. LAWRENCE: THE CRITICAL HERITAGE.   London:
      Routledge, 1970.
      Gathers over eighty contemporary reviews of
      DHL's fiction, paintings, poetry, and prose,
      as well as a number of obituaries and final
      assessments. The items included, while se-
      lected for their representativeness or intrin-
      sic value, are generally favorable and often
      perceptive. Includes Draper's general essay
      on DHL's critical reputation (E16), the fol-
      lowing articles: H36, H64, H107, H120, H127,
      H267, H316, H339, H340, H356, H376, H391, L36,
      P8, U46, U53, X16, Y8, Y59, Y99, Y104, Y105,
      Z27, Z28, Z75, Z120, and extracts from F120,
      H106, H142, and Y7. Also see H226.

G35   Ebbatson, Roger. LAWRENCE AND THE NATURE TRADITION: A
      THEME IN ENGLISH FICTION, 1859-1914. Atlantic Highlands,
      N.J.: Humanities Press, 1980.
      Full study of the later nineteenth- and early
      twentieth-century novelists' inheritance of a
      dual conception of nature, the joint product
      of the Romantic and American transcendentalist
      exaltation of nature and the scientific, Dar-
      winian conception of nature as ordeal. Ebbat-
      son sees DHL as the "great inheritor" of the
      literary tradition which attempted to synthe-
      size these two views, examines his view of na-
      ture as potent and liberating in THE WHITE PEA-
      COCK and THE TRESPASSER, argues his achieve-
      ment of synthesis in his movement toward na-
      ture mysticism in R and beyond, and traces the
      chief influences on his view of nature (the
      English Romantics, Emerson, and the novelists
      Meredith, Hardy, Jeffries, White, and Forster).
      His comments on DHL bracket chapter-length
      essays on each of the above named novelists.

G36 Eisenstein, Samuel A. BOARDING THE SHIP OF DEATH: D.H.
LAWRENCE'S QUESTER HEROES. The Hague: Mouton, 1974.
Jungian exploration of DHL's "monomyth" of the
"quester hero," his repeated use of central
characters who pursue wholeness of being, with
varying degrees of success. While Eisenstein's
external frame of reference is wide, from Hindu
mysticism, to St. John of the Cross and the an-
thropologist-critic Joseph Campbell, he focuses
on DHL's "less successful" works on the dubious
grounds that they best illustrate the processes
and pitfalls of the archetypal quest. Thus, he
tells us more about myth than about DHL. Readings of THE TRESPASSER, THE LOST GIRL, AARON'S
ROD, KANGAROO, and "The Man Who Died," among
other works.

G37 Fedder, Norman J. THE INFLUENCE OF D.H. LAWRENCE ON TEN-
NESSEE WILLIAMS. The Hague: Mouton, 1966.
Fedders covers Williams's poetry, fiction and
drama searching out Lawrencean elements and
borrowings. He concludes, not too surpris-
ingly, that DHL is the better novelist, Williams the better dramatist, and neither a major poet. See F162, H322, and V182. Also
see H174 and V94.

G38 Fishawy, Wagdy. D.H. LAWRENCE: A CRITICAL STUDY. Cairo:
Daral-Sakafa, 1975.
Essentially an extended study of John Middleton
Murry's criticism of DHL, and of DHL's works at
one remove. An ardent admirer of Murry, Fishawy's comments on DHL's works, when they are
discussed, essentially reaffirm Murry's criticisms (see F119-F121, G84, G85, H270, and H271).

G39 Ford, George H. DOUBLE MEASURE: A STUDY OF THE NOVELS AND
STORIES OF D.H. LAWRENCE. New York: Holt, 1965.
Brief remarks on the early novels and eight
shorter fictions, and intensive readings of
the two major works: R and WL. Ford's analyses concentrate on the thematic and structural
double rhythms which he finds most characteristic of DHL (e.g., life-death, Persephone-
Pluto, mother-father, communion-isolation).
The best fiction "portrays conflicts, one
force pitted against another, in which a dramatic testing is more significant than a

simplified evaluation, especially a consistently righteous evaluation, of the protagonists."
In the two masterworks the dualistic tensions
are never resolved, to the benefit of the works.
Excellent analyses of R and WL with especially
fine commentaries on their backgrounds (the influences of the Bible and the War respectively).
Extracts reprinted in L1, L3, M2, M4, and N3.

G40   Freeman, Mary. D.H. LAWRENCE: A BASIC STUDY OF HIS IDEAS.
Gainesville: Univ. of Florida Press, 1955.
DHL's developing philosophy of individualism,
with emphasis on his systematic, affirmative
message rather than on his art. Freeman considers each novel in turn, violating chronology
only in treating SL first, as the "best introduction," to document DHL's social, economic,
moral, and literary radicalism. Some good discussion of DHL's intellectual context, but little critical insight and too tendentious in the
search for system in DHL's thought. Extract
reprinted in M2.

G41   Galinsky, Hans. DEUTSCHLAND IN DER SICHT VON D.H. LAWRENCE
UND T.S. ELIOT: EINE STUDIE ZUM ANGLO-AMERIKANISCHEN DEUT-
SCHLANDBILD DES 20. JAHRHUNDERTS [GERMANY AS SEEN BY D.H.
LAWRENCE AND T.S. ELIOT: A STUDY OF THE ANGLO-AMERICAN PIC-
TURE OF GERMANY IN THE TWENTIETH CENTURY]. Mainz: Akademie
der Wissenschaften und der Literatur, 1956.
Specialized monograph (46 pp.). Galinsky briefly summarizes the pre- and post-World War I perspectives on Germany, in modern British and
American literature, and surveys the remarkable
and peculiar ("eigentümliche") views of Germany
and the influence of German thought in selected
writings by DHL (early novels, essays, travel
works, and letters) and Eliot (poetry and criticism). [In German.]

G42   Garcia, Reloy. STEINBECK AND D.H. LAWRENCE: FICTIVE VOICES
AND THE ETHICAL IMPERATIVE. Muncie, Ind.: John Steinbeck
Society of America, 1972.
Frail comparative study based on two assumptions: both novelists believed art must be
moral and both declined after their masterworks, THE GRAPES OF WRATH (1939) and WL.

G43 Gomme, Andor, ed. D.H. LAWRENCE: A CRITICAL STUDY OF THE
MAJOR NOVELS AND OTHER WRITINGS. New York: Barnes and
Noble, 1978.
Collects ten essays (one previously published)
on DHL's art and writings, generally representing the discursive approach popular among the
present generation of British academics. The
essays, on a peculiar range of subjects, do not
constitute a very balanced survey of DHL's "major" work. Includes H296, H312, L31, M15, N26,
U69, V49, V86, W9, and Y33.

G44 Goodheart, Eugene. THE UTOPIAN VISION OF D.H. LAWRENCE.
Chicago: Univ. of Chicago Press, 1963.
Excellent study of DHL's thought, in relation
"to the central concerns of his time and to
the intellectual and cultural movements with
which his work has affinity." Reacting against
the provincial view of DHL as the culmination
of the English literary tradition, Goodheart
suggests correspondences to DHL in the thought
and writings of Nietzsche, Rilke, Mann, Freud,
and others. As a visionary iconoclast (cf.
Blake), DHL foresaw a return to the physical
and psychic health he found in the "pre-civil-
ized past." The effects of this primitivist,
utopian vision are measured in DHL's views of
"nature, myth and religious experience." Discusses AARON'S ROD, KANGAROO, "St. Mawr," and
"The Man Who Died," among other works. Extract
reprinted in G5. See H355.

G45 Goodman, Richard. FOOTNOTE TO LAWRENCE. London: White
Owl Press, 1932.
DHL's "mystical" solution to man's divided nature acceptable, but limited because he "never
knew, never really understood anyone other than
himself." (Pamphlet--21 pp.)

G46 Gottwald, Johannes. DIE ERZÄHLFORMEN DER ROMANE VON ALDOUS
HUXLEY UND DAVID HERBERT LAWRENCE [NARRATIVE TECHNIQUES IN
THE NOVELS OF ALDOUS HUXLEY AND DAVID HERBERT LAWRENCE].
Munich: Univ. of Munich, 1964.
Extended contrast, with some comparison, of
DHL's and Huxley's approaches to fiction.
Gottwald distinguishes Huxley's contrapuntal
organization in his novels ("mosaic") from
DHL's rhythmic process ("stream"), Huxley's

concern with a society or a network of ideas
("Der Roman ohne Held," "Die Romanfigur im
Ideengefüge") from DHL's focus on the individual character or on individualized characters in relationship, Huxley's play with
ideas from DHL's studies of psychic and emo-
tional development, and Huxley's inorganic
structural frameworks ("Gefüge") from DHL's
organic, structural fabrics ("Gewebe"). [In
German.]

G47   Gregory, Horace. D.H. LAWRENCE: PILGRIM OF THE APOCALYPSE.
      1933. Rev. ed. New York: Grove Press, 1957.
      Interesting, still useful examination of DHL's
      life and work. Gregory recognizes DHL's ances-
      tors as Blake and Shelley, rather than the Vic-
      torian novelists, and presents him as primarily
      a poetic novelist and "a twentieth century poet
      of major proportions." DHL turned to prose
      only as the less convention-bound genre. Greg-
      ory surprises us with his negative opinion of
      WL and his view of the late works, with the
      exception of PS, as unqualified triumphs. Ex-
      tract reprinted in G53.

G48   Hamalian, Leo, ed. D.H. LAWRENCE: A COLLECTION OF CRITI-
      CISM. New York: McGraw-Hill, 1973.
      Twelve previously published essays on DHL, plus
      DHL's "Autobiographical Sketch" (reprinted from
      A75). Includes Hamalian's elementary "Introduc-
      tion" (pp. 1-14), four essays: H194, L34, V13,
      Y50, and extracts from F87, G9, G16, G18, G56, G88,
      G104, and G130.

G49   Herzinger, Kim A. D.H. LAWRENCE IN HIS TIME: 1908-1915.
      Lewisburg, Pa.: Bucknell Univ. Press, [1982].
      "This study approaches Lawrence by placing him
      in the cultural matrix of his time. The author
      shows how Lawrence's work displays both an im-
      pulse toward community and a reaction away from
      the community and toward the enclave." (Quoted
      from publisher's announcement--not seen.) In-
      cludes discussions of DHL's relations with his
      contemporary culture and events (Edwardians and
      Georgians, futurists, imagists, and vorticists,
      the Bloomsbury group, and World War I). An-
      nounced for publication late in 1982.

G50 Hess, Elisabeth. DIE NATURBETRACHTUNG IM PROSAWERK VON
D.H. LAWRENCE [THE VISION OF NATURE IN THE FICTION OF
D.H. LAWRENCE]. Bern: Francke, 1957.
   Traces the development of DHL's vision of nature through his major works. Hess sees DHL
   moving in distinct stages from the youthful,
   sentimental, and impassioned presentation of
   nature in THE WHITE PEACOCK ("Natureckstase"),
   the tension between reality and reverie in SL
   (resolved in the direction of realism), the
   fulfillment of nature in R ("Realismus" evolving into "Natursymbolik"), the turn toward pessimism in WL, the discovery of the dark gods of
   the earth in KANGAROO, and the achievement of a
   fully matured vision of nature in PS, particularly in its descriptive passages and hymns to
   nature. Useful observations, but too prescrip-
   tive a thesis. [In German.]

G51 Hobsbaum, Philip. A READER'S GUIDE TO D.H. LAWRENCE.
London: Thames and Hudson, 1981.
   Summarizes, with some general critical commentary, all the novels and (very briefly) the
   novellas, a large number of the poems and short
   stories (approached volume-by-volume), and the
   major nonfiction prose. Hobsbaum also provides
   a brief note on the plays, which are otherwise
   dismissed from consideration. Useful, perhaps,
   to the beginning student, but too little original observation to be of value to the experi-
   enced reader of DHL.

G52 Hochman, Baruch. ANOTHER EGO: THE CHANGING VIEW OF SELF
AND SOCIETY IN THE WORK OF D.H. LAWRENCE. Columbia: Univ.
of South Carolina Press, 1970.
   Study of the development of DHL's ideas, rely-
   ing extensively on the expository prose, especially the "Study of Thomas Hardy" (in B16),
   "The Crown" (A60), and the psychoanalytic essays (A62, A63). Hochman's purpose, to clarify the backgrounds of DHL's "vision" and to
   explore his "critique of the modern world,"
   is primarily extra-literary in emphasis. He
   sees a twofold pattern in DHL's developing
   vision, from the concern with the emerging
   self, the ego, which ultimately fails in WL,
   to the assertion of a "radical communalism,"
   "another ego," in the later work (e.g., PS

and APOCALYPSE). Particularly interesting comments on DHL's relation to nineteenth- and twentieth-century philosophic trends. See T29.

G53   Hoffman, Frederick J., and Harry T. Moore, eds.   THE
      ACHIEVEMENT OF D.H. LAWRENCE. Norman: Univ. of Oklahoma
      Press, 1953.
            Earliest and still the best anthology of crit-
            icism, coinciding with the revival of interest
            in DHL during the 1950s. Contains the editors'
            fine introductory survey of DHL and his critics
            (E26), and eighteen previously published essays,
            including biographical commentaries, documents
            in the Eliot-Leavis controversy, and studies of
            several of the novels, the stories, the poetry,
            and the travel books. Includes F153, H105, H185,
            H191, H218, H390, L16, M58, N88, U77, V7, Y19,
            Z125, and extracts from G47, G62, G80, G120,
            and G125.

G54   Holderness, Graham. D.H. LAWRENCE: HISTORY, IDEOLOGY AND
      FICTION. London: Gill and MacMillan, 1982.
            "A critical study which examines the work of
            D.H. Lawrence from a historical as well as a
            literary perspective." (Quoted from publisher's
            announcement--not seen.)

G55   -----.   WHO'S WHO IN D.H. LAWRENCE. New York: Taplinger,
      1976.
            Alphabetical, annotated listing of DHL's char-
            acters (limited to the novels, "most important"
            novellas, and collected stories), a similar
            brief list of "animals and other non-human char-
            acters," and an index of characters "book-by-
            book." A dubious enterprise.

G56   Hough, Graham. THE DARK SUN: A STUDY OF D.H. LAWRENCE.
      New York: Macmillan, 1957.
            An excellent general assessment of DHL as a
            prophet and as artist. Hough closely examines
            nine of DHL's novels (THE TRESPASSER is "al-
            most an irrelevance") arguing, for example,
            that SL is a masterpiece in "the central tra-
            dition of the novel" and that R weakens at the
            end, as DHL unsuccessfully strives to "explain
            the inexplicable." WL, however, his masterful
            critique of modern industrial society, announces
            the arrival of the "prophet." PS, treated to-
            gether with the 'better' story, "The Woman Who

Rode Away," is only a partially successful
ritualization of his prophecy and LCL, a
"careful, consistent" novel, is no great ad-
vance in idea. Hough also briefly surveys
the short fiction (less effective than the
novels) and the poetry (an organic whole).
He concludes with an excellent description
of DHL's doctrine. One of the finest studies of DHL. Extracts reprinted in G48, G115,
and L5.

G57 ------. TWO EXILES: LORD BYRON AND D.H. LAWRENCE. Notting-
ham: Univ. of Nottingham Press, 1956.
Original and interesting brief comparison.
(Pamphlet--26 pp.) Reprinted in Hough's
IMAGE AND EXPERIENCE: STUDIES IN A LITERARY
REVOLUTION (Lincoln: Univ. of Nebraska Press,
1960).

G58 Howe, Marguerite Beede. THE ART OF THE SELF IN D.H. LAW-
RENCE. Athens: Ohio Univ. Press, 1977.
Distinguished critical analyses of seven major
novels in light of DHL's evolving "ego psychology," his developing "concept of self" which
governs characterization, theme, and structure
in the works (the first two novels are briefly
treated as preparations for SL; THE LOST GIRL
is dismissed as regressive). Each novel, in
turn, bears the seed for DHL's subsequent mod-
ifications of his views of personality. Howe
finds the early works, through R, concerned
with the "coming into being" of the self in
"relationship to other individuals, to society,
and to nature"; WL through KANGAROO consider
how the self is "maintained" in relationship
and in isolation; PS views the self confronted
with death; LCL, like THE LOST GIRL a regressive work, is a lapse into "summary and recap-
itulation."

G59 Huttar, Charles A., ed. LITERATURE AND RELIGION: VIEWS
ON D.H. LAWRENCE. Holland, Mich.: Hope College, 1968.
Contains six papers, "Collected for MLA Sem-
inar 15," exemplifying "various forms of what
might be called 'Christian criticism,'" as ap-
plied to DHL. Several interesting contributions. Includes H363, H392, H411, M60, M77,
and Y39.

G60   Inniss, Kenneth.   D.H. LAWRENCE'S BESTIARY.   The Hague:
      Mouton, 1971.
            DHL's use of the animal trope in his prose,
            poetry, and fiction, as archetype and as cre-
            ative symbol.   Inniss traces the typological
            significance of DHL's beasts from the obvious
            (e.g., Lion=nobility) to the idiosyncratic
            (e.g., porcupine=egoism).   He notes a move-
            ment through the career away from the tradi-
            tional animal metaphors, culminating in the
            "savage" celebration of wild animals (e.g.,
            foxes, snakes, stallions) in the post-war
            fiction, followed by the exaltation of the
            "pure animal man" in the more serene late
            work.   Useful, but limited study.

G61   Jaensson, Knut B.   D.H. LAWRENCE.   Stockholm: Tidens För-
      lag, 1934.
            Introductory study of DHL which deviates into
            specialized commentaries within its general
            overview of DHL's life and work.   Jaensson
            briefly retells DHL's life and surveys his
            major fiction (SL, R, WL, AARON'S ROD, KANG-
            AROO, PS, "The Man Who Died," LCL), chiefly
            analyzing DHL's major characters therein, and
            introduces commentaries on the psychoanalytic
            and other essays, on DHL's responses to Freud,
            Bergson, Croce, and Ortega y Gasset, and on
            his synthesis of evangelical enthusiasm and
            social-political ideas.   Jaensson concludes
            with discussions of DHL's relations with J.M.
            Murry (see F121), Murry's criticism of DHL,
            and DHL's artistic techniques in his poetry
            and fiction (with several references to THE
            LOST GIRL and with comparisons to Dostoevsky,
            Tolstoy, Whitman, and Nietzsche).   [In Swedish.]

G62   Jarrett-Kerr, Martin [Father William Tiverton].   D.H. LAW-
      RENCE AND HUMAN EXISTENCE.   1951.   Rev. ed.   London: Rock-
      liff, 1961.
            Important study of DHL "specifically from a
            Christian angle."   Jarrett-Kerr sees DHL akin
            to the Christian existentialists in his moral
            view of art and in his belief in the necessity
            of "engagement" in life.   DHL's most valuable
            message, however, is in his demand for a *liv-
            ing* religion and a *vital* godhead.   Although
            DHL is fundamentally ignorant of Christian

doctrine, his pantheism and pan-sexualism (influenced by Rozanov) are closer to the spirit
of Christianity than first appears. Jarrett-
Kerr concentrates on DHL's intellectual formation and central themes rather than on detailed
literary analysis of specific works. Generally,
he finds the novels more successful art, because less personal than the poetry. Extracts
reprinted in G53 and Ll. Also see H218. Includes a "Foreword" by T.S. Eliot (see H105).

G63 Johnsson, Melker. D.H. LAWRENCE: ETT MODERNT TANKEÄVENTYR
[D.H. LAWRENCE: A MODERN ADVENTURE IN THOUGHT]. Stockholm:
Albert Bonniers, 1939.
Chronological reading of DHL's principal writings, his "thought adventures," summarizing his
leading themes and ideas and attributing his vitalism to the deprivations of his lower-middle
class, industrial childhood. Johnsson anticipates several of the leading concerns of subsequent critics (the Oedipal conflict in SL, the
new conception of character in R, the impact of
the war on WL the varieties of "flights" and
"quests" characterizing the writings of the
twenties), with the exception of his high estimate of LCL as, in many ways, DHL's most complete statement of his ideas, and, despite its
apocalyptic melancholy, his most hopeful work.
Throughout Johnsson draws insightful illustrations from DHL's novels, contemporary essays,
poetry (chiefly LOOK! WE HAVE COME THROUGH!),
and (rarely) short fiction. [In Swedish.]

G64 Joost, Nicholas, and Alvin Sullivan. D.H. LAWRENCE AND
THE DIAL. Carbondale: Southern Illinois Univ. Press, 1970.
Curious historical and critical study. Joost
and Sullivan trace DHL's insubstantial relationship with the American avant-garde journal
of the twenties so far as to number the adver-
tisements for his works, yet offer little original comment on "The Fox" and "The Woman Who
Rode Away," the two most important DHL stories
published in THE DIAL (1922, 1925).

G65 Kermode, Frank. D.H. LAWRENCE. New York: Viking, 1973.
Introduction to DHL as a "modern master." Kermode explicates the philosophy of DHL and its
operation in the novels and a few shorter works

"to show how the visionary is contained by the
novelist." He finds DHL's "metaphysic" nearly
as systematic as Yeats's, with the conflict between "doctrine" and "tale" and its reconciliation the chief characteristic of the canon. DHL
achieves true equilibrium in a few works (e.g.,
R, WL, and "St. Mawr"), where his metaphysic,
compared to the male principle (God the Father,
or the Law), reaches communion with his art,
the female principle (God the Son, or Love), to
"usher in the Holy Ghost," the spirit of reconciliation that holds the "opposites in tension."
Ingenious thesis, yet haphazardly developed.
See H203 and H317.

G66   THE LAUGHING HORSE. No. 13 (Apr. 1926), 1-30. "D.H. Lawrence Number."
        Contains three portraits of DHL, three essays
        and two poems by DHL, and four slight essays
        concerning DHL: "The Bite of Mr. Lawrence" (by
        Frederic W. Leighton), "Black Magic" (by Idella
        Purnell), "THE PLUMED SERPENT" (review, by Ma-
        bel Dodge Luhan), and "Animals and Ideas" (by
        Walter Wiggington). Includes extracts from A89
        and B16.

G67   Leavis, F.R.   D.H. LAWRENCE. Cambridge, Engl.: Minority
        Press, 1930.
        Early demand that DHL be recognized as a "gen-
        ius" and a "great artist," by one of his most
        vocal champions. Leavis's eccentric judgments
        of individual works are considerably modified
        in his later studies (see below). Reprinted
        in Leavis's FOR CONTINUITY (Cambridge: Heffer,
        1933). Extract reprinted in G20. Also see
        below and H226.

G68   -----.   D.H. LAWRENCE: NOVELIST. New York: Knopf, 1956.
        The most controversial study of DHL's achieve-
        ment. Intending "to win clear recognition for
        the nature of Lawrence's greatness," Leavis
        examines in detail DHL's "presentment" of so-
        ciety in R and WL, placing him in the same
        "ethical and religious tradition" as George
        Eliot. The two novels are considered as en-
        tirely separate entities, despite their common
        origin, which succeed in objectively "render-
        ing the continuity and rhythm of life." In R,

DHL emphasizes the "transmission of the spiritual heritage," or tradition of a society
through several generations, while in WL he
presents a broad, comprehensive picture of
the moral disintegration of modern society.
The balance of Leavis's study considers three
shorter works ("The Daughters of the Vicar,"
"The Captain's Doll," and "St. Mawr"). Leavis's focus on DHL's fundamentally religious
social conscience has been influential, but
his insistently moral basis for judgment, his
hyperbolic rhetoric, his occasionally eccentric valuations, his hysterical preoccupation
with T.S. Eliot as his (and DHL's) enemy, and
his often vacuous criticism, making the self-
evident seem profound, all seriously weaken
his credibility. Extracts reprinted in G20.
Also see G18, G53, G85, H41, H50, H151, H171,
H301, H311, H355, H381, H395, V155, Z2, Z3,
and AA124.

G69   ------. THOUGHT, WORDS AND CREATIVITY: ART AND THOUGHT IN
       LAWRENCE. New York: Oxford Univ. Press, 1976.
            Valedictory study of DHL, and final "swipe"
            at T.S. Eliot, by the late Dr. Leavis. Lea-
            vis defines DHL's synthesis of thought and
            creativity, as distinguished from Eliot's
            "intellectuality," shows his supreme "capa-
            city for thought" in the prose, and examines
            DHL's achievement of his "profounder thought
            about life" in PS (retracting his earlier
            dismissal of the novel), WL (his most "fully
            creative" novel), "The Captain's Doll," and
            R. Specialized, yet fuzzy thesis and irra-
            tating preoccupation with Eliot as *bête
            noire*. Also see above, G53, and H104.

G70   LITERATURE/FILM QUARTERLY. 1 (1973), 3-70.
            Special issue on DHL's attitude toward cinema
            and the film adaptations of his fiction. In-
            cludes eight original articles: H259, H345,
            L13, N106, U61, V63, V129, and V179.

G71   Littlewood, J.C.F. D.H. LAWRENCE. Vol. 1. 1885-1914.
       London: Longman, 1976.
            Replaces Young's earlier monograph for Long-
            mans, on the "writer and his work" (see G129).
            Brief commentary on the early life and on

"Odour of Chrysanthemums," and extended dis-
cussion of the autobiographical dimensions of
SL. Vol. 2 had not appeared through 1982.
See L38.

G72 Marnat, Marcel. DAVID-HERBERT LAWRENCE. Paris: Éditions
Universitaires, 1966.
Fine overview of DHL's thought and principal
novels. Marnat laments the scarcity and nar-
rowness of French criticism of DHL (here sur-
veyed) and argues that the French have falsely
labeled him merely an erotic writer, or sen-
sualist (e.g., Malraux; see U46). In a series of brief discussions of the novels, chiefly
THE WHITE PEACOCK, SL, R, WL, AARON'S ROD, and
PS (considered DHL's finest achievement), Marnat summarizes DHL's psychological, social,
and political themes, admires his frankness
and vitality, and stresses his modern, inqui-
sitive analyses of a contemporary world "qu'il
jugeait aberrant." Marnat's commentaries al-
ternate with his valuable chronologies for the
major periods of DHL's life, which, like his
text, emphasize DHL's modernity, relating his
works to contemporary international events in
letters, music, painting, film, politics, and
technology. [In French.]

G73 Meyers, Jeffrey. D.H. LAWRENCE AND THE EXPERIENCE OF
ITALY. Philadelphia: Univ. of Pennsylvania Press, [1982].
Studies of DHL's Italian travel books (and
"Introduction" to MEMOIRS OF THE FOREIGN LE-
GION; see A66), his translations of Verga and
Grazzini, and his poetry, paintings, and novels
(THE LOST GIRL through LCL) of the 'twenties.
(Announced for 1982 publication--not seen.)

G74 Michaels-Tonks, Jennifer. D.H. LAWRENCE: THE POLARITY OF
NORTH AND SOUTH--GERMANY AND ITALY IN HIS PROSE WORKS.
Bonn: Bouvier, 1976.
Narrow but thorough survey of DHL's attitudes
toward Germany and Italy, and their cultures,
and of the German influence on his works.
Michaels-Tonks examines DHL's shifting views
of the two countries (in the letters), his evident knowledge of their languages and cultures,
his German and Italian literary allusions, his
assimilation of the German psychoanalysts

(Freud and Gross) and Nietzsche, and his dualistic use of German and Italian settings to sym-
bolize two modes of life in his fiction and
travel narratives.

G75   Miko, Stephen J. TOWARD *WOMEN IN LOVE*: THE EMERGENCE OF
A LAWRENTIAN AESTHETIC. New Haven, Conn.: Yale Univ.
Press, 1972.
          DHL's aesthetic evolution through the first
     five novels, in light of his important prose
     works: "Study of Thomas Hardy" (in B16) and
     "The Crown" (A60). Miko sees DHL's fiction
     as a "search for coherence," a "continual
     struggle for relation" through the consistent
     reconciliation of opposites, often by means
     of paradoxical philosophic or theological
     formulations. DHL develops ideological and
     personal conflicts throughout the early fic-
     tion, culminating in his character of Birkin,
     his spokesman as anti-intellectual intellec-
     tual. Miko's thesis, therefore, could encom-
     pass all inherent contradictions and incon-
     sistencies in DHL's thought, but it is not
     used injudiciously.

G76   Miles, Kathleen M. THE HELLISH MEANING: THE DEMONIC MOTIF
IN THE WORKS OF D.H. LAWRENCE. Carbondale: Southern Illinois Univ. Press, 1969.
          Study of DHL's demonic characters, chiefly in
     WL and later works. To exhibit "the destruc-
     tive tendencies in modern man" DHL creates two
     kinds of male demons, "The Fatal Man" (e.g.,
     Gerald Crich, in WL), who prostitutes his vital
     self to his intellect, and "The Demon Lover"
     (e.g., Cipriano, in PS) who seeks sensation to
     the exclusion of the intellect. While he por-
     trays his blood-conscious figures more sympa-
     thetically than his mind-conscious automatons,
     DHL condemns them nonetheless for their failure
     to achieve true unity of being, the balanced
     psyche that can be attained only through a
     creative relationship with the female. Unor-
     iginal.

G77   Miller, Henry. THE WORLD OF LAWRENCE: A PASSIONATE APPRE-
CIATION. Ed. Evelyn J. Hinz and John J. Teunissen. Santa
Barbara, Calif.: Capra Press, 1980.
          "Passionate, prejudiced" commentaries, written
     in the early thirties, treating DHL's personal-
     ity, his "soil and climate," his views of

death, resurrection, destiny, and the "sacred
body," and his philosophy and literary use of
form and symbol. Testifies to Miller's emphatic appreciation of DHL, though tells us more
about Miller than DHL. Includes editorial commentary on the origins of Miller's uncompleted
study (pp. 11-24). Also see H252, H253, and
Q1.

G78   MODERN FICTION STUDIES. 5 (1959), 3-98. "D.H. Lawrence
Number."
Special issue, containing three general studies,
four commentaries on individual works, and a
bibliographical checklist. Includes E7, H393,
J11, M67, Q6, and extracts from G24, G83, and
V5.

G79   MODERNIST STUDIES: LITERATURE & CULTURE 1920-1940. 4
(1982), 3-122. "A Special Issue on D.H. Lawrence, 1885-
1930."
Gathers eight essays on DHL's works. Includes
H143, H280, M14, M33, M42, V59, Y62, and Y68.

G80   Moore, Harry T. D.H. LAWRENCE: HIS LIFE AND WORKS. 1951.
2nd ed. New York: Twayne, 1964.
Insistently biographical, critical study of DHL's
career. Moore usefully relates DHL's writings
to contemporary events, yet strays from his announced intention to concentrate on the works,
compulsively retelling the life. Nevertheless,
Moore insightfully compares DHL's use of symbol
to the *symbolistes* (especially well in R and
WL). Also, his discussions of DHL's "belief
in the blood" as the unifying theme of all the
writings are lucid and informative. Indexes
and appendices on DHL's critical reputation,
the "Genesis of SONS AND LOVERS," and "the
Lawrence country" (map). Extracts reprinted
in G53, L7, and V130.

G81   -----, ed. A D.H. LAWRENCE MISCELLANY. Carbondale: Southern Illinois Univ. Press, 1959.
Valuable gathering of twenty-three critical
and seven biographical essays, with first publication of DHL's early version of "The Fox"
(see A34). Only nine items previously published. Includes F2, F69, F79, F100, F104,
F130, F132, H1, H224, H263, H270, H329, H412,
J3, M56, N11, T14, U52, V33, V52, V107, V119,
Y9, Y27, Y56, Y125, Z29, Z59, and extracts
from V5 and H383.

G82 Moore, Olive. FURTHER REFLECTIONS ON THE DEATH OF A PORC-
UPINE. London: Blue Moon, 1932.
Attacks the spate of memoirs by "cultists,"
finding DHL, *sans* myth, "one of the finest
imaginative prose writers in English letters."
(Pamphlet--34 pp.)

G83 Moynahan, Julian. THE DEED OF LIFE: THE NOVELS AND TALES
OF D.H. LAWRENCE. Princeton, N.J.: Princeton Univ. Press,
1963.
Close readings and technical analyses of the
novels and tales. Assuming that DHL is a
writer of fiction "first and last," a great
though uneven novelist, Moynahan considers
the first three novels as apprentice works
("The Search for Form"), while R and WL are
his highest achievement, his "discovery of
form." The last five novels document two re-
actions to the shattering experience of war.
AARON'S ROD, KANGAROO and PS are angry, poorly
constructed, and increasingly futile attempts
to change the world ("The Breaking of Form"),
but the two pastorals, THE LOST GIRL and LCL,
effectively "replac[e] the ruined world" with
an affirmation of life ("The Deed of Life").
The tales on the whole are consistent artistic successes, following the same develop-
mental scheme as the novels. Consistently
rewarding analyses, though straying at times
from the announced concern to form. Extract
originally published in G78. Extracts reprinted in G115, L3, M2, and N3. Also see
H355.

G84 Murry, John Middleton. D.H. LAWRENCE (TWO ESSAYS). Cambridge, Engl.: Minority Press, 1930.
Contains U53 and Y40. Also see F120.

G85 ------. LOVE, FREEDOM AND SOCIETY: AN ANALYTIC COMPARISON
OF D.H. LAWRENCE AND ALBERT SCHWEITZER. London: Cape,
1957.
Response to the devaluation of DHL's later
work, by Leavis and others. Murry attempts
to show DHL's progressive development from
impasse, at the prospect of civilization's
imminent destruction, to the discovery of a
new religious consciousness, the realization
that salvation "depends upon opening up new

sources of love" (cf. Schweitzer). Murry reads
DHL's later works as prophecies of much that
has since come to pass; however, he too force-
fully imposes his own mystic tendencies on DHL.
(DHL chiefly considered, pp. 23-123). Extract
reprinted in L3. See H138 and H151.

G86   Nahal, Chaman Lal. D.H. LAWRENCE: AN EASTERN VIEW.   South
Brunswick, N.J.: Barnes, 1970.
Study of several remarkable similarities between DHL's personal philosophy and Eastern
religious thought (also see G127). DHL's vitalism and Indian thought alike maintain the
reverence for life and for man's "relatedness"
to the universe, the importance of sex for
man's spiritual well-being, and the necessity
for full self-realization in life. Nahal thus
examines DHL's fiction, from his early "delight of creation" (THE WHITE PEACOCK), through
his evolution of the "love and marriage" ethic
(SL, R, WL, AARON'S ROD), to his advocacy of
intuitive self-consciousness as a positive
ideal in the late works (especially "The Man
Who Died"). Hindu philosophy provides the
framework for Nahal's original "view," but is
never imposed as a formula to explain DHL, or
for narrow critical exegesis. Includes a useful index of DHL's ideas and attitudes.

G87   Negriolli, Claude. LA SYMBOLIQUE DE D.H. LAWRENCE.   Paris:
Presses Universitaires de France, 1970.
Extended structuralist study of DHL's use of
symbols, "d'établir une systématique des sym-
boles, véhicules quasi obligatoires de la pensée, dans l'oeuvre de D.H. Lawrence." Negriolli finds a system "cohérent, équilibré et
stable" in DHL's employment of natural symbols
in his long and short fiction, and in a series
of chapters details DHL's symbolism of air and
fire (space, wind, sun, moon, stars, light and
darkness), water (purifying, violent, and destructive), earth (direction, journeys, topog-
raphy, architecture), bodies (physiognomy, sexuality, types, language, clothes), animals
(e.g., insects, fish, birds, reptiles, mam-
mals), and vegetation (e.g., grain, flowers,
trees, fruits). Systematic and, regrettably,
often self-evident commentary. [In French.]

G88   Nin, Anais.   D.H. LAWRENCE: AN UNPROFESSIONAL STUDY. Paris:
      Titus, 1932.
              Impressionistic, gushing appreciation, with
              some interesting insights. Discussing DHL
              from her own perspective as a professional
              writer, Nin shows remarkable sensitivity to
              the texture of DHL's language. Her views of
              DHL as the great modern "mystic" and as an
              androgynous writer anticipate some recent
              trends. Extract reprinted in G48. See H180.

G89   Niven, Alastair.   D.H. LAWRENCE: THE NOVELS. Cambridge:
      Cambridge Univ. Press, 1978.
              Readings of the ten major novels, concentrat-
              ing on their themes and language, intended as
              an introduction for the nonspecialist. Niven
              shows more enthusiasm for the first two novels
              than most commentators and argues for a higher
              estimate of the frequently dismissed KANGAROO.
              A creditable survey.

G90   -----.   D.H. LAWRENCE: THE WRITER AND HIS WORK. Harlow,
      Essex: Longman, 1980.
              Extended biographical and critical introduction
              to the "writer and his work." Slight critical
              value.

G91   Panichas, George A.   ADVENTURE IN CONSCIOUSNESS: THE MEAN-
      ING OF D.H. LAWRENCE'S RELIGIOUS QUEST. The Hague: Mouton,
      1964.
              Eight essays on DHL's progressive, yet unsys-
              tematic development of his religious ideas,
              his pursuit of a "fuller awareness of man's
              role in and contribution to life." Panichas
              finds DHL eventually transcending the secular
              "conflicts and fatality" of the modern world
              through an anti-materialist exaltation of the
              human spirit. He appraises DHL's inherited,
              nonconformist religious concepts, notes his
              identification with Christ and his love of
              Scripture, persuasively compares his and
              Dostoevsky's visions of evil (WL and CRIME
              AND PUNISHMENT [1867]), and analyzes his fas-
              cination with death in the later works. Use-
              ful, but not very well integrated commentaries.
              Extract reprinted in G5.

G92   Partlow, Robert B., and Harry T. Moore, eds. D.H. LAW-
       RENCE: THE MAN WHO LIVED: PAPERS DELIVERED AT THE D.H.
       LAWRENCE CONFERENCE AT SOUTHERN ILLINOIS UNIVERSITY, CAR-
       BONDALE, APRIL 1979. Carbondale: Southern Illinois Univ.
       Press, 1980.
              Twenty-six essays on DHL, his stories, his
              ideas and techniques, his major works, and
              his views of women, and on the textual edi-
              tions of his works. Indexed. (For Charles
              Rossman's report on the Carbondale conference
              on "D.H. Lawrence Today," where the papers in
              this volume were presented, see DHLR, 12
              [1979], 326-31). Includes F8, F134, H43,
              H66, H78, H261, H321, H324, H352, H373, L21,
              N12, N50, N81, R17, S5, U6, U66, V20, V25,
              V48, Y23, Z90, Z93, Z96, and Z100.

G93   Patmore, Derek. D.H. LAWRENCE AND THE DOMINANT MALE.
       London: Covent Garden Press, 1970.
              Suggests that DHL was "fascinated" by the dom-
              inant male type because of his own physical
              frailty. (Pamphlet--7 pp.)

G94   PAUNCH. No. 26 (1966), pp. 5-68. "D.H. Lawrence Number."
              Collects a brief note (by Arthur Efron, the
              editor), and five good essays on DHL's ideas,
              fiction, and reputation. Includes H408, L26,
              Q4, U12, and Z21.

G95   Pinion, F.B. A D.H. LAWRENCE COMPANION: LIFE, THOUGHT,
       AND WORKS. New York: Barnes and Noble, 1979.
              Brief biography, critical overviews of the
              major essays ("thought-adventures"), the po-
              etry, the shorter stories, the "other writ-
              ings" (fragments, travel, drama, literary
              criticism), and commentaries on the ten major
              novels (largely summaries, with slight, gen-
              eral criticism). Among various appendices is
              a useful listing of DHL's prototypes for char-
              acters and settings in the novels. Handy ref-
              erence work.

G96   Pinto, Vivian de Sola. D.H. LAWRENCE: PROPHET OF THE MID-
       LANDS. Nottingham: Univ. of Nottingham Press, 1951.
              Lecture on the formative influences of the mid-
              lands' culture, society, and nonsectarianism on
              DHL. (Pamphlet--24 pp.)

G97   Poole, Roger Henry. LAWRENCE AND EDUCATION. Nottingham:
       Univ. of Nottingham Press, 1968.
              On DHL's educational ideas as a manifestation
              of his general concern for the individual in
              mass society. (Pamphlet--14 pp.)

G98   Potter, Stephen. D.H. LAWRENCE: A FIRST STUDY. New York:
       Cape and Smith, 1930.
              Traces the impact of DHL's anti-intellectual
              intellectualism, his vitalist philosophy, on
              his works and his world view. Potter's crit-
              icisms are somewhat limited by his contempor-
              ary perspective, but several judgments remain
              sound. Incidentally, *not* a "first study"
              (see G108).

G99   Prasad, Madhusudan. D.H. LAWRENCE: A STUDY OF HIS NOVELS.
       Bareilly, India: Prakash Book Depot, 1980.
              Traces the autobiographical dimension of DHL's
              ten novels, with the assumption that "every
              character, theme and episode is based on the
              personal experiences of a fictionist." Prasad
              ploddingly relates figures and events in DHL's
              novels to prototypes he finds in the biograph-
              ical literature about DHL, occasionally sug-
              gesting an interesting sidelight on a partic-
              ular work, but in no way increasing our appre-
              ciation of DHL's fiction as art. A critically
              naive study, written in labored, unidiomatic
              English.

G100   Prasad, Suman Prabha. THOMAS HARDY AND D.H. LAWRENCE:
       A STUDY OF THE TRAGIC VISION IN THEIR NOVELS. London:
       Arnold-Heinemann, 1976.
              Analyses of six works each by Hardy and DHL
              (THE WHITE PEACOCK, THE TRESPASSER, SL, R,
              WL, LCL), arguing that, despite differences,
              Hardy and DHL present an essentially tragic
              vision of life. Prasad distinguishes their
              modern conceptions of tragedy, derived from
              Schopenhauer and Nietzsche, in terms of their
              conceptions of the tragic hero who is ulti-
              mately aware of the futility of human life.
              Hardy accepts his vision; DHL asserts a dog-
              matic optimism in his philosophy, but his
              works betray his fundamentally tragic sense
              of life. Well done, but not very profound.

G101 Pritchard, Ronald E. D.H. LAWRENCE: BODY OF DARKNESS.
      London: Hutchinson, 1971.
           Arm-chair Freudian study of the novels, tales,
           and poetry, based on the assumption that anal-
           eroticism provides the key to understanding
           DHL's personality and fiction. Thus, his
           statement of his "carbon" theme in the famous
           letter on R (reprinted in M2), becomes a typ-
           ically revealing trope: "by burrowing into the
           underworld, the bowels of the earth, is dis-
           covered the black primary material and living
           body of darkness associated with his father."
           Pritchard, too, relentlessly probes every
           "dark" episode in the works, adding slightly
           to our understanding of DHL. See H317 and U64.

G102 Rees, Richard. BRAVE MEN: A STUDY OF D.H. LAWRENCE AND
      SIMONE WEIL. London: Gollancz, 1958.
           Comparison of DHL and Simone Weil, a French
           mystic. Both DHL and Weil have a deep rev-
           erence for the "quality" of human life; both
           attribute the malaise of modern existence to
           the "uprooting effect of contemporary mass
           civilization"; and both attempt to counteract
           this disintegration of modern man by empha-
           sizing a vitalistic religion of love. Rees
           provides interesting insights into DHL's es-
           sentially "feminine" point of view and writes
           illuminatingly on THE LOST GIRL, to him "in
           some ways Lawrence's most perfect novel."
           See H198.

G103 Reul, Paul de. L'OEUVRE DE D.H. LAWRENCE. Paris: Vrin,
      1937.
           Broad survey of DHL's long and short fiction,
           poetry, and nonfiction, in roughly chronologi-
           cal order. Reul seeks, with frequent disap-
           pointment, a coherent philosophy in DHL, ana-
           lyzing the fiction and poetry with uninspired
           conventionality, often lapsing into apprecia-
           tion; nevertheless, his approach is marked by
           a balance of sympathy and judgment rarely
           achieved in mid-thirties' criticism of DHL.
           [In French.]

G104 Sagar, Keith. THE ART OF D.H. LAWRENCE. Cambridge: Cam-
      bridge Univ. Press, 1966.
           A "spiritual-artistic biography," examining
           the relationship between DHL's life and his

imaginative work.. Sagar traces DHL's periods
of growth (early fiction), maturity (through
WL), uncertainty (the post-war fiction), and
regeneration (LCL and the last writings),
with exhaustive documentation and, at times,
exhausting citation; however, he avoids the
danger of misreading the fiction as autobiography. Includes a primary and an extensive
secondary bibliography, and prefatory, chronological bibliographies before each subsection. Extracts reprinted in G48, L1, L5, and
M4.

G105   Salgādo, Gāmini.   A PREFACE TO D.H. LAWRENCE.   London:
       Longmans, [1983].
              Announced for 1983 publication. Not seen and
              publication unconfirmed.

G106   Sanders, Scott.   D.H. LAWRENCE: THE WORLD OF FIVE MAJOR
       NOVELS. New York: Viking, 1974.
              Correlates DHL's style, themes, and "the basic
              categories of his thought" with contemporary
              economic, political, and social developments.
              While DHL's thought shifted constantly through-
              out his works, his ideas are ultimately reduc-
              ible to a radical conflict between "nature and
              culture," the permutations of which Sanders
              traces in the social analyses of SL and R, the
              political contrasts of WL, the "religious and
              anthropological distinctions" of PS, and the
              final, aesthetic vision of LCL. Sanders con-
              cludes with a succinct and perceptive essay
              on the impact of the tensions between "liter-
              ary consciousness and social reality" on DHL's
              conception of the novel. Excellent insights
              throughout. See H407.

G107   Seillière, Ernest.   DAVID-HERBERT LAWRENCE ET LES RE-
       CÉNTES IDÉOLOGIES ALLEMANDES. Paris: Bovin, 1936.
              An important study of DHL's assimilation and
              synthesis of major elements of French and Ger-
              man Romanticism (and one of over fifty volumes
              by Baron Seillière tracing the pernicious ef-
              fects of Romanticism in the later nineteenth
              and early twentieth centuries). Seillière
              opens with an extended survey of those writers
              who "influenced" DHL, from the often-noted
              figures of Rousseau, Stendhal, Baudelaire,

Flaubert, Schopenhauer, Nietzsche, and Spengler, to the less frequently suggested names of Sand, Fénelon, Zola, and Ludwig Klages, the Bavarian romantic pantheist and irrationalist. The largest portion of Seillière's book examines, with disapproval, DHL's political, social, and sexual theories in his major fiction and essays. See Praz's review (H295) of Seillière's earlier work, NÉOROMANTISME EN ALLEMAGNE (1931), which might have provoked this thesis-ridden and argumentative, yet vividly written and illuminating study of DHL. [In French.]

G108 Seligmann, Herbert J. D.H. LAWRENCE: AN AMERICAN INTERPRETATION. New York: Seltzer, 1924.
Contemporary study, surveying a great many of DHL's writings, through KANGAROO, in a small space. Seligmann rates STUDIES IN CLASSIC AMERICAN LITERATURE highly and provides some interesting criticism on WL. Extracts reprinted in G20.

G109 Simpson, Hilary. D.H. LAWRENCE AND FEMINISM. Dekalb: Northern Illinois Univ. Press, [1982].
A "thorough investigation" of DHL's "relation to the feminist movement of his time" and "a balanced historical account of his attitudes toward women and sexual relations." (Quoted from publisher's advertisement--not seen.) Announced for late 1982 publication.

G110 Sinzelle, Claude M. THE GEOGRAPHICAL BACKGROUND OF THE EARLY WORKS OF D.H. LAWRENCE. Paris: M. Didier, 1964.
DHL's use of Eastwood and the mining countryside for symbol and setting, in THE WHITE PEACOCK, SL, two plays (A COLLIER'S FRIDAY NIGHT and THE WIDOWING OF MRS. HOLROYD), and several early tales. Much unnecessary biographical summary, but useful comments on animism, environmental determinism, and topographical accuracy in DHL's use of nature.

G111 Slade, Tony. D.H. LAWRENCE. New York: Arco, 1969.
Admirable brief study of DHL, written primarily for the non-academic audience. Hence, two rather pedestrian opening chapters are devoted to his life and background, and his "philosophy"

(i.e., DHL's ideas on sex). Slade's commentary
improves considerably with his considerations
of the novels (special emphasis on SL, R, and
WL), a sampling of the short fiction, and a
number of the major poems. A readable introductory volume.

G112 Smith, Anne, ed. LAWRENCE AND WOMEN. London: Vision,
1978.
Nine generally sensitive and for the most part
sensible essays on the inflammatory topic of
DHL's attitudes toward women. One essay previously published. Includes F150, H206, H258,
H265, H386, L54, M16, T3, and U65.

G113 Spender, Stephen, ed. D.H. LAWRENCE: NOVELIST, POET,
PROPHET. London: Weidenfeld and Nicolson, 1973.
Fifteen generally superficial, though pleasant
essays and memoirs (one previously published),
generously illustrated. A handsome academic
coffee-table volume. Includes F13, F62, F78,
H57, H165, H203, H249, H341, H347, H384, V30,
W11, Y9, Y35, and Z92.

G114 Spilka, Mark. THE LOVE ETHIC OF D.H. LAWRENCE. Bloomington: Indiana Univ. Press, 1955.
DHL seen as a profoundly religious, if non-
Christian novelist. His best works, Spilka
argues, follow a recurring pattern of spiritual self-discovery, embodied in the Lawrencean central character. DHL expertly blends
art and doctrine, making discovery the chief
structural component of the novels through
his repeated, ritualistic depiction of the
"resurrection or destruction of the human
soul, within the living body." The vehicle
of rebirth is DHL's "love ethic": the "radical commitment to spontaneous life, and to
'phallic marriage' as the fount of life itself." Spilka examines in detail major ritual scenes in SL, R, WL, LCL, and "The Man
Who Died," with some forcing to make the works
conform. Extracts reprinted in L1, L3, L7,
N3, and below. Also see V34.

G115 -----, ed. D.H. LAWRENCE: A COLLECTION OF CRITICAL ES-
SAYS. Englewood Cliffs, N.J.: Prentice-Hall, 1963.
Thirteen critical essays, all but one pre-
viously published. Contains studies of the

five major novels (SL, R, WL, PS, LCL), four
commentaries on the tales, and four essays
on "other genres." Excellent selection. Includes H412, L65, M56, N88, T17, V13, V147,
X7, Y43, Z29, and extracts from G56, G83,
and above.

G116 Stoll, John E. THE NOVELS OF D.H. LAWRENCE: A SEARCH
FOR INTEGRATION. Columbia: Univ. of Missouri Press,
1971.
Psychological study of DHL, differing little
from others in considering his writing a therapeutic search for psychic integration. Stoll
distinguishes DHL's vitalistic view of the unconscious from Freud and differentiates his
belief in the ultimately irreconcilable polar-
ities of the psyche from Jung, maintaining
that regeneration, for DHL, means the "destruction" of consciousness. To Stoll the
entire career assumes the pattern of recognition of psychological abnormality (early fiction), rejection of simple psychic integration
(R and WL), suggested salvation through disintegration (AARON'S ROD, KANGAROO, PS), and
idyllic completion of the quest for regeneration (LCL). Valuable account of the chaotic
post-war fiction, as a reflection of psychic
destruction, yet an overstated thesis which
violently orders the fiction into a "patterned
whole." Incorporates Stoll's D.H. LAWRENCE'S
"SONS AND LOVERS": SELF-ENCOUNTER AND THE UN-
KNOWN SELF (Muncie, Ind.: Ball State Univ.
Press, 1968). See H407.

G117 Swigg, Richard. LAWRENCE, HARDY, AND AMERICAN LITERATURE.
London: Oxford Univ. Press, 1972.
Relationships among DHL's "Study of Thomas
Hardy" (in B16), his two versions of STUDIES
IN CLASSIC AMERICAN LITERATURE, and his writing of R and WL. Closely analyzing several
major works by five authors, Swigg shows the
"tragic mode" of Hardy, Poe, Hawthorne, Melville, and Cooper merging with DHL's native
"sense of passive fatalism" in his developing
art. Too limited, too discursive, and too
dependent upon questionable assumptions of
influence.

G118 Tedlock, Ernest W. D.H. LAWRENCE: ARTIST AND REBEL: A
STUDY OF LAWRENCE'S FICTION. Albuquerque: Univ. of New
Mexico Press, 1963.
    A solid and scholarly study of DHL's entire
career. Tedlock ranges throughout the shorter
fiction and novels, discussing the works in
chronological order and following the by now
orthodox four-phase approach to his development: "Patterns of Revolt" (through SL),
"Alienation and Exile" (through AARON'S ROD),
"Search for a New World" (through PS), and
"Mediterranean and English Salvations" (LCL
and last works). No startlingly original
thesis, yet this study may be recommended for
its sobriety, its synthesis of viewpoints,
and its complete coverage of the fiction.
Extract reprinted in V130. See H355.

G119 Temple, Frédéric J. DAVID HERBERT LAWRENCE: L'OEUVRE ET
LA VIE. Paris: Seghers, 1960.
    Enthusiastic biographical reading of DHL's
major works, offering little original insight, confused synopses of DHL's "ideas,"
and too frequent factual errors. [In French.]
See H7.

G120 Tindall, William York. D.H. LAWRENCE AND SUSAN HIS COW.
New York: Columbia Univ. Press, 1939.
    Unsympathetic reading of DHL, partly influ-
enced by contemporary politics, partly by the
exaggerated claims of cultists. Tindall ex-
plains the evolution of DHL's spiritual temper
(symbolized in his "pursuit" of Susan, his cow
at Taos), and, through an examination of his
reading and sources, places him within the
"intellectual, social and literary movements
of his time." He finds DHL an anti-intellec-
tual, proto-fascist, animistic-theosophist
megalomaniac, and a sensual and evocative,
yet second-rate writer. Tindall considers
KANGAROO and PS, the "best novel," at some
length, although he generally avoids critical
commentary on the works. For Tindall's mod-
ified and revised judgments, see his post-war
FORCES IN MODERN BRITISH LITERATURE (H378).
Extract reprinted in G53. Also see H19.

G121 Vivas, Eliseo. D.H. LAWRENCE: THE FAILURE AND THE TRI-
      UMPH OF ART. Evanston, Ill.: Northwestern Univ. Press,
      1960.
          One of the most challenging books on DHL, a
          full exploration of the view of DHL implicit
          in T.S. Eliot's criticisms (see H104-H107).
          Vivas, a distinguished aesthetician, analyzes
          the works to determine the nature of DHL's
          weaknesses and strengths, unoriginally con-
          cluding that DHL fails when he sacrifices his
          art to his doctrine. His individual analyses,
          however, are consistently thoughtful. Vivas
          first examines the four major "failures,"
          AARON'S ROD, KANGAROO, PS, and LCL, finding
          much to admire but ultimately dismissing them
          as unintegrated. SL, R, and WL, DHL's most
          mature works, successfully synthesize art and
          message through his use of the "constitutive
          symbol" (here defined). Imaginative yet ul-
          timately arbitrary judgments. Extracts re-
          printed in L5 and N3. See H172, H208, H254,
          and H407.

G122 Weidner, Ingeborg. BOTSCHAFTSVERKÜNDIGUNG UND SELBSTAUS-
      DRUCK IM PROSAWERK VON D.H. LAWRENCE [MESSAGE AND SELF-
      EXPRESSION IN THE FICTION OF D.H. LAWRENCE]. Braunschweig:
      Serger and Hempel, 1938.
          Impressive survey of DHL's ideas, arranged
          topically and illustrated thoroughly from his
          letters, fiction, and essays (the poetry is
          dismissed as too impressionistic and unrelia-
          ble). Following a prefatory summary of the
          backgrounds of DHL's representative, modern
          quest to express the ineffable, to explore
          soul-knowledge and life-knowledge (which grew
          out of his predecessors' exhaustion of mate-
          rialist and psychological naturalism), Weidner
          surveys the personal, self-expressive dimen-
          sions of DHL's writings and paintings (e.g.,
          his self-criticism, revision, self-contradic-
          tion, self-therapy through art, consciousness
          of mission). The largest portion of her study
          classifies, discusses, and documents DHL's
          leading ideas (e.g., his concern for contemp-
          orary issues, quest for a "new world," wonder
          for life, affirmative view of sexuality, du-
          alistic vision of human nature, proposed rem-
          edies, etc.). Though scarce, this study of

"England's Nietzsche" remains valuable as a
serious, objective, and nonpolitical consideration of DHL, unique for its place and time.
[In German.]

G123 Weiss, Daniel A. OEDIPUS IN NOTTINGHAM: D.H. LAWRENCE.
Seattle: Univ. of Washington Press, 1962.
Rigorously Freudian reading of DHL. Weiss's
opening chapter suggests a balanced psycho-
analytic-critical approach to DHL and his
discussion of SL, the major part of his book,
is judicious and illuminating. Weiss argues
the early fiction confronts the Oedipus complex and the later works elaborate an "anti-
oedipal" vision; however, his application of
SL as a guidebook to DHL, in a brief overview
of the rest of the career, leads to a distorted, reductive interpretation of much of
the best fiction. Extracts reprinted in L1,
L7, and N3. See H146 and H355.

G124 Wesslau, Werner. DER PESSIMISMUS BEI D.H. LAWRENCE.
Greifswald: Hans Adler, 1931.
The first of many German studies of DHL.
Wesslau surveys DHL's "pessimism" (defined
as his view of existence, the world, and life
as so miserable that nonexistence would be
preferable), with extensive reference to DHL's
expression of pessimistic attitudes, principally through his characters in his major
fiction. Under three general headings, Wesslau describes and documents DHL's pessimistic
psychological, sociological, and philsophic
views (re: relationships, marriage, the family, industry, politics, etc.), for the most
part overlooking DHL's affirmations. He does
admit, however, in his final assessment of
DHL's personal philosophy, that, while ex-
pressing little hope, DHL suggests some remote
possibility of a more fulfilling creative
existence, that DHL's pessimism is relative,
a product of his time, and critically con-
structive ("relativer, temporärer, kritischer
Pessimismus"). [In German.]

G125 West, Anthony. D.H. LAWRENCE. 1950. 2nd ed. London:
Barker, 1966.
Biographical and critical introduction. West
sees DHL as an "extreme romantic" who succeeded

best when his temperament was confined (e.g.,
in the short fiction). Dated opinions. (2nd
ed. only slightly altered.) Extract reprinted
in G53.

G126 Wettern, Regina. D.H. LAWRENCE: ZUR FUNKTION UND FUNK-
TIONS-WEISE VON LITERARISCHEM IRRATIONALISMUS [D.H. LAW-
RENCE: ON THE FUNCTION AND STRATEGY OF LITERARY IRRATION-
ALISM]. Heidelberg: C. Winter, 1979.
Densely-written study of DHL's evolving myst-
ical-metaphysical *"symbolsystem,"* in R, WL,
and PS, as it arises out of Romantic tradi-
tions of irrationalism and matures as a re-
placement for reality in his work (the func-
tional strategy of the system). Wettern
traces DHL's irrationalism in his ideological
studies of the origins of *"regressiv"* social
behavior in his essays, and in his delinea-
tion of regressive behavior in his fiction,
relating R to "Study of Thomas Hardy" (in
B16), WL to "The Crown" (A60) and FANTASIA
OF THE UNCONSCIOUS (A63), among other works,
and PS, the completion of his system's evolution, again to FANTASIA OF THE UNCONSCIOUS.
Useful observations on DHL's intellectual
forebears, his critical reputation as a sym-
bolist, his craft of fiction, and his systematic use of structural symbols.

G127 Wickramasinghe, Martin. THE MYSTICISM OF D.H. LAWRENCE.
Colombo, Ceylon [Sri Lanka]: Gunasena, 1951.
Interesting, but unfortunately scarce study.
Wickramasinghe compares DHL's mystical accep-
tance of an "irrational truth," his view of
sex as beyond sensuality, and his "noble philosophic conceptions" mixed with ritual and
magic, to the Indian mystic philosophy of
Tantricism. He expertly discusses PS to illustrate his thesis that DHL's unsystematic
philosophy is not especially original (Tantricism dates from the eighth century). He suggests, less convincingly, the possibility that
DHL was exposed to Tantric literature during
his Eastern travels, or through the translations of Sir John Woodroffe (c. 1918). Also
see G86.

G128 Worthen, John. D.H. LAWRENCE AND THE IDEA OF THE NOVEL.
      Totowa, N.J.: Rowman and Littlefield, 1979.
             Reconstructs the development of DHL's ten
             novels, from conception to publication, rely-
             ing principally on biographical documents and
             curiously omitting any substantive commentary
             on the manuscripts or texts. Worthen argues,
             reasonably, that DHL always wrote for an audi-
             ence. However simple-minded, his assertion
             does lead him to several useful discussions
             of DHL's changing relationship with his audi-
             ence, his ideal of a unity between artist and
             audience despite his own sense of isolation,
             and his developing ideas of how to achieve
             this symbolic union. While neither an account
             of the novel's textual evolution, nor, strictly
             speaking, a study of DHL's theories of fiction,
             a moderately useful history of the composition
             of the major fiction.

G129 Young, Kenneth. D.H. LAWRENCE. London: Longmans, 1952.
             Brief introduction to DHL's life and work.
             Most of Young's critical opinions are dated
             (e.g., "Lawrence obeys no rules"). See G71.

G130 Yudhishtar, M. CONFLICT IN THE NOVELS OF D.H. LAWRENCE.
      New York: Barnes and Noble, 1969.
             Quarrelsome and idolatrous book. When he is
             not attacking previous, "unenlightened" crit-
             ics, Yudhishtar traces through each of the
             novels his central thesis that the key to
             DHL's meaning is his theme of conflict be-
             tween men, or between man and the universe.
             This axiom is general enough to apply to all
             narrative forms, so it clearly "works" with
             DHL. Adds little to our understanding of
             DHL. Extract reprinted in G48.

G131 Zytaruk, George J. D.H. LAWRENCE'S RESPONSE TO RUSSIAN
      LITERATURE. The Hague: Mouton, 1971.
             Specialized investigation into DHL's reading,
             criticism, and translation of Russian writers,
             especially Tolstoy, Dostoevsky, and Rozanov.
             Zytaruk makes some tentative judgments of the
             Russian influence on DHL as artist and pursues
             effectively the influence of Rozanov's "phallic
             vision" on "The Man Who Died," as already noted
             by Jarrett-Kerr (see G62).

H. GENERAL CRITICAL ARTICLES OR CHAPTERS ON LAWRENCE

Also see Appendix A, parts ii-iii.

H1 Abel, Patricia, and Robert Hogan. "D.H. Lawrence's Singing
    Birds." NS, 2 (1958), 49-56.
        DHL's bird imagery illustrates his "assimilation
        of the use of myth and archetype." Reprinted in
        G81.

H2 Abrams, M.H. "Four Versions of the Circuitous Return: Marx,
    Nietzsche, Eliot, Lawrence." In NATURAL SUPERNATURALISM:
    TRADITION AND REVOLUTION IN ROMANTIC LITERATURE. New York:
    Norton, 1971. Pp. 313-24.
        DHL's share in the development of the Romantic
        themes of alienation and "the persisting quest
        for connection, community," now obsessive con-
        cerns of the modern era.

H3 Adamowski, T.H. "Character and Consciousness: D.H. Law-
    rence, Wilhelm Reich, and Jean-Paul Sartre." UTQ, 43
    (1974), 311-34.
        DHL's view of human psychology, in light of re-
        cent theories on the "nature of character." Also
        see N5.

H4 -----. "Self/Body/Other: Orality and Ontology in Lawrence."
    DHLR, 13 (1980), 193-208.
        DHL's "themes of existence" discussed from the
        perspectives of Sartrean Existentialism and
        psychoanalytic theories of "pre-oedipal," or
        "oral" psychic development. See G28. Also
        see N5.

H5 Albright, Daniel. "D.H. Lawrence." In PERSONALITY AND
    IMPERSONALITY: LAWRENCE, WOOLF, AND MANN. Chicago: Univ.
    of Chicago Press, 1978. Pp. 17-95.
        DHL's views of personality and his innovative
        creation of characters suffused with his own
        personality.

H6   Alcorn, John. THE NATURE NOVEL FROM HARDY TO LAWRENCE.
        New York: Columbia Univ. Press, 1977. Pp. 75-102 and
        passim.
                DHL's early fiction imitative of Hardy and his
                mid-career works (R and WL) adaptations of pas-
                toral conventions to modern themes.

H7   Aldington, Richard. "D.H. Lawrence." 1960. In SELECTED
        CRITICAL WRITINGS, 1928-1960. Ed. Alister Kershaw. Car-
        bondale: Southern Illinois Univ. Press, 1970. Pp. 130-37.
                The distortions of DHL's reputation in France
                (originally a preface to Temple's critical
                study [G119]).

H8   Alexander, Edward. "Thomas Carlyle and D.H. Lawrence: A
        Parallel." UTQ, 37 (1968), 248-67.
                Both writers seen as intellectually confused
                misanthropes who refused to learn from contemp-
                orary moral philosophers, J.S. Mill and Ber-
                trand Russell.

H9   Alexander, Henry. "Lawrence and Huxley." QQ, 42 (1935),
        96-108.
                Despite their comparable concern for the rela-
                tions of the sexes, the two writers offer drastic
                contrasts in their works.

H10   Alexander, John C. "D.H. Lawrence and Teilhard de Chardin:
        A Study in Agreements." 1966. DHLR, 2 (1969), 138-56.
                Similarities in their views of human sexuality.

H11   Allen, Walter. AS I WALKED DOWN NEW GRUB STREET: MEMORIES
        OF A WRITING LIFE. Chicago: Univ. of Chicago Press, 1981.
        Pp. 17-19 and passim.
                Allen recalls his discovery of DHL during his
                adolescence and records his lasting conviction
                that DHL "remains the greatest *English* writer
                of the century...a virtuoso" in the numerous
                "literary forms he commanded."

H12   -----. THE ENGLISH NOVEL: A SHORT CRITICAL HISTORY.   New
        York: Dutton, 1954. Pp. 431-39.
                DHL a "great romantic poet" in prose, England's
                nonconformist "genius" (cf. Joyce).

H13   -----. THE MODERN NOVEL IN BRITAIN AND THE UNITED STATES.
        New York: Dutton, 1964. Pp. 21-29.
                DHL's essential "Englishness" extraordinary fac-
                ulty for "primitive thinking and feeling," sym-
                bolic techniques, and social insight.

H14   Amado, Éliane Lévy-Valensi. "L'en-deçà de la connaissance:
      Le péché et les voies du salut dans l'ontologie Lawrenci-
      enne" ["On This Side of Consciousness: Sin and the Means
      of Salvation in the Lawrencean Ontology"]. In LES NIVEAUX
      DE L'ÊTRE, LA CONNAISSANCE, ET LA MAL [LEVELS OF BEING,
      CONSCIOUSNESS, AND EVIL]. Paris: Presses Universitaires
      de France, 1962. Pp. 280-333.
          Extended study of DHL's vitalistic world view
          (cf. Schopenhauer). [In French.]

H15   Ananthamurthy, U.R. "D.H. Lawrence as an Indian Writer
      Sees Him." LCrit, 16, No. 2 (1981), 1-17.
          Suggests several sources for DHL's strong ap-
          peal to Indian readers (e.g., class conscious-
          ness, the mystical strain).

H16   Anderson, Sherwood. "A Man's Song of Life." VQR, 9
      (1933), 108-14.
          Views DHL as the "greatest" writer "who has
          lived in my times."

H17   Appleman, Philip. "D.H. Lawrence and the Intrusive Knock."
      MFS, 3 (1957-58), 328-32.
          DHL's subtle and varied use of the "device" of
          the "intrusive knock," for sudden contrast,
          viewed in light of DeQuincey's essay "On the
          Knocking at the Gate in MACBETH" (1823). (Re:
          "The Prussian Officer," THE TRESPASSER, SL,
          THE FIRST LADY CHATTERLEY).

H18   Armytage, W.H.G. "The Disenchanted Mecanophobes in Twen-
      tieth Century England." EXTRAPOLATION, 9 (1968), 33-60.
          DHL, Auden, Huxley, and Orwell as antiutopians.

H19   Auden, W.H. "Heretics (Rimbaud and Lawrence)." 1939.
      In LITERARY OPINION IN AMERICA. Ed. Morton Dauwen Zabel.
      1937. Rev. ed. New York: Harpers, 1951. Pp. 256-59.
          Notes parallels in lives and attitudes of
          the two writers (unsympathetic review of Tin-
          dall [see G120] and Enid Starkie's ARTHUR RIM-
          BAUD [1939]).

H20   -----. "Some Notes on D.H. Lawrence." NATION, 164 (1947),
      482-84.
          Selective praise for a DHL whose "answers do
          not mean much to us any more; [but] his ques-
          tions still disturb a good deal." Review of
          B19. Extract reprinted in G5.

H21 Baim, Joseph. "D.H. Lawrence's Social Vision." In IN
HONOR OF AUSTIN WRIGHT. Ed. Baim, et al. Pittsburgh:
Carnegie-Mellon Univ. Press, 1972. Pp. 1-9.
DHL's distrust of political distractions and
his social ideal, based on revived personal
relations.

H22 Baker, Ernest A. "D.H. Lawrence." In THE HISTORY OF THE
ENGLISH NOVEL. Vol. 10. YESTERDAY. New York: Barnes and
Noble, 1939. Pp. 345-91.
Judicious historical account of DHL's "uneven"
achievement.

H23 Baldanza, Frank. "D.H. Lawrence's Song of Songs." MFS,
7 (1961), 106-14.
Influence of Biblical language on DHL's style
(R, WL, and other works).

H24 Ballin, Micheal. "The Third Eye: The Relationship Between
D.H. Lawrence and Maurice Maeterlinck." In THE PRACTICAL
VISION: ESSAYS IN ENGLISH LITERATURE IN HONOUR OF FLORA
ROY. Ed. Jane Campbell and James Doyle. Waterloo, Ont.:
Wilfrid Laurier Univ. Press, 1978. Pp. 87-102.
DHL's and Maeterlinck's comparable assimilation
of occult symbolism (especially the horse sym-
bol).

H25 Bantock, G.H. "D.H. Lawrence and the Nature of Freedom."
In FREEDOM AND AUTHORITY IN EDUCATION: A CRITICISM OF
MODERN CULTURAL AND EDUCATIONAL ASSUMPTIONS. London:
Faber, 1952. Pp. 133-81.
DHL an unsystematic, yet penetrating critic of
modern educational ideas.

H26 Baron, Carl E. "Lawrence's Influence on Eliot." CAMBRIDGE
QUARTERLY, 5 (1971), 235-48.
Lawrencean elements in THE FOUR QUARTETS (1936-
42).

H27 -----. "The Nottingham Festival D.H. Lawrence Exhibition,
1972." DHLR, 7 (1974), 19-57.
Comments principally on the influence of the
visual arts in DHL's "cultural heritage." Includes a valuable portfolio of fifty photographs, chiefly of art works by or admired by
DHL. Also see E19.

H28   Bartlett, Norman. "Aldous Huxley and D.H. Lawrence."
      AusQ, 36, No. 1 (1964), 76-84.
      "Huxley was always trying to justify intellect-
      ually D.H. Lawrence's instinctive religion of
      sensuality."

H29   Bayley, John. THE CHARACTERS OF LOVE: A STUDY IN THE LIT-
      ERATURE OF PERSONALITY. London: Constable, 1960. Pp. 24-
      29 and passim.
      DHL a prime example of the paradox of the Ro-
      mantic's attack on love "in the head." The
      clarity of DHL's romantic mysticism and the
      "unity and intensity" of his intelligence make
      his emphasis on visceral experience in "his
      world of love more...purely abstract" and cere-
      bral "than that of any other great author."

H30   -----. THE USES OF DIVISION: UNITY AND DISHARMONY IN LIT-
      ERATURE. New York: Viking, 1976. Pp. 27-50.
      DHL, Forster, and Kipling as divided personali-
      ties both manipulating art to "speak on their
      behalf" and struggling to "emancipate their art
      from themselves."

H31   Beach, Joseph Warren. "Impressionism: Lawrence." In THE
      TWENTIETH-CENTURY NOVEL: STUDIES IN TECHNIQUE. New York:
      Appleton, 1932. Pp. 366-84.
      Thematic rather than technical examination of
      SL, R, and WL.

H32   Beauvoir, Simone de. "D.H. Lawrence or Phallic Pride."
      In THE SECOND SEX. Trans. and ed. H.M. Parshley. New
      York: Knopf, 1953. Pp. 214-24.
      Woman in DHL's works "is not evil, she is even
      good--but subordinated" to man. Classic discus-
      sion of DHL's passionate belief "in the supre-
      macy of the male," both extended in implication
      and diminished in critical perspicuity by Mil-
      lett (see H255). Also see H233, H319, and AA55.

H33   Bedient, Calvin. ARCHITECTS OF THE SELF: GEORGE ELIOT,
      D.H. LAWRENCE, AND E.M. FORSTER. Berkeley: Univ. of
      California Press, 1972. Pp. 98-195.
      The inevitable frustration of DHL's "transcen-
      dent" ideal of the vital, non-social self as
      "sacred being." Includes essays on DHL and
      George Eliot, on SL, WL, PS, and LCL, and on
      DHL and Forster.

H34 Beer, John. "'The Last Englishman': Lawrence's Apprecia-
tion of Forster." In E.M. FORSTER: A HUMAN EXPLORATION:
CENTENARY ESSAYS. Ed. G.K. Das and John Beer. New York:
New York Univ. Press, 1979. Pp. 245-68.
> Demonstrates a number of similarities between
> DHL and Forster, and documents DHL's admiration
> for A PASSAGE TO INDIA (1924).

H35 Bell, Michael. PRIMITIVISM. London: Methuen, 1972. Passim.
> Comments throughout on primitivist elements in
> DHL's writings.

H36 Bennett, Arnold. "[A Tribute of Admiration]." 1930. In
D.H. LAWRENCE: THE CRITICAL HERITAGE. Ed. Ronald P. Draper. Pp. 340-42. See G34.
> Last of Bennett's several admiring comments on
> DHL, praising his frankness and his fiction (as
> opposed to his "philosophy"), yet noting his
> lack of "discipline."

H37 Bentley, Eric. "D.H. Lawrence, John Thomas, and Dionysos."
In A CENTURY OF HERO WORSHIP. 1944. 2nd ed. Boston: Bea-
con Press, 1957. Pp. 215-36.
> Influence of Carlyle and Nietzsche on DHL, the
> "heroic vitalist." General survey with passing
> reference to KANGAROO, PS, LCL, and APOCALYPSE.

H38 Bentley, Joseph. "Aldous Huxley's Ambivalent Responses
to the Ideas of D.H. Lawrence." TCL, 13 (1967), 139-53.
> Huxley's dualistic, satiric view of man pre-
> vents him from accepting DHL's pleas for "un-
> ity of being."

H39 Bergonzi, Bernard. HEROES' TWILIGHT: A STUDY OF THE LIT-
ERATURE OF THE GREAT WAR. New York: Coward-McCann, 1965.
Pp. 141-44.
> Slight commentary on the effect of the war on
> DHL.

H40 Bersani, Leo. "Lawrencian Stillness." In A FUTURE FOR
ASTYANAX: CHARACTER AND DESIRE IN LITERATURE. Boston:
Little, Brown, 1976. Pp. 156-85.
> Contrast between "agitation" and the Lawren-
> cean "ideal of stillness" in DHL's symbolism,
> themes, and characterization.

H41   Bilan, R.P.   "Leavis on Lawrence."   In THE LITERARY CRIT-
      ICISM OF F.R. LEAVIS.   Cambridge: Cambridge Univ. Press,
      1979.   Pp. 195-272.
           Extended discussion of Leavis's interest in and
           writings on DHL, in the contexts of Leavis's
           thought and of the central issues in modern
           literary criticism.   See G68.

H42   Black, Michael H.   THE LITERATURE OF FIDELITY.   London:
      Chatto and Windus, 1975.   Pp. 169-211.
           Finds DHL embarrassingly shallow in his treat-
           ment of marriage and fidelity, in comparison
           to Tolstoy (R, WL, LCL and ANNA KARENINA
           [1877]).

H43   ------.   "The Works of D.H. Lawrence: The Cambridge Edi-
      tion."   In D.H. LAWRENCE: THE MAN WHO LIVED.   Ed. Robert
      B. Partlow and Harry T. Moore.   Pp. 49-57.   See G92.
           Supervising editor of the Cambridge edition
           (see B1) describes and accounts for the deplor-
           able state of DHL's texts and summarizes the
           Press's editorial principles (with examples).

H44   Blanchard, Lydia.   "Love and Power: A Reconsideration of
      Sexual Politics in D.H. Lawrence."   MFS, 21 (1975), 431-43.
           Illustrates DHL's attack on destructive, male
           domination (contra Millet, see H255).   Also
           see H233.

H45   Blisset, William.   "D.H. Lawrence, D'Annunzio, Wagner."
      WSCL, 7 (1966), 21-46.
           DHL's sustained motivic style influenced di-
           rectly and indirectly (through D'Annunzio) by
           Wagner.

H46   Bloom, Alice.   "The Larger Connection: The Communal Vision
      in D.H. Lawrence."   YR, 68 (1979), 176-91.
           DHL's thirst for community, in his travels and
           in his writings.

H47   Bodkin, Maud.   ARCHETYPAL PATTERNS IN POETRY: PSYCHOLOGI-
      CAL STUDIES OF IMAGINATION.   London: Oxford Univ. Press,
      1934.   Pp. 289-99.
           Discusses DHL's use of the "rebirth" archetype
           in his *fiction*.

H48   Bolsterli, Margaret. "Studies in Context: The Homosexual
      Ambience of Twentieth Century Literary Culture." DHLR,
      6 (1973), 71-85.
            Welcomes a number of recent studies which clar-
            ify DHL's cultural context by discussing more
            openly than earlier works "the influence of
            homosexuality on English intellectual and so-
            cial life." (Reviews F44, among several other
            works not directly concerned with DHL).

H49   Bowen, Elizabeth. "D. H. Lawrence." 1947. In her COL-
      LECTED IMPRESSIONS. New York: Knopf, 1950. Pp. 156-59.
            Foresees the post-war recovery of DHL's reputa-
            tion: "...this is his day. He has outlived his
            denouncers."

H50   Boyers, Robert. "Leavis and the Novel: 2. D.H. Lawrence."
      In F. R. LEAVIS: JUDGMENT AND THE DISCIPLINE OF THOUGHT.
      Columbia: Univ. of Missouri Press, 1978. Pp. 100-22.
            Examines Leavis's extraordinary and not always
            convincing, partisan criticism of DHL. See G68.

H51   Bramley, J.A. "The Significance of D.H. Lawrence." Con-
      tempR, 195 (1959), 304-07.
            DHL's preoccupations with the relations between
            the sexes and the "horrors of industrialism"
            potentially fruitful, yet his influence has
            been largely "wild and irresponsible, if not
            actually destructive and pernicious."

H52   Bredsdorff, Elias. "D.H. Lawrence." In FREMMEDE DIGTERE
      I DET 20 ÅRHUNDREDE. Ed. Sven M. Kristensen. Copenhagen:
      G.E.C. Gads, 1968. II, 19-41.
            Biographical summary, survey of the fiction
            (principally the novels), and conclusion that
            "The Man Who Died" is a central book for under-
            standing DHL's idea of the art of living. [In
            Danish.]

H53   Broembsen, F. von. "Mythic Identification and Spatial
      Inscendence: The Cosmic Vision of D.H. Lawrence." WHR,
      29 (1975), 137-54.
            The failure of most readers and critics to rec-
            ognize the mythic dimensions of DHL's fiction,
            reducing his works to, and judging his works
            by, the "categories" of conventional fiction.

H54   Brown, Ivor.   "Brother Lawrence"; "Belly and Brain."   In
I COMMIT TO THE FLAMES.   London: Hamilton, 1934.   Pp. 78-
94; 95-109.
  Extremely contemptuous attack on DHL's ideas,
  rhetoric, sentimentality, primitivism, and fascism.

H55   Brunsdale, Mitzi M.   "Lawrence and the Myth of Brynhild."
WHR, 31 (1977), 342-48.
  Influence of Ibsen on DHL's "view of woman as
  a sexual mediatrix" to creativity, in his early
  fiction (through SL).

H56   Bullett, Gerald.   MODERN ENGLISH FICTION.   London: Jenkins,
1926.   Pp. 93-99.
  DHL not a "barbarian" but a civilized man who
  "worships instinct."   His later prose style
  "ineffectual verbiage."

H57   Carey, John.   "D.H. Lawrence's Doctrine."   In D.H. LAW-
RENCE.   Ed. Stephen Spender.   Pp. 122-34.   See G113.
  Superficial outlines of DHL's thought on "epis-
  temology, morals, religion, sociology and sex."

H58   Caudwell, Christopher.   "D.H. Lawrence: A Study of the
Bourgeois Artist."   In STUDIES IN A DYING CULTURE.   New
York: Dodd, Mead, 1938.   Pp. 44-72.
  Distinguished, though heavy-handed Marxist in-
  terpretation of DHL as a fascist.   Influential.
  See H189 and H405.

H59   Cavaliero, Glen.   "Phoenix and Serpent: D.H. Lawrence and
John Cowper Powys."   THE POWYS REVIEW, No. 2 (1977), pp.
51-58; No. 3 (1978), p. 103.
  Strong similarities in the two authors' "comple-
  mentary approaches to reality."

H60   -----.   THE RURAL TRADITION IN THE ENGLISH NOVEL, 1900-
1939.   Totowa, N.J.: Rowman and Littlefield, 1977.   Pp.
206-08 and passim.
  DHL's tangential relation to the rural novelists
  of modern England (e.g., the Powys brothers,
  among others).

H61   Chaning-Pearce, Melville.   THE TERRIBLE CRYSTAL: STUDIES
IN KIERKEGAARD AND MODERN CHRISTIANITY.   New York: Oxford
Univ. Press, 1941.   Pp. 179-89.
  Magic, myth, and the supernatural as religion
  surrogates in DHL (cf. J.C. Powys).

H62   Chesterton, G.K. "The End of the Moderns." LONDON MER-
       CURY, 27 (1933), 228-33.
               "There was something grand about D.H. Lawrence
               groping blindly in the dark; but he really was
               in the dark, not only about the Will of God,
               but about the will of D.H. Lawrence."

H63   -----. "The Spirit of the Age in Literature." BOOKMAN
       (New York), 72 (1930), 97-103.
               Though DHL "started cock-sure that he was
               right, [he] gradually grew more and more
               fruitful and human as he discovered that he
               was wrong." Unusual conservative perspective
               on DHL, among other moderns (e.g., James
               Joyce and Rebecca West).

H64   Chevalley, Abel. "D.H. Lawrence." In THE MODERN ENGLISH
       NOVEL. Trans. B.R. Redman. New York: Knopf, 1927. Pp.
       236-38.
               DHL's "fierce" feeling for nature, "sensual
               emotion," and awkward treatment of sexuality
               (through SL). Reprinted in G34. Also see
               AA60.

H65   Clark, L.D. "D.H. Lawrence and the American Indian."
       DHLR, 9 (1976), 305-72.
               DHL's fascination with and ambivalence toward
               the American Indian (includes twenty-seven re-
               lated photographs).

H66   -----. "Immediacy and Recollection: The Rhythm of the
       Visual in D.H. Lawrence." In D.H. LAWRENCE: THE MAN WHO
       LIVED. Ed. Robert B. Partlow and Harry T. Moore. Pp.
       121-35. See G92.
               DHL's repetition of "key images" in visual
               scenes parallels the "continual, slightly mod-
               ified repetition" he described as characteriz-
               ing his prose style (WL, p. viii). Supple-
               mented with five passages from DHL and sixteen
               photographs by Laverne Harrell Clark.

H67   Cockshut, A.O.J. MAN AND WOMAN: A STUDY OF LOVE AND THE
       NOVEL, 1740-1940. London: Collins, 1977. Pp. 152-60,
       199-204.
               Superficial and inaccurate summary of DHL's
               sexual attitudes in R, WL, and "The Fox."

H68   Collins, Arthur S.   ENGLISH LITERATURE OF THE TWENTIETH
      CENTURY.   1951.   4th ed.   London: University Tutorial
      Press, 1961.   Pp. 203-10.
            General overview and comparison with E.M. For-
            ster.

H69   Collins, Joseph.   "Even Yet It Can't Be Told--The Whole
      Truth About D.H. Lawrence."   In THE DOCTOR LOOKS AT LIT-
      ERATURE.   London: Allen and Unwin, 1923.   Pp. 256-88.
            DHL a depraved and sterile pornographer.   Col-
            lins's essay is a valuable index to the atti-
            tudes DHL had to confront.

H70   Collins, Norman.   "The Case Against D.H. Lawrence."   In
      THE FACTS OF FICTION.   London: Gollancz, 1932.   Pp. 237-48.
            Severely negative view of DHL's "frantic in-
            tensity," "fantastic conception of mankind,"
            "dismal" style, obscure meaning, and "contempt
            for the world."

H71   Collis, John Stewart.   "An Inevitable Prophet."   In FARE-
      WELL TO ARGUMENT.   London: Cassell, 1935.   Pp. 156-95.
            DHL, the anti-rationalist, a logical and inev-
            itable result of modern intellectualism: if he
            "had not existed he would have been invented."
            (Also see Collis's contrast of DHL and Gandhi,
            pp. 50-54.)

H72   Connolly, Cyril.   "Under Which King?"   LIVING AGE, 341
      (1932), 533-38.
            Discounts both DHL and Aldous Huxley from ser-
            ious consideration as artists.

H73   Cook, Albert S.   THE MEANING OF FICTION.   Detroit: Wayne
      State Univ. Press, 1960.   Pp. 171-75.
            The novelist and the prophet are mutually sup-
            portive in DHL's best fiction.

H74   Cook, Ian G.   "Consciousness and the Novel: Fact or Fic-
      tion in The Works of D.H. Lawrence."   In HUMANISTIC GEOG-
      RAPHY AND LITERATURE: ESSAYS ON THE EXPERIENCE OF PLACE.
      Ed. Douglas C.D. Pocock.   Totowa, N.J.: Barnes and Noble,
      1981.   Pp. 66-84.
            From the perspective of the humanistic geogra-
            pher, DHL "strongest in the portrayal of place"
            and "weakest...in his description, or lack of
            description, of the links between the individ-
            ual and society," in his "coalfield novels"
            (THE WHITE PEACOCK, SL, R, WL, LCL).

H75 Core, Deborah. "'The Closed Door': Love Between Women in the Works of D.H. Lawrence." DHLR, 11 (1978), 114-31.
DHL shows "disdain" for female friendships incompatible with his exaltation of male relationships.

H76 Cornwell, Ethel F. "The Sex Mysticism of D.H. Lawrence." In THE "STILL POINT": THEME AND VARIATIONS IN THE WRITINGS OF T.S. ELIOT, COLERIDGE, YEATS, HENRY JAMES, VIRGINIA WOOLF, AND D.H. LAWRENCE. New Brunswick, N.J.: Rutgers Univ. Press, 1962. Pp. 208-41.
Equilibrium achieved through balanced, dynamic tensions in DHL's works.

H77 Coveney, Peter. THE IMAGE OF CHILDHOOD. THE INDIVIDUAL AND SOCIETY: A STUDY OF THE THEME IN ENGLISH LITERATURE. 1957. Rev. ed. Baltimore, Md.: Penguin, 1967. Pp. 320-36.
General examination of the child in DHL, concentrating on SL, R, and "The Rocking-Horse Winner."

H78 Cowan, James C. "D.H. Lawrence and the Resurrection of the Body." In D.H. LAWRENCE: THE MAN WHO LIVED. Ed. Robert B. Partlow and Harry T. Moore. Pp. 94-104. See G92.
DHL's use of "the Christian mystery of resurrection as a profound symbol for the emergence into living sensuality."

H79 -----. "Lawrence's Phoenix: An Introduction." DHLR, 5 (1972), 187-99.
DHL's use of the phoenix archetype of death and rebirth as "emblem" and as "process" in his fiction and poetry. See G25.

H80 Crump, G.B. "D.H. Lawrence and the Immediate Present: Kurt Vonnegut, Jr., Ken Kesey, and Wright Morris." DHLR, 10 (1977), 103-41.
Similarities of attitude and idea between DHL and the three "recognizably romantic" modern Americans.

H81 Dahlberg, Edward, and Herbert Read. "On D.H. Lawrence." In TRUTH IS MORE SACRED: A CRITICAL EXCHANGE ON MODERN LITERATURE. New York: Horizon, 1961. Pp. 69-117.
Debate on DHL's ethics.

H82 Daiches, David. "D.H. Lawrence." In THE NOVEL AND THE
MODERN WORLD. 1939. Rev. ed. Chicago: Univ. of Chicago
Press, 1960. Pp. 138-86.
    DHL an innovative novelist who transforms the
    conventions of fiction to sustain his dynamic
    vision of life against the deadness of the
    modern world. Surveys major fiction. Extract
    reprinted in L5.

H83 Danby, John F. "D.H. Lawrence." CAMBRIDGE JOURNAL, 4
(1951), 273-89.
    DHL wrote within the Romantic "tradition of
    no-tradition."

H84 Davies, Rosemary Reeves. "The Mother as Destroyer: Psychic
Divisions in the Writings of D.H. Lawrence." DHLR, 13
(1980), 220-38.
    DHL's destructive relationship with his mother,
    as reflected in his works (notably SL and "The
    Ladybird"), discussed in light of Erich Fromm's
    theories in THE ANATOMY OF HUMAN DESTRUCTIVE-
    NESS (1974). See G28.

H85 Davis, Herbert. "The Poetic Genius of D.H. Lawrence."
UTQ, 3 (1934), 439-53.
    In the lyric intensity of his fiction, DHL is
    in the tradition of Shelley and the great Eng-
    lish Romantics who refused to distinguish be-
    tween poetry and prose.

H86 Delavenay, Émile. "D.H. Lawrence and Sacher-Masoch."
Trans. Katherine M. Delavenay. DHLR, 6 (1973), 119-48.
    Literary and psychological correspondences be-
    tween DHL and Sacher-Masoch. See AA62.

H87 -----. "Sur un exemplaire de Schopenhauer annoté par
D.H. Lawrence." REVUE ANGLO-AMÉRICAINE, 13 (1935), 234-
38.
    DHL's early reading of Schopenhauer, assimila-
    tion of his ideas, and annotations in his texts
    of Schopenhauer's essays (particularly "The
    Metaphysics of Love" [Engl. trans., 1891]).
    [In French.] DHL's notes reprinted in F123.

H88 Dervin, Daniel A. "D.H. Lawrence and Freud." AI, 36
(1979), 95-117.
    Parallels between the artist and psychoanalyst,
    particularly between DHL's "use of symbols" and
    "Freud's approach to instincts."

H89   -----. "Rainbow, Phoenix, and Plumed Serpent: D.H. Lawrence's Great Composite Symbols and Their Vicissitudes."
PsyR, 67 (1981), 515-41.
        DHL's three major symbols of union and consum-
        mation arise from his probable witnessing of
        the "primal scene" (they stand both for "mytho-
        logical composites" and for the "sexually-com-
        bined or quarrelling parents").

H90   D'Heurle, Adma, and Joel N. Feimer. "The Tender Connection." AR, 37 (1979), 293-310.
        DHL's view of "sexual-love as a force that
        could save man from mechanized death" acquits
        him from the charges of anti-feminism.

H91   DiGaetani, John Louis. "Situational Myths: Richard Wag-
ner and D.H. Lawrence." In RICHARD WAGNER AND THE MODERN
BRITISH NOVEL. Rutherford, N.J.: Fairleigh Dickinson
Univ. Press, 1978. Pp. 58-89.
        DHL's response to Wagner, correspondences be-
        tween their beliefs, and "Wagnerism" in DHL's
        fiction (several stories, THE TRESPASSER, and
        WL).

H92   Dobrée, Bonamy. "D.H. Lawrence." In THE LAMP AND THE
LUTE: STUDIES IN SEVEN AUTHORS. 1929. 2nd ed. London:
Cass, 1963. Pp. 82-98.
        General survey of life and work, with slight
        critical comment.

H93   Donoghue, Denis. "Prometheus in Straits." In THIEVES OF
FIRE. New York: Oxford Univ. Press, 1974. Pp. 111-39.
        Patterns of the myth of Prometheus and the in-
        evitably frustrated, Promethean imagination
        in DHL's fiction.

H94   Draper, Ronald P. "Satire as a Form of Sympathy: D.H.
Lawrence as a Satirist." In RENAISSANCE AND MODERN ES-
SAYS. Ed. George R. Hibbard. London: Routledge, 1966.
Pp. 189-97.
        Good general consideration of a neglected ele-
        ment of DHL's art.

H95   -----. "The Sense of Reality in the Work of D.H. Lawrence."
RLV, 33 (1967), 461-70.
        Varying degrees of realism in DHL's fiction
        modify his characters' shifting states of mind.

H96   Eaglestone, Arthur A. [Dataller, Roger]. "Eastwood in
        Taos." ADELPHI, 28 (1952), 673-81.
             Influences of his nonconformist upbringing re-
             main with DHL (e.g., relations between his
             style and hymn rhythms).

H97   -----. "Elements of D.H. Lawrence's Prose Style." EIC,
        3 (1953), 416-24.
             DHL's style finest in those works set in the
             Eastwood environment. Reprinted in G5.

H98   Eagleton, Mary, and David Pierce. ATTITUDES TO CLASS
        AND THE ENGLISH NOVEL, FROM WALTER SCOTT TO DAVID STOREY.
        London: Thames and Hudson, 1979. Pp. 101-08 and passim.
             Origins of DHL's dualism lie in "his own fam-
             ily background" and his experience of class
             division. Surveys major fiction.

H99   Eagleton, Terry. "D.H. Lawrence." In EXILES AND EMIGRÉS:
        STUDIES IN MODERN LITERATURE. New York: Schocken, 1970.
        Pp. 191-218.
             DHL an exception among modern writers, exiling
             himself from his own culture without sacrific-
             ing his rich personal involvement in it.

H100   Edgar, Pelham. "Omissions and Conclusions: Chiefly Law-
        rence." In THE ART OF THE NOVEL: FROM 1700 TO THE PRE-
        SENT TIME. New York: Macmillan, 1933. Pp. 352-64.
             Though technically conventional (and thus ex-
             cluded from the main body of Edgar's study),
             DHL a "brilliant and significant" writer of
             "great books."

H101   Edge, John. "D.H. Lawrence and the Theme of Comradeship."
        SOUTHERN REVIEW (Adelaide, Australia), 9 (1976), 34-49.
             Argues with and extends Haegert's analysis of
             male friendship in DHL (see H162), with empha-
             sis on the later works. See Haegert's reply
             (H163).

H102   Edwards, Duane. "D.H. Lawrence: Tragedy in the Modern
        Age." LITERARY REVIEW, 24 (1980), 71-88.
             While maintaining that "ours is essentially a
             tragic age" (in LCL), the burden of DHL's work
             emphasizes that man's fate need not be tragic.

H103   Ehrstine, John W. "The Dialectic in D.H. Lawrence." RS,
        33 (1965), 11-26.
             DHL's effective, yet unsystematic use of his
             "sexual theme" (in SL, R, WL, LCL).

H104 Eliot, T.S. AFTER STRANGE GODS: A PRIMER OF MODERN
HERESY. London: Faber, 1934. Pp. 31-38, 58-62, and
passim.
Famous derogatory commentary on DHL's ethics
and source for Eliot's notorious observation
of DHL's "incapacity for what we ordinarily
call thinking." This intellectual "high-
churchman's" reaction to DHL's artistic "non-
conformity" is typical of the slighting treatment accorded DHL by Eliot (also see next
three entries), THE CRITERION critics, and
Bloomsbury, which provoked the equally self-
righteous fulminations of Leavis and the SCRU-
TINY critics (see G68, G69, and H218). Also
see H41, H208, H218, H263, H282, H403, M45,
R4, and Y125.

H105 -----. "Foreword." In Martin Jarrett-Kerr's D.H. LAW-
RENCE AND HUMAN EXISTENCE. Pp. vii-viii. See G62.
Eliot's provocative, condescending description
of DHL as "an ignorant man in the sense that
he was unaware of how much he did not know."
See above. Reprinted in G53. Also see H208,
H218, and H398.

H106 -----. "Le Roman anglais contemporain." NOUVELLE REVUE
FRANÇAISE, 28 (1927), 669-75.
DHL, an often brilliant and insightful novelist, deteriorates through his career, from the
high point of SL, as he becomes preoccupied
with a pseudo-psychology of man's primitive
impulses. [In French.] Extract reprinted,
from original unpublished English text, in
G34. Also see H208 and H218.

H107 -----. "SON OF WOMAN." CRITERION, 10 (1931), 768-74.
Review of Murry's study of DHL (F121) and
early, central statement of Eliot's objections to DHL: (1) that his "false prophecy"
egotistically centered on his own sensations,
"kills" his art and wastes his talent; (2)
that he is "ignorant" in the sense of lacking
a "wise and large capacity for orthodoxy
[which would have preserved him] from the
solely centrifugal impulse of heresy"; (3)
that his "craving for greater intimacy than
is possible between human beings [arises
from] his unusual incapacity for being inti-
mate at all"; (4) and that his work since

FANTASIA OF THE UNCONSCIOUS (1922) shows a
marked decline and waste of his potentially
"great powers of understanding and tenderness." Reprinted in G20 and G34. Also see
H208, H218, and H398.

H108   Ellis, Geoffrey U. TWILIGHT ON PARNASSUS: A SURVEY OF
POST-WAR FICTION AND PRE-WAR CRITICISM. London: Michael
Joseph, 1939. Pp. 287-329 and passim.
Balanced and judicious summary of DHL's movement toward visionary and mystic fiction, assessment of his beliefs, and suggestions of
his influence.

H109   Elsbree, Langdon. "D.H. Lawrence, *Homo Ludens*, and the
Dance." DHLR, 1 (1968), 1-30.
DHL's use of the English folk dance as "a
means of apprehending and diagnosing a deeper
self."

H110   -----. "The Purest and Most Perfect Form of Play: Some
Novelists and the Dance." CRITICISM, 14 (1972), 361-72.
Symbolic value of the dance in Austen, George
Eliot, Hardy, and DHL.

H111   -----. THE RITUALS OF LIFE: PATTERNS IN NARRATIVE. Port
Washington, N.Y.: Kennikat, 1982. Pp. 111-17 and passim.
Several of DHL's short-stories and novels (SL,
R) briefly discussed as illustrations of the
central archetypal patterns found in prose nar-
ratives.

H112   -----, ed. "On the Teaching of D.H. Lawrence: A Forum."
DHLR, 8 (1975), 63-79.
Four comments on the difficulties and rewards
of teaching DHL. Includes Elsbree's brief
introduction and notes by Joanne Trautmann
("The Body Electric"), Sanford Pinsker ("Con-
fessions of a Lawrentian Manqué"), William
Lowery ("Trivium"), and James Cox ("Pollyana-
lytics and Pedagogy: Teaching Lawrence's Short
Stories").

H113   Enroth, Clyde. "Introduction." In JOYCE AND LAWRENCE.
Ed. Enroth. New York: Holt, 1969. Pp. 1-7.
Joyce and DHL contrasted as "Apollonian" and
"Dionysian" writers. Introduces a modest
anthology of their fiction and poetry, in-
tended for secondary schools.

H114 Evans, B. Ifor. "D.H. Lawrence." In ENGLISH LITERATURE
      BETWEEN THE WARS. London: Methuen, 1948. Pp. 49-57.
          DHL the most "fiercely original mind" and
          "most powerful personality" in the literature
          of his time.

H115 Fairbanks, N. David. "'Strength Through Joy' in the
      Novels of D.H. Lawrence." LITERATURE & IDEOLOGY, No. 8
      (1971), pp. 67-78.
          Correlates DHL's views of class betrayal and
          social rejuvenation to Nazi ideological pro-
          grammes.

H116 Fergusson, Francis. "D.H. Lawrence's Sensibility." HOUND
      AND HORN, 6 (1933), 447-63.
          Mildly patronizing general survey.

H117 Firchow, Peter. "Wells and Lawrence in Huxley's BRAVE
      NEW WORLD." JML, 5 (1976), 260-78.
          Huxley's novel a "Lawrencean" response to
          Wells's utopianism.

H118 Fluchère, Henri. "D.H. Lawrence: Travaux d'approche."
      CAHIERS DU SUD, 18 (1931), 86-108.
          Critical survey and appreciation of DHL's fic-
          tion. [In French.]

H119 Ford, Ford Madox. "A Haughty and Proud Generation." YR,
      11 (1922), 703-17.
          DHL "indulges his moods too much" in his fic-
          tion (cf. Joyce, Wyndham Lewis, Mansfield, and
          Richardson).

H120 Forster, E.M. "D.H. Lawrence." LISTENER, 3 (1930), 753-
      54.
          Insists on the inseparability of DHL's art and
          his message: "Disbelieve his theories, if you
          like, but never brush them aside." Considers
          PS his most beautifully made and effective
          novel. Reprinted in F127 (extract) and G34.
          Also see F61.

H121 Fraenkel, Michael. "The Otherness of D.H. Lawrence." In
      DEATH IS NOT ENOUGH: ESSAYS IN ACTIVE NEGATION. London:
      Daniel, 1939. Pp. 73-108.
          DHL's "escape from the deadness of society in
          his *otherness*...a kind of mystico-sexual aware-
          ness" is, in effect, another kind of death which
          disowns the human in humanity.

H122   Fricker, Robert. "David Herbert Lawrence." In DER MOD-
       DERNE ENGLISCHE ROMAN. 1958. 2nd ed. Göttingen: Van-
       denhoeck and Ruprecht, 1966. Pp. 123-38.
              Useful general introduction to DHL's fiction
              and ideas. [In German.]

H123   -----. "David Herbert Lawrence (1885-1930)." In ENG-
       LISCHE DICHTER DER MODERNE: IHR LEBEN UND WERK. Ed.
       Rudolf Sühnel and Dieter Riesner. Berlin: Schmidt, 1971.
       Pp. 338-50.
              Surveys DHL's exploration of his contemporary
              culture and original application of the prin-
              ciples of depth-psychology for the analysis
              of human motivations. Touches on an impres-
              sive number of stories and novellas, as well
              as the major novels. [In German.]

H124   Friedman, Alan. "The Other Lawrence." PR, 37 (1970),
       239-53.
              DHL no less a technical innovator than Joyce.

H125   Frierson, William C. THE ENGLISH NOVEL IN TRANSITION,
       1885-1940. Norman: Univ. of Oklahoma Press, 1942. Pp.
       229-34 and passim.
              DHL's search for "harmony" and "vitality" in
              his fiction indebted to Whitman.

H126   Garcia, Reloy. "The Quest for Paradise in the Novels of
       D.H. Lawrence." DHLR, 3 (1970), 93-114.
              DHL's developing vision of Paradise in his
              fiction, emerging from the conventional city-
              country antithesis.

H127   Garnett, Edward. "Mr. D.H. Lawrence and the Moralists."
       1916. In FRIDAY NIGHTS. New York: Knopf, 1922. Pp.
       145-60.
              DHL's higher sense of morality informs his
              portraits of human behavior and instinct as
              they are, not as they "should be." Extracts
              reprinted in G20, G34, and L1.

H128   Garrett, Peter K. "D.H. Lawrence: The Revelation of the
       Unconscious." In SCENE AND SYMBOL FROM GEORGE ELIOT TO
       JAMES JOYCE: STUDIES IN CHANGING FICTIONAL MODE. New
       Haven, Conn.: Yale Univ. Press, 1969. Pp. 181-213.
              Symbolic scenes as revelations of characters'
              unconscious states in SL and R, evolve into the
              highly original "symbolic fictional mode" that
              distinguishes WL.

H129 George, Walter L. "Mr. D.H. Lawrence." In A NOVELIST
ON NOVELS. London: Collins, 1918. Pp. 90-101.
DHL's fiction and verse "the fruit of personal
[and class] angers and hatreds."

H130 Gerard, David E., comp. "Glossary of Eastwood Dialect
Words Used by D.H. Lawrence in His Poems, Plays, and
Fiction." DHLR, 1 (1968), 215-37.
Useful reference tool. Reprinted in E41.

H131 Ghiselin, Brewster. "D.H. Lawrence and a New World." WR,
11 (1947), 150-59.
The quest for a "new world" a characteristic
motif in DHL's life and work.

H132 -----. "D.H. Lawrence and the Peacocks of Atrani." MICH-
IGAN QUARTERLY REVIEW, 14 (1975), 119-34.
DHL's bird symbolism influenced by his study
of Italian church ornamentation.

H133 Gifford, Henry, and Raymond Williams. "D.H. Lawrence and
ANNA KARENINA." 1960-61. In RUSSIAN LITERATURE AND MOD-
ERN ENGLISH FICTION: A COLLECTION OF CRITICAL ESSAYS. Ed.
Donald Davie. Chicago: Univ. of Chicago Press, 1965.
Pp. 148-63.
Conversation concerning DHL's debts to and
critical rejection of Tolstoy. Also see H414.

H134 Gill, Richard. HAPPY RURAL SEAT: THE ENGLISH COUNTRY-
HOUSE AND THE LITERARY IMAGINATION. New Haven, Conn:
Yale Univ. Press, 1972. Pp. 151-55 and passim.
The country house as symbol in DHL.

H135 Gillie, Christopher. "D.H. Lawrence (1885-1930)." In
MOVEMENTS IN ENGLISH LITERATURE, 1900-1940. Cambridge:
Cambridge Univ. Press, 1975. Pp. 47-64.
Survey of DHL as a novelist "who understood
the social scene from within as thoroughly as
Wells [and] possessed an insight into the hu-
man consciousness comparable to that of James
or Conrad."

H136 Gindin, James. "D.H. Lawrence." In HARVEST OF A QUIET
EYE: THE NOVEL OF COMPASSION. Bloomington: Indiana Univ.
Press, 1971. Pp. 205-21.
DHL's essentially compassionate attitude toward
society in his novels.

H137   Gindre, M. "Points de vue sur D.H. Lawrence." EA, 11
       (1958), 229-39.
              Welcomes the major new trend in the critical
              study of DHL in the 1950s, away from passion-
              ate controversy and toward "compréhension plus
              exacte et impartiale." Review essay on sev-
              eral British and American studies. [In
              French.]

H138   Girard, Denis. "John Middleton Murry, D.H. Lawrence et
       Albert Schweitzer." EA, 12 (1959), 212-21.
              Murry's inability ultimately to accept or to
              understand DHL's and Schweitzer's "reverence
              for life" as divorced from traditional Christi-
              anity. [In French.] See G85.

H139   Glicksberg, Charles I. "D.H. Lawrence: The Prophet of
       Surrealism." NINETEENTH CENTURY, 143 (1948), 229-37.
              DHL anticipates André Breton, the founder of
              the surrealist movement, in his explorations
              of "psychic landscape."

H140   -----. "D.H. Lawrence and Science." SCIENTIFIC MONTHLY,
       73 (1951), 99-104.
              DHL's brilliant, influential, and misguided
              repudiation of science as an "intellectualiza-
              tion of the creative process."

H141   -----. "D.H. Lawrence and the Religion of Sex." In THE
       SEXUAL REVOLUTION IN MODERN ENGLISH LITERATURE. The
       Hague: Martinus Nijhoff, 1973. Pp. 88-117.
              DHL's attacks on both Puritanism and hedonism
              traced in the sexual themes of the major fic-
              tion.

H142   Goldring, Douglas. "The Later Work of D.H. Lawrence."
       In REPUTATIONS: ESSAYS IN CRITICISM. New York: Seltzer,
       1920. Pp. 67-78.
              Registers disappointment with DHL's R (a
              "splendid...failure"), and his poetry and
              essays (1915-20), though recognizing the
              nobility of his ambitions. Reprinted in F66,
              F123, G20, and G34 (extract).

H143   Gontarski, S.E. "Filming Lawrence." MODERNIST STUDIES,
       4 (1982), 87-95.
              Describes the unfulfilled plans to film DHL's
              works, in the early 1930s, and the six film
              adaptations that have been produced since 1949.
              See G79.

H144 Goode, John. "D.H. Lawrence." In THE TWENTIETH CENTURY.
Ed. Bernard Bergonzi. London: Barrie and Jenkins, 1970.
Pp. 106-52.
> Fine historical survey of DHL's achievement.

H145 Goodheart, Eugene. "Lawrence and Christ." In THE CULT
OF THE EGO: THE SELF IN MODERN LITERATURE. Chicago: Univ.
of Chicago Press, 1968. Pp. 161-82.
> DHL's fierce, radically subversive anti-
> Christianity (e.g., "The Man Who Died,"
> APOCALYPSE, among other works). Like Blake
> and Nietzsche, DHL messianic and misunder-
> stood.

H146 -----. "Lawrence and the Critics." ChiR, 16, No. 3
(1963), 127-37.
> Regrets the tendency of Leavis-inspired crit-
> ics who place DHL in the great "moral" tradi-
> tion to underplay or overlook the equally im-
> portant, "radical and subversive elements" in
> his life and thought. Review essay, welcoming
> studies by Weiss (G123) and Widmer (V5).

H147 Goonetilleke, D.C.R.A. "D.H. Lawrence: Primitivism?"
In DEVELOPING COUNTRIES IN BRITISH FICTION. London:
Macmillan, 1977. Pp. 170-98.
> DHL a "chronological" primitivist in his view
> of history and a "cultural" primitivist in
> his attraction toward developing peoples.
> Chiefly on the Mexican works.

H148 Gordon, David J. "D.H. Lawrence's Dual Myth of Origin."
SR, 89 (1981), 83-94.
> DHL's Rousseauistic view of human nature as
> fundamentally "good, innocent, pristine" in
> his psychoanalytic essays, balanced by his
> antithetical vision of inevitable degenera-
> tion in his fiction.

H149 -----. "Two Anti-Puritan Puritans: Bernard Shaw and D.H.
Lawrence." YR, 56 (1966),76-90.
> Comparative discussion.

H150 Gould, Gerald. "Mr. Lawrence and Mr. Joyce." In THE
ENGLISH NOVEL OF TODAY. London: Castle, 1924. Pp. 19-
27.
> DHL's early promise perverted by his "sinis-
> ter" descent into the unconscious (cf. Joyce).

H151   Grant, Douglas. "England's Phoenix." UTQ, 27 (1957),
       216-25.
                Excellent synopsis of the conflicting back-
                grounds, attitudes, and approaches to art in
                the hieratic traditionalist Eliot and the de-
                motic nonconformist DHL, noting the academic
                critic's tendency to find Eliot the safer,
                more reassuring, hence better artist. Reviews
                B23, F123, G68, and G85.

H152   Green, Eleanor H. "Blueprints for Utopia: The Political
       Ideas of Nietzsche and D.H. Lawrence." RMS, 18 (1974),
       141-61.
                Several strong parallels to Nietzsche's ideas
                in DHL's political thought, particularly in
                the "leadership" novels. See H155.

H153   -----. "Lawrence, Schopenhauer, and the Dual Nature of
       the Universe." SAB, 42, No. 4 (1977), 84-92.
                Asserts Schopenhauer's direct influence on
                DHL's concepts of duality in his fiction.
                See below.

H154   -----. "Schopenhauer and D.H. Lawrence on Sex and Love."
       DHLR, 8 (1975), 329-45.
                DHL's rejection of Schopenhauer's pessimistic
                view of human sexuality and incorporation of
                several key elements of the philosopher's
                thought into his own affirmative "conception
                of the role and nature and passion." See G26
                and above.

H155   -----. "The WILLE ZUR MACHT and D.H. Lawrence." MAS-
       SACHUSETTS STUDIES IN ENGLISH, 5, No. 2 (1975), 25-30.
                DHL's misconception of Nietzsche's term led
                to his outspoken condemnation of the German
                philosopher, while his own ideas on the "will
                to power" are roughly parallel. See H152.

H156   Green, Martin. TRANSATLANTIC PATTERNS: CULTURAL COMPAR-
       ISONS OF ENGLAND WITH AMERICA. New York: Basic Books,
       1977. Pp. 15-24, 33-36, 173-78, and passim.
                Considers DHL's attitudes toward marriage (cf.
                Howells, and Anna Wulf) and toward society in
                the twenties (cf. American post-1945 attitudes).

H157   Greene, Thomas. "Lawrence and the Quixotic Hero." SR,
       59 (1951), 559-73.
                DHL a "Quixote of the flesh."

H158 Gregor, Ian, and Mark Kinkead-Weekes. "Lawrence and
      Joyce: A Critical Comparison." In THE ENGLISH NOVEL.
      Ed. Cedric Watts. London: Sussex Books, 1976. Pp.
      135-52.
          Initial discussion of "Odour of Chrysanthe-
          mums" and "The Dead" leads to illuminating
          comparisons and contrasts of the two writers,
          by two distinguished critics. (Presented in
          dialogue-form.)

H159 Gunn, Drewey, W. "Lawrence's Search for the Great Sun."
      In AMERICAN AND BRITISH WRITERS IN MEXICO, 1556-1973.
      Austin: Univ. of Texas Press, 1974. Pp. 123-44.
          Knowledgeability, force, and insight of DHL's
          Mexican writings (fiction and nonfiction).

H160 Gutierrez, Donald. "The Ancient Imagination of D.H.
      Lawrence." TCL, 27 (1981), 178-96.
          The element of "hylozoism" (the "archaic pre-
          Socratic conception that all matter is alive")
          in SL, WL, "St. Mawr," and LCL. See Z119.

H161 Guyard, Marius F. LA GRANDE BRETAGNE DANS LE ROMAN FRAN-
      ÇAIS: 1914-1940. Paris: Didier, 1954. Pp. 86-101 and
      passim.
          DHL made significant contributions, along with
          Wilde, Joyce, and others, to the changing view
          of England and English literature in France,
          in the 1920s. [In French.]

H162 Haegert, John W. "Brothers and Lovers: D.H. Lawrence
      and the Theme of Friendship." SOUTHERN REVIEW (Adelaide,
      Australia), 8 (1975), 39-50.
          The consistent "dramatic purpose and thematic
          relevance" of DHL's portrayal of male comrade-
          ship (through WL). See H101 and below.

H163 -----. "Turning One's Back on Lawrence: Or, The Function
      of Friendship Once More." SOUTHERN REVIEW (Adelaide,
      Australia), 11 (1978), 72-89.
          Rejects John Edge's contention that DHL's view
          of male friendship was conditioned by repressed
          homosexuality and proto-fascist phallic worship
          (see H101).

H164 Hardy, Barbara. "Truthfulness and Schematicism: D.H.
      Lawrence." In THE APPROPRIATE FORM: AN ESSAY ON THE
      NOVEL. London: Univ. of London Press, 1964. Pp. 132-73.
          DHL's movement from developmental to symbolic
          structures in his novels (SL and WL) and his

unsuccessful, confused, partial return to con-
ventional form in LCL.

H165   -----. "Women in D.H. Lawrence's Works." In D.H. LAW-
RENCE. Ed. Stephen Spender. Pp. 90-98, 115-21. See
G113.
DHL's insightful portrayals of women as human
beings.

H166   Harris, Janice H. "Sexual Antagonism in D.H. Lawrence's
Early Leadership Fiction." MODERN LANGUAGE STUDIES, 7
(1977), 43-52.
DHL's leadership fiction credible only when
he places the "intelligent female" in the
"role of skeptical follower" (e.g., "The Captain's Doll").

H167   Harris, Wendell V. "Molly's 'Yes': The Transvaluation
of Sex in Modern Fiction." TSLL, 10 (1968), 107-18.
Sex as an affirmation of life (e.g., DHL's
works, among others).

H168   Harrison, A.W. "The Philosophy of D.H. Lawrence." HIB-
BERT JOURNAL, 32 (1934), 554-63.
Skeptical survey of DHL as an anti-intellec-
tual prophet, whose "so-called philosophy rep-
resents the bankruptcy of clear thinking."
Comments on THE TRESPASSER, AARON'S ROD, "St.
Mawr," and several short stories.

H169   Harrison, John R. "D.H. Lawrence." In THE REACTIONARIES:
YEATS, LEWIS, POUND, ELIOT, LAWRENCE: A STUDY OF THE ANTI-
DEMOCRATIC INTELLIGENTSIA. New York: Schocken, 1967. Pp.
163-89.
DHL's social criticism and primitivist "phallic consciousness" compared to fascist racial
exclusivism, with little subtlety.

H170   Hawkins, Desmond. "Introduction." In STORIES, ESSAYS,
AND POEMS: D.H. LAWRENCE. Ed. Hawkins. Pp. v-ix. See
B28.
DHL and Byron both men "of great *personal*
genius and of revolutionary significance."

H171   Hayman, Ronald. "D.H. Lawrence." In LEAVIS. Totowa,
N.J.: Rowman and Littlefield, 1976. Pp. 101-10.
Summarizes the theoretical basis of and chief
contentions in Leavis's championship of DHL
as "our last great writer." Discusses G68.

H172 Heilman, Robert B. "Nomad, Monads, and the Mystique of the Soma." SR, 68 (1960), 635-59.
>   Approving review of Vivas's attempt to establish a "tenable" aesthetic position for the criticism of DHL's achievement (in G121), prefaced by an intriguing comparison of Joyce's Stephen Dedalus and DHL as artists in quest of "the word made flesh, and the flesh made word." Extract reprinted in N3.

H173 Henderson, Philip. "The Primitivism of D.H. Lawrence." In THE NOVEL TODAY: STUDIES IN CONTEMPORARY ATTITUDES. London: Lane, 1936. Pp. 60-73.
>   DHL's fiction rooted in violent sexual antagonism, not "communion."

H174 Hendrick, George. "'10' and the Phoenix." DHLR, 2 (1969), 162-67.
>   Reviews recent studies of Tennessee Williams and DHL and comments on Williams' debt to DHL. See G37.

H175 Henig, Suzanne. "D.H. Lawrence and Virginia Woolf." DHLR, 2 (1969), 265-71.
>   Traces Woolf's ultimately admiring critical opinions of DHL (see L69 and P8).

H176 Henry, Graeme. "D.H. Lawrence: Objectivity and Belief." CR, 22 (1980), 32-43.
>   Not seen.

H177 Heppenstall, Rayner. THE FOURFOLD TRADITION: NOTES ON THE FRENCH AND ENGLISH LITERATURES. New York: New Directions, 1961. Pp. 132-38.
>   Compares DHL's and Joyce's backgrounds and views of each other, and contrasts their art.

H178 Heywood, Christopher. "Olive Schreiner's THE STORY OF AN AFRICAN FARM: Prototype of Lawrence's Early Novels." ELN, 14 (1976), 44-50.
>   Influence of Schreiner's novel (1883) on the method and content of DHL's fiction (principally SL, R, and WL). Expanded version published as "Olive Schreiner's Influence on George Moore and D.H. Lawrence," in ASPECTS OF SOUTH AFRICAN LITERATURE, ed. Heywood (London: Heinemann, 1976), pp. 42-53.

H179 Higashida, Chiaki. "On the Prose Style of D.H. Lawrence."
      STUDIES IN ENGLISH LITERATURE (Tokyo), 19 (1939), 545-56.
      DHL's style the closest approach to colloquial
      English in modern fiction (analysis of selected
      passages).

H180 Hinz, Evelyn J. "A Word about Influences and Unprofes-
      sional Studies: D.H. LAWRENCE: AN UNPROFESSIONAL STUDY."
      In THE MIRROR AND THE GARDEN: REALISM AND REALITY IN THE
      WRITINGS OF ANAIS NIN. Columbus: The Ohio State Univ.
      Libraries, Publications Committee, 1971. Pp. 15-32.
      Examines the premises and judgments of Nin's
      "essentially creative rather than critical"
      essay on DHL (G88), noting the similarity in
      both authors' approaches to literary criticism.

H181 -----. "D.H. Lawrence and 'Something Called "*Canada*".'"
      DR, 54 (1974), 240-50.
      DHL's varying use of Canada as a symbolic es-
      cape or a promised land.

H182 -----. "D.H. Lawrence's Clothes Metaphor." DHLR, 1
      (1968), 87-113.
      Full survey of DHL's use of clothing both for
      characterization and as a "vehicle" for social
      comment (chiefly SL, WL, LCL).

H183 -----. "Hierogamy versus Wedlock: Types of Marriage Plots
      and Their Relationship to Genres of Prose Fiction." PMLA,
      91 (1976), 900-13.
      Distinguishes works concerned with the rela-
      tions of the sexes (e.g., WUTHERING HEIGHTS
      [1847], R, WL, LCL) from novels concerned with
      the conventional moral and social concerns of
      marriage (e.g., PRIDE AND PREJUDICE [1813]).

H184 Hoare, Dorothy M. "The Novels of D.H. Lawrence." In
      SOME STUDIES IN THE MODERN NOVEL. London: Chatto and
      Windus, 1938. Pp. 97-112.
      DHL's awesome power "forces us to listen to
      him and to think," despite his "incoherence"
      and unevenness.

H185 Hoffman, Frederick J. "Lawrence's Quarrel with Freud."
      In FREUDIANISM AND THE LITERARY MIND. 1945. 2nd ed.
      Baton Rouge: Louisiana State Univ. Press, 1957. Pp.
      151-76.
      DHL's writings reflect his exposure to, aware-
      ness of, and independence from Freud. Reprinted
      in G53 and L7 (extract).

H186   -----. "From Surrealism to 'The Apocalypse': A Development in Twentieth Century Irrationalism." ELH, 15 (1948),
147-65.
          DHL's emphasis upon the value of the irrational
          element in human nature (as opposed to Freud)
          and his influence on subsequent apocalyptic
          writers (e.g., Huxley, Dylan Thomas).

H187   -----. "'The Book of Himself': Joyce and Lawrence." In
THE MORTAL NO: DEATH AND THE MODERN IMAGINATION. Princeton, N.J.: Princeton Univ. Press, 1964. Pp. 393-423.
          Death and rebirth secular metaphors for self-
          realization in both authors as they adapt
          Christian myth and traditional views of mor-
          tality to their personal ideologies. (DHL:
          pp. 408-23).

H188   Hogan, Robert. "D.H. Lawrence and His Critics." EIC, 9
(1959), 381-87.
          Regrets that DHL has become "too critically
          fashionable" in the 1950s, prompting much
          "trivial" criticism. Objects to three con-
          temporary articles: L27, V121, and Z22.

H189   Hoyles, John. "D.H. Lawrence and the Counter-Revolution:
An Essay in Socialist Aesthetics." DHLR, 6 (1973), 173-
200.
          Finds Caudwell, the Marxist (see H58), and
          Millett, the feminist (see H255), make posi-
          tive contributions to DHL criticism, but lack
          a cohesive "socialist aesthetic."

H190   Humma, John B. "D.H. Lawrence as Friedrich Nietzsche."
PQ, 53 (1974), 110-20.
          Despite DHL's outspoken criticisms of Nietzsche,
          their central beliefs "differ only inconsequen-
          tially."

H191   Huxley, Aldous. "Introduction." In THE LETTERS OF D.H.
LAWRENCE. Ed. Huxley. Pp. ix-xxxiv. See C10.
          Memoir and ambivalent critique, with dispro-
          portionate emphases on DHL's spontaneous writ-
          ing and "dislike of abstract knowledge." Re-
          printed in C2 and C8. Extracts reprinted in
          F127, G5, G20, and G53.

H192   -----. "To the Puritan all Things are Impure." In MUSIC
AT NIGHT, AND OTHER ESSAYS. London: Chatto and Windus,
1943. Pp. 173-83.
          Attacks the "Grundyism" of the English censorship

of DHL and notes the irony that DHL himself
waged war on "unnatural vice," though with
higher motives.

H193   Irwin, W.R. "The Survival of Pan." PMLA, 76 (1961),
        159-67.
            The Pan myth in DHL's novels.

H194   Jacobson, Dan. "D.H. Lawrence and Modern Society." JOUR-
        NAL OF CONTEMPORARY HISTORY, 2 (1967), 81-92.
            DHL's hatred of modern society and his search
            for a more fulfilling social and political
            philosophy (WL, KANGAROO, and other works).
            Reprinted in G48.

H195   Joad, C.E.M. "Lawrence and Determination by the Uncon-
        scious." In GUIDE TO MODERN THOUGHT. New York: Stokes,
        1933. Pp. 252-58.
            DHL's view of "human consciousness as a regis-
            ter...of unconscious forces" originates in
            psychoanalytic theory.

H196   John, Brian. "D.H. Lawrence and the Quickening Word."
        In SUPREME FICTIONS: STUDIES IN THE WORK OF WILLIAM
        BLAKE, THOMAS CARLYLE, W.B. YEATS, AND D.H. LAWRENCE.
        Montreal: McGill-Queen's Univ. Press, 1974. Pp. 231-309.
            DHL's ultimate optimism, firmly within and,
            though tested, triumphantly faithful to the
            tradition of romantic vitalism.

H197   Johnson, Reginald Brimley. "D.H. Lawrence." In SOME
        CONTEMPORARY NOVELISTS (MEN). London: Parsons, 1922.
        Pp. 121-29.
            Despite great imaginative gifts, DHL's "rav-
            ings" drag his fiction through the deep and
            black "mud" of perverted sex.

H198   Johnsson, Melker. EN KLOSTERRESSA: FÄRDER OCH FRÅGOR
        [A CLOISTER-TOUR: JOURNEY AND INQUIRY.] Stockholm: Natur
        och Kultur, 1960. Pp. 83-115.
            Collects five previously published essays
            (1957-59), including an article on DHL's town,
            Nottingham, and two review essays each on
            DHL's biography and on his and Simone Weil's
            views of "man's condition," provoked by Nehls's
            biography (F123) and Rees's study (G102), re-
            spectively. [In Swedish.]

H199 Jones, W.S. Handley. "D.H. Lawrence and the Revolt
      Against Reason." In THE PRIEST AND THE SIREN, AND OTHER
      LITERARY STUDIES. London: Epworth, 1953. Pp. 114-26.
          Ambivalent view of DHL as a remarkable genius,
          but at root a misanthrope who "cultivated mind-
          lessness and made a religion of sexuality."

H200 Kaplan, Harold J. "The Naturalist Theology of D.H. Law-
      rence." In THE PASSIVE VOICE: AN APPROACH TO MODERN FIC-
      TION. Athens: Ohio Univ. Press, 1966. Pp. 159-85.
          DHL's vitalistic theology.

H201 Karl, Frederick R., and Marvin Magalaner. "D.H. Lawrence."
      In A READER'S GUIDE TO GREAT TWENTIETH-CENTURY ENGLISH
      NOVELS. New York: Noonday, 1959. Pp. 150-204.
          Brief life and overview of the fiction, fol-
          lowed by introductory analyses of SL, R, and
          WL.

H202 Kay, Wallace G. "The Cortege of Dionysus: Lawrence and
      Giono." SOUTHERN QUARTERLY, 4 (1966), 159-71.
          Stylistic and biographical similarities be-
          tween DHL and the French Provençal novelist,
          Jean Giono.

H203 Kermode, Frank. "The Novels of D.H. Lawrence." In D.H.
      LAWRENCE. Ed. Stephen Spender. Pp. 77-89. See G113.
          Brief essay rehearsing many of the judgments
          made in his book (see G65).

H204 Kessler, Jascha. "D.H. Lawrence's Primitivism." TSLL,
      5 (1964), 467-88.
          Important study of DHL's primitivist ideas.

H205 Kiely, Robert. BEYOND EGOTISM: THE FICTION OF JAMES
      JOYCE, VIRGINIA WOOLF, AND D.H. LAWRENCE. Cambridge,
      Mass.: Harvard Univ. Press, 1980. Pp. 23-29, 61-68,
      87-91, 103-19, 150-68, 209-21, and passim.
          Distinguished study of the three novelists
          who, despite numerous particular differences,
          both share similar backgrounds and basic as-
          sumptions, and reflect comparable thematic
          and technical concerns.

H206 Kinkead-Weekes, Mark. "Eros and Metaphor: Sexual Rela-
      tionship in the Fiction of Lawrence." 1969. In LAWRENCE
      AND WOMEN. Ed. Anne Smith. Pp. 101-21. See G112.
          Sexual activity becomes a metaphor, in DHL's
          work, "for exploring wider relationships,

within people, between them, throughout
society, and the connection of man to the
universe."

H207   ------. "The Marble and the Statue: The Exploratory Imag-
ination of D.H. Lawrence." In IMAGINED WORLDS: ESSAYS ON
SOME ENGLISH NOVELS AND NOVELISTS IN HONOUR OF JOHN BUTT.
Ed. Maynard Mack and Ian Gregor. London: Methuen, 1968.
Pp. 371-418.
        The evolution of DHL's art toward R and WL,
        demonstrating how the manuscript fragments of
        "The Sisters I, II" and "The Wedding Ring"
        (early versions of the novels, 1913-16), and
        "Study of Thomas Hardy" (in B16), reflect the
        development of DHL's fiction and "religion."
        Extract reprinted in M4.

H208   Kirk, Russell. "Vivas, Lawrence, Eliot, and the Demon."
In ¡VIVA VIVAS! ESSAYS IN HONOR OF ELISEO VIVAS. Ed.
Henry Regnery. Indianapolis, Ind.: Liberty, 1976. Pp.
227-49.
        Vivas's and Eliot's ambivalent responses to
        DHL. See G121, H104-H107.

H209   Kirkham, Michael. "D.H. Lawrence and Social Consciousness." MOSAIC, 12, No. 1 (1978), 79-92.
        Disparity between DHL's insightful diagnoses
        of modern man's "sicknesses" and his limited
        remedy of sound sexual relationships.

H210   Klein, Robert C. "I, Thou, and You in Three Lawrencian
Relationships." PAUNCH, No. 31 (1968), pp. 52-70.
        The Paul-Miriam (SL), the Will-Anna (R), and
        the Connie-Mellors (LCL) relationships.

H211   Knight, G. Wilson. "Lawrence, Joyce, and Powys." EIC,
11 (1961), 403-17.
        Sadism and anal-eroticism in the works of the
        three novelists. Reprinted in Knight's NE-
        GLECTED POWERS (New York: Barnes and Noble,
        1971), pp. 142-55, and in M2 (extract). Also
        see U64.

H212   Kohler, Dayton. "D.H. Lawrence." SR, 29 (1931), 25-38.
        DHL's "new valuation of human relationships"
        in his fiction never fully developed: "his
        conclusions lack the quality of final purpo-
        siveness." SL his most satisfactory novel.

H213 Langbaum, Robert. "Reconstitution of Self: Lawrence: The Religion of Love." In THE MYSTERIES OF IDENTITY: A THEME IN MODERN LITERATURE. New York: Oxford Univ. Press, 1977. Pp. 251-353.
  Distinguished commentary on DHL's analyses of "the modern sexual problem" as "an identity problem" and on his attempt to fashion a new concept of the ego. Includes extended discussions of R and WL.

H214 Lavrin, Janko. "Sex and Eros (On Rozanov, Weininger and D.H. Lawrence)." 1934. In ASPECTS OF MODERNISM, FROM WILDE TO PIRANDELLO. London: Nott, 1935. Pp. 141-59.
  Rozanov is DHL's Russian "counterpart" in his "yearning for sexual 'monism,'" and Weininger is DHL's antithesis in his "intense but suppressed sexuality" and advocacy of a *"conscious* cleavage between Sex and Love."

H215 Lea, Frank A. "David Herbert Lawrence, 1885-1930." In VOICES IN THE WILDERNESS: FROM POETRY TO PROPHECY IN BRITAIN. London: Brentham Press, 1975. Pp. 120-66.
  Valuable summary and evaluation of the social and political philosophy of DHL, "incomparably the greatest of modern English Writers," chiefly discussing R, WL, PS, FANTASIA OF THE UNCONSCIOUS, and other essays, and describing DHL's life-long campaign against Utilitarian Materialism (he was "Carlyle" to Bertrand Russell's "Mill").

H216 Leaver, Florence B. "The Man-Nature Relationship of D.H. Lawrence's Novels." UKCR, 19 (1953), 241-48.
  DHL's shift in emphasis from nature viewed for its "inherent worth" in the early fiction (THE WHITE PEACOCK, SL), to nature used as a vehicle for Lawrencean ideology in the later works (WL, PS).

H217 Leavis, F.R. "ANNA KARENINA." CAMBRIDGE QUARTERLY, 1 (1965-66), 5-27.
  Several comments, in passing, on DHL's responses to Tolstoy's novel. Reprinted in *ANNA KARENINA*, AND OTHER ESSAYS (London: Chatto and Windus, 1967).

H218 -----. "Mr. Eliot and Lawrence." SCRUTINY, 18 (June 1951), 66-72.
  Attack on T.S. Eliot and assertion of DHL's place within the English cultural tradition.

(Review of Aldington [F1] and Jarrett-Kerr
[G62]). Reprinted in G53. Also see H41,
H104-H107.

H219   Lee, Robin. "A True Relatedness: Lawrence's View of Morality." ESA, 10 (1967), 178-85.
DHL's morality defined as both an individual
and a social concept.

H220   -----. "Irony and Attitude in George Eliot and D.H. Lawrence." ESA, 16 (1973), 15-21.
Dubious argument that, after SL, DHL "largely
avoids irony" (cf. Eliot).

H221   Lerner, Laurence. "D.H. Lawrence." In THE TRUTHTELLERS:
JANE AUSTEN, GEORGE ELIOT, AND D.H. LAWRENCE. New York:
Schocken, 1967. Pp. 66-83, 172-235.
Curious commentaries on the moral values in-
culcated by DHL's major fiction, the most edi-
fying works consistently being found the better art. Extracts reprinted in L5 and M4.

H222   Levine, George L. "Lawrence, FRANKENSTEIN, and the Re-
versal of Realism." In THE REALISTIC IMAGINATION: ENG-
LISH FICTION FROM *FRANKENSTEIN* TO *LADY CHATTERLEY*.
Chicago: Univ. of Chicago Press, 1981. Pp. 317-28.
DHL's rejection of the conventions of realism,
seen by him as a substitution of mechanism for
life, embodies and completes the same recognition found in Mary Shelley's FRANKENSTEIN
(1817).

H223   Lewis, Wyndham. "D.H. Lawrence." 1929. In ENEMY SALVOES:
SELECTED LITERARY CRITICISM. Ed. C.J. Fox. London:
Vision, 1976. Pp. 118-25.
Attacks DHL's romanticization of the savage
and the primitive. Reprinted from Lewis's
PALEFACE (London: Chatto and Windus, 1929).
Extract reprinted in L1. Also see H297.

H224   Lindenberger, Herbert. "Lawrence and the Romantic Tradition." In A D.H. LAWRENCE MISCELLANY. Ed. Harry T.
Moore. Pp. 326-41. See G81.
DHL an expressive, Romantic artist rather than
a social novelist in the Victorian tradition,
with extended comparison between Wordsworth's
PRELUDE (1850) and DHL's major fiction.

H225 Liscano Velutini, Juan. "D.H. Lawrence, predicador apoca-
líptico." In ESPIRITUALIDAD Y LITERATURA: UNA RELACIÓN
TORMENTOSA. Barcelona: Seix Barral, 1976. Pp. 137-62.
Finds DHL a vital and affirmative, though dying writer in his last years (1925-30), describes his synthesis of eroticism and religion, and notes his recurrent resurrection
theme (PS, "The Man Who Died," APOCALYPSE).
[In Spanish.]

H226 Littlewood, J.C.F. "Lawrence Old and New." EIC, 21
(1971), 195-204.
Finds the majority of contemporary criticisms
of DHL (representative selections collected
by Draper in G34) and of recent academic criticism (e.g., Cavitch; see G16), devoid of
merit, arguing that the crucial period of DHL
criticism is during the years 1930-36 (first
work of Leavis, and others). Review essay.

H227 Lovett, Robert M., and Helen S. Hughes. "D.H. Lawrence
(1885-1930)." In THE HISTORY OF THE NOVEL IN ENGLAND.
Boston: Houghton Mifflin, 1932. Pp. 421-27.
Survey of career, noting DHL's intensity of
feeling (a weakness) and his psychoanalytic
themes.

H228 MacCarthy, Desmond. "D.H. Lawrence." In CRITICISM.
London: Putnam, 1932. Pp. 247-59.
Posthumous appreciations of DHL's works, de-
spite their technical flaws, his "reverence
for sex," and his impassioned rhetoric (cf.
Carlyle).

H229 McCormick, John. CATASTROPHE AND IMAGINATION: AN INTER-
PRETATION OF THE RECENT ENGLISH AND AMERICAN NOVEL. London: Longmans, 1937. Pp. 51-55, 244-47, and passim.
The absurdities and "enormous defects" of DHL,
an "obsessive" novelist, lacking form or ideas.

H230 MacDonald, Robert H. "'The Two Principles': A Theory of
the Sexual and Psychological Symbolism of D.H. Lawrence's
Later Fiction." DHLR, 11 (1978), 132-55.
The cosmos and the psyche, fire and water,
union and opposition in the fiction and essays of the twenties.

H231   Macy, John A. "D.H. Lawrence." In THE CRITICAL GAME.
       New York: Boni and Liveright, 1922. Pp. 325-35.
           DHL achieves a balance between lyrically in-
           tense style and philosophic substance.

H232   Maes-Jelinek, Hena. "D.H. Lawrence." In CRITICISM OF
       SOCIETY IN THE ENGLISH NOVEL BETWEEN THE WARS. Paris:
       Societé d'Éditions "Les Belles Lettres," 1970. Pp. 11-
       100.
           Superficial survey of social themes in DHL's
           pre- and post-war novels.

H233   Mailer, Norman. THE PRISONER OF SEX. Boston: Little,
       Brown, 1971. Pp. 134-60 and passim.
           Thoroughly devastates Millett's either simple-
           minded or disingenuous reading of DHL (see
           H255), yet presents an equally misleading
           counterargument. For the best responses to
           "feminist" misreadings, see H44, H189, H319,
           M18, M80, N12, and T3.

H234   Marks, W.S., III. "D.H. Lawrence and His Rabbit Adolph:
       Three Symbolic Permutations." CRITICISM, 10 (1968),
       200-16.
           Progressively vicious animal imagery in
           "Adolph" (in B16), SL, and WL.

H235   Marshall, Percy. "David Herbert Lawrence." In MASTERS
       OF THE ENGLISH NOVEL. London: Dobson, 1962. Pp. 199-213.
           The only twentieth-century figure included in
           Marshall's selection of masters, DHL is re-
           viewed as an original, powerful, and poetic
           novelist. Survey, with biographical and crit-
           ical commentary.

H236   Martin, Dexter. "D.H. Lawrence and Pueblo Religion: An
       Inquiry into Accuracy." ArQ, 9 (1953), 219-34.
           DHL remarkably accurate in his observation of
           Indian religions.

H237   Mason, Michael. THE CENTRE OF HILARITY: A PLAY UPON
       IDEAS ABOUT LAUGHTER AND THE ABSURD. London: Sheed and
       Ward, 1959. Passim.
           DHL's "titanism" counterpointed to Eliot's
           Christianity throughout.

H238   Mather, Rodney. "Patrick White and Lawrence: A Contrast."
       CR, 13 (1970), 34-50.
           The Australian novelist White suffers in this
           comparison with DHL.

H239 Mauriac, François. "D.H. Lawrence." In SECOND THOUGHTS:
REFLECTIONS ON LITERATURE AND ON LIFE. Trans. Adrienne
Foulke. New York: World, 1961. Pp. 122-25.
    Admires the logic of DHL's fundamental ques-
tion: "How can man rediscover the Universe if
he neglects the strength, the elemental poten-
cy of blood and flesh?"

H240 Maurois, André. "D.H. Lawrence." In PROPHETS AND POETS.
Trans. Hamish Miles. New York: Harper, 1935. Pp. 245-83.
    Asserts the profound influence of DHL's work,
although his philosophy is "flimsy" and his
fiction often tiresome. Reprinted in his
POINTS OF VIEW (New York: Ungar, 1968), pp.
243-83. Also see AA83.

H241 May, Keith M. "The Living Self: Integration of the Personality in Lawrence and Jung." In OUT OF THE MAELSTROM:
PSYCHOLOGY AND THE NOVEL IN THE TWENTIETH CENTURY. London: Elek, 1977. Pp. 43-61.
    Jung's and DHL's comparable visions, and paral-
lels to Jungian ideas in DHL's work.

H242 Mayhall, Jane. "D.H. Lawrence: The Triumph of Texture."
WHR, 19 (1965), 161-74.
    The "texture" of DHL's language.

H243 Mégroz, Rodolphe L. "David Herbert Lawrence." In THE
POST VICTORIANS. Ed. William R. Inge. London: Nicholson
and Watson, 1933. Pp. 317-28.
    Accurately predicts that "about 1955" the sig-
nificance of DHL's "educational purpose," if
not his literary achievement, will begin to be
recognized.

H244 -----. "D.H. Lawrence." In FIVE NOVELIST POETS OF TO-
DAY. London: Joiner and Steele, 1933. Pp. 189-255.
    DHL essentially a poet of nature and human
nature in prose (cf. Hardy), creating in his
novels before LCL a *Comedie Humaine* of the
"rushing stream...of modern life."

H245 Melchiori, Giorgio. "The Lotus and the Rose." In THE
TIGHTROPE WALKERS: STUDIES OF MANNERISM IN MODERN ENG-
LISH LITERATURE. London: Routledge, 1956. Pp. 89-103.
    Influence of DHL on Eliot's FOUR QUARTETS
(1936-42).

H246   Mendel, Sydney. "Shakespeare and D.H. Lawrence: Two
       Portraits of the Hero." WASCANA REVIEW, 3, No. 2 (1968),
       49-60.
              DHL's development from SL to LCL "is in cer-
              tain important respects very similar" to Shake-
              speare's from HAMLET to ANTONY AND CLEOPATRA
              (e.g., widening focus of interests, themes).

H247   Merivale, Patricia. "D.H. Lawrence and the Modern Pan
       Myth." In PAN THE GOAT-GOD: HIS MYTH IN MODERN TIMES.
       Cambridge, Mass.: Harvard Univ. Press, 1969. Pp. 194-
       219.
              DHL the "chief creator of the modern Pan myth,"
              particularly in the Mexican works, THE WHITE
              PEACOCK, and WL.

H248   Mesnil, Jacques. "A Prophet: D.H. Lawrence." Trans.
       Frieda Lawrence. SWR, 31 (1946), 257-59.
              DHL's religious intensity, primitivism, and
              irrationalism.

H249   Meyers, Jeffrey. "D.H. Lawrence." In HOMOSEXUALITY AND
       LITERATURE, 1890-1930. Montreal: McGill-Queen's Univ.
       Press, 1977. Pp. 131-61.
              Superficial discussion of DHL's "search for
              satisfactory masculine relationships" as an al-
              ternative to mutually destructive heterosexual
              relations, in THE WHITE PEACOCK, WL, AARON'S
              ROD, and PS. Originally published in G113.

H250   Michaels [-Tonks], Jennifer. "The Horse as a Life-Symbol
       in the Prose Works of D.H. Lawrence." INTERNATIONAL FIC-
       TION REVIEW, 5 (1978), 116-23.
              Variable symbolic significance of horses in
              DHL's long and short fiction.

H251   Miles, Rosalind. THE FICTION OF SEX: THEMES AND FUNC-
       TIONS OF SEX DIFFERENCE IN THE MODERN NOVEL. London:
       Vision, 1974. Pp. 16-21 and passim.
              Typical of the recent "feminist" misconstruc-
              tion of DHL's views, claiming that DHL "artic-
              ulated one of the most potent myths of our
              time, that of fundamental and irreconcilable
              opposition of male and female."

H252   Miller, Henry. "Creative Death"; "Into the Future." In
       THE WISDOM OF THE HEART. Norfolk, Conn.: New Directions,
       1941. Pp. 1-12; 159-72.
              DHL as a "dionysian" artist (influenced by Dos-
              toevsky), and as a prophet-martyr. Sympathetic

essays, written at the low-point of DHL's reputation. Also see G77.

H253   -----. "The Apocalyptic Lawrence." SWR, 31 (1946),
254-56.
DHL, "a writer outside all time...will be
fully understood" only when we overcome "our
own obtuseness, our own blindness, and our
own deadness." Also see G77.

H254   Miller, Nolan. "The 'Success' and 'Failure' of D.H. Lawrence." AR, 22 (1962), 380-92.
Speculates that DHL's later works fail because
"he could no longer find exactly the form his
passion wanted" and because he was surrounded
by uncritical, worshipful admirers. But, "only
the best writers 'fail.'" Review of several
publications, including C2, F123, and G121.

H255   Millett, Kate. "D.H. Lawrence." In SEXUAL POLITICS.
Garden City, N.Y.: Doubleday, 1970. Pp. 237-93.
Outspoken, tendentious, and distorted discussion of DHL's religious and political belief
in male supremacy, from SL to LCL. See H32,
H44, H189, H233, H319, H386, M18, M80, N12,
and T3.

H256   Mirsky, Dmitri. "D.H. Lawrence." In THE INTELLIGENTSIA
OF GREAT BRITAIN. Trans. Alec Brown. London: Gollancz,
1935. Pp. 120-22.
Marxist view of DHL as "the principal exponent
of that strain of bourgeois decadence which is
'attracted to the primitive'...one of the forms
taken by bourgeois civilization as it col-
lapses." See AA85.

H257   Moore, Harry T. AGE OF THE MODERN, AND OTHER LITERARY
ESSAYS. Carbondale: Southern Illinois Univ. Press, 1971.
Pp. viii-xvi, 9-12, 28-31, 70-72.
Moore comments on his life-long support of DHL
studies and reprints an early appeal for recognition of DHL's genius (H260), a review of the
unexpurgated LCL (NYTBR, 1959; see U52), and a
response to Leavis's splenetic attacks on his
scholarship (Z97).

H258   -----. "Bert and Lawrence and Lady Jane." In LAWRENCE
AND WOMEN. Ed. Anne Smith. Pp. 178-88. See G112.
In his relationships and presentations of women
DHL "sometimes 'wrong,' but he tried to be
right." Limp defense.

H259   -----. "D.H. Lawrence and the Flicks." LFQ, 1 (1973),
       3-11.
              DHL's dislike of the film, cinematic qualities
              in his fiction, and comments on the screen
              adaptations of his works. See G70.

H260   -----. "The Great Unread." SatR, 21 (2 Mar. 1940), 8, 17.
              Summarizes DHL's career and, at the time of
              his reputation's lowest point, calls for re-
              newed interest in his works. Reprinted in
              H257.

H261   -----. "The Prose of D.H. Lawrence." In D.H. LAWRENCE:
       THE MAN WHO LIVED. Ed. Robert B. Partlow and Moore. Pp.
       245-57. See G92.
              Overview of the several kinds of prose style
              and stylistic techniques in DHL's writing.

H262   Moore, Ruth F. "Spades and D.H. Lawrence." BOOKMAN (New
       York), 72 (1930), 118-25.
              Forcefully rejects both DHL's cultist admirers
              and his tyrannical, "impuritan" zealotry. Obit-
              uary condemnation.

H263   Morris, Wright. "Lawrence and the Immediate Present."
       In THE TERRITORY AHEAD. New York: Harcourt, 1957. Pp.
       217-31.
              A rejoinder to T.S. Eliot's comments on DHL in
              AFTER STRANGE GODS (see H104), defending DHL's
              concern with life rather than with conscious
              artistry. Reprinted in G81.

H264   Morse, Stearns. "The Phoenix and the Desert Places."
       MR, 9 (1968), 773-84.
              Comparison of DHL and Frost.

H265   Moynahan, Julian. "Lawrence, Woman, and the Celtic
       Fringe." In LAWRENCE AND WOMEN. Ed. Anne Smith. Pp.
       122-35. See G112.
              DHL's attraction to the supposed sensitivity
              of the Celtic race and his "equation" of Celt
              and woman.

H266   Mudrick, Marvin. "Lawrence." HudR, 27 (1974), 424-42.
              Anticipations of and similarities to DHL in
              the Russian novelists (especially Tolstoy).
              Reprinted in his THE MAN IN THE MACHINE (New
              York: Horizon, 1977), pp. 37-60.

H267   Muir, Edwin. "D.H. Lawrence." In TRANSITION: ESSAYS ON CONTEMPORARY LITERATURE. New York: Viking, 1926. Pp. 49-63.
         DHL's strength and weakness alike related to his "splendour...of the senses." He has written "greatly," but has produced no "completely satisfying work." Reprinted in G34.

H268   Muller, Herbert J. "D.H. Lawrence." In MODERN FICTION: A STUDY OF VALUES. New York: Funk and Wagnalls, 1937. Pp. 262-87.
         Admires the "sheer force" of DHL's originality and passion; however, only SL is a great work.

H269   Murfin, Ross C. SWINBURNE, HARDY, LAWRENCE, AND THE BURDEN OF BELIEF. Chicago: Univ. of Chicago Press, 1978. Pp. 170-220.
         DHL's debts to, criticism of, and similarities to Swinburne and Hardy. Surveys the poetry and two novels: THE WHITE PEACOCK and R. Also see Y88.

H270   Murry, John Middleton. "D.H. Lawrence: Creative Iconoclast." 1956. In A D.H. LAWRENCE MISCELLANY. Ed. Harry T. Moore. Pp. 3-6. See G81.
         DHL's "reactionary" views on education.

H271   ------. "On the Significance of D.H. Lawrence." In ADAM AND EVE: AN ESSAY TOWARDS A NEW AND BETTER SOCIETY. London: Dakers, 1944. Pp. 88-101 and passim.
         DHL's gospel, though "revolutionary and right," inherently weakened by its rejection of the "love idealism" of Christianity.

H272   Myers, Walter L. THE LATER REALISM: A STUDY OF CHARACTERIZATION IN THE BRITISH NOVEL. Chicago: Univ. of Chicago Press, 1927. Pp. 63-70, 87-93, and passim.
         The deliberate "incongruity" of DHL's characters. DHL essentially a realist, informed by an altered conception of the ego and the unconscious in his approach to characterization.

H273   Nardi, Piero. "Introduzione." In Lawrence's TUTTE LE POESIE [THE COMPLETE POEMS]. Milan: Mondadori, 1959. Pp. xvii-xxxviii.
         Most substantial of DHL's Italian biographer's numerous introductions to his works in translation, published by Mondadori (1947-75). See B29 and F122.

H274   Nathan, Peter W. "D.H. Lawrence." In RETREAT FROM REA-
       SON: AN ESSAY ON THE INTELLECTUAL LIFE OF OUR TIME. Lon-
       don: Heinemann, 1955. Pp. 109-30.
              Sees woman/mother hatred and advocacy of male
              dominance as DHL's chief preoccupation and as
              the logical outgrowth both of his family situ-
              ation and class status, and of his and our cul-
              ture.

H275   Nazareth, Peter. "D.H. Lawrence and Sex." TRANSITION,
       2, Nos. 6-7 (1962), 54-57; 3, No. 8 (1963), 38-43.
              DHL's reverence for the sexual experience as
              the access to "the immediate non-mental know-
              ledge of divine otherness."

H276   Nicholson, Norman. "Lawrence." In MAN AND LITERATURE.
       London: Macmillan, 1943. Pp. 64-86 and passim.
              DHL the chief progenitor of the modern literary
              cult of the "Natural" man, i.e., the amoral
              conception of man as a "highly developed animal
              fulfilling his natural impulses or being frus-
              trated in them."

H277   "Notes on D.H. Lawrence and One Reader." PAUNCH, No. 33
       (1968), pp. 10-21.
              Personal responses to DHL's dualistic theories
              of human personality and to the novels (SL, R,
              WL) and stories ("England, My England" and "The
              Blind Man").

H278   Nulle, Stebelton H. "D.H. Lawrence and the Fascist Move-
       ment." NEW MEXICO QUARTERLY, 10 (1940), 3-15.
              DHL a "great prophet and teacher...fated to be
              interpreted in terms of a lower order of real-
              ity," whose "impratical" ideals must not be
              confused with the visciously pragmatic fascist
              ideology.

H279   Pachmuss, Temira. "Dostoevsky, D.H. Lawrence, and Carson
       McCullers: Influences and Confluences." GERMANO-SLAVICA,
       No. 4 (1974), pp. 59-68.
              Traces several superficial resemblances between
              Dostoevsky's works and numerous titles by DHL
              and McCullers.

H280   Padhi, Bibhu. "Lawrence's Idea of Language." MODERNIST
       STUDIES, 4 (1982), 65-76.
              The tentative, exploratory nature of DHL's fic-
              tion reflected and embodied in his handling of
              dialogue and conversations. See G79.

H281 Panichas, George A. "E.M. Forster and D.H. Lawrence: Their Views on Education." In RENAISSANCE AND MODERN ESSAYS. Ed. George R. Hibbard. London: Routledge, 1966. Pp. 199-213.
> Forster and DHL often embody their social themes within their depictions of modern education.

H282 -----. "Notes on Eliot and Lawrence, 1915-1924"; "D.H. Lawrence and the Ancient Greeks." In THE REVERENT DIS-CIPLINE: ESSAYS IN LITERARY CRITICISM AND CULTURE. Knoxville: Univ. of Tennessee Press, 1974. Pp. 135-56; 335-50.
> Eliot and DHL, despite vast differences, both reacting to the horror of World War I in their search for visionary faith. Second essay on DHL's use of Greek life and myths in his work.

H283 Parkes, H.B. "D.H. Lawrence and Irving Babbitt." NEW ADELPHI, 9 (1935), 328-31.
> The puritanical Babbitt, "in terms of pure in-tellect," and the Rousseauistic DHL, "in terms of pure feeling," akin in their condemnation of the dehumanizing modern industrial civiliza-tion.

H284 Paterson, John. "D.H. Lawrence: The One Bright Book of Life." In THE NOVEL AS FAITH: THE GOSPEL ACCORDING TO JAMES, HARDY, CONRAD, JOYCE, LAWRENCE AND VIRGINIA WOOLF. Boston: Gambit, 1973. Pp. 143-83.
> Surveys the profound impact of DHL's noncon-formist heritage on his view of the novel as a "missionary enterprise," to be pursued with a near-religious zeal in search of an "entire-ly new world."

H285 Peach, Linden. "Powys, Lawrence, and a New Sensibility: A Reading of Two Neglected Prose [Works] by John Cowper Powys." THE ANGLO-WELSH REVIEW, 26, No. 59 (1977), 32-41.
> DHL's and Powys's similar views of sensuality and psychic health.

H286 Peterson, Richard F. "Steinbeck and D.H. Lawrence." In STEINBECK'S LITERARY DIMENSION: A GUIDE TO COMPARATIVE STUDIES. Ed. Tetsumaro Hayashi. Metuchen, N.J.: Scare-crow Press, 1973. Pp. 67-82.
> Superficial parallels between the authors' works.

H287   Petre, M.D. "Some Reflections on D.H. Lawrence from the
       Catholic Point of View." NEW ADELPHI, 6 (1933), 337-45.
              DHL a frustrated "seeker after reality" who,
              in rejecting a personal God, failed to recog-
              nize that he was seeking "Him in whom is all
              reality."

H288   Peyre, Henri. "D.H. Lawrence, le message d'un prophète."
       In HOMMES ET OEUVRES DU XXe SIÈCLE. Paris: Éditions R.A.
       Corrêa, 1938. Pp. 275-98.
              DHL in the tradition of English "non-conform-
              istes obstinés." Biographical criticism of
              DHL's works, emphasizing his revolt against
              English literary, moral, and social conventions
              and his "nouveau message d'amour." [In French.]

H289   Phelps, Gilbert. THE RUSSIAN NOVEL IN ENGLISH FICTION.
       London: Hutchinson, 1956. Pp. 180-84.
              DHL's debts to and critical repudiation of Dos-
              toevsky and Tolstoy.

H290   Pinto, Vivian de Sola. "D.H. Lawrence." In THE POLITICS
       OF TWENTIETH-CENTURY NOVELISTS. Ed. George A. Panichas.
       New York: Hawthorne Books, 1971. Pp. 30-50.
              Intelligent rebuttal to the view of DHL as a
              fascist.

H291   -----. "William Blake and D.H. Lawrence." In WILLIAM
       BLAKE: ESSAYS FOR S. FOSTER DAMON. Ed. Alvin H. Rosen-
       feld. Providence, R.I.: Brown Univ. Press, 1969. Pp.
       84-106.
              "Further exploration of the points of contact"
              between the "two prophetic artists."

H292   Plowman, Max. "The Significance of D.H. Lawrence." 1930.
       In THE RIGHT TO LIVE: ESSAYS. London: Dakers, 1942. Pp.
       122-30.
              Praises DHL's attacks on modern mechanization
              of relationships ("blasphemy against life")
              as the first, essential protest in the "move-
              ment" for an affirmative, creative vision of
              life.

H293   Poole, Roger H., and P.J. Shepherd. "Introductory Es-
       says." In D.H. LAWRENCE: A SELECTION. Ed. Poole and
       Shepherd. Pp. 1-60. See B7.
              A series of six essays on DHL and travel, on
              DHL and education, and on DHL and religion,

by Poole, on DHL and politics, on DHL and sex,
and a general introduction by Shepherd. Good
introductory commentaries.

H294   Powys, John Cowper. "Modern Fiction." In SEX IN THE
ARTS: A SYMPOSIUM. Ed. John F. McDermott and Kendall
B. Taft. New York: Harper, 1932. Pp. 34-63.
DHL's important contributions to the emancipa-
tion of sex in modern fiction (pp. 57-63).

H295   Praz, Mario. "Nota su D.H. Lawrence nel quadro del Ro-
manticismo europeo" ["Note on D.H. Lawrence in the Con-
text of European Romanticism"]. 1931. In CRONACHE LET-
TERARIE ANGLOSASSONI. Vol. 1. CRONACHE INGLESI. Rome:
Edizioni di storia e letteratura, 1950. Pp. 198-202.
DHL's reflection of the anti-intellectualism
("L'anti-cerebralismo") and anti-Christianity
of the European Romantic tradition. Review
of Ernest Seillière's NÉO-ROMANTISME EN AL-
LEMAGNE (1931; also see Seillière study of
DHL, G107). [In Italian.]

H296   Pritchard, Ronald E. "The Way of Freedom...Furtive Pride
and Slinking Singleness." In D.H. LAWRENCE: A CRITICAL
STUDY. Ed. Andor Gomme. Pp. 94-119. See G43.
DHL's projection of his own struggles and personality on to all he read or saw, his loss of
objective reality, traced in the works of the
twenties and attributed to his general failure
to achieve "relationship."

H297   Pritchard, William H. "Lawrence and [Wyndham] Lewis."
AGENDA, 7, No. 3, and 8, No. 1 (1969-70), 140-47.
Compares the two writers, their antipathetic
views of one another, and their critical repu-
tations. (Reprinted in IOWA REVIEW [1971]).
See H223.

H298   -----. SEEING THROUGH EVERYTHING: ENGLISH WRITERS, 1918-
1940. New York: Oxford Univ. Press, 1977. Pp. 70-89,
123-33, and passim.
Sober and distinguished reservations about
DHL's achievement in fiction (chiefly WL and
"St. Mawr") and poetry.

H299   Quennell, Peter. "D.H. Lawrence and Aldous Huxley." In
THE ENGLISH NOVELISTS: A SURVEY OF THE NOVEL BY TWENTY
CONTEMPORARY NOVELISTS. London: Chatto and Windus, 1936.
Pp. 247-57.
Intellectual and artistic contrasts and a

fundamental similarity (their disdain for
form) between Huxley and DHL.

H300   -----. "The Later Period of D.H. Lawrence." In SCRUTI-
NIES. Comp. Edgell Rickword. London: Wishart, 1931.
II, 124-37.
      Regrets the pronounced *"feminist* bias" in
      DHL's late fiction: "the overwhelming exhala-
      tions of this worser and female self."

H301   Rahv, Philip. "On F.R. Leavis and D.H. Lawrence." 1968.
In LITERATURE AND SIXTH SENSE. Boston: Houghton Mifflin,
1969. Pp. 289-306.
      Considers DHL overrated and Leavis's champion-
      ship of DHL's work both motivated by class re-
      sentment and "lacking in disinterestedness and
      even a minimum of objectivity." See G68.

H302   Raleigh, John Henry. "Victorian Morals and the Modern
Novel." PR, 25 (1958), 241-64.
      Despite vast differences, both DHL and Joyce
      were rebels against Victorianism.

H303   Rascoe, Burton. "D.H. Lawrence." In PROMETHEANS: ANCIENT
AND MODERN. New York: Putnam's, 1933. Pp. 221-38.
      Extremely unfavorable character sketch of DHL
      as "the most weakly endowed intellectually of
      the writers of major importance" in our cen-
      tury.

H304   Read, Herbert. "D.H. Lawrence." In A COAT OF MANY COL-
OURS. 1945. Rev. ed. London: Routledge, 1956. Pp.
262-64.
      Of his generation, DHL had "the greatest gen-
      ius...the most prophetic knowledge...and the
      greatest influence on the younger generation."

H305   -----. "D.H. Lawrence." 1950. In THE CULT OF SINCERITY.
London: Faber, 1968. Pp. 160-77.
      DHL is both a writer of "peculiar power" and
      sincerity and an "irregular genius" who lacks
      the discipline to achieve a coherent philoso-
      phy.

H306   Reade, Arthur R. "The Intelligentsia and D.H. Lawrence."
In MAIN CURRENTS IN MODERN LITERATURE. London: Nicholson
and Watson, 1935. Pp. 179-96.
      Finds DHL's later works the product of the
      deep psychic wounds of the First World War

and the contemporary censorship of R, and speculates on the reasons for his appeal to the
young, post-war intelligentsia.

H307 Rieff, Philip. "The Therapeutic as Mythmaker: Lawrence's
True Christian Philosophy." In THE TRIUMPH OF THE THERA-
PEUTIC: USES OF FAITH AFTER FREUD. New York: Harper,
1966. Pp. 189-231.
  DHL's assimilation of both Freud and Christi-
  anity into his thought.

H308 -----. "Two Honest Men." LISTENER, 63 (1960), 794-96.
  Distinguishes DHL's affirmative from Freud's
  negative view of the unconscious. Reprinted
  in L3.

H309 Roberts, John H. "Huxley and Lawrence." VQR, 13 (1937),
546-57.
  Huxley's conversion to DHL's ideology, in POINT
  COUNTER POINT (1928) and after.

H310 Roberts, William H. "D.H. Lawrence: A Study of a Free
Spirit in Literature." 1928. RMS, 18 (1974), 7-16.
  Early critical article reprinted with a letter
  of acknowledgment to the author by DHL and a
  prefatory comment by James T. Boulton.

H311 Robertson, P.J.M. "F.R. Leavis and D.H. Lawrence." In
THE LEAVISES ON FICTION. New York: St. Martin's Press,
1981. Pp. 76-98.
  Overview and evaluation of Leavis's "quest for
  self-knowledge" in his critical writings on
  DHL. See G68.

H312 Robinson, Ian. "D.H. Lawrence and English Prose." In
D.H. LAWRENCE: A CRITICAL STUDY. Ed. Andor Gomme. Pp.
13-29. See G43.
  Techniques (e.g., phrase rhythms), purposes,
  and influence of DHL's remarkable innovations
  in prose style.

H313 Robson, W.W. MODERN ENGLISH LITERATURE. London: Oxford
Univ. Press, 1970. Pp. 82-92 and passim.
  DHL's "desire was not only to write, but to
  live, as if his doctrine of spontaneity were
  true." Surveys fiction.

H314   Rogers, Katherine M. THE TROUBLESOME HELPMATE: A HISTORY
       OF MISOGYNY IN LITERATURE. Seattle: Univ. of Washington
       Press, 1966. Pp. 237-47.
              DHL's "fear of mom," awe of the "power of
              motherhood," and resulting misogyny.

H315   Rosenfeld, Paul. "D.H. Lawrence." In MEN SEEN: TWENTY
       FOUR MODERN AUTHORS. New York: Dial Press, 1925. Pp.
       45-62.
              DHL, "the Minnesinger returned in a modern
              day," a major writer and thinker who, like
              Wagner, speaks for and epitomizes his age.
              Reprinted in G20.

H316   ------. "D.H. Lawrence." NEW REPUBLIC, 62 (1930), 155-56.
              Laudatory obituary tribute to DHL as a great
              contemporary "realistic mystic." Reprinted
              in G20 and G34.

H317   Ross, Charles L. "Art and 'Metaphysic' in D.H. Lawrence's
       Novels." DHLR, 7 (1974), 206-17.
              Warns against a recent tendency in DHL criti-
              cism to read his fiction as direct embodiment
              of the ideas found in the essays, or as "al-
              legorization of the pollyanalytics." Reviews
              G65 and G101.

H318   Rossman, Charles. "Myth and Misunderstanding D.H. Law-
       rence." BuR, 22, No. 2 (1976), 81-101.
              DHL's later works not mythic, but essentially
              personal expressions of resentment against as-
              sertive women. See below.

H319   ------. "'You are the call and I am the answer': D.H. Law-
       rence and Women." DHLR, 8 (1975), 255-328.
              Thoughtful evaluation of DHL's attitudes toward
              "the second sex" in his works, dismissing the
              assertion that he advocates male supremacy as
              "reductive" and arguing that, despite "reac-
              tionary, even unpalatable, facets," his works
              dramatize a far more sympathetic and liberat-
              ing attitude toward women than his feminist
              critics would admit (e.g., Beauvoir and Mil-
              lett; see H32 and H255). Also see G26, N83,
              and above.

H320 Sagar, Keith. "Beyond D.H. Lawrence." In D.H. LAWRENCE:
      THE MAN WHO LIVED. Ed. Robert B. Partlow and Harry T.
      Moore. Pp. 258-66. See G92.
              Though some of DHL's "battles have been won,"
              he remains a vital force, a "beacon of san-
              ity," and a brave participant in the unending
              "process of evolving human consciousness."

H321 -----. THE ART OF TED HUGHES. Cambridge: Cambridge Univ.
      Press, 1975. Pp. 38-45 and passim.
              DHL's influence on Hughes's poetry.

H322 -----. "What Mr. Williams Has Made of D.H. Lawrence."
      TWENTIETH CENTURY, 168 (1960), 143-53.
              Summarizes Williams's tributes to DHL and his
              several debts to DHL for characters and situa-
              tions in his works. See F162, G37, and V182.

H323 Sale, Roger. "D.H. Lawrence, 1910-1916." In MODERN HERO-
      ISM: ESSAYS ON D.H. LAWRENCE, WILLIAM EMPSON, AND J.R.R.
      TOLKIEN. Berkeley: Univ. of California Press, 1973. Pp.
      16-106.
              Recounts in detail DHL's heroic struggle toward
              artistic maturity and suggests the sources of
              his imaginative failure in the later career.

H324 Sanders, Scott. "D.H. Lawrence and the Resacralization
      of Nature." In D.H. LAWRENCE: THE MAN WHO LIVED. Ed.
      Robert B. Partlow and Harry T. Moore. Pp. 159-67. See
      G92.
              DHL's chief effect on his audience a revital-
              ization of the awareness of living, a partic-
              ipation in "the sacred, unified surge of life,"
              achieved through his "*de*sacralization" and sub-
              sequent "*re*sacralization" of nature.

H325 Sarvan, Charles, and Liebetraut Sarvan. "D.H. Lawrence
      and Doris Lessing's THE GRASS IS SINGING." MFS, 24
      (1978-79), 533-37.
              Draws several parallels between DHL's long and
              short fiction and Lessing's novel (1950), find-
              ing his influence "sustained and significant."

H326 Savage, Derek S. "D.H. Lawrence: A Study in Dissolution."
      In THE PERSONAL PRINCIPLE: STUDIES IN MODERN POETRY. Lon-
      don: Routledge, 1944. Pp. 131-54.
              DHL's rejection of spiritual values in his "bi-
              ologism," or retrogressive dissolution back in-
              to primary life (considers fiction as well as
              poetry).

H327   Schneider, Daniel J. "The Symbolism of the Soul: D.H.
        Lawrence and Some Others." DHLR, 7 (1974), 107-26.
                DHL's "search for symbolism adequate to grasp
                the soul's complexities" (cf. Hawthorne, Con-
                rad, Mann, Stevens, and others).

H328   Schorer, Mark. "D.H. Lawrence: Then, During, Now." ATLAN-
        TIC, 233 (Mar. 1974), 84-88.
                DHL's rejection by critics and poverty in life
                compared to his recent critical esteem and the
                prosperity of his estate.

H329   -----. "Poste Restante: Lawrence as Traveler." In Harry
        T. Moore's POSTE RESTANTE. Pp. 1-18. See F111.
                Importance of place as an agent of spiritual
                renewal or as a symbol of transformation in
                DHL's fiction. Reprinted in G81 and below.

H330   -----. THE WORLD WE IMAGINE: SELECTED ESSAYS. New York:
        Farrar, Straus and Giroux, 1968. Pp. 3-23, 107-21, 122-
        46, 147-61, 195-218.
                Collects five of Schorer's most important es-
                says on DHL. Includes H329, H331, L57, N88,
                and U59.

H331   -----. "Two Houses, Two Ways: The Florentine Villas of
        Lewis and Lawrence, Respectively." NEW WORLD WRITING,
        No. 4 (1953), pp. 136-54.
                Useful and interesting comparison of Sinclair
                Lewis and DHL on the basis of their two con-
                siderably different life-styles in Florence.
                Reprinted above and in F123 (extract).

H332   Schwartz, Murray M. "D.H. Lawrence and Psychoanalysis:
        An Introduction." DHLR, 10 (1977), 215-22.
                On the reflection of Lawrencean attitudes in
                current psychoanalytic theory (lists twenty-
                five titles) and the value of approaching DHL
                through psychoanalytic criticism. See V1.

H333   Scott, Nathan A. "D.H. Lawrence: Chartist of the *Via
        Mystica*." In REHEARSALS OF DISCOMPOSURE: ALIENATION AND
        RECONCILIATION IN MODERN LITERATURE. New York: King's
        Crown Press, 1952. Pp. 112-77.
                DHL a mystic modern "saint" whose profound de-
                spair hovers "on the verge of prayer." A good
                general survey of his "radical heresy" from a
                rigorously Christian viewpoint.

H334   Scott-James, Rolfe A. FIFTY YEARS OF ENGLISH LITERATURE, 1900-1950; WITH A POSTSCRIPT 1951-1955. London: Longmans, 1955. Pp. 125-31.
        DHL's reaction to literary realism in his fiction of "interior vision" (cf. Joyce, Dorothy Richardson, and Woolf).

H335   Sellers, W.H. "New Light on Auden's THE ORATORS." PMLA, 82 (1967), 455-64.
        Explores the "primary dependence" of Auden's second book (1932) on DHL's works, particularly emphasizing the theme of England's social illness found in both writers.

H336   Sen, M.K. "D.H. Lawrence and the Language of the 'Locks.'" In FRESH GROUNDS IN ENGLISH LITERATURE. New Delhi: Chand, 1974. Pp. 104-25.
        DHL's hair "fetish" and decided preference for long hair evident in his fiction (related to contemporary fashion for "bobbed" hair).

H337   Seward, Barbara. THE SYMBOLIC ROSE. New York: Columbia Univ. Press, 1960. Pp. 137-43.
        The "highly subjective" rose symbolism of DHL's "personal creed."

H338   Shanks, Edward. "Friends of D.H. Lawrence." LONDON MERCURY, 29 (1933), 142-50.
        DHL done a disservice by his friends and critics who have "lost their heads." (Shanks claims to have had an early and sustained admiration for DHL, but see below.)

H339   -----. "Mr. D.H. Lawrence." In SECOND ESSAYS ON LITERATURE. London: Collins, 1927. Pp. 62-83.
        DHL "lives at the bottom of a dark pit." Equivocally surveys his "shapeless, ragged, diffuse," yet "genuine" writings. See above. Reprinted in G34.

H340   Sherman, Stuart P. "D.H. Lawrence Cultivates His Beard." In CRITICAL WOODCUTS. New York: Scribner's, 1926. Pp. 18-31.
        Admires the potency and power of DHL's fiction, with equivocal respect for his dark primitivism and alienation (symbolized by his beard). Reprinted in G34.

H341   Sillitoe, Alan.   "D.H. Lawrence and His District."   In
       D.H. LAWRENCE.   Ed. Stephen Spender.   Pp. 42-50, 67-70.
       See Gll3.
              DHL's psychologically and artistically crip-
              pling preoccupation with and ambivalence toward
              his home district of Nottinghamshire.   Re-
              printed in Sillitoe's MOUNTAINS AND CAVERNS:
              SELECTED ESSAYS (London: Allen, 1975), pp.
              128-44.

H342   Slochower, Harry.   "D.H. Lawrence."   In NO VOICE IS WHOLLY
       LOST...: WRITERS AND THINKERS IN WAR AND PEACE.   New York:
       Creative Age Press, 1945.   Pp. 136-43.
              DHL's awareness of the futility of his revolt
              against convention.

H343   Smith, Elton.   "Redemptive Snobbishness in Nietzsche, Law-
       rence, and Eliot."   C&L, 18, No. 3 (1969), 30-35.
              The three "spiritual aristocrats" alike find
              Biblical sanction for "human distinctions."

H344   Soames, Jane.   "The Modern Rousseau."   LIFE AND LETTERS,
       8 (1932), 451-70.
              Intriguing parallels between DHL and Rousseau
              ("to a great extent [their] ideas coincided").

H345   Solecki, Sam.   "D.H. Lawrence's View of Film."   LFQ, 1
       (1973), 12-16.
              DHL's dislike of movies largely an objection
              to their primary appeal to the non-vital "men-
              tal consciousness" of the spectator.   See G70.

H346   Speirs, John.   POETRY TOWARDS NOVEL.   London: Faber, 1971.
       Pp. 326-33.
              In his "individual vision of life," DHL the
              "culmination" of the "19th-century line of
              great novelist poets," the successors of
              Shakespeare (e.g., Dickens, Eliot, Hardy,
              Conrad).

H347   Spender, Stephen.   "D.H. Lawrence, England and the War."
       In D.H. LAWRENCE.   Ed. Spender.   Pp. 71-76.   See Gll3.
              DHL's pastoral vision of England demolished
              by the war, yet he retained the hope that the
              country might survive.   Similar to below.

H348   -----. "English Threnody, American Tragedy: Lawrentian
        Love-Hate for England." In LOVE-HATE RELATIONS: ENGLISH
        AND AMERICAN SENSIBILITIES. New York: Random House, 1974.
        Pp. 234-42.
            DHL's nostalgic idealization of primitive Eng-
            land and hatred of modern industrial England.

H349   -----. "Notes on D.H. Lawrence." In THE DESTRUCTIVE
        ELEMENT: A STUDY OF MODERN WRITERS AND BELIEFS. London:
        Cape, 1935. Pp. 176-86.
            DHL primarily a prophet and a preacher. His
            fiction neither very experimental nor intel-
            lectually profound, yet his power of observa-
            tion great.

H350   -----. "Pioneering the Instinctive Life." In THE CREA-
        TIVE ELEMENT: A STUDY OF VISION, DESPAIR, AND ORTHODOXY
        AMONG SOME MODERN WRITERS. London: Hamilton, 1953. Pp.
        92-107.
            DHL's creative anti-intellectualism, his real-
            istic rather than idealistic assertion of the
            value of instinctual life over mere conscious-
            ness.

H351   Spilka, Mark. "Lawrence Up-tight, or the Anal Phase Once
        Over." NOVEL, 4 (1971), 252-67.
            Amusing objection to the recent critical pre-
            occupation with anal-eroticism as central to
            DHL's art. (Review of Clarke; see G18). Also
            see responses by George Ford, Frank Kermode,
            and Colin Clarke, and a final rejoinder by
            Spilka, in NOVEL, 5 (1971), 54-70. Also see
            G101, H211, and U64.

H352   -----. "Lawrence versus Peeperkorn on Abdication; or,
        What Happens to a Pagan Vitalist When the Juice Runs Out?"
        In D.H. LAWRENCE: THE MAN WHO LIVED. Ed. Robert B. Part-
        low and Harry T. Moore. Pp. 105-20. See G92.
            Sees DHL's resistance to treatment for tuber-
            culosis and his literary responses to the sex-
            ual impotency of his last years, in the light
            of the story of Peeperkorn in Mann's DER ZAU-
            BERBERG (1924), as his refusal to abdicate
            from life.

H353   -----. "Lawrence's Quarrel with Tenderness." CritQ, 9
        (1967), 363-77.
            Traces the "quarrel" (SL) through its recon-
            ciliation (LCL).

H354   -----. "Lessing and Lawrence: The Battle of the Sexes."
        ConL, 16 (1975), 218-40.
                In THE GOLDEN NOTEBOOK (1962) Lessing "both
                undercuts yet refuses to abandon Lawrencean
                values" in her treatment of sexual relations.

H355   -----. "Post-Leavis Lawrence Critics." MLQ, 25 (1964),
        212-17.
                Observes the inevitable influence of Leavis's
                criticism, in both the application and the
                rejection of his ideas in subsequent critical
                studies. Reviews G44, G83, G118, G123, and
                V5. See G68.

H356   Squire, John C. "[the 'precious residuum']." 1930. In
        D.H. LAWRENCE: THE CRITICAL HERITAGE. Ed. Ronald P. Dra-
        per. Pp. 330-34. See G34.
                DHL an "exasperated...very self-centered" mis-
                anthrope, degenerating philosophically in his
                later years, yet the best of his works are
                unique achievements which "will live." Obit-
                uary critique. See G8.

H357   Stavrou, Constantine N. "D.H. Lawrence's 'Psychology'
        of Sex." L&P, 6 (1956), 90-95.
                DHL's affirmation of the sexual impulses as
                creative "seems undesirable hedonism only
                when we read 'with' and not 'through' our
                minds."

H358   -----. "William Blake and D.H. Lawrence." UKCR, 22
        (1956), 235-40.
                Notes "echoes" of Blake's style, imagery, and
                "principal doctrines" and ideas throughout
                DHL's writings.

H359   Stewart, Garrett. "Lawrence, 'Being,' and the Allotropic
        Style." NOVEL, 9 (1976), 217-42.
                Rhetorical analysis of DHL's vocabulary, gram-
                mar, and imitative style. Important and well-
                done. Reprinted in TOWARDS A POETICS OF FIC-
                TION, ed. Mark Spilka (Bloomington: Indiana
                Univ. Press, 1977), pp. 331-56.

H360   Stewart, Jack F. "Lawrence and Gauguin." TCL, 26 (1980),
        385-401.
                DHL's "primitivism" and "painterly vision"
                (in his writings) compared to Gauguin's.

H361 Stewart, J.I.M. "Lawrence." In EIGHT MODERN WRITERS.
      Oxford: Clarendon Press, 1963. Pp. 484-593, 686-94.
            Good critical survey of the novels, featuring
            extended commentary on the major works, and
            brief analyses of selected short stories and
            poems. Checklist of DHL studies (pp. 686-94).

H362 Stoehr, Taylor. "'Mentalized Sex' in D.H. Lawrence."
      NOVEL, 8 (1975), 101-22.
            The ironic relationship between DHL's attacks
            on "mentalized sex" and his intellectual treat-
            ment of sex in literature.

H363 Stohl, Johan H. "Man and Society: Lawrence's Subversive
      Vision." In LITERATURE AND RELIGION. Ed. Charles A. Hut-
      tar. [Pp. 55-62.] See G59.
            DHL's social vision not a traditional attempt
            to find "accommodation for man within society,"
            but a revolutionary argument for man's need to
            preserve integrity within the community.

H364 Stonier, George Walter. "D.H. Lawrence." In GOG MAGOG, AND
      OTHER CRITICAL ESSAYS. London: Dent, 1933. Pp. 70-87.
            Representative posthumous rejection of DHL as
            an unprofound and unoriginal, minor Romantic
            prophet, predicting "no reader in twenty-years'
            time will be likely to take...[him] seriously."

H365 Stubbs, Patricia. "Mr. Lawrence and Mrs. Woolf." In
      WOMEN AND FICTION: FEMINISM AND THE NOVEL, 1880-1920.
      New York: Barnes and Noble, 1979. Pp. 225-35.
            Distorted view of DHL's complex treatment of
            women in his fiction (cf. Woolf's failed "fem-
            inism").

H366 Sturm, Ralph D. "Lawrence: Critic of Christianity."
      CathW, 208 (1968), 75-79.
            Summarizes DHL's attitudes toward organized
            religion, from his repudiation through his
            attempted reconstruction of Christianity.

H367 Suckow, Ruth. "Modern Figures of Destiny: D.H. Lawrence
      and Frieda Lawrence." DHLR, 3 (1970), 1-30.
            Critical estimate by a middle-American novel-
            ist, emphasizing the importance of Frieda in
            shaping DHL's work as well as his life.

H368   Sutherland, James R. ON ENGLISH PROSE. Toronto: Toronto
Univ. Press, 1966. Pp. 105-09.
> DHL's prose shares the "same abhorence of airs
> and graces and decoration of any kind" found
> in the great Puritan writers.

H369   Swinden, Patrick. "Growing Pains: Romanticism and the
Novel: D.H. Lawrence, Richard Hughes." In UNOFFICIAL
SELVES: CHARACTER IN THE NOVEL FROM DICKENS TO THE PRES-
ENT DAY. London: Macmillan, 1973. Pp. 158-202.
> Considers DHL's development of the internal as
> well as the social dimensions of character and
> personality (pp. 160-81).

H370   Swinnerton, Frank. "David Herbert Lawrence." In THE
GEORGIAN LITERARY SCENE, 1910-1935. 1934. 2nd ed.
London: Hutchinson, 1969. Pp. 312-24.
> DHL an original genius, a prophet, a poet, and
> an impressionist whose reputation has suffered
> from the "sophisticates or cranks" among his
> followers.

H371   Taylor, Anne Robinson. "Modern Primitives: Molly Bloom
and James Joyce, with a Note on D.H. Lawrence." In MALE
NOVELISTS AND THEIR FEMALE VOICES: LITERARY MASQUERADES.
Troy, N.Y.: Whitston, 1981. Pp. 189-222.
> Woman, in both Joyce and DHL, seen ambivalently
> as a symbol of the primitive consciousness and
> as a source of the archetypal qualities of "un-
> consciousness, irrationality, undifferentiated
> acceptance, mother love, and sex."

H372   Tedlock, Ernest W. "D.H. Lawrence's Annotation of Ous-
pensky's TERTIUM ORGANUM." TSLL, 2 (1960), 206-18.
> Transcribes DHL's running marginal debate with
> Ouspensky's "key to the enigmas of the world"
> (1911), a book by which he was nevertheless
> influenced.

H373   -----. "Lawrence's Voice: A Keynote Address." In D.H.
LAWRENCE: THE MAN WHO LIVED. Ed. Robert B. Partlow and
Harry T. Moore. Pp. 5-12. See G92.
> Stresses importance of listening "attentively
> to the complexities of tone and diction" in
> DHL's writings "before we can say we under-
> stand what Lawrence is saying," and surveys
> recent critical commentaries on DHL's "voice."

H374   Terry, C.J.   "Aspects of D.H. Lawrence's Struggle with
       Christianity."   DR, 54 (1974), 112-29.
              The "anxiety, adventurousness and oscillation
              incurred by his search for a fresh set of non-
              Christian...values" traced in DHL's fiction.

H375   Thomas, John Heywood.   "The Perversity of D.H. Lawrence."
       CRITERION, 10 (1930), 5-22.
              DHL's essential abhorrence of the physical
              world and dedication to "contradicting at
              every turn the man he is in the main."   Pa-
              tronizing misreading.

H376   Thompson, Alan R.   "D.H. Lawrence: Apostle of the Dark
       God."   BOOKMAN (New York), 73 (1931), 492-99.
              Modest attempt at an objective evaluation of
              DHL's dualistic philosophy, which inverts Pla-
              tonic values, espousing the subrational in na-
              ture.   Reprinted in G34.

H377   Thompson, Leslie M.   "D.H. Lawrence and Judas."   DHLR, 4
       (1971), 1-19.
              The Judas theme and fears of betrayal in DHL's
              later fiction.

H378   Tindall, William York.   FORCES IN MODERN BRITISH LITER-
       ATURE, 1885-1956.   New York: Knopf, 1956.   Pp. 222-27
       and passim.
              Modification of Tindall's earlier, outspoken
              disapproval of DHL (see G120), finding his
              dire prophecies more legitimate in a post-war
              perspective.

H379   -----.   "Introduction."   In THE LATER D.H. LAWRENCE.   Ed.
       Tindall.   Pp. v-xvii.   See B13.
              Especially good commentary on the kinds and
              qualities of DHL's symbolism.

H380   -----.   "Transcendentalism in Contemporary Literature."
       In THE ASIAN LEGACY AND AMERICAN LIFE.   Ed. Arthur E.
       Christy.   New York: Day, 1945.   Pp. 175-92.
              Influence of theosophy and oriental religion
              on DHL, Yeats, and Huxley.

H381   Traversi, Derek.   "Dr. Leavis and the Case of D.H. Law-
       rence."   MONTH, 15 (1956), 166-71.
              F.R. Leavis's program for establishing DHL as
              the great Modern English novelist appraised:

DHL is "an even greater writer than Dr. Leavis'
restricted treatment of him would indicate; he
is also one with more faults" (e.g., his limitations of experience and "sense of failure").
Reviews G68.

H382 Trient, René. "Lawrence panthéiste et l'antiquité païenne." CAHIERS DU SUD, 20 (1933), 614-21.
      Commentary on DHL's primitivism in light of
      contemporary fascist ideologies. [In French.]

H383 Trilling, Diana. "A Letter of Introduction." In THE
SELECTED LETTERS OF D.H. LAWRENCE. Ed. Trilling. Pp.
xi-xxxvii. See C14.
      An open "letter" to Norman Podhoretz, represen-
      tative of the younger generation, noting her
      equivocal responses to DHL and DHL's own ambiv-
      alence toward sex and love. Extract reprinted
      in G81.

H384 -----. "D.H. Lawrence and the Movements of Modern Culture." In D.H. LAWRENCE. Ed. Stephen Spender. Pp. 1-7.
See G113.
      DHL would have been unsympathetic to contempo-
      rary social and sexual liberation movements.
      Reprinted in her WE MUST MARCH MY DARLINGS
      (New York: Harcourt, 1977), pp. 293-303.

H385 -----. "Introduction." In THE PORTABLE D.H. LAWRENCE.
Ed. Trilling. Pp. 1-32. See B19.
      Apologetic and dated critical estimate.

H386 Tristram, Philippa. "Eros and Death (Lawrence, Freud
and Women)." In LAWRENCE AND WOMEN. Ed. Anne Smith.
Pp. 136-55. See G112.
      Intelligently drawn parallels between Freud's
      thought and DHL's progress, in R, WL, and
      AARON'S ROD. See H233.

H387 Troy, William. "D.H. Lawrence as Hero"; "The Lawrence
Myth." 1933; 1938. In his SELECTED ESSAYS. Ed. Stanley
Edgar Hyman. New Brunswick, N.J.: Rutgers Univ. Press,
1967. Pp. 110-19; 120-33.
      A valuable early review of Huxley's edition of
      the letters (C10), with a general estimate of
      DHL, and a discussion of DHL's "Dionysian" be-
      lief in the blood (APOCALYPSE [A76] and other
      works).

H388 Turnell, Martin. MODERN LITERATURE AND CHRISTIAN FAITH.
      London: Darton, Longman, and Todd, 1961. Pp. 30-34.
          DHL's search "for something absolute" in this
          life, "a realm where, in the nature of things,
          it could not exist."

H389 Ulmer, Gregory L. "Rousseau and D.H. Lawrence: 'Philoso-
      phies' of the 'Gelded' Age." CANADIAN REVIEW OF COMPARA-
      TIVE LITERATURE, 4 (1977), 68-80.
          Pervasive Rousseauistic elements in DHL's
          thought despite DHL's condemnations of the
          "so-called Father of Romanticism."

H390 Undset, Sigrid. "D.H. Lawrence." In MEN, WOMEN, AND
      PLACES. Trans. Arthur G. Chater. New York: Knopf, 1939.
      Pp. 33-53.
          The Norwegian novelist's excellent portrait of
          DHL as a genius and as a prophet of the con-
          temporary crises of civilization. Reprinted
          in G53. Also see AA99.

H391 Untermeyer, Louis. "D.H. Lawrence." NEW REPUBLIC, 23
      (1920), 314-15.
          "Frustration the keynote of all" DHL's work,
          as he fails to find "fulfillment through the
          flesh." Reprinted in G34.

H392 Vanderlip, E.C. "The Morality of D.H. Lawrence." In
      LITERATURE AND RELIGION. Ed. Charles A. Huttar. [Pp.
      47-54.] See G59.
          Call for a "disinterested" Christian criticism
          of DHL's avowedly "moral" art, acknowledging
          his obvious divergence from Christianity, yet
          balancing ethical and aesthetic judgment.

H393 Vickery, John B. "D.H. Lawrence: The Mythic Elements."
      In THE LITERARY IMPACT OF *THE GOLDEN BOUGH.*" Princeton,
      N.J.: Princeton Univ. Press, 1973. Pp. 294-325.
          Archtype and ritual in DHL's fiction (e.g.,
          the Scapegoat figure, animal and totemic myths,
          virgin sacrifice). Earlier version originally
          published in G78. Also see Y65.

H394 Vivante, Leone. "Reflections on D.H. Lawrence's Insight
      Into the Concept of Potentiality." In A PHILOSOPHY OF
      POTENTIALITY. London: Routledge, 1955. Pp. 79-111.
          Important general philosophic inquiry examin-
          ing DHL's employment of spontaneity to suggest

individuality in opposition to both "mechanism" and "deliberate will." Excellent comments on the "living potentiality" and the "quick" of DHL's characters. Extract reprinted in N3.

H395   Vivas, Eliseo. "Mr. Leavis on D.H. Lawrence." SR, 65 (1957), 123-36.
Extended negative review of Leavis's D.H. LAWRENCE: NOVELIST (G68), admitting the value in Leavis's attempt to establish the quality of DHL's art but objecting chiefly to his lack of critical discipline: "Mr. Leavis's critical practice...consists of extended exhortations."

H396   Wagenknecht, Edward. "D.H. Lawrence, Pilgrim of the Rainbow." In CAVALCADE OF THE ENGLISH NOVEL. New York: Holt, 1954. Pp. 494-504.
DHL a "passionate Puritan" and potentially a "great moral liberator," diminished by his sex hatred and primitivism.

H397   Wais, Kurt. "D.H. Lawrence, Valéry, Rilke in ihrer Auseinandersetzung mit den bildenden Künsten: Eine vergleichende Betrachtung" ["D.H. Lawrence, Valéry, and Rilke--Their Testament of the Pictoral Arts: A Comparative Study"]. 1951. In AN DEN GRENZEN DER NATIONALLITERATUREN: VERGLEICHENDE AUFSÄTZE. Berlin: Walter de Gruyter, 1958. Pp. 271-312.
DHL's response to visual arts, his comments on artists, and visual symbolism in his works. [In German.]

H398   Waldron, Philip. "The Education of D.H. Lawrence." AUMLA, No. 24 (1965), pp. 239-52.
Stresses importance of fuller recognition of the extensiveness, but limited quality of DHL's education, a refinement upon Eliot's often abused reservations concerning DHL's intellectual qualifications (see H104-H107).

H399   Walsh, William. "The Writer as Teacher: The Educational Ideas of D.H. Lawrence." In THE USE OF THE IMAGINATION: EDUCATIONAL THOUGHT AND THE LITERARY MIND. London: Chatto and Windus, 1959. Pp. 199-228.
DHL's didacticism and his attitudes toward education. Also see M82.

H400 Ward, Alfred C. "D.H. Lawrence." In THE NINETEEN-TWEN-
      TIES: LITERATURE AND IDEAS IN THE POST-WAR DECADE. Lon-
      don: Methuen, 1930. Pp. 109-15.
           Comments on DHL as a "tormented" revolutionary.

H401 Warner, Rex. "The Cult of Power." In THE CULT OF POWER:
      ESSAYS. London: Lane, 1946. Pp. 7-20.
           DHL, always "uneasily conscious" of the inade-
           quacy of his reverence for the blood, "would
           have been appalled" by the logical extension
           of his ideas in fascist ideology.

H402 Watson, George. "The Politics of D.H. Lawrence." In
      POLITICS AND LITERATURE IN MODERN BRITAIN. London: Mac-
      millan, 1977. Pp. 110-19.
           Sees DHL's affinities greater with the working-
           class novelists of the left than with the fa-
           scist writers on the right.

H403 Weatherby, H.L. "Old Fashioned Gods: Eliot on Lawrence
      and Hardy." SR, 75 (1967), 301-16.
           Fundamental differences in the social visions
           of DHL and Hardy, unnoticed by Eliot (see H104),
           or by DHL himself.

H404 Werner, Alfred. "Lawrence and Pascin." KR, 23 (1961),
      217-28.
           Compares DHL and the artist Jules Pascin as
           modernists.

H405 West, Alick. "D.H. Lawrence." In CRISIS AND CRITICISM,
      AND SELECTED LITERARY ESSAYS. London: Lawrence and Wis-
      hart, 1975. Pp. 259-82.
           Marxist response to Caudwell's rejection of
           DHL (see H58), arguing the political insight
           and significance of DHL's "revolt against
           bourgeois relations."

H406 Wicker, Brian. "Lawrence and the Unseen Presences." In
      THE STORY-SHAPED WORLD: FICTION AND METAPHYSICS: SOME
      VARIATIONS ON A THEME. Notre Dame, Ind.: Univ. of Notre
      Dame Press, 1975. Pp. 120-33.
           DHL approaches tragedy in his preoccupation
           with the classical concern for "man's place
           in Nature" and for "the 'unseen presences'
           to be found there."

H407 Widmer, Kingsley. "Lawrence as Abnormal Novelist." DHLR,
      8 (1975), 220-32.
           Notes with concern that several major studies
           of DHL which appear discriminating are flawed
           by a fundamental lack of "sympathy with what
           Lawrence is doing even at his best." Comment
           on Vivas (G121) and review of Sanders (G106)
           and Stoll (G116).

H408 -----. "Notes on the Literary Institutionalization of
      D.H. Lawrence: An Anti-Review of the Current State of
      Lawrence Studies." PAUNCH, No. 26 (1966), pp. 5-13.
           Devastating attack on the recent critical fal-
           sifications of DHL by "official liberal human-
           ists, to serve the wrong gods." Comments on
           numerous studies of DHL (c. 1955-65). See G94.

H409 Wildi, Max. "The Birth of Expressionism in the Work of
      D.H. Lawrence." ES, 19 (1937), 241-59.
           Good survey of expressionistic elements in DHL.

H410 Williams, Charles. "'Sensuality and Substance': A Study
      of D.H. Lawrence." 1939. In THE IMAGE OF THE CITY, AND
      OTHER ESSAYS. Comp. Anne Ridler. London: Oxford Univ.
      Press, 1968. Pp. 68-75.
           The "romantic" theologian and novelist Williams'
           appreciation of DHL's "natural," undesirably
           violent, and erroneous reaction against the
           Christian pietists' rejection of sensuality:
           "The Church owes more to heretics [such as
           DHL] than she is ever likely (on this earth)
           to admit."

H411 Williams, Hubertien H. "Lawrence's Concept of Being."
      In LITERATURE AND RELIGION. Ed. Charles A. Huttar. [Pp.
      40-46.] See G59.
           DHL's evolving conception of "Being in the
           World" achieves a "remarkable amalgamation
           of pre-Socratic philosophy and traditional
           Christian belief."

H412 Williams, Raymond. "D.H. Lawrence." In CULTURE AND
      SOCIETY, 1780-1850. New York: Columbia Univ. Press,
      1958. Pp. 199-215.
           Evaluates DHL's influence on modern social
           thought and values, as an advocate of "com-
           munity" as opposed to isolation (e.g., R),
           who has provided us with disturbing critiques
           of contemporary social disintegration (e.g.,
           WL). Reprinted in G81 and G115.

H413   -----. "D.H. Lawrence." In THE ENGLISH NOVEL FROM DICK-
       ENS TO LAWRENCE. London: Chatto and Windus, 1970. Pp.
       169-84.
               Places DHL within the realistic tradition of
               English fiction and fixes his transformation
               into a modern novelist in the second half of
               SL.

H414   -----. "Social and Personal Tragedy: Tolstoy and Law-
       rence." In MODERN TRAGEDY. London: Chatto and Windus,
       1966. Pp. 121-38.
               DHL's assimilation of Tolstoy's tragic vision
               and his variations upon it. Also see H133.

H415   Wilson, Colin. "D.H. Lawrence." In THE STRENGTH TO
       DREAM: LITERATURE AND THE IMAGINATION. Boston: Houghton
       Mifflin, 1962. Pp. 180-86.
               DHL's aesthetic "uncertainty" and failure as
               a mystical visionary.

H416   -----. "Existential Criticism." 1959. In EAGLE AND
       EARWIG: ESSAYS ON BOOKS AND WRITERS. London: Baker,
       1965. Pp. 55-85.
               The difficulties in applying existentialist
               criticism to DHL (especially pp. 65-69).

H417   Wilt, Judith, "D.H. Lawrence: Ghosts in the Daylight."
       In GHOSTS OF THE GOTHIC: AUSTEN, ELIOT, & LAWRENCE.
       Princeton, N.J.: Princeton Univ. Press, 1980. Pp. 231-92.
               DHL's assimilation and "modernist" adaptation
               of Gothic conventions (e.g., vampirism) in
               his major fiction (R, WL, PS, and selected
               short stories).

H418   Winegarten, Renee. "Revolutionary Resurrection: D.H.
       Lawrence." In WRITERS AND REVOLUTION: THE FATAL LURE
       OF ACTION. New York: New Viewpoints, 1974. Pp. 248-60.
               DHL's apocalyptic belief in the creative pos-
               sibilities of destructive revolution, not a
               political but a metaphysical ideal.

H419   Witcutt, W.P. "The Cult of D.H. Lawrence." AMERICAN
       REVIEW, 3 (1934), 161-66.
               DHL's malign influence "a solvent of tradi-
               tional things, and his thought an agent of
               destruction." Typical mid-thirties alarm
               at DHL's ideas.

H420   Wood, Frank. "Rilke and D.H. Lawrence." GERMANIC REVIEW, 15 (1940), 213-23.
> Compares Rilke and DHL as writers who share "a common emotive direction [and] an approach to experience" based on remarkably similar metaphysical views.

H421   Woodcock, George. "Mexico and the English Novelist." WR, 21 (1956), 21-32.
> DHL's Mexico experience a "radical test" of his primitivist ideas.

H422   Wright, Raymond. "Lawrence's Non-Human Analogues." MLN, 76 (1961), 426-32.
> DHL's application of animal metaphors to human situations.

H423   Young, Richard O. "'Where Even the Trees Come and Go': D.H. Lawrence and the Fourth Dimension." DHLR, 13 (1980), 30-44.
> DHL's assimilation of the idea of a fourth dimension from several sources (most notably Peter D. Ouspensky's TERTIUM ORGANUM [1911]) and increasing use of the concept to suggest the "timelessness and spaciousness" of the perfected relationship, in his works after 1923. See G27.

H424   Zeraffa, Michel. PERSONNE ET PERSONNAGE: LE ROMANESQUE DES ANNÉES 1920 AUX ANNÉES 1950. Paris: Éditions Klincksieck, 1971. Pp. 227-34 and passim.
> DHL's insistence on the interrelationship of individual human psychology and collective human society ("L'homme de Lawrence est essentiellement psycho-social"). [In French.]

H425   Zoll, Allan R. "Vitalism and the Metaphysics of Love: D.H. Lawrence and Schopenhauer." DHLR, 11 (1978), 1-20.
> Schopenhauer's "claim for the primacy of the sensuous as the final basis of knowledge" and his view of "polarity in the individual" assimilated and modified by DHL.

J. STUDIES OF *THE WHITE PEACOCK* (1911)

Since there are no books, essay collections, monographs, or
pamphlets on THE WHITE PEACOCK, this section consists entirely
of critical articles or chapters on the novel.

For a textual edition of THE WHITE PEACOCK, see A1. Another
textual edition, in progress, will be published in THE CAM-
BRIDGE EDITION (B1--ed. Andrew Robertson).

For bibliographical information on THE WHITE PEACOCK, see Roberts (E39) and Sagar (E40), and, for biographical backgrounds
to the novel, see Moore (F112), Murry (F121), Nehls (F123),
and Neville (F124).

For additional critical commentaries and information on THE
WHITE PEACOCK, see the following books, in Section G above:
Alldritt (G3), Beal (G9), Ben-Ephraim (G11), Brunsdale (G14),
Burns (G15), Colin (G19), Daleski (G24), Dix (G29), Donnerstag
(G30), Draper (G33), Ebbatson (G35), Eisenstein (G36), Ford
(G39), Freeman (G40), Galinsky (G41), Gottwald (G46), Hess
(G50), Hobsbaum (G51), Holderness (G55), Hough (G56), Howe
(G58), Inniss (G60), Johnsson (G63), Littlewood (G71), Marnat
(G72), Miko (G75), Moore (G80), Moynahan (G83), Nahal (G86),
Negriolli (G87), Niven (G89), Pinion (G95), Potter (G98),
M. Prasad (G99), S. Prasad (G100), Pritchard (G101), Reul
(G103), Sagar (G104), Sanders (G106), Seligmann (G108), Sin-
zelle (G110), Slade (G111), Stoll (G116), Swigg (G117), Ted-
lock (G118), Weidner (G122), Wesslau (G124), West (G125),
Worthen (G128); the following critical articles, in section
H above: Albright (H5), Alcorn (H6), Brunsdale (H55), Cava-
liero (H60), Cook (H74), Goode (H144), Kiely (H205), Leaver
(H216), Maes-Jelinek (H232), Merivale (H247), Meyers (H249),
Murfin (H269), Rossman (H319), Stewart (H361), Vickery (H393);
and the following study, entered elsewhere in this bibliography: Reuter (V4).

For additional, foreign-language studies of THE WHITE PEACOCK,
see the following entries in Appendix A: Fujiwara (AA149), Itô
(AA167), Kitazaki (AA182), Koga (AA189), Mori (AA220), Nishikawa (AA231), Sugiyama (AA274), Yoshida (AA292), and Yoshimura
(AA298).

J1 Brown, Christopher. "As Cyril Likes It: Pastoral Reality
    and Illusion in THE WHITE PEACOCK." ESSAYS IN LITERATURE,
    6 (1979), 187-93.
        DHL's unacknowledged emphasis of "the darker,
        equivocal side of the pastoral tradition" seen
        in his picture of the "post-lapsarian domain" of
        Nethermere.

J2 Gajdusek, Robert E. "A Reading of 'A Poem of Friendship,'
    a Chapter in Lawrence's THE WHITE PEACOCK." DHLR, 3 (1970),
    47-62.
        DHL's early mythic exploration of the relation-
        ships among life, death, and the "creation of a
        work of art."

J3 -----. "A Reading of THE WHITE PEACOCK." In A D.H. LAW-
    RENCE MISCELLANY. Ed. Harry T. Moore. Pp. 188-203. See
    G81.
        Novel a successful formal experiment and a bet-
        ter anticipation of the later work, in theme and
        symbolism, than is generally recognized.

J4 Hinz, Evelyn J. "Juno and THE WHITE PEACOCK: Lawrence's
    English Epic." DHLR, 3 (1970), 115-35.
        Reevaluation of the novel stressing DHL's use of
        classical myth.

J5 Keith, W.J. "D.H. Lawrence's THE WHITE PEACOCK: An Essay
    in Criticism." UTQ, 37 (1968), 230-47.
        Novel's purported weaknesses not signs of "sla-
        vish imitation" (of Hardy), nor "anticipations"
        of DHL's later works, but conscious experimental
        deviations from conventions by an independent
        and confident young novelist.

J6 Mason, H.A. "D.H. Lawrence and THE WHITE PEACOCK." CAM-
    BRIDGE QUARTERLY, 7 (1977), 216-31.
        Attempts to find the kernel of DHL's later work
        in his first novel.

J7 Meyers, Jeffrey. "Maurice Greiffenhagen and THE WHITE PEA-
    COCK." In PAINTING AND THE NOVEL. Manchester, Engl.: Man-
    chester Univ. Press, 1975. Pp. 46-52.
        DHL's use of Greiffenhagen's painting "An Idyll"
        (1891) as a visual symbol.

J8 Morrison, Kristin. "Lawrence, Beardsley, Wilde: THE WHITE
    PEACOCK and Sexual Ambiguity." WHR, 30 (1976), 241-48.
        Homosexual implications in DHL's peacock symbol.

J9   Sepčić, Višnja. "THE WHITE PEACOCK Reconsidered." STUDIA
     ROMANICA ET ANGLICA ZAGRABIENSIA, No. 38 (1975), pp. 105-
     14.
          Not seen.

J10 Squires, Michael. "THE WHITE PEACOCK: 'Fit for Old Theo-
     critus.'" In THE PASTORAL NOVEL: STUDIES IN GEORGE ELIOT,
     THOMAS HARDY, AND D.H. LAWRENCE. Charlottesville: Univ.
     Press of Virginia, 1974. Pp. 174-95.
          DHL's adaptations of classical pastoral conven-
          tions and his four distinguishable "attitudes
          toward rural life" traced in the novel.

J11 Stanford, Raney. "Thomas Hardy and Lawrence's THE WHITE
     PEACOCK." MFS, 5 (1959), 19-28.
          Hardy's and DHL's use of "symbolic scenes as
          structural devices" and their fascination with
          "feminine psychology." See G78.

K. STUDIES OF *THE TRESPASSER* (1912)

Since there are no books, essay collections, monographs, or
pamphlets on THE TRESPASSER, this section consists entirely
of critical articles or chapters on the novel.

For the textual edition of THE TRESPASSER, see A2.

For bibliographical information on THE TRESPASSER, see Roberts
(E39) and Sagar (E40), and, for biographical backgrounds to
the novel, see Corke (F36, F38), Moore (F112), Muggeridge and
Corke (F118), and Nehls (F123).

For additional critical commentaries and information on THE
TRESPASSER, see the following books, in section G above: Beal
(G9), Ben-Ephraim (G11), Brunsdale (G14), Clark (G17), Colin
(G19), Daleski (G24), Draper (G33), Ebbatson (G35), Eisenstein
(G36), Ford (G39), Freeman (G40), Galinsky (G41), Gottwald
(G46), Gregory (G47), Hobsbaum (G51), Holderness (G55), Howe
(G58), Johnsson (G63), Littlewood (G71), Michaels-Tonks (G74),
Miko (G75), Moore (G80), Moynahan (G83), Negriolli (G87),
Niven (G89), Pinion (G95), Potter (G98), M. Prasad (G99),
S. Prasad (G100), Pritchard (G101), Reul (G103), Sagar (G104),
Seligmann (G108), Slade (G111), Stoll (G116), Swigg (G117),
Tedlock (G118), Weidner (G122), Wesslau (G124), Worthen (G128),
Yudhishtar (G130); and the following critical articles, in sec-
tion H above: Albright (H5), Appleman (H17), Brunsdale (H55),
Core (H75), DiGaetani (H91), Harrison (H168), Kiely (H205),
Rossman (H319), and Vickery (H393).

For additional, foreign-language studies of THE TRESPASSER,
see the following entries in Appendix A: Fujiwara (AA151),
Itô (AA167), Kitazaki (AA184), Sugiyama (AA273), and Yoshimura
(AA297).

K1   Corke, Helen. "The Writing of THE TRESPASSER." DHLR, 7
     (1974), 227-39.
          Memories of DHL (1909-12), and backgrounds to
          his writing THE TRESPASSER based on her unfor-
          tunate love affair. Material covered similarly,
          but more diffusely in her IN OUR INFANCY (F38).

K2   Gurko, Leo. "THE TRESPASSER: D.H. Lawrence's Neglected
     Novel." CE, 24 (1962), 29-35.
          For "all its erratically verbalized emotional
          sludge," the novel "is at once an essential pre-
          figurement of the later work and a striking
          achievement in itself."

K3   Hinz, Evelyn J. "THE TRESPASSER: Lawrence's Wagnerian Trag-
     edy and Divine Comedy." DHLR, 4 (1971), 122-41.
          Mythic elements in the novel.

K4   Howarth, Herbert. "D.H. Lawrence from Island to Glacier."
     UTQ, 37 (1968), 215-29.
          DHL's movement away from the Flaubertain con-
          scious artistry of THE TRESPASSER seen in "The
          Captain's Doll."

K5   Kestner, Joseph A. "The Literary Wagnerism of D.H. Law-
     rence's THE TRESPASSER." MODERN BRITISH LITERATURE, 2
     (1977), 123-38.
          Various kinds of literary Wagnerism in the "un-
          derrated" novel, including the Wagnerian use of
          myth and structural motifs.

K6   Mansfield, Elizabeth. "Introduction." In D.H. LAWRENCE:
     THE TRESPASSER. Ed. Mansfield. Pp. 3-37. See A2.
          Backgrounds to the novel's composition and pub-
          lication. Mansfield also includes explanatory
          notes for THE TRESPASSER (pp. 233-43), textual
          apparatus for the edition (pp. 247-78), and six
          appendixes: extracts from Helen Corke's diary
          (pp. 281-92), her "Freshwater Diary" (pp. 293-
          301; reprinted from F38), two extracts from
          earlier manuscript versions of the novel (pp.
          302-23), a background newsclipping (p. 324),
          and notes on Wagner's influence on THE TRESPAS-
          SER (pp. 325-27).

K7   Millett, Robert. "Great Expectations: D.H. Lawrence's THE
     TRESPASSER." In TWENTY SEVEN TO ONE. Ed. B. Broughton.
     Ogdensburg, N.Y.: Ryan Press, 1970. Pp. 125-32.
          Novel anticipates the later DHL, particularly in
          the character of Helena, a "female seeker."

K8   Sepčić, Višnja. "A Link Between D.H. Lawrence's THE TRES-
      PASSER and THE RAINBOW." STUDIA ROMANICA ET ANGLICA ZAG-
      RABIENSIA, No. 24 (1967), pp. 113-26.
            Compares DHL's symbolism in the two novels.
            Not seen.

K9   Steele, Bruce. "The Manuscript of D.H. Lawrence's 'Saga
      of Siegmund.'" SB, 33 (1979), 193-205.
            Describes the early manuscript version of the
            novel in the Bancroft Library (Univ. of Cali-
            fornia, Berkeley).

K10   Wright, Louise. "Lawrence's THE TRESPASSER: Its Debt to
      Reality." TSLL, 20 (1978), 230-48.
            DHL's novel "deeply rooted" in his own life,
            despite debts to Helen Corke's life and writ-
            ings.

K11   Zuckerman, Elliott. "Wagnerizing on the Isle of Wight."
      In THE FIRST HUNDRED YEARS OF WAGNER'S *TRISTAN*. New York:
      Columbia Univ. Press, 1964. Pp. 124-27.
            On DHL's use of Wagner's TRISTAN UND ISOLDE
            (1865). Not seen.

L. STUDIES OF *SONS AND LOVERS* (1913)

The following section is subdivided into two parts: i. Books
and Essay Collections on SL; and ii. Critical Articles or Chapters on SL.

For facsimiles of SL's holograph manuscript and the surviving
manuscript fragments of the novel's early version, "Paul Morel,"
see A14. A textual edition of SL will be published in THE CAM-
BRIDGE EDITION (B1--ed. Carl E. Baron [tent.]).

For bibliographical information on SL, see Roberts (E39) and
Sagar (E40), and for biographical backgrounds to the novel, see
Chambers (F29), Delavenay (F43, F44), Ehrenzweig (F51), Lawrence and Gelder (F85), Moore (F112), Murry (F121), Nehls (F123),
and Neville (F124, F125).

For additional critical commentaries and information on SL, see
the following books, in section G above: Alldritt (G3), Allendorf (G4), Beal (G9), Becker (G10), Ben-Ephraim (G11), Boadella
(G12), Brunsdale (G14), Burns (G15), Cavitch (G16), Clark (G17),
Colin (G19), Daleski (G24), Dix (G29), Draper (G32, G33), Eb-
batson (G35), Ford (G39), Freeman (G40), Gottwald (G46), Greg-
ory (G47), Hess (G50), Hobsbaum (G51), Hochman (G52), Holder-
ness (G55), Hough (G56), Howe (G58), Jaensson (G61), Johnsson
(G63), Kermode (G65), Leavis (G68), Littlewood (G71), Marnat
(G72), Michaels-Tonks (G74), Miko (G75), Moore (G80), Moynahan
(G83), Nahal (G86), Negriolli (G87), Niven (G89), Pinion (G95),
Potter (G98), M. Prasad (G99), S. Prasad (G100), Prichard (G101),
Reul (G103), Sagar (G104), Sanders (G106), Seligmann (G108),
Sinzelle (G110), Slade (G111), Spilka (G114), Stoll (G116),
Swigg (G117), Tedlock (G118), Vivas (G121), Weidner (G122),
Weiss (G123), Wesslau (G124), Worthen (G128), Yudhishtar (G130);
the following critical articles, in section H above: Albright
(H5), Alcorn (H6), Appleman (H17), Beach (H31), Bedient (H33),
Brunsdale (H55), Cook (H74), Coveny (H77), Davies (H84), Dela-
venay (H86), Eaglestone (H97), Eagleton and Pierce (H98), Ea-
gleton (H99), Ehrstine (H103), Eliot (H106), Elsbree (H111),
Garrett (H128), Gillie (H135), Gindin (H136), Glicksberg (H141),
Goode (H144), Gutierrez (H160), Hardy (H164), Heywood (H178),

Hinz (H182), Hoffman (H185, H187), Karl and Magalaner (H201),
Kiely (H205), Kinkead-Weekes (H206), Klein (H210), Kohler (H212),
Leaver (H216), Lee (H220), Maes-Jelinek (H232), Marks (H234),
Maurois (H240), Millett (H255), Muller (H268), "Notes..."
(H277), Rossman (H319), Sale (H323), Scott (H333), Spilka
(H353), Stewart (H361), Swinden (H369), Vickery (H393), Wil-
liams (H413); and the following studies, entered in other sec-
tions of this bibliography: Kinkead-Weekes (M4), Alinei (M11),
Engelberg (M30), Reuter (V4), Ruderman (V68), Pearsall (W7),
Gilbert (Y1), Aiken (Z8), and Gilbert (AB4).

L, i. Books and Essay Collections on SONS AND LOVERS

Also see the following "Study Guides" for SL, listed in Appendix B: Fielding (AB3), Handley (AB5), Rothkopf (AB8), Shaw
(AB9), and *SONS AND LOVERS* (AB10).

L1 Farr, Judith, ed. TWENTIETH CENTURY INTERPRETATIONS OF
    SONS AND LOVERS: A COLLECTION OF CRITICAL ESSAYS. Engle-
    wood Cliffs, N.J.: Prentice-Hall, 1970.
        Useful casebook of previously published material,
        containing six essays and ten brief "View Points"
        on SL (including some of DHL's letters), together
        with Farr's biographical-critical "Introduction"
        (pp. 1-23). Includes L34, L69, and extracts from
        C6, F87, G39, G62, G104, G114, G123, H127, H223,
        L48, L57, and V5.

L2 Hanson, Christopher. *SONS AND LOVERS* (D.H. LAWRENCE). Ox-
    ford: Blackwell, 1967.
        Competent critical overview of SL's "aims and
        structure," "setting," and "characters and re-
        lationships," intended for secondary school stu-
        dents and undergraduates.

L3 Moynahan, Julian, ed. *SONS AND LOVERS*: TEXT, BACKGROUND,
    AND CRITICISM. New York: Viking, 1968.
        Although labeled as a "critical edition," not an
        edited text. In the casebook section of the vol-
        ume Moynahan reprints three representative early
        reviews, five extracts from memoirs, selections
        from DHL's relevant letters, prose, and poetry,
        Freud's essay on the Oedipus complex, and eight
        essays on SL. Good teaching or term-paper text.
        Includes A74, H308, L34, L37, L65, and extracts
        from A55, F29, F85, F86, F123, G39, G83, G85,
        and G114.

L4   Salgādo, Gāmini.   D.H. LAWRENCE: *SONS AND LOVERS*.   London:
     Arnold, 1966.
          Chapter-by-chapter commentary on SL, emphasizing
          DHL's handling of point of view and arguing for
          a greater appreciation of the book's structure.
          Primarily useful as an introductory study guide.

L5   -----, ed.   D.H. LAWRENCE: *SONS AND LOVERS*: A CASEBOOK.
     London: Macmillan, 1969.
          Useful gathering of extracts from DHL's letters
          and poems, pertinent biographical information,
          five contemporary reviews, and fourteen reprint-
          ed essays on SL.   Includes Salgādo's general,
          brief "Introduction" (pp. 11-17), six essays:
          L15, L16, L36, L37, L48, L65, and extracts from
          F29, F121, G24, G56, G104, G121, H82, H221, and
          L57.

L6   Talon, Henri A.   D.H. LAWRENCE: *SONS AND LOVERS*: LES AS-
     PECTS SOCIAUX ET ECONOMIQUES, LA VISION DE L'ARTISTE.
     Paris: Archives des Lettres Modernes, 1965.
          Introductory study, devoting chapters to the geo-
          graphical, social, and economic factors in Paul's
          environment which leave their "empreintes dans
          son espirit et dans son coeur," of the symbolic
          structure of Paul's home and society, of DHL's
          and Paul's passionately intense vision of nature,
          and of "l'affirmation originaire" of the novel's
          conclusion.   [In French.]

L7   Tedlock, Ernest W., ed.   D.H. LAWRENCE AND *SONS AND LOVERS*:
     SOURCES AND CRITICISM.   New York: New York Univ. Press,
     1965.
          Three-part casebook of previously published
          source materials on SL's "Origins," "Freudian
          Connections," and "Techniques and Values."   In-
          cludes Tedlock's brief general and sectional
          introductions, slight commentaries on the manu-
          script of SL, by Harry T. Moore and Tedlock
          (pp. 63-69), pertinent extracts from DHL's let-
          ters, five essays: L30, L34, L36, L48, L65, and
          extracts from F29, F87, F121, G80, G114, G123,
          H185, and L57.

L, ii. Critical Articles or Chapters on SONS AND LOVERS

For additional, foreign-language articles on SL, see the fol-
lowing entries in Appendix A: IL VERRI (AA44), Gorlier (AA68),
Gozzi (AA70), Kamihata (AA77), Fujiwara (AA150), Imaizumi
(AA166), Itô (AA167), Kamitami (AA178), Kitazaki (AA183),
Kumbatović (AA193), Laurent (AA200), Milatović (AA217), Nish-
ida (AA230), Okano (AA238), Okumura (AA241, AA244), Requardt
(AA254), Sepčić (AA264), Yoshida (AA293), and Yoshimura (AA296).

L8   Adamowski, T.H. "Intimacy at a Distance: Sexuality and
      Orality in SONS AND LOVERS." MOSAIC, 13, No. 2 (1980),
      71-89.
            SL examined in light of the psychoanalytic
            theories of "oral," pre-oedipal development.
            See below.

L9   -----. "The Father of All Things: The Oral and the Oedi-
      pal in SONS AND LOVERS." MOSAIC, 14, No. 4 (1981), 69-88.
            Extends his earlier investigation (see above)
            of the "pre-oedipal motifs" of SL (e.g., cas-
            tration anxiety, the "primal scene").

L10   Alinei, Tamara. "D.H. Lawrence's Natural Imagery: A Non-
      Vitalist Reading." DUTCH QUARTERLY REVIEW, 6 (1976), 116-
      38.
            As early as SL, DHL uses moon and flower ima-
            gery to "communicate meaning symbolically"
            about his characters.

L11   -----. "Three Times Morel: Recurrent Structure in SONS
      AND LOVERS." DUTCH QUARTERLY REVIEW, 5 (1975), 39-53.
            Repetitive form in the related stories of Wil-
            liam, Arthur, and, most important, Paul Morel.

L12   Balbert, Peter H. "Forging and Feminism: SONS AND LOVERS
      and the Phallic Imagination." DHLR, 11 (1978), 93-113.
            Discounts recent feminist criticism of DHL,
            finding SL a persuasive treatment of the at-
            tainment of "mature and healthy sexuality."

L13   Baldanza, Frank. "SONS AND LOVERS: Novel to Film as a
      Record of Cultural Growth." LFQ, 1 (1973), 64-70.
            Cinematic compromises, despite faith to the
            original spirit of DHL, in the successful
            screen adaptation of SL (1960). See G70.

L14   Beards, Richard D.   "SONS AND LOVERS as *Bildungsroman*."
      COLLEGE LITERATURE, 1 (1974), 204-17.
           Paul's aesthetic, sexual, and spiritual develop-
           ment traced by DHL within the traditional *Bil-
           dungsroman* conventions for self-realization.

L15   Beebe, Maurice.   IVORY TOWERS AND SACRED FOUNTS: THE ART-
      IST AS HERO IN FICTION FROM GOETHE TO JOYCE.   New York:
      New York Univ. Press, 1964.   Pp. 103-13.
           SL a "Sacred Fount" novel, emphasizing the cre-
           ative, sensual relationship of art to life.   Re-
           printed in L5.

L16   Betsky, Seymour.   "Rhythm and Theme: D.H. Lawrence's SONS
      AND LOVERS."   In THE ACHIEVEMENT OF D.H. LAWRENCE.   Ed.
      Frederick J. Hoffman and Harry T. Moore.   Pp. 131-43.
      See G53.
           Rhythmic, wave-like, rather than conventional,
           climactic development a structural and thematic
           characteristic of the novel.   Reprinted in L5.

L17   Buckley, Jerome H.   "D.H. Lawrence: The Burden of Apology."
      In SEASON OF YOUTH: THE *BILDUNGSROMAN* FROM DICKENS TO GOLD-
      ING.   Cambridge, Mass.: Harvard Univ. Press, 1974.   Pp.
      204-24.
           Through the conventions of the *Bildungsroman*
           DHL transcends "the distortions of a personal
           apology" in SL.

L18   Burrell, Angus.   "D.H. Lawrence: SONS AND LOVERS."   In his
      and Dorothy Brewster's MODERN FICTION.   New York: Columbia
      Univ. Press, 1934.   Pp. 137-54.
           SL, written before the "hysteria" of sexual mal-
           adjustment set in, DHL's best novel.   Some good
           insights.

L19   Burwell, Rose Marie.   "Schopenhauer, Hardy, and Lawrence:
      Toward a New Understanding of SONS AND LOVERS."   WHR, 28
      (1974), 105-17.
           DHL's treatment of Paul's quest for self-inte-
           gration seen in light of his reading of Schopen-
           hauer and his "Study of Thomas Hardy" (in B16).

L20   D'Avanzo, Mario L.   "On the Naming of Paul Morel and the
      Ending of SONS AND LOVERS."   SOUTHERN REVIEW (Adelaide,
      Australia), 12 (1979), 103-07.
           Paul's change from a "morel" (parasite "fungus"),
           to a seed of independent development, by the
           novel's end.

L21 Delavenay, Émile. "Lawrence's Major Work." In D.H. LAW-
     RENCE: THE MAN WHO LIVED. Ed. Robert B. Partlow and Harry
     T. Moore. Pp. 139-42. See G92.
          SL deemed DHL's most important work in its ca-
          pacity "both to shock the reader into recogni-
          tion of greatness and to communicate a wide
          range of human experience."

L22 DeNitto, Dennis. "SONS AND LOVERS (1913), D.H. Lawrence:
     Jack Cardiff, 1960: All Pasion Spent." In THE ENGLISH
     NOVEL AND THE MOVIES. Ed. Michael Klein and Gillian Parker.
     New York: Ungar, 1981. Pp. 235-47.
          On the extraordinary difficulty of translating
          the "inner realities" of a character's psycho-
          logy to film, as seen in the admirable, but only
          partially successful Cardiff adaptation of SL.

L23 Dervin, Daniel. "Play, Creativity and Matricide: The Im-
     plications of Lawrence's 'Smashed Doll' Episode." MOSAIC,
     14, No. 3 (1981), 81-94.
          The psychoanalytic theory of play, the first
          "important stage in the development of creativ-
          ity," suggests that the doll-burning scene is
          Paul's "acted-out" identification "with the
          sexual father."

L24 Dietz, Susan. "Miriam." RECOVERING LITERATURE, 6, No. 3
     (1978), 15-22.
          Miriam succumbs to the despair Paul narrowly
          avoids, in "her impotence, her inability to
          respond to the instinctual longings within her-
          self."

L25 DiMaggio, Richard. "A Note on SONS AND LOVERS and Emer-
     son's 'Experience.'" DHLR, 6 (1973), 214-16.
          DHL indebted to Emerson's essay (1844) for his
          novel's title and for his recognition of "the
          insufficiency of grief to lead one...to the
          very axis of reality." Same discovery reported
          by Gary Sloan, in AMERICAN NOTES AND QUERIES,
          16 (1978), 160-61, and by Wise (see L67).

L26 Doheny, John. "The Novel is the Book of Life: D.H. Law-
     rence and a Revised Version of Polymorphous Perversity."
     PAUNCH, No. 26 (1966), pp. 40-59.
          Applies to SL the Freudian critical theories
          of Norman O. Brown (LIFE AGAINST DEATH [1959])
          and Herbert Marcuse (EROS AND CIVILIZATION
          [1955]), themselves anticipated in DHL's crit-
          icism. See G94.

L27   Draper, Ronald P.   "D.H. Lawrence on Mother Love."   EIC,
      8 (1958), 285-89.
           DHL's recognition of mother-wife-submissiveness
           as a "deadly form of domination" in FANTASIA OF
           THE UNCONSCIOUS (A63), already implicitly demon-
           strated in SL.   See H188.

L28   Eichrodt, John M.   "Doctrine and Dogma in SONS AND LOVERS."
      ConnR, 4 (1970), 18-32.
           SL a heavily religious parable which antici-
           pates R's pleas for the revivification of a
           moribund Christianity.

L29   Fleishman, Avrom.   "The Fictions of Autobiographical Fic-
      tion."   GENRE, 9 (1976), 73-86.
           DAVID COPPERFIELD (1848-50), THE MILL ON THE
           FLOSS (1860), and SL representative of three
           kinds of "symbolic self-creation" in autobio-
           graphical fiction.   The self in SL structured
           on archetypal patterns (pp. 82-86).

L30   Fraiberg, Louis.   "The Unattainable Self: D.H. Lawrence's
      SONS AND LOVERS."   In TWELVE ORIGINAL ESSAYS ON GREAT
      ENGLISH NOVELS.   Ed. Charles Shapiro.   Detroit: Wayne
      State Univ. Press, 1960.   Pp. 175-201.
           Weaknesses in SL, arising from conflicts be-
           tween technique and meaning.   Reprinted in L7.

L31   Gomme, Andor.   "Jessie Chambers and Miriam Leivers: An
      Essay on SONS AND LOVERS."   In D.H. LAWRENCE: A CRITICAL
      STUDY.   Ed. Gomme.   Pp. 30-52.   See G43.
           Claims DHL intended Mrs. Morel to be seen in a
           positive light, though modern readers tend to
           sympathize with Miriam.

L32   Hardy, John Edward.   "SONS AND LOVERS: The Artist as Sav-
      ior."   In MAN IN THE MODERN NOVEL.   Seattle: Univ. of
      Washington Press, 1964.   Pp. 52-66.
           SL documents the emergence in DHL of the "art-
           ist-hero" who needs isolation and detachment
           in order to create.

L33   Hinz, Evelyn J.   "SONS AND LOVERS: The Archetypal Dimen-
      sions of Lawrence's Oedipal Tragedy."   DHLR, 5 (1972),
      26-53.
           Thorough tracing of SL's Oedipal pattern.

L34   Kazin, Alfred. "Sons, Lovers, and Mothers." PR, 29
       (1962), 373-85.
            Important psychological reading of the novel,
            seeing DHL's career as a life-long quest to
            recreate the "living bond" of the mother-son
            relationship depicted in SL. Reprinted as
            "Introduction" to Lawrence's SONS AND LOVERS
            (New York: Modern Library, 1962), and in G48,
            L1, L3, and L7.

L35   Kleinbard, David J. "Laing, Lawrence, and the Maternal
       Cannibal." PsyR, 58 (1971), 5-13.
            Paul Morel seen as an "ontologically insecure"
            personality in the terms of R.D. Laing's DI-
            VIDED SELF (1969).

L36   Kuttner, Alfred Booth. "SONS AND LOVERS: A Freudian Ap-
       preciation." PsyR, 3 (1916), 295-317.
            Valuable early recognition of SL's Oedipal
            theme and the therapeutic value to DHL of its
            composition. Reprinted in G34, L5, and L7.

L37   Lesser, Simon O. FICTION AND THE UNCONSCIOUS. Boston:
       Beacon Press, 1957. Pp. 173-78.
            Relationship between Freud's and DHL's versions
            of the Oedipus complex. Reprinted in L3 and L5.

L38   Littlewood, J.C.F. "Son and Lover." CAMBRIDGE QUARTERLY,
       4 (1969-70), 323-61.
            Biographical backgrounds to and criticism of
            SL, partially assimilated into Littlewood's
            monograph on DHL (see G71). Reprinted in G20.

L39   Martz, Louis L. "Portrait of Miriam: A Study in the De-
       sign of SONS AND LOVERS." In IMAGINED WORLDS: ESSAYS ON
       SOME ENGLISH NOVELS AND NOVELISTS IN HONOUR OF JOHN BUTT.
       Ed. Maynard Mack and Ian Gregor. London: Methuen, 1968.
       Pp. 343-69.
            The pivotal psychological, structural, and the-
            matic importance of SL's central section (chap-
            ters 7-11), developing Paul's tormented rela-
            tionship with Miriam.

L40   Melchiori, Barbara. "'Objects in the powerful light of
       emotion.'" ARIEL, 1 (1970), 21-30.
            DHL's "camera technique."

L41   Meyer, Kurt Robert. "D.H. Lawrence (1885-1930)." In ZUR
      ERLEBTEN REDE IM ENGLISCHEN ROMAN DES ZWANZIGSTEN JAHR-
      HUNDERTS. Bern: Franke, 1957. Pp. 44-65.
            DHL's use of *erlebten rede*, or indirect free
            style of narration, examined principally in SL
            and AARON'S ROD. [In German.]

L42   Mitchell, Giles R. "SONS AND LOVERS and the Oedipal Pro-
      ject." DHLR, 13 (1980), 209-19.
            Failure to accept death seen as a primary ele-
            ment in the "tragic" fates of Paul and Oedipus
            (in OEDIPUS REX). See G28.

L43   Mortland, Donald E. "The Conclusion of SONS AND LOVERS:
      A Reconsideration." SNNTS, 3 (1971), 305-15.
            Paul Morel's 'turn toward town' temporary and
            SL's ending negative.

L44   Moseley, Edwin M. "Christ as Artist and Lover: D.H. Law-
      rence's SONS AND LOVERS." In PSEUDONYMS OF CHRIST IN THE
      MODERN NOVEL. Pittsburgh: Univ. of Pittsburgh Press, 1962.
      Pp. 69-86.
            Paul a Christ figure torn between the creative
            love of the mother and the spiritual love of
            Miriam.

L45   Muggeridge, Malcolm. "Lawrence's SONS AND LOVERS." NEW
      STATESMAN AND NATION, 49 (1955), 581-82.
            DHL "the most significant novelist of the first
            decades of this century," though SL becomes
            "irretrievably foolish" when DHL "gets on to
            the sex life of his hero, Paul Morel."

L46   Nadel, Ira B. "From Fathers and Sons to Sons and Lovers."
      DR, 59 (1979), 221-38.
            SL concludes a century-long "shift from fathers
            and sons as the basis of family conflict to mo-
            thers and sons, and, then, sons and lovers."

L47   New, William H. "Character and Symbol: Annie's Role in
      SONS AND LOVERS." DHLR, 1 (1968), 31-43.
            Annie, too, instrumental in the development of
            Paul.

L48   O'Connor, Frank. "D.H. Lawrence: SONS AND LOVERS." In
      THE MIRROR IN THE ROADWAY: A STUDY OF THE MODERN NOVEL.
      New York: Knopf, 1956. Pp. 270-79.
            DHL's change of direction in the middle trans-
            forms SL from a traditional to a modern novel.
            Reprinted in L1 (extract), L5, and L7.

L49   Panken, Shirley. "Some Psychodynamics in SONS AND LOVERS:
      A New Look at the Oedipal Theme." PsyR, 61 (1974-75),
      571-89.
           Investigates the "entire family matrix" in SL
           for its influence on Paul's development.

L50   Entry deleted.

L51   Pascal, Roy. "The Autobiographical Novel and the Autobi-
      ography." EIC, 9 (1959), 134-50.
           Old men write autobiographies (e.g., Wells),
           while young writers transmute and objectify
           their selves through fiction (e.g., C. Bronte,
           DHL, and Joyce).

L52   Phillips, Danna. "Lawrence's Understanding of Miriam
      through Sue." RECOVERING LITERATURE, 7, No. 1 (1979),
      46-56.
           DHL's portrait of Miriam influenced by Hardy's
           Sue Bridehead (in JUDE THE OBSCURE [1895]).

L53   Pritchett, V.S. "SONS AND LOVERS." In THE LIVING NOVEL
      AND LATER APPRECIATIONS. New York: Random House, 1964.
      Pp. 182-89.
           DHL, representative of an uprooted and disori-
           ented generation, "ceased to be a novelist"
           after his "patchy," only partially satisfactory
           SL.

L54   Pullin, Faith. "Lawrence's Treatment of Women in SONS
      AND LOVERS." In LAWRENCE AND WOMEN. Ed. Anne Smith.
      Pp. 49-74. See G112.
           DHL arrested in the "infantile state in which
           other people are merely instruments," as illu-
           strated in his "ruthless" use of women in SL.

L55   Rossman, Charles. "The Gospel According to D.H. Lawrence:
      Religion in SONS AND LOVERS." DHLR, 3 (1970), 31-41.
           Religion informing DHL's allusions, images,
           symbols, and themes.

L56   Sagar, Keith. "Introduction"; "Notes." In Lawrence's
      SONS AND LOVERS. Harmondsworth, Engl.: Penguin, 1981.
      Pp. 11-28; 493-500.
           History of the novel's genesis and composition,
           account of its biographical backgrounds, and
           commentary on DHL's "transformation of autobi-
           ography into art." Sagar's notes clarify his-
           torical and literary references and identify a

number of DHL's poems which treat materials
related to the novel. Sagar also includes a
glossary of dialect words and phrases and
Penguin provides an introductory chronology
of DHL's life and works.

L57 Schorer, Mark. "Technique as Discovery." HudR, 1 (1948),
67-87.
A fundamental conflict between DHL's intention
and his achievement observed in SL and attributed to the incomplete auto-therapy of its
composition. DHL's self-discovery and objective distance from his experience are both
insufficient. One of the landmark modern
studies of the relationship between the artist
and his material. Reprinted in H330. Extracts
reprinted in L1, L5, and L7.

L58 Schwarz, Daniel R. "Speaking of Paul Morel: Voice, Unity,
and Meaning in SONS AND LOVERS." SNNTS, 8 (1976), 255-77.
DHL's subtle, complex, and "exciting" use of
the omniscient narrator for form and meaning.

L59 Sepčić, Višnja. "Realism Versus Symbolism: The Double
Patterning of SONS AND LOVERS." STUDIA ROMANICA ET ANG-
LICA ZAGRABIENSIA, Nos. 33-36 (1972-73), pp. 185-208.
Not seen.

L60 Shealy, Ann. "The Epiphany Theme in Modern Fiction: E.M.
Forster's HOWARDS END and D.H. Lawrence's SONS AND LOVERS."
In THE PASSIONATE MIND: FOUR STUDIES. Philadelphia: Dor-
rance, 1976. Pp. 3-27.
Uninspired view of Paul's grasp of "the 'one-
ness' or 'otherness' of selfhood."

L61 Smith, Grover. "The Doll-Burners: D.H. Lawrence and Louisa
Alcott." MLQ, 19 (1958), 28-32.
Source (in LITTLE MEN [1871]) and symbolic mean-
ing of the doll-burning scene.

L62 Spacks, Patricia Meyer. THE ADOLESCENT IDEA: MYTHS OF
YOUTH AND THE ADULT IMAGINATION. New York: Basic Books,
1981. Pp. 243-51 and passim.
Unlike their Victorian predecessors, Joyce (in
A PORTRAIT OF THE ARTIST AS A YOUNG MAN [1916]),
and DHL (in SL), write "as though from deep in-
side the experience of adolescence" and demonstrate the modern writer's identification with
the adolescent as "hero."

L63   Taylor, John A. "The Greatness in SONS AND LOVERS."   MP,
       71 (1974), 380-87.
            Paul's heroic struggles presented against the
            background of the "great world."

L64   Tomlinson, T.B. "D.H. Lawrence: SONS AND LOVERS, WOMEN
       IN LOVE." In THE ENGLISH MIDDLE-CLASS NOVEL. London:
       Macmillan, 1976. Pp. 185-98.
            DHL technically remains within the middle-class
            tradition, though his best fiction presents a
            non-traditional, despairing vision of the fu-
            ture of society and the human race. Earlier
            version reprinted in G5.

L65   Van Ghent, Dorothy. "Lawrence: SONS AND LOVERS." In THE
       ENGLISH NOVEL: FORM AND FUNCTION. New York: Rinehart,
       1953. Pp. 245-61, 454-62.
            Apparent formal irregularities attributable to
            the novel's organization upon "elementary bio-
            logical rhythms," rathern than upon a rigid
            structure. Includes "study questions" in ap-
            pendix. Essay reprinted in G115, L3, L5, and
            L7.

L66   Wahl, Jean. "Sur D.H. Lawrence." NOUVELLE REVUE FRAN-
       ÇAISE, 42 (1934), 115-21.
            DHL's "dialectique de l'amour" in his late
            works (chiefly LCL) already fully developed,
            implicitly, in SL. [In French.]

L67   Wise, James N. "Emerson's 'Experience' and SONS AND LOV-
       ERS." COSTERUS, 6 (1972), 179-221.
            Parallels between the authors' ideas in their
            two works, but no argument for influence. See
            L25.

L68   Wolf, Howard R. "British Fathers and Sons, 1773-1913:
       From Filial Submissiveness to Creativity." PsyR, 52
       (1965), 197-214.
            Antagonism toward the father in Mill, Gosse,
            and DHL (pp. 210-14).

L69   Woolf, Virginia. "Notes on D.H. Lawrence." 1931. In her
       COLLECTED ESSAYS. Ed. Leonard Woolf. London: Hogarth,
       1966-67. I, 352-55.
            DHL's anxiety to rise above his class and his
            lack of a literary tradition make SL an unsta-
            ble, unconventional, yet peculiarly dynamic
            book. Also see H175 and V121. Reprinted in
            G5 and L1.

M. STUDIES OF *THE RAINBOW* (1915)

The following section is subdivided into two parts: i. Books
and Essay Collections on R; and ii. Critical Articles or Chapters on R.

A textual edition of R, in progress, will be published in THE
CAMBRIDGE EDITION (B1--ed. Mark Kinkead-Weekes).

For bibliographical information on R, see Roberts (E39) and
Sagar (E40), and, for biographical backgrounds to the novel,
see LAWRENCE IN LOVE (C6), Delany (F41), Delavenay (F43, F44),
Holroyd (F75), Lunn (F96), Moore (F110, F112), Murry (F121),
and Nehls (F123).

For additional critical commentaries and information on R, see
the following books, in section G above: Alldritt (G3), Arnold
(G7), Beal (G9), Becker (G10), Ben-Ephraim (G11), Boadella
(G12), Burns (G15), Cavitch (G16), Clark (G17), Clarke (G18),
Colin (G19), Daleski (G24), Dix (G29), Donnerstag (G30), Dra-
per (G32, G33), Ebbatson (G35), Ford (G39), Freeman (G40),
Gottwald (G46), Gregory (G47), Hess (G50), Hobsbaum (G51),
Hochman (G52), Holderness (G55), Hough (G56), Howe (G58),
Jaensson (G61), Jarrett-Kerr (G62), Johnsson (G63), Kermode
(G65), Leavis (G68, G69), Marnat (G72), Miko (G75), Miles
(G76), Miller (G77), Moore (G80), Moynahan (G83), Nahal (G86),
Negriolli (G87), Nin (G88), Niven (G89), Pinion (G95), Potter
(G98), M. Prasad (G99), S. Prasad (G100), Pritchard (G101),
Reul (G103), Sagar (G104), Sanders (G106), Seligmann (G108),
Slade (G111), Spilka (G114), Stoll (G116), Swigg (G117), Ted-
lock (G118), Vivas (G121), Weidner (G122), Wesslau (G124),
Wettern (G126), Worthen (G128), Yudhishtar (G130), Zytaruk
(G131); the following critical articles, in section H above:
Albright (H5), Alcorn (H6), Baker (H22), Baldanza (H23), Ban-
tock (H25), Beach (H31), Bedient (H33), Black (H42), Cockshut
(H67), Cook (H74), Core (H75), Cornwell (H76), Coveny (H77),
Donoghue (H93), Eagleton and Pierce (H98), Eagleton (H99),
Ehrstine (H103), Elsbree (H109, H111), Garcia (H126), Garrett
(H128), Gifford and Williams (H133), Gindin (H136), Glicksberg
(H141), Goldring (H142), Goode (H144), Heywood (H178), Hinz
(H183), Hoffman (H187), Kaplan (H200), Karl and Magalaner (H201),

Kiely (H205), Kinkead-Weekes (H206, H207), Klein (H210), Langbaum (H213), Lea (H215), Lerner (H221), Lindenberger (H224),
Maes-Jelinek (H232), Millett (H255), Murfin (H269), "Notes..."
(H277), Panichas (H281), Rossman (H319), Sale (H323), Scott
(H333), Stewart (H361), Swinden (H369), Tristram (H386), Vickery (H393), Williams (H412), Wilt (H417); and the following
studies, entered in other sections of this bibliography: Eichrodt (L28), Ruderman (Q9), Gilbert (Y1), Pinto (Y44), and Gilbert (AB4).

M, i. Books and Essay Collections on THE RAINBOW

Also see the following "study guides" for R, listed in Appendix B: Aylwin (AB1), Bunnell (AB2), and Martin (AB7).

M1   Balbert, Peter H. D.H. LAWRENCE AND THE PSYCHOLOGY OF RHY-
     THM: THE MEANING OF FORM IN *THE RAINBOW*. The Hague: Mouton,
     1974.
          Reconciliation of message and medium in R. Adapt-
          ing the terms "psychology" and "rhythm" to sig-
          nify the content and form of Lawrencean fiction,
          Balbert argues their synthesis ("the meaning of
          form") in R through DHL's use of a structural
          metaphor of conception, gestation, and birth
          which governs the novel's social content and
          its pulsating, rhythmic style. Justifies the
          "formalist" approach to R, but fails to suggest
          any wider applicability of the critical method
          for DHL's fiction.

M2   Clarke, Colin, ed. D.H. LAWRENCE: *THE RAINBOW* AND *WOMEN
     IN LOVE*: A CASEBOOK. London: Macmillan, 1969.
          Valuable critical source book. Clarke collects
          fourteen essays and reviews, all previously pub-
          lished, a section of pertinent quotations from
          DHL's letters, DHL's cancelled "Prologue" to WL,
          and his "Foreword" to the same novel. Clarke's
          "Introduction" (pp. 11-22) briefly describes the
          novels' composition and subsequent reputations.
          Includes A35, A78, M35, M67, N32, N56, and ex-
          tracts from F120, F121, G18, G24, G39, G40, G83,
          H211, and N44.

M3   D.H. LAWRENCE REVIEW. 13 (1980), 150-86. "Special Sec-
     tion: The End of THE RAINBOW."
          Collects three approaches to the interpretation
          of the second half and the concluding chapter of
          the novel. Includes M51, M63, and M68.

M4   Kinkead-Weekes, Mark, ed. TWENTIETH CENTURY INTERPRETA-
     TIONS OF *THE RAINBOW*: A COLLECTION OF CRITICAL ESSAYS.
     Englewood Cliffs, N.J.: Prentice-Hall, 1971.
          Judicious selection of seven previously pub-
          lished essays, organized into three sections:
          examining the work in "Perspective," critically
          interpreting the novel, and analyzing the evo-
          lution of R from its prototypes. Kinkead-
          Weekes's "Introduction" (pp. 1-10) usefully de-
          scribes the relationship of the book to both SL
          and WL. Includes M56, M82, and extracts from
          G24, G39, G104, H207, and H221.

M5   Obler, Paul C. D.H. LAWRENCE'S WORLD OF *THE RAINBOW*. Mad-
     ison, N.J.: Drew University, 1955.
          Brief, general critical essay. (Pamphlet--19 pp.)

M6   Ross, Charles L. THE COMPOSITION OF *THE RAINBOW* AND *WOMEN
     IN LOVE*: A HISTORY. Charlottesville: Univ. Press of Vir-
     ginia, 1979.
          Lays to rest the myth of DHL's "spontaneous"
          techniques of composition. Ross discusses thor-
          oughly DHL's developing vision and painstaking
          revision of each novel, through several drafts,
          evaluating both the textual and the creative
          evolution of the two related masterpieces. Lo-
          cates, orders, dates, and describes, with analy-
          sis of "their textual peculiarities," all the
          available manuscripts and typescripts. Also
          see N82.

M7   Smith, Frank Glover. D.H. LAWRENCE: *THE RAINBOW*. London:
     Arnold, 1971.
          Excellent, insightful brief introduction. Smith
          discusses R's upward spiraling structure, its
          narrowing of focus from the patriarchal society
          to the individual, and its expansive inclusion
          of religious and cultural traditions. DHL's use
          of archetype and symbol raises R "from a regional
          English context into a fully European one."

M, ii.   Critical Articles or Chapters on THE RAINBOW

For additional, foreign-language articles on R, see the following entries in Appendix A: Mori (AA223), Okumura (AA241, AA242),
Yamakawa (AA290), and Yoshii (AA294).

M8   Adam, Ian. "Lawrence's Anti-Symbol: The Ending of THE
      RAINBOW." JNT, 3 (1973), 77-84.
            Ursula's encounter with the horses elemental
            and real.

M9   Adamowski, T.H. "THE RAINBOW and 'Otherness.'" DHLR, 7
      (1974), 58-77.
            Distinguishes DHL's concept of "otherness"
            from the sentimental "cant" of modern psycho-
            therapists, and analyzes its function in R.

M10   Alinei, Tamara. "Imagery and Meaning in D.H. Lawrence's
      THE RAINBOW." YES, 2 (1972), 205-11.
            DHL's suggestion of "'human' meaning" in his
            non-human imagery of "root, wind, and flower."

M11   -----. "The Beginning of THE RAINBOW: Novel within a
      Novel?" LINGUA E STILE, 12 (1977), 161-66.
            Opening of R "a highly concentrated recapitu-
            lation" of SL. DHL "transferred *en bloc* to
            Tom Brangwen his personal history as he had
            worked it out in his autobiographical novel."

M12   Armytage, W.H.G. "The Novel as the Hole in the Wall: D.H.
      Lawrence's [THE] RAINBOW." In YESTERDAY'S TOMORROWS: A
      HISTORICAL SURVEY OF FUTURE SOCIETIES. Toronto: Univ. of
      Toronto Press, 1968. Pp. 106-08.
            DHL's prophetic strain attributed to his read-
            ing of Nietzsche.

M13   Barry, J. "Oswald Spengler and D.H. Lawrence." ESA, 12
      (1969), 151-61.
            R and WL present a "microcosm of the Spengler-
            ian world picture."

M14   Bell, Elizabeth S. "Slang Associations of D.H. Lawrence's
      Image Patterns in THE RAINBOW." MODERNIST STUDIES, 4
      (1982), 77-86.
            Part of the "effectiveness" of DHL's imagery
            in R dependent on "sexual slang" and "associ-
            ations" with which "he and his audience were
            familiar." See G79.

M15 Berthoud, Jacques. "THE RAINBOW as Experimental Novel."
     In D.H. LAWRENCE: A CRITICAL STUDY. Ed. Andor Gomme.
     Pp. 53-69. See G43.
            DHL's "disturbing" experimentation with a new
            mode of expressing feeling and sexuality, with-
            in a generally conventional context, creates
            "strain and incoherence."

M16 Blanchard, Lydia. "Mothers and Daughters in D.H. Lawrence:
     THE RAINBOW and Selected Shorter Works." In LAWRENCE AND
     WOMEN. Ed. Anne Smith. Pp. 75-100. See G112.
            DHL's insight into the tensions of the mother-
            daughter relationship, principally in R and
            "St. Mawr."

M17 Brandabur, A.M. "The Ritual Corn Harvest Scene in THE
     RAINBOW." DHLR, 6 (1973), 284-302.
            Harvest rituals and archetypes.

M18 Brookesmith, Peter. "The Future of the Individual: Ursula
     Brangwen and Kate Millett's SEXUAL POLITICS." HUMAN WORLD,
     No. 10 (1973), pp. 42-65.
            Extended defense of Ursula as a sympathetically
            positive, three-dimensional character, not DHL's
            "sabotage [of] the new breed of female," as seen
            by Millett (see H255).

M19 Brown, Homer O. "'The Passionate Struggle Into Conscious
     Being': D.H. Lawrence's THE RAINBOW." DHLR, 7 (1974),
     275-90.
            DHL not an advocate of "a kind of mindless
            blood-intimacy with the universe," but a su-
            premely "conscious" narrator chronicling his
            characters' struggle to a consciousness "through
            close relationship with the unknown other."

M20 Burns, Robert. "The Novel as a Metaphysical Statement:
     Lawrence's THE RAINBOW." SOUTHERN REVIEW (Adelaide,
     Australia), 4 (1971), 139-60.
            DHL's metaphysical claustrophobia: life in the
            novel "oppressive."

M21 Chapple, J.A.V. DOCUMENTARY AND IMAGINATIVE LITERATURE,
     1880-1920. New York: Barnes and Noble, 1970. Pp. 72-83,
     88-90, and passim.
            Rural themes in DHL's fiction and poetry, es-
            pecially his vision of the desolation of the
            countryside in R.

M22   Cross, Barbara. "Lawrence and the Unbroken Circle." PER-
      SPECTIVE, 11 (1959), 81-89.
            Circle symbolism in R.

M23   Cushman, Keith. "'I am going through a transition stage':
      THE PRUSSIAN OFFICER and THE RAINBOW." DHLR, 8 (1975),
      176-97.
            DHL's final revisions of the stories in THE
            PRUSSIAN OFFICER volume (1914) a major compon-
            ent of his significant maturation as a novel-
            ist, from SL to R. Surveys the overlapping
            composition of, and describes relationships
            between, the stories and R. See comment by
            Evelyn J. Hinz in DHLR, 8 (1975), 213-19.

M24   Davis, Edward. "THE RAINBOW." In READINGS IN MODERN FIC-
      TION. Cape Town, S. Africa: Simondium, 1964. Pp. 258-69.
            A "common sense" reading of DHL's traditional
            view of sexual love in R as a "war between the
            sexes."

M25   Delany, Paul. "Lawrence and E.M. Forster: Two Rainbows."
      DHLR, 8 (1975), 54-62.
            DHL's and Forster's similar use of rainbow sym-
            bolism (R and HOWARDS END [1910]).

M26   Ditsky, John M. "'Dark, Darker than Fire': Thematic Par-
      allels in Lawrence and Faulkner." SHR, 8 (1974), 497-505.
            DHL's treatment of "dark forces" in R paral-
            leled in several Faulkner novels.

M27   Dougherty, Adelyn. "The Concept of Person in D.H. Law-
      rence's THE RAINBOW." C&L, 21, No. 4 (1972), 15-22.
            Correspondences between DHL's and Teilhard de
            Chardin's views of the "search for fulfillment."

M28   Draper, Ronald P. "THE RAINBOW." CritQ, 20, No. 3 (1978),
      49-64.
            Novel's transcendent ending forced, since its
            body demonstrates that "growth is slow, tortu-
            ous and constantly perilous."

M29   Efron, Arthur. "Toward a Dialectic of Sensuality and
      Work." PAUNCH, Nos. 44-45 (1976), pp. 152-70.
            Parallels Marx's and DHL's realization that
            "new changing social conditions" have dis-
            rupted the traditional familial relationship,
            "a dialectic of work and sex." (DHL, pp. 165-
            70).

M30 Engelberg, Edward. "Escape from the Circles of Experience:
D.H. Lawrence's THE RAINBOW as a Modern *Bildungsroman*."
PMLA, 78 (1963), 103-13.
> R succeeds as a *Bildungsroman*, where SL fails,
> showing Ursula prepared by her experiences to
> face life. Reprinted in G5.

M31 Ford, George H. "The Eternal Moment: D.H. Lawrence's THE
RAINBOW and WOMEN IN LOVE." In THE STUDY OF TIME, III.
Ed. Julius T. Fraser, Nathaniel Lawrence, and David A.
Park. Berlin and New York: Springer Verlag, 1978. Pp.
512-36.
> DHL's companion novels concerned with time past,
> present, and future, yet most distinctive for
> their focus on a succession of present moments,
> when "clock time" is suspended. Followed by
> A.A. Mendilow's "Discussion and Comment" (pp.
> 537-39).

M32 Friedman, Alan. "D.H. Lawrence: 'The Wave Which Cannot
Halt.'" In THE TURN OF THE NOVEL. New York: Oxford Univ.
Press, 1966. Pp. 130-78.
> Technical open-endedness and thematic inconclu-
> siveness of R and WL consistent with their
> themes: conclusions are sterile, while organic
> expansion is a sign of health. Extract re-
> printed in N3.

M33 Gamache, Lawrence B. "Husband Father: D.H. Lawrence's Use
of Character in Structuring a Narrative." MODERNIST STUD-
IES, 4 (1982), 36-51.
> Uninspired comments on Tom Brangwen as a model
> for the male struggle for "fullness of life,"
> in DHL. See G79.

M34 -----. "The Making of an Ugly Technocrat: Character and
Structure in Lawrence's THE RAINBOW." MOSAIC, 12, No. 1
(1978), 61-78.
> Young Tom Brangwen, from embryo to adult, rep-
> resents the "dehumanization which each major
> character must struggle to overcome."

M35 Goldberg, S.L. "THE RAINBOW: Fiddle-Bow and Sand." EIC,
11 (1961), 418-34.
> DHL's intrusive assertion of his own will, his
> prophetic voice, in the second half of the
> novel contradicts the "moral intent" of the
> tale. Reprinted in M2.

M36 Heilbrun, Carolyn G. TOWARDS ANDROGYNY: ASPECTS OF MALE
     AND FEMALE IN LITERATURE. London: Gollancz, 1973. Pp.
     101-10 and passim.
            The "myth of the new female creation born into
            a world the male spirit had despoiled," the re-
            creation of Eve, one of three central myths in
            R.

M37 Heldt, Lucia Henning. "Lawrence on Love: The Courtship
     and Marriage of Tom Brangwen and Lydia Lensky." DHLR,
     8 (1975), 358-70.
            The dynamics of the first courtship in R ex-
            amined as "the standard by which all of the
            other sexual involvements" of R and WL "can
            be judged." Tom and Lydia provide "a rare,
            fully developed example of exactly what Law-
            rence has in mind when he speaks of love."
            See G26.

M38 Hill, Ordelle G., and Potter Woodbery. "Ursula Brangwen
     of THE RAINBOW: Christian Saint or Pagan Goddess?" DHLR,
     4 (1971), 274-79.
            Ursula sustained not by her Christian namesake,
            St. Ursula, but by her "spiritual inheritance"
            from the saint's pagan prototypes, Venus and
            Horsel.

M39 Hinz, Evelyn J. "ANCIENT ART AND RITUAL and THE RAINBOW."
     DR, 58 (1978-79), 617-37.
            DHL's views of the "communalizing function of
            ritual" and the relationship between "loss of
            religious faith and the beginnings of secular
            art" influenced by Ellen Harrison's ANCIENT ART
            AND RITUAL (1913).

M40 -----. "The Paradoxical Fall: Eternal Recurrence in D.H.
     Lawrence's THE RAINBOW." ENGLISH STUDIES IN CANADA, 3
     (1977), 466-81.
            DHL's theme of man's "Fall from a cosmic to an
            historical or egocentric point of view" (cf.
            Mircea Eliade's theories of social conscious-
            ness).

M41 -----. "THE RAINBOW: Ursula's 'Liberation.'" ConL, 17
     (1976), 24-43.
            DHL's "accurate insights into the frustrated
            needs that motivate liberationist tendencies"
            the actual, emotionally sensitive cause for his
            rejection by feminist critics: he is the "enemy
            within the ranks."

M42 Hyde, Virginia. "Toward 'The Earth's New Architecture':
     Triads, Arches, and Angles in THE RAINBOW." MODERNIST
     STUDIES, 4 (1982), 3-35.
          The structural and visual architecture of R, a
          novel which proceeds by chapter "triads" and
          develops a symbolic tension between the curved
          (positive) and angular (negative). See G79.

M43 -----. "Will Brangwen and Paradisal Vision in THE RAIN-
     BOW and WOMEN IN LOVE." DHLR, 8 (1975), 346-57.
          Affirmative view of Will's character, seeing
          in him the source for Ursula's "capacity for
          visionary experience." See G26.

M44 Kay, Wallace G. "Lawrence and THE RAINBOW: Apollo and
     Dionysus in Conflict." SOUTHERN QUARTERLY, 10 (1972),
     209-22.
          R's ending suggests reconciliation. Also see
          N55.

M45 Kennedy, Andrew. "After Not So Strange Gods in THE RAIN-
     BOW." ES, 63 (1982), 220-30.
          Examines the "function" of DHL's biblical lan-
          guage, the "quality of Lawrence's post-Chris-
          tian 'heterodoxy'" (see Eliot, H104), and their
          relation to DHL's presentation of the religious
          heritage of the Brangwens.

M46 Kettle, Arnold. "D.H. Lawrence: THE RAINBOW." In AN IN-
     TRODUCTION TO THE ENGLISH NOVEL. Vol. 2. HENRY JAMES TO
     THE PRESENT. London: Hutchinson, 1951. Pp. 111-34.
          Various characters' struggles to realize them-
          selves both as individuals and, through personal
          relationships, as social beings in R, DHL's most
          representative fiction.

M47 Kleinbard, David J. "D.H. Lawrence and Ontological Inse-
     curity." PMLA, 89 (1974), 154-63.
          Will Brangwen's unstable ego in light of "R.D.
          Laing's concept of ontological insecurity and
          Erik Erikson's analysis of identity confusion."

M48 Lainoff, Seymour. "THE RAINBOW: The Shaping of Modern
     Man." MFS, 1, No. 4 (1955), 23-27.
          The three generations of R parallel the evolu-
          tion of the "modern outlook."

M49   Latta, William. "Lawrence's Debt to Rudolph, Baron von
      Hube." DHLR, 1 (1968), 60-62.
             DHL's source for some details in the portrait
             of Baron Skrebensky, Anton's father.

M50   Lenz, William E. "The 'Organic Connexion' of THE RAINBOW
      with WOMEN IN LOVE." SAB, 43, No. 1 (1978), 5-18.
             Argues against the critical tendency to see
             R and WL separately, demonstrating several "dis-
             tinct continuities" between them.

M51   McLaughlin, Ann L. "The Clenched and Knotted Horses in
      THE RAINBOW." DHLR, 13 (1980), 179-86.
             Horses seen as symbols of vitality "enslaved,"
             appropriate to Ursula's situation. See M3.

M52   Marković, Vida E. "Ursula Brangwen." In THE CHANGING
      FACE: DISINTEGRATION OF PERSONALITY IN THE TWENTIETH-CEN-
      TURY BRITISH NOVEL, 1900-1950. Carbondale: Southern Ill-
      inois Univ. Press, 1970. Pp. 19-37.
             Traces Ursula's progress through R and WL, find-
             ing her DHL's chief embodiment of his "idea of
             life and human existence."

M53   Mendilow, A.A. "The Multi-dimensional Present in D.H.
      Lawrence's World-Picture." HUSL, 5 (1977), 465-78.
             R and WL dramatize in their rhythmic "time-
             structure and perspectives" DHL's philosophi-
             cal thesis that modern man is situated within
             "that unseizable moment between a past that
             no longer is and a future that is not yet,"
             the "pure present."

M54   Meyers, Jeffrey. "Fra Angelico and THE RAINBOW." In
      PAINTING AND THE NOVEL. Manchester, Engl.: Manchester
      Univ. Press, 1975. Pp. 53-64.
             Angelico's fifteenth-century painting "The Last
             Judgement" used as a visual symbol in R.

M55   Mori, Haruhide. "Lawrence's Imagistic Development in THE
      RAINBOW and WOMEN IN LOVE." ELH, 31 (1964), 460-81.
             Transformation in DHL's technique, from poetic
             vision to prosaic philosophizing.

M56   Mudrick, Marvin. "The Originality of THE RAINBOW." SPEC-
      TRUM, 3 (1959), 3-28.
             DHL's original attempt to present a "normal,"
             fully developed, and *interesting* woman in
             fiction. Reprinted in G81, G115, and M4.

M57 Mueller, William R. "The Paradisal Quest." In CELEBRA-
     TION OF LIFE: STUDIES IN MODERN FICTION. New York: Sheed
     and Ward, 1972. Pp. 148-68.
          The search for a fulfilling human relationship
          is DHL's central theme.

M58 Nicholes, E.L. "The 'Symbol of the Sparrow' in THE RAIN-
     BOW by D.H. Lawrence." MLN, 64 (1949), 171-74.
          The sparrow as well as the horses, at the end
          of the novel, archetypal symbols of rebirth.
          Reprinted in G53.

M59 Nixon, Cornelia. "To Procreate Oneself: Ursula's Horses
     in THE RAINBOW." ELH, 49 (1982), 123-42.
          DHL's ambivalence toward procreation as an in-
          hibiting factor in self-development, underlies
          the symbolism of labor and birth in the scene
          of Ursula and the horses, at the novel's con-
          clusion.

M60 O'Connell, Adelyn, RSCJ. "The Concept of Person in D.H.
     Lawrence's THE RAINBOW." In LITERATURE AND RELIGION. Ed.
     Charles A. Huttar. Pp. 1-7. See G59.
          DHL's correlation of self-awareness with self-
          fulfillment similar to that found in recent
          theological definitions of "person" (cf. Robert
          Johann and Teilhard de Chardin).

M61 Raddatz, Volker. "Lyrical Elements in D.H. Lawrence's THE
     RAINBOW." RLV, 40 (1974), 235-42.
          DHL's rhythmic use of time and lyric descrip-
          tions of the "flux of sensations."

M62 Raina, M.L. "The Wheel and the Centre: An Approach to THE
     RAINBOW." LCrit, 9, No. 2 (1970), 41-55.
          Narrative structure of primitive myth in R.

M63 Rosenzweig, Paul J. "A Defense of the Second Half of THE
     RAINBOW: Its Structure and Characterization." DHLR, 13
     (1980), 150-60.
          Argues the "thematic appropriateness" of the
          novel's split structure and changes in form,
          characterization, and style in its second half.
          See M3.

M64 Ross, Charles L. "D.H. Lawrence's Use of Greek Tragedy:
     Euripides and Ritual." DHLR, 10 (1977), 1-19.
          DHL's study of Classical tragedy and its impact
          on R and WL.

M65 Ruthven, K.K. "The Savage God: Conrad and Lawrence."
CritQ, 10 (1968), 39-54.
The savage primitivism of "Heart of Darkness"
(1899), R, and WL, *fin de siècle* "decadence
in its most ferocious form."

M66 Sagar, Keith. "The Genesis of THE RAINBOW and WOMEN IN
LOVE." DHLR, 1 (1968), 179-99.
Stresses vast differences between the works
despite their common origins.

M67 Sale, Roger. "The Narrative Technique of THE RAINBOW."
MFS, 5 (1959), 29-38.
Attributes deterioration of later chapters to
DHL's loss of objective narrative detachment.
See G78. Reprinted in M2.

M68 Schleifer, Ronald. "Lawrence's Rhetoric of Vision: The
Ending of THE RAINBOW." DHLR, 13 (1980), 161-78.
In R's final chapter, DHL achieves a masterful,
"delicate balance between language and vision,
continuity and discontinuity...the known and
the unknown." See M3.

M69 Schwarz, Daniel R. "Lawrence's Quest in THE RAINBOW."
ARIEL, 11, No. 3 (1980), 43-66.
The quests for values, appropriate form, self-
definition, and fulfillment in R viewed as DHL's
"efforts to clarify his own ideas and feelings."

M70 Sepčić, Višnja. "A Link Between D.H. Lawrence's THE TRES-
PASSER and THE RAINBOW." STUDIA ROMANICA ET ANGLICA ZAG-
RABIENSIA, No. 24 (1967), pp. 113-26.
See K8.

M71 Shepherd, P.J. "Introductory Commentary." In Lawrence's
THE RAINBOW. London: Heinemann, 1968. Pp. ix-xxxvi.
R the transitional work in DHL's career and his
finest novel. Surveys themes and discusses major characters.

M72 Spano, Joseph. "A Study of Ursula (of THE RAINBOW) and
H.M. Daleski's Commentary." PAUNCH, No. 33 (1968), pp.
22-31.
Ursula's egoism and perversity make her less
than the "model" Lawrencean character Daleski
suggests (in G24).

M73 Speirs, Logan. "Lawrence's Debt to Tolstoy in THE RAIN-
BOW." In TOLSTOY AND CHEKHOV. Cambridge: Cambridge Univ.
Press, 1971. Pp. 227-37.
> The "intimate" and extensive relationship be-
> tween DHL's and Tolstoy's "massive studies of
> marriage," in R and ANNA KARENINA (1878).

M74 Squires, Michael. "Recurrence as a Narrative Technique
in THE RAINBOW." MFS, 21 (1975), 230-36.
> DHL's counterpoint of recurrent and "singular"
> scenes (i.e., scenes which "occur only once and
> possess unusual power and immediacy").

M75 -----. "Scenic Construction and Rhetorical Signals in
Hardy and Lawrence." DHLR, 8 (1975), 125-46.
> Compares structural techniques in JUDE THE OB-
> SCURE (1895) and R.

M76 Stewart, Jack F. "Expressionism in THE RAINBOW." NOVEL,
13 (1980), 296-315.
> DHL's "verbal emulation" of the expressionist
> painters' drive "towards inner being and its
> source" (distinguished from the techniques of
> literary expressionism in Joyce and Kafka).

M77 Tischler, Nancy M. "The Rainbow and the Arch." In LIT-
ERATURE AND RELIGION. Ed. Charles A. Huttar. [Pp. 8-29.]
See G59.
> Explicit religious symbols and implicit Chris-
> tian themes in R and WL (e.g., the searches for
> the "Christ-husband" and the "Promised Land").

M78 Tobin, Patricia D. "The Cycle Dance: D.H. Lawrence, THE
RAINBOW." In TIME AND THE NOVEL: THE GENEALOGICAL IMPER-
ATIVE. Princeton, N.J.: Princeton Univ. Press, 1978.
Pp. 81-106.
> DHL's unique structural adaptation of the fam-
> ily-saga convention, to show the repeated pat-
> tern of self-discovery, allows him to assert
> the autonomy of the ego within the usually
> deterministic genealogical novel.

M79 Twitchell, James. "Lawrence's Lamias: Predatory Women in
THE RAINBOW and WOMEN IN LOVE." SNNTS, 11 (1979), 23-42.
> The motifs of the vampire and the vampire's
> female victim ("lamia") in DHL's male-female
> relationships.

M80   Tysdahl, Bjørn J. "Kvinnesak og skjønnlitteratur: D.H. Lawrence: THE RAINBOW" ["Feminism and Fiction: D.H. Lawrence: THE RAINBOW"]. EDDA, 75 (1975), 29-36.
          Sees Kate Millett's misconstruction of DHL's view of women in R (in H255), as a false concentration on a single, possible interpretation in a novel of multiple meanings. [In Norwegian.]

M81   Unrue, Darlene H. "Lawrence's Vision of Evil: The Power-Spirit in THE RAINBOW and WOMEN IN LOVE." DR, 55 (1975-76), 643-54.
          DHL's concept of the "power-spirit" as "that force for evil, generated by man's lust for power, which interferes with the achievement of cosmic harmony."

M82   Walsh, William. "The Writer and the Child: Ursula in THE RAINBOW." In THE USE OF THE IMAGINATION: EDUCATIONAL THOUGHT AND THE LITERARY MIND. London: Chatto and Windus, 1959. Pp. 163-74.
          Environmental determinism in DHL's description of the formative influences upon Ursula. Also see H399. Reprinted in M4.

M83   Wasson, Richard. "Comedy and History in THE RAINBOW." MFS, 13 (1967), 465-77.
          R's comic structure and historical dynamics.

M84   Wilding, Michael. "THE RAINBOW: 'smashing the great machine.'" In POLITICAL FICTIONS. London: Routledge, 1980. Pp. 127-49.
          R "an acute analysis of the failures of capitalist industrial society and of the conventional ways of criticizing that society."

M85   Worthen, John. "Introduction"; "Notes." In Lawrence's THE RAINBOW. Harmondsworth, Engl.: Penguin, 1981. Pp. 11-33; 551-71.
          History of the novel's composition, publication, and reception, and review of the central critical issues for its interpretation. Worthen's endnotes identify, among other concerns, a large number of DHL's biblical allusions. Worthen also includes a chronology for R's events and a glossary of dialect words and phrases. Penguin provides an introductory chronology of DHL's life and works.

N.   STUDIES OF *WOMEN IN LOVE* (1920)

The following section is subdivided into two parts: i. Books
and Essay Collections on WL; and ii. Critical Articles or Chapters on WL.

A textual edition of WL, in progress, will be published in THE
CAMBRIDGE EDITION (B1--ed. David R. Farmer).   Also see A35, A36,
and A78.

For bibliographical information on WL, see Roberts (E39) and
Sagar (E40), and, for biographical backgrounds to the novel,
see Delany (F41, F42), Delavenay (F44), Gray (F68), Huxley
(F76), Moore (F112), Morrell (F116), Murry (F120, F121), and
Nehls (F123).

For additional critical commentaries and information on WL, see
the following books, in section G above: Alldritt (G3), Beal
(G9), Becker (G10), Ben-Ephraim (G11), Boadella (G12), Breds-
dorff (G13), Burns (G15), Cavitch (G16), Clark (G17), Clarke
(G18), Colin (G19), Daleski (G24), Dix (G29), Draper (G32, G33),
Ebbatson (G35), Eisenstein (G36), Ford (G39), Freeman (G40),
Garcia (G42), Goodheart (G44), Gottwald (G46), Gregory (G47),
Hess (G50), Hobsbaum (G51), Hochman (G52), Holderness (G55),
Hough (G56), Howe (G58), Inniss (G60), Jaensson (G61), Jarrett-
Kerr (G62), Johnsson (G63), Kermode (G65), Leavis (G68, G69),
Marnat (G72), Michaels-Tonks (G74), Miko (G75), Miles (G76),
Moore (G80), Moynahan (G83), Nahal (G86), Negriolli (G87), Nin
(G88), Niven (G89), Panichas (G91), Pinion (G95), Potter (G98),
M. Prasad (G99), S. Prasad (G100), Pritchard (G101), Reul (G103),
Sagar (G104), Sanders (G106), Seillière (G107), Seligmann (G108),
Slade (G111), Spilka (G114), Stoll (G116), Swigg (G117), Ted-
lock (G118), Tindall (G120), Vivas (G121), Weidner (G122), Weiss
(G123), Wesslau (G124), Wettern (G126), Worthen (G128), Yudhi-
shtar (G130); the following critical articles, in section H
above: Albright (H5), Alcorn (H6), Baldanza (H23), Ballin (H24),
Bayley (H30), Beach (H31), Beauvoir (H32), Bedient (H33), Ber-
sani (H40), Black (H42), Cockshut (H67), Collins (H69), Cook
(H74), Cornwell (H76), DiGaetani (H91), Donoghue (H93), Eagleton and Pierce (H98), Eagleton (H99), Ehrstine (H103), Garrett
(H128), Gindin (H136), Goode (H144), Goonetilleke (H147),

Gutierrez (H160), Haegert (H162), Hardy (H164), Heywood (H178),
Hinz (H182, H183), Hoffman (H187), Jacobson (H194), Karl and
Magalaner (H201), Kiely (H205), Kinkead-Weekes (H206, H207),
Knight (H211), Langbaum (H213), Lea (H215), Leaver (H216), Ler-
ner (H221), Lindenberger (H224), MacDonald (H230), Maes-Jelinek
(H232), Marks (H234), Merivale (H247), Meyers (H249), Michaels-
Tonks (H250), Millett (H255), Mudrick (H266), "Notes..." (H277),
Pinto (H290), R. Pritchard (H296), W. Pritchard (H298), Rossman
(H319), Sale (H323), Scott (H333), Spilka (H351), Stewart (H361),
Tristram (H386), Vickery (H393), Vivante (H394), Williams (H412,
H414), Wilt (H417), Wright (H422); and the following studies,
entered in other sections of this bibliography: Kinkead-Weekes
(M4), Ruderman (Q9), Reuter (V4), Craig (V11), Gilbert (Y1),
Oates (Y5), Pinto (Y44), Aiken (Z8), and Gilbert (AB4).

N, i. Books and Essay Collections on WOMEN IN LOVE

Also see Kai's RORENSU KENKYU: *WOMEN IN LOVE* (AA21).

N1   Clarke, Colin, ed. D.H. LAWRENCE: *THE RAINBOW* AND *WOMEN
     IN LOVE*: A CASEBOOK. London: Macmillan, 1969.
          For annotation see M2.

N2   Fraisse, Anne-Marie, ed. RÉFLEXIONS ET DIRECTIVES POUR
     L'ÉTUDE DE D.H. LAWRENCE: *WOMEN IN LOVE*. Paris: Lettres
     Modernes, 1970.
          Workbook for the study of WL, containing numer-
          ous extracts from the novel and related writings
          by DHL, with questions for study, sample discus-
          sions of "Sickness in WOMEN IN LOVE," "Gerald
          and his Symbols," "Communion with Nature," "Sym-
          bolical-Structure," and a concluding dialogue
          on DHL and Freud (by Françoise-Marie Barbier and
          Simone Rozenberg). [In French; sample discus-
          sions and quotations from DHL's related writings
          in English.]

N3   Miko, Stephen J., ed. TWENTIETH CENTURY INTERPRETATIONS
     OF *WOMEN IN LOVE*: A COLLECTION OF CRITICAL ESSAYS. Engle-
     wood Cliffs, N.J.: Prentice-Hall, 1969.
          Balanced collection of six critical essays and
          four brief "View Points" on WL, together with
          Miko's informative "Introduction" to the novel
          and its reputation (pp. 1-19). All but one se-
          lection reprinted from earlier publication. In-
          cludes N43, N51, and extracts from G39, G83,
          G114, G121, G123, H172, H394, and M32.

N4   Ross, Charles L. THE COMPOSITION OF *THE RAINBOW* AND *WO-
       MEN IN LOVE*: A HISTORY. Charlottesville: Univ. Press of
       Virginia, 1979.
              For annotation see M6.

N, ii. Critical Articles or Chapters on WOMEN IN LOVE

For additional, foreign-language articles on WL, see the fol-
lowing entries in Appendix A: Bareiss (AA54), Barrière (AA110),
Brugière (AA117), Imaizumi (AA165), Kéry (AA181), Madonna
(AA204), Mikhal'skaya (AA216), Mori (AA222), Okumura (AA241),
Sepčić (AA263), and Tetsumura (AA277).

N5   Adamowski, T.H. "Being Perfect: Lawrence, Sartre, and
       WOMEN IN LOVE." CRITICAL INQUIRY, 2 (1975), 345-68.
              Sartre and DHL on man's quest for perfect be-
              ing. Also see H3 and H4.

N6   Barber, David S. "Can a Radical Interpretation of WOMEN
       IN LOVE Be Adequate?" DHLR, 3 (1970), 168-74.
              Questions the New University Conference's es-
              sentially political "evaluation of the novel
              [based] on economic values," as reported in
              DHLR, 3 (1970), 63-69.

N7   ------. "Community in WOMEN IN LOVE." NOVEL, 5 (1971),
       32-41.
              Birkin and Ursula ready to reenter the commun-
              ity at WL's end.

N8   Barry, J. "Oswald Spengler and D.H. Lawrence." ESA, 12
       (1969), 151-61.
              On R and WL. For annotation see M13.

N9   Bassoff, Bruce. "Metaphysical Desire in WOMEN IN LOVE."
       RLV, 42 (1976), 227-36.
              Adapts René Girard's term "metaphysical desire"
              (from DECEIT, DESIRE, AND THE NOVEL, 1965), to
              describe the Lawrencean ideal of "relation" to
              the cosmos in WL.

N10   Beker, Miroslav. "'The Crown,' 'The Reality of Peace,'
       and WOMEN IN LOVE." DHLR, 2 (1969), 254-64.
              Argues significant relations between DHL's two
              essays (A60, A61) on "the forces of corruption
              and dissolution" and WL.

N11   Bertocci, Angelo P. "Symbolism in WOMEN IN LOVE." In A
       D.H. LAWRENCE MISCELLANY. Ed. Harry T. Moore. Pp. 83-102.
       See G81.
            Key to DHL's symbolism his "religious vision"
            of destruction and creation.

N12   Blanchard, Lydia. "The 'Real Quartet' of WOMEN IN LOVE:
       Lawrence on Brothers and Sisters." In D.H. LAWRENCE: THE
       MAN WHO LIVED. Ed. Robert B. Partlow and Harry T. Moore.
       Pp. 199-206. See G92.
            DHL's intelligent treatment of the woman-to-
            woman relationship, the fourth but regrettably
            least discussed major relationship in WL, dis-
            proves Millett's claim that he dreaded "female
            alliances of any kind" (see H255).

N13   -----. "WOMEN IN LOVE: Mourning Becomes Narcissism." MO-
       SAIC, 15, No. 1 (1982), 105-18.
            DHL's and Freud's shared recognition that the
            failure to find a new love-object, "when the
            work of mourning is completed," will result
            in a destructive turn toward self love. (Quote
            from Freud's "On Transience" [1916].

N14   Bonds, Diane S. "Going into the Abyss: Literalization in
       WOMEN IN LOVE." ESSAYS IN LITERATURE, 8 (1981), 189-202.
            Permutations of the metaphor of the figure
            standing at the edge of an abyss, woven sys-
            tematically through the descriptions and sit-
            uations of WL.

N15   Branda, Eldon S. "Textual Changes in WOMEN IN LOVE." TSLL,
       6 (1964), 306-21.
            The first, privately printed American edition
            a far better text than the several available
            trade editions.

N16   Brookesmith, Peter. "The Future of the Individual: Ursula
       Brangwen and Kate Millett's SEXUAL POLITICS." HUMAN WORLD,
       No. 10 (1973), pp. 42-65.
            On R and WL. For annotation see M18.

N17   Cain, William E. "Lawrence's 'Purely Destructive' Art in
       WOMEN IN LOVE." THE SOUTH CAROLINA REVIEW, 13 (1980),
       38-47.
            DHL's "self-criticism" in WL less a sign of his
            objectivity than of his self-destruction.

N18 Caserio, Robert L. PLOT, STORY, AND THE NOVEL. Princeton, N.J.: Princeton Univ. Press, 1979. Pp. 255-64.
DHL's "desperate" struggle to create a new kind
of fictional plot at odds with traditional,
formally structured narrative forms.

N19 Chamberlain, Robert L. "Pussum, Minette, and the Africo-
Nordic Symbol in Lawrence's WOMEN IN LOVE." PMLA, 78
(1963), 407-16.
Antithetical Arctic and African ways to destruction control the theme, characterization,
and symbolism of the novel.

N20 Clark, L.D. "Lawrence/WOMEN IN LOVE: The Contravened
Knot." In APPROACHES TO THE TWENTIETH CENTURY NOVEL. Ed.
John Unterecker. New York: Crowell, 1965. Pp. 51-78.
Similarities between DHL's evangelistic love
ethic and primitive Christian ideals; WL an
ultimately affirmative study of the varieties
of amatory relationships.

N21 Crump, G.B. "WOMEN IN LOVE: Novel and Film." DHLR, 4
(1971), 28-41.
WL's film adaptation (1970), though only a
"partial success," still faithful to DHL's
spirit and an excellent "perspective" from
which to view the novel.

N22 Cushman, Keith. "A Note on Lawrence's 'Fly in the Ointment.'" ELN, 15 (1977), 47-51.
The "psycho-sexual undercurrent" in DHL's early
story (1913; see A16), anticipates the cancelled "Prologue to WOMEN IN LOVE" (A35).

N23 Davis, Edward. "WOMEN IN LOVE." In READINGS IN MODERN
FICTION. Cape Town, S. Africa: Simondium, 1964. Pp.
270-81.
Itemizes the "defects" of the novel and asserts
DHL's conservative, traditional view of sexual
love.

N24 Davis, Herbert. "WOMEN IN LOVE: A Corrected Typescript."
UTQ, 27 (1957), 34-53.
DHL's methodical revisions demonstrate his con-
scious artistry.

N25   Doherty, Gerald. "The Salvator Mundi Touch: Messianic
       Typology in D.H. Lawrence's WOMEN IN LOVE." ARIEL, 13, No.
       3 (1982), 53-71.
              Finds a veiled "meta-structure" in the novel,
              provided by DHL's paralleling of Birkin's ca-
              reer and the archetypal schema of the messiah's
              progress.

N26   Drain, Richard L. "WOMEN IN LOVE." In D.H. LAWRENCE: A
       CRITICAL STUDY. Ed. Andor Gomme. Pp. 70-93. See G43.
              Surveys complexities and paradoxes of WL and
              of DHL's view of human personalities and rela-
              tionships.

N27   Drew, Elizabeth. "WOMEN IN LOVE." In THE NOVEL: A MODERN
       GUIDE TO FIFTEEN ENGLISH MASTERPIECES. New York: Dell,
       1963. Pp. 208-23.
              Thematic and structural pattern of the novel
              determined by the conflict between creation
              and destruction.

N28   Eastman, Donald R. "Myth and Fate in the Characters of
       WOMEN IN LOVE." DHLR, 9 (1976), 177-93.
              The "aesthetic function...of the half-submerged
              allusions to myth" in WL.

N29   Erlich, Richard D. "Catastrophism and Coition: Universal
       and Individual Development in WOMEN IN LOVE." TSLL, 9
       (1967), 117-28.
              Sources in the literature of catastrophism for
              DHL's thematic counterpoint of destruction and
              creation in WL.

N30   Farber, Stephen. "WOMEN IN LOVE." HudR, 23 (1970), 321-
       26.
              What makes WL great, the "urgency" and impor-
              tance of DHL's ideas for his time, "is exactly
              what makes it untranslatable" as a film. (Re-
              view of Russell's film version, 1970.)

N31   Farmer, David R. "WOMEN IN LOVE: A Textual History and
       Premise for a Critical Edition." In EDITING BRITISH AND
       AMERICAN LITERATURE, 1880-1920. PAPERS GIVEN AT THE TENTH
       ANNUAL CONFERENCE ON EDITORIAL PROBLEMS, UNIVERSITY OF
       TORONTO, NOVEMBER 1974. Ed. Eric W. Domville. New York:
       Garland, 1976. Pp. 77-92.
              The editor of the forthcoming textual edition
              describes the multitude of textual variations

among WL's eleven published impressions, its
corrected page proofs, typescripts, and manuscripts, and suggests principles for a critical edition.

N32 Ford, George H. "An Introductory Note to D.H. Lawrence's
     'Prologue' to WOMEN IN LOVE." TQ, 6, No. 1 (1963), 92-97.
          Clarifies the homoerotic theme in the novel and
          suggests that the "Prologue" (1916) was cancel-
          led both in fear of censorship and for aesthe-
          tic reasons. Precedes first publication of the
          "Prologue" (see A35). Reprinted in M2.

N33 -----. "Shelley or Schiller? A Note on D.H. Lawrence at
     Work." TSLL, 4 (1962), 154-56.
          DHL's confusion of Shelley and Schiller in WL.

N34 -----. "The Eternal Moment: D.H. Lawrence's THE RAINBOW
     and WOMEN IN LOVE." In THE STUDY OF TIME, III. Ed. Julius
     T. Fraser, Nathaniel Lawrence, and David A. Park. Berlin
     and New York: Springer Verlag, 1978. Pp. 512-36.
          For annotation see M31.

N35 French, A.L. "'The Whole Pulse of Social England': WOMEN
     IN LOVE." CR, 21 (1979), 57-71.
          Not seen.

N36 Friedman, Alan. "D.H. Lawrence: 'The Wave Which Cannot
     Halt.'" In THE TURN OF THE NOVEL. New York: Oxford Univ.
     Press, 1966. Pp. 130-78.
          On R and WL. For annotation see M32.

N37 Gerber, Stephen. "Character, Language, and Experience in
     'Water Party.'" PAUNCH, Nos. 36-37 (1973), pp. 3-29.
          Close analysis of DHL's language and his modes
          of "perceiving and relating to the social and
          natural environment."

N38 Gill, Stephen. "Lawrence and Gerald Crich." EIC, 27
     (1977), 231-47.
          DHL's failure to present Crich as a convincing
          or coherent embodiment of subjugated, modern
          industrial man.

N39 Gillie, Christopher. CHARACTER IN ENGLISH LITERATURE.
     New York: Barnes and Noble, 1965. Pp. 187-202.
          Birkin illustrates DHL's theory of allotropic
          characterization.

N40   Goldknopf, David. "Realism in the Novel." In THE LIFE
       OF THE NOVEL. Chicago: Univ. of Chicago Press, 1972.
       Pp. 177-98.
            ULYSSES (1922), WL, and the higher realism of
            modern fiction.

N41   Gomez, Joseph A. "WOMEN IN LOVE (1920), D.H. Lawrence;
       Ken Russell, 1969: Russell's Images of Lawrence's Vision."
       In THE ENGLISH NOVEL AND THE MOVIES. Ed. Michael Klein
       and Gillian Parker. New York: Ungar, 1981. Pp. 248-56.
            Similarities between the technique (counter-
            pointing) and treatment (extremity and shock
            to provoke a balanced attitude in the audience)
            of DHL's WL and Russell's film version. Abridges
            Gomez's discussion of "WOMEN IN LOVE: Novel into
            Film," in KEN RUSSELL: THE ADAPTOR AS CREATOR
            (London: Muller, 1976), pp. 78-95.

N42   Gordon, David J. "Sex and Language in D.H. Lawrence."
       TCL, 27 (1981), 362-75.
            Despite his ambivalence toward "verbal con-
            sciousness," DHL realized that sex and lan-
            guage are both "incomplete but supreme means
            of contact between persons." Examines WL
            and LCL.

N43   -----. "WOMEN IN LOVE and the Lawrencean Aesthetic." In
       TWENTIETH CENTURY INTERPRETATIONS OF *WOMEN IN LOVE*. Ed.
       Stephen J. Miko. Pp. 50-60. See N3.
            Balanced and judicious study of WL as both a
            traditional and an innovative novel, strength-
            ened and weakened alike by DHL's personal in-
            volvement.

N44   Gray, Ronald D. "English Resistance to German Literature
       from Coleridge to D.H. Lawrence." In THE GERMAN TRADITION
       IN LITERATURE, 1871-1945. Cambridge: Cambridge Univ.
       Press, 1967. Pp. 327-54.
            The influence and rejection, in WL (pp. 341-53),
            of German ideas (e.g., *Blutbruderschaft*, *Wille
            zur Macht*, *Götterdämmerung*). Extract reprinted
            in M2.

N45   Gregor, Ian. "Towards a Christian Literary Criticism."
       MONTH, 219 (1965), 239-49.
            DHL's novel and Iris Murdoch's A SEVERED HEAD
            (1961) similarly suggest "that it is in the
            union of man and woman that human existence
            approaches its unobtainable completion."

N46   Haegert, John W. "D.H. Lawrence and the Ways of Eros."
      DHLR, 11 (1978), 199-233.
            Intensive analysis of the "pattern" of erotic
            initiation and consummation in DHL's major fic-
            tion and its fullest development in the "Star-
            Equilibrium" theme in WL. See U1.

N47   Hall, William F. "The Image of the Wolf in Chapter XXX
      of D.H. Lawrence's WOMEN IN LOVE." DHLR, 2 (1969), 272-74.
            Shakespearian parallel to DHL's wolf-image
            found in TROILUS AND CRESSIDA.

N48   Harper, Howard M. "FANTASIA and the Psychodynamics of
      WOMEN IN LOVE." In THE CLASSIC BRITISH NOVEL. Ed. Harper
      and Charles Edge. Athens: Univ. of Georgia Press, 1972.
      Pp. 202-19.
            WL interpreted in light of DHL's 'explanation'
            of human nature in FANTASIA OF THE UNCONSCIOUS
            (A63).

N49   Heldt, Lucia Henning. "Lawrence on Love: The Courtship
      and Marriage of Tom Brangwen and Lydia Lensky." DHLR, 8
      (1975), 358-70.
            On R and WL. For annotation see M37.

N50   Hinz, Evelyn J., and John J. Teunissen. "WOMEN IN LOVE
      and the Myth of Eros and Psyche." In D.H. LAWRENCE: THE
      MAN WHO LIVED. Ed. Robert B. Partlow and Harry T. Moore.
      Pp. 207-20. See G92.
            Eros and Psyche, seen by DHL as the archetypal
            myth of "woman becoming individual, self-re-
            sponsible, taking her own initiative," the in-
            forming myth of WL.

N51   Honig, Edwin. DARK CONCEIT: THE MAKING OF ALLEGORY. Evan-
      ston, Ill.: Northwestern Univ. Press, 1959. Pp. 166-69
      and passim.
            Pastoral and allegorical elements in DHL (chief-
            ly WL). Extract reprinted in N3.

N52   Hyde, Virginia. "Will Brangwen and Paradisal Vision in
      THE RAINBOW and WOMEN IN LOVE." DHLR, 8 (1975), 346-57.
            For annotation see M43.

N53   Jacobson, Sibyl. "The Paradox of Fulfillment: A Discus-
      sion of WOMEN IN LOVE." JNT, 3 (1973), 53-65.
            DHL's subtle creation of "double perspective"
            in WL's narration.

N54   Jones, David A. "The Third Unrealized Wonder: The Reality
      of Relation in D.H. Lawrence and Martin Buber." RELIGION
      IN LIFE, 44 (1975), 178-87.
            Similarities in Buber's and DHL's "analyses of
            modern life" (WL and LCL).

N55   Kay, Wallace G. "WOMEN IN LOVE and "The Man Who Died":
      Resolving Apollo and Dionysus." SOUTHERN QUARTERLY, 10
      (1972), 325-39.
            The balance of polar oppositions attempted in
            WL and achieved in "The Man Who Died." Also
            see M44.

N56   Kermode, Frank. "Lawrence and the Apocalyptic Types."
      CritQ, 10 (1968), 14-38.
            WL exhibits all the "apocalyptic types" in DHL.
            Also notes influence of MIDDLEMARCH (1872) on
            WL. Reprinted in M2.

N57   Kestner, Joseph A. "Sculptural Character in Lawrence's
      WOMEN IN LOVE." MFS, 21 (1975), 543-53.
            DHL's attempts to give his characters "sculp-
            tural coestensive volume," or almost visual
            roundness, under the influence of both Cézanne
            and the Futurists.

N58   Krieger, Murray. "The State of Monologue in D.H. Law-
      rence." In THE TRAGIC VISION: VARIATIONS ON A THEME IN
      LITERARY INTERPRETATION. Chicago: Univ. of Chicago Press,
      1966. Pp. 37-49.
            Examines the dramatic monologues in the "Moony"
            chapter.

N59   Langham, F.H. "WOMEN IN LOVE." EIC, 17 (1967), 183-206.
            Birkin and Ursula not presented as the ideal,
            but favorably treated because they are open to
            a number of possibilities in life. Reprinted
            in G5.

N60   Lee, Robin. "Darkness and 'A Heavy Gold Glamour': Law-
      rence's WOMEN IN LOVE." THEORIA, 42 (1974), 57-64.
            DHL's use of imagery to suggest the symbolic,
            "almost mythic dimension" of his characters'
            search for the self within a social community.

N61   Lenz, William E. "The 'Organic Connexion' of THE RAINBOW
      with WOMEN IN LOVE." SAB, 43, No. 1 (1978), 5-18.
            For annotation see M50.

N62 Lucente, Gregory L. "WOMEN IN LOVE and 'The Man Who Died':
     From Realism to the Mythopoeia of Passion and Rebirth." In
     THE NARRATIVE OF REALISM AND MYTH: VERGA, LAWRENCE, FAULK-
     NER, PAVESE. Baltimore, Md.: Johns Hopkins Univ. Press,
     1981. Pp. 107-23.
          Excellent overview of DHL's use of myth "to
          shade and fulfill his characters in a seemingly
          real world" and "to provide depth for [his]
          psychological realism," in WL. DHL's method
          degenerates, however, into a dogmatism, domi-
          nant mythism, and "thoroughly allegorized sys-
          tem" in "The Man Who Died."

N63 Marković, Vida E. "Ursula Brangwen." In THE CHANGING
     FACE: DISINTEGRATION OF PERSONALITY IN THE TWENTIETH-
     CENTURY BRITISH NOVEL, 1900-1950. Carbondale: Southern
     Illinois Univ. Press, 1970. Pp. 19-37.
          On R and WL. For annotation see M52.

N64 Martin, W.R. "'Freedom Together' in D.H. Lawrence's WOMEN
     IN LOVE." ESA, 8 (1965), 111-20.
          Birkin's and DHL's ideal of "freedom together,"
          involving whole relationships both with the
          self and with another, variously reflected by
          the many relationships in WL.

N65 Mendilow, A.A. "The Multi-dimensional Present in D.H.
     Lawrence's World-Picture." HUSL, 5 (1977), 265-78.
          On R and WL. For annotation see M53.

N66 Meyers, Jeffrey. "Mark Gertler and WOMEN IN LOVE." In
     PAINTING AND THE NOVEL. Manchester, Engl.: Manchester
     Univ. Press, 1975. Pp. 65-82.
          Gertler's avant garde painting, "Merry-Go-Round"
          (1916), used as an aesthetic model and a unify-
          ing symbol in WL.

N67 Miles, Thomas H. "Birkin's Electro-Mystical Body of Re-
     ality: D.H. Lawrence's Use of Kundalini." DHLR, 9 (1976),
     194-212.
          DHL's assimilation of the "mystical doctrine of
          Hindu yogis" into his phallic mysticism in WL
          ("Excurse").

N68 Mori, Haruhide. "Lawrence's Imagistic Development in THE
     RAINBOW and WOMEN IN LOVE." ELH, 31 (1964), 460-81.
          For annotation see M55.

N69 Newman, Paul B. "The Natural Aristocrat in Letters." UR, 31 (1964), 23-31.
> The tension between union and polarity in WL viewed as DHL's attempt to restore "aristocratic values within a new synthesis with the democratic" (cf. Yeats, and others).

N70 Oates, Joyce Carol. "Lawrence's *Götterdämmerung*: The Tragic Vision of WOMEN IN LOVE." CRITICAL INQUIRY, 4 (1978), 559-78.
> DHL's analysis of the "curious self-destructive condition of the spirit" in a rootless modern world.

N71 Pirenet, Colette. "La Structure symbolique de WOMEN IN LOVE." EA, 22 (1969), 137-51.
> Distinguishes DHL's structural symbols (sun, snow, horses, water, etc.), from his recurring symbols (e.g., birds, rodents, insects, colors, clothes) and his "social" symbols (e.g., houses, furniture, the cat). [In French.]

N72 Procopiow, Norma. "The Narrator's Stratagem in WOMEN IN LOVE." COLLEGE LITERATURE, 5 (1978), 114-24.
> DHL's deliberate creation of Gerald Crich as an "inscrutable" character through manipulation of style and narrative voice.

N73 Rachman, Shalom. "Art and Value in D.H. Lawrence's WOMEN IN LOVE." DHLR, 5 (1972), 1-25.
> Little practical or moral value in WL, despite DHL's evident technical success.

N74 Ragussis, Michael. "Lawrence, Freud, and 'Verbal Consciousness'"; "D.H. Lawrence." In THE SUBTERFUGE OF ART: LANGUAGE AND THE ROMANTIC TRADITION. Baltimore, Md.: Johns Hopkins Univ. Press, 1978. Pp. 1-5; 172-225.
> DHL's view of art as "subterfuge" and its impact on language and silence, vocabulary and communication in WL.

N75 Raskin, Jonah. THE MYTHOLOGY OF IMPERIALISM: RUDYARD KIPLING, JOSEPH CONRAD, E.M. FORSTER, D.H. LAWRENCE, AND JOYCE CARY. New York: Random House, 1971. Pp. 252-56.
> Simple-minded Marxist praise for WL as a "revolutionary" work.

N76   Reddick, Bryan D. "Point of View and Narrative Tone in
      WOMEN IN LOVE: The Portrayal of Interpsychic Space."
      DHLR, 7 (1974), 156-71.
           Varieties of narrative technique in WL.

N77   ------. "Tension at the Heart of WOMEN IN LOVE." ELT, 19
      (1976), 73-86.
           Central focus of WL found in counterpoint of
           "Excurse" and "Death in Love" chapters.

N78   Remsbury, John. "WOMEN IN LOVE as a Novel of Change."
      DHLR, 6 (1973), 149-72.
           Finds the "true drama" of WL in the Gudrun,
           Gerald, and Loerke relationships, and sees
           Gudrun as "by no means" corrupt.

N79   Robson, W.W. "D.H. Lawrence and WOMEN IN LOVE." In THE
      MODERN AGE. Ed. Boris Ford. 1961. 3rd ed. Baltimore,
      Md.: Penguin, 1973. Pp. 280-300.
           Survey of work, with special emphasis on WL.
           Birkin's and the novel's inadequacies insep-
           arable from DHL's.

N80   Ross, Charles L. "D.H. Lawrence's Use of Greek Tragedy:
      Euripides and Ritual." DHLR, 10 (1977), 1-19.
           On R and WL. For annotation see M64.

N81   ------. "Homoerotic Feeling in WOMEN IN LOVE: Lawrence's
      'Struggle for Verbal Consciousness' in the Manuscripts."
      In D.H. LAWRENCE: THE MAN WHO LIVED. Ed. Robert B. Part-
      low and Harry T. Moore. Pp. 168-82. See G92.
           Rather than being diverted and partially sup-
           pressed in the final version, as commonly ar-
           gued, the homosexual dimensions of Rupert's
           attraction to Gerald grow and mature in the
           successive drafts of WL.

N82   ------. "Introduction"; "Notes." In Lawrence's WOMEN IN
      LOVE. Harmondsworth, Engl.: Penguin, 1982. Pp. 13-48;
      585-93.
           History of the novel's composition, publica-
           tion, and reception, a commentary on the rela-
           tionship of the cancelled "Prologue" (not re-
           printed here; see A35), and the final text,
           and a survey of the central critical issues
           for WL's interpretation. Ross's notes iden-
           tify historical, literary, and mythological

references and translate foreign phrases. Ross
also includes a brief chronology for DHL's composition of "The Sisters" (based on his full
study; see M6) and Penguin provides an introductory chronology of DHL's life and works.

N83   Rossman, Charles. "D.H. Lawrence, Women, and WOMEN IN
      LOVE." CAHIERS VICTORIENS & ÉDOUARDIENS, No. 8 (1979),
      pp. 93-115.
            WL shows DHL's "growing hostility toward women"
            and, in casting Birkin in the role of Ursula's
            teacher, demonstrates "pronounced (if subtle...)
            assumptions of masculine superiority." See H319.

N84   Rudrum, Alan. "Philosophical Implication in Lawrence's
      WOMEN IN LOVE." DR, 51 (1971), 240-50.
            Excellent on the philosophic backgrounds to
            the novel.

N85   Ruthven, K.K. "The Savage God: Conrad and Lawrence."
      CritQ, 10 (1968), 39-54.
            On R and WL. For annotation see M65.

N86   Sagar, Keith. "The Genesis of THE RAINBOW and WOMEN IN
      LOVE." DHLR, 1 (1968), 179-99.
            For annotation see M66.

N87   Salgādo, Gāmini. "Taking a Nail for a Walk: On Reading
      WOMEN IN LOVE." In THE MODERN ENGLISH NOVEL: THE READER,
      THE WRITER, AND THE WORK. Ed. Gabriel Josipovici. New
      York: Barnes and Noble, 1976. Pp. 95-112.
            WL "positively invites and even compels" flag-
            rantly contradictory reading because it is
            "shot through" with the "tension between the
            necessity of articulating a vision and its
            impossibility."

N88   Schorer, Mark. "WOMEN IN LOVE and Death." HudR, 6 (1953),
      34-47.
            Important examination of WL's unconventional
            use of character, as *fate*, and its rhythmic
            form. Reprinted in G53, G115, and H330.

N89   Scott, James F. "'Continental': The Germanic Dimension
      of WOMEN IN LOVE." LITERATUR IN WISSENSCHAFT UND UNTER-
      RICHT (Kiel), 12 (1979), 117-34.
            Not seen.

N90 Smailes, Thomas A. "Plato's 'Great Lie of Ideals': Func-
     tion in WOMEN IN LOVE." In GENEROUS CONVERSE: ENGLISH ES-
     SAYS IN MEMORY OF EDWARD DAVIS. Ed. Brian Green. Cape
     Town: Oxford Univ. Press, 1980. Pp. 133-35.
         Gerald's ideas paralleled with Plato's in THE
         REPUBLIC, and "the fall of the house of Crich"
         seen as DHL's "comment on the Platonic ideal
         community."

N91 -----. "The Mythical Bases of WOMEN IN LOVE." DHLR, 1
     (1968), 129-36.
         Gerald Crich as Hermes and as archetypal "Ger-
         manic Hero."

N92 Spanier, Sandra Whipple. "Two Foursomes in THE BLITHEDALE
     ROMANCE and WOMEN IN LOVE." CLS, 16 (1979), 58-68.
         Similarities of "characters, scenery, and theme"
         in WL and Hawthorne's THE BLITHEDALE ROMANCE
         (1852).

N93 Stewart, Jack F. "Primitivism in WOMEN IN LOVE." DHLR,
     13 (1980), 45-62.
         Explores sources and significance of DHL's fas-
         cination with primitive visions of degeneration
         and primitivist art. See G27.

N94 -----. "Rhetoric and Image in Lawrence's 'Moony.'" STUD-
     IES IN THE HUMANITIES, 8, No. 1 (1980), 33-37.
         Not seen.

N95 Tatar, Maria M. SPELLBOUND: STUDIES IN MESMERISM AND LIT-
     ERATURE. Princeton, N.J.: Princeton Univ. Press, 1978.
     Pp. 243-55 and passim.
         Mesmeric motifs in WL, particularly in DHL's
         analysis of the "magnetic and electrical qual-
         ities of characters."

N96 Tenenbaum, Elizabeth Brody. "D.H. Lawrence." In THE
     PROBLEMATIC SELF: APPROACHES TO IDENTITY IN STENDHAL,
     D.H. LAWRENCE, AND MALRAUX. Cambridge, Mass.: Harvard
     Univ. Press, 1977. Pp. 65-112.
         DHL, in WL, in the romantic tradition of Rous-
         seau and Stendhal ("free reign to impulse"),
         as opposed to the antithetical romanticism of
         Byron and Nietzsche (the power of will).

N97 Tischler, Nancy M. "The Rainbow and the Arch." In LITER-
     ATURE AND RELIGION. Ed. Charles A. Huttar. [Pp. 8-29.]
     See G59.
         On R and WL. For annotation see M77.

N98   Tomlinson, T.B. "D.H. Lawrence: SONS AND LOVERS, WOMEN
        IN LOVE." In THE ENGLISH MIDDLE-CLASS NOVEL. London:
        Macmillan, 1976. Pp. 185-98.
            For annotation see L64.

N99   Torgovnick, Marianna. "Pictorial Elements in WOMEN IN
        LOVE: The Uses of Insinuation and Visual Rhyme." ConL,
        21 (1980), 420-34.
            Develops terminology to describe DHL's pur-
            poses and techniques for presenting highly
            visualized scenes in WL.

N100   Twitchell, James. "Lawrence's Lamias: Predatory Women
        in THE RAINBOW and WOMEN IN LOVE." SNNTS, 11 (1979),
        23-42.
            For annotation see M79.

N101   Unrue, Darlene H. "Lawrence's Vision of Evil: The Power-
        Spirit in THE RAINBOW and WOMEN IN LOVE." DR, 55 (1975-
        76), 643-54.
            On R and WL. For annotation see M81.

N102   Vichy, Thérèse. "Symbolisme et structures dans WOMEN IN
        LOVE." EA, 33 (1980), 400-13.
            Gerald's character a model for the analysis
            of WL's structural tension between progres-
            sive and primitivist symbols (viewed in light
            of Paul Ricoeur's theories of symbolism in LE
            CONFLIT DES INTERPRÉTATIONS [1969]). [In
            French.]

N103   Vitoux, Pierre. "The Chapter 'Excurse' in WOMEN IN LOVE:
        Its Genesis and the Critical Problem." TSLL, 17 (1976),
        821-36.
            Interpretive problems of the "Excurse" chapter
            attributed to DHL's changing intentions, evi-
            dent in successive manuscript drafts.

N104   -----. "WOMEN IN LOVE: From Typescripts into Print."
        TSLL, 23 (1981), 577-93.
            Comparison of WL's two surviving typescripts
            and its published text, and commentary on
            DHL's revisions.

N105   Yetman, Michael G. "The Failure of the Un-Romantic Imagi-
        nation in WOMEN IN LOVE." MOSAIC, 9, No. 3 (1976), 83-96.
            Studies Gudrun's failure to realize DHL's
            "organicist" belief in the "connection be-
            tween life and art."

N106 Zambrano, Ana Laura. "WOMEN IN LOVE: Counterpoint on
      Film." LFQ, 1 (1973), 46-54.
            Ken Russell's contrapuntal reinforcement of
            DHL's themes, in his screen adaptation of WL
            (1970), one artist's successful interpreta-
            tion of another. See G70.

N107 Zytaruk, George J. "What Happened to D.H. Lawrence's
      GOATS AND COMPASSES?" DHLR, 4 (1971), 280-86.
            Identifies DHL's projected "philosophical
            work" (so described in F68), as, in fact,
            an early version of WL (c. 1916). Also see
            Charles L. Ross's emphatic objection to this
            identification and Zytaruk's rejoinder in
            DHLR, 6 (1973), 33-46, and Keith Sagar's sug-
            gestion that GOATS AND COMPASSES was an ear-
            lier version of "The Reality of Peace" (A61),
            in DHLR, 6 (1973), 303-08.

P. STUDIES OF *THE LOST GIRL* (1920)

Since there are no books, essay collections, monographs, or
pamphlets on THE LOST GIRL, this section consists entirely of
critical articles or chapters on the novel.

For the textual edition of THE LOST GIRL, see A6.

For bibliographical information on THE LOST GIRL, see Roberts
(E39) and Sagar (E40), and, for biographical backgrounds to
the novel, see Moore (F112), Murry (F120, F121), and Nehls
(F123).

For additional critical commentaries and information on THE
LOST GIRL, see the following books, in section G above: All-
dritt (G3), Beal (G9), Clark (G17), Colin (G19), Daleski (G24),
Dix (G29), Draper (G33), Eisenstein (G36), Freeman (G40), Gott-
wald (G46), Hobsbaum (G51), Holderness (G55), Hough (G56),
Howe (G58), Jaensson (G61), Johnsson (G63), Kermode (G65),
Meyers (G73), Michaels-Tonks (G74), Moore (G80), Moynahan (G83),
Negriolli (G87), Niven (G89), Pinion (G95), Prasad (G99), Prit-
chard (G101), Rees (G102), Reul (G103), Sagar (G104), Seligmann
(G108), Slade (G111), Tedlock (G118), Weidner (G122), Wesslau
(G124), Worthen (G128), Yudhishtar (G130); and the following
critical articles, in section H above: Albright (H5), Goode
(H144), Kiely (H205), Millett (H255), Pritchard (H296), and
Vickery (H393).

P1   Delbaere-Garant, Jeanne. "The Call of the South: WHERE
     ANGELS FEAR TO TREAD and THE LOST GIRL." RLV, 29 (1963),
     336-57.
            Sexual, class, and cultural confrontations in
            Forster and DHL.

P2   Gurko, Leo. "THE LOST GIRL: D.H. Lawrence as 'Dickens of
     the Midlands.'" PMLA, 78 (1963), 601-05.
            DHL as a gifted satirist.

P3 Hafley, James. "THE LOST GIRL: Lawrence Really Real." ArQ,
    10 (1954), 312-22.
        Argues for a higher opinion of the work, a real-
        istic "masterpiece."

P4 Herring, Phillip F. "Caliban in Nottingham: D.H. Lawrence's
    THE LOST GIRL." MOSAIC, 12, No. 4 (1979), 9-19.
        The brilliance and blunders of the novel sur-
        veyed, with its failures attributed to the con-
        fused circumstances of its composition.

P5 Heywood, Christopher. "D.H. Lawrence's THE LOST GIRL and
    Its Antecedents by George Moore and Arnold Bennett." ES,
    47 (1966), 131-34.
        Slight similarities among DHL's novel, Bennett's
        ANNA OF THE FIVE TOWNS (1902), and Moore's A
        MUMMER'S WIFE (1885).

P6 Ruderman, Judith G. "Rekindling the 'Father-Spark': Law-
    rence's Ideal of Leadership in THE LOST GIRL and THE PLUMED
    SERPENT." DHLR, 13 (1980), 239-59.
        DHL's correlation of familial and political dom-
        inance traced in the opening and closing works
        of his "leadership period." THE LOST GIRL de-
        picts "invidious" mother-domination; PS "re-
        stores the rightful leader...the father." See
        G28.

P7 Russell, John. "D.H. Lawrence: THE LOST GIRL, KANGAROO."
    In STYLE IN MODERN BRITISH FICTION: STUDIES IN JOYCE, LAW-
    RENCE, FORSTER, LEWIS, AND GREEN. Baltimore, Md.: Johns
    Hopkins Univ. Press, 1978. Pp. 43-88.
        Close stylistic analysis of DHL's vocabulary,
        syntax, and structure in his most stylistically
        antithetical novels.

P8 Woolf, Virginia. "Postscript or Prelude?" In her CONTEMP-
    ORARY WRITERS. Comp. Jean Guiguet. New York: Harcourt,
    1966. Pp. 158-60.
        Though a disappointing novel, THE LOST GIRL
        shows DHL occasionally infusing the method of
        a Bennett with the momentary insight of a Tol-
        stoy. Also see H175. Reprinted in G20 and
        G34.

P9   Worthen, John. "Introduction." In D.H. LAWRENCE: THE LOST
     GIRL. Ed. Worthen. Pp. xix-liv. See A6.
          Backgrounds to the novel's composition and pub-
          lication. Worthen also includes a previously
          unpublished manuscript fragment related to THE
          LOST GIRL, "Elsa Culverwell" (pp. 343-58), ex-
          planatory notes for the novel (pp. 361-401,
          426), and textual apparatus for the edition
          (pp. 405-25).

Q. STUDIES OF *AARON'S ROD* (1922)

The following section is subdivided into two parts: i. Books
and Essay Collections on AARON'S ROD; and ii. Critical Articles or Chapters on AARON'S ROD.

A textual edition of AARON'S ROD, in progress, will be published in THE CAMBRIDGE EDITION (Bl--ed. Mara Kalnins).

For bibliographical information on AARON'S ROD, see Roberts
(E39) and Sagar (E40), and, for biographical backgrounds to
the novel, see Firchow (F55), Moore (F112), Murry (F120, F121),
Nehls (F123), and Weintraub (F158).

For additional critical commentaries and information on AARON'S
ROD, see the following books, in section G above: Alldritt (G3),
Beal (G9), Boadella (G12), Bredsdorff (G13), Cavitch (G16),
Clark (G17), Colin (G19), Corsani (G21), Daleski (G24), Dix
(G29), Draper (G33), Eisenstein (G36), Freeman (G40), Goodheart
(G44), Gottwald (G46), Gregory (G47), Hobsbaum (G51), Holder-
ness (G55), Hough (G56), Howe (G58), Jaensson (G61), Jarrett-
Kerr (G62), Johnsson (G63), Kermode (G65), Leavis (G68), Mar-
nat (G72), Meyers (G73), Michaels-Tonks (G74), Miller (G77),
Moore (G80), Moynahan (G83), Nahal (G86), Negriolli (G87),
Niven (G89), Panichas (G91), Pinion (G95), Potter (G98), Pra-
sad (G99), Pritchard (G101), Reul (G103), Sagar (G104), San-
ders (G106), Seligmann (G108), Slade (G111), Stoll (G116),
Tedlock (G118), Vivas (G121), Weidner (G122), Wesslau (G124),
Worthen (G128), Yudhishtar (G130); the following critical art-
icles, in section H above: Albright (H5), Alcorn (H6), Bedient
(H33), Garcia (H126), Gindin (H136), Glicksberg (H141), Green
(H152), Harrison (H168), Kiely (H205), Maes-Jelinek (H232),
Meyers (H249), Millett (H255), Pinto (H290), Pritchard (H296),
Rossman (H319), Stewart (H361), Tristram (H386), Vickery (H393);
and the following studies, entered in other sections of this
bibliography: Gilbert (Y1) and Kim (AC5).

Q, i.   Books and Essay Collections on AARON'S ROD

Q1   Miller, Henry. NOTES ON *AARON'S ROD*, AND OTHER NOTES ON
     LAWRENCE FROM THE PARIS NOTEBOOKS. Ed. Seamus Cooney.
     Santa Barbara, Calif.: Black Sparrow Press, 1980.
          Miller's notes (1933) for a proposed, yet never
          written essay on DHL, principally concerning
          AARON'S ROD. Cooney's brief "Introduction"
          (pp. 7-12) describes Miller's interest in DHL.
          Also see G77.

Q, ii. Critical Articles or Chapters on AARON'S ROD

For additional, foreign-language articles on AARON'S ROD, see
the following entries in Appendix A: Mori (AA219), Okumura
(AA240), and Yoshii (AA295).

Q2   Baker, Paul G. "Profile of an Anti-Hero: Aaron Sisson Re-
     considered." DHLR, 10 (1977), 182-92.
          DHL's distanced portrait of Aaron's aloof and
          alienated character as "emblematic of the ma-
          laise inflecting an entire society."

Q3   Barr, William R. "AARON'S ROD as D.H. Lawrence's Picares-
     que Novel." DHLR, 9 (1976), 213-25.
          Novel employs formal conventions of the picares-
          que.

Q4   Barry, Sandra. "Singularity of Two; the Plurality of One."
     PAUNCH, No. 26 (1966), pp. 34-39.
          DHL's ideal of "equilibrium" within and between
          individuals. See G94.

Q5   Debu-Bridel, Jacques. "LA VERGE D'AARON, par D.H. Law-
     rence." NOUVELLE REVUE FRANÇAISE, 46 (1936), 606-08.
          Extraordinary parallels between the theses of
          Hitler's MEIN KAMPF (1925), "et les vues dévelop-
          pées dans ce roman par" DHL. [In French.]

Q6   Hogan, Robert. "The Amorous Whale: A Study in the Symbol-
     ism of D.H. Lawrence." MFS, 5 (1959), 39-46.
          DHL's assimilation of Melville and Whitman the
          key to the "firm, though subtle" structures of
          AARON'S ROD and KANGAROO. Unusual point of
          view. See G78.

Q7   Mayhead, Robin. UNDERSTANDING LITERATURE.   Cambridge: Cam-
     bridge Univ. Press, 1965. Pp. 30-34.
          Discusses the "universal significance" of the
          novel's family Christmas scene as an illustra-
          tion of "the most usual kind of relation be-
          tween literature" and the reader's personal
          experience.

Q8   Meyer, Kurt Robert. "D.H. Lawrence (1885-1930)." In ZUR
     ERLEBTEN REDE IM ENGLISCHEN ROMAN DES ZWANGISTEN JAHRHUN-
     DERTS. Bern: Francke, 1957. Pp. 44-65.
          On SL and AARON'S ROD. For annotation see L41.

Q9   Ruderman, Judith G. "The 'Trilogy' That Never Was: THE RAIN-
     BOW, WOMEN IN LOVE, and AARON'S ROD." PBSA, 74 (1980),
     76-80.
          Describes the misimpression of DHL's American
          publisher, Thomas Seltzer, that AARON'S ROD was
          the completion of a trilogy including R and WL
          (apparently a notion DHL accepted).

Q10 Wagner, Jeanie. "A Botanical Note on AARON'S ROD."   DHLR,
     4 (1971), 287-90.
          Novel's title both a biblical allusion and a
          common name for the yellow mullein plant, a
          phallic-shaped "healing agent as well as an
          insect trap."

R. STUDIES OF *KANGAROO* (1923)

The following section is subdivided into two parts: i. Books
and Essay Collections on KANGAROO; and ii. Critical Articles
or Chapters on KANGAROO.

A textual edition of KANGAROO will be published in THE CAM-
BRIDGE EDITION (B1--ed. John Grover [tent.]).

For bibliographical information on KANGAROO, see Roberts (E39)
and Sagar (E40), and, for biographical backgrounds to the novel,
see Moore (F112), Murry (F121), Nehls (F123), Weintraub (F158),
and Wilding (F161).

For additional critical commentaries and information on KANGA-
ROO, see the following books, in section G above: Alldritt (G3),
Beal (G9), Bredsdorff (G13), Cavitch (G16), Clark (G17), Colin
(G19), Daleski (G24), Draper (G33), Eisenstein (G36), Freeman
(G40), Goodheart (G44), Gottwald (G46), Hess (G50), Hobsbaum
(G51), Hochman (G52), Holderness (G55), Hough (G56), Howe (G58),
Inniss (G60), Jaensson (G61), Jarrett-Kerr (G62), Johnsson
(G63), Kermode (G65), Leavis (G68), Meyers (G73), Michaels-
Tonks (G74), Moore (G80), Moynahan (G83), Murry (G85), Nahal
(G86), Negriolli (G87), Nin (G88), Niven (G89), Panichas (G91),
Pinion (G95), Potter (G98), Prasad (G99), Pritchard (G101),
Reul (G103), Sagar (G104), Sanders (G106), Seillière (G107),
Seligmann (G108), Slade (G111), Stoll (G116), Tedlock (G118),
Tindall (G120), Vivas (G121), Weidner (G122), Wesslau (G124),
West (G125), Worthen (G128), Yudhishtar (G130); the following
critical articles, in section H above: Baker (H22), Bedient
(H33), Bentley (H37), Green (H152), Harrison (H169), Jacobson
(H194), Kiely (H205), Maes-Jelinek (H232), Millett (H255),
Pinto (H290), Rossman (H319), Stewart (H361), Vickery (H393);
and the following study, entered elsewhere in this bibliogra-
phy: Kim (AC5).

R, i.   Books and Essay Collections on KANGAROO

R1   Darroch, Robert.   D.H. LAWRENCE IN AUSTRALIA.   Melbourne:
     Macmillan, 1981.
          "A study of the time that D.H. Lawrence spent
          in Australia and the works that resulted from
          this visit." (Quoted from publisher's annouce-
          ment--not seen). Presumably chiefly concerned
          with KANGAROO and THE BOY IN THE BUSH.

R2   Schickele, René.   LIEBE UND ÄRGERNIS DES D.H. LAWRENCE [THE
     LOVE AND SORROW OF D.H. LAWRENCE].   Amsterdam: Allert de
     Lange, n.d. [1934].
          Discursive commentary on DHL's politics, born
          of the nightmare of the First World War, as
          they emerge from KANGAROO and PS. Schickele
          summarizes DHL's theories of natural aristoc-
          racy and his rejection of fascism in KANGAROO
          (with an aside on Kangaroo's symbolically ap-
          propriate Judaism) and devotes the largest
          portion of his book to the magnificent, im-
          probable revolution in PS, which he considers
          DHL's strongest novel. Schickele offers a
          unique view of Mabel Dodge Luhan's role in
          providing a comic dimension to PS, finding
          satiric portraits of her and her husband Tony
          in the novel.

R, ii.   Critical Articles or Chapters on KANGAROO

For additional, foreign-language articles on KANGAROO, see the
following entries in Appendix A: Mori (AA219) and Okumura
(AA240).

R3   Alexander, John.   "D.H. Lawrence's KANGAROO: Fantasy, Fact,
     or Fiction?" MEANJIN, 24 (1965), 179-96.
          Historical elements in the novel. See R5.

R4   Alter, Robert.   "Eliot, Lawrence and the Jews: Two Versions
     of Europe." 1970. In DEFENSES OF THE IMAGINATION: JEWISH
     WRITERS AND MODERN HISTORICAL CRISIS. Philadelphia: Jewish
     Publication Society of America, 1978. Pp. 137-51.
          DHL's purported anti-semitism in the novel act-
          ually a symbolic renunciation of "the living

source of the Judeo-Christian religious tradition" (cf. Eliot's indefensible anti-semitism).
See H104.

R5   Atkinson, Curtis. "Was There Fact in D.H. Lawrence's
      KANGAROO? MEANJIN, 24 (1965), 358-59.
           Fact and fiction in the novel. See R3. Re-
           printed in G5.

R6   Friederich, Werner P. AUSTRALIA IN WESTERN IMAGINATIVE
      PROSE WRITINGS 1600-1960: AN ANTHOLOGY AND A HISTORY OF
      LITERATURE. Chapel Hill: Univ. of North Carolina Press,
      1967. Pp. 226-35.
           Weakness of DHL's sense of Australia only mar-
           ginally redeemed by "his poetic and sensitive
           descriptions of the Australian coastline and
           the nearby bush," peripheral elements in the
           novel.

R7   Gaya Nuño, Juan Antonio. "El lider fascista en la novela
      inglesa de nuestro tiempo." CUADERNOS HISPANOAMERICANOS,
      72, No. 216 (1967), 632-40.
           Fascist elements in KANGAROO and Huxley's POINT
           COUNTER POINT (1928). [In Spanish.]

R8   Gurko, Leo. "KANGAROO: D.H. Lawrence in Transit." MFS,
      10 (1964), 349-58.
           KANGAROO primarily a novel of place and Aus-
           tralia itself the most important element of
           the book.

R9   Guttmann, Allen. "D.H. Lawrence: The Politics of Irra-
      tionality." WSCL, 5 (1964), 151-63.
           DHL's "fascism" in KANGAROO and PS.

R10   Heuzenroeder, John. "D.H. Lawrence's Australia." AUS-
      TRALIAN LITERARY STUDIES, 4 (1970), 319-33.
           DHL's unfavorable treatment of Australia,
           chiefly in KANGAROO, but also in THE BOY IN
           THE BUSH.

R11   Hogan, Robert. "The Amorous Whale: A Study in the Sym-
      bolism of D.H. Lawrence." MFS, 5 (1959), 39-46.
           On AARON'S ROD and KANGAROO. For annotation
           see Q6.

R12   Hope, A.D. "D.H. Lawrence's KANGAROO: How It Looks to
      an Australian." In THE AUSTRALIAN EXPERIENCE: CRITICAL
      ESSAYS ON AUSTRALIAN NOVELS. Ed. William S. Ramson.
      Canberra: Australian National Univ. Press, 1974. Pp.
      157-73.
            Novel a "fantasy," a dream in which DHL "dram-
            atises his personal problems on a world screen
            and preaches a solution which he never tries
            to put even into imaginary action."

R13   Jarvis, F.P. "A Textual Comparison of the First British
      and American Editions of D.H. Lawrence's KANGAROO." PBSA,
      59 (1965), 400-24.
            DHL continued revisions between the English
            and the American editions; the later Seltzer
            text is clearly superior.

R14   Lee, Robert. "D.H. Lawrence and the Australian Ethos."
      SOUTHERLY, 33 (1973), 144-51.
            Finds a superior, intuitive grasp of the Aus-
            tralian ethos in DHL's KANGAROO (especially
            re: ideas of sexual versus fraternal love).

R15   Myers, Neil. "Lawrence and the War." CRITICISM, 4 (1962),
      44-58.
            General account of the impact of the war on
            DHL, focusing on the "Nightmare" chapter.

R16   Ocampo, Victoria. "El hombre que murió (D.H. Lawrence)."
      SUR, No. 329 (1971), pp. 33-56.
            Skeptical summary of DHL's theme of "blood
            consciousness" and superstition of sexuality
            in KANGAROO and LCL ("en realidad la super-
            stición del sexo"). [In Spanish.]

R17   Roberts, Warren. "Problems in Editing D.H. Lawrence."
      In D.H. LAWRENCE: THE MAN WHO LIVED. Ed. Robert B. Part-
      low and Harry T. Moore. Pp. 58-61. See G92.
            Considers "in detail" the "extensive textual
            difficulties" in editing KANGAROO and the
            poems, for THE CAMBRIDGE EDITION (see B1).

R18   Russell, John. "D.H. Lawrence: THE LOST GIRL, KANGAROO."
      In STYLE IN MODERN BRITISH FICTION: STUDIES IN JOYCE,
      LAWRENCE, FORSTER, LEWIS, AND GREEN. Baltimore, Md.:
      Johns Hopkins Univ. Press, 1978. Pp. 43-88.
            For annotation see P7.

R19   Samuels, Marilyn S.   "Water, Ships, and the Sea: Unifying
       Symbols in Lawrence's KANGAROO." UR, 37 (1970), 46-57.
              Though a weak novel, KANGAROO unified by sev-
              eral related symbols.

R20   Sepčić, Višnja.   "The Category of Landscape in D.H. Law-
       rence's KANGAROO." STUDIA ROMANICA ET ANGLICA ZAGRABIEN-
       SIA, Nos. 27-28 (1969), pp. 129-52.
              Symbolic landscape in the novel.   Not seen.

R21   Wilding, Michael.   "Between Scylla and Charybdis: KANGAROO
       and the Form of the Political Novel." AUSTRALIAN LITERARY
       STUDIES, 4 (1970), 334-48.
              Novel's chaotic form an appropriate reflection
              of its chaotic politics.

R22   -----.   "KANGAROO: 'a new show.'"   In POLITICAL FICTIONS.
       London: Routledge, 1980.   Pp. 150-91.
              While strikingly unconventional as political
              fiction and approaching the anti-political in
              its attitudes, KANGAROO develops important
              original connections between political and
              "sexual and domestic concerns."

S.   STUDIES OF *THE BOY IN THE BUSH* (1924)

The following section is subdivided into two parts: i. Books
and Essay Collections on THE BOY IN THE BUSH; and ii. General
Critical Articles or Chapters on THE BOY IN THE BUSH.

A textual edition of THE BOY IN THE BUSH will be published in
THE CAMBRIDGE EDITION (B1--ed. P. Eggert [tent.]).

For bibliographical information on the work, see Roberts (E39)
and Sagar (E40), and, for biographical backgrounds to the novel,
see Moore (F112), Murry (F121), Nehls (F123), and Skinner (F149).

DHL's novel collaboration with Mollie L. Skinner, THE BOY IN
THE BUSH, has received scant attention from his critics.   For
some additional critical commentaries and information on THE
BOY IN THE BUSH, however, see the following books, in section
G above: Clark (G17), Ford (G39), Hobsbaum (G51), Kermode (G65),
Michaels-Tonks (G74), Negriolli (G87), Sagar (G104), and Ted-
lock (G118).

S, i.   Books and Essay Collections on THE BOY IN THE BUSH

S1   Darroch, Robert.   D.H. LAWRENCE IN AUSTRALIA.   Melbourne:
     Macmillan, 1981.
          On KANGAROO and THE BOY IN THE BUSH.   For an-
          notation see R1.

S, ii.   Critical Articles or Chapters on THE BOY IN THE BUSH

S2   Gay, Harriet.   "Mollie Skinner: D.H. Lawrence's Australian
     Catalyst."   BIOGRAPHY, 3 (1980), 331-47.
          Biographical sketch of DHL's most unlikely col-
          laborator, "a middle-aged Quaker spinster...in
          a remote backwater of Western Australia."   Also
          see F149.

S3   Heuzenroeder, John. "D.H. Lawrence's Australia." AUSTRAL-
     IAN LITERARY STUDIES, 4 (1970), 319-33.
          On KANGAROO and THE BOY IN THE BUSH. For anno-
          tation see R10.

S4   Moore, Harry T. "Preface." In Lawrence's and Mollie L.
     Skinner's THE BOY IN THE BUSH. Carbondale: Southern Illi-
     nois Univ. Press, 1971. Pp. vii-xxviii.
          Background and origins of DHL's collaboration
          with Skinner, and the literary merits of their
          novel.

S5   Rossman, Charles. "THE BOY IN THE BUSH in the Lawrence
     Canon." In D.H. LAWRENCE: THE MAN WHO LIVED. Ed. Robert
     B. Partlow and Harry T. Moore. Pp. 185-94. See G92.
          Argues for a greater acceptance of the novel,
          unfairly disclaimed because it is a collabor-
          ation, and suggests DHL's significant imprint
          on the portrait of its hero, Jack Grant.

S6   Skinner, Mollie L. "D.H. Lawrence and THE BOY IN THE BUSH."
     MEANJIN, 9 (1950), 260-63.
          DHL's collaborator's account of their collabor-
          ation. Reprinted in F123 (extract) and F149.

T. STUDIES OF *THE PLUMED SERPENT* (1926)

The following section is subdivided into two parts: i. Books
and Essay Collections on PS; and ii. Critical Articles or Chapters on PS.

A textual edition of PS, in progress, will be published in THE
CAMBRIDGE EDITION (Bl--ed. L.D. Clark).

For bibliographical information on PS, see Roberts (E39) and
Sagar (E40), and, for biographical backgrounds to the novel,
see Moore (F112), Murry (F121), and Nehls (F123). The numerous
memoirs of DHL's sojourn in the American Southwest should also
be consulted (see, particularly, F6, F20, F22, F23, F49, F54,
F59, F91, F95, F106, F117, and F152).

For additional critical commentaries and information on PS, see
the following books, in section G above: Alldritt (G3), Arnold
(G7), Beal (G9), Boadella (G12), Bredsdorff (G13), Cavitch (G16),
Clark (G17), Clarke (G18), Colin (G19), Cowan (G22), Daleski
(G24), Dix (G29), Donnerstag (G30), Draper (G33), Freeman (G40),
Gottwald (G46), Gregory (G47), Hess (G50), Hobsbaum (G51), Hoch-
man (G52), Holderness (G55), Hough (G56), Howe (G58), Inniss
(G60), Jaensson (G61), Johnsson (G63), Kermode (G65), Leavis
(G68, G69), Marnat (G72), Meyers (G73), Michaels-Tonks (G74),
Miles (G76), Moore (G80), Moynahan (G83), Murry (G85), Nahal
(G86), Negriolli (G87), Niven (G89), Panichas (G91), Pinion
(G95), Potter (G98), Prasad (G99), Pritchard (G101), Reul (G103),
Sagar (G104), Sanders (G106), Seillière (G107), Slade (G111),
Spilka (G114), Stoll (G116), Tedlock (G118), Tindall (G120),
Vivas (G121), Weidner (G122), Wesslau (G124), West (G125),
Wickramasinghe (G127), Worthen (G128), Yudhishtar (G130); the
following critical articles, in section H above: Albright (H5),
Baker (H22), Bedient (H33), Bentley (H37), Clark (H65), Corn-
well (H76), Dervin (H89), Forster (H120), Garcia (H126), Gindin
(H136), Goonetilleke (H147), Green (H152), Gunn (H159), Harri-
son (H169), John (H196), Kiely (H205), Lea (H215), Leaver (H216),
Lerner (H221), Liscano Velutini (H225), MacDonald (H230), Maes-
Jelinek (H232), Martin (H236), Meyers (H249), Millett (H255),   •
Pinto (H290), Quennell (H300), Rossman (H319), Scott (H333),
Stewart (H361), Tindall (H379), Vickery (H393), Wilt (H417),

Winegarten (H418), Woodcock (H421); and the following studies,
entered in other sections of this bibliography: Humma (V137),
Gilbert (Y1), Marshall (Y3), Rexroth (Y50), Gilbert (AB4), and
Kim (AC5).

T, i.   Books and Essay Collections on THE PLUMED SERPENT

T1   Clark, L.D.   DARK NIGHT OF THE BODY: D.H. LAWRENCE'S *THE
     PLUMED SERPENT*.   Austin: Univ. of Texas Press, 1964.
          Informative study of the sources of PS and the
          alien culture it reconstructs, illustrating sub-
          stantial and unrecognized realistic elements in
          the work.   DHL's synthesis of this realism and
          his mysticism (cf. St. John of the Cross), his
          union of doctrine and art, ultimately determines
          PS's integration theme, its circular symbolism,
          and its spiral structure.   While Clark does not
          entirely convince the reader of PS's "bril-
          liance," he does argue persuasively for a con-
          siderably higher critical estimate of this dis-
          turbing book.

T2   Schickele, René.   LIEBE UND ÄRGERNIS DES D.H. LAWRENCE [THE
     LOVE AND SORROW OF D.H. LAWRENCE].   Amsterdam: Allert de
     Lange, n.d. [1934].
          On KANGAROO and PS.   For annotation see R2.

T, ii.   Critical Articles or Chapters on THE PLUMED SERPENT

For additional, foreign-language articles on PS, see the following entries in Appendix A: Filippi (AA142), Mori (AA224),
Okumura (AA240), and Soulie-Lapeyre (AA271).

T3   Apter, T.E.   "Let's Hear What the Male Chauvinist is Say-
     ing: THE PLUMED SERPENT."   In LAWRENCE AND WOMEN.   Ed. Anne
     Smith.   Pp. 156-77.   See G112.
          PS a sensitive and sane analysis of the inade-
          quacy of sexual stereotypes, showing the "depth"
          lacking in so many of the feminist critics who
          share DHL's premise, yet attack him.   See H255.

T4   Baldwin, Alice. "The Structure of the Coatl Symbol in THE
       PLUMED SERPENT." STYLE, 5 (1971), 138-50.
                The novel and its symbols fail to achieve bal-
                ance.

T5   Ballin, Micheal. "Lewis Spence and the Myth of Quetzal-
       coatl in D.H. Lawrence's THE PLUMED SERPENT." DHLR, 13
       (1980), 63-78.
                DHL's incorporation of elements of the Egyptian
                Osiris myth derived from articles on Atlantis
                and Mexico, familiar to DHL. See G27.

T6   Baron, Carl E. "Forster on Lawrence." In E.M. FORSTER:
       A HUMAN EXPLORATION: CENTENARY ESSAYS. Ed. G.K. Das and
       John Beer. New York: New York Univ. Press, 1979. Pp.
       186-95.
                Surveys and clarifies Forster's responses
                to DHL, noting his admiration for THE PLUMED
                SERPENT, a novel resembling in its cultural
                themes his own A PASSAGE TO INDIA (1924).

T7   Brotherston, J.G. "Revolution and the Ancient Literature
       of Mexico, For D.H. Lawrence and Antonin Artaud." TCL,
       18 (1972), 181-89.
                DHL's and Artaud's comparable responses to post-
                revolutionary Mexico (e.g., their rejection of
                Marxism; viz. Artaud's 1936 articles on Mexico,
                reprinted in MÉXICO [1962]).

T8   Clark, L.D. "The Making of a Novel: The Search for the
       Definitive Text of D.H. Lawrence's THE PLUMED SERPENT."
       In VOICES FROM THE SOUTHWEST: A GATHERING IN HONOR OF
       LAWRENCE CLARK POWELL. Ed. Donald C. Dickinson, et al.
       Flagstaff, Ariz: Northland Press, 1976. Pp. 113-30.
                History of the "conception, composition, and
                publication" of PS, with comparisons between
                its unpublished first draft ("Quetzalcoatl")
                and its final version.

T9   Diaz de León, Martha. "El México visto por D.H. Lawrence."
       CUADERNOS AMERICANOS, 24, No. 2 (1965), 262-83.
                Interesting Mexican response to DHL's vision
                of her land and people in PS. [In Spanish.]

T10   Glicksberg, Charles I. "Myth in Lawrence's Fiction." In
       MODERN LITERARY PERSPECTIVISM. Dallas, Tex.: Southern
       Methodist Univ. Press, 1970. Pp. 139-48.
                Mostly on DHL's narrative technique and use of
                myth in PS.

T11   Guttmann, Allen. "D.H. Lawrence: The Politics of Irration-
      ality." WSCL, 5 (1964), 151-63.
            On PS and KANGAROO. For annotation see R9.

T12   Harris, Janice H. "The Moulting of THE PLUMED SERPENT: A
      Study of the Relationship between the Novel and Three Con-
      temporary Tales." MLQ, 39 (1978), 154-68.
            DHL's increasing concern with and variations
            upon the questing woman figure in "The Woman
            Who Rode Away," "St. Mawr," "The Princess,"
            and principally PS.

T13   Jones, Keith. "Two Morning Stars." WR, 17 (1952), 15-25.
            DHL achieves in the art of PS, a novel about
            human communion, "a more immediate and endur-
            ing contact" with his fellow man than he was
            able to achieve elsewhere in his fiction or
            in his life.

T14   Kessler, Jascha. "Descent in Darkness: The Myth of THE
      PLUMED SERPENT." In A D.H. LAWRENCE MISCELLANY. Ed.
      Harry T. Moore. Pp. 239-61. See G81.
            PS centered around Kate's rebirth, her discov-
            ery of a figurative fountain of youth.

T15   Meyers, Jeffrey. "THE PLUMED SERPENT and the Mexican Rev-
      olution." JML, 4 (1974), 55-72.
            DHL "attempts to transcend and redeem" recent
            Mexican history (here surveyed) through myth-
            ology in PS.

T16   Michener, Richard L. "Apocalyptic Mexico: THE PLUMED SER-
      PENT and THE POWER AND THE GLORY." UR, 34 (1968), 313-16.
            Suggests "germane points of comparison and con-
            trast" and "ultimately antagonistic resolutions"
            in the "social criticisms and ethical solutions"
            of DHL's PS and Greene's novel (1940).

T17   Moore, Harry T. "THE PLUMED SERPENT: Vision and Language."
      In D.H. LAWRENCE. Ed. Mark Spilka. Pp. 61-71. See G115.
            Superficial critical comments, with remarks on
            recent criticism of PS and its place in DHL's
            career.

T18   Moravia, Alberto. "Il mito del Messico" ["The Myth of
      Mexico"]. IL CORRIERE DELLA SERA, 20 Nov. 1966, p. 3.
            Finds DHL's presentation of Mexican religion
            in PS inconsistent with the harsh reality of

Aztec cruelty (also noted by DHL in MORNINGS
IN MEXICO [1927], but evidently not to Moravia's knowledge).

T19   Porter, Katherine Anne. "Quetzalcoatl." 1926. In THE
DAYS BEFORE. New York: Harcourt, 1952. Pp. 262-67.
Sees PS as DHL's failed attempt to find "a cen-
ter and meaning to life" in an alien race, his
pretentious invasion of the mystery of an alien
culture "that remained a mystery to him." Porter has never much cared for DHL (also see U9
and U57).

T20   Powell, Lawrence Clark. "THE PLUMED SERPENT." In SOUTH-
WEST CLASSICS: THE CREATIVE LITERATURE OF THE ARID LANDS,
ESSAYS ON THE BOOKS AND THEIR WRITERS. Los Angeles: Ward
Ritchie, 1974. Pp. 81-91.
DHL's experiences in the southwest briefly re-
counted and all the southwest fictions briefly
described (chiefly PS).

T21   Ramey, Frederick. "Words in the Service of Silence: Preverbal Language in Lawrence's THE PLUMED SERPENT." MFS,
27 (1981-82), 613-21.
DHL's creation of a "language of myth in his
attempt to find the verbal structures that
would allow him the greatest expressiveness
in the presentation of preverbal experience."

T22   Ruderman, Judith G. "Rekindling the 'Father-Spark': Law-
rence's Ideal of Leadership in THE LOST GIRL and THE PLUMED
SERPENT." DHLR, 13 (1980), 239-59.
For annotation see P6.

T23   Tindall, William York. "Introduction." In Lawrence's THE
PLUMED SERPENT (QUETZALCOATL). New York: Knopf, 1951. Pp.
v-xv.
Indispensable, controversial argument for con-
sidering DHL's synthesis of myth and symbol in
PS "one of the great creations of our time."

T24   Veitch, Douglas W. "D.H. Lawrence's Elusive Mexico." In
LAWRENCE, GREENE AND LOWRY: THE FICTIONAL LANDSCAPE OF
MEXICO. Waterloo, Ont.: Wilfrid Laurier Univ. Press, 1978.
Pp. 14-57.
DHL's symbolic exploitation of the Mexican
culture and setting. Kate's "mythic journey"
traced through six "landscapes."

T25 Vickery, John B. "THE PLUMED SERPENT and the Eternal Paradox." CRITICISM, 5 (1963), 119-34.
> Man's paradoxical states of being not the weakness of the novel; they are its theme.

T26 -----. "THE PLUMED SERPENT and the Reviving God." JML, 2 (1972), 505-32.
> Kate's attraction toward and repulsion from the Mexican myths are characteristic of Frazer's ambivalence toward the myth-rituals he describes (i.e., scientific curiosity and enlightened scorn), in THE GOLDEN BOUGH (3rd ed. 1907-15).

T27 Walker, Ronald G. INFERNAL PARADISE: MEXICO AND THE MODERN ENGLISH NOVEL. Berkeley: Univ. of California Press, 1978. Pp. 21-104 and passim.
> Surveys DHL's experiences in and attitudes toward the American Southwest and Mexico, his essays and stories involving Mexico, and, at length, PS as DHL's "Mexican nightmare."

T28 Waters, Frank. "Quetzalcoatl Versus D.H. Lawrence's PLUMED SERPENT." WESTERN AMERICAN LITERATURE, 3 (1968), 103-13.
> DHL's fundamental misunderstanding of his mythic material (e.g., Quetzalcoatl an Aztec vulgarization of a Toltec myth).

T29 Wiley, Paul L. "D.H. Lawrence." ConL, 13 (1972), 245-54.
> Review essay on three studies of DHL's fiction, noting the increasing interest in PS in recent criticism and focusing on Cavitch's, Cowan's, and Hochman's ultimate judgment of the "worth of the novel." See G16, G22, and G52.

U. STUDIES OF *LADY CHATTERLEY'S LOVER* (1928)

The following section is subdivided into two parts: i. Books and Essay Collections on LCL; and ii. Critical Articles or Chapters on LCL.

A textual edition of LCL with DHL's companion essay "A Propos of LADY CHATTERLEY'S LOVER," in progress, will be published in THE CAMBRIDGE EDITION (Bl--ed. Michael Squires). Also see the two earlier manuscript versions of LCL, THE FIRST LADY CHATTERLEY (A12) and JOHN THOMAS AND LADY JANE (A13).

For bibliographical information on LCL, see Roberts (E39), Sagar (E40), and Tedlock (E49), and, for biographical backgrounds to the novel, see Aldington (F1), Ehrenzweig (F51), MacKensie (F98), Moore (F110, F112), Murry (F120, F121), and Nehls (F123).

For additional critical commentaries and information on LCL, see the following books, in section G above: Alldritt (G3), Beal (G9), Becker (G10), Cavitch (G16), Clark (G17), Clarke (G18), Colin (G19), Daleski (G24), Dix (G29), Draper (G33), Ebbatson (G35), Freeman (G40), Gottwald (G46), Gregory (G47), Hobsbaum (G51), Hochman (G52), Holderness (G55), Hough (G56), Howe (G58), Inniss (G60), Jaensson (G61), Jarrett-Kerr (G62), Johnsson (G63), Kermode (G65), Meyers (G73), Miles (G76), Miller (G77), Moore (G80), Moynahan (G83), Nahal (G86), Negriolli (G87), Nin (G88), Niven (G89), Pinion (G95), Potter (G98), M. Prasad (G99), S. Prasad (G100), Pritchard (G101), Reul (G103), Sagar (G104), Sanders (G106), Seillière (G107), Slade (G111), Spilka (G114), Stoll (G116), Tedlock (G118), Vivas (G121), Weidner (G122), Weiss (G123), Wesslau (G124), West (G125), Wettern (G126), Worthen (G128), Yudhishtar (G130); the following critical articles, in section H above: Albright (H5), Appleman (H17), Beauvoir (H32), Bedient (H33), Bentley (H37), Black (H42), Cook (H74), Cowan (H78), Donoghue (H93), Eagleton and Pierce (H98), Eagleton (H99), Ehrstine (H103), Garcia (H126), Gill (H134), Glicksberg (H141), Goode (H144), Gutierrez (H160), Hardy (H164), Hinz (H182, H183), Hoffman (H185), Huxley (H192), John (H196), Kinkead-Weekes (H206), Klein (H210), Knight (H211), Lerner (H221), Levine (H222),

Maes-Jelinek (H232), Millett (H255), Powys (H294), Pritchard (H298), Quennell (H300), Rossman (H319), Spilka (H351-H353), Stewart (H361); and the following studies, entered in other sections of this bibliography: Haegert (N46), Murry (V104), and Gilbert (Y1).

U, i. Books and Essay Collections on LADY CHATTERLEY'S LOVER

Also see Napolitano's *L'AMANTE DI LADY CHATTERLEY O DEL PUDORE* (AA30), Kim's A STUDY OF D.H. LAWRENCE (AC6), and Squires' forthcoming textual study of LCL (see U66, below).

U1   D.H. LAWRENCE REVIEW. 11 (1978), 199-271, 294-300.
     "LADY CHATTERLEY and Eros."
           Collects four articles and two notes on erotic
           themes in DHL's major works, principally LCL.
           Includes N46, U9, U30, U63, and U68.

U2   Orliac, Jehanne d'. LADY CHATTERLEY'S SECOND HUSBAND.
     Trans. Warre Bradley Wells. New York: McBride, 1935.
           Flattery in the form of imitation. D'Orliac's
           continuation of LCL has Constance (divorced)
           and Mellors (divorce refused) fleeing to France,
           and further explores the psychological and so-
           cial significance of their relationship. The
           most significant of the several adaptations,
           continuations, and parodies of LCL (see A11).
           Also see AA35.

U3   Rolph, C.H., ed. THE TRIAL OF LADY CHATTERLEY. Harmonds-
     worth, Engl.: Penguin, 1961.
           A brief historical introduction followed by a
           journalistic transcript of the 1960 trial (Re-
           gina vs. Penguin Books Ltd.). Prominent among
           the witnesses for the defense are Graham Hough,
           Joan Bennett, Rebecca West, Vivian de Sola
           Pinto, E.M. Forster, and Walter Allen. Con-
           spicuously absent, however, is F.R. Leavis,
           for reasons he details in U41 below. Also see
           U8, U11, U13, U41, U45, U49, U50, U58, U64,
           and AA23.

U, ii. Critical Articles or Chapters on LADY CHATTERLEY'S LOVER

For additional, foreign-language articles on LCL, see the fol-
lowing entries in Appendix A: Konishi (AA23), Lucia (AA27),
Gandon (AA66), Lagerkrantz (AA79), Arellano-Salgado (AA107),
Fluchère (AA144), Gillet (AA155), Jaloux (AA169), Kuramochi
(AA194, AA195), Mauriac (AA214), Nardi (AA227), Okumura (AA243),
Orsini (AA246), Radica (AA251), Sorani (AA270), and Yanada
(AA291).

U4   Adams, Elsie B. "A 'Lawrentian' Novel by Bernard Shaw."
     DHLR, 2 (1969), 245-53.
          Notes parallel situations in Shaw's CASHEL BY-
          RON'S PROFESSION (1885-86) and LCL.

U5   Amorós, Andrés. "Vitalismo Sexual." In INTRODUCCIÓN A LA
     NOVELA CONTEMPORÁNEA. 1966. 2nd ed. Salamanca, Spain:
     Ediciones Anaya, 1971. Pp. 201-06.
          DHL's and Henry Miller's attempts to present
          human sexuality in their fiction (LCL and Mil-
          ler's "tropics" novels), in "una manera equi-
          librada y comprensiva." [In Spanish.]

U6   Balbert, Peter H. "The Loving of Lady Chatterley: D.H.
     Lawrence and the Phallic Imagination." In D.H. LAWRENCE:
     THE MAN WHO LIVED. Ed. Robert B. Partlow and Harry T.
     Moore. Pp. 143-58. See G92.
          DHL's primary preoccupation in LCL not Connie's
          fulfillment, but, as his title suggests, the
          "modes of belief and manners of sex which men
          display in their various ways of 'loving' Lady
          Chatterley."

U7   Beck, Rudolf. "Die drei Versionen von LADY CHATTERLEY'S
     LOVER." ANGLIA, 96 (1978), 409-29.
          Examines the transformations in DHL's charac-
          ters, narrative technique, and style in LCL's
          three versions. [In German.]

U8   Bedford, Sybille. "The Last Trial of Lady Chatterley."
     ESQUIRE, 55 (Apr. 1961), 132-36, 138, 141-55.
          Extended report of the British censorship
          trial. See U3.

U9   Blanchard, Lydia. "Women Look at Lady Chatterley: Feminine
     Views of the Novel." DHLR, 11 (1978), 246-59.
          Surveys LCL's disfavor among women critics (e.g.,
          Virginia Woolf, Katherine Anne Porter, Anais Nin,
          Joyce Carol Oates, and others). See U1.

U10   Bradbury, Malcolm. POSSIBILITIES: ESSAYS ON THE STATE
       OF THE NOVEL. New York: Oxford Univ. Press, 1973. Pp.
       81-90.
              The liberties of LCL one aspect of the "Pha-
              ses of Modernism."

U11   Bryan, Frederick van Pelt. "United States District Court
       Decision on LADY CHATTERLEY'S LOVER." In SEX, LITERATURE,
       AND CENSORSHIP. Ed. Harry T. Moore. Pp. 122-28. See
       B26.
              Expresses no doubt about DHL's "honesty and
              sincerity of purpose, artistic integrity and
              lack of intention to appeal to prurient inter-
              est" in LCL. Extracts reprinted in first un-
              expurgated American edition of LCL (New York:
              Grove Press, 1959). See A11.

U12   Burns, Wayne. "LADY CHATTERLEY'S LOVER: A Pilgrim's Prog-
       ress for Our Time." PAUNCH, No. 26 (1966), pp. 16-33.
              LCL a poignant and masterful statement of DHL's
              central statement, throughout his fiction: "be
              human in our 'insentient iron world.'" See G94.

U12a   Charney, Maurice. "Sexuality and the Life Force: LADY
       CHATTERLEY'S LOVER and TROPIC OF CANCER." In SEXUAL
       FICTION. London: Methuen, 1981. Pp. 93-112.
              Discusses DHL's and Miller's differing treat-
              ments of the same theme: the recovery of the
              instinctual life through "the fructifying
              power of sex," in LCL and TROPIC OF CANCER
              (1934).

U13   Cox, C.B., et al. "Symposium: Pornography and Obscenity."
       CritQ, 3 (1961), 99-122.
              Post-LCL trial discussion of obscenity in lit-
              erature, only generally related to the novel.
              Includes editorial comment, a survey of the
              legal problems involved, and individual re-
              marks by Donald Davie, Martin Jarrett-Kerr,
              and C.S. Lewis. Also see U3.

U14   Craig, G. Armour. "D.H. Lawrence on Thinghood and Self-
       hood." MR, 1 (1959), 56-60.
              DHL's calculated exploitation of traditional
              fictional conventions.

U15   Croft-Cooke, Rupert. "At Sea." In THE WINTRY SEA. Lon-
       don: Allen, 1964. Pp. 166-78.
              DHL's resentment of the upper-classes, "para-
              noid" obsession with himself, pathetically

wish-fulfilling identification with the sex-
ually potent Mellors, and humorlessness in
his ultimately "trivial" and "tiresome" LCL,
a "book for vapid teenagers."

U16 Delavenay, Émile. "Les Trois Amants de Lady Chatterley."
EA, 29 (1976), 46-63.
The conflict between DHL as "romancier" and as
"théoricien," between his art and his propaganda, which cripples the second version of
LCL, is resolved in the final version as DHL
abandons his social and moral schemes, even
his conception of the new ego of character,
in his creation of Mellors. [In French.]

U17 Doheny, John. "Lady Chatterley and Her Lover." WEST COAST
REVIEW, 8, No. 3 (1974), 51-56.
Finds the novel's second draft in several ways
superior to its final version.

U18 Doherty, Gerald. "Connie and the Chakras: Yogic Patterns
in D.H. Lawrence's LADY CHATTERLEY'S LOVER." DHLR, 13
(1980), 79-93.
Yoga symbolism in the "seven love-encounters"
in LCL. See G27.

U19 Ebbatson, Roger. "Thomas Hardy and Lady Chatterley."
ARIEL, 8, No. 2 (1977), 85-95.
Argues influence of Hardy's TWO ON A TOWER
(1882) on the plot situation in LCL.

U20 Friedland, Ronald. "Introduction." In Lawrence's LADY
CHATTERLEY'S LOVER [Orioli text]. New York: Bantam,
1968. Pp. xiii-xxiv.
Good, brief account of LCL's composition and
"painful" publishing history. Note: This Bantam edition also includes a slight "Preface"
by Lawrence Durrell (pp. vii-xi) and a reprint
of DHL's "A Propos of LADY CHATTERLEY'S LOVER"
(pp. 329-60; see A72).

U21 Gill, Stephen. "The Composite World: Two Versions of LADY
CHATTERLEY'S LOVER." EIC, 21 (1971), 347-64.
Weaknesses of the final version not present in
the first draft.

U22   Gomes, Eugênio. "D.H. Lawrence." In D.H. LAWRENCE E
      OUTROS. Pôrto Alegre, Brazil: Livraria do Globo, 1937.
      Pp. 7-39.
          Describes DHL's completed social vision and
          analysis of human sexuality and psychology
          in LCL. [In Portugese.]

U23   Gordon, David J. "Sex and Language in D.H. Lawrence."
      TCL, 27 (1981), 362-75.
          On WL and LCL. For annotation see N42.

U24   Gregor, Ian, and Brian Nicholas. "The Novel as Prophecy:
      LADY CHATTERLEY'S LOVER." In THE MORAL AND THE STORY.
      London: Faber, 1962. Pp. 217-48.
          Ethical questions in the novel.

U25   Hanlon, Lindley. "LADY CHATTERLEY'S LOVER (1928), D.H.
      Lawrence, Marc Allegret, 1955: Sensuality and Simplifi-
      cation." In THE ENGLISH NOVEL AND THE MOVIES. Ed. Mi-
      chael Klein and Gillian Parker. New York: Ungar, 1981.
      Pp. 268-78.
          Allegret's "delicate" adaptation of LCL sub-
          limates the novel's eroticism and elegantly
          translates DHL's themes into visual symbolism.

U26   Hartogs, Renatus (with Hans Fantel). "Intercourse with
      Lady Chatterley." In FOUR LETTER WORD GAMES: THE PSYCHO-
      LOGY OF OBSCENITY. New York: M. Evans and Delacorte Press,
      1967. Pp. 11-24.
          A discussion of DHL's liberating use of four-
          letter words in LCL opens a psychiatrist's en-
          tertaining and perceptive study of the cultural
          significance of profanity and obscenity.

U27   Hays, Peter L. THE LIMPING HERO: GROTESQUES IN LITERATURE.
      New York: New York Univ. Press, 1971. Pp. 35-38, 77-79,
      and passim.
          The emasculated hero in DHL (particularly in
          "The Man Who Died" and LCL).

U28   Henriot, Émile. "Dire ou ne pas dire." LES NOUVELLES
      LITTÉRAIRES, No. 490 (5 Mar. 1932), p. 1.
          DHL shares the experience of contemporary op-
          probrium felt by de Sade, Louys, Flaubert, and
          Malraux. [In French.]

U29   Henry, G.B. McK. "Carrying On: LADY CHATTERLEY'S LOVER."
      CR, 10 (1967), 46-62.
          LCL not successful, nor a "triumphant affirma-
          tion of life," yet DHL does make "tenderness" a
          viable alternative. Reprinted in G5.

U30   Higdon, David Leon. "Bertha Coutts and Bertha Mason: A
        Speculative Note." DHLR, 11 (1978), 294-96.
                Mellors' wife based on Bertha Mason, Roches-
                ter's mad wife in JANE EYRE (1847). See U1.

U31   -----. "D.H. Lawrence's JOHN THOMAS AND LADY JANE: 'the
        line of fulfillment.'" In TIME AND ENGLISH FICTION.
        Totowa, N.J.: Rowman and Littlefield, 1977. Pp. 23-29.
                Examines the second version of LCL as an il-
                lustration of DHL's characteristic use of
                "linear time" in his fiction.

U32   Hinz, Evelyn J. "Pornography, Novel, Mythic Narrative:
        The Three Versions of LADY CHATTERLEY'S LOVER." MODERN-
        IST STUDIES, 3 (1979), 35-47.
                Each version of LCL written in essentially a
                different literary genre.

U33   Holbrook, David. "The Fiery Hill: LADY CHATTERLEY'S
        LOVER." In THE QUEST FOR LOVE. London: Methuen, 1964.
        Pp. 192-366.
                Crotchety study of the love "need" in Chaucer
                and Shakespeare, followed by an extended and
                embarrassed reading of DHL's "bravest book"
                and "greatest falsification."

U33a   Humma, John B. "The Interpenetrating Metaphor: Nature
        and Myth in LADY CHATTERLEY'S LOVER." PMLA, 98 (1983),
        77-86.
                Comparisons with the earlier novels and with
                LCL's second version demonstrate DHL's inno-
                vative use of "interpenetrating" imagery and
                increasing use of myth, both to reinforce his
                central themes and to provide structural un-
                ity in LCL's final version.

U34   Jackson, Dennis. "The 'Old Pagan Vision': Myth and Rit-
        ual in LADY CHATTERLEY'S LOVER." DHLR, 11 (1978), 260-71.
                Like DHL's later works generally, but not as
                explicitly, LCL contains numerous allusions
                to myth and ritual (cf. Frazer's THE GOLDEN
                BOUGH [3rd ed., 1907-15]). See U1.

U35   Jones, David A. "The Third Unrealized Wonder: The Re-
        ality of Relation in D.H. Lawrence and Martin Buber."
        RELIGION IN LIFE, 44 (1975), 178-87.
                On WL and LCL. For annotation see N54.

U36 Kayser, Rudolf. "D.H. Lawrence und sein erotisches Evan-
     gelium." NEUE RUNDSCHAU, 42, pt. 1 (1931), 569-70.
         The infernal eroticism of Joyce's ULYSSES
         (1922) contrasted to the evangelical anti-
         Puritanism of DHL's "erotische Philosophie
         [und] soziale Kritik" in LCL. [In German.]

U37 Kazin, Alfred. "LADY CHATTERLEY in America." 1959. In
     CONTEMPORARIES. Boston: Little, Brown, 1962. Pp. 105-13.
         DHL's healthy veneration of love contrasted
         to the contemporary preoccupation with sex.

U38 King, Dixie. "The Influence of Forster's MAURICE on LADY
     CHATTERLEY'S LOVER." ConL, 23 (1982), 65-82.
         On dubious grounds, argues that DHL read For-
         ster's 1913 novel in manuscript (it was first
         published in 1971), identified strongly with
         its homosexual theme, and "drew on it heavily
         as a source" for LCL.

U39 Knoepflmacher, U.C. "The Rival Ladies: Mrs. Ward's LADY
     CONNIE and Lawrence's LADY CHATTERLEY'S LOVER." VS, 4
     (1960), 141-58.
         LCL an inversion of Victorian fictional and
         ethical conventions (cf. Ward's novel,1916).

U40 Lacher, Walter. "David Herbert Lawrence." In L'AMOUR ET
     LE DIVIN. Geneva: Perret-Gentil, 1961. Pp. 63-102.
         On DHL's treatment of love in his writings
         (cf. Marceline Desbordes-Valmore, Anna de
         Noailles, and Charles Morgan). [In French.]

U41 Leavis, F.R. "The New Orthodoxy." SPECTATOR, 206 (1961),
     229-30.
         LCL "a bad novel" which should be published
         without expurgation since it "serves as a foil
         to his successful and great art" (an "essen-
         tial" point, overlooked by the defense in the
         censorship trial [1960]; see U3). Reprinted
         in G20.

U42 Littlewood, J.C.F. "Lawrence, Last of the English." THEO-
     RIA, No. 7 (1955), pp. 79-92.
         DHL unappreciated, especially in America, for
         his "intense realization of the fineness of
         the old English civilization--of the qualities
         it fostered--[which] showed itself [in his]
         predominating concern for the future" (chiefly
         LCL).

U43   McIntosh, Angus. "A Four-Letter Word in LADY CHATTERLEY'S
      LOVER." In PATTERNS OF LANGUAGE: PAPERS IN GENERAL, DE-
      SCRIPTIVE, AND APPLIED LINGUISTICS. By McIntosh and Mi-
      chael A.K. Halliday. London: Longmans, 1966. Pp. 151-64.
          Linguist's analysis of DHL's use of the word
          "know" (293 instances in LCL).

U44   MacKenzie, Compton. LITERATURE IN MY TIME. London: Rich
      and Cowan, 1933. Pp. 189-98.
          Despite early promise, DHL "unbalanced" by the
          time he wrote LCL, a novel "unworthy of Law-
          rence's genius."

U45   -----. "The Case of LADY CHATTERLEY'S LOVER." In ON MORAL
      COURAGE. London: Collins, 1962. Pp. 120-38.
          Summarizes the testimony for the defense in
          the censorship trial (1960) and argues that,
          while DHL's supporters showed "moral courage"
          in testifying, he himself showed little in
          writing the book (a petty attempt to insult
          Bloomsbury and to rival Joyce). Also see F98
          and U3.

U46   Malraux, André. "D.H. Lawrence and Eroticism." 1932.
      Trans. Bert M-P. Leefmans. In FROM THE *N.R.F.*: AN IMAGE
      OF THE TWENTIETH CENTURY FROM THE PAGES OF THE *NOUVELLE
      REVUE FRANÇAISE*. Ed. Justin O'Brien. New York: Farrar,
      Straus and Cudahy, 1958. Pp. 194-98.
          With DHL the development of eroticism in West-
          ern thought reaches completion: it "ceases to
          be the *expression* of the individual [and] be-
          comes a state of soul, a condition of life."
          Originally a preface to Roger Cornaz's French
          translation of LCL (1932). Also translated by
          Charles K. Colhoun in CRITERION, 12 (1933),
          215-19, and reprinted in G34. Also see G72
          and AA207.

U47   Mandel, Jerome. "Medieval Romance and LADY CHATTERLEY'S
      LOVER." DHLR, 10 (1977), 20-33.
          DHL's adaptation of the Tristan and Isolde
          legend.

U48   Mandel, Oscar. "Ignorance and Privacy." ASch, 29 (1960),
      509-19.
          LCL's effect the opposite of DHL's intention
          (e.g., DHL's explicitness, in fact, removes
          the senses of awe, importance, discovery, and
          mystery from sexuality). See a response by
          Jean Giles, ASch, 30 (1961), 454, 456.

U49   Marcuse, Ludwig. "LADY CHATTERLEY'S LOVER." In OBSCENE:
      THE HISTORY OF AN INDIGNATION. Trans. Karen Gershon. Lon-
      don: MacGibbon and Kee, 1965. Pp. 215-54.
            Not seen. See AA81.

U50   [Michel-] Michot, Paulette. "D.H. Lawrence: A Belated
      Apology." RLV, 27 (1961), 290-305.
            Surveys England's fitful reacknowledgement of
            DHL (chiefly re: the LCL trial, 1960; see U3).

U51   Moore, Harry T. "Afterword: LADY CHATTERLEY'S LOVER: The
      Novel as Ritual." In Lawrence's LADY CHATTERLEY'S LOVER.
      New York: New American Library, 1962. Pp. 285-99.
            DHL the "great continuator" of the medieval
            romance tradition and LCL the "only important
            romance of the twentieth century." See below.

U52   -----. "LADY CHATTERLEY'S LOVER as Romance." 1959.   In
      A D.H. LAWRENCE MISCELLANY. Ed. Harry T. Moore. Pp. 262-
      64. See G81.
            LCL a great modern variation upon the "Sleep-
            ing Beauty" motif. Assimilated into essay
            above. Reprinted in H257.

U53   Murry, John Middleton. "The Doctrine of D.H. Lawrence."
      1929. In his D.H. LAWRENCE (TWO ESSAYS). Pp. 9-15.
      See G84.
            The "world is not fit for" DHL's "most 'appal-
            ling' book." LCL "not merely obscene but non-
            sense as well." Reprinted in F120 and G34.

U54   Ober, William B. "Lady Chatterley's What?" In BOSWELL'S
      CLAP, AND OTHER ESSAYS: MEDICAL ANALYSES OF LITERARY MEN'S
      AFFLICTIONS. Carbondale: Southern Illinois Univ. Press,
      1979. Pp. 89-117.
            Relates DHL's treatment of love in LCL to his
            psychosexual development and impulses, and his
            final illness.

U55   Ocampo, Victoria. "El hombre que murió (D.H. Lawrence)."
      SUR, No. 329 (1971), pp. 33-56.
            On KANGAROO and LCL. For annotation see R16.

U56   Parker, David. "Lawrence and Lady Chatterley: The Teller
      and the Tale." CR, 20 (1978), 31-41.
            First version of LCL more satisfactory, espe-
            cially in presenting DHL's affirmation of mar-
            riage, than the "reductive" final version.

U57   Porter, Katherine Anne. "A Wreath for the Gamekeeper."
       SHENANDOAH, 11 (1959), 3-12.
              Apoplectic attack on DHL's "tiresome," senti-
              mentalized view of obscenity. Also see T19.

U58   Rembar, Charles. THE END OF OBSCENITY: THE TRIALS OF
       LADY CHATTERLEY, TROPIC OF CANCER, AND *FANNY HILL.* New
       York: Random House, 1968. Pp. 59-160.
              Commentary on the American trial of LCL, by a
              participating attorney, with edited trial tran-
              script. Also see U3 and U11.

U59   Schorer, Mark. "On LADY CHATTERLEY'S LOVER." EVERGREEN
       REVIEW, 1 (1957), 149-78.
              Important, laudatory essay on LCL as a tri-
              umphant, moving tragedy of modern society.
              Reprinted as introduction to first unexpur-
              gated American edition (New York: Grove Press,
              1959), pp. ix-xxxix (see A11). Also reprinted
              in H330.

U60   Schotz, Myra Glazer. "For the Sexes: Blake's Hermaphrodite
       in LADY CHATTERLEY'S LOVER." BuR, 24, No. 1 (1978), 17-26.
              LCL's "very Blakean" conception of the tensions
              between sexes.

U61   Scott, James F. "The Emasculation of LADY CHATTERLEY'S
       LOVER." LFQ, 1 (1973), 37-45.
              The unsuccessful, almost "prissy" French screen
              adaptation: L'AMANT DE LADY CHATTERLEY (1955).
              See G70.

U62   Sepčić, Višnja. "The Dialogue in LADY CHATTERLEY'S LOVER."
       STUDIA ROMANICA ET ANGLICA ZAGRABIENSIA, Nos. 29-32 (1970-
       71), pp. 461-80.
              Not seen.

U63   Sheerin, Daniel J. "John Thomas and the King of Glory:
       Two Analogues to D.H. Lawrence's Use of Psalm 24:7 in
       Chapter XIV of LADY CHATTERLEY'S LOVER." DHLR, 11 (1978),
       297-300.
              DHL's "blasphemously droll" allusion to the
              psalms in Mellors' apostrophe to his phallus.
              See U1.

U64 Sparrow, John. "Regina v. Penguin Books Ltd.: An Undis-
     closed Element in the Case"; "Afterthoughts on Regina v.
     Penguin Books, Ltd." 1962. In CONTROVERSIAL ESSAYS. New
     York: Chilmark, 1966. Pp. 40-58; 59-70.
          Influential commentary on DHL's anal eroticism
          (also see G18, G101, H211, and H351). Sparrow
          discovers DHL's veiled description of anal
          intercourse in LCL, contends that "buggery"
          is an important yet "unsuspected element" in
          DHL's "beliefs and feelings about sex," notes
          the prosecution's failure to exploit this as-
          pect of LCL in the censorship trial (see U3),
          and argues that DHL contradicts his own creed
          by doing "dirt" on sex. Sparrow's second es-
          say reflects on the controversy prompted by
          his first.

U65 Spilka, Mark. "On Lawrence's Hostility to Wilful Women:
     The Chatterley Solution." In LAWRENCE AND WOMEN. Ed.
     Anne Smith. Pp. 189-211. See G112.
          DHL threatened by wilfullness in women and in
          himself, until securing his own male identity
          (achieved by the time of and evident in the
          attitudes of LCL).

U66 Squires, Michael. "Editing LADY CHATTERLEY'S LOVER." In
     D.H. LAWRENCE: THE MAN WHO LIVED. Ed. Robert B. Partlow
     and Harry T. Moore. Pp. 62-70. See G92.
          Defends and explains his use of two distinct
          editorial strategies in preparing LCL's text
          for THE CAMBRIDGE EDITION (see B1). Squires's
          study of the evolution of the three stages of
          LCL, THE CREATION OF *LADY CHATTERLEY'S LOVER*,
          is scheduled for publication in 1983, by Johns
          Hopkins Univ. Press (Baltimore).

U67 -----. "LADY CHATTERLEY'S LOVER: 'Pure Seclusion.'" In
     THE PASTORAL NOVEL: STUDIES IN GEORGE ELIOT, THOMAS HARDY,
     AND D.H. LAWRENCE. Charlottesville: Univ. Press of Vir-
     ginia, 1974. Pp. 196-212.
          LCL "more than sexual: it is [a] pastoral...
          novel that embodies the attitudes, techniques,
          and patterns of traditional pastoral romance"
          against a real background of "despair and
          doom."

U68 -----. "New Light on the Gamekeeper in LADY CHATTERLEY'S
LOVER." DHLR, 11 (1978), 234-45.
Four manuscripts of LCL (three versions and
corrected typescript) illustrate DHL's substantial modification of Mellors' character
and the operation of DHL's "critical judgment."
See U1.

U69 Strickland, G.R. "The First LADY CHATTERLEY'S LOVER."
1971. In D.H. LAWRENCE: A CRITICAL STUDY. Ed. Andor
Gomme. Pp. 159-74. See G43.
Argues the earliest draft of the novel far
superior to its final version.

U70 Sullivan, J.P. "Lady Chatterley in Rome." PACIFIC COAST
PHILOLOGY, 15, No. 1 (1980), 53-62.
DHL's creation of the modern archetype for the
sexual woman, anticipated by the emancipated
female in Roman literature (c. 100 B.C.-A.D.
150; Catullus's Lesbia and Horace's Cleopatra).

U71 Tedlock, Ernest W. "The Three Versions of LADY CHATTER-
LEY'S LOVER." In THE FRIEDA LAWRENCE COLLECTION OF MANU-
SCRIPTS. Ed. Tedlock. Pp. 279-316. See E48.
Description, rather than evaluation, of the
"salient variations" among the three versions
of the novel.

U72 Trilling, Lionel. "D.H. Lawrence: A Neglected Aspect."
SYMPOSIUM, 1 (1930), 361-70.
Connections between FANTASIA OF THE UNCONSCIOUS
(A63) and LCL.

U73 Voelker, Joseph C. "The Spirit of No-Place: Elements of
the Classical Ironic Utopia in D.H. Lawrence's LADY CHAT-
TERLEY'S LOVER." MFS, 25 (1979), 223-39.
DHL's conscious employment of the utopia genre
and its conventions in exploring the contrasts
between Wragby Hall ("anti-Utopia") and Wragby
Wood ("Utopia").

U74 Wahl, Jean. "Sur D.H. Lawrence." NOUVELLE REVUE FRAN-
ÇAISE, 42 (1934), 115-21.
On SL and LCL. For annotation see L66.

U75 Welker, Robert H. "Advocate for Eros: Notes on D.H. Lawrence." ASch, 30 (1961), 191-202.
"Offering heterosexual love as the way to salvation for humankind," LCL is "in the best
sense, erotic propaganda."

U76   Widmer, Kingsley. "The Pertinence of Modern Pastoral: The
      Three Versions of LADY CHATTERLEY'S LOVER." SNNTS, 5 (1973),
      298-313.
            DHL's development of a modified pastoral vision
            of the "regenerative love affair" examined in
            the three published versions of LCL.

U77   Wilson, Edmund. "Signs of Life: LADY CHATTERLEY'S LOVER."
      1929.   In THE SHORES OF LIGHT: A LITERARY CHRONICLE OF THE
      TWENTIES AND THIRTIES.   New York: Farrar, Straus and Gir-
      oux, 1952.   Pp. 403-07.
            Early, admiring review of the novel as "one of
            Lawrence's best books," a "parable of post-war
            England." Reprinted in G20 and G53.

V. STUDIES OF THE NOVELLAS AND SHORT STORIES

The following section is subdivided into three parts: i. Books
and Essay Collections on the Novellas and Short Stories; ii.
General Critical Articles or Chapters on the Novellas and
Short Stories; and iii. Studies of Individual Novellas, Short
Stories, and Story Collections (arranged alphabetically, by
title).

For the textual edition of ST. MAWR AND OTHER STORIES, see B8.
Textual editions of the remaining novellas and story collections will be published in THE CAMBRIDGE EDITION (B1) as follows (editors of editions-in-progress identified in parentheses): LOVE AMONG THE HAYSTACKS AND OTHER STORIES, THE PRUSSIAN
OFFICER AND OTHER STORIES (ed. John Worthen), ENGLAND MY ENG-
LAND AND OTHER STORIES, THE LADYBIRD, THE WOMAN WHO RODE AWAY
AND OTHER STORIES, and THE ESCAPED COCK AND OTHER STORIES (ed.
Lindeth Vasey). DHL's unfinished novel, "Mr. Noon," of which
only a brief portion has been published (in B18), is also being edited for THE CAMBRIDGE EDITION by Lindeth Vasey.

For a concordance to the textually unreliable American edition
of THE COMPLETE SHORT STORIES (B4), see Garcia and Karabatsos
(D2).

For bibliographical information on the novellas and short
stories, see Roberts (E39) and Sagar (E40), and, for biographical backgrounds to the shorter fiction, see Moore (F112),
Murry (F121), and Nehls (F123).

For additional, general critical commentaries and information
on the novellas and short stories, see the following books,
in section G above: Beal (G9), Brunsdale (G14), Cavitch (G16),
Clark (G17), Clarke (G18), Corsani (G21), Cowan (G22), Draper
(G33), Ford (G39), Galinsky (G41), Hobsbaum (G51), Holderness
(G55), Hough (G56), Johnsson (G63), Leavis (G68), Michaels-
Tonks (G74), Moore (G80), Moynahan (G83), Nahal (G86), Negri-
olli (G87), Pinion (G95), Pritchard (G101), Reul (G103), Sagar
(G104), Seillière (G107), Seligmann (G108), Sinzelle (G110),
Slade (G111), Tedlock (G118), Weidner (G122), Weiss (G123),
West (G125), Worthen (G128); the following critical articles,

in section H above: Albright (H5), Baker (H22), DiGaetani
(H91), Elsbree (H111), Cox (in H112), Fricker (H123), Gerard
(H130), Goode (H144), Goonetilleke (H147), Harrison (H168),
John (H196), Kaplan (H200), MacDonald (H230), Merivale (H247),
Michaels-Tonks (H250), Millett (H255), Moynahan (H265), Prit-
chard (H298), Rossman (H318, H319), Stewart (H361), Vickery
(H393), Wicker (H406), Wilt (H417); and the following studies,
entered in other sections of this bibliography: Blanchard
(M16) and Gutierrez (Z4).

V, i.   Books and Essay Collections on the Novellas and Short
        Stories

Also see the following books and essay collections on individ-
ual stories and story collections: Cushman's D.H. LAWRENCE AT
WORK (V124--on THE PRUSSIAN OFFICER AND OTHER STORIES), Bar-
rett's and Erskine's FROM FICTION TO FILM: D.H. LAWRENCE'S
"THE ROCKING-HORSE WINNER"(V128), Consolo's D.H. LAWRENCE:
"THE ROCKING-HORSE WINNER" (V130), Mackenzie's "THE FOX"
(AB6), and Kim's A STUDY OF D.H. LAWRENCE (AC6--on "The Man
Who Died").

V1   D.H. LAWRENCE REVIEW. 10 (1977), 215-76.   "Psychoanalytic
     Criticism of the Short Stories."
          Contains four essays applying psychoanalytic
          criticism to selected stories, and a useful
          introduction by the issue's guest editor, Murry
          M. Schwartz, on DHL and psychoanalytic theory
          (see H332).   Includes V17, V68, V110, and V172.

V2   Hsia, Adrian Rue Chun.   D.H. LAWRENCE: DIE CHARAKTERE IN
     DER HANDLUNG UND SPANNUNG SEINER KURZGESCHICHTEN.   Bonn:
     Bouvier, 1968.
          Useful discussion of DHL's fictional techniques
          in his short fiction.   Hsia's introduction sur-
          veys the criticism of DHL's stories, regret-
          ting the tendency of critics to see them as
          offshoots of the novels and arguing that they
          deserve independent consideration, for, partic-
          ularly during the last phase of DHL's career
          (1920 and after), the stories often differ
          considerably in method and content from the
          long fiction.   Hsia examines DHL's story-tell-
          ing under three headings: character (surveying
          the varieties of DHL's narrative techniques

and approaches to characterization), character
and plot (on the interrelations of character,
event, and meaning), and suspense ("Spannung").
This final section, which reviews DHL's skill-
ful manipulation of the reader's curiosity and
creation of suspense through scenery, characterization, narrative technique, and structure,
is a particularly valuable reader's-response
analysis of DHL's fiction. [In German.]

V3   Krishnamurthi, M.G.   D.H. LAWRENCE: TALE AS A MEDIUM.   My-
sore: Rao and Raghavan, 1979.
Commentaries on seventeen stories, grouped into
categories to illustrate some of DHL's characteristic themes: that idealism perverts the development of the individual (e.g., "The Princess"), that self-discovery is "holy" (e.g.,
"The Virgin and the Gipsy"), that man must
strive to achieve "true relatedness" in life
(e.g., "England, My England"), love (e.g., "The
Fox") and marriage (e.g., "The Woman Who Rode
Away"), and that DHL himself achieved a "true
relatedness" through the auto-therapy of his
fiction (e.g., "The Lovely Lady"). Krishnamurthi assumes, via Leavis (see G68), that all
DHL's stories are fundamentally moral statements.

V4   Reuter, Irmgard.   STUDIEN ÜBER DIE PERSÖNLICHKEIT UND DIE
KUNSTFORM VON D.H. LAWRENCE [STUDIES OF D.H. LAWRENCE'S
PERSONALITY AND ART].   Marburg: H. Pöppinghaus, 1934.
Studies of the chief themes and techniques of
DHL's short fiction (with occasional references
to THE WHITE PEACOCK, SL, and WL). Reuter focuses on DHL's treatment of man-woman relations
(the tensions between love and power, communion
and integrity, blood and mind), his use of the
moment ("Augenblick")--the dynamic highpoint in
a love experience (cf. Browning)--his various
stylistic techniques for intensifying meaning
(e.g., specific words, situations, gestures),
and his "impressionismus" (e.g., uses of nuance,
narrative technique, and symbolism). Specific
illustrations drawn from most of the stories
and novellas. [In German.]

V5   Widmer, Kingsley. THE ART OF PERVERSITY: D.H. LAWRENCE'S
     SHORTER FICTION. Seattle: Univ. of Washington Press, 1962.
          Systematic survey of the novellas and tales,
          "Lawrence's central writings," as expressions
          of a profound nihilism. Although the stories
          are consistently suffused with a sense of de-
          struction and negation, Widmer finds them ul-
          timately positive in a perverse way. They il-
          lustrate "the wisdom of...waywardness," the
          negative "ways to his affirmations." Widmer's
          five-chapter explication of the tales illu-
          strates DHL's chief preoccupations: the longing
          for annihilation, the demonic lover, the de-
          structive woman, erotic conflict, and spiritual
          regeneration. Individual interpretations fre-
          quently penetrating, occasionally forced. Ex-
          tracts originally published in G78 and G81.
          Extracts reprinted in L1 and V130. Also see
          H146 and H355.

V, ii.   General Critical Articles or Chapters on the Novellas
         and Short Stories

For additional, general foreign-language articles on the
novellas and short stories, see the following entries in Appendix A: IL VERRI (AA44) and Nogueira (AA88).

V6   Allen, Walter. THE SHORT STORY IN ENGLISH. Oxford: Clar-
     endon, 1981. Pp. 99-109 and passim.
          High praise for DHL as the modern English mas-
          ter of the short story and review of several
          tales, disputing the common contentions that
          the stories are necessarily superior to the
          novels, or simply more constrained treatments
          of the same subject matter.

V7   Amon, Frank. "D.H. Lawrence and the Short Story." In THE
     ACHIEVEMENT OF D.H. LAWRENCE. Ed. Frederick J. Hoffman
     and Harry T. Moore. Pp. 222-34. See G53.
          Theme of initiation in several of the stories.
          Extract reprinted in V130.

V8   Bates, Herbert E. "Lawrence and the Writers of Today."
     In THE MODERN SHORT STORY: A CRITICAL SURVEY. New York:
     Nelson, 1943. Pp. 194-213.
          DHL's "rejection" of form in the short story
          seen in its contemporary context. Dated.

V9   Beachcroft, Thomas O. THE MODEST ART: A SURVEY OF THE
      SHORT STORY IN ENGLISH. New York: Oxford Univ. Press,
      1968. Pp. 204-09.
          DHL "at his own best when the limitations of
          the short-story form force some shape and brev-
          ity on him." Brief survey.

V10   Craig, David. "Love and Society: MEASURE FOR MEASURE and
      Our Own Time." In SHAKESPEARE IN A CHANGING WORLD: ESSAYS.
      Ed. Arnold Kettle. New York: International, 1964. Pp.
      195-216.
          Compares Shakespeare's and DHL's affirmation
          of values (love, fulfillment, personal free-
          dom, integrity) and triumphant rejection of
          "anti-life" forces in MEASURE FOR MEASURE and
          several of DHL's tales ("The Captain's Doll,"
          "Daughters of the Vicar," "St. Mawr," and "The
          Virgin and the Gipsy"). See below.

V11   -----. "Shakespeare, Lawrence, and Sexual Freedom"; "Law-
      rence and Democracy." In THE REAL FOUNDATIONS: LITERATURE
      AND SOCIAL CHANGE. London: Chatto and Windus, 1973. Pp.
      17-38 ; 143-67.
          Comparisons of Shakespeare's and DHL's "free
          and open spirit" toward humanity and sexuality
          (MEASURE FOR MEASURE and several DHL tales--
          similar to above), and discriminating discus-
          sion of DHL's rejection of social egalitarian-
          ism.

V12   Cushman, Keith. "The Young Lawrence and the Short Story."
      MODERN BRITISH LITERATURE, 3 (1978), 101-12.
          DHL's early study and application of short-
          story techniques, learned chiefly from Gorki,
          Maupassant, and less well-known turn of the
          century writers.

V13   Engel, Monroe. "The Continuity of Lawrence's Short Novels."
      HudR, 11 (1958), 201-09.
          The short novels are more regular in form while
          presenting similar themes and employing many of
          the same technical devices as the longer fic-
          tion. Considers "The Captain's Doll," "The
          Fox," "The Ladybird," "The Man Who Died," and
          "St. Mawr." Reprinted in G48 and G115.

V14   Goodman, Charlotte. "Henry James, D.H. Lawrence, and the
      Victimized Child." MODERN LANGUAGE STUDIES, 10, No. 1
      (1979-80), 43-51.
               DHL's and James's comparable dramatizations of
               the child as victim of his elders, in several
               short stories by each.

V15   Harris, Janice H. "Insight and Experiment in D.H. Law-
      rence's Early Short Fiction." PQ, 55 (1976), 418-35.
               DHL's unrecognized but substantial experimen-
               tation with form and content in his early re-
               alistic tales.

V16   -----. "The Moulting of THE PLUMED SERPENT: A Study of
      the Relationship between the Novel and Three Contemporary
      Tales." MLQ, 39 (1978), 154-68.
               On PS and "The Woman Who Rode Away," "St. Mawr,"
               and "The Princess." For annotation see T12.

V17   Hirsch, Gordon D. "The Laurentian Double: Images of D.H.
      Lawrence in the Stories." DHLR, 10 (1977), 270-76.
               DHL's tendency to cope with the "maternal"
               threat in his stories by doubling his male
               characters, projecting his own "unresolved
               ambivalence" toward women. See V1.

V18   Jones, William M. "Growth of a Symbol: The Sun in Law-
      rence and Eudora Welty." UKCR, 26 (1959), 68-73.
               In her fiction Welty adapts the "manipulated"
               and obviously "artifical" sun symbolism found
               in several of DHL's later stories.

V19   Littlewood, J.C.F. "D.H. Lawrence's Early Tales." CAM-
      BRIDGE QUARTERLY, 1 (1966), 107-24.
               Sees the best of DHL's early tales ("Daughters
               of the Vicar," "Odour of Chrysanthemums," "The
               Thorn in the Flesh,") benefitting from the
               "crucial development in his work as a novelist,"
               between SL and R (i.e., his greater command of
               style and character). Also see further comment
               by G.H. Earl, CAMBRIDGE QUARTERLY, 1 (1966),
               273-75.

V20   MacNiven, Ian S. "D.H. Lawrence's Indian Summer." In
      D.H. LAWRENCE: THE MAN WHO LIVED. Ed. Robert B. Partlow
      and Harry T. Moore. Pp. 42-46. See G92.
               DHL's mixture of primitivism and optimism in
               four late stories: "The Man Who Died," "The
               Man Who Loved Islands," "Sun," and "The Woman
               Who Rode Away."

V21   Marnat, Marcel. "L'Envers d'un conte de fées" ["Fairy-
      Tales in Reverse"]. LA QUINZAINE LITTÉRAIRE, No. 47
      (1968), pp. 3-4.
            Finds "le plus grand Lawrence: dense, concis,
            'moderne,'" in his short fiction (THE LOVELY
            LADY volume, "The Horse Dealer's Daughter,"
            and "The Princess"). [In French.]

V22   Martin. Richard. "Abgeschiedenheit und Auferstehung: Die
      Entfaltung eines Motivs in D.H. Lawrence's letzten Kurz-
      geschichten" ["Seclusion and Resurrection: The Develop-
      ment of a Theme in D.H. Lawrence's Last Short Stories"].
      POETICA, 2 (1968), 70-78.
            The movement toward seclusion in "The Man Who
            Was Through with the World" and "The Man Who
            Loved Islands," redirected in the resurrection
            theme of "The Man Who Died." [In German.]

V23   Moynahan, Julian. "Foreword." In Lawrence's A MODERN
      LOVER AND OTHER STORIES. New York: Ballantine Books,
      1969. Pp. ix-xxiii.
            The scope and style of DHL's short fiction.
            Introduces an excellent collection of twenty-
            two stories, now unfortunately out of print.

V24   O'Connor, Frank. "The Writer Who Rode Away." In THE
      LONELY VOICE: A STUDY OF THE SHORT STORY. Cleveland,
      Ohio: World, 1963. Pp. 143-55.
            Comments on DHL's themes and techniques as a
            short story writer (cf. A.E. Coppard). Ex-
            tract reprinted in V130.

V25   Poynter, John S. "The Early Short Stories of Lawrence."
      In D.H. LAWRENCE: THE MAN WHO LIVED. Ed. Robert B. Part-
      low and Harry T. Moore. Pp. 39-41. See G92.
            DHL's early stories reflect his personal rela-
            tionships with women, his developed sense of
            class conflict, and his emerging "search" for
            his personal and social "self."

V26   Rose, Shirley. "Physical Trauma in D.H. Lawrence's Short
      Fiction." ConL, 16 (1975), 73-83.
            DHL uses physical pain to suggest the "dulling
            of sensitivity," not the route to wisdom.

V27   Scott, James F. "D.H. Lawrence's *Germania:* Ethnic Psy-
      chology and Cultural Crisis in the Shorter Fiction."
      DHLR, 10 (1977), 142-64.
            DHL's love-hate of Germany traced in setting,
            character, and theme in the shorter fiction.

V28 Serraillier, Ian. "Introduction." In Lawrence's SELECTED
     TALES. London: Heinemann, 1963. Pp. vii-xi.
          Argues the "best approach" to DHL's works is
          through his short fiction. Introduces a col-
          lection of eleven major tales.

V29 Springer, Mary Doyle. FORMS OF THE MODERN NOVELLA. Chi-
     cago: Univ. of Chicago Press, 1975. Pp. 25-32, 142-48,
     and passim.
          DHL's use of allegory and treatment of charac-
          ter, principally in "The Fox," "The Virgin and
          the Gipsy," and "The Woman Who Rode Away."

V30 Tanner, Tony. "D.H. Lawrence and America." In D.H. LAW-
     RENCE. Ed. Stephen Spender. Pp. 170-74, 187-96. See
     G113.
          Traces DHL's American experiences and their
          impact on "St. Mawr," "The Woman Who Rode
          Away," and "The Princess."

V31 Temple, J. "The Definition of Innocence: A Consideration
     of the Short Stories of D.H. Lawrence." STUDIA GERMANICA
     GANDENSIA, 20 (1979), 105-18.
          "Principle of innocence either present in the
          young or rediscovered" in tales such as "The
          Border Line," "Glad Ghosts," "You Touched Me,"
          and others.

V32 Travis, Leigh. "D.H. Lawrence: The Blood-Conscious Art-
     ist." AI, 25 (1968), 163-90.
          The triumph of blood over intellect in "The
          Daughters of the Vicar," "The Man Who Died,"
          "The Princess," and "The Woman Who Rode Away."

V, iii.   Studies of Individual Novellas, Short Stories, and
          Story Collections

Titles of all of DHL's novellas, stories, collections, and
fictional fragments and sketches are listed, alphabetically,
in this section, regardless of whether there have been significant critical studies published on them individually.
The headnotes for each title will identify substantial critical commentary on the work to be found in studies located
elsewhere in this bibliography.

Note: The dates following individual published story titles
indicate date(s) of composition ("w"), date of first separate
publication prior to collected publication, if any ("s"), and
date of first collected publication ("v"), with the collection identified by brief title in brackets. The dating information has been drawn from Roberts (E39) and Sagar (E40).

"Adolf" (w. 1919; s. 1920; v. 1936 [PHOENIX])

There are no essential critical studies principally concerned
with this sketch. For commentary on the work, see Hobsbaum
(G51), Gillie (H135), and Marks (H234).

"The Baker's Man." Working title of "The Christening" (q.v.)

"The Blind Man" (w. 1918; s. 1920; v. 1922 [ENGLAND, MY ENG-
LAND])

For additional commentary on this story, see Delany (F41),
Negriolli (G87), Spilka (G114), Tedlock (G118), "Notes..."
(H277), Hsia (V2), Krishnamurthi (V3), Reuter (V4), Widmer
(V5), and Mackenzie (V49).

V33   Abolin, Nancy. "Lawrence's 'The Blind Man': The Reality
      of Touch." In A D.H. LAWRENCE MISCELLANY. Ed. Harry T.
      Moore. Pp. 215-20. See G81.
            Story illustrates the essential DHL theme of
            conflict in its fictional techniques.

V34   Fadiman, Regina. "The Poet as Choreographer: Lawrence's
      'The Blind Man.'" JNT, 2 (1972), 60-67.
            Story not focused on Maurice Pervin's experi-
            ence, as Spilka argues (in G114), but on "sym-
            bolic" actions among all three of its charac-
            ters.

V35   Marks, W.S., III. "The Psychology of Regression in D.H.
      Lawrence's 'The Blind Man.'" L&P, 17 (1967), 177-92.
            Jungian analysis, finding the story's three
            characters doomed to "the same spiritual iso-
            lation."

V36   Ross, Michael L. "The Mythology of Friendship: D.H. Law-
      rence, Bertrand Russell, and 'The Blind Man.'" In ENGLISH
      LITERATURE AND BRITISH PHILOSOPHY: A COLLECTION OF ESSAYS.
      Ed. Stanford P. Rosenbaum. Chicago: Univ. of Chicago
      Press, 1971. Pp. 285-315.
            DHL's antagonism toward Russell transcended in
            the story. See F33.

V37   Warschausky, Sidney. "'The Blind Man.'" In INSIGHT II:
      ANALYSES OF MODERN BRITISH LITERATURE. Ed. John V. Hago-
      pian and Martin Dolch. Frankfurt: Hirschgraben, 1964.
      Pp. 221-28.
            Story synopsis, critique, and study questions.

V38   West, Ray. "Point of View and Authority in 'The Blind
      Man.'" In THE ART OF WRITING FICTION. New York: Crowell,
      1968. Pp. 223-36.
            Useful perspective on DHL's technique.

V39   Wheeler, Richard P. "Intimacy and Irony in 'The Blind
      Man.'" DHLR, 9 (1976), 236-53.
            Psychoanalytic interpretation, concentrating
            on the psychic needs of Maurice and his male
            relationship with Bertie.

"The Blue Moccasins" (w. 1928; s. 1929; v. 1933 [LOVELY LADY])

There are no essential critical studies principally concerned
with this story. For commentary on the work, see Moore (G80),
Tedlock (G118), Hsia (V2), Krishnamurthi (V3), Reuter (V4),
and Widmer (V5).

"The Border Line" (w. 1924, 1928; s. 1924; v. 1928 [WOMAN WHO RODE AWAY])

For additional commentary on this story, see Murry (F121), Clark (G17), Cowan (G22), Michaels-Tonks (G74), Moore (G80), Negriolli (G87), Tedlock (G118), West (G125), Vickery (H393), Hsia (V2), Reuter (V4), Widmer (V5), Scott (V27), Temple (V31), and Kamimura (AA175).

V40 Hudspeth, Robert N. "Duality as Theme and Technique in
     D.H. Lawrence's 'The Border Line.'" SSF, 4 (1966), 51-56.
     Self-explanatory title.

"The Burns Novel" (w. 1912; s. 1957; v. 1968 [PHOENIX II])

There are no essential critical studies principally concerned with this novel fragment. For commentary on the work, see Sagar (E40) and Nehls (F123).

"The Captain's Doll" (w. 1921; v. 1923 [LADYBIRD])

For additional commentary on this novella, see Clark (G17), Draper (G33), Goodheart (G44), Hough (G56), Leavis (G68, G69), Michaels-Tonks (G74), Pritchard (G101), Slade (G111), Tedlock (G118), Harris (H167), Pritchard (H298), Stewart (H361), Vickery (H393), Hsia (V2), Reuter (V4), Widmer (V5), Craig (V10), Engel (V13), Scott (V27), Daleski (V86), and Gurko (V87).

V41 Dawson, Eugene W. "Love Among the Mannikins: 'The Cap-
     tain's Doll.'" DHLR, 1 (1968), 137-48.
     Novella influenced by DHL's reading of the
     American psychoanalyst, Dr. Trigant Burrow.

V42 Howarth, Herbert. "D.H. Lawrence from Island to Glacier."
     UTQ, 37 (1968), 215-29.
     On THE TRESPASSER and "The Captain's Doll."
     For annotation see K4.

V43 Mellown, Elgin W. "'The Captain's Doll': Its Origins and
     Literary Allusions." DHLR, 9 (1976), 226-35.
     Compares novella to its earlier version, "The
     Mortal Coil" (1917; see A19), and describes
     DHL's allusions to a play by Hauptmann (HAN-
     NELES HIMMELFAHRT [1892]).

THE CAPTAIN'S DOLL: THREE NOVELETTES. Variant title for THE
LADYBIRD (q.v.)

"A Chapel Among the Mountains" (w. 1912; v. 1930 [LOVE AMONG
THE HAYSTACKS])

There are no essential critical studies concerned with this
semi-fictional travel sketch, which is related to materials
subsequently incorporated into TWILIGHT IN ITALY (q.v.). For
notes on its composition see Sagar (E40), Moore (F112), and
Nehls (F123).

"The Christening" (w. 1912; v. 1914 [PRUSSIAN OFFICER])

There are no essential critical studies principally concerned
with this story. For commentary on the work, see Hobsbaum
(G51), Tedlock (G118), Weiss (G123), Vickery (H393), Hsia (V2),
Reuter (V4), Widmer (V5), Harris (V15), Cushman (V124, V125),
and Finney (V126).

"Christs in the Tirol" (w. 1912; s. 1913; v. 1930 [LOVE AMONG
THE HAYSTACKS--Amer. ed.])

There are no essential critical studies concerned with this
semi-fictional travel sketch, which was also published with
revisions as "The Crucifix Across the Mountains" in TWILIGHT
IN ITALY (q.v.). For notes on its composition, see Sagar
(E40), Moore (F112), and Nehls (F123).

"The Daughters of the Vicar" (w. 1911, 1913; v. 1914 [PRUSSIAN OFFICER])

For additional commentary on this story, see Brunsdale (G14), Leavis (G68), Littlewood (G71), Pritchard (G101), Sinzelle (G110), Slade (G111), Tedlock (G118), Vivas (G121), Weiss (G123), Vickery (H393), Hsia (V2), Reuter (V4), Widmer (V5), Craig (V10), Harris (V15), Littlewood (V19), Travis (V32), Cushman (V124, V125), and Finney (V126).

V44   Kalnins, Mara. "D.H. Lawrence's 'Two Marriages' and
       'Daughters of the Vicar.'" ARIEL, 7, No. 1 (1976), 32-49.
           DHL's technical and imaginative growth evident
           in comparing the early and finished versions
           of the story (1911, 1913; see A29).

V45   Padhi, Bibhu. "An Instrument of Sympathy: Irony in Law-
       rence's 'The Daughters of the Vicar.'" JOURNAL OF LITER-
       ARY STUDIES (Utkal Univ.), 4, No. 2 (1981), 53-61.
           Story's ironies in situation, setting, symbol-
           ism, and tone, control the reader's sympathies.

"The Dead Rose." Working title of "The Shades of Spring"(q.v.)

"Delilah and Mr. Bircumshaw" (w. 1912; s. 1940; v. 1968 [PHOE-
NIX II])

There are no essential critical studies principally concerned
with this story. For commentary on the work, see Widmer (V5).

"Elsa Culverwell" (w. 1912; s. 1980 [LOST GIRL])

For commentary on this novel fragment, which treats materials
DHL subsequently developed in THE LOST GIRL, see Worthen (P9).

"England, My England" (w. 1915; s. 1915; v. 1922 [ENGLAND, MY ENGLAND])

For additional commentary on this story, see Delany (F41), Clarke (G18), Hobsbaum (G51), Leavis (G68), Pritchard (G101), Tedlock (G118), "Notes..." (H277), Rossman (H318), Vickery (H393), Hsia (V2), Krishnamurthi (V3), Reuter (V4), Widmer (V5), and Mackenzie (V49).

V46   Lodge, David. "D.H. Lawrence." In THE MODES OF MODERN
      WRITING: METAPHOR, METONYMY, AND THE TYPOLOGY OF MODERN
      LITERATURE. London: Arnold, 1977. Pp. 160-76.
            DHL, more concerned with flow and continuity
            than with counterpoint and irony, a "meto-
            nymic" stylist (cf. Eliot, Hemingway, and
            Joyce). Close analysis of DHL's style in
            "England, My England" (pp. 164-76).

V47   Lucas, Barbara. "Apropos of 'England, My England.'"
      TWENTIETH CENTURY, 169 (1961), 288-93.
            Offers several reasonable objections to Moore's
            identification of her father, Percy Lucas, as
            the original of Egbert (see F112). Reprinted
            in G20.

ENGLAND, MY ENGLAND AND OTHER STORIES (1922)

For additional commentary on this collection, see Hobsbaum (G51), Hough (G56), Moore (G80), Pritchard (G101), Sinzelle (G110), Tedlock (G118), Hsia (V2), Reuter (V4), and Widmer (V5).

V48   Cushman, Keith. "The Achievement of ENGLAND, MY ENGLAND
      AND OTHER STORIES." In D.H. LAWRENCE: THE MAN WHO LIVED.
      Ed. Robert B. Partlow and Harry T. Moore. Pp. 27-38.
      See G92.
            Finds the stories in the collection imagina-
            tively unified by their wartime background,
            mythic dimension, ambiguous attitude, and
            sardonic tone.

V49   Mackenzie, D. Kenneth M. "Ennui and Energy in ENGLAND,
      MY ENGLAND." In D.H. LAWRENCE: A CRITICAL STUDY. Ed.
      Andor Gomme. Pp. 120-41. See G43.
            Themes of disillusion, vigour, and sensibility
            in the ten stories of the ENGLAND, MY ENGLAND
            volume.

"Ephraim's Half Sovereign." Working title of "Strike Pay" (q.v.)

"The Escaped Cock." Original title of "The Man Who Died" (q.v.)

"Fanny and Annie" (w. 1919; s. 1921; v. 1922 [ENGLAND, MY ENGLAND])

For additional commentary on this story, see Hobsbaum (G51), Tedlock (G118), Hsia (V2), Reuter (V4), Widmer (V5), and Mackenzie (V49).

V50   Secor, Robert. "Language and Movement in 'Fanny and Annie.'" SSF, 6 (1969), 395-400.
          Close attention to DHL's language suggests a
          positive reading of Fanny's fate.

"The Fly in the Ointment" (w. 1910; s. 1913; v. 1968 [PHOENIX II])

For additional commentary on this story, see Sagar (in B14), Brunsdale (G14), Tedlock (G118), and Widmer (V5).

V51   Cushman, Keith. "A Note on Lawrence's 'Fly in the Ointment.'" ELN, 15 (1977), 47-51.
          On WL and DHL's early story. For annotation
          see N22.

"The Flying Fish" (w. 1925; v. 1936 [PHOENIX])

There are no essential critical studies principally concerned with this unfinished story. For commentary on the work, see Cavitch (G16), Clark (G17), Cowan (G22), and Widmer (V5).

"The Fox" (w. 1918; s. 1922; v. 1923 [LADYBIRD])

For additional commentary on this novella, see Clark (G17),
Colin (G19), Goodheart (G44), Hobsbaum (G51), Hough (G56),
Inniss (G60), Joost and Sullivan (G64), Leavis (G68, G69),
Miles (G76), Moore (G80), Moynahan (G83), Negriolli (G87),
Sagar (G104), Slade (G111), Tedlock (G118), Cockshut (H67),
Core (H75), Hinz (H181), Pritchard (H298), Hsia (V2), Krish-
namurthi (V3), Reuter (V4), Widmer (V5), Engel (V13), Springer
(V29), Daleski (V86), and Gurko (V87). Also see the pub-
lished manuscript version of "The Fox" (A34) and Mackenzie's
"Study Guide" for the novella (AB6).

V52   Bergler, Edmund. "D.H. Lawrence's 'The Fox' and the Psy-
      choanalytic Theory on Lesbianism." 1958. In A D.H. LAW-
      RENCE MISCELLANY. Ed. Harry T. Moore. Pp. 49-55. See
      G81.
              DHL's "intuitive" yet "clinically correct ob-
              servations" of the lesbian relationship.

V53   Boren, James L. "Commitment and Futility in 'The Fox.'"
      UR, 31 (1965), 301-04.
              Novella a "study in defeat."

V54   Brayfield, Peggy. "Lawrence's 'Male and Female Principles'
      and the Symbolism of 'The Fox.'" MOSAIC, 4, No. 3 (1971),
      41-51.
              The inner struggle of the androgynous March.

V55   Brown, Christopher. "The Eyes Have It: Vision in 'The
      Fox.'" WASCANA REVIEW, 15, No. 2 (1980), 61-68.
              DHL's strategic use of vision in the novella
              ("to see is to dominate, to be seen is to be
              dominated"), suggests that Henry's "victory"
              is superficial and "equivocal at best."

V56   Davis, Patricia. "Chicken Queen's Delight: D.H. Lawrence's
      'The Fox.'" MFS, 19 (1973), 565-71.
              DHL's unconvincing treatment, indeed confusion,
              of his characters' psychology and sexuality.

V57   Draper, Ronald P. "The Defeat of Feminism: DHL's 'The
      Fox' and 'The Woman Who Rode Away.'" SSF, 3 (1966), 186-
      98.
              DHL ultimately relents in his antifeminism.

V58 Fulmer, O. Bryan. "The Significance of the Death of the
     Fox in D.H. Lawrence's 'The Fox.'" SSF, 5 (1968), 275-82.
          The relationship of Henry and March dead at
          the story's end.

V59 Gontarski, S.E. "Mark Rydell and the Filming of 'The
     Fox': An Interview with S.E. Gontarski." MODERNIST STUD-
     IES, 4 (1982), 96-104.
          The director of the film version of "The Fox"
          (1968) describes its production, direction,
          and "scandalous" reputation. See G79.

V60 Gregor, Ian. "'The Fox': A Caveat." EIC, 9 (1959),10-21.
          Conflict between DHL's evident intention and
          his creation painfully clear in the unsatis-
          factory ending of the tale.

V61 Jones, Lawrence. "Physiognomy and the Sensual Will in
     'The Ladybird' and 'The Fox.'" DHLR, 13 (1980), 1-29.
          The symbolic implications of the physical fea-
          tures of DHL's characters, examined in light
          of his analysis of sexual psychology in FANTA-
          SIA OF THE UNCONSCIOUS (A63). See G27.

V62 Levin, Gerald. "The Symbolism of Lawrence's 'The Fox.'"
     CLAJ, 11 (1967), 135-41.
          "The Fox" a "nearly perfect story--consistent
          in symbolism and meaning."

V63 Mellen, Joan. "Outfoxing Lawrence: Novella into Film."
     LFQ, 1 (1973), 17-27.
          The departures of the film version of the nov-
          ella (1968) make it "almost a cartoon version
          of the story." See G70.

V64 Rossi, Patrizio. "Lawrence's Two Foxes: A Comparison of
     the Texts." EIC, 22 (1972), 265-78.
          Novella's "artistic and structural inconsisten-
          cies" attributed to DHL's haphazard expansion
          of its early version (see A34).

V65 -----. "'The Fox' e 'La Lupa': D.H. Lawrence lettore di
     Verga." EM, 24 (1973-74), 299-320.
          Influences of DHL's reading and translation
          of Verga on his novella. See below.

V66 Ruderman, Judith G. "Lawrence's 'The Fox' and Verga's 'The She-Wolf': Variations on the Theme of the 'Devouring Mother.'" MLN, 94 (1979), 153-65.
Increasing violence in DHL's fiction in the twenties influenced by his reading and translation of Verga. See above and V68.

V67 ------. "Prototypes for Lawrence's 'The Fox.'" JML, 8 (1980), 77-98.
Originals for the story's characters, setting, and circumstances, drawn from DHL's sojourns in rural England (c. 1918-19).

V68 ------. "'The Fox' and the 'Devouring Mother.'" DHLR, 10 (1977), 251-69.
Story demonstrates DHL's continued preoccupation with "unresolved pre-oedipal conflicts," well after the supposed resolution of SL, in its emphasis on "male lordship...as a necessary corrective to female domination." See V1 and V66.

V69 ------. "Tracking Lawrence's 'Fox': An Account of its Composition, Evolution, and Publication." SB, 33 (1979), 206-21.
Traces DHL's growing concern with the "ideal of leadership" in the early twenties, reflected in the textual evolution of his novella.

V70 Shields, E.F. "Broken Vision in Lawrence's 'The Fox.'" SSF, 9 (1972), 353-63.
Story, seriously flawed by revisions, not an integrated work.

V71 Sobchack, Thomas. "'The Fox': The Film and the Novel." WHR, 23 (1969), 73-78.
The failure of the film version (1968) "to capture the essential quality" of the novella: DHL's "evocation of the ambiguous and enigmatic nature of the relationships between men and women."

V72 Wolkenfeld, Suzanne. "'The Sleeping Beauty' Retold: D.H. Lawrence's 'The Fox.'" SSF, 14 (1977), 345-52.
DHL's use of the folk-tale archetype of death and rebirth.

"A Fragment of Stained Glass" (w. 1907; s. 1911; v. 1914 [PRUS-SIAN OFFICER])

For additional commentary on this story, see Brunsdale (G14), Ford (G39), Moore (G80), Tedlock (G118), Vickery (H393), Hsia (V2), Reuter (V4), Widmer (V5), Cushman (V125), and Finney (V126).

V73   Baim, Joseph. "Past and Present in D.H. Lawrence's 'A
      Fragment of Stained Glass.'" SSF, 8 (1971), 323-26.
          Story's early treatment of a characteristic
          Lawrencean concern for the tensions between
          the "primitive" past and "modern industrial-
          ized England."

V74   Baker, P.G. "By the Help of Certain Notes: A Source for
      D.H. Lawrence's 'A Fragment of Stained Glass.'" SSF, 17
      (1980), 317-26.
          Walter Pater's "Denys L'Auxerrois" (in IMAGIN-
          ARY PORTRAITS [1886]) a source for DHL's title
          and "elaborate framing device" for his story.

"Glad Ghosts" (w. 1925; s. 1926; v. 1928 [WOMAN WHO RODE AWAY])

There are no essential critical studies principally concerned with this story. For commentary on the work, see Murry (F121), Ford (G39), Moore (G80), Tedlock (G118), Vickery (H393), Hsia (V2), Reuter (V4), Widmer (V5), and Temple (V31).

"Goose Fair" (w. 1909; s. 1910; v. 1914 [PRUSSIAN OFFICER])

There are no essential critical studies principally concerned with this story. For commentary on the work, see Brunsdale (G14), Hobsbaum (G51), Tedlock (G118), Hsia (V2), Reuter (V4), Widmer (V5), Cushman (V125), and Finney (V126).

"Hadrian." Working title of "You Touched Me" (q.v.)

"A Hay Hut Among the Mountains" (w. 1912; v. 1930 [LOVE AMONG THE HAYSTACKS])

There are no essential critical studies concerned with this semi-fictional travel sketch, which is related to materials subsequently incorporated into TWILIGHT IN ITALY (q.v.). For notes on its composition, see Sagar (E40), Moore (F112), and Nehls (F123).

"Her Turn" (w. 1912; s. 1913; v. 1934 [MODERN LOVER])

There are no essential critical studies principally concerned with this story. For commentary on the work, see Tedlock (G118), Hsia (V2), and Widmer (V5).

"A Hole in the Window." Working title of "A Fragment of Stained Glass" (q.v.)

"Honour and Arms." Pre-publication title of "The Prussian Officer" (q.v.)

"The Horse Dealer's Daughter" (w. 1916, 1921; s. 1922; v. 1922 [ENGLAND, MY ENGLAND])

For additional commentary on this story, see Ford (G39), Leavis (G68), Sinzelle (G110), Tedlock (G118), Vickery (H393), Hsia (V2), Krishnamurthi (V3), Reuter (V4), Widmer (V5), Marnat (V21), Mackenzie (V49), and Férnandez (AA141).

V75 Betsky-Zweig, Sara. "'Floutingly in the Fine Black Mud': D.H. Lawrence's 'The Horse Dealer's Daughter.'" DUTCH QUARTERLY REVIEW, 3 (1973), 159-64.
        Story's act of symbolic sexual intercourse precedes the recognition of love.

V76 Gullason, Thomas A. "Revelation and Evolution: A Neglected Dimension of the Short Story." SSF, 10 (1973), 347-56.
        Story (discussed pp. 348-52), as much based on a "moral evolution" in its characters as on a situation revealed in its climax.

V77 Junkins, Donald. "D.H. Lawrence's 'The Horse Dealer's
     Daughter.'" SSF, 6 (1969), 210-12.
          Story's monster-maiden archetype.

V78 McCabe, Thomas H. "Rhythm as Form in Lawrence's 'The
     Horse Dealer's Daughter.'" PMLA, 87 (1972), 64-68.
          Rhythmic structure of story reflects the char-
          acters' discovery of the vital rhythms of life.

V79 Phillips, Stephen R. "The Double Pattern of D.H. Law-
     rence's 'The Horse Dealer's Daughter.'" SSF, 10 (1973),
     94-97.
          Mabel's "rebirth" doubled by Fergusson's.

V80 -----. "The Monomyth and Literary Criticism." COLLEGE
     LITERATURE, 2 (1975), 1-16.
          Applies Joseph Campbell's concept of "mono-
          myth" (viz. THE HERO WITH A THOUSAND FACES
          [1949]) to Conrad's "The Secret Sharer" (1910),
          Yeats's "Sailing to Byzantium" (1926), and
          "The Horse Dealer's Daughter."

V81 Ryals, Clyde de L. "D.H. Lawrence's 'The Horse Dealer's
     Daughter.'" L&P, 12 (1962), 39-43.
          Discusses the Jungian rebirth archetype in the
          story.

"In Love" (w. 1926; s. 1927; v. 1928 [WOMAN WHO RODE AWAY])

There are no essential critical studies principally concerned
with this story. For commentary on the work, see Tedlock
(G118), Hsia (V2), Reuter (V4), and Widmer (V5).

"Intimacy." Working title of "The Witch à la Mode" (q.v.)

"Jimmy and the Desperate Woman" (w. 1924; s. 1924; v. 1928
[WOMAN WHO RODE AWAY])

There are no essential critical studies principally concerned
with this story. For commentary on the work, see Cowan (G22),
Hobsbaum (G51), Moore (G80), Tedlock (G118), Vickery (H393),
Hsia (V2), Reuter (V4), and Widmer (V5).

"The Ladybird" (w. 1921; v. 1923 [LADYBIRD])

For additional commentary on this novella, see Murry (F121), Clarke (G18), Hobsbaum (G51), Negriolli (G87), Pinion (G95), Tedlock (G118), Davies (H84), Vickery (H393), Hsia (V2), Reuter (V4), Widmer (V5), Engel (V13), Scott (V27), Daleski (V86), Gurko (V87), and Hyde (Z5).

V82   Cowan, James C. "D.H. Lawrence's Dualism: The Apollonian-
      Dionysian Polarity and 'The Ladybird.'" In FORMS OF MODERN
      BRITISH FICTION. Ed. Alan W. Friedman. Austin: Univ. of
      Texas Press, 1975. Pp. 73-99.
            "The Ladybird" illustrates DHL's characteristic
            creation of a "dialectical tension" between op-
            posed forces.

V83   Finney, Brian H. "Two Missing Pages from 'The Ladybird.'"
      RES, 24 (1973), 191-92.
            Publishes two pages of DHL's manuscript, "omit-
            ted by mistake in all subsequent published
            texts."

V84   Jones, Lawrence. "Physiognomy and the Sensual Will in
      'The Ladybird' and 'The Fox.'" DHLR, 13 (1980), 1-29.
            For annotation see V61.

V85   Scott, James F. "Thimble into Ladybird: Nietzsche, Fro-
      benius, and Bachofen in Later Work of D.H. Lawrence."
      ARCADIA, 13 (1978), 161-76.
            Traces in the novella DHL's "assimilation of
            motifs" gleaned from a decade's reading of
            Germanic literature and philosophy.

THE LADYBIRD, THE FOX, THE CAPTAIN'S DOLL (1923)

For additional commentary on this collection, see Hobsbaum (G51), Hough (G56), Moore (G80), Tedlock (G118), Hsia (V2), Reuter (V4), and Widmer (V5).

V86   Daleski, H.M. "Aphrodite of the Foam and THE LADYBIRD
      Tales." In D.H. LAWRENCE: A CRITICAL STUDY. Ed. Andor
      Gomme. Pp. 142-58. See G43.
            The three LADYBIRD novellas demonstrate the
            necessity for female submission in the sexual
            relationship and for abandoning sentimental
            conceptions of love.

V87 Gurko, Leo. "D.H. Lawrence's Greatest Collection of Short
     Stories--What Holds it Together." MFS, 18 (1972), 173-82.
         The three novellas clearly illustrate the tran-
         sition between DHL's early and later fiction.

"The Last Laugh" (w. 1924; s. 1925; v. 1928 [WOMAN WHO RODE
AWAY])

For additional commentary on this story, see Clark (G17), Cowan
(G22), Moore (G80), Negriolli (G87), Tedlock (G118), Merivale
(H247), Vickery (H393), Hsia (V2), Reuter (V4), and Widmer (V5).

V88 Baim, Joseph. "The Second Coming of Pan: A Note on D.H.
     Lawrence's 'The Last Laugh.'"   SSF, 6 (1968), 98-100.
         Each character in the story "symbolic of a dif-
         ferent response to the essential nature and
         spirit of life," rendered by DHL "in the figure
         of Pan."

"Legend." Working title of "A Fragment of Stained Glass" (q.v.)

"Lessford's Rabbits" and "A Lesson on a Tortoise" (w. 1908;
v. 1968 [PHOENIX II])

There are no essential critical studies principally concerned
with these early, semi-fictional companion pieces. For commentary on the sketches, see Brunsdale (G14) and Hobsbaum (G51).

"Love Among the Haystacks" (w. 1908-11 [?]; v. 1930 [LOVE AMONG
THE HAYSTACKS]

For additional commentary on this story, see Ford (G39), Moore
(G80), Sinzelle (G110), Tedlock (G118), Hsia (V2), Reuter (V4),
and Widmer (V5).

V89 Holloway, John. NARRATIVE AND STRUCTURE. Cambridge: Cam-
     bridge Univ. Press, 1979. Pp. 57-62, 67-73.
         Structural analysis of the story, in compari-
         son with tales by Chekhov and James.

LOVE AMONG THE HAYSTACKS AND OTHER PIECES (1930)

There are no essential critical studies principally concerned with this collection. For commentary on the volume, see Hobsbaum (G51), Moore (G80), and Tedlock (G118).

"The Lovely Lady" (w. 1927; s. 1927; v. 1933 [LOVELY LADY])

For additional commentary on this story, see Ford (G39), Moore (G80), Nahal (G86), Tedlock (G118), Vickery (H393), Hsia (V2), Krishnamurthi (V3), Reuter (V4), Widmer (V5), and Marnat (V21).

V90   Finney, Brian H. "A Newly Discovered Text of D.H. Law-
      rence's 'The Lovely Lady.'" YULG, 49 (1974), 245-52.
      Compares the condensed and carefully revised
      published text of DHL's murder story with the
      considerably longer holograph manuscript
      (1927), housed at Yale.

THE LOVELY LADY (1933)

There are no essential critical studies principally concerned with this collection. For commentary on the volume, see Hobsbaum (G51), and Marnat (V21).

"The Man Who Died" (w. 1927-28; s. 1928, 1929; v. 1934 [TALES])

For additional commentary on this novella, see Moore and Montague (F113), Murry (F121), Clark (G17), Donnerstag (G30), Draper (G33), Eisenstein (G36), Ford (G39), Goodheart (G44), Hobsbaum (G51), Hough (G56), Jaensson (G61), Jarrett-Kerr (G62), Kermode (G65), Moore (G80), Nahal (G86), Negriolli (G87), Panichas (G91), Pinion (G95), Pritchard (G101), Reul (G103), Sagar (G104), Spilka (G114), Tedlock (G118), Zytaruk (G131), Bredsdorff (H52), Cowan (H78), Goodheart (H145), Hoffman (H187), John (H196), Liscano Velutini (H225), Murry (H271), Rossman (H319), Sturm (H366), Vickery (H393), Wicker (H406), Williams (H410), Hsia (V2), Reuter (V4), Widmer (V5), Engel (V13), MacNiven (V20), Martin (V22), Travis (V32), Gilbert (Y1), Pinto (Y44), Gutierrez (Z4), Sorani (AA270), Tetsumura (AA278), and Kim (AC6).

V91 Butler, Gerald J. "'The Man Who Died' and Lawrence's
     Final Attitude Towards Tragedy." RECOVERING LITERATURE,
     6, No. 3 (1977), 1-14.
         DHL's ultimate, anti-tragic attitude toward
         death and life.

V92 Fiderer, Gerald. "D.H. Lawrence's 'The Man Who Died':
     The Phallic Christ." AI, 25 (1968), 91-96.
         Story a "perfectly realized work of art."

V93 Hays, Peter L. THE LIMPING HERO: GROTESQUES IN LITERA-
     TURE. New York: New York Univ. Press, 1971. Pp. 35-38,
     77-79, and passim.
         On LCL and "The Man Who Died." For annotation
         see U27.

V94 Hendrick, George. "Jesus and the Osiris-Isis Myth: Law-
     rence's 'The Man Who Died' and Williams's THE NIGHT OF
     THE IGUANA." ANGLIA, 84 (1966), 398-406.
         Williams's play (1962), indebted to DHL's
         novella in several respects, including its
         "central theme" of "how to live beyond de-
         spair and still live."

V95 Hinz, Evelyn J., and John J. Teunissen. "Savior and Cock:
     Allusion and Icon in Lawrence's 'The Man Who Died.'" JML,
     5 (1976), 279-96.
         The cock as classical symbol for healer and in
         the "iconography of ancient phallic worship."

V96 Kay, Wallace G. "WOMEN IN LOVE and 'The Man Who Died':
     Resolving Apollo and Dionysus." SOUTHERN QUARTERLY, 10
     (1972), 325-39.
         For annotation see N55.

V97 Krook, Dorothea. "Messianic Humanism: D.H. Lawrence's
     'The Man Who Died.'" In THREE TRADITIONS OF MORAL THOUGHT.
     Cambridge: Cambridge Univ. Press, 1959. Pp. 255-92.
         The fundamental conflict between the Christian
         and Humanist traditions of moral thought in
         the novella.

V98 Kunkel, Francis L. "Lawrence's 'The Man Who Died': The
     Heavenly Cock." In PASSION AND THE PASSION: SEX AND RE-
     LIGION IN MODERN LITERATURE. Philadelphia: Westminster
     Press, 1975. Pp. 37-57.
         DHL's synthesis of carnality and spirituality
         in the novella healthy, though arising from

his love-hate relationship with Christianity
and his neurotic, ultimately Oedipal desire
to gain "revenge on the father, [by] bringing
low the supreme father figure in the universe."

V99   Lacy, Gerald M. "Commentary." In Lawrence's THE ES-
CAPED COCK. Ed. Lacy. Pp. 123-70. See B11.
Intensive analysis of the story's backgrounds,
composition, publication history, literary
quality, and text.

V100   LeDoux, Larry V. "Christ and Isis: The Function of the
Dying and Reviving God in 'The Man Who Died.'" DHLR, 5
(1972), 132-47.
DHL's counterpoint of the physical renewal of
man and woman with the "symbolic renewal of
an increasingly sterile Christianity."

V101   Lucente, Gregory L. "WOMEN IN LOVE and 'The Man Who
Died': From Realism to the Mythopoeia of Passion and
Rebirth." In THE NARRATIVE OF REALISM AND MYTH: VERGA,
LAWRENCE, FAULKNER, PAVESE. Baltimore, Md.: Johns Hop-
kins Univ. Press, 1981. Pp. 107-23.
For annotation see N62.

V102   MacDonald, Robert H. "The Union of Fire and Water: An
Examination of the Imagery of 'The Man Who Died.'" DHLR,
10 (1977), 34-51.
Rhetorical analysis of DHL's integration of
language and theme.

V103   Miller, Milton. "Definition by Comparison: Chaucer,
Lawrence, and Joyce." EIC, 3 (1953), 369-81.
Shared vitalism of DHL and Chaucer; the
shared sense of the past in Joyce and Chaucer ("The Man Who Died" and "The Dead").

V104   Murry, John Middleton. "'The Escaped Cock.'" CRITERION,
10 (1930), 183-88.
Reviews DHL's novella as his tender and profound "swan song," his reassertion of his
"love of the world against his hate of it"
expressed in LCL.

V105   Steinhauer, H. "Eros and Psyche: A Nietzschean Motif
in Anglo-American Literature." MLN, 64 (1949), 217-28.
DHL "espouses Nietzsche's irrationalism to
a degree that would have embarrassed the master" (cf. Eugene O'Neill).

V106   Thompson, Leslie M.   "The Christ Who Didn't Die: Analogues
       to D.H. Lawrence's 'The Man Who Died.'"   DHLR, 8 (1975),
       19-30.
              DHL's story the culmination of a series of
              unorthodox views of the Christian resurrec-
              tion, dating from the mid-nineteenth century.

"The Man Who Loved Islands" (w. 1926; s. 1927; v. 1928 [WOMAN
WHO RODE AWAY--Amer. ed.])

For additional commentary on this story, see Clark (G17), Ford
(G39), Hobsbaum (G51), Moore (G80), Moynahan (G83), Negriolli
(G87), Tedlock (G118), Draper (H94), Hsia (V2), Krishnamurthi
(V3), Reuter (V4), Widmer (V5), MacNiven (V20), Martin (V22),
and Kamimura (AA176).

V107   Karl, Frederick R.   "Lawrence's 'The Man Who Loved Is-
       lands': The Crusoe Who Failed."   In A D.H. LAWRENCE MIS-
       CELLANY.   Ed. Harry T. Moore.   Pp. 265-79.   See G81.
              Story a modern fable of the failure of the
              cerebral Englishman, the Crusoe figure, il-
              lustrating DHL's essential strengths and
              weaknesses.

V108   Squires, Michael.   "Teaching a Story Rhetorically: An
       Approach to a Short Story by D.H. Lawrence."   CCC, 24
       (1973), 150-56.
              DHL's "rhetorical problem" is his need to
              "win our respect" for his story's attack on
              egoism, preventing the reader's identifica-
              tion with its egoistic central character.

V109   Toyokuni, Takashi.   "A Modern Man Obsessed by Time: A
       Note on 'The Man Who Loved Islands.'"   DHLR, 7 (1974),
       78-82.
              Cathcart's "self-dissolution" reinforced by
              DHL's use of three perceptions of time: cyc-
              lic, linear, and discontinuous.

V110   Willbern, David.   "Malice in Paradise: Isolation and
       Projection in 'The Man Who Loved Islands.'"   DHLR, 10
       (1977), 223-41.
              Story a projection of DHL's senses of isola-
              tion and failure in relationships and of his
              ultimate withdrawal from meaning in the
              story's conclusion.   See V1.

"The Man Who Was Through With the World" (w. 1927; s. 1959; v. 1971 [PRINCESS AND OTHER WORKS])

There are no essential critical studies principally concerned with this unfinished story. For commentary on the work, see Elliott (in A33), Sagar (in B20), Widmer (V5), and Martin (V22).

"Mercury" (w. 1926; s. 1927; v. 1936 [PHOENIX])

There are no essential critical studies principally concerned with this allegorical sketch. For commentary on the work, see Roberts (E39), Nehls (F123), Moore (G80), and Widmer (V5).

"The Miner at Home" (w. 1912; s. 1912; v. 1936 [PHOENIX])

There are no essential critical studies principally concerned with this sketch. For commentary on the work, see Widmer (V5).

"The Miracle." Working title of "The Horse Dealer's Daughter" (q.v.)

"Mr. Noon" (w. 1920-21; v. 1934 [MODERN LOVER])

There are no essential critical studies principally concerned with this novel fragment. For commentary on the work, see Neville (F124), Tedlock (G118), Worthen (G128), and the head-notes to sections A, i, and V of this bibliography.

"A Modern Lover" (w. 1909; s. 1933; v. 1934 [MODERN LOVER])

For additional commentary on this story, see Brunsdale (G14), Tedlock (G118), Hsia (V2), Reuter (V4), and Widmer (V5).

V111   Sagar, Keith. "The Best I Have Known: Lawrence's 'A Modern Lover' and 'The Shades of Spring.'" SSF, 4 (1967), 144-51.
            The recurrent theme of the displaced lover in DHL's long and short fiction.

A MODERN LOVER (1934)

There are no essential critical studies principally concerned
with this collection. For commentary on the volume, see Hobsbaum (G51) and Tedlock (G118).

"Monkey Nuts" (w. 1919; s. 1922; v. 1922 [ENGLAND, MY ENGLAND])

There are no essential critical studies principally concerned
with this story. For commentary on the work, see Slade (G111),
Tedlock (G118), Hsia (V2), Reuter (V4), Widmer (V5), and Mackenzie (V49).

"More Modern Love." Working title of "In Love" (q.v.)

"The Mortal Coil" (w. 1913, 1916; s. 1917; v. 1968 [PHOENIX II])

For commentary on this original version of "The Captain's Doll"
see Mellown (V43).

"Mother and Daughter" (w. 1928; s. 1929; v. 1933 [LOVELY LADY])

For additional commentary on this story, see Leavis (G68),
Moore (G80), Tedlock (G118), Blanchard (M16), Hsia (V2), Krishnamurthi (V3), Reuter (V4), and Widmer (V5).

V112   Meyers, Jeffrey. "Katherine Mansfield, Gurdjieff and
       Lawrence's 'Mother and Daughter.'" TCL, 22 (1976),
       444-53.
              DHL's story an "allegory" of Mansfield's
              "seduction by the mysticism of Gurdjieff"
              in the last months of her life.

"The New Eve." Working title of "New Eve and Old Adam" (below)

"New Eve and Old Adam" (w. 1913; v. 1934 [MODERN LOVER])

There are no essential critical studies principally concerned with this story. For commentary on the work, see Tedlock (G118), Hsia (V2), and Widmer (V5).

"None of That" (w. 1927; v. 1928 [WOMAN WHO RODE AWAY])

There are no essential critical studies principally concerned with this story. For commentary on the work, see Moore (G80), Tedlock (G118), Vickery (H393), Hsia (V2), Krishnamurthi (V3), Reuter (V4), and Widmer (V5).

"Odour of Chrysanthemums" (w. 1909-10; s. 1911; v. 1914 [PRUS-SIAN OFFICER])

For additional commentary on this story, see Ford (F56), Bruns-dale (G14), Draper (G33), Ford (G39), Hobsbaum (G51), Little-wood (G71), Moore (G80), Moynahan (G83), Pinion (G95), Pritchard (G101), Sagar (G104), Sinzelle (G110), Slade (G111), Tedlock (G118), Gregor and Weekes (H158), Hsia (V2), Reuter (V4), Wid-mer (V5), Amon (V7), Littlewood (V19), Moynahan (V23), Cushman (V124, V125), Finney (V126), Marland (X11), Coniff (X19), and Williams (X22). Also see the early manuscript version of "Odour of Chrysanthemums," published with a commentary by Boulton in A37.

V113   Donoghue, Denis. "Action is Eloquence." In THE ORDINARY
       UNIVERSE: SOUNDINGS IN MODERN LITERATURE. New York: Mac-
       millan, 1968. Pp. 169-79.
            Slight. Compares story to J.C. Ransom's poem
            "Prelude to an Evening" (1962).

V114   Hudspeth, Robert N. "Lawrence's 'Odour of Chrysanthe-
       mums': Isolation and Paradox." SSF, 6 (1969), 630-36.
            The paradoxical isolations of Elizabeth, as
            wife and as widow.

V115   Kalnins, Mara. "D.H. Lawrence's 'Odour of Chrysanthe-
       mums': The Three Endings." SSF, 13 (1976), 471-79.
            DHL's revisions reveal his maturing under-
            standing of Elizabeth Bates's psychology.

V116 McGinnis, Wayne D. "Lawrence's 'Odour of Chrysanthemums'
      and Blake." RS, 44 (1976), 251-52.
            DHL's "creative vision" of marriage related
            to Blake's proverbs in THE MARRIAGE OF HEAVEN
            AND HELL (c. 1793).

"The Old Adam" (w. 1911; v. 1934 [MODERN LOVER])

There are no essential critical studies principally concerned
with this story. For commentary on the work, see Tedlock
(G118), Weiss (G123), Hsia (V2), and Widmer (V5).

"Once" (w. 1912; v. 1930 [LOVE AMONG THE HAYSTACKS])

There are no essential critical studies principally concerned
with this story. For commentary on the work, see Tedlock
(G118), Hsia (V2), and Widmer (V5).

"The Overtone" (w. 1924; v. 1933 [LOVELY LADY])

For additional commentary on this story, see Tedlock (G118),
Merivale (H247), Hsia (V2), Reuter (V4), and Widmer (V5).

V117 Neumarkt, Paul. "Pan and Christ: An Analysis of the
      Hieros Gamos Concept in D.H. Lawrence's Short Story
      'The Overtone.'" DOS CONTINENTES, 9-10 (1971-72), 27-48.
            Not seen.

"A Prelude" (w. 1907; s. 1907; v. 1968 [PHOENIX II])

For additional commentary on this story, see Roberts (E39),
Chambers (F29), Moore (F112), Nehls (F123), Brunsdale (G14),
Pinion (G95), Hsia (V2), and Widmer (V5).

V117a   Wadsworth, P. Beaumont. "Introduction." In A PRELUDE,
        BY D.H. LAWRENCE: HIS FIRST AND PREVIOUSLY UNRECORDED
        WORK. Thames Ditton, Engl.: Merle Press, 1949. Pp.
        7-25.
                Wadsworth recounts his discovery of DHL's
                first publication, which appeared as a
                prize-winning story, under Jessie Chambers's
                name, in the NOTTINGHAMSHIRE GUARDIAN (see
                A15).

"The Primrose Path" (w. 1913; v. 1922 [ENGLAND, MY ENGLAND])

There are no essential critical studies principally concerned
with this story. For commentary on the work, see Tedlock
(G118), Hsia (V2), Reuter (V4), Widmer (V5), and Mackenzie
(V49).

"The Princess" (w. 1924; s. 1925; v. 1934 [TALES])

For additional commentary on this story, see Cavitch (G16),
Clark (G17), Cowan (G22), Hough (G56), Leavis (G68), Moore
(G80), Nin (G88), Pinion (G95), Tedlock (G118), Goonetilleke
(H147), Gunn (H159), Merivale (H247), Rossman (H318), Vickery
(H393), Woodcock (H421), Clark (T1), Harris (T12), Powell
(T20), Walker (T27), Hsia (V2), Krishnamurthi (V3), Reuter
(V4), Widmer (V5), Marnat (V21), Tanner (V30), Travis (V32),
and Férnandez (AA141).

V118   MacDonald, Robert H. "Images of Negative Union: The
        Symbolic World of D.H. Lawrence's 'The Princess.'"
        SSF, 16 (1979), 289-93.
                Symbols of negative opposition reinforce the
                destructive relationship in the story.

V119   Weiner, S. Ronald. "Irony and Symbolism in 'The Prin-
        cess.'" In A D.H. LAWRENCE MISCELLANY. Ed. Harry T.
        Moore. Pp. 221-38. See G81.
                DHL's irony in the story "symbolic." Vague.

"Prologue to WOMEN IN LOVE" (w. 1916; s. 1963; v. 1968 [PHOE-NIX II])

For commentary on this cancelled opening chapter to WL, see Ford (G39), Clarke (M2), Ross (M6), Ford (N32), and Ross (N82).

"The Prussian Officer" (w. 1913; s. 1914; v. 1914 [PRUSSIAN OFFICER])

For additional commentary on this story, see Delany (F41), Draper (G33), Ford (G39), Hobsbaum (G51), Moore (G80), Panichas (G91), Tedlock (G118), Weiss (G123), Appleman (H17), Haegert (H162), Kaplan (H200), Sale (H323), Vickery (H393), Hsia (V2), Reuter (V4), Widmer (V5), Amon (V7), Scott (V27), Cushman (V124, V125), and Finney (V126).

V120   Adelman, Gary.   "Beyond the Pleasure Principle: An Ana-
       lysis of D.H. Lawrence's 'The Prussian Officer.'"   SSF,
       1 (1963), 8-15.
            Story an allegory of mankind's perverse and
            perverting "denial of life."

V121   Eaglestone,Arthur A. [Roger Dataller].   "Mr. Lawrence
       and Mrs. Woolf."   EIC, 8 (1958), 48-59.
            Disputes Woolf's criticism of DHL's "inade-
            quate technique" (see L69), showing his con-
            scientious revision of two stories: "The
            Prussian Officer" and "The Thorn in the
            Flesh."   See H188.

V122   Englander, Ann.   "'The Prussian Officer': The Self Di-
       vided."   SR, 71 (1963), 605-19.
            DHL's theory "rides roughshod" over the
            story.   A bewildered and confused essay.

V123   Humma, John B.   "Melville's BILLY BUDD and Lawrence's
       'The Prussian Officer': Old Adams and New."   ESSAYS IN
       LITERATURE, 1 (1974), 83-88.
            "Curious" correspondences between the central
            situations of the two stories, despite the
            impossibility of DHL knowing Melville's BILLY
            BUDD (not published until 1924).

THE PRUSSIAN OFFICER AND OTHER STORIES (1914)

For additional commentary on this collection, see Brunsdale
(G14), Hobsbaum (G51), Hough (G56), Moore (G80), Pritchard
(G101), Sinzelle (G110), and Tedlock (G118).

V124   Cushman, Keith.   D.H. LAWRENCE AT WORK: THE EMERGENCE
       OF THE *PRUSSIAN OFFICER* STORIES.   Charlottesville: Univ.
       Press of Virginia, 1978.
              Careful study of DHL's textual revisions of
              several stories collected in THE PRUSSIAN
              OFFICER volume, indicating both the radical
              changes in his view of his materials and
              the development of his craftsmanship during
              his critical apprenticeship years (1907-14).
              Includes general history of the stories and
              close analyses of "The Daughters of the Vi-
              car," "Odour of Chrysanthemums," "The Prus-
              sian Officer," "The Shades of Spring," "The
              Thorn in the Flesh," and "The White Stock-
              ing."   Several portions previously published.

V125   -----.   "'I am going through a transition stage': THE
       PRUSSIAN OFFICER and THE RAINBOW."   DHLR, 8 (1975),
       176-97.
              For annotation see M23.

V126   Finney, Brian H.   "D.H. Lawrence's Progress to Maturity:
       From Holograph Manuscript to Final Publication of THE
       PRUSSIAN OFFICER AND OTHER STORIES."   SB, 28 (1975),
       321-32.
              Comparison of the holograph versions of the
              stories (c. 1907 and after) with their re-
              vised final versions (1913-14), illustrates
              DHL's "astonishing growth" between 1912 and
              1915.

V127   Orwell, George.   "Review of THE PRUSSIAN OFFICER AND
       OTHER STORIES by D.H. Lawrence."   1945.   In THE COLLECTED
       ESSAYS, JOURNALISM AND LETTERS OF GEORGE ORWELL.   Ed.
       Sonia Orwell and Ian Angus.   New York: Harcourt, 1969.
       IV, 30-33.
              DHL's "faults" less troubling in his short
              stories, yet his strengths most evident: his
              lyricism, his "undisciplined enthusiasm" for
              nature, and his "power of understanding...
              people totally different from himself."

"Rawdon's Roof" (w. 1927, 1928; s. 1928; v. 1933 [LOVELY LADY])

There are no essential critical studies principally concerned
with this story. For commentary on the work, see Tedlock
(G118), Hsia (V2), and Widmer (V5).

"Renegade Eve." Working title of "New Eve and Old Adam" (q.v.)

"Rex" (w. 1919 [?]; s. 1921; v. 1936 [PHOENIX])

There are no essential critical studies principally concerned
with this sketch. For commentary on the work, see Moore (F112),
Nehls (F123), and Moore (G80).

"The Rocking-Horse Winner" (w. 1926; s. 1926; v. 1933 [LOVELY
LADY])

For additional commentary on this story, see Moore (G80), Ted-
lock (G118), Ballin (H24), Coveny (H77), Michaels-Tonks (H250),
Vickery (H393), Hsia (V2), Widmer (V5), Amon (V7), and Goodman
(V14).

V128   Barrett, Gerald R., and Thomas L. Erskine, eds.   FROM
       FICTION TO FILM: D.H. LAWRENCE'S "THE ROCKING-HORSE
       WINNER." Encino, Calif.: Dickenson, 1974.
              Reprints story text, three previously-pub-
              lished critical discussions of the story,
              the film's final shooting script, with tech-
              nical annotations and numerous "stills,"
              and three critical essays (two not pre-
              viouly published) on the film adaptation.
              Includes study questions, suggestions for
              papers, a bibliography, Barrett's "Intro-
              duction" (pp. 2-33)--a general consideration
              of the relationship between film and fic-
              tion--and V129, V140, V143, V146, and V147.

V129   Becker, Henry, III.   "'The Rocking-Horse Winner': Film
       as Parable." LFQ, 1 (1973), 55-63.
              Summarizes Anthony Pelissier's cinematic
              techniques in his faithful and unsuccessful
              screen adaptation of the story (1949).   See
              G70.   Reprinted above.

V130 Consolo, Dominick P., ed. D.H. LAWRENCE: "THE ROCKING-
      HORSE WINNER." Columbus, Ohio: Merrill, 1969.
            Reprints story text, with Consolo's brief
            "Introduction" (pp. 1-5), the standard case-
            book apparatus (e.g., suggestions for papers),
            and fifteen critical essays, notes, and ex-
            tracts concerning the story (all but one item
            previously published). Includes V131, V134,
            V135, V140, V141, V142, V147, V148, and ex-
            tracts from G80, G118, V5, V7, and V24.

V131 Davis, Robert G. "Observations on 'The Rocking-Horse
      Winner.'" In INSTRUCTOR'S MANUAL FOR *TEN MODERN MASTERS*.
      1953. 2nd ed. New York: Harcourt, 1959. Pp. 49-50.
            Good brief comment on themes and symbols in
            the story. Reprinted above.

V132 Fraiberg, Selma. "Two Modern Incest Heroes." PR, 28
      (1961), 646-61.
            Freud's influence on DHL's "The Rocking-Horse
            Winner," among other works.

V133 Goldberg, Michael. "Lawrence's 'The Rocking-Horse Win-
      ner': A Dickensian Fable?" MFS, 15 (1969), 525-36.
            DHL's symbolism Dickensian rather than Freud-
            ian (cf. DOMBEY AND SON [1848]).

V134 Gordon, Carolyn, and Allen Tate. THE HOUSE OF FICTION.
      Ed. Gordon and Tate. New York: Scribner's, 1950. Pp.
      227-30.
            The symbolism of the horse. Reprinted in V130.

V135 Hepburn, James G. "Disarming and Uncanny Visions: Freud's
      'The Uncanny' with Regard to Form and Content in Stories
      by Sherwood Anderson and D.H. Lawrence." L&P, 9 (1959),
      9-12.
            Applies Freud's theory of the "uncanny" to
            DHL's story and Anderson's "Death in the
            Woods" (1926). Reprinted in V130.

V136 Holland, Norman N. THE DYNAMICS OF LITERARY RESPONSE.
      New York: Oxford Univ. Press, 1968. Pp. 255-58.
            DHL's employment of the Great Mother arche-
            type in the story (Oscar = Osiris; Esther =
            Ishtar).

V137 Humma, John B. "Pan and 'The Rocking-Horse Winner.'"
ESSAYS IN LITERATURE, 5 (1978), 53-60.
> Story's allusions to the myth of Pan (god of
> luck), consonant with DHL's use of the Pan
> myth in the twenties (e.g., in "St. Mawr"
> and PS).

V138 Issacs, Neil D. "The Autoerotic Metaphor in Joyce,
Sterne, Lawrence, Stevens, and Whitman." L&P, 15 (1965),
92-106.
> Undertones of self-abuse in DHL's story, among
> other works.

V139 Koban, Charles. "Allegory and the Death of the Heart
in 'The Rocking-Horse Winner.'" SSF, 15 (1978), 391-96.
> Story echoes the Biblical parables in style
> and subject.

V140 Lamson, Roy, et al. "Critical Analysis of 'The Rocking-
Horse Winner.'" In THE CRITICAL READER. 1949. Rev.
ed. Ed. Roy Lamson, et al. New York: Norton, 1962.
Pp. 542-47.
> Introductory criticism of the story. Reprint-
> ed in V128 and V130.

V141 Marks, W.S., III. "The Psychology of the Uncanny in
Lawrence's 'The Rocking-Horse Winner.'" MFS, 11 (1966),
381-92.
> Analogies to Paul's behavior in selected
> Freudian case studies familiar to DHL. Re-
> printed in V130.

V142 Martin, W.R. "Fancy or Imagination? 'The Rocking-Horse
Winner.'" CE, 24 (1962), 64-65.
> Defends story as representative of DHL's most
> inspired work, prompting replies and amplifi-
> cations in a later issue of CE (24 [1962],
> 323-24). Note and replies reprinted in V130.

V143 Mellen, Joan. "'The Rocking-Horse Winner' as Cinema."
In FROM FICTION TO FILM. Ed. Gerald R. Barrett and
Thomas L. Erskine. Pp. 214-23. See V128.
> Technical critique of the story's film adap-
> tation.

V144 Rohrberger, Mary. "D.H. Lawrence: 'The Rocking-Horse Winner.'" In HAWTHORNE AND THE MODERN SHORT STORY: A STUDY IN GENRE. The Hague: Mouton, 1966. Pp. 74-80.
Fairy-tale conventions and symbolism in the story (cf. Hawthorne's fictional techniques).

V145 San Juan, Epifanio. "Theme Versus Imitation: D.H. Lawrence's 'The Rocking-Horse Winner.'" DHLR, 3 (1970), 136-40.
On the "dialectical interplay of fantasy... and the worldly" in the story. Reprinted in V128.

V146 Smith, Julian. "The Social Architecture of 'The Rocking-Horse Winner.'" In FROM FICTION TO FILM. Ed. Gerald R. Barrett and Thomas L. Erskine. Pp. 224-30. See V128.
Story's and its film adaptation's social themes excellently communicated through the "environment of its characters."

V147 Snodgrass, W.D. "A Rocking-Horse: The Symbol, the Pattern, the Way to Live." HudR, 11 (1958), 191-200.
Story dramatizes a masturbation fantasy. Reprinted in Snodgrass's THE RADICAL PURSUIT (New York: Harper, 1975), pp. 128-40, and in G115, V128, and V130.

V148 Turner, Frederick W. "Prancing in to a Purpose: Myths, Horses, and True Selfhood in Lawrence's 'The Rocking-Horse Winner.'" In D.H. LAWRENCE: "THE ROCKING-HORSE WINNER." Ed. Dominick P. Consolo. Pp. 95-106. See V130.
Paul's death the destruction of the "societal instinct" in a "world populated with egomaniacs."

V149 Warschausky, Sidney. "'The Rocking-Horse Winner.'" In INSIGHT II: ANALYSES OF MODERN BRITISH LITERATURE. Ed. John V. Hagopian and Martin Dolch. Frankfurt: Hirschgraben, 1964. Pp. 228-33.
Story synopsis, critique, and study questions.

"St. Mawr" (w. 1924; s. 1925; v. 1934 [TALES])

For additional commentary on this novella, see Cavitch (G16),
Clark (G17), Colin (G19), Cowan (G22), Draper (G33), Goodheart
(G44), Hobsbaum (G51), Hough (G56), Inniss (G60), Kermode (G65),
Leavis (G68), Michaels-Tonks (G74), Miles (G76), Moore (G80),
Murry (G85), Nahal (G86), Negriolli (G87), Pinion (G95), Sagar
(G104), Seillière (G107), Slade (G111), Tedlock (G118), Tin-
dall (G120), Vivas (G121), Albright (H5), Ballin (H24), Goone-
tilleke (H147), Gunn (H159), Gutierrez (H160), Harrison (H168),
Irwin (H193), John (H196), Kaplan (H200), Lerner (H221), Meri-
vale (H247), Michaels-Tonks (H250), Moynahan (H265), Pritchard
(H298), Sherman (H340), Stewart (H361), Tindall (H379), Vickery
(H393), Wicker (H406), Woodcock (H421), Clark (T1), Harris
(T12), Powell (T20), Walker (T27), Hsia (V2), Reuter (V4),
Widmer (V5), Craig (V10), Engel (V13), Tanner (V30), Humma
(V137), and Koljević (AA191).

V150 Blanchard, Lydia. "Mothers and Daughters in D.H. Lawrence:
     THE RAINBOW and Selected Shorter Works." In LAWRENCE AND
     WOMEN. Ed. Anne Smith. Pp. 75-100. See G112.
         On R and "St. Mawr," chief among the "se-
         lected shorter works." For annotation see
         M16.

V151 Bodenheimer, Rosemarie. "'St. Mawr,' A PASSAGE TO INDIA,
     and the Question of Influence." DHLR, 13 (1980), 134-49.
         "Remarkable similarities in structure and con-
         cern" traced in the two works. (DHL was read-
         ing Forster's novel [1924] while writing his
         novella.)

V152 Brown, Keith. "Welsh Red Indian: D.H. Lawrence and 'St.
     Mawr.'" EIC, 32 (1982), 158-79.
         DHL's unnoticed interweaving of primitive Cel-
         tic and American Indian myths and allusions
         into his novella.

V153 Cary, Joyce. ART AND REALITY: WAYS OF THE CREATIVE PRO-
     CESS. Garden City, N.Y.: Doubleday, 1958. Pp. 107-09,
     117-18, 174-76, 183-85, and passim.
         Comments on the power and revolutionary orig-
         inality of DHL's style and symbolism, with
         special praise for "St. Mawr," his "master-
         piece" (cf. Tolstoy).

V154   Gidley, Mick. "Antipodes: D.H. Lawrence's 'St. Mawr.'"
       ARIEL, 5, No. 1 (1974), 25-41.
              Dualistic themes and symbols in the novella.

V155   Liddell, Robert.   "Lawrence and Dr. Leavis: The Case
       of 'St. Mawr.'" EIC, 4 (1954), 321-27.
              Leavis's high estimate of "St. Mawr" a dis-
              tortion of DHL (see G68).

V156   Oppel, Horst. "D.H. Lawrence: 'St. Mawr.'" In DER
       MODERNE ENGLISCHE ROMAN: INTERPRETATIONEN. Ed. Oppel.
       Berlin: Schmidt, 1965. Pp. 115-34.
              Surveys DHL's unique fictional techniques
              (characterization, style, point of view),
              special form of realism, and metaphysical
              themes in the novella. [In German.]

V157   Poirier, Richard. A WORLD ELSEWHERE: THE PLACE OF STYLE
       IN AMERICAN LITERATURE. New York: Oxford Univ. Press,
       1966. Pp. 37-50 and passim.
              DHL's "St. Mawr" paradoxically the best ex-
              pression of a major struggle in *American*
              writing "of the last century," the struggle
              "to find a voice, a personal style appropri-
              ate to what he calls in the story the 'on-
              ward pushing spirit.'" Notes association
              between the novella's major motifs and the
              American themes explored by DHL in STUDIES
              IN CLASSIC AMERICAN LITERATURE (A65).

V158   Ragussis, Michael. "The False Myth of 'St. Mawr': Law-
       rence and the Subterfuge of Art." PLL, 11 (1975), 186-96.
              Ironic reading, seeing novella as implicitly
              critical of the Pan myth and of Lou's "ful-
              fillment" through escape.

V159   Scholtes, M. "'St. Mawr': Between Degeneration and Re-
       generation." DUTCH QUARTERLY REVIEW, 5 (1975), 253-69.
              Novella DHL's most effective vision of the
              transition from cultural dissolution to the
              generation of a new and "higher culture."

V160   Smith, Bob L. "D.H. Lawrence's'St. Mawr': Transposition
       of Myth." ArQ, 24 (1968), 197-208.
              The Pan myth in America.

V161 Wasserman, Jerry. "'St. Mawr' and the Search for Com-
      munity." MOSAIC, 5, No. 2 (1972), 113-23.
          Novella rejects the earlier fiction's sug-
          gestion of sexual fulfillment as an alter-
          native to the break-down of community, to
          postulate a higher sense of community through
          a "quasi-sexual," mystical union with the
          landscape.

V162 Wilde, Alan. "The Illusion of 'St. Mawr': Technique and
      Vision in D.H. Lawrence's Novel." PMLA, 79 (1964), 164-
      70.
          The symbolic journey provides the novel's
          structural integrity; the ending is delib-
          erately and significantly open.

"Samson and Delilah" (w. 1916; s. 1917; v. 1922 [ENGLAND, MY
ENGLAND])

There are no essential critical studies principally concerned
with this story. For commentary on the work, see Tedlock
(G118), Hsia (V2), Reuter (V4), Widmer (V5), and Mackenzie
(V49).

"Second Best" (w. 1911; s. 1912; v. 1914 [PRUSSIAN OFFICER])

There are no essential critical studies principally concerned
with this story. For commentary on the work, see Brunsdale
(G14), Tedlock (G118), Vickery (H393), Hsia (V2), Reuter (V4),
Widmer (V5), Harris (V15), Cushman (V125), and Finney (V126).

"The Shades of Spring" (w. 1911, 1914; s. 1913; v. 1914 [PRUS-
SIAN OFFICER])

For additional commentary on this story, see Brunsdale (G14),
Moore (G80), Tedlock (G118), Weiss (G123), Delavenay (H86),
Vickery (H393), Hsia (V2), Reuter (V4), Widmer (V5), Cushman
(V124, V125), and Finney (V126).

V163 Sagar, Keith. "The Best I Have Known: Lawrence's 'A
      Modern Lover' and 'The Shades of Spring.'" SSF, 4 (1967),
      144-51.
          For annotation see V111.

"The Shadow in the Rose Garden" (w. 1908, 1914; s. 1914; v. 1914 [PRUSSIAN OFFICER])

For additional commentary on this story, see Brunsdale (G14), Moore (G80), Tedlock (G118), Eliot (H104), Kiely (H205), Melchiori (H245), Hsia (V2), Reuter (V4), Widmer (V5), Cushman (V125), and Finney (V126).

V164   Cushman, Keith. "D.H. Lawrence at Work: 'The Shadow in the Rose Garden.'" DHLR, 8 (1975), 31-46.
        Describes DHL's revisions of two earlier versions of the story (1908, 1914), to heighten the "intensity" of the narrative.

V165   Martz, Louis L. THE POEM OF THE MIND. New York: Oxford Univ. Press, 1966. Pp. 111-13.
        Shadows of DHL's story in T.S. Eliot's "Burnt Norton" (1936) and THE FAMILY REUNION (1939).

"A Sick Collier" (w. 1912; s. 1913; v. 1914 [PRUSSIAN OFFICER])

There are no essential critical studies principally concerned with this story. For commentary on the work, see Hobsbaum (G51), Tedlock (G118), Vickery (H393), Hsia (V2), Reuter (V4), Widmer (V5), Cushman (V125), and Finney (V126).

"Smile" (w. 1925; s. 1926; v. 1928 [WOMAN WHO RODE AWAY])

There are no essential critical studies principally concerned with this story. For commentary on the work, See Cowan (G22), Moore (G80), Tedlock (G118), Hsia (V2), Reuter (V4), and Widmer (V5).

"The Soiled Rose." Original title of "The Shades of Spring" (q.v.)

"Strike Pay" (w. 1912; s. 1913; v. 1934 [MODERN LOVER])

There are no essential critical studies principally concerned with this story. For commentary on the work, see Tedlock (G118), Hsia (V2), and Widmer (V5).

"Strike Pay I, Her Turn." Original title of "Her Turn" (q.v.)

"Strike Pay II, Ephraim's Half Sovereign." Original title of "Strike Pay" (q.v.)

"Sun" (w. 1925, 1926; s. 1926, 1928; v. 1928 [WOMAN WHO RODE AWAY])

For additional commentary on this story, see Sagar (in B20), Clark (G17), Hobsbaum (G51), Leavis (G68), Moore (G80), Sagar (G104), Tedlock (G118), Vickery (H393), Hsia (V2), Krishnamurthi (V3), Reuter (V4), Widmer (V5), Jones (V18), MacNiven (V20), and Oppel (Y116).

V166   Ross, Michael L. "Lawrence's Second 'Sun.'" DHLR, 8
        (1975), 1-18.
                Compares the widely anthologized, inferior
                earlier version of the story and the prefer-
                able, unexpurgated, 1928 text. Also see
                Brian Finney's response and Ross's rejoinder
                in DHLR, 8 (1975), 371-74.

"The Thimble" (w. 1915; s. 1917; v. 1968 [PHOENIX II])

There are no essential critical studies principally concerned with this original version of "The Ladybird." For commentary on the work, see Widmer (V5) and Scott (V85).

"Things" (w. 1927; s. 1928; v. 1933 [LOVELY LADY])

There are no essential critical studies principally concerned
with this story. For commentary on the work, see Hobsbaum
(G51), Leavis (G68), Moore (G80), Tedlock (G118), Hsia (V2),
Krishnamurthi (V3), and Widmer (V5).

"The Thorn in the Flesh" (w. 1913; s. 1914; v. 1914 [PRUSSIAN
OFFICER])

For additional commentary on this story, see Tedlock (G118),
Vickery (H393), Hsia (V2), Reuter (V4), Widmer (V5), Little-
wood (V19), Scott (V27), Cushman (V124, V125), and Finney
(V126).

V167   Eaglestone, Arthur A. [Roger Dataller]. "Mr. Lawrence
        and Mrs. Woolf." EIC, 8 (1958), 48-59.
                On "The Prussian Officer" and "The Thorn in
                the Flesh." For annotation see V121.

"Tickets, Please" (w. 1918; s. 1919; v. 1922 [ENGLAND, MY
ENGLAND])

For additional commentary on this story, see Slade (G111),
Tedlock (G118), Hsia (V2), Reuter (V4), Widmer (V5), and Mackenzie (V49).

V168   Kegel-Brinkgreve, E. "The Dionysian Tramline." DUTCH
        QUARTERLY REVIEW, 5 (1975), 180-94.
                Story's parallel to Euripides' treatment of
                the myth of Dionysus, in THE BACCHAE.

V169   Lainoff, Seymour. "The Wartime Setting of Lawrence's
        'Tickets, Please.'" SSF, 7 (1970), 649-51.
                Story's undercurrent of "lawlessness and
                bleakness."

V170   Michel-Michot, Paulette. "D.H. Lawrence's 'Tickets,
        Please': The Structural Importance of the Setting."
        RLV, 41 (1975), 464-70.
                Significance of story's wartime setting and
                "covert criticism of modern society."

V171 Trilling, Lionel. "D.H. Lawrence: 'Tickets, Please.'"
      1967. In PREFACES TO *THE EXPERIENCE OF LITERATURE*. New
      York: Harcourt, 1979. Pp. 123-27.
           Story explores the contrast between the old
           and the new ways, in style as well as in sub-
           ject matter.

V172 Wheeler, Richard P. "'Cunning in his overthrow': Law-
      rence's Art in 'Tickets, Please.'" DHLR, 10 (1977),
      242-50.
           DHL, like his character John Thomas, cunningly
           achieves "a measure of dignity and power...
           proud autonomy and mystery" by precipitating
           guilt in those who pervert and brutalize
           "longings for intimate contact." See V1.

"Two Blue Birds" (w. 1926; s. 1927; v. 1928 [WOMAN WHO RODE
AWAY])

There are no essential critical studies principally concerned
with this story. For commentary on the work, see Leavis (G68),
Tedlock (G118), Vickery (H393), Hsia (V2), Krishnamurthi (V3),
Reuter (V4), and Widmer (V5).

"Two Marriages" (w. 1911; s. 1934)

For commentary on this original version of "The Daughters of
the Vicar," see Kalnins (V44).

"The Undying Man" (w. 1927; v. 1936 [PHOENIX])

For additional commentary on this story fragment, see Sagar
(in B20) and Widmer (V5).

V173 Zytaruk, George J. "'The Undying Man': D.H. Lawrence's
      Yiddish Story." DHLR, 4 (1971), 20-27.
           Story DHL's "reworking" of Koteliansky's
           translation of a Yiddish folktale: "Maimo-
           nides and Aristotle" (c. 1926).

"The Vicar's Garden." Working title of "The Shadow in the
Rose Garden" (q.v.)

"Vin Ordinaire." Working title of "The Thorn in the Flesh"
(q.v.)

"The Virgin and the Gipsy" (w. 1926; s. 1930; v. 1934 [TALES])

For additional commentary on this novella, see Clark (G17),
Draper (G33), Hobsbaum (G51), Hough (G56), Leavis (G68), Moyn-
ahan (G83), Negriolli (G87), Tedlock (G118), Albright (H5),
Vickery (H393), Hsia (V2), Krishnamurthi (V3), Reuter (V4),
Widmer (V5), Craig (V10, V11), Springer (V29), Gutierrez (Z4),
and Koljević (AA191).

V174 Crump, G.B. "Gopher Prairie or Papplewick?: 'The Virgin
      and the Gipsy' as Film." DHLR, 4 (1971), 142-53.
            Imaginative failures and distortions of DHL's
            admittedly weak novella in the blundering
            screen adaptation (1970).

V175 Gontarski, S.E. "'The Virgin and the Gypsy' (1930),
      D.H. Lawrence; Christopher Miles, 1970: An English Water-
      color." In THE ENGLISH NOVEL AND THE MOVIES. Ed. Mi-
      chael Klein and Gillian Parker. New York: Ungar, 1981.
      Pp. 257-67.
            Reviews the novella's film "reinterpretation"
            (film title spelled "Gypsy"), a "delicate
            period piece, significantly different in
            theme and structure" from DHL's novella, yet
            a "faithful transformation" of DHL's "spirit."

V176 Guttenberg, Barnett. "Realism and Romance in Lawrence's
      'The Virgin and the Gipsy.'" SSF, 17 (1980), 99-103.
            DHL's "theoretical and formal impasse" be-
            tween the modes of realism and romance, seen
            in his novella, "reflects a critical junc-
            ture" in DHL's development.

V177 Hesse, Hermann. "Erinnerung an ein paar Bücher." NEUE
      RUNDSCHAU, 45, pt. 1 (1934), 454-58.
            Notes similarities between DHL's novella and
            Knut Hamsun's THE ROAD LEADS ON (1933). [In
            German.]

V178   Meyers, Jeffrey.   "'The Voice of Water': Lawrence's 'The
       Virgin and the Gipsy.'"   EM, 21 (1970), 199-207.
           Novella an exploration of three variations
           on DHL's characteristic love themes.

V179   Smith, Julian.   "Vision and Revision: 'The Virgin and
       the Gipsy' as Film."   LFQ, 1 (1973), 28-36.
           The novella's screen adaptation (1970) suc-
           cessfully expands and amplifies DHL's story.
           See G70.

"The White Stocking" (w. 1907, 1910; v. 1914 [PRUSSIAN OFFICER])

There are no essential critical studies principally concerned
with this story.   For commentary on the work, see Brunsdale
(G14), Hobsbaum (G51), Leavis (G68), Tedlock (G118), Hsia (V2),
Krishnamurthi (V3), Reuter (V4), Widmer (V5), Cushman (V124,
V125), and Finney (V126).

"The White Woman."   Working title of "The Witch à la Mode"
(q.v.)

"The Wilful Woman" (w. 1922; v. 1971 [PRINCESS AND OTHER
STORIES])

There are no essential critical studies principally concerned
with this novel fragment.   For commentary on the work, see
Finney (in B8) and Sagar (in B20).

"Wintry Peacock" (w. 1919; s. 1921; v. 1922 [ENGLAND, MY ENG-
LAND])

There are no essential critical studies principally concerned
with this story.   For commentary on the work, see Tedlock
(G118), Vickery (H393), Hsia (V2), Reuter (V4), Widmer (V5),
and Mackenzie (V49).

"The Witch à la Mode" (w. 1911, 1913; s. 1934; v. 1934 [MODERN LOVER])

There are no essential critical studies principally concerned with this story. For commentary on the work, see Brunsdale (G14), Tedlock (G118), Hsia (V2), Widmer (V5), and Harris (V15).

"The Woman Who Rode Away" (w. 1924; s. 1925; v. 1928 [WOMAN WHO RODE AWAY])

For additional commentary on this story, see Murry (F121), Cavitch (G16), Clark (G17), Cowan (G22), Draper (G33), Eisenstein (G36), Goodheart (G44), Hobsbaum (G51), Hough (G56), Joost and Sullivan (G64), Leavis (G68), Negriolli (G87), Pinion (G95), Pritchard (G101), Tedlock (G118), Albright (H5), Clark (H65), Goonetilleke (H147), Gunn (H159), John (H196), Martin (H236), Merivale (H247), Millett (H255), Rossman (H318, H319), Stewart (H361), Vickery (H393), Wicker (H406), Woodcock (H421), Clark (T1), Harris (T12), Powell (T20), Walker (T27), Hsia (V2), Krishnamurthi (V3), Reuter (V4), Widmer (V5), Jones (V18), MacNiven (V20), Springer (V29), Tanner (V30), and Travis (V32).

V180   Draper, Ronald P. "The Defeat of Feminism: D.H. Lawrence's 'The Fox' and 'The Woman Who Rode Away.'" SSF, 3 (1966), 186-98.
            For annotation see V57.

V181   Wasserstrom, William. "Phoenix on Turtle Island: D.H. Lawrence in Henry Adams' America." GaR, 32 (1978), 173-97.
            Parallels between DHL's and Adams' analyses of the "problem of American progress."

THE WOMAN WHO RODE AWAY AND OTHER STORIES (1928)

There are no essential critical studies principally concerned with this collection. For commentary on the volume, see Hobsbaum (G51), Moore (G80), and Tedlock (G118).

"You Touched Me" (w. 1919; s. 1920; v. 1922 [ENGLAND, MY ENG-
LAND])

For additional commentary on this story, see Hobsbaum (G51),
Leavis (G68), Tedlock (G118), Lerner (H221), Hsia (V2), Krish-
namurthi (V3), Reuter (V4), Widmer (V5), Temple (V31), and
Mackenzie (V49).

V182   Williams, Tennessee (and Donald Windham). YOU TOUCHED
        ME! A ROMANTIC COMEDY IN THREE ACTS, SUGGESTED BY A
        SHORT STORY OF THE SAME NAME BY D.H. LAWRENCE. New York:
        French, 1947.
            Adaptation of DHL's story, first produced in
        1945. See F162, G37, and H322.

W.   STUDIES OF THE PAINTINGS

The following section is subdivided into two parts; i. Books
and Essay Collections on the Paintings; and ii. Critical Articles or Chapters on the Paintings.

At present, there are no plans to republish DHL's paintings
in THE CAMBRIDGE EDITION (B1).

For the dates of and information concerning the paintings,
see Sagar (E40), and, for locations of some of the art works,
see Edwards and Phillips (E19) and Welch (E50). For biographical backgrounds to the paintings, see Moore (F112), Murry
(F121), and Nehls (F123).

For additional commentaries on the paintings and art works,
see Lindsay (F93), Draper (G34), Meyers (G73), Sagar (G104),
Weidner (G122), Baron (H27), Earp (Z27), and Rubenstein (Z70).

W, i. Books and Essay Collections on the Paintings

W1   Farmer, David. "ETRUSCAN PLACES." McFarlin Library Keep-
     sake, No. 6. Tulsa, Okla.: McFarlin Library, 1981.
          First separate publication (in facsimile), of
          DHL's 1927 needlepoint figure, based on Etru-
          scan tomb motifs, enclosed with a brief histor-
          ical note by Farmer. (Pamphlet--2 pp.)

W2   Levy, Mervyn, ed. THE PAINTINGS OF D.H. LAWRENCE. New
     York: Viking, 1964.
          Includes DHL's "Making Pictures" (from A75),
          reproductions of forty-seven paintings by DHL
          (see B15), and three essays on DHL as an art-
          ist: W5, W6, and W8.

W, ii.   Critical Articles or Chapters on the Paintings

W3   Baron, Carl E. "D.H. Lawrence's Early Paintings." In
     YOUNG BERT. Comp. Lucy I. Edwards and David Phillips. Pp.
     32-39. See E19.
          The limitations of DHL's provincial cultural
          background seen in his apprentice work as an
          artist. Almost all his early paintings are
          copies and studies of minor English water-
          colorists and predate "the remarkable expan-
          sion of his consciousness from 1912 onwards."

W4   Crehan, Hubert. "Lady Chatterley's Painter: The Banned
     Pictures of D.H. Lawrence." ART NEWS, 55 (Feb. 1957), 38-
     41, 63-64, 66.
          A "first attempt to consider seriously both the
          meaning and the quality" of DHL's paintings.
          Includes photographs of nine of the paintings.

W5   Lindsay, Jack. "The Impact of Modernism on Lawrence." In
     THE PAINTINGS OF D.H. LAWRENCE. Ed. Mervyn Levy. Pp. 35-
     53. See W2.
          DHL's movement toward primitivism in his paint-
          ings, a reaction against modernism.

W6   Moore, Harry T. "D.H. Lawrence and His Paintings." In
     THE PAINTINGS OF D.H. LAWRENCE. Ed. Mervyn Levy. Pp. 17-
     34. See W2.
          General commentary, relating DHL's paintings
          to his writing and his life.

W7   Pearsall, Robert Brainard. "The Second Art of D.H. Law-
     rence." SAQ, 63 (1964), 457-67.
          Painting, for DHL, an uncomplicated "release"
          from his personal and creative preoccupations
          in his first art (e.g., in his paintings dur-
          ing the period of SL he seeks "his mother as
          before"; in his last paintings he celebrated
          life in the face of death).

W8   Read, Herbert. "Lawrence as a Painter." In THE PAINTINGS
     OF D.H. LAWRENCE. Ed. Mervyn Levy. Pp. 55-64. See W2.
          Skillful technical analyses of several of the
          individual paintings.

W9   Remsbury, John, and Ann Remsbury. "Lawrence and Art."
      1971. In D.H. LAWRENCE: A CRITICAL STUDY. Ed. Andor
      Gomme. Pp. 190-218. See G43.
            Stresses influence of Cézanne on DHL's paint-
            ings and art criticism.

W10   Rosenthal, T.G. "The Writer as Painter." LISTENER, 68
      (1962), 349-50.
            DHL's "essentially literary" paintings less
            interesting than his essay "Introduction to
            These Paintings" (A71).

W11   Russell, John. "D.H. Lawrence and Painting." In D.H.
      LAWRENCE. Ed. Stephen Spender. Pp. 234-43. See G113.
            DHL an insignificant, intentionally provoca-
            tive, but earnest painter.

X. STUDIES OF THE PLAYS

The following section is subdivided into three parts: i. Books
and Essay Collections on the Plays; ii. General Critical Articles or Chapters on the Plays; and iii. Studies of Individual
Plays (arranged alphabetically, by play title).

A two-volume textual edition of the plays, in progress, will
be published in THE CAMBRIDGE EDITION (B1--ed. Hans Schwarze
and H. Wilderotter).

For bibliographical information on the plays, see Hepburn (E25),
Roberts (E39), and Sagar (E40, E41), and, for biographical
backgrounds to the drama, see Delany (F41), Moore (F112), Murry
(F121), Nehls (F123), and Neville (F124).

For additional, general critical commentaries and information
on the plays, see the following books, in section G above:
Brunsdale (G14), Clark (G17), Hobsbaum (G51), Moore (G80),
Panichas (G91), Pinion (G95), and Sinzelle (G110).

X, i. Books and Essay Collections on the Plays

X1 Nath, Suresh. D.H. LAWRENCE, THE DRAMATIST. Ghaziabad,
    India: Vimal Prakashan, 1979.
            A thematic study of DHL's eight completed plays,
        offering few useful or striking insights. Nath
        discusses, in successive chapters, DHL's "theme
        of human relationships" and "criticism of modern
        civilization," and surveys his plays' structure,
        characterization, realism and naturalism, sym-
        bolism, "tragic vision," "comic genius," and
        performance history. Far inferior to Sklar's
        study, below.

X2   Sklar, Sylvia. THE PLAYS OF D.H. LAWRENCE: A BIOGRAPHICAL
     AND CRITICAL STUDY. New York: Barnes and Noble, 1975.
          Excellent study of DHL's eight plays and two
          play-fragments. Sklar opens with an introduc-
          tory survey of DHL's interest in drama and
          dramatists (e.g., Chekhov and Shaw) and an ac-
          count of the contemporary theatrical tastes
          and conventions which either prevented his
          plays from being performed, or made their per-
          formances fail. In the body of her study
          Sklar examines the individual plays in turn,
          grouping A COLLIER'S FRIDAY NIGHT, THE WIDOW-
          ING OF MRS. HOLROYD, and THE DAUGHTER-IN-LAW
          as naturalist dramas in the manner of Chekhov
          (and too "advanced" for their time), and THE
          MERRY-GO-ROUND, THE MARRIED MAN, and THE FIGHT
          FOR BARBARA as tragi-comedies in which DHL
          deftly achieves a remarkable "formal distance"
          despite his own "personal involvement" in the
          events and themes they present. TOUCH AND GO
          and DAVID are admirable examples of their re-
          spective genres, the political and the biblical
          drama, and ALTITUDE, a social satire, and NOAH'S
          FLOOD, a preparation for DAVID, are fragments
          demonstrating DHL's mature command of dramatic
          form. Sklar's analyses, approaching the plays
          from the director's point of view, skillfully
          assess DHL's dramaturgy and sense of his audi-
          ence. Her conclusion is a useful summary of
          the critical reputation of DHL's plays. This
          is an important study not only for its stress
          on DHL's stagecraft, but also for its implicit
          and valid assumption that DHL's dramatic skills
          are evident in his fiction as well.

X, ii. General Critical Articles or Chapters on the Plays

For additional, foreign-language articles on the plays, see
the following entries in Appendix A: Mori (AA221) and Sandulescu (AA260).

X3   DeFilippis, Simonetta. "Minatori e anime superiori: con-
     flitti famigliari e lotta delle classi nel teatro autobi-
     ografico di D.H. Lawrence" ["Miners and Superior Souls:
     Family Conflicts and Class Struggle in D.H. Lawrence's
     Autobiographical Drama"]. ANNALI ISTITUTO ORIENTALE NAPOLI,
     SEZIONE GERMANICA-ANGLISTICA, 17 (1974), 7-59.
          Biographical sources for DHL's familial and so-
          cial themes in A COLLIER'S FRIDAY NIGHT, THE
          DAUGHTER-IN-LAW, and THE WIDOWING OF MRS. HOL-
          ROYD. [In Italian.]

X4   French, Philip. "Major Miner Dramatist." NEW STATESMAN,
     75 (1968), 390.
          DHL a "major dramatist in the naturalistic tra-
          dition" in A COLLIER'S FRIDAY NIGHT, THE DAUGH-
          TER-IN-LAW, and THE WIDOWING OF MRS. HOLROYD.

X5   Pritchett, V.S. "Lawrence's Laughter." NEW STATESMAN, 72
     (1966), 18-19.
          DHL "loses most of his force in his plays," but
          shows "a surprising gift for farce and low com-
          edy." Review of THE COMPLETE PLAYS (B2), among
          other publications.

X6   Sagar, Keith. "D.H. Lawrence: Dramatist." DHLR, 4 (1971),
     154-82.
          DHL's naturalist plays "clearly the work of a
          major English twentieth century dramatist."
          Concentrates on A COLLIER'S FRIDAY NIGHT, THE
          DAUGHTER-IN-LAW, and THE WIDOWING OF MRS. HOL-
          ROYD.

X7   Waterman, Arthur E. "The Plays of D.H. Lawrence." MD, 2
     (1960), 349-57.
          Enthusiastic survey of the plays and their re-
          lation to DHL's general artistic development.
          Reprinted in Gl15.

X8   Williams, Raymond. "Introduction." In Lawrence's THREE
       PLAYS: A COLLIER'S FRIDAY NIGHT, THE-DAUGHTER-IN-LAW, THE
       WIDOWING OF MRS. HOLROYD. Harmondsworth, Engl.: Penguin,
       1969. Pp. 7-14.
             DHL's difficulty in subordinating his materials
             to dramatic form and convention in his early
             treatment of his "decisive experience--of love,
             of a family, of working life."

X, iii. Studies of Individual Plays

Titles of all of DHL's plays and play fragments are listed,
alphabetically, in this section, regardless of whether there
have been significant critical studies published on them individually. The headnotes for each title will identify substantial critical commentary on the work to be found in studies located elsewhere in this bibliography.

Note: The dates following individual play titles indicate
date(s) of composition ("w"), date of first separate publication prior to collected publication, if any ("s"), and date
of first collected publication ("v"), with the collection
identified by brief title in brackets. The dating information has been drawn from Roberts (E39) and Sagar (E40).

"Altitude" (w. 1924; s. 1938; v. 1965 [COMPLETE PLAYS])

There are no essential critical studies principally concerned
with this play fragment. For commentary on the work, see
Johnson (in A45), Tedlock (E48), and Sklar (X2).

A COLLIER'S FRIDAY NIGHT (w. 1906, 1909; s. 1934; v. 1965
[COMPLETE PLAYS])

For additional commentary on this play, see Brunsdale (G14),
Sinzelle (G110), Nath (X1), Sklar (X2), DeFilippis (X3),
French (X4), Sagar (X6), Waterman (X7), and Williams (X8).

X9   Garnett, Edward. "Introduction." In Lawrence's A COLLIER'S
       FRIDAY NIGHT. London: Secker, 1934. Pp. v-vii.
             Despite the immaturities of his early play, DHL
             shows "sureness of touch and penetrating direct-
             ness" in his "dramatic chronicle of family life."

X10 O'Casey, Sean. "A Miner's Dream of Home." 1934. In
     BLASTS AND BENEDICTIONS: ARTICLES AND STORIES. Ed. Ronald
     Ayling. London: Macmillan, 1967. Pp. 222-25.
          DHL "shows the makings of a fine dramatist,"
          but the English "theatre received him not."

THE DAUGHTER-IN-LAW (w. 1913; v. 1965 [COMPLETE PLAYS])

For additional commentary on this play, see Brunsdale (G14),
Nath (X1), Sklar (X2), DeFilippis (X3), French (X4), Sagar
(X6), and Williams (X8).

X11 Marland, Michael. "Introduction." In Lawrence's *THE*
     WIDOWING OF MRS. HOLROYD AND *THE DAUGHTER-IN-LAW*. London:
     Heineman Educational, 1968. Pp. xi-xxxvi.
          Backgrounds to the plays' composition and com-
          ment on their place in DHL's canon (e.g., a
          comparison of THE WIDOWING OF MRS. HOLROYD and
          "Odour of Chrysanthemums"). Marland also pro-
          vides a glossary of Nottinghamshire dialect
          and mining terms.

X12 Sagar, Keith. "The Strange History of THE DAUGHTER-IN-
     LAW." DHLR, 11 (1978), 175-84.
          Summarizes play's composition and curious per-
          formance history, questioning why Walter Green-
          wood's 1936 stage adaptation ("My Son's My
          Son") was falsely publicized as the completion
          of an unfinished manuscript. See below.

X13 Sklar, Sylvia. "THE DAUGHTER-IN-LAW and 'My Son's My
     Son.'" DHLR, 9 (1976), 254-65.
          "My Son's My Son," heretofore believed to be
          Walter Greenwood's completion of an unfinished
          play by DHL (1936), actually his revision and
          adaptation of THE DAUGHTER-IN-LAW for perfor-
          mance. See above.

DAVID (w. 1925; s. 1926; v. 1933 [PLAYS])

For additional commentary on this play, see Murry (F121),
Clark (G17), Panichas (G91), Patmore (G93), R. Pritchard
(G101, H296), W. Pritchard (H298), Nath (X1), Sklar (X2),
Waterman (X7), and Mori (AA221). Also see the facsimile of
DHL's "Music for DAVID," published in G81.

X14 DeFilippis, Simonetta. "La fiamma e il volto: Studio
     filologico dell'ideologia del DAVID di D.H. Lawrence"
     ["The Flame and the Face: A Philological Study of the
     Ideology of D.H. Lawrence's DAVID"]. ANNALI ISTITUTO
     ORIENTALE NAPOLI, SEZIONE GERMANICA-ANGLISTICA, 18
     (1975), 7-84.
          Studies DHL's assimilation and adaptation of
          his biblical sources for DAVID. [In Italian.]

X15 Roston, Murray. "W.B. Yeats and D.H. Lawrence." In BIB-
     LICAL DRAMA IN ENGLAND: FROM THE MIDDLE AGES TO THE PRES-
     ENT DAY. Evanston, Ill.: Northwestern Univ. Press, 1968.
     Pp. 264-79.
          The paradoxically pagan appeal of the Bible
          for Yeats and DHL in their Biblical plays.

X16 West, Edward Sackville. "A Modern Isaiah." NEW STATES-
     MAN, 27 (1926), 360-61.
          Selective praise for DHL's "The Crown" (A61),
          and the title essay in REFLECTIONS ON THE
          DEATH OF A PORCUPINE (A69; cf. Blake), and
          admiring review of DHL's unperformable DAVID
          (cf. André Gide's SAÜL [1896]). Reprinted
          in G34.

THE FIGHT FOR BARBARA (w. 1912; s. 1933; v. 1965 [COMPLETE
PLAYS])

There are no essential critical studies principally concerned
with this play. For commentary on the work, see Nath (X1) and
Sklar (X2).

"Keeping Barbara." Title given to THE FIGHT FOR BARBARA (q.v.)
for periodical publication in 1933.

THE MARRIED MAN (w. 1912; s. 1940; v. 1965 [COMPLETE PLAYS])

There are no essential critical studies principally concerned with this play. For commentary on the work, see Neville (F124), Brunsdale (G14), Nath (X1), Sklar (X2), and Waterman (X7).

THE MERRY-GO-ROUND (w. 1910; s. 1941; v. 1965 [COMPLETE PLAYS])

There are no essential critical studies principally concerned with this play. For commentary on the work, see Nath (X1), Sklar (X2), and Waterman (X7).

"My Son's My Son." Title of Walter Greenwood's revision of THE DAUGHTER-IN-LAW (q.v.)

"Noah's Flood" (w. 1925; v. 1936 [PHOENIX])

There are no essential critical studies principally concerned with this play fragment. For commentary on the work, see Sklar (X2).

THE PLAYS OF D.H. LAWRENCE (1933)

There are no essential critical studies principally concerned with this collection. For commentary on the volume, see Nath (X1) and Sklar (X2).

TOUCH AND GO (w. 1918; s. 1920; v. 1933 [PLAYS])

For additional commentary on this play, see Delany (F41), Clark (G17), Panichas (G91), Nath (X1), Sklar (X2), Waterman (X7), and Mori (AA221).

X17 DeFilippis, Simonetta. "Sociologia e ideologia della classe operaia in TOUCH AND GO di D.H. Lawrence" ["Sociology and Ideology of the Working Class in Lawrence's TOUCH AND GO"]. ANNALI ISTITUTO ORIENTALE NAPOLI, SEZIONE GERMANICA, 15 (1972), 185-206.
     Examines the sources and significance of DHL's political themes in his play. [In Italian.]

X18 Lowell, Amy. "A Voice Cries in Our Wilderness (D.H. Law-
     rence)." 1926. In POETRY AND POETS: ESSAYS. Boston:
     Houghton Mifflin, 1930. Pp. 175-86.
          Praises DHL's insight into the conflict be-
          tween capital and labor, his utopian solution
          ("if only it were workable"), and his in-
          sightful preface to his play. Review.

THE WIDOWING OF MRS. HOLROYD (w. 1910, 1913; s. 1914; v. 1933
[PLAYS])

For additional commentary on this play, see Brunsdale (G14),
Hobsbaum (G51), Moore (G80), Sinzelle (G110), Nath (X1), Sklar
(X2), DeFilippis (X3), French (X4), Sagar (X6), Waterman (X7),
Williams (X8), and Mori (AA221).

X19 Coniff, Gerald. "The Failed Marriage: Dramatization of a
     Lawrentian Theme in THE WIDOWING OF MRS. HOLROYD." DHLR,
     11 (1978), 21-37.
          Examines DHL's adjustments in his materials,
          used elsewhere in his fiction (e.g., "Odour
          of Chrysanthemums"), for dramatic presenta-
          tion.

X20 Hartman, Geoffrey H. "The Concept of Character in Law-
     rence's First Play." BULLETIN OF THE MIDWEST MODERN
     LANGUAGE ASSOCIATION, 10, No. 1 (1977), 38-43.
          DHL's play not primarily a realistic study of
          Mrs. Holroyd's character but a drama symboliz-
          ing modern woman's need to reject the child
          in the man.

X21 Marland, Michael. "Introduction." In Lawrence's *THE
     WIDOWING OF MRS. HOLROYD* AND *THE DAUGHTER-IN-LAW*. London:
     Heinemann Educational, 1968. Pp. xi-xxxvi.
          For annotation see X11.

X22 Williams, Raymond. "D.H. Lawrence: THE WIDOWING OF MRS.
     HOLROYD." In DRAMA FROM IBSEN TO BRECHT. London: Chatto
     and Windus, 1968. Pp. 257-60.
          DHL's play, written "outside the modes of the
          contemporary theatre," an extension and comp-
          lication of his story "Odour of Chrysanthemums."

Y. STUDIES OF THE POETRY

The following section is subdivided into three parts: i. Books
and Essay Collections on the Poetry; ii. General Critical Articles or Chapters on the Poetry; and iii. Studies of Individual
Poems and Collections.

A two-volume textual edition of the poems, in progress, will
be published in THE CAMBRIDGE EDITION (B1--ed. Carole Ferrier
and Warren Roberts).

For a concordance to the first edition of THE COMPLETE POEMS
(1964), see Garcia and Karabatsos (D1).

For bibliographical information on the poetry, see Ferrier
(E21), Roberts (E39), and Sagar (E40), and, for biographical
backgrounds to the poems, see Delany (F41), Moore (F112),
Murry (F121), Nehls (F123), and Rhys (F136).

For additional, general critical commentaries and information
on the poetry, see the following books, in section G above:
Allendorf (G4), Arnold (G7), Beal (G9), Brunsdale (G14),
Cavitch (G16), Clark (G17), Clarke (G18), Corsani (G21),
Donnerstag (G30), Draper (G33, G34), Eisenstein (G36),
Goodheart (G44), Gregory (G47), Hobsbaum (G51), Hough (G56),
Johnsson (G63), Meyers (G73), Moore (G80), Murry (G85),
Nahal (G86), Negriolli (G87), Nin (G88), Panichas (G91),
Pinion (G95), Potter (G98), Pritchard (G101), Reul (G103),
Sagar (G104), Seligmann (G108), Slade (G111); the following
critical articles, in section H above: Albright (H5),
Cowan (H79), Gerard (H130), Goldring (H142), Hardy (H165),
Lerner (H221), Murfin (H269), Nardi (H273), Pritchard (H298),
Sagar (H320), Savage (H326), Speirs (H346), Stewart (H361),
Vickery (H393); and the following studies, entered in other
sections of this bibliography: Sagar (L56), Chapple (M21),
and Nardi (AA226).

Y, i.   Books and Essay Collections on the Poetry

Also see Konishi's D.H. RORENSU (AA23).

Y1   Gilbert, Sandra M.   ACTS OF ATTENTION: THE POEMS OF D.H.
     LAWRENCE.   Ithaca, N.Y.: Cornell Univ. Press, 1972.
          Attempt to give DHL's poetry the full examina-
          tion it deserves but has not received, "to ac-
          count *for*" the verse in the full view of his
          writing career.   Gilbert opens her study with
          an examination of DHL's "neo-Romantic" defini-
          tion of poetry as an act of attending to a
          visionary experience (in DHL's "Introduction"
          [1929] to Harry Crosby's CHARIOT OF THE SUN
          [1931]; collected in B16), which would neces-
          sarily preclude any conscious attention to
          form, poetic tradition, or certain calculated
          rhetorical techniques (e.g., irony).   In the
          rest of her book she pursues DHL's self-dis-
          covery through constant self-examination, the
          coherent pattern of his development as a poet
          throughout his career, and argues that DHL
          matures from uncertain artistry to visionary
          insight.   Gilbert surveys the poems and vol-
          umes chronologically, with frequently excellent
          analyses of individual poems.   See Y10.

Y2   Kenmare, Dallas.   FIRE-BIRD: A STUDY OF D.H. LAWRENCE.   Lon-
     don: Barrie, 1951.
          Adulatory and generally uninformative "new-
          critical" reading of the poetry.

Y3   Marshall, Tom.   THE PSYCHIC MARINER: A READING OF THE POEMS
     OF D.H. LAWRENCE.   New York: Viking, 1970.
          Study of DHL's poetic development in isolation
          from his fiction, asserting that DHL continued
          to mature as a poet long after his growth as a
          novelist was arrested.   Marshall summarizes
          the "mixed" critical reputation of the poetry
          briefly and surveys the poems chronologically,
          blending interpretation, biographical remarks,
          and discussion of DHL's psychic development
          and beliefs.   Valuable commentaries on individ-
          ual poems, yet overall a less satisfactory
          study than Gilbert's book (Y1), which is equally
          insightful but more methodical in approach and
          treatment.

Y4   Murfin, Ross C. THE POETRY OF D.H. LAWRENCE. Lincoln:
      Univ. of Nebraska Press, [1983].
           Announced for 1983 publication.   Not seen.

Y5   Oates, Joyce Carol. THE HOSTILE SUN: THE POETRY OF D.H.
      LAWRENCE.   Los Angeles: Black Sparrow Press, 1973.
           Brief study. Oates finds DHL's collected poems
           "more powerful, more emotionally combative,
           than even the greatest of his novels" and
           praises their qualities of spontaneity and
           evanescence. Appreciations and extensive ci-
           tations, rather than full analyses. Reprinted
           in her NEW HEAVEN, NEW EARTH: THE VISIONARY EX-
           PERIENCE IN LITERATURE (New York: Vanguard,
           1974), pp. 39-81.

Y6   Smailes, Thomas A. SOME COMMENTS ON THE VERSE OF D.H. LAW-
      RENCE. Port Elizabeth, South Africa: Univ. of Port Eliza-
      beth, 1970.
           Discursive monograph (110 pp.) on DHL's poetry,
           examining DHL's growth and achievement through
           close readings of several of the poems.

Y, ii. General Critical Articles or Chapters on the Poetry

For additional, general, foreign-language articles on the poe-
try, see the following entries in Appendix A: Elektorowicz
(AA137), Friedrich (AA146, AA148), Gillès (AA153), Kobayashi
(AA186, AA187), Marcel (AA210), Michelis (AA215), Nardi (AA228),
Okumura (AA239), Perosa (AA247), and Truchlar (AA282).

Y7   Aiken, Conrad. "The Melodic Line: D.H. Lawrence." In
      SCEPTICISMS: NOTES ON CONTEMPORARY POETRY. New York: Knopf,
      1919. Pp. 91-104.
           DHL a "brilliant poet," but largely unaware of
           the value and importance of the melodic line in
           poetry. Extract reprinted in G34.

Y8   Aldington, Richard. "D.H. Lawrence as Poet." SatR, 2
      (1926), 749-50.
           Praises DHL's artistry with words, his "essen-
           tially poetical way of seeing and feeling,"
           and his talent for composing the "life of the
           senses and the mind...in poetic symbols." Re-
           printed in G34.

Y9   Alvarez, A. "D.H. Lawrence: The Single State of Man."
       In THE SHAPING SPIRIT: STUDIES IN MODERN ENGLISH AND AMER-
       ICAN POETS. London: Chatto and Windus, 1958. Pp. 140-61.
            Champions DHL as the "only native English poet
            of any importance to survive the First World
            War." Reprinted in G81 and G113.

Y10   Bair, Hebe. "Lawrence as Poet." DHLR, 6 (1973), 313-25.
            Acclaims the recent scholarly interest in the
            wider publication, textual study, and critical
            assessment of DHL's poetry. Describes and tab-
            ulates the revisions in 1971 edition of COM-
            PLETE POEMS (B3), here reviewed together with
            B24 and Y1.

Y11   Baker, James R. "Lawrence as Prophetic Poet." JML, 3
       (1974), 1219-38.
            Only in DHL's poems "does one find a synopsis
            of his [prophetic] ideas on the fate of the
            modern age."

Y12   Blackmur, R.P. "D.H. Lawrence and Expressive Form." 1935.
       In LANGUAGE AS GESTURE. New York: Harcourt, 1952. Pp.
       286-300.
            Influential indictment of DHL's poetry, and in-
            directly his entire canon, for illustrating
            "the fallacy of the faith in expressive form."
            Also see Y16, Y20, Y43, and Y125.

Y13   Bogan, Louise. "The Poet Lawrence." 1948. In her SE-
       LECTED CRITICISM: PROSE, POETRY. New York: Noonday, 1955.
       Pp. 346-49.
            Hails DHL's "poetic contribution...as one of
            the most important, in any language, of our
            time." Review of B25.

Y14   Bullough, Geoffrey. THE TREND OF MODERN POETRY. 1934.
       3rd ed. Edinburgh: Oliver and Boyd, 1949. Pp. 145-52.
            DHL an "important poet," despite "his occasional
            turgidity, hysteria, crudities, [and] imitations
            of Whitman's barbaric yawp."

Y15   Daiches, David. "Georgian Poetry." In POETRY AND THE
       MODERN WORLD: A STUDY OF POETRY IN ENGLAND BETWEEN 1900
       and 1939. Chicago: Univ. of Chicago Press, 1940. Pp.
       36-60.
            DHL a Georgian poet chronologically, but in his
            poems he is "obviously out of place" among his
            Georgian contemporaries (pp. 51-53 and passim).

Y16 Davie, Donald. "A Doggy Demos: Hardy and Lawrence." In
     THOMAS HARDY AND BRITISH POETRY. London: Routledge, 1973.
     Pp. 130-51.
          DHL turns "to profit the confessional mode which
          Hardy bequeathed" to him. Debates Roxroth's
          (Y50) and Blackmur's (Y12) criticisms of DHL.

Y17 Deutsch, Babette. "The Burden of Mystery." In THIS MODERN
     POETRY. New York: Norton, 1935. Pp. 187-209.
          DHL's poetry severely flawed, yet his vision
          of the tragedy of life makes him comparable
          to Blake, Rimbaud, and Whitman (cf. Jeffers
          and Yeats).

Y18 Drew, Elizabeth A., and John L. Sweeney. "D.H. Lawrence."
     In DIRECTIONS IN MODERN POETRY. New York: Norton, 1940.
     Pp. 113-33.
          General overview of DHL's themes and weaknesses
          as a "poet of affirmation."

Y19 Ellmann, Richard. "Barbed Wire and Coming Through." 1953.
     In THE ACHIEVEMENT OF D.H. LAWRENCE. Ed. Frederick J.
     Hoffman and Harry T. Moore. Pp. 253-67. See G53.
          The toughening effect of World War I on DHL's
          poetry.

Y20 Enright, Dennis Joseph. "A Haste for Wisdom: The Poetry
     of D.H. Lawrence." In CONSPIRATORS AND POETS. London:
     Chatto and Windus, 1966. Pp. 95-101.
          DHL's greatness as a poet rejected only by
          those formalists who have narrowed "the con-
          ception of poetry and poetic possibilities"
          (e.g., Blackmur; see Y12). Review of B3.
          Reprinted in G20.

Y21 Fairchild, Hoxie N. RELIGIOUS TRENDS IN ENGLISH POETRY.
     Vol. 5: 1880-1920. New York: Columbia Univ. Press, 1962.
     Pp. 276-84.
          Impact of DHL's Protestantism on his both wise
          and absurd poetry.

Y22 Fisher, William J. "Peace and Passivity: The Poetry of
     D.H. Lawrence." SAQ, 55 (1956), 337-48.
          Unusual view of DHL's poems as the antithesis
          to his rebelliously individualistic fiction:
          in the poems the "passive conception and the
          passive image prevail."

Y23   Gilbert, Sandra M. "D.H. Lawrence's Uncommon Prayers."
      In D.H. LAWRENCE: THE MAN WHO LIVED. Ed. Robert B. Part-
      low and Harry T. Moore. Pp. 73-93. See G92.
             Examines and defends the Blakean, diabolic di-
             mension of DHL's poetry.

Y24   Glicksberg, Charles I. "The Poetry of D.H. Lawrence."
      NEW MEXICO QUARTERLY, 18 (1948), 289-303.
             DHL's "organically felt and sensuously com-
             municated" ideas in his poetry contrast with
             the ideological "middle" of his fiction. Com-
             ments on DHL's major themes.

Y25   Grigson, Geoffrey. "The Poet in D.H. Lawrence." In POEMS
      AND POETS. London: Macmillan, 1969. Pp. 186-92.
             Reasonably expressed objections to DHL's ideas
             and literary techniques, chiefly in his poetry.
             DHL turned "idea into feeling and feeling into
             idea, at times falsifying both."

Y26   Harmer, J.B. VICTORY IN LIMBO: IMAGISM, 1908-1917. Lon-
      don: Secker and Warburg, 1975. Pp. 99-103 and passim.
             DHL's poems (1909-23) show "remarkable insight
             and power," but they are hardly Imagist works
             despite his personal association with several
             Imagist writers. Also see Y29.

Y27   Hassall, Christopher. "D.H. Lawrence and the Etruscans."
      EDH, 31 (1962), 61-78.
             Excellent study of the Etruscan influence on
             DHL's late poetry (1923 and after). Earlier
             version published in G81.

Y28   Hehner, Barbara. "'Kissing and Horrid Strife': Male and
      Female in the Early Poetry of D.H. Lawrence." FOUR DEC-
      ADES OF POETRY, 1890-1930, 1 (1976), 3-26.
             Not seen.

Y29   Hughes, Glenn. "D.H. Lawrence: The Passionate Psycholo-
      gist." In IMAGISM AND THE IMAGISTS: A STUDY IN MODERN
      POETRY. Stanford: Stanford Univ. Press, 1931. Pp. 167-96.
             Broad review of DHL's poetic themes and tech-
             niques, and clarification of his strictly ac-
             cidental connection with the Imagist movement.
             Also see Y26. Extract reprinted in F123.

Y30 Hyman, Stanley Edgar. "The Lawrence Mob." 1965. In his THE CRITIC'S CREDENTIALS: ESSAYS AND REVIEWS. Ed. Phoebe Pettingell. New York: Atheneum, 1978. Pp. 130-34.
> DHL has "seven" poetic voices, "six of them in various degress objectionable." Review of B3.

Y31 Janik, Del Ivan. "Toward 'Thingness': Cézanne's Painting and Lawrence's Poetry." TCL, 19 (1973), 119-28.
> DHL's comments on Cézanne in "Art and Morality" (A67) and "Introduction to These Paintings" (A71), asserting "the supreme artistic importance of immediacy and intuitive knowledge," reflect DHL's own ambitions for his poetry.

Y32 Jennings, Elizabeth. "D.H. Lawrence: A Vision of the Natural World." In SEVEN MEN OF VISION: AN APPRECIATION. London: Vision, 1976. Pp. 45-80.
> DHL's ecstatic loss of self into nature: animals, trees, and flowers, in his ultimately visionary poetry.

Y33 Jones, R.T. "D.H. Lawrence's Poetry: Art and the Apprehension of Fact." In D.H. LAWRENCE: A CRITICAL STUDY. Ed. Andor Gomme. Pp. 175-89. See G43.
> Relation of fact and creative imagination in DHL's poetry.

Y34 "Lawrence the Poet: Achievement and Irrelevance." TLS, 26 Aug. 1965, pp. 725-27.
> The autobiographical interest of DHL's poetry also its chief limitation. Admiring review of B3.

Y35 Lucie-Smith, Edward. "The Poetry of D.H. Lawrence--With a Glance at Shelley." In D.H. LAWRENCE. Ed. Stephen Spender. Pp. 224-33. See G113.
> DHL a modernist as well as a traditionalist in his poetry.

Y36 Miller, James E., Jr. "Four Cosmic Poets." UKCR, 23 (1957), 312-20.
> The "myth" of a schematic universe and the affirmation of the spirit unite Walt Whitman, DHL, Hart Crane, and Dylan Thomas in a tradition of "religious" poetry. Assimilated into studies below.

Y37   Miller, James E., Jr., Karl Shapiro, and Bernice Slote.
      START WITH THE SUN: STUDIES IN COSMIC POETRY. Lincoln:
      Univ. of Nebraska Press, 1960. Pp. 57-134, 229-38.
            Essays on DHL and "the Whitman tradition" in
            poetry, by Shapiro (pp. 57-70), Slote (pp. 71-
            98, 229-38), and Miller (pp. 99-134), with
            passing reference to the fiction. See above.

Y38   Moorthy, P. Rama. "The Poetry of D.H. Lawrence." COMMON-
      WEALTH QUARTERLY, 2, No. 7 (1978), 69-78.
            DHL's poetic exploration of "'other worlds'
            and 'unknown modes of being.'"

Y39   Murray, James G. "Screaming in Pentecost." In LITERATURE
      AND RELIGION. Ed. Charles A. Huttar. [Pp. 30-39.] See
      G59.
            Discernible, modern, and meaningful Christian
            dimensions in DHL's work explored in his poems,
            particularly in the reverent nature poetry
            (e.g., BIRDS, BEASTS AND FLOWERS).

Y40   Murry, John Middleton. "The Poems of D.H. Lawrence."
      1928. In his D.H. LAWRENCE (TWO ESSAYS). Pp. 3-8. See
      G84.
            Read in chronological order, DHL's poems lose
            their richness and their wisdom seems "absolute
            foolishness."

Y41   Perkins, David. A HISTORY OF MODERN POETRY: FROM THE
      1890s TO THE HIGH MODERNIST MODE. Cambridge, Mass: Har-
      vard Univ. Press, 1976. Pp. 439-45 and passim.
            Beginning under the influence of Hardy and the
            Pre-Raphaelites, DHL evolves into a modernist
            poet through his career.

Y42   Pinto, Vivian de Sola. "D.H. Lawrence Letter-Writer and
      Craftsman in Verse." RMS, 1 (1957), 5-34.
            Commentary on the early versions of ten poems
            by DHL (including "Piano," published here in
            manuscript facsimile) and letters from DHL to
            his sister and niece.

Y43   -----. "Introduction: 'D.H. Lawrence: Poet Without a
      Mask.'" 1961. In THE COMPLETE POEMS OF D.H. LAWRENCE.
      Ed. Pinto and Warren Roberts. Pp. 1-21. See B3.
            Refutes Blackmur (see Y12), seeing DHL's in-
            tense personal involvement and spontaneity as
            a deliberate reaction against "traditional
            form," the "mask" convention. Earlier version
            reprinted in G115.

Y44   -----. "The Burning Bush: D.H. Lawrence as Religious
Poet." In MANSIONS OF THE SPIRIT: ESSAYS IN LITERATURE
AND RELIGION. Ed. George A. Panichas. New York: Haw-
thorn, 1967. Pp. 213-38.
     DHL "religious" in the sense of his constant
     searching for "truth," "transcendence," and
     "the divine."

Y45   Potts, Abbie Findlay. "Pipings of Pan: D.H. Lawrence."
In THE ELEGIAC MODE: POETIC FORM IN WORDSWORTH AND OTHER
ELEGISTS. Ithaca, N.Y.: Cornell Univ. Press, 1967. Pp.
359-432.
     DHL the "undeniable elegiac successor of Hardy
     and Yeats." Traces affinities with the classi-
     cal elegiac tradition in DHL's major poetry,
     particularly stressing his Pan-like vitalism.

Y46   Powell, Dilys. "D.H. Lawrence." In DESCENT FROM PARNAS-
SUS. New York: Macmillan, 1935. Pp. 3-54.
     DHL a "great" poet, creating intrinsically
     beautiful poetry, significant within its own
     right and in relation to his prose.

Y47   Presley, John. "D.H. Lawrence and the Resources of Poetry."
LANGUAGE AND STYLE, 12 (1979), 3-12.
     Sometimes excellent effects of DHL's "inter-
     esting" stylistic experiments in poetry.

Y48   Press, John. "D.H. Lawrence." In A MAP OF MODERN ENGLISH
VERSE. London: Oxford Univ. Press, 1969. Pp. 93-104.
     DHL's "main contribution [is] his extraordinary
     skill in discovering and embodying in verse the
     rhythm that would correspond exactly with the
     subtle yet overwhelmingly powerful rhythm of
     his sensual perceptions and emotional life."
     Reprints extracts from several criticisms by
     and about DHL, and four poems.

Y49   Reeves, James. "Introduction." In Lawrence's SELECTED
POEMS. Ed. Reeves. London: Heinemann, 1966. Pp. 1-9.
     DHL "exciting and original," but neither
     "great" nor technically "good" as a poet.
     Introduces an anthology of eighty-one poems.

Y50   Rexroth, Kenneth. "Introduction." In Lawrence's SELECTED
POEMS. Ed. Rexroth. Pp. 1-23. See B25.
     Balanced estimate of DHL's poetic strengths
     and weaknesses, with special praise for his
     lack of manner and affectation. Reprinted
     in G48. Also see Y16.

Y51   Rich, Adrienne. "Reflections on D.H. Lawrence." POETRY,
      106 (1965), 218-25.
            DHL "a major poet" who created his own, "or-
            ganic" forms: "he knows what he is doing with
            line-length, with diction, with pause, repeti-
            tion, termination." Comments briefly on each
            of the volumes in THE COMPLETE POEMS (B3). Re-
            view.

Y52   Roberts, Warren. "Problems in Editing D.H. Lawrence."
      In D.H. LAWRENCE: THE MAN WHO LIVED. Ed. Robert B. Part-
      low and Harry T. Moore. Pp. 58-61. See G92.
            On KANGAROO and the poems. For annotation see
            R17.

Y53   Rosenthal, M.L. "D.H. Lawrence." In THE MODERN POETS:
      A CRITICAL INTRODUCTION. New York: Oxford Univ. Press,
      1960. Pp. 160-68.
            General summary of DHL's chief themes and con-
            cerns, emphasizing his interests "in the de-
            tails of life among the most ordinary men and
            women."

Y54   Ross, Robert H. THE GEORGIAN REVOLT, 1910-1922: RISE AND
      FALL OF A POETIC IDEAL. Carbondale, Ill.: Southern Illi-
      nois Univ. Press, 1965. Pp. 89-91 and passim.
            DHL's defense of his *verse libre* and objections
            to conventional poetic meter and form: "I read
            my poetry more by length than by stress." Sev-
            eral additional comments on DHL's relations to
            the Georgians and their "ideals."

Y55   Shakir, Evelyn. "'Secret Sin': Lawrence's Early Verse."
      DHLR, 8 (1975), 155-75.
            Psycho-sexual analysis of DHL's sublimation of
            his "secret feelings, secret fantasies" in his
            early poetry and in the late volume PANSIES ("a
            regression of sorts"). See response by Evelyn
            J. Hinz, in DHLR, 8 (1975), 213-19.

Y56   Shapiro, Karl. "The Unemployed Magician." POETRY, 91
      (1957), 194-209.
            Imaginary conversation with the god of poetry,
            defending DHL among contemporary poets for his
            lack of affectation. Reprinted in G81.

Y57 Solomon, Gerald. "The Banal, and the Poetry of D.H. Lawrence." EIC, 23 (1973), 254-67.
    DHL's fear of self-questioning at the source of
    his rhetorical banality in poetry.

Y58 Spender, Stephen. "Form and Pressure in Poetry." TLS,
23 Oct. 1970, pp. 1226-28.
    The timelessness of free verse (e.g., DHL's
    poetry), a modern "response to pressure of the
    time," creating a "chaotic inner life" which
    reflects "chaotic outward circumstances."

Y59 Squire, John C. "[Review of COLLECTED POEMS]." OBSERVER,
7 Oct. 1928, p. 6.
    DHL "a limited, a writhing, a bewildered poet,"
    but also a "man of genius" who "will never be
    dull" in his poetry. Reprinted in G34.

Y60 Stanzel, Franz. "G.M. Hopkins, W.B. Yeats, D.H. Lawrence,
und die Spontaneität der Dichtung." In ANGLISTISCHE STU-
DIEN: FESTSCHRIFT ZUM 70. GEBURTSTAG VON PROFESSOR FRIED-
RICH WILD. Ed. Karl Brunner, Herbert Kozoil, and Sieg-
fried Korninger. Vienna: Bramüller, 1958. Pp. 179-93.
    Compares the three poets' approaches to the idea
    of poetic spontaniety. [In German.]

Y61 Sullivan, Alvin. "D.H. Lawrence and POETRY: The Unpublished Manuscripts." DHLR, 9 (1976), 266-77.
    Publishes two letters from DHL to Harriet Mon-
    roe and substantial manuscript variants for
    ten of the forty-five DHL poems published in
    her influential journal.

Y62 Thesing, William B. "D.H. Lawrence's Poetic Response to
the City: Some Continuities with Nineteenth-Century Poets."
MODERNIST STUDIES, 4 (1982), 52-64.
    Traces the varieties of traditional responses
    to the city, chiefly London, in DHL's poetry,
    observing his movement from early, impression-
    istic cityscapes, to rejection of the urban
    mechanism, and, ultimately, to a "vision of
    the golden city" in his late works. See G79.

Y63 Thwaite, Anthony. "D.H. Lawrence." In TWENTIETH-CENTURY
ENGLISH POETRY: AN INTRODUCTION. London: Heinemann, 1978.
Pp. 39-42.
    DHL, "seldom a great poet," writes best when
    "describing or evoking" an object, "without too
    much of a didactic or moralizing burden."

Y64 Tiedje, Egon. "D.H. Lawrence's Early Poetry: The Compo-
     sition-Dates of the Drafts in MS E317." DHLR, 4 (1971),
     227-52.
            Determines composition dates (with a chronolog-
            ical chart) for the numerous poems and fragments
            (1905-11), preserved in DHL's Nottingham Univer-
            sity College exercise-book (Roberts, ms. no.
            E317; see E39). Also see E21, Carole Ferrier's
            serious reservations about this article, and
            Tiedje's response, in DHLR, 5 (1972), 149-57.

Y65 Vickery, John B. "D.H. Lawrence: The Evidence of the
     Poetry." In THE LITERARY IMPACT OF *THE GOLDEN BOUGH*.
     Princeton, N.J.: Princeton Univ. Press, 1973. Pp. 280-93.
            Myth and archetype in DHL's poetry. Also see
            H393.

Y66 -----. "D.H. Lawrence's Poetry: Myth and Matter." DHLR,
     7 (1974), 1-18.
            DHL's "best poetry" motivated by "a delicately
            balanced sense of the realities of matter and
            the potentialities of myth." Examines mythic
            dimensions of several poems.

Y67 Waugh, Arthur. "Mr. D.H. Lawrence." In TRADITION AND
     CHANGE: STUDIES IN CONTEMPORARY LITERATURE. New York:
     Dutton, 1919. Pp. 131-37.
            Attacks DHL's poetry: his "fancy is half-asleep
            upon a foetid hot-bed of moods."

Y68 Whalen, Terry. "Lawrence and Larkin: The Suggestion of
     an Affinity." MODERNIST STUDIES, 4 (1982), 105-22.
            Argues and illustrates Larkin's extensive debt
            to DHL's poetry and ideas. See G79.

Y69 Wilder, Amos N. "The Primitivism of D.H. Lawrence." In
     THE SPIRITUAL ASPECTS OF THE NEW POETRY. New York: Har-
     per's, 1940. Pp. 153-65.
            DHL's "pantheism" and "irrationalism."

Y70 Williams, George G. "D.H. Lawrence's Philosophy as Ex-
     pressed in His Poetry." RICE INSTITUTE PAMPHLET, 38,
     No. 1 (1951), 73-94.
            DHL's poems, concerned with "philosophical
            ideas only after those ideas have matured and
            fixed themselves in Lawrence's mind, are a
            better source" for the study of his thought
            "than are his prose works."

Y71   Youngblood, Sarah. "Substance and Shadow: The Self in
       Lawrence's Poetry." DHLR, 1 (1968), 114-28.
            Not seen.

Y, iii. Studies of Individual Poems and Collections

Relatively few of DHL's over 1,000 poems have been discussed
individually in critical publications. These few poems, which
are possibly his best as well as his best known poetry, are
listed alphabetically in this section along with the titles
of *all* DHL's poetry collections. The collections are listed
regardless of whether there have been significant critical
studies published on them individually. The headnotes for
each title will identify substantial critical commentary on
the work to be found in studies located elsewhere in this
bibliography.

Note: The dates following individual poems indicate date(s)
of composition ("w"), date of first separate publication prior
to collected publication, if any ("s"), and date of first
collected publication ("v"), with the collection identified
by brief title in brackets. The dating information has been
drawn from Roberts (E39) and Sagar (E40).

AMORES (1916)

For additional commentary on this collection, see Ferrier
(E21), Murry (F121), Gregory (G47), Hobsbaum (G51), Moore
(G80), Gilbert (Y1), Kenmare (Y2), Marshall (Y3), Murfin (Y4),
Aldington (Y8), Hehner (Y28), and Tiedje (Y64).

Y72   Bartlett, Phyllis. "Lawrence's COLLECTED POEMS: The
       Demon Takes Over." PMLA, 66 (1951), 583-93.
            Assesses the significance of DHL's "liberal"
            revisions of his poetry in the winter of 1927-
            28, chiefly the early poems in LOVE POEMS AND
            OTHERS and AMORES, for publication in THE
            COLLECTED POEMS (A55).

"Bavarian Gentians" (w. 1929; v. 1932 [LAST POEMS])

For additional commentary on this poem, see Hobsbaum (G51),
Hough (G56), Moore (G80), Gilbert (Y1), Kenmare (Y2), Marshall
(Y3), Oates (Y5), Pinto (Y43), Rexroth (Y50), Vickery (Y66),
Cipolla (Y90), Janik (Y92), Kirkham (Y93), Gutierrez (Z4),
Tiedje (AA98), and Sonoi (AA269).

Y73 Cox, C.B., and A.E. Dyson. "'Bavarian Gentians,' by D.H.
     Lawrence." In MODERN POETRY: STUDIES IN PRACTICAL CRITI-
     CISM. London: Arnold, 1963. Pp. 66-71.
          In his constant revision to achieve "rhythmic
          effects," DHLR "developed a new kind of poetic
          expression." Analyzes the poem's rhythms and
          imagery.

Y74 Harvey, R.W. "On Lawrence's 'Bavarian Gentians.'" WAS-
     CANA REVIEW, 1, No. 1 (1966), 74-86.
          Search for "the kind of law that lies behind
          the sensitively fluctuating style of free-
          verse" in DHL's successive drafts of his poem.

Y75 Sagar, Keith. "The Genesis of 'Bavarian Gentians.'" DHLR,
     8 (1975), 47-53.
          Clarifies the poem's textual history and ar-
          gues the superiority of the less known, later
          version.

BAY (1919)

There are no essential critical studies principally concerned
with this collection. For commentary on the volume, see Ferrier (E21), Moore (G80), Gilbert (Y1), Marshall (Y3), and Murfin (Y4).

BIRDS, BEASTS AND FLOWERS (1923)

For additional commentary on this collection, see Ferrier (E21),
Murry (F121), Donnerstag (G30), Hobsbaum (G51), Inniss (G60),
Moore (G80), Pinion (G95), Pritchard (G101), Sagar (G104), Slade
(G111), Gilbert (Y1), Kenmare (Y2), Marshall (Y3), Murfin (Y4),
Oates (Y5), Smailes (Y6), Aldington (Y8), Gilbert (Y23), Harmer
(Y26), Lucie-Smith (Y35), Murray (Y39), Pinto (Y43, Y44), Rex-
roth (Y50), and Vickery (Y66).

Y76   Aiken, Conrad. "D.H. Lawrence." 1924, 1929. In A RE-
      VIEWER'S ABC. New York: Meridian, 1958. Pp. 256-61;
      266-68.
            Despite considerable merit in his poems, DHL's
            "conspicuous" preoccupations with himself and
            his theme of "sex-crucifixion" irritating and
            "infantile." Review of volume (first essay)
            and brief comment on THE COLLECTED POEMS (A55).

Y77   Auden, W.H. "D.H. Lawrence." In THE DYER'S HAND AND
      OTHER ESSAYS. New York: Random House, 1962. Pp. 277-95.
            DHL's concern for "genuineness of feeling" and
            "belief that art is the true religion." Ex-
            amines BIRDS, BEASTS AND FLOWERS, "the peak of
            Lawrence's achievement as a poet." Reprinted
            in Auden's SELECTED ESSAYS (London: Faber,
            1964), pp. 123-44. Extract reprinted in G20.

Y78   Gilbert, Sandra M. "Hell on Earth: BIRDS, BEASTS AND
      FLOWERS as Subversive Narrative." DHLR, 12 (1979), 256-74.
            Volume "organized and unified by a submerged
            narrative structure," DHL's "subversive" and
            "revisionary synthesis of a group of myths of
            darkness" (Persephone, Orpheus, Osiris, Diony-
            sus, Lucifer).

Y79   Henderson, Philip. "BIRDS, BEASTS AND FLOWERS." In THE
      POET AND SOCIETY. London: Secker and Warburg, 1939. Pp.
      172-201.
            Eliot's "cerebral" poetry a retreat from the
            "painful...experience of living"; DHL's vis-
            ceral poems a retreat from the "modern world"
            in search of more vital "modes of life."

Y80   Pinto, Vivian de Sola. "Imagists and D.H. Lawrence." In
      CRISIS IN ENGLISH POETRY, 1880-1940. London: Hutchinson,
      1951. Pp. 151-57.
            DHL's affinities with the imagist poets, in
            BIRDS, BEASTS AND FLOWERS.

Y81   Rajiva, Stanley F. "The Empathetic Vision." LHY, 9, No.
      2 (1968), 49-70.
              The "sensitivity and compassion" of DHL's ap-
              proach to the natural world make him "one of
              the world's great nature poets." Comments on
              a number of the poems in the volume.

Y82   Trail, George Y. "West by East: The Psycho-Geography of
      BIRDS, BEASTS AND FLOWERS." DHLR, 12 (1979), 241-55.
              DHL uses both the "thematic" structure of the
              poems in the volume and the movement eastward
              to reflect his "personal quest for regenera-
              tion."

"Cherry Robbers" (w. 1905-06, 1910; v. 1913 [LOVE POEMS])

For additional commentary on this poem, see Ferrier (E21),
Moore (G80), Gilbert (Y1), Marshall (Y3), Rexroth (Y50), and
Tiedje (Y64).

Y83   Brooks, Emily Potter. "D.H. Lawrence: A Day in the Coun-
      try and a Poem in Autograph." DHLR, 9 (1976), 278-82.
              Memoir and comment on DHL's early poem. For
              annotation see F21.

THE COLLECTED POEMS OF D.H. LAWRENCE (1928)

There are no essential critical studies principally concerned
with this collection. For commentary on the volumes, see Ferrier (E21), Donnerstag (G30), Moore (G80), Gilbert (Y1), Marshall (Y3), Murfin (Y4), Murry (Y40), Pinto (Y43), Roberts
(Y52), Shakir (Y55), Squire (Y59), Bartlett (Y72), Aiken (Y76),
Green (Y84), and Farmer (Y128).

"Dreams Old and Nascent" (w. 1909, 1916, 1928; s. 1909; v. 1916 [AMORES])

For additional commentary on this poem, see Ferrier (E21), Gilbert (Y1), Marshall (Y3), and Tiedje (Y64).

Y84   Green, Eleanor H.   "Nietzsche, Helen Corke, and D.H. Lawrence." AMERICAN NOTES AND QUERIES, 15 (1976), 56-59.
            Analogues between the development of thought in
            a poem by Nietzsche, "Einsiedlers Sehnsucht"
            (DHL gave Corke a copy of the poem in 1912),
            and the development discernible in two versions
            of "Dreams" (1909, 1928--in THE COLLECTED POEMS
            [A55]).

"Fish" (w. 1921; s. 1922; v. 1923 [BIRDS, BEASTS AND FLOWERS])

For additional commentary on the poem, see Ferrier (E21), Gilbert (Y1), Marshall (Y3), Oates (Y5), and Blackmur (Y12).

Y85   Cavitch, David.   "Merging--with Fish and Others."   DHLR, 7 (1974), 172-78.
            Poem closely analyzed to demonstrate DHL's re-
            pudiation of "his strong narcissistic drift"
            in his struggle "to readjust his connections
            to the object world" in the early 1920s.

Y86   Langbaum, Robert.   "The New Nature Poetry."   In THE MODERN SPIRIT: ESSAYS ON THE CONTINUITY OF NINETEENTH AND TWENTIETH CENTURY LITERATURE. New York: Oxford Univ. Press, 1970. Pp. 101-26.
            The modern adaptation of the nature poem. Com-
            ments on Robert Frost, Dylan Thomas, DHL (espe-
            cially "Fish" and "Snake"), Marianne Moore, W.S.
            Merwin, and Wallace Stevens.

"How Beastly the Bourgoisie Is" (w. 1928-29; v. 1929 [PANSIES])

For additional commentary on this poem, see Gilbert (Y1) and Marshall (Y3).

Y87   Lerner, Laurence.   "'How Beastly the Bourgoisie Is.'"
      CRITICAL SURVEY, 1 (1963), 87-89.
            Explication and appreciation of the poem.

"Hymn to Priapus" (w. 1917; s. 1917; v. 1917 [LOOK! WE HAVE COME THROUGH!])

For additional commentary on this poem, see Ferrier (E21), Gilbert (Y1), Marshall (Y3), Ellmann (Y19), Rexroth (Y50), and Vickery (Y65).

Y88   Murfin, Ross C.   "'Hymn to Priapus': Lawrence's Poetry of
      Difference."   CRITICISM, 22 (1980), 214-29.
            DHL's poem a revision of Swinburne's "Hymn to
            Proserpine" (1866), "that half develops and
            half covers over the traces of a Victorian or-
            iginal." Also see H269 and Y4.

LAST POEMS (1932)

For additional commentary on this collection, see Donnerstag (G30), Gregory (G47), Hobsbaum (G51), Inniss (G60), Sagar (G104), Gilbert (Y1), Marshall (Y3), Hassall (Y27), Pinto (Y44), Vickery (Y66), Gutierrez (Z4), and Truchlar (AA282).

Y89   Aldington, Richard.   "Introduction."   In Lawrence's LAST
      POEMS.   Ed. Aldington and Giuseppi Orioli.   Pp. xi-xxii.
      See A58.
            Notes on the manuscripts for DHL's last volume
            of poems, contrast of the static Joyce and the
            dynamic DHL, and appreciation of the "fluid
            ego," the flow, and the individual qualities
            of DHL's late poetry. Reprinted in B3.

Y90 Cipolla, Elizabeth. "The LAST POEMS of D.H. Lawrence."
DHLR, 2 (1969), 103-19.
> Notes DHL's turn toward death in the collection
> and surveys the chief themes of the poems.

Y91 Gomes, Eugênio. "D.H. Lawrence (O Poeta)." In D.H. LAW-
RENCE E OUTROS. Pôrto Alegre, Brazil: Livraria do Globo,
1937. Pp. 40-58.
> Summary and critique of a number of the LAST
> POEMS, stressing DHL's resemblances to Robert
> Browning. [In Portugese.]

Y92 Janik, Del Ivan. "D.H. Lawrence's 'Future Religion': The
Unity of LAST POEMS." TSLL, 16 (1975), 739-54.
> DHL's "very personal religious understanding
> of life as a preparation for death and rebirth"
> in his LAST POEMS.

Y93 Kirkham, Michael. "D.H. Lawrence's LAST POEMS." DHLR,
5 (1972), 97-120.
> Reads LAST POEMS as a "loosely connected se-
> quence of thought," demonstrating DHL's "spir-
> itual preparation" for death, comments gen-
> erally on DHL's "central themes," and provides
> close readings of several poems.

Y94 Mace, Hebe Riddick. "The Achievement of Poetic Form: D.H.
Lawrence's LAST POEMS." DHLR, 12 (1979), 275-88.
> Presents a theory for the rhythmic analysis
> of free verse and examines the formal quali-
> ties of several poems in the volume.

Y95 Nahal, Chaman Lal. "The Colour Ambience of Lawrence's
Early and Later Poetry." DHLR, 8 (1975), 147-54.
> DHL's subtle and varied use of color in his
> early poems (LOOK! WE HAVE COME THROUGH!)
> "becomes rigid and dogmatic," as does his
> thought, by the time of his LAST POEMS. See
> response by Evelyn J. Hinz, in DHLR, 8 (1975),
> 213-19.

Y96 Smailes, Thomas A. "MORE PANSIES and LAST POEMS: Variant
Readings Derived from MS. Roberts E192." DHLR, 1 (1968),
200-13.
> Suggests a number of corrigenda for THE COM-
> PLETE POEMS (B3). Also see Vivian de Sola
> Pinto's and Warren Roberts's brief response
> following, pp. 213-14.

Y97   Southworth, James G. "D.H. Lawrence: Poet; 'A Note on
      His Political Ideology.'" In SOWING THE SPRING: STUDIES
      IN BRITISH POETRY FROM HOPKINS TO MACNEICE. Oxford:
      Blackwell, 1940. Pp. 64-75.
          DHL's LAST POEMS permeated by "his thesis of
          political freedeom," in statement and technique.

"Lightning" (w. 1906-07; s. 1911; v. 1913 [LOVE POEMS])

For additional commentary on this poem, see Ferrier (E21),
Gilbert (Yl), Marshall (Y3), Hehner (Y28), Shakir (Y55), and
Tiedje (Y64).

Y98   Gutierrez, Donald. "The Pressures of Love: Kinesthetic
      Action in an Early Lawrence Poem." CONTEMPORARY POETRY,
      1 (1973), 6-20.
          Not seen.

LOOK! WE HAVE COME THROUGH! (1917)

For additional commentary on this collection, see Ferrier (E21),
Delany (F41), Murry (F121), Donnerstag (G30), Gregory (G47),
Hobsbaum (G51), Hough (G56), Inniss (G60), Johnsson (G63),
Pritchard (G101), Hardy (H165), Gilbert (Yl), Kenmare (Y2),
Marshall (Y3), Murfin (Y4), Oates (Y5), Aiken (Y7), Aldington
(Y8), Blackmur (Yl2), Davie (Yl6), Ellmann (Yl9), Pinto (Y43),
Rexroth (Y50), and Okumura (AA239).

Y99   Fletcher, John Gould. "A Modern Evangelist." POETRY,
      12 (1918), 269-74.
          DHL's poetry formally flawed, though profound,
          important, and powerful, since it depends "on
          the extension of emotion [rather] than on its
          minute concentration." Review of volume. Re-
          printed in G20 (extract) and G34.

Y100 Lowell, Amy. "The Poetry of D.H. Lawrence." 1919. In
      POETRY AND POETS: ESSAYS. Boston: Houghton Mifflin, 1930.
      Pp. 161-74.
          DHL's "perfectly original and perfectly sin-
          cere" style in LOOK! WE HAVE COME THROUGH!
          Quotes several selections from the volume and
          considers the collection "a greater novel even"
          than SL. Review essay.

Y101   Nahal, Chaman Lal. "The Colour Ambience of Lawrence's
       Early and Later Poetry." DHLR, 8 (1975), 147-54.
           On LAST POEMS and LOOK! WE HAVE COME THROUGH!
           For annotation see Y95.

Y102   Rubin, Merle R. "'Not I, but the Wind That Blows through
       Me': Shelleyan Aspects of Lawrence's Poetry." TSLL, 23
       (1981), 102-22.
           Documents DHL's rarely noted appreciation for
           Shelley and discusses traces of Shelley's in-
           fluence in the themes of the volume.

LOVE POEMS AND OTHERS (1913)

For additional commentary on this collection, see Ferrier (E21),
Gregory (G47), Hobsbaum (G51), Gilbert (Y1), Kenmare (Y2), Mar-
shall (Y3), Murfin (Y4), Ellmann (Y19), Hehner (Y28), and
Tiedje (Y64).

Y103   Bartlett, Phyllis. "Lawrence's COLLECTED POEMS: The Demon
       Takes Over." PMLA, 66 (1951), 583-93.
           On AMORES and LOVE POEMS AND OTHERS. For an-
           notation see Y72.

Y104   Pound, Ezra. "LOVE POEMS AND OTHERS, by D.H. Lawrence."
       POETRY, 2 (1913), 149-51.
           Separates the Lawrencean wheat (his "low-life"
           narratives) from the chaff (the love poems:
           "pre-raphaelitish slush"). Review. Slightly
           revised version (from NEW FREEWOMAN, 1 [1913])
           reprinted in G20 and G34.

Y105   Thomas, Edward. "More Georgian Poetry." BOOKMAN (London),
       44 (1913), 47.
           DHL's "intensity" and "absolute" concentration
           in his poems. Reprinted in G20, G34, and in A
           LANGUAGE NOT TO BE BETRAYED: SELECTED PROSE OF
           EDWARD THOMAS, ed. Edna Longley (New York: Per-
           sea Books, 1981), pp. 105-08.

MORE PANSIES. Subtitle of second part of LAST POEMS (q.v.)

NETTLES (1930)

There are no essential critical studies principally concerned with this collection. For commentary on the volume, see Moore (G80), Gilbert (Y1), Marshall (Y3), Murfin (Y4), and Hassall (Y27).

NEW POEMS (1918)

There are no essential critical studies principally concerned with this collection. For commentary on the volume, see Ferrier (E21), Moore (G80), Gilbert (Y1), Marshall (Y3), Murfin (Y4), and Hassall (Y27).

PANSIES (1929)

For additional commentary on this collection, see Ghiselin (F64), Murry (F121), Colin (G19), Donnerstag (G30), Gregory (G47), Hobsbaum (G51), Hough (G56), Inniss (G60), Moore (G80), Pinion (G95), Sagar (G104), Gilbert (Y1), Marshall (Y3), Murfin (Y4), Oates (Y5), Ellmann (Y19), and Hassall (Y27).

Y106   Farmer, David. "An Unpublished Version of D.H. Lawrence's Introduction to 'Pansies.'" RES, 21 (1970), 181-84.
         Publishes (pp. 183-84) an early draft of DHL's second introduction to PANSIES, his "basis for expanding his ideas" in the published version.

Y107   Praz, Mario. "Poesie di D.H. Lawrence" ["D.H. Lawrence's Poems"]. 1929. In CRONACHE LETTERARIE ANGLOSASSONI. Vol. 1. CRONACHE INGLESI. Rome: Edizioni di storia e letteratura, 1950. Pp. 193-97.
         Notes the Blakean qualities and Nietzschean thought in DHL's PANSIES. Review essay. [In Italian.]

Y108   Shakir, Evelyn. "'Secret Sin': Lawrence's Early Verse." DHLR, 8 (1975), 155-75.
         On the early poems and PANSIES. For annotation see Y55.

"Piano" (w. 1913; v. 1918 [NEW POEMS])

For additional commentary on this poem, see Ferrier (E21), Hobsbaum (G51), Slade (G111), Gilbert (Y1), Marshall (Y3), Pinto (Y42), and Rexroth (Y50).

Y109　Bleich, David.　"The Determination of Literary Value." L&P, 17 (1967), 19-30.
　　　　　　"Piano" is "about the reluctant release of emotion" and provokes a corresponding defensiveness in its readers, which is not, however, to be considered a weakness in the poem (contra Richards; see below).

Y110　Richards, I.A.　"Poem 8."　In PRACTICAL CRITICISM.　1929. New York: Harcourt, 1966.　Pp. 99-112.
　　　　　　Quotes a variety of readers' mostly dissatisfied responses to "Piano."　See above.

RHYMING POEMS.　Title of first volume of THE COLLECTED POEMS (q.v.)

"The Ship of Death" (w. 1929; v. 1932 [LAST POEMS])

For additional commentary on this poem, see Clark (G17), Hobsbaum (G51), Hough (G56), Moore (G80), Nahal (G86), Gilbert (Y1), Marshall (Y3), Oates (Y5), Ellmann (Y19), Pinto (Y43, Y44), Rexroth (Y50), Cipolla (Y90), Janik (Y92), Kirkham (Y93), and Gutierrez (Z4).

Y111　Honig, Edwin.　"Lawrence: 'The Ship of Death.'"　In MASTER POEMS OF THE ENGLISH LANGUAGE.　Ed. Oscar Williams. New York: Washington Square Press, 1967.　Pp. 954-57.
　　　　　　Discussion of DHL's poetic techniques and theme, finding in the poem a possible "final healing of the rift between body and soul."

"Snake" (w. 1920; s. 1921; v. 1923 [BIRDS, BEASTS AND FLOWERS])

For additional commentary on the poem, see Ferrier (E21), Ca-vitch (G16), Hobsbaum (G51), Hough (G56), Inniss (G60), Moore (G80), Sagar (G104), Slade (G111), Gilbert (Y1), Marshall (Y3), Alvarez (Y9), and Ellmann (Y19).

Y112   Brashear, Lucy M. "Lawrence's Companion Poems: 'Snake' and TORTOISES." DHLR, 5 (1972), 54-62.
       Similarities and a common theme, the coexis-
       tence of the mortal and the divine in nature,
       in poems which DHL evidently considered com-
       panion pieces.

Y113   Dalton, Robert O. "'Snake': A Moment of Consciousness." BRIGHAM YOUNG UNIVERSITY STUDIES, 4 (1962), 243-53.
       DHL in complete control of his materials in
       "Snake'; his free form appropriate to the
       poem's theme of naturalness.

Y114   Deutsch, Babette. POETRY IN OUR TIME. New York: Holt, 1952. Pp. 86-91.
       Impressionistic comments on DHL's rhythms and
       imagery, chiefly in "Snake."

Y115   Langbaum, Robert. "The New Nature Poetry." In THE MOD-ERN SPIRIT: ESSAYS ON THE CONTINUITY OF NINETEENTH AND TWENTIETH CENTURY LITERATURE. New York: Oxford Univ. Press, 1970. Pp. 101-26.
       On "Fish" and "Snake." For annotation see Y86.

Y116   Oppel, Horst. "D.H. Lawrence: 'Snake.'" In DIE MODERNE ENGLISCHE LYRIK: INTERRETATIONEN. Ed. Oppel. Berlin: Schmidt, 1967. Pp. 117-36.
       Close reading of the poem, discussion of its
       'organic form,' and introductory comment on
       the snake as a life symbol in DHL (cf. "The
       Reality of Peace" [A61] and "Sun" [A23]).
       [In German.]

Y117   Ramos Suárez, Jorge. "El poema 'Snake,' de D.H. Lawrence, y la 'Elegía a un moscardón azul,' de Dámaso Alonzo: Una influencia admitida y dos sensibilidades diferentes." CUADERNOS HISPANOAMERICANOS, Nos. 280-82 (1973), pp. 274-83.
       Comparative readings of DHL's "Snake" and
       Dámaso Alonzo's "Elegy for a Blue Mosquito"
       (1969).

Y118   Smith, L.E.W. "'Snake.'" CRITICAL SURVEY, 1 (1963),
       81-86.
              Explication and appreciation of the poem.

Y119   Tarinayya, M. "Lawrence's 'Snake': A Close Look." LCrit,
       16, No. 1 (1981), 67-77.
              Explication, attending to the poem's rhythms,
              sound qualities, and vocabulary.

Y120   Trail, George Y. "The Psychological Dynamics of D.H.
       Lawrence's 'Snake.'" AI, 36 (1979), 345-56.
              "'Snake' begins as a deliberate, even careful
              repudiation of Freudian theory...then breaks
              down under the pressures of a severe confronta-
              tion with castration anxieties."

Y121   Young, Archibald M. "Rhythm and Meaning in Poetry: D.H.
       Lawrence's 'Snake.'" ENGLISH, 17 (1968), 41-47.
              Analysis of DHL's achievement of form, through
              various rhythmic patterns, in the ostensibly
              formless poem "Snake."

"Song of a Man Who Has Come Through" (w. 1914; v. 1917 [LOOK!
WE HAVE COME THROUGH!])

For additional commentary on this poem, see Ferrier (E21),
Gilbert (Y1), Marshall (Y3), and Aldington (Y8).

Y122   Steinberg, Erwin R. "'Song of a Man Who Has Come
       Through'--A Pivotal Poem." DHLR, 11 (1978), 50-62.
              Poem a deliberately unresolved reflection of
              DHL's "hopes and fears" at the time of his
              marriage, when his "whole life hung in the
              balance."

Y123   Zanger, Jules. "D.H. Lawrence's Three Strange Angels."
       PLL, 1 (1965), 184-87.
              The poem's "triumphant conclusion" DHL's ref-
              erence to his marriage with Frieda, in 1914.

"Sorrow" (w. 1913; s. 1914; v. 1916 [AMORES])

For additional commentary on this poem, see Ferrier (E21), Gilbert (Y1), and Marshall (Y3).

Y124   Arbur, Rosemarie. "'Lilacs' and 'Sorrow': Whitman's
       Effect on the Early Poems of D.. H. Lawrence." WALT
       WHITMAN REVIEW, 24 (1978), 17-21.
              DHL's dependence on Whitman's great elegy,
              "When Lilacs Last in the Dooryard Bloom'd"
              (1865), in composing his poems about his
              mother's death (e.g., "Sorrow").

TORTOISES (1921)

For additional commentary on this collection, see Ferrier (E21), Murry (F121), Hobsbaum (G51), Hough (G56), Inniss (G60), Sagar (G104), Gilbert (Y1), Kenmare (Y2), Marshall (Y3), Murfin (Y4), Blackmur (Y12), Ellmann (Y19), and Pinto (Y44).

Y125   Bloom, Harold. "Lawrence, Blackmur, Eliot, and the
       Tortoise." In A D. H. LAWRENCE MISCELLANY. Ed. Harry
       T. Moore. Pp. 360-69. See G81.
              Examines the tortoise poems, arguing that the
              obsolete critical dicta of Blackmur (Y12) and
              Eliot (see H104) fail to account for the emo-
              tional and intellectual energy of DHL's poetry.

Y126   Brashear, Lucy M. "Lawrence's Companion Poems: 'Snake'
       and TORTOISES." DHLR, 5 (1972), 54-62.
              For annotation see Y112.

Y127   Sagar, Keith. "'Little Living Myths': A Note on
       Lawrence's TORTOISES." DHLR, 3 (1970), 161-67.
              Argues for reading DHL's tortoise poems
              as "one long poem in six sections."

"The Turning Back" (w. 1915; s. 1972)

For additional commentary on this poem, see Ferrier (E21).

Y128   Farmer, David.   "D. H. Lawrence's 'The Turning Back':
        The Text and Its Genesis in Correspondence."   DHLR,
        5 (1972), 121-31.
            Introduces and publishes for the first
            time the complete text of DHL's poem ("an
            expression of ideas and feelings about
            World War I"), which appears in fragmen-
            tary form as "We Have Gone Too Far" in THE
            COLLECTED POEMS (A55).

UNRHYMING POEMS.   Title of second volume of THE COLLECTED
POEMS (q.v.)

"We Have Gone Too Far."   Original title of "The Turning Back"
(q.v.)

Z.   STUDIES OF THE MISCELLANEOUS WRITINGS

The following section is subdivided into six parts: i. Books
and Essay Collections on the Miscellaneous Writings; ii. Critical Articles or Chapters on the Essays and Introductions;
iii. Critical Articles or Chapters on the Letters; iv. Critical Articles or Chapters on MOVEMENTS IN EUROPEAN HISTORY;
v. Critical Articles or Chapters on the Translations; and
vi. Critical Articles or Chapters on the Travel Writings.

For information on textual editions, bibliographical and
biographical backgrounds, and additional critical commentaries
concerning the miscellaneous writings, see the headnotes to
sections Z, i, through Z, vi, below.

Z, i.   Books and Essay Collections on the Miscellaneous
        Writings

Also see Boulton's PROSPECTUS AND NOTES (Z90) and Lucia's
"A PROPOSITIO DI *L'AMANTI DI LADY CHATTERLEY*" DI D. H.
LAWRENCE (AA27).

Z1   Arnold, Armin. D. H. LAWRENCE AND GERMAN LITERATURE:
       WITH TWO HITHERTO UNKNOWN ESSAYS BY D. H. LAWRENCE.
       Montreal: Mansfield Book Mart, Heinemann, 1963.
             Reprints two of DHL's reviews of German literature
             (1912--also collected in PHOENIX II [B18]), with
             introduction, postscript, and three appendixes
             (on German translations and criticism of DHL, on
             Mann's influence on his views of German literature
             [for earlier publication, see AA109], and on the
             English expurgation of DHL's German letters
             [first published in AA108; later expanded--see
             Z89]).

Z2   Cura-Sazdanić, Ileana. D. H. LAWRENCE AS CRITIC. Delhi:
       Munshiram Manoharlal, 1969.
             Examination of DHL as the bridge in the
             critical "great tradition" from Matthew

Arnold to F. R. Leavis. However, too much
energy is spent explicating Arnold's ethical
criticism, in CULTURE AND ANARCHY (1869),
"The Arnoldian Succession," DHL's contemporary
critics and champions, and Leavis's writings
on DHL, to survey adequately either DHL's
social ideals, or his "Conception of Art,
Morality, and the Novel." Poorly focused,
highly derivative, and badly in need of post-
dissertation revision. See Z3 and Z7.

Z2a Douglas, Norman. D. H. LAWRENCE AND MAURICE MAGNUS:
A PLEA FOR BETTER MANNERS. Florence: Privately
printed, 1924.
Vituperative attack on DHL by a former friend,
in reaction to DHL's too candid portrait of
Magnus, written as a preface to Magnus's
MEMOIRS OF THE FOREIGN LEGION (1924; see
A66). Douglas's pamphlet reprinted in his
EXPERIMENTS (London: Chapman and Hall,
1925). Also see Z30.

Z3 Gordon, David J. D. H. LAWRENCE AS A LITERARY CRITIC.
New Haven, Conn.: Yale Univ. Press, 1966.
Examines DHL's literary criticism as a significant
"*expression* of his achievement," as a complement to, rather than a commentary on, his art.
Taking the middle position between Leavis's
unqualified praise and Eliot's scorn of DHL's
critical abilities, Gordon evaluates the
relationship of DHL's modernism to the expressive, "Romantic tradition," and elucidates
DHL's conception of the critic's role, his
aesthetic theories (e.g., on form, symbol,
fiction), his "quarrel" with the tragic mode,
and his apocalyptic historiography and mythology. Gordon concludes with a judicious
assessment of the limitations of DHL's
ideological criticism, using the example of
his essay on Whitman, from STUDIES IN CLASSIC
AMERICAN LITERATURE (A65), where ideology
obscures subject. Far better study than Cura-
Sazdanić 's (Z2) or Sitesh's (Z7).

Z4 Gutierrez, Donald. LAPSING OUT: EMBODIMENTS OF DEATH
AND REBIRTH IN THE LAST WRITINGS OF D. H. LAWRENCE.
Rutherford, N. J.: Fairleigh Dickinson Univ. Press, 1980.
Argues the autonomy and excellence of the
works of DHL's "post-1925 phase" (APOCALYPSE,

ETRUSCAN PLACES, LAST POEMS, "The Man Who Died,"
"The Virgin and the Gipsy," and other late
stories--LCL unconvincingly excluded), finding
an organic unity among the writings in DHL's
insistent use of the death-rebirth pattern.
Gutierrez persuasively links DHL's "apocalyp-
tical and resurrectional" cast of mind to his
near death in Oaxaca, Mexico, in 1925, but
does not finally account for the uniqueness
of these last works by tracing in them a
pattern which, though intensified, also
characterizes DHL's earlier writings.

Z5   Hyde, G. M.   D. H. LAWRENCE AND THE ART OF TRANSLATION.
New York: Barnes and Noble, 1981.
Examines "those translations which are beyond doubt" by DHL, noting also a number of
texts which he may have participated in
translating, principally to gauge his fidelity to the original language and to the spirit
of the author (both uniformly excellent) and
to estimate the reasons for his attraction to
particular languages and writers. Hyde's
opening chapter assesses DHL's responses to
Italian and Russian literatures, focusing on
his and Koteliansky's 1920 translation of Leo
Shestov's ALL THINGS ARE POSSIBLE (A80).
He devotes two chapters to the analysis of
DHL's translations of Verga's stories (A83,
A84), and novel, MASTRO-DON GESUALDO (A82),
and a concluding chapter to his and "Kot's"
version of Ivan Bunin's "The Gentleman from
San Francisco" (A81). Hyde also notes a
trace of Bunin's influence on DHL's "The Ladybird," in an appendix. Assimilates Z109.

Z6   Janik, Del Ivan. THE CURVE OF RETURN: D. H. LAWRENCE'S
TRAVEL BOOKS. Victoria, B.C.:   Univ. of Victoria
English Literary Studies, 1981.
Studies, in chronological order, the composition and content of DHL's four travel
narratives, as "often seminal statements" of
the "directions taken" by DHL's imagination
through his career. Arising from the dualistic tension between "his need for community
and his need for separateness," DHL prescribes
for his culture a psychological and philosophic paradox, a "swerve or curve of return
toward primitive modes of perception," to

revitalize the present and direct man into the
future. TWILIGHT IN ITALY, SEA AND SARDINIA,
and MORNINGS IN MEXICO, "essentially diagnos-
tic" works, examine the conflicts between the
separateness of the modern mechanistic world
and the lost communion of the primitive past,
while ETRUSCAN PLACES, a "tentative prescrip-
tion," explores the possibility of reviving
our culture through the recapture of the
primitive's "spontaneous sense of wonder."
Useful study and strong thesis.

Z7   Sitesh, Aruna. D. H. LAWRENCE: THE CRUSADER AS CRITIC.
Delhi: Macmillan, 1975.
Study of DHL's critical and social theories,
drawing widely from the prose. Sitesh distinguishes her approach from those of Cura-
Sazdanić (Z2) and Gordon (Z3), who derive
DHL's critical attitudes from Arnold and the
Romantic tradition respectively, relating his
views to the Puritan tradition ("the solitary
individual's" search for "self-realization"
and "transcendental values"), with differences
(e.g., DHL's attitude toward human nature).
Within this broad framework and despite some
tortured writing, Sitesh usefully examines
the tension between individual and social
consciousness, emotions and intellect, and
isolation and "relatedness" in DHL's critical
writings.

Z, ii. Critical Articles or Chapters on the Essays and
Introductions

For the textual edition of *APOCALYPSE* AND THE WRITINGS ON
REVELATION, see B6. Textual editions of the remaining
essays and introductions will be published in six additional
volumes in THE CAMBRIDGE EDITION (B1), as follows (editors
of editions-in-progress identified in parentheses):   STUDIES
IN CLASSIC AMERICAN LITERATURE (ed. H. Shapiro), STUDY OF
THOMAS HARDY AND OTHER ESSAYS (ed. D. Steele), INTRODUCTIONS,
PREFACES AND REVIEWS, *FANTASIA OF THE UNCONSCIOUS* AND
PSYCHOANALYSIS AND THE UNCONSCIOUS, *REFLECTIONS ON THE
DEATH OF A PORCUPINE* AND OTHER ESSAYS, 1915-25 (ed. M. Herbert),
and *ASSORTED ARTICLES* AND OTHER ESSAYS, 1926-30 (ed. Elizabeth
Mansfield). Several additional travel essays, previously
published in the PHOENIX collections (B16 and B18), will be
placed in the textual editions of the travel writings (see
section Z, vi, below).

For bibliographical information on the essays and introductions,
see Roberts (E39) and Sagar (E40), and, for biographical backgrounds to the prose writings, see Carter (F27), Corke (F36),
Delany (F41), Delavenay (F44), Moore (F112), Murry (F121),
and Nehls (F123).

For additional critical commentary and information on the
essays and introductions, see the following books, in section
G above: Allendorf (G4), Arnold (G7), Beal (G9), Bredsdorff
(G13), Brunsdale (G14), Burns (G15), Cavitch (G16), Clark
(G17), Clarke (G18), Corsani (G21), Cowan (G22), Daleski (G24),
Dix (G29), Draper (G34), Ebbatson (G35), Freeman (G40),
Galinsky (G41), Goodheart (G44), Gregory (G47), Hobsbaum (G51),
Hochman (G52), Hough (G56), Howe (G58), Inniss (G60),
Jaensson (G61), Jarrett-Kerr (G62), Johnsson (G63), Kermode
(G65), Leavis (G68, G69), Meyers (G73), Michaels-Tonks (G74),
Miko (G75), Miller (G77), Moore (G80), Nahal (G86),
Negriolli (G87), Nin (G88), Pinion (G95), Potter (G98),
Pritchard (G101), Reul (G103), Sagar (G104), Seillière (G107),
Seligmann (G108), Slade (G111), Swigg (G117), Tedlock (G118),
Tindall (G120), Weidner (G122), Wettern (G126), Worthen (G128),
Zytaruk (G131); the following critical articles, in section H
above: Albright (H5), Alcorn (H6), Baker (H22), Bentley (H37),
Clark (H65), Cornwell (H76), Cowan (H78), Eliot (H104),
Glicksberg (H141), Goldring (H142), Goode (H144), Goodheart
(H145), Gunn (H159), Hinz (H180), Hoffman (H185, H187),
John (H196), Kinkead-Weekes (H207), Lea (H215), Lerner (H221),
Liscano Velutini (H225), MacDonald (H230), Marks (H234),
Panichas (H281), Poole and Shepherd (H293), Pritchard (H296),
Rieff (H308), Ross (H317), Rossman (H319), Schwartz (H332),
Tristram (H386), Troy (H387), Vickery (H393), Young (H423);
the following books, in section Z, i, above: Arnold (Z1),
Cura-Sazdanić (Z2), Douglas (Z2a), Gordon (Z3), Gutierrez (Z4),
Sitesh (Z7); and the following studies, entered in other
sections of this bibliography: Walker (T27), Widmer (V5),
Gilbert (Y1), Marshall (Y3), Oates (Y5), Oppel (Y116),
Nogueira (AA88), Comellini (AA121), Grassi (AA158),
Kamimura (AA177), and Vuković (AA285).

Z8   Aiken, Conrad. "D. H. Lawrence." 1924, 1927. In A
       REVIEWER'S ABC. New York: Meridian, 1958. Pp. 261-63;
       263-66.
               Considers DHL's STUDIES IN CLASSIC AMERICAN
       LITERATURE (A65) and MORNINGS IN MEXICO (A89)
       confused, objects to their "semi-mystic, semi-
       psychological jargon," and regrets the decline
       of DHL's style from the heights of SL and WL to
       "slipshod and journalistic prose." Two review
       essays. First essay reprinted in G5.

Z9   Aldington, Richard. "Introduction." In Lawrence's
      APOCALYPSE. New York: Viking, 1931. Pp. v–xxxii.
          The disservice done DHL both by his admirers
          and by his detractors, and the place of
          APOCALYPSE (A76) in his campaign against
          the dehumanization of man. An "open-letter"
          to Frieda, added to the second American
          impression of APOCALYPSE.

Z10   Anderson, Sherwood. "A Man's Mind." NEW REPUBLIC,
      63 (1930), 22–23.
          Anderson's account of his shock and distress
          at DHL's death and appreciation of the
          vitality of his mind, as seen in his essays.
          Review of ASSORTED ARTICLES (A75).

Z11   Arnold, Armin. "Introduction." In Lawrence's THE
      SYMBOLIC MEANING. Ed. Arnold. Pp 1–11. See A77.
          Clarifies the textual history of STUDIES
          IN CLASSIC AMERICAN LITERATURE (A65) for his
          edition of earlier versions of the essays.

Z12   Axelrad, Allen M. "The Order of the Leatherstocking
      Tales: D. H. Lawrence, David Noble, and the Iron Trap
      of History." AMERICAN LITERATURE, 54 (1982), 189–211.
          Though acknowledging DHL's "primacy in
          Cooper studies," disputes DHL's chrono-
          logical ordering of Cooper's Leatherstocking
          tales, in STUDIES IN CLASSIC AMERICAN LITER-
          ATURE (A65).

Z13   Baron, Carl E. "Two Hitherto Unknown Pieces by D. H.
      Lawrence." ENCOUNTER, 33, No. 2 (1969), 3–5.
          Locates DHL's first critical review (ENGLISH
          REVIEW, Nov. 1911, pp. 721–24) and an over-
          looked essay ("With the Guns," MANCHESTER
          GUARDIAN, 18 Aug. 1914).

Z14   Beards, Richard D. "D. H. Lawrence and the 'Study of
      Thomas Hardy,' His Victorian Predecessor." DHLR, 2 (1969),
      210–29.
          Hardy's and DHL's "similar vision," "shared
          concern for the importance of sexual relation-
          ships in human development," and "mutual
          sympathy" for the uncommon hero.   Examines
          DHL's essay on Hardy (in B16).

Z15 Beker, Miroslav. "'The Crown,' 'The Reality of Peace,'
     and WOMEN IN LOVE." DHLR, 2 (1969), 254-64.
          On DHL's two philosophic essays (A60, A61)
          and WL. For annotation see N10.

Z16 Chomel, Luisetta. "Verga: A Note on Lawrence's Criti-
     cism." DHLR, 13 (1980), 275-81.
          DHL's highly subjective comments on Verga,
          in the introductions to his translations
          (A82-A84), "substantially valid" and echoed
          in much subsequent criticism.

Z17 Clark, L. D. "The Apocalypse of Lorenzo." DHLR, 3
     (1970), 141-60.
          Influence of the Book of Revelation on DHL's
          APOCALYPSE (A76) and "The Crown" (A60).

Z18 Cohen, Marvin R. "The Prophet and the Critic: A Study
     in Classic Lawrentian Literature." TSLL, 22 (1980), 1-21.
          The tensions between critic and prophet in
          DHL's thought, and the nature of his prophecy.

Z19 Colacurcio, Michael J. "The Symbolic and the Symptomatic:
     D. H. Lawrence in Recent American Criticism." AMERICAN
     QUARTERLY, 27 (1975), 486-501.
          DHL's STUDIES IN CLASSIC AMERICAN LITERATURE
          (A65) the seminal influence on significant
          trends in recent American literary criticism.

Z20 Davies, J. V. "Introduction." In LAWRENCE ON HARDY AND
     PAINTING: "STUDY OF THOMAS HARDY" AND "INTRODUCTION TO
     THESE PAINTINGS." Ed. Davies. London: Heinemann, 1973.
     Pp. 1-9.
          In his critical and aesthetic essays DHL
          "alive to the thought of his time" (e.g.,
          Cézanne, Hardy, and Nietzsche). Intro-
          duces two reprinted essays (see A71 and B16).

Z21 Dawson, Eugene W. "Lawrence's Pollyanalytic Esthetic
     for the Novel." PAUNCH, No. 2 (1966), pp. 60-68.
          Examines DHL's critical statements on the
          novel form. See G94.

Z22 Deakin, William. "D. H. Lawrence's Attacks on Proust
     and Joyce." EIC, 7 (1957), 383-403.
          DHL's untenable indictment of extremes of
          self-conscious artistry in "Surgery for the
          Novel, or a Bomb" (A64). See H188.

Z23 Delavenay, Émile. "Le Phénix et ses cendres." EA, 21
     (1968), 373-80.
            The publication of PHOENIX II (B18), a
            compromise between what is needed (DHL's
            uncollected writings collected) and what is
            practical to publish. Regrets omission,
            for example, of early drafts of the stories.
            Review essay. [In French.]

Z24 Dennis, Nigel. "Angry Visitor: The Landscape and D. H.
     Lawrence." In AN ESSAY ON MALTA. New York: Vanguard,
     1972. Pp. 28-42.
            The harshness of Malta's landscape in
            summer, aptly described by DHL in "Intro-
            duction to MEMOIRS OF THE FOREIGN LEGION" (A66).

Z25 Entry deleted.

Z26 Draper, Ronald P. "D. H. Lawrence on Mother Love." EIC,
     8 (1958), 285-89.
            On SL and FANTASIA OF THE UNCONSCIOUS (A63).
            For annotation see L27.

Z27 Earp, T. W. "Mr. Lawrence on Painting." NEW STATESMAN,
     33 (1929), 578.
            Chiefly concerned with DHL's "Introduction to
            These Paintings" (A71). Since DHL is a great
            novelist "we are interested in his views on
            painting," but his own pictures "do not give
            him interest as a painter." Reprinted in G34.

Z28 Forster, E. M. "PORNOGRAPHY AND OBSCENITY." NATION AND
     ATHENAEUM, 46 (1930), 508-09.
            Finds merit in DHL's important and novel
            definition of acts which encourage "any turning-
            inward upon itself of the spirit," any rejec-
            tion of the "passionate outer life of
            personal interchange," as obscene. Reviews
            DHL's essay (A73). Reprinted in G34. Also
            see F61.

Z29 Foster, Richard. "Criticism as Rage: D. H. Lawrence."
     In A D. H. LAWRENCE MISCELLANY. Ed. Harry T. Moore.
     Pp. 312-25. See G81.
            DHL an intemperate, doctrinaire, iconoclastic
            critic. Unpleasantly patronizing. Reprinted
            in G115.

Z30   Fraser, Keath.   "Norman Douglas and D. H. Lawrence:
       A Sideshow in Modern Memoirs."   DHLR, 9 (1976), 283-95.
             Summary of Douglas's feud with DHL and com-
             parison of his "flat" portrait of Magnus and
             DHL's "round" one, in "Introduction" to
             Magnus's MEMOIRS OF THE FOREIGN LEGION (A66).
             Also see Z2a.

Z31   Gass, William H.   "From Some Ashes No Bird Rises."   1968.
       In FICTION AND THE FIGURES OF LIFE. New York: Knopf,
       1970.   Pp. 212-21.
             Impressionistic commentary on DHL's person-
             ality, as revealed in his essays.   Review of
             PHOENIX II (B18).

Z32   Gatti, Hilary.   "D. H. Lawrence and the Idea of Education."
       EM, 21 (1970), 209-31.
             Though proposing unrealizable remedies, DHL
             a persistent and acute critic both of old
             methods and of new educational ideals in
             "Education of the People" (in B16).

Z33   Green, Martin.   "STUDIES IN CLASSIC AMERICAN LITERATURE."
       In REAPPRAISALS: SOME COMMONSENSE READINGS IN AMERICAN
       LITERATURE.   New York: Norton, 1965.   Pp. 231-47.
             Surveys DHL's "brilliant" but misleading
             critiques of American authors (A65).

Z34   Gregory, Horace.   "The Speaking Voice of D. H. Lawrence."
       1942.   In SPIRIT OF TIME AND PLACE: COLLECTED ESSAYS.
       New York: Norton, 1973.   Pp. 180-85.
             DHL's "vision and insight" the "mark of
             genius" in his essays; yet he was, it appears,
             an ineffective teacher.

Z35   Gurling, Freda E.   "D. H. Lawrence's Apology for the
       Artist."   LONDON MERCURY, 33 (1936), 596-603.
             DHL attacks pretentiousness in his critical
             essays, demanding that art ("evanescent")
             and the artist (quite mortal) be put in their
             "humble" place.

Z36   Harper, Howard M.   "FANTASIA and the Psychodynamics of
       WOMEN IN LOVE."   In THE CLASSIC BRITISH NOVEL.   Ed.
       Harper and Charles Edge.   Athens: Univ. of Georgia
       Press, 1972.   Pp. 202-19.
             For annotation see N48.

Z37 Hinz, Evelyn J. "The Beginning and the End: D. H.
     Lawrence's PSYCHOANALYSIS and FANTASIA." DR, 52 (1972),
     251-65.
          PSYCHOANALYSIS AND THE UNCONSCIOUS (A62)
          attempts to be a clinical study; FANTASIA
          OF THE UNCONSCIOUS (A63), the more personal
          statement, is far more successful.

Z38 Howe, Irving. "Sherwood Anderson and D. H. Lawrence."
     FURIOSO, 5, No. 4 (1950), 21-33.
          Anderson's Freudianism came to him via
          DHL's psychoanalytic treatises, PSYCHO-
          ANALYSIS AND THE UNCONSCIOUS (A62) and
          FANTASIA OF THE UNCONSCIOUS (A63).

Z39 Janik, Del Ivan. "Toward 'Thingness': Cézanne's
     Painting and Lawrence's Poetry." TCL, 19 (1973), 119-28.
          On DHL's views in "Art and Morality" (A67),
          "Introduction to These Paintings" (A71),
          and his poetry. For annotation see Y31.

Z40 Jarrett-Kerr, Martin. "D. H. Lawrence and 'The Spirit
     of Place.'" In DER ENGLISCHE ESSAY: ANALYSEN. Ed.
     Horst Weber. Darmstadt: Wissenschaftliche Buchgesell-
     schaft, 1975. Pp. 308-19.
          Examines DHL's "Foreword" to STUDIES IN
          CLASSIC AMERICAN LITERATURE (A65) and
          defines three catagories for classifying
          DHL's essays: literary criticism, prophecy,
          and description (the "search into the
          heart of objects or scenes observed").

Z41 Jones, Lawrence. "Physiognomy and the Sensual Will in
     'The Ladybird' and 'The Fox.'" DHLR, 13 (1980), 1-29.
          On FANTASIA OF THE UNCONSCIOUS (A63) and
          the two novellas. For annotation see V61.

Z42 Kalnins, Mara. "Introduction." In D. H. LAWRENCE:
     APOCALYPSE AND THE WRITINGS ON REVELATION. Ed. Kalnins.
     Pp. 3-38. See B6.
          Discusses the origins, composition, and
          editing of APOCALYPSE, its publication
          and reviews, its relations to DHL's
          other writings on the Book of Revelation,
          and its reflection of DHL's interests
          and ideas in the late 'twenties.

Z43 Kaplan, Harold J. "Cooper, Poe, and D. H. Lawrence: The Myth of America." In DEMOCRATIC HUMANISM AND AMERICAN LITERATURE. Chicago: Univ. of Chicago Press, 1972. Pp. 103-28.
> Exalted praise for and useful commentary on DHL's rich, "rare and valuable" analyses of Cooper and Poe in STUDIES IN CLASSIC AMERICAN LITERATURE (A65).

Z44 Kermode, Frank. "Spenser and the Allegorists." In SHAKESPEARE, SPENSER, DONNE: RENAISSANCE ESSAYS. New York: Viking, 1971. Pp. 12-32.
> Compares and contrasts DHL's apocalyptic vision and allegorical technique with Spenser's (chiefly re: APOCALYPSE [A76]).

Z45 Kinkead-Weekes, Mark. "Lawrence on Hardy." In THOMAS HARDY AFTER FIFTY YEARS. Ed. Lance St.J. Butler. Totowa, N. J.: Rowman and Littlefield, 1977. Pp. 90-103.
> Analysis of DHL's inchoate, "sadly neglected," yet illuminating "Study of Thomas Hardy" (in B16).

Z46 -----. "This Old Maid: Jane Austen Replies to Charlotte Bronte and D. H. Lawrence." NCF, 30 (1975), 399-419.
> Responds to Bronte's and DHL's criticisms of Austen.

Z47 Klingopulos, G. D. "Lawrence's Criticism." EIC, 7 (1957), 294-303.
> Admires the insights and independence of DHL's literary criticism, but considers his radically original approach to the unconscious significance of the writer ("Never trust the artist. Trust the tale") his greatest contribution. Review of SELECTED LITERARY CRITICISM (B23).

Z48 Leavis, F. R. "Genius as Critic." SPECTATOR, 206 (1961), 412, 414.
> PHOENIX (B16) "immeasurably the finest body of criticism in existence." Review of reissued edition (1961). Reprinted in G20.

Z49 -----. "The Wild, Untutored Phoenix." 1937. In THE COMMON PURSUIT. New York: Stewart, 1952. Pp. 233-39.
> Essay review of PHOENIX (B16) and of DHL's criticism in general.

Z50 Lee, Brian. "America, My America." In RENAISSANCE AND
MODERN ESSAYS. Ed. George R. Hibbard. London: Routledge, 1966. Pp. 181-88.
     DHL and America (especially STUDIES IN
     CLASSIC AMERICAN LITERATURE [A65]).

Z51 Longville, Timothy. "The Longest Journey: D. H. Lawrence's PHOENIX." CritQ, 4 (1962), 82-87.
     DHL's indecisiveness about his vision of
     an earth "reparadised," his "confusion
     between Eden and oblivion." Review of
     reissued edition of PHOENIX (B16, 1961).

Z52 McDonald, Edward D. "Introduction." In Lawrence's
PHOENIX. Ed. McDonald. Pp. ix-xxvii. See B16.
     "Information and comment . . . likely to
     contribute to a fuller understanding of
     some of the numerous selections which make
     up the volume."

Z53 Mann, Charles W., ed. "D. H. Lawrence: Notes on Reading
Hawthorne's THE SCARLET LETTER." In NATHANIEL HAWTHORNE
JOURNAL 1973. Ed. C. E. Frazer Clark, Jr. Englewood,
Colo.: Microcard Editions Books, 1973. Pp. 9-11, 13-15.
     Introduction to and transcription and
     reproduction of DHL's notes on Hawthorne
     (1917-18), his workbook for an essay on
     Hawthorne (1919) which he later incorpor-
     ated into STUDIES IN CLASSIC AMERICAN
     LITERATURE (A65).

Z54 Maud, Ralph N. "D. H. Lawrence: True Emotion as the
Ethical Control in Art." WHR, 9 (1955), 233-40.
     Usefully compares Babbitt and DHL as critics.

Z55 Morrison, Claudia. "D. H. Lawrence and American
Literature." In FREUD AND THE CRITIC: THE EARLY USE
OF DEPTH PSYCHOLOGY IN LITERARY CRITICISM. Chapel Hill:
Univ. of North Carolina Press, 1968. Pp. 203-25.
     On the influence of DHL's psychoanalytic tracts
     on his critical views in STUDIES IN CLASSIC
     AMERICAN LITERATURE (A65).

Z56 Paterson, John. "Lawrence's Vital Source: Nature and
Character in Thomas Hardy." In NATURE AND THE VICTORIAN
IMAGINATION. Ed. U. C. Knoepflmacher and G. B. Tennyson.
Berkeley: Univ. of California Press, 1977. Pp. 455-69.
     Hardy "dear" to DHL because he rehabilitated
     both man and nature as sources of "mystery

and miracle" (chiefly on Hardy). Some
comment on DHL's "Study of Thomas Hardy"
(in B16).

Z57   Peckham, Morse. ART AND PORNOGRAPHY: AN EXPERIMENT IN
      EXPLANATION. New York: Basic Books, 1969. Pp. 19-27.
           DHL's "obvious strategy of semantic confu-
           sion" in his use of the terms "Pornography"
           and "Obscenity" (see A73). Examines impli-
           cations of DHL's intellectually silly,
           "antisexual justification of sexual behavior"
           (cf. Margaret Mead's "Sex and Censorship in
           Contemporary Society" [1953]).

Z58   Pierle, Robert C. "D. H. Lawrence's STUDIES IN CLASSIC
      AMERICAN LITERATURE: An Evaluation." SOUTHERN QUARTERLY,
      6 (1968), 333-40.
           Not seen.

Z59   Pinto, Vivian de Sola. "Lawrence and the Nonconformist
      Hymns." In A D. H. LAWRENCE MISCELLANY. Ed. Harry T.
      Moore. Pp. 103-13. See G81.
           Description of the manuscript of "Hymns in
           a Man's Life"(in A75) and commentary on
           DHL's nonconformist heritage.

Z60   Pittock, Malcolm. "Lawrence's 'Art and the Individual.'"
      EA, 26 (1973), 312-19.
           Early and lasting influence of Tolstoy on
           DHL's views of the nature and purpose of
           art (traced in a 1908 essay, "Art and the
           Individual," collected in B18).

Z61   Poirier, Richard. A WORLD ELSEWHERE: THE PLACE OF
      STYLE IN AMERICAN LITERATURE. New York: Oxford Univ.
      Press, 1966. Pp. 37-50 and passim.
           On "St. Mawr" and STUDIES IN CLASSIC
           AMERICAN LITERATURE (A65). For annota-
           tion see V157.

Z62   Remsbury, John. "'Real Thinking': Lawrence and Cézanne."
      CAMBRIDGE QUARTERLY, 2 (1967), 117-47.
           DHL's "absorption in" and assimilation
           of Cézanne's attempt "to paint the real
           existence of the body" (viz. DHL's essays,
           especially "Introduction to These Paintings"
           [A71]).

Z63 Remsbury, John, and Ann Remsbury. "Lawrence and Art."
     1971. In D. H. LAWRENCE: A CRITICAL STUDY. Ed. Andor
     Gomme. Pp. 190-218. See G43.
         On DHL's paintings and art criticism. For
         annotation see W9.

Z64 Richardson, John Adkins, and John I. Ades. "D. H.
     Lawrence on Cézanne: A Study in the Psychology of
     Critical Intuition." JAAC, 28 (1970), 441-53.
         On both the aesthetic problems posed by
         DHL's criticism and the intuitive insight
         of his discussion of Cézanne in "Introduc-
         tion to These Paintings" (A71).

Z65 Rieff, Philip. "A Modern Mythmaker." In MYTH AND MYTH-
     MAKING. Ed. Henry A. Murray. New York: Braziller,
     1960. Pp. 240-75.
         In PSYCHOANALYSIS AND THE UNCONSCIOUS (A62)
         and FANTASIA OF THE UNCONSCIOUS (A63), DHL's
         philosophy-mythology "encompasses within
         rational science the irrational, from which
         the specifically religious emotion grows."

Z66 -----. "Introduction." In Lawrence's PSYCHOANALYSIS
     AND THE UNCONSCIOUS AND FANTASIA OF THE UNCONSCIOUS.
     New York: Viking, 1960. Pp. vii-xxiii.
         Fine analysis of DHL's treatises (A62 and
         A63), counterpointing the "incoherent and
         revolutionary imagination" of DHL with the
         "coherent and conservative" rationalism
         of Freud.

Z67 Roberts, Mark. "D. H. Lawrence and the Failure of Energy:
     FANTASIA OF THE UNCONSCIOUS; PSYCHOANALYSIS AND THE
     UNCONSCIOUS." In THE TRADITION OF ROMANTIC MORALITY.
     London: Macmillan, 1973. Pp. 322-48.
         DHL's psychological tracts (A62, A63),
         present, better than the fiction, "the
         fullness and the *balance*"of DHL's thought.

Z68 Roberts, Warren, and Harry T. Moore. "Introduction."
     In Lawrence's PHOENIX II. Ed. Roberts and Moore.
     Pp. ix-xv. See B18.
         DHL's essays always stimulating and often
         useful "commentaries on the imaginative
         work."

Z69   Rosenthal, T. G. "The Writer as Painter." LISTENER,
      68 (1962), 349-50.
            On DHL's paintings and his views in
            "Introduction to These Paintings" (A71).
            For annotation see W10.

Z70   Rubenstein, H. F. "The Law Versus D. H. Lawrence." In
      Lawrence's SEX, LITERATURE, AND CENSORSHIP. Ed. Harry
      T. Moore. London: Heinemann, 1955. Pp. 39-54.
            Compares Shaw, the "dramatist of unusual
            ideas," and DHL, both the "novelist (and
            painter) of innocent sexuality" and the
            critic of censorship, as similar victims
            of the narrow-minded modern censor ("Dog-
            berry").

Z71   Salgādo, Gāmini. "D. H. Lawrence as Literary Critic."
      LONDON MAGAZINE, 7, No. 2 (1960), 49-57.
            DHL's passion and subjectivity as a critic
            (cf. Pound).

Z72   Salter, K. W. "Lawrence, Hardy, and 'The Great Tradi-
      tion.'" ENGLISH, 22 (1973), 60-65.
            Discusses DHL's high estimate and thought-
            ful analysis of Hardy in "Study of Thomas
            Hardy" (in B16), and similarities in their
            thought.

Z73   Schneiderman, Leo. "Notes on D. H. Lawrence's STUDIES
      IN CLASSIC AMERICAN LITERATURE." ConnR, 1, No. 2 (1968),
      57-71.
            Attempts "to trace the process" by which
            DHL "identifies the central conflict" in
            Cooper, Hawthorne, Poe, Dana, Whitman,
            and Melville, in his study of American
            literature (A65).

Z74   [Schotz], Myra Glazer. "Sex and the Psyche: William
      Blake and D. H. Lawrence." HUSL, 9 (1981), 196-229.
            Echoes of Blake's style and ideas in DHL
            (e.g., the four-fold conception of the
            psyche and the nature of human sexuality),
            chiefly illustrated from DHL's essays.
            Presumably this essay, or a related version,
            has also been published as "Why the Sons of God
            Want Daughters of Men: On William Blake
            and D. H. Lawrence," in WILLIAM BLAKE AND THE
            MODERNS, ed. Robert J. Bertholf and Annette
            S. Levitt (Albany: State Univ. of New York
            Press, 1982); not seen.

Z75 Sherman, Stuart P. "America is Discovered." NEW YORK
     EVENING POST LITERARY REVIEW, 20 Oct. 1923, pp. 143-44.
          Sees DHL discovering his own "cave-man
          philosophy" in his STUDIES IN CLASSIC
          AMERICAN LITERATURE (A65), and notes,
          with amusement, his adoption of an
          idiomatic "American" prose style. Re-
          printed in G34.

Z76 Small, Michel. "The Tale the Critic Tells: D. H. Law-
     rence on Nathaniel Hawthorne." PAUNCH, Nos. 40-41
     (1975), pp. 40-58.
          Hawthorne's THE SCARLET LETTER (1850)
          succeeds despite the author's imposed
          morality and DHL's distorted, equally
          "imposed" interpretation in STUDIES
          IN CLASSIC AMERICAN LITERATURE (A65).

Z77 Spender, Stephen. "D. H. Lawrence: PHOENIX." 1936.
     In THE THIRTIES AND AFTER: POETRY, POLITICS, PEOPLE,
     1933-1970. New York: Random House, 1978. Pp. 26-29.
          Writing during his communist phase,
          Spender finds DHL's "isolation and his
          desperate originality of thought . . .
          forced onto him by his social position."
          DHL's essays demonstrate that "the revolt
          of his genius against bourgeois society was
          complete." Review of PHOENIX (B16).

Z78 Tanner, Michael. "The Total Work of Art." In THE
     WAGNER COMPANION. Ed. Peter Burbidge and Richard Sutton.
     London: Faber, 1979. Pp. 140-224.
          Invokes DHL's theories of fiction and
          criticism to clarify Wagner's theory of
          the *Gesamtkunstwerk* (chiefly pp. 147-54,
          222-24).

Z79 Thornham, Susan. "Lawrence and Freud." DURHAM UNIVERSITY
     JOURNAL, 39, No. 1 (1977), 73-82.
          The essential contrasts between Freud's
          and DHL's views of the unconscious (re:
          DHL's psychoanalytic tracts; A62 and A63).

Z80 Trilling, Lionel. "D. H. Lawrence: A Neglected Aspect."
     SYMPOSIUM, 1 (1930), 361-70.
          On LCL and FANTASIA OF THE UNCONSCIOUS (A63).
          For annotation see U72.

Z81   Ulmer, Gregory L.   "D. H. Lawrence, Wilhelm Worringer,
      and the Aesthetics of Modernism."   DHLR, 10 (1977), 165-81.
          DHL's criticism "less eccentric" when
          related to the German tradition in art
          history which played an important, little
          acknowledged role in the shaping of
          modern aesthetics.

Z82   Unger, Leonard.   "Now, *Now*, the Bird is on the Wing."
      In ELIOT'S COMPOUND GHOST: INFLUENCE AND CONFLUENCE.
      University Park: Pennsylvania State Univ. Press, 1981.
      Pp. 73-76.
          Parallels between DHL's preface to the
          American edition of NEW POEMS ("Poetry
          of the Present"; see A51) and the ideas
          and imagery of Eliot's "Burnt Norton" (1936).

Z83   West, Edward Sackville.   "A Modern Isaiah."   NEW STATESMAN,
      27 (1926), 360-61.
          On DAVID and REFLECTIONS ON THE DEATH OF A
          PORCUPINE (A69).   For annotation see X16.

Z84   West, Paul.   "D. H. Lawrence: Mystical Critic."   SoR,
      1 (1965), 210-28.
          Discerning comparison of the more
          satisfactory earlier versions of
          STUDIES IN CLASSIC AMERICAN LITER-
          ATURE (A65) with its published text,
          contained in a favorable review of
          Arnold's edition of THE SYMBOLIC
          MEANING (A77) and five other studies
          of DHL.   Reprinted in West's THE
          WINE OF ABSURDITY: ESSAYS ON
          LITERATURE AND CONSOLATION (Univer-
          sity Park: Pennsylvania State Univ.
          Press, 1966), pp. 19-38.

Z85   Westbrook, Max.   "The Poetical Spirit, Sacrality and the
      American West."   WESTERN AMERICAN LITERATURE, 3 (1968),
      193-205.
          DHL's western American, "symbolic apprehension
          of sacred reality" in APOCALYPSE (A76; cf.
          Whitman and others).

Z86   White, Richard L.   "D. H. Lawrence as Critic: Theories
      of English and American Fiction."   DHLR, 11 (1978), 156-74.
          DHL's theoretical distinction between the
          "motivating impulses" of English ("harmony

and reconciliation") and American
fiction ("disharmony and division"),
in a number of his critical pronounce-
ments, anticipates important trends in
recent academic criticism (e.g., Richard
Chase and Leslie Fiedler on the American
novel).

Z87 Williams, Raymond. "Introduction." In D. H. LAWRENCE
ON EDUCATION. Ed. Joy Williams and Raymond Williams.
Pp. 7-13. See B10.
DHL, as "one of the first English writers
to have direct experience of ordinary
teaching," an informed critic of education.

Z88 Zytaruk, George J. "What Happened to D. H. Lawrence's
GOATS AND COMPASSES?" DHLR, 4 (1971), 280-86.
On an untraced philosophical essay (1916).
For fuller annotation, see N107.

Z, iii. Critical Articles or Chapters on the Letters

For the various editions of DHL's correspondence, see section
C of this bibliography. As of 1983, the first two volumes
of the projected eight-volume edition of THE LETTERS OF D. H.
LAWRENCE have appeared (see C11), an integral part of THE
CAMBRIDGE EDITION (B1). For information on the texts and
locations of the letters, their biographical backgrounds,
and their recipients, see THE LETTERS (C11) and the still
useful COLLECTED LETTERS OF D. H. LAWRENCE (C2).

The introductions to the various collections of DHL's correspondence invariably comment on his qualities as a letter
writer, while primarily discussing the biographical, literary,
and historical backgrounds to his letters. See THE COLLECTED
LETTERS (C2), LETTERS TO BERTRAND RUSSELL (see C2), "Letters
to Dorothy Brett" (C4), "Letters to Catherine Carswell" (C5),
THE LETTERS (C11), Boulton (F18), Levin and Levin (F92),
Zytaruk (F165), Huxley (H191), and Trilling (H383).

For additional commentary and information on the letters, see
Allott and Allott (F4), Delavenay (F46), D. H. LAWRENCE REVIEW
(F48), Mason (F103), Pollak (F133), Worthen (F164), Galinsky
(G41), Gregory (G47), Michaels-Tonks (G74), Weidner (G122),
Troy (H387), Cushman (Z103), Rossi (Z111), Guéhenno (AA159),
and Nishimura (AA236).

Z89   Arnold, Armin. "The German Letters of D. H. Lawrence."
      CLS, 3 (1966), 285-98.
            DHL's German letters were censored by Frieda
            when translated. Expanded version of appen-
            dix in Arnold's study of D. H. LAWRENCE AND
            GERMAN LITERATURE (see Z1). Also see AA108.

Z90   Boulton, James T. "The Cambridge University Press
      Edition of Lawrence's Letters, Part 4." In D. H. LAW-
      RENCE: THE MAN WHO LIVED. Ed. Robert B. Partlow and
      Harry T. Moore. Pp. 223-28. See G92.
            Statement of editorial principles for
            presenting the texts of DHL's letters in
            the Cambridge edition (see C11). For a
            fuller, though less available statement of
            principles, see Boulton's PROSPECTUS AND
            NOTES FOR VOLUME EDITORS: THE LETTERS
            OF D. H. LAWRENCE (Cambridge: Cambridge
            Univ. Press, 1973). (Pamphlet--18 pp.)

Z91   Cazamian, Louis. "D. H. Lawrence and Katherine Mansfield
      as Letter-Writers." UTQ, 3 (1934), 286-307.
            DHL more earnest and profound, but less
            coherent and appealing than Mansfield,
            as artist as well as correspondent.

Z92   Donoghue, Denis. "'Till the Fight Is Finished': D. H.
      Lawrence in His Letters." In D. H. LAWRENCE. Ed.
      Stephen Spender. Pp. 197-209. See G113.
            DHL's letters "among the most achieved . . .
            in English literature," though too many are
            regrettable "essays in self pity."

Z93   Farmer, David. "The Cambridge University Press Edition
      of THE LETTERS OF D. H. LAWRENCE: Sources for the Edi-
      tion." In D. H. LAWRENCE: THE MAN WHO LIVED. Ed.
      Robert B. Partlow and Harry T. Moore. Pp. 239-41. See
      G92.
            Backgrounds on the editors' procedures for
            locating and cataloging DHL's vast correspon-
            dence, in preparation for the edition (see C11).

Z94   Gillet, Louis. "D. H. Lawrence d'après sa correspon-
      dance." REVUE DES DEUX MONDES, 8th Series, 12 (1932),
      685-98.
            Surveys DHL's quest for "purification
            et . . . rédemption," as seen in his early

life and in his letters (the finest cor-
respondence in English literature since
Byron and Shelley). Reviews C10 and F85.
[In French.]

Z95 Gomes, Eugênio. "D. H. Lawrence--(A Correspondência de)."
In D. H. LAWRENCE E OUTROS. Pôrto Alegre, Brazil:
Livraria do Globo, 1937. Pp. 59-77.
Review of Huxley's edition of DHL's correspondence (C10), finding in the letters a
number of DHL's central statements of his
beliefs and particularly valuable information on DHL's conception of and intention
for his works ("gênese e . . . intenção de
suas obras"). [In Portugese.]

Z96 Lacy, Gerald M. "The Case for an Edition of the Letters
of D. H. Lawrence." In D. H. LAWRENCE: THE MAN WHO
LIVED. Ed. Robert B. Partlow and Harry T. Moore.
Pp. 229-33. See G92.
Chief among the several justifiable reasons
for a new edition of DHL's letters is the
fact that approximately 2,000 known letters
have never been published (see C11).

Z97 Leavis, F. R. "'Lawrence Scholarship' and Lawrence."
SR, 71 (1963), 25-35.
Splenetic attack on Harry T. Moore's
"qualifications as a critic" or an
editor of DHL (reviews Moore's edition
of the letters; see C2), and general
assault on American literary scholarship. Reprinted in Leavis's *ANNA
KARENINA* AND OTHER ESSAYS (London:
Chatto and Windus, 1967). Moore's
rejoinder (SR, 71 [1963], 347-48)
reprinted in H257.

Z98 McDowall, Arthur S. "Letters of D. H. Lawrence." 1933.
In A DETACHED OBSERVER: ESSAYS AND SKETCHES. Ed. Mary
McDowall. London: Oxford Univ. Press, 1934. Pp. 115-27.
Equivocal review of DHL's ideas, but un-
equivocal praise for the vitality and
intensity of his letters. Reviews Huxley's
edition of the letters (see C10).

Z99   Panichas, George A. "D. H. Lawrence's War Letters."
        TSLL, 5 (1963), 398-409.
                DHL's inability to maintain an affirmative
                attitude in the midst of international
                cataclysm seen in his contemporary cor-
                respondence.

Z100   Zytaruk, George J. "Editing Lawrence's Letters: The
        Strategy of Volume Division." In D. H. LAWRENCE: THE
        MAN WHO LIVED. Ed. Robert B. Partlow and Harry T. Moore.
        Pp. 234-48. See G92.
                The seven volumes of the Cambridge edition
                to be divided so as to remain roughly
                equal in size, retain the chronology of the
                letters, and break, as nearly as possible,
                according to the major phases of DHL's life.
                (Volume eight will contain appendixes and
                indexes; see C11).

Z, iv. Critical Articles or Chapters on MOVEMENTS IN EUROPEAN
        HISTORY (1921)

At present, there are no plans to republish DHL's history in
THE CAMBRIDGE EDITION (B1).

For bibliographical information on the history, see Roberts
(E39) and Sagar (E40), and, for biographical backgrounds to
the work, see Moore (F112) and Nehls (F123).

For additional commentary and information on MOVEMENTS IN
EUROPEAN HISTORY, see Clark (G17), Cowan (G22), Moore (G80),
Sagar (G104), Goonetilleke (H147), Scott (V27), Gordon (Z3),
and Terada (AA276).

Z101   Boulton, James T. "Introduction to the New Edition."
        In Lawrence's MOVEMENTS IN EUROPEAN HISTORY. London:
        Oxford Univ. Press, 1971. Pp. vii-xxiv.
                While not a satisfactory history, DHL's
                text a significant part of his canon.

Z102   Crumpton, Philip. "D. H. Lawrence's 'mauled history':
        The Irish Edition of MOVEMENTS IN EUROPEAN HISTORY."
        DHLR, 13 (1980), 105-18.
                Describes the Irish publication (1926), with
                DHL's consent, of a heavily censored version
                of his European history, and accounts for its
                modest sales.

Z103 Cushman, Keith. "D. H. Lawrence and Nancy Henry: Two
Unpublished Letters and a Lost Relationship." DHLR, 6
(1963), 21-32.
Describes DHL's correspondence with Henry
(eight letters, 1918-19, two newly published here), a typist and editor with
whom he worked on his MOVEMENTS IN
EUROPEAN HISTORY.

Z104 Hinz, Evelyn J. "History as Education and Art: D. H.
Lawrence's MOVEMENTS IN EUROPEAN HISTORY." MODERN
BRITISH LITERATURE, 2 (1977), 139-52.
Parallels between DHL's approach to history
and his fictional perspectives and techniques.

Z, v. Critical Articles or Chapters on the Translations

At present, there are no plans to republish DHL's several
translations in THE CAMBRIDGE EDITION (B1).

For bibliographical information on the translations, see
Roberts (E39) and Sagar (E40), and, for biographical back-
grounds to the works, see THE QUEST FOR RANANIM (C13),
Moore (F112), Nehls (F123), and Zytaruk (F165).

Hyde's D. H. LAWRENCE AND THE ART OF TRANSLATION is an important, full critical study of the translations (Z5 above).
For additional critical commentary and information on the
translations, see the following books, in section G above:
Corsani (G21), Hobsbaum (G51), Jarrett-Kerr (G62),
Meyers (G73), Michaels-Tonks (G74), Sagar (G104), Zytaruk
(G131); and the following studies, located in other sections
of this bibliography: Mayer (F104), Rossi (V65), Chomel (Z16),
and Wilkin (AA289).

Z105 Arnold, Armin. "D. H. Lawrence, the Russians, and
Giovanni Verga." CLS, 2 (1965), 249-57.
DHL's disaffection from the Russians and
sustained interest in translating Verga.

Z106 -----. "Genius with a Dictionary: Reevaluating D. H.
Lawrence's Translations." CLS, 5 (1968), 389-401.
DHL's translations of Verga still the best
available.

Z107   Cecchetti, Giovanni. "Verga and D. H. Lawrence's
       Translations." CL, 9 (1957), 333-44.
       Recent translator of Verga attacks DHL's
       versions.

Z108   Corsani, Mary. "D. H. Lawrence traduttore dall'
       italiano." EM, 17 (1966), 249-78.
       Extends her analysis of DHL's translations
       of Verga and Grazzini (see her D. H.
       LAWRENCE E L'ITALIA [G21]), to examine
       DHL's assimilation of their Italianate world
       view. [In Italian.]

Z109   Hyde, G. M. "D. H. Lawrence as Translator." DELOS,
       No. 4 (1970), pp. 146-74.
       DHL's absorption and translation of
       "kindred spirits" in Russian and Italian
       literature (especially Shestov and Verga).
       Assimilated into Z5.

Z110   McWilliam, G. H. "Verga and 'Verismo.'" HERMATHENA,
       95 (1961), 3-20.
       Praises DHL's translations of Verga.

Z111   Rossi, Patrizio. "Verga e l'Italia nella corrispondenza
       di D. H. Lawrence" ["Verga and Italy in the Correspon-
       dence of D. H. Lawrence"]. ANNALI ISTITUTO ORIENTALE
       NAPOLI, SEZIONE ROMANZA, 15 (1973), 25-43.
       Backgrounds to DHL's interest in and
       translation of Verga.

Z, vi.   Critical Articles or Chapters on the Travel Writings

Textual editions of DHL's four travel books and several
related essays will be published, in four volumes, in THE
CAMBRIDGE EDITION (B1), as follows (editor of edition-in-
progress identified in parentheses):   *TWILIGHT IN ITALY*
AND OTHER ESSAYS, *SEA AND SARDINIA*, *MORNINGS IN MEXICO* AND
OTHER ESSAYS, and *ETRUSCAN PLACES* AND OTHER ESSAYS (ed.
Simonetta DeFilippis).

For bibliographical information on the travel writings, see
Roberts (E39) and Sagar (E40), and, for biographical back-
grounds to the works, see Delany (F41), James (F78),
Moore (F112), Murry (F121), Nehls (F123), and Palmer (F128).

Janik's THE CURVE OF RETURN is an important, full critical
study of the travel works (Z6 above). For additional critical
commentary and information on the travel writings, see the
following books, in section G above: Cavitch (G16), Clark
(G17), Corsani (G21), Draper (G33), Galinsky (G41), Hobsbaum
(G51), Kermode (G65), Meyers (G73), Michaels-Tonks (G74),
Moore (G80), Negriolli (G87), Nin (G88), Pinion (G95),
Pritchard (G101), Reul (G103), Sagar (G104); the following
critical articles, in section H above: Bedient (H33),
Bloom (H46), Ghiselin (H132), Gunn (H159), Lewis (H223),
Schorer (H329), Woodcock (H421); and the following studies,
entered in other sections of this bibliography: Walker (T27),
Farmer (W1), Gilbert (Y1), Hassall (Y27), Gutierrez (Z4),
Cavallone (AA119), Kobayashi (AA188), and Linati (AA203).

Z112   Aiken, Conrad. "D. H. Lawrence." 1924, 1927. In A
       REVIEWER'S ABC. New York: Meridian, 1958. Pp. 261-63;
       263-66.
            On STUDIES IN CLASSIC AMERICAN LITERATURE
            (A65) and MORNINGS IN MEXICO (A89). For
            annotation see Z8.

Z113   Bonadeo, Barbara Bates. "D. H. Lawrence's View of the
       Italians." EM, 24 (1973-74), 271-97.
            DHL's view of Italians as arrested in the
            pre-Renaissance condition of the medieval
            man (in the three Italian travel books).

Z114   Burgess, Anthony. "Introduction." In D. H. LAWRENCE
       AND ITALY: *TWILIGHT IN ITALY, SEA AND SARDINIA,
       ETRUSCAN PLACES*. New York: Viking, 1972. Pp. vii-xiii.
            DHL's "highly idiosyncratic" response to
            place makes his travel works "an indispensable
            guide to the sensibility of one of the most
            astonishing writers of our century." Intro-
            duces collected reprinting of three of the
            travel books.

Z115   Ellis, David. "Reading Lawrence: The Case of SEA AND
       SARDINIA." DHLR, 10 (1977), 52-63.
            Analysis of DHL's artful creation of an
            apparently "casual" narrative.

Z116   Fahey, William A. "Lawrence's San Gaudenzio Revisited."
       DHLR, 1 (1968), 51-59.
            Backgrounds to the San Gaudenzio chapters
            in TWILIGHT IN ITALY (A87).

Z117   Fussell, Paul. "The Places of D. H. Lawrence." In
        ABROAD: BRITISH LITERARY TRAVELING BETWEEN THE WARS.
        New York: Oxford Univ. Press, 1980. Pp. 141-64.
                DHL's travels in the twenties, the response
                to place in his fiction, and, chiefly, the
                art of his travel books.

Z118   Gersh, Gabriel. "In Search of D. H. Lawrence's SEA AND
        SARDINIA." QQ, 80 (1973), 581-88.
                The vividness and fascination of DHL's
                travel book, a "remarkable" work, though
                hastily written.

Z119   Gutierrez, Donald. "The Ideas of Place: D. H. Law-
        rence's Travel Books." UNIVERSITY OF DAYTON REVIEW,
        15, No. 1 (1981), 143-52.
                Discusses the three most distinctive
                qualities of DHL's travel books: their
                concept of the spirit of place ("the
                totality of interaction of man and his
                natural and social environment"), their
                concept of "hylozoism" (the pre-Socratic
                doctrine that "all matter[is] alive or
                animate"), and their ideal of organic
                community. See H160.

Z120   Hackett, Francis. "A Week in D. H. Lawrence." NEW
        REPUBLIC, 29 (1922), 184-85.
                Review of DHL's beautiful, yet "inept
                and silly" SEA AND SARDINIA (A88). The
                volume's strengths and weaknesses alike
                attributed to DHL's preoccupation with
                his own feelings. Reprinted in G34.

Z121   Leavis, F. R. "The Necessary Opposite, Lawrence:
        Illustration--The Opposed Critics on HAMLET."
        In ENGLISH LITERATURE IN OUR TIME AND THE UNIVERSITY.
        London: Chatto and Windus, 1969. Pp. 135-57.
                Compares T. S. Eliot's and DHL's views of
                HAMLET (viz. "The Theatre" in TWILIGHT IN
                ITALY). Extract reprinted in G20.

Z122   Mayne, Richard. "SEA AND SARDINIA Revisited." NEW
        STATESMAN AND NATION, 59 (1960), 899-900.
                DHL's fascination with the "shock of
                really meeting the past" and the "gulf"
                between modern and primitive man, in
                his journal of his tour of Sardinia (A88).

Z123   Mitchell, Peter Todd. "Lawrence's SEA AND SARDINIA
       Revisited." TQ, 8, No. 1 (1965), 67-80.
              Record of Todd's retracing "every step" of
              DHL in Sardinia (A88). Includes eleven of
              Mitchell's paintings of Sardinian subjects.

Z124   Morris, Tom. "On ETRUSCAN PLACES." PAUNCH, Nos. 40-41
       (1975), pp. 8-39.
              DHL's praise for the Etruscan life-
              affirming attitudes toward personal and
              social life make ETRUSCAN PLACES his strongest
              statement against contemporary Fascism.

Z125   Nehls, Edward. "D. H. Lawrence: The Spirit of Place."
       In THE ACHIEVEMENT OF D. H. LAWRENCE. Ed. Frederick J.
       Hoffman and Harry T. Moore. Pp. 268-90. See G53.
              Still the best introduction to the travel
              writings.

Z126   Nichols, Ann Eljenholm. "Syntax and Style: Ambiguities
       in Lawrence's TWILIGHT IN ITALY." CCC, 16 (1965), 261-66.
              "Epic" syntax of TWILIGHT IN ITALY appropriate
              for its "heroic" subject.

Z127   Swan, Michael. "D. H. Lawrence: Italy and Mexico."
       In A SMALL PART OF TIME. London: Cape, 1957. Pp. 279-87.
              In his travel works DHL misses more than
              he sees, for he prefers to make his "vision
              of the world about [him] consonant with"
              his theories and preconceptions.

Z128   Tenebaum, Louis. "Two Views of the Modern Italian:
       D. H. Lawrence and Sean O'Faolain." ITALICA, 37 (1960),
       118-25.
              DHL's views of the Italians "challenged"
              by O'Faolain's A SUMMER IN ITALY (1949) and
              AN AUTUMN IN ITALY (1953).

Z129   Tracy, Billy T. "D. H. Lawrence and the Travel Book
       Tradition." DHLR, 11 (1978), 272-93.
              DHL's travel books written firmly within
              a "well-established" late Victorian and
              Edwardian "tradition of travel literature."

Z130   -----. "'Reading up the Ancient Etruscans': Lawrence's
       Debt to George Dennis." TCL, 23 (1977), 437-50.
              Dennis's THE CITIES AND CEMETERIES OF
              ETRURIA (1848) enjoyed by DHL and used
              in ETRUSCAN PLACES (A90).

Z131   -----. "The Failure of the Flight: D. H. Lawrence's
       Travels." DENVER QUARTERLY, 12, No. 1 (1977), 205-17.
           DHL's frustrated search for "sanctuary in
           the real world, among peasant . . . peoples"
           ends in his "imaginary" asylum with the
           ancient Etruscans, in ETRUSCAN PLACES (A90).

Z132   Wagner, Jeanie. "D. H. Lawrence's Neglected 'Italian
       Studies.'" DHLR, 13 (1980), 260-74.
           DHL's revisions of earlier versions of
           several essays in TWILIGHT IN ITALY (A87)
           show an important change in his "attitude
           towards the world," from 1913 to 1916.

Z133   Weiner, S. Ronald. "The Rhetoric of Travel: The
       Example of SEA AND SARDINIA." DHLR, 2 (1969), 230-44.
           DHL's idiosyncratic development of the
           travel book as a work of rhetorical art.

Z134   Whitaker, Thomas R. "Lawrence's Western Path: MORNINGS
       IN MEXICO." CRITICISM, 3 (1961), 219-36.
           DHL's travel work organized literarily
           (the thematic significance of the stages
           of the journey), rather than chronologically.

Appendixes

APPENDIX A: FOREIGN-LANGUAGE STUDIES OF LAWRENCE

The following appendix is subdivided into three parts:
i. Book-Length Critical Studies and Essay Collections concerning DHL; ii. Chapters and Essays on DHL, in Books and
Essay Collections not exclusively concerned with DHL; and
iii. Periodical Articles concerning DHL, published in
languages other than English. Cross-reference numbers have
been provided, in lieu of annotations, for the numerous
foreign-language titles which are entered elsewhere in this
guide and annotated, from original publication or from
subsequent publication in English translation. Several
other entries have been briefly annotated to indicate the
subject or coverage of the study, if not evident from the
title, when this information has been available. Translations of titles have been provided for works appearing in
less familiar languages and for those French, German, and
Italian titles which might present some translation difficulties. In rare cases the language of the publication
is identified at the conclusion of the entry, if it is not
evident from either the title or the place of publication.
For additional studies see Mauriac (H239) and Mesnil (H248),
for whom original foreign-language publication data (if
any) have not been located, and Beutmann (AC1), Kéry (AC2),
and Vallese (AC8), whose publications have not been located.

AA, i. Book-Length Critical Studies and Essay Collections

AA1 Allendorf, Otmar. DIE BEDEUTUNG THOMAS HARDYS FÜR DAS
     FRÜWERK VON D. H. LAWRENCE [THE INFLUENCE OF THOMAS
     HARDY ON THE EARLY WORK OF D. H. LAWRENCE]. Marburg:
     Lahn, 1969.
          See G4.

AA2 Arnold, Armin. D. H. LAWRENCE. Berlin: Colloquium,
     1972.
          See G6.

AA2a Beck, Rudolf. D. H. LAWRENCE. Heidelberg: Winter, 1978.

AA3   Bredsdorff, Elias. D. H. LAWRENCE: ET FORSØG PAA
       EN POLITISK ANALYSE [D. H. LAWRENCE: AN ATTEMPT AT
       A POLITICAL ANALYSIS]. Copenhagen: Levin and
       Munksgaard, 1937.
       See G13.

AA4   Colin, Saul. NATURALISME ET MYSTICISME CHEZ D. H.
       LAWRENCE. Paris: Librairie Lipschutz, 1932.
       See G19.

AA5   Corsani, Mary. D. H. LAWRENCE E L'ITALIA. Milan:
       Mursia, 1965.
       See G21.

AA6   Couaillac, Maurice. D. H. LAWRENCE: ESSAI SUR LA
       FORMATION ET LE DÉVELOPPEMENT DE SA PENSÉE D'APRÈS
       SON OEUVRE EN PROSE. Toulouse: Imprimerie du
       Commerce, 1937.

AA7   Delavenay, Émile. D. H. LAWRENCE: L'HOMME ET LA GENÈSE
       DE SON OEUVRE. LES ANNÉES DE FORMATION, 1885-1919.
       2 vols. Paris: Éditions Klinckseick, 1969.
       See F43.

AA8   Donnerstag, Jürgen. DIE STILENTWICKLUNG IM WERK VON
       D. H. LAWRENCE [STYLISTIC DEVELOPMENT IN THE WORK OF
       D. H. LAWRENCE]. Cologne: Univ. of Cologne, 1969.
       See G30.

AA9   Fabre-Luce, Alfred. LA VIE DE D. H. LAWRENCE. Paris:
       Bernard Grasset, 1935.
       See F52.

AA10   Fraisse, Anne-Marie, ed. RÉFLEXIONS ET DIRECTIVES POUR
       L'ÉTUDE DE D. H. LAWRENCE: *WOMEN IN LOVE*. Paris:
       Lettres Modernes, 1970.
       See N2.

AA11   Galinsky, Hans. DEUTSCHLAND IN DER SICHT VON D. H.
       LAWRENCE UND T. S. ELIOT: EINE STUDIE ZUM ANGLO-
       AMERIKANISCHEN DEUTSCHLANDBILD DES 20. JAHRHUNDERTS
       [GERMANY AS SEEN BY D. H. LAWRENCE AND T. S. ELIOT:
       A STUDY OF THE ANGLO-AMERICAN PICTURE OF GERMANY IN
       THE TWENTIETH CENTURY]. Mainz: Verlag der Akademie
       der Wissenschaften und der Literatur, 1956.
       See G41.

AA12   Gillès, Daniel. D. H. LAWRENCE, OU, LE PURITAIN
       SCANDALEUX. Paris: René Julliard, 1964.
       See F65.

AA13   Gottwald, Johannes. DIE ERZÄHLFORMEN DER ROMANE VON
       ALDOUS HUXLEY UND DAVID HERBERT LAWRENCE [NARRATIVE
       TECHNIQUES IN THE NOVELS OF ALDOUS HUXLEY AND DAVID
       HERBERT LAWRENCE]. Munich: Univ. of Munich, 1964.
       See G46.

AA14   Haya, Kenichi. D. H. ROSENSU NO SEKAI [THE WORLD OF
       D. H. LAWRENCE]. Tokyo: Hyoronsha, 1978.

AA15   Hess, Elisabeth. DIE NATURBETRACHTUNG IM PROSAWERK
       VON D. H. LAWRENCE [THE VISION OF NATURE IN THE FICTION
       OF D. H. LAWRENCE]. Bern: Francke, 1957.
       See G50.

AA16   Hsia, Adrian Rue Chun. D. H. LAWRENCE: DIE CHARAKTERE
       IN DER HANDLUNG UND SPANNUNG SEINER KURZGESCHICHTEN.
       Bonn: Bouvier, 1968.
       See V2.

AA17   Irie, Takanori. KENJA RORENSU [LAWRENCE THE SEER].
       Tokyo: Kodansha, 1974.
       A biography. Not seen.

AA18   Itô, R., ed. RORENSU. Tokyo: Orion Press, 1978.
       Anthology of three DHL works in translation
       (LCL, "The Man Who Died," and "The Woman Who
       Rode Away"), with biographical backgrounds and
       critical comment. Not seen.

AA19   Jaensson, Knut B. D. H. LAWRENCE. Stockholm:
       Tidens Förlag, 1934.
       See G61.

AA20   Johnsson, Melker. D. H. LAWRENCE: ETT MODERNT
       TANKEÄVENTYR [D. H. LAWRENCE: A MODERN ADVENTURE IN
       THOUGHT]. Stockholm: Albert Bonniers, 1939.
       See G63.

AA21   Kai, Sadanobu, et al. RORENSU KENKYU: WOMEN IN LOVE
       Tokyo: Asahi Shuppansha, 1979.

AA22   Kitazawa, Shigehisa. D. H. RORENSU: SONO BUNAKU TO
       JINSEI [D. H. LAWRENCE: LIFE AND WORKS]. Tokyo:
       Bokusui Shobo, 1973.

AA23   Konishi, Nagatomo. D. H. RORENSU: SHIJIN TO "CHAT-
       TERLEY" SAIBAN [D. H. LAWRENCE: THE POET AND THE
       "CHATTERLEY" TRIAL]. Tokyo: Ubunshoin, 1975.

AA24   Kuramochi, Saburô. D. H. RORENSU: SHOSETSU NO KENKYU
       [D. H. LAWRENCE: A STUDY OF THE NOVELS]. Tokyo:
       Aratake Shuppan, 1976.
       Presumably assimilates several previously
       published articles (see AA194-AA196). Not seen.

AA25   -----. RORENSU: AI NO YOGENSHA [LAWRENCE: THE
       PROPHET OF LOVE]. Tokyo: Tojusha, 1978.

AA26   LES LANGUES MODERNES. 62 (1968), 186-205. "Dossier
       D. H. Lawrence."
       Contains three articles and two short notes on
       DHL. Includes AA117, AA135, and AA204.

AA27   Lucia, Dino. "A PROPOSITIO DI L'AMANTI DI LADY
       CHATTERLEY" DI D. H. LAWRENCE. Matera, Italy:
       Motemurro, 1951.
       Pamphlet (20 pp.) on DHL's essay. Not seen.

AA28   Marnat, Marcel. DAVID-HERBERT LAWRENCE. Paris:
       Éditions Universitaires, 1966.
       See G72.

AA29   Mori, Haruhide. RORENSU NO BUTAI: CHOHEN SHOSETSU
       NO BUNTAI TO KOZO [THE WORLD OF LAWRENCE: THE STYLE
       AND STRUCTURE OF HIS NOVELS]. Kyôto: Yamaguchi, 1978.
       Presumably assimilates several previously
       published articles (see AA219-AA224). Not seen.

AA30   Napolitano, Giovanni. L'AMANTI DI LADY CHATTERLEY
       O DEL PUDORE. Naples: Miccoli, 1948.
       Monograph (91 pp.). Not seen.

AA31   Nardi, Piero. LA VITA DI D. H. LAWRENCE. Milan:
       Mondadori, 1947.
       See F122.

AA32   Negriolli, Claude. LA SYMBOLIQUE DE D. H. LAWRENCE.
       Paris: Presses Universitaires de France, 1970.
       See G87.

AA33   Nishimura, Kôji. RORENSU [LAWRENCE]. Tokyo:
       Kenkyusha, 1972.

AA34 -----. RORENSU NO SEKAI: GENDAI NO SHONIN TO SHITE [THE WORLD OF LAWRENCE: WITNESS TO THE MODERN WORLD]. Tokyo: Chuoshinsho, 1970.

AA35 Orliac, Jehanne d'. LE DEUXIÈME MARI DE LADY CHATTER-LEY. Paris: Albin Michel, 1934.
See U2.

AA36 Reul, Paul de. L'OEUVRE DE D. H. LAWRENCE. Paris: Vrin, 1937.
See G103.

AA37 Reuter, Irmgard. STUDIEN ÜBER DIE PERSÖNLICHKEIT UND DIE KUNSTFORM VON D. H. LAWRENCE [STUDIES OF D. H. LAWRENCE'S PERSONALITY AND ART]. Marburg: H. Pöppinghaus, 1934.
See V4.

AA38 Sasaki, Manabu. D. H. RORENSU NO BUNGAKU TO SHISO [D. H. LAWRENCE'S WRITINGS AND THOUGHT]. Tokyo: Shohakusha, 1976.

AA39 Schickele, René. LIEBE UND ÄRGERNIS DES D. H. LAW-RENCE [THE LOVE AND SORROW OF D. H. LAWRENCE]. Amsterdam: Allert de Lange, n.d. [1934].
See R2.

AA40 Seillière, Ernest. DAVID-HERBERT LAWRENCE ET LES RÉCENTES IDÉOLOGIES ALLEMANDES. Paris: Boivin, 1936.
See G107.

AA41 Shibata, Takaji. RORENSU BUNGAKU NO SEKAI [THE WORLD OF LAWRENCE'S WRITINGS]. Tokyo: Yashio Shuppansha, 1975.

AA42 Talon, Henri A. D. H. LAWRENCE: *SONS AND LOVERS*: LES ASPECTS SOCIAUX ET ECONOMIQUES, LA VISION DE L'ARTISTE. Paris: Archives des Lettres Modernes, 1965.
See L6.

AA43 Temple, Frédéric J. DAVID HERBERT LAWRENCE: L'OEUVRE ET LA VIE. Paris: Seghers, 1960.
See G119.

AA44 IL VERRI: REVISTA DI LETTERATURA (Milan), 17 (1980), 37-152. "D. H. Lawrence."
Collects six essays on DHL's stories, psychology, idea of nature, and relation to modernist movements (futurism and vor-ticism), and on SL. Not seen.

AA45   Wada, Shizuo. D. H. RORENSU BUNGAKU NO RONRI [THE
       LOGIC OF LAWRENCE'S WRITINGS]. Tokyo: Nanundo, 1972.

AA46   Weidner, Ingeborg. BOTSCHAFTSVERKÜNDIGUNG UND
       SELBSTAUSDRUCK IM PROSAWERK VON D. H. LAWRENCE
       [MESSAGE AND SELF-EXPRESSION IN THE FICTION OF
       D. H. LAWRENCE]. Braunschweig: Serger & Hempel,
       1938.
       See G122.

AA47   Wesslau, Werner. DER PESSIMISMUS BEI D. H. LAWRENCE.
       Greifswald: Hans Adler, 1931.
       See G124.

AA48   Wettern, Regina. D. H. LAWRENCE: ZUR FUNKTION UND
       FUNKTIONSWEISE VON LITERARISCHEM IRRATIONALISMUS
       [D. H. LAWRENCE: ON THE FUNCTION AND STRATEGY OF
       LITERARY IRRATIONALISM]. Heidelberg: C. Winter, 1979.
       See G126.

AA49   Wulfsberg, Fredrik. D. H. LAWRENCE FRA NOTTINGHAM-
       SHIRE: EN STUDIE I DIKTERENS OPRINNELSE [D. H.
       LAWRENCE FROM NOTTINGHAMSHIRE: A STUDY OF THE ORIGIN
       OF THE POET]. Oslo: Det Mallingske Bogtrykkeri, 1937.
       Biographical study. Not seen.

AA50   Yamakawa, Kozo. SHISO NO BOKEN: RORENSU NO SHOSETSU
       [ADVENTURES IN THOUGHT: LAWRENCE'S FICTION]. Tokyo:
       Kenkyusha, 1974.

AA, ii. Chapters and Essays on DHL, in Books and Essay
         Collections

AA51   Amado, Éliane Lévy-Valensi. "L'en-deçà, de la
       conaissance. Le péché et les voies du salut dans
       l'ontologie Lawrencienne" ["On this Side of Cons-
       ciousness. Sin and the Means of Salvation in the
       Lawrencean Ontology"]. In LES NIVEAUX DE L'ÊTRE,
       LA CONAISSANCE, ET LA MAL [LEVELS OF BEING, CONS-
       CIOUSNESS, AND EVIL]. Paris: Presses Universitaires
       de France, 1962. Pp. 280-333.
       See H14.

AA52   Amorós, Andrés. "Vitalismo Sexual." In INTRODUCCIÓN
       A LA NOVELA CONTEMPORÁNEA. 1966. 2nd ed. Salamanca,
       Spain: Ediciones Anaya, 1971. Pp. 201-06.
       See U5.

AA53 Astaldi, Maria Luisa. "Ancora intorno a Lawrence"["On Lawrence Again"]. In LETTURE INGLESI. Venice: Neri Pozza, 1953. Pp. 106-33.

AA54 Bareiss, Dieter. DIE VIERPERSONENKONSTELLATION IM ROMAN: STRUKTURUNTERSUCHUNGEN ZUR PERSONENFÜHRUNG, DARGESTELLET AN N. HAWTHORNES THE BLITHEDALE ROMANCE, G. ELIOTS DANIEL DERONDA, H. JAMES THE GOLDEN BOWL UND D. H. LAWRENCES WOMEN IN LOVE [THE NOVEL WITH FOUR PRINCIPAL CHARACTERS: STUDIES OF CHARACTER-GROUPING IN N. HAWTHORNE'S THE BLITHEDALE ROMANCE, G. ELIOT'S DANIEL DERONDA, H. JAMES'S THE GOLDEN BOWL AND D. H. LAWRENCE'S WOMEN IN LOVE]. Berlin: Lang, 1969.

AA55 Beauvoir, Simone de. "D. H. Lawrence ou l'orgeuil phallique." In LE DEUXIÈME SEXE. Vol. 1. LES FAITS ET LES MYTHES. Paris: Gallimard, 1949. Pp. 331-43. See H32.

AA56 Beker, Miroslav. "Lawrenceov obraćun sa svojim suvremenicima" ["Lawrence's Dispute with his Contem-poraries"]. In MODERNA KRITIKA U ENGLESKOJ I AMERICI. Zagreb: Liber Mladost, 1973. Pp 225-49.

AA57 Blöcker, Günter. "D. H. Lawrence." In DIE NEUEN WIRKLICHKEITEN: LINIEN UND PROFILE DER MODERNEN LITERATUR. Berlin: Argon, 1957. Pp. 187-97.

AA58 Bredsdorff, Elias. "D. H. Lawrence." In FREMMEDE DIGTERE I DET 20 ÅHRHUNDREDE. Ed. Sven M. Kristensen. Copenhagen: G.E.C. Gads, 1968. II, 19-41. See H52.

AA59 Cecchi, Emilio. SCRITTORI INGLESI E AMERICANI. Milano: Il Saggiatore, 1976. Pp. 70-84. Gathers four previously published essays.

AA60 Chevalley, Abel. "D. H. Lawrence." In LE ROMAN ANGLAIS DE NOTRE TEMPS. London: H. Milford, 1921. Pp. 229-32. See H64.

AA61 Croce, Benedetto. "A Proposito del 'misticismo' del Lawrence" ["On Lawrence's 'Mysticism'"]. In PAGINE SPARSE. Vol. 3. POSTILLE: OSSERVAZIONI SU LIBRI NUOVI. Naples: R. Ricciardi, 1943. Pp. 9-11.

AA62   Delavenay, Émile. "D. H. Lawrence et Sacher-Masoch:
        Contribution à l'étude d'une sensibilité moderne."
        In LE ROMANTISME ANGLO-AMÉRICAIN: MÉLANGES OFFERTS
        À LOUIS BONNEROT. Ed. Roger Asselineau, et al.
        Paris: Didier, 1971. Pp. 345-70.
        See H86.

AA63   Ehrenzweig, Robert [Robert Lucas]. FRIEDA VON
        RICHTHOFEN: IHR LEBEN MIT D. H. LAWRENCE. Munich:
        Kindler, 1972.
        See F51.

AA64   Fricker, Robert. "David Herbert Lawrence." In DER
        MODERNE ENGLISCHE ROMAN. 1958. 2nd ed. Göttingen:
        Vandenhoeck and Ruprecht, 1966. Pp. 123-38.
        See H122.

AA65   -----. "David Herbert Lawrence (1885-1930)."
        In ENGLISCHE DICHTER DER MODERNE: IHR LEBEN UND
        WERK. Ed. Rudolf Sühnel and Dieter Riesner.
        Berlin: Schmidt, 1971. Pp. 338-50.
        See H123.

AA66   Gandon, Yves. "L'Illumination de D. H. Lawrence,
        ou la genèse de Lady Chatterley." In IMAGERIES
        CRITIQUES. Paris: Société Française d'éditions
        littéraires et techniques, 1933. Pp. 171-80.

AA67   Gomes, Eugênio. D. H. LAWRENCE E OUTROS. Pôrto
        Alegre, Brazil: Livraria do Globo, 1937.
            Contains three essays on DHL, among other
            writers. See U22, Y91, and Z95.

AA68   Gorlier, Claudio. "Introduzione." In Lawrence's
        FIGLI E AMANTI [SONS AND LOVERS]. Milan: Mondadori,
        1976. Pp. vii-xxxii.

AA69   Gouirand, Jacqueline. "Tradition et innovation: D. H.
        Lawrence, romancier de l'inexprimé." In ACTES DU
        CONGRÈS DE NANCY DE LA S.A.E.S. Paris: Didier, 1972.
        Pp. 219-41.

AA70   Gozzi, Francesco. "La forma organica di SONS AND
        LOVERS." In CRITICAL DIMENSIONS: ENGLISH, GERMAN
        AND COMPARATIVE LITERATURE ESSAYS IN HONOUR OF
        AURELIO ZANCO. Ed. Mario Curreli and Alberto Martino.
        Cuneo, Italy: SASTE, 1978. Pp. 493-511.

AA71   Guyard, Marius F. LA GRANDE BRETAGNE DANS LE ROMAN
        FRANÇAIS: 1914-1940. Paris: Didier, 1954. Pp. 86-
        101 and passim.
            See H161.

AA72   Hoops, Reinald. "D. H. Lawrence." In DER EINFLUSS
        DER PSYCHOANALYSE AUF DIE ENGLISCHE LITERATUR.
        Heidelberg: C. Winter, 1934. Pp. 59-93.

AA73   Hortmann, Wilhelm. "D. H. Lawrence." In ENGLISCHE
        LITERATUR IM 20. JAHRHUNDERT. Bern: Francke, 1965.
        Pp. 52-57.

AA74   Iwasaki, Soji. "KINSHI-HEN To Dento no Kannen: Eliot
        to Frazer to Lawrence" ["THE GOLDEN BOUGH and the Sense
        of Tradition: Eliot and Frazer and Lawrence"]. In
        ELIOT TO DENTO [ELIOT AND TRADITION]. Ed. Shoichiro
        Yasuda. Tokyo: Kenkyusha, 1977. Pp. 25-47.

AA75   Iwata, Noboru. "Haha to Koibito: D. H. Lawrence no
        Joseitachi" ["Mothers and Lovers: Women in D. H. Law-
        rence"]. In EIBUNGAKU NO HEROINE-TACHI [HEROINES IN
        ENGLISH LITERATURE]. Ed. Yoshinobu Aoyama. Tokyo:
        Hyoronsha, 1977. Pp. 253-89.

AA76   Johnsson Melker. EN KLOSTERRESSA: FÄRDER OCH FRÅGOR
        [A CLOISTER-TOUR: JOURNEY AND INQUIRY]. Stockholm:
        Natur och Kultur, 1960. Pp. 83-115.
            See H198.

AA77   Kamihata, Yoshikazu. "MUSUKO TO KOIBITO to Sogo-
        Shutaisei" ["SONS AND LOVERS and Mutual Independence"].
        In GENGO TO BUNTAI: HIGASHIDA CHIAKI KYOJU KANREKI
        KINEN RONBUNSHU [LANGUAGE AND STYLE: COLLECTED ESSAYS
        COMMEMORATING THE 60TH BIRTHDAY OF PROF. CHIAKI
        HIGASHIDA]. Ed. Chiaki Higashida. Osaka: Osaka
        Kyoiku Tosho, 1975. Pp. 156-65.

AA78   Lacher, Walter. "David Herbert Lawrence." In L'AMOUR
        ET LE DIVIN. Geneva: Perret-Gentil, 1961. Pp. 63-
        102.
            See U40.

AA79   Lagercrantz, Olof. "D. H. Lawrences LADY CHATTERLEYS
        ÄLSKARE." In FÖRBJUDNA BÖCKER OCH NORDISK DEBATT OM
        TRYCKFRIHET OCH SEDLIGHET [FORBIDDEN BOOKS AND THE
        SCANDINAVIAN DEBATE ON CENSORSHIP AND MORALITY]. Ed.
        Karl-Erik Lundevall. Stockholm: Wahlström and Wid-
        strand, 1958. Pp. 113-25.

AA80   Liscano Velutini, Juan. "D. H. Lawrence, predicador
       apocalíptico." In ESPIRITUALIDAD Y LITERATURA: UNA
       RELACIÓN TORMENTOSA. Barcelona: Seix Barral, 1976.
       Pp. 137-62.
       See H225.

AA81   Marcuse, Ludwig. "London 1960: D. H. Lawrence oder
       purissimus penis (Kaiser Augustus über Horaz)"
       ["London 1960: D. H. Lawrence or *purissimus penis*
       (Caesar Augustus on Horace)"]. In OBSZÖN: GESCHICHTE
       EINER ENTRÜSTUNG. Munich: P. List, 1962. Pp. 265-311.
       See U49.

AA82   Marković, Vida E. "David Herbert Lorens." In ENGLESKI
       ROMAN XX VEKA. Vol. 1. Belgrade: Naučna, 1963.
       Pp. 78-99, 170-73.

AA83   Maurois, André. "D. H. Lawrence." In MAGICIENS ET
       LOGICIENS. Paris: Bernard Grasset, 1935. Pp. 279-317.
       See H240.

AA84   Meyer, Kurt Robert. "D. H. Lawrence (1885-1930)."
       In ZUR ERLEBTEN REDE IM ENGLISCHE ROMAN DES ZWANZIG-
       STEN JAHRHUNDERTS. Bern: Francke, 1957. Pp. 44-65.
       See L41.

AA85   Mirsky, Dmitri. INTELLIGENTSIA. Moscow: Sovetskaya
       Literatura, 1934.
       See H256.

AA86   Monteiro Grillo, Joaquim. TRADIÇÃO E CRISE NO ROMANCE
       INGLÊS CONTEMPORÂNEO [TRADITION AND CRISIS IN THE
       COMTEMPORARY ENGLISH NOVEL]. Lisbon: Edições
       Broteria, 1963. Passim.

AA87   Nardi, Piero. "Introduzione." In Lawrence's TUTTE LE
       POESIE [THE COMPLETE POEMS]. Milan: Mondadori,
       1959. Pp. xvii-xxxviii.
       See H273.

AA88   Nogueira, Albano. "Miniatura Inacabada De David-
       Herbert Lawrence" ["D. H. Lawrence's Unfinished Short
       Works"]. In IMAGENS EM ESPELHO CÔNCAVO [REFLECTIONS
       IN A CONCAVE MIRROR]. Coimbra, Port.: Editorial
       Livraria Gonçalves, 1940. Pp. 11-32.

AA89   Nojima, Hidekatsu. EGUZAILU NO BUNGAKU: JOISU,
       ERIOTTO, RORENZU NO BA'AI [THE LITERATURE OF EXILE:
       THE CASES OF JOYCE, ELIOT, LAWRENCE]. Tokyo: Nanundo,
       1963.

AA90 Okunishi, Akira. "Rorensu ni okeru Kyushinteki
      Shiko to sono Hyogen" ["Centripetal Thought and
      Expression in Lawrence"]. In GENGO TO BUNTAI:
      HIGASHIDA CHIAKI KYOJU KANREKI KINEN RONBUNSHU
      [LANGUAGE AND STYLE: COLLECTED ESSAYS COMMEMORATING
      THE 60TH BIRTHDAY OF PROF. CHIAKI HIGASHIDA]. Ed.
      Chiaki Higashida. Osaka: Osaka Kyoiku Tosho, 1975.
      Pp. 166-84.

AA91 Oppel, Horst. "D. H. Lawrence: 'St. Mawr.'" In
      DER MODERNE ENGLISCHE ROMAN: INTERPRETATIONEN. Ed.
      Oppel. Berlin: Schmidt, 1965. Pp. 115-34.
      See V156.

AA92 -----. "D. H. Lawrence: 'Snake.'" In DIE MODERNE
      ENGLISCHE LYRIK: INTERPRETATIONEN. Ed. Oppel. Berlin:
      Schmidt, 1967. Pp. 117-36.
      See Y116.

AA93 Peyre, Henri. "D. H. Lawrence, le message d'un
      prophète." In HOMMES ET OEUVRES DU XXe SIÈCLE. Paris:
      Éditions R. A. Corrêa, 1938. Pp. 275-98.
      See H288.

AA94 Praz, Mario. "Lorenzo in Taos." 1932. In STUDI E
      SVAGHI INGLESI. Florence: Sansoni, 1937. Pp. 149-56.

AA95 -----. "Poesie di D. H. Lawrence"; "Nota su D. H.
      Lawrence nel quadro del Romanticismo europeo" ["D. H.
      Lawrence's Poems"; "Note on D. H. Lawrence in the
      Context of European Romanticism"]. 1929, 1931. In
      CRONACHE LETTERARIE ANGLOSASSONI. Vol. 1. CRONACHE
      INGLESI. Rome: Edizioni di storia e letteratura,
      1950. Pp. 193-97; 198-202.
      See Y107 and H295.

AA96 Simões, João Gaspar. TENDÊNCIAS DO ROMANCE CONTEMPOR-
      ÂNEO. Coimbra, Port.: Edicões Presença, 1933. Passim.

AA97 Stanzel, Franz. "G. M. Hopkins, W. B. Yeats, D. H.
      Lawrence, und die Spontaneität der Dichtung." In
      ANGLISTISCHE STUDIEN: FESTSCHRIFT ZUM 70. GEBURTSTAG
      VON PROFESSOR FRIEDRICH WILD. Ed. Karl Brunner,
      Herbert Kozoil, and Siegfried Korninger. Vienna:
      Braumüller, 1958. Pp. 179-93.
      See Y60.

AA98   Tiedje, Egon. "D. H. Lawrence: 'Bavarian Gentians.'"
       In DIE ENGLISCHE LYRIK VON DER RENAISSANCE BIS ZUR
       GEGENWART. Ed. Karl Heinz Göller. Düsseldorf:
       Bagel, 1968. II, 321-35.

AA99   Undset, Sigrid. "D. H. Lawrence." In SELVPORTRETTER
       OG LANDSKAPSBILLEDER. Oslo: H. Aschehoug, 1938.
       See H390.

AA100 Villeneuve-Trans, Romée François, Compte de.
       CHRONIQUES ET ROMANS SOCIAUX. Avignon: Aubanel
       père, 1965. Pp. 243-63.

AA101 Wais, Kurt. "D. H. Lawrence, Valéry, Rilke in
       ihrer Auseinandersetzung mit den bildenden Künsten:
       Eine vergleichende Betrachtung" ["D. H. Lawrence,
       Valéry, and Rilke--Their Testament of the Pictorial
       Arts: A Comparative Study"]. 1951. In AN DEN
       GRENZEN DER NATIONALLITERATUREN: VERGLEICHENDE
       AUFSÄTZE. Berlin: Walter de Gruyter, 1958.
       Pp. 271-312.
       See H397.

AA102 Weineck, Kurt. "D. H. Lawrence." In DEUTSCHLAND
       UND DER DEUTSCHE IM SPIEGEL DER ENGLISCHEN ERZÄHLENDEN
       LITERATUR SEIT 1830. Halle: Akademischer Verlag,
       1938. Pp. 176-80.

AA103 Wild, Friedrich. DIE ENGLISCHE LITERATUR DER
       GEGENWART SEIT 1870. Vol. 2. VERSDICHTUNGEN.
       Leipzig: Im Dioskuren-verlag, 1931. Pp. 256-61.

AA104 Wolpers, Theodor. "Formen mythisierenden Erzählens
       in der modernen Prosa: Joseph Conrad im Vergleich
       mit Joyce, Lawrence, und Faulkner" ["Myth-Making
       in Modern Prose Narrative: Joseph Conrad Compared
       with Joyce, Lawrence, and Faulkner"]. In LEBENDE
       ANTIKE: SYMPOSION FÜR RUDOLF SÜHNEL. Ed. Horst
       Meller and Hans-Joachim Zimmermann. Berlin:
       Schmidt, 1967. Pp. 397-422.

AA105 Yagyu, Naoyuki. "D. H. Rorensu to Kirisutokyō"
       ["D. H. Lawrence and Christianity"]. In KIRISUTOKYŌ
       TO BUNGAKU (DAI 3 SHU) [CHRISTIANITY AND LITERATURE
       (No. 3)]. Ed. Tomoichi Sasbuchi. Tokyo: Kasama
       Shoin, 1975. Pp. 135-54.

AA106   Zeraffa, Michel. PERSONNE ET PERSONNAGE: LE ROMAN-
        ESQUE DES ANNÉES 1920 AUX ANNÉES 1950. Paris: Éditions
        Klincksieck, 1971. Pp. 227-34 and passim.
           See H424.

AA, iii.   Periodical Articles

AA107   Arellano Salgado, Olga. "El Sentido del amor en
        EL AMANTE DE LADY CHATTERLEY." NUEVA REVISTA DEL
        PACÍFICO, 9 (1978), 1-4.

AA108   Arnold, Armin. "Die deutschen Briefe von D. H.
        Lawrence." NEUE ZÜRCHER ZEITUNG, No. 3342
        (25 Aug. 1963), pp. 1-2.
           See Z1 and Z89.

AA109   -----. "D. H. Lawrence und Thomas Mann." NEUE
        ZÜRCHER ZEITUNG, No. 3696 (29 Nov. 1959), pp. 1-2.
           See Z1.

AA110   Barrière, Françoise. "WOMEN IN LOVE ou le roman de
        l'antagonisme." LES LANGUES MODERNES, 63 (1969),
        293-303.

AA111   Bechot, J. "Sur D. H. Lawrence: Psychologie de
        D. H. Lawrence." CAHIERS DU SUD, 26 (July 1939),
        588-94.

AA112   Beck, Rudolf. "Die drei Versionen von LADY CHATTER-
        LEY'S LOVER." ANGLIA, 96 (1978), 409-29.
           See U7.

AA113   Beker, Miroslav. "Estetika Bloomsbury grupe" ["The
        Aesthetics of the Bloomsbury Group"]. UMJETNÓST
        RIJEČI, No. 3 (1957), pp. 177-86.
           DHL and Bloomsbury.

AA114   Blanche, J. E. "D. H. Lawrence et Mabel Dodge."
        REVUE DE PARIS, 39 (1932), 325-41.

AA115   Blöcker, Günter. "D. H. Lawrence nach dreissig
        Jahren" ["D. H. Lawrence After Thirty Years"].
        MERKUR, 11 (1957), 480-86.

AA116   Breton, Georges Le. "D. H. Lawrence et l'architecture
        du roman." PREUVES, No. 189 (1966), pp. 70-73.

AA117   Brugière, Bernard. "Lecture critique d'un passage
        de WOMEN IN LOVE." LES LANGUES MODERNES, 62 (1968),
        197-203.
            On the "Moony" chapter. See AA26.

AA118   Cathelin, J. "La litterature d'un Lawrence."
        CORRESPONDANCES, 2 (1955), 257-61.

AA119   Cavallone, Anna Anzi. "Lawrence a Gargnano."
        STUDI INGLESI (Rome), 2 (1975), 401-23.
            On TWILIGHT IN ITALY.

AA120   Cecchi, Emilio. "La morte di Lawrence." L'ITALIA
        LETTERARIA, 9 Mar. 1930, p. 1.
            Obituary.

AA121   Comellini, Carla. "D. H. Lawrence e i classici
        americani: 'Un rinnegato fra i rinnegati'" ["D. H.
        Lawrence and the American Classics: 'A Renegade
        among the Renegades'"]. LETTORE DI PROVINCIA, 39
        (1979), 47-60.

AA122   Corsani, Mary. "D. H. Lawrence traduttore dall'
        italiano." EM, 17 (1966), 249-78.
            See Z108.

AA123   Crémieux, B. "David-Herbert Lawrence." LES ANNALES
        POLITIQUES ET LITTÉRAIRES, 98 (1932), 150.

AA124   Curčin, Ivo. "D. H. Lawrence i Dr. F. R. Leavis"
        ["D. H. Lawrence and Dr. F. R. Leavis"]. UMJETNOST
        RIJEČI, No. 3 (1957), pp. 187-206.

AA125   -----. "Meštrović i D. H. Lawrence" ["Meštrović and
        D. H. Lawrence"]. KNJIŽEVNA SMOTRA, No. 23 (1976),
        pp. 22-28.

AA126   Debu-Bridel, Jacques. "LA VERGE D'AARON, par D. H.
        Lawrence." NOUVELLE REVUE FRANÇAISE, 46 (1936),
        606-08.
            See Q5.

AA127   De Filippis, Simonetta. "La fiamma e il volto:
        studio filologico dell'ideologia del DAVID di D. H.
        Lawrence" ["The Flame and the Face: A Philological
        Study of the Ideology of D. H. Lawrence's DAVID"].
        ANNALI ISTITUTO ORIENTALE NAPOLI, SEZIONE GERMANICA-
        ANGLISTICA, 18 (1975), 7-84.
            See X14.

AA128 -----. "Minatori e anime superiori: conflitti famigliari e lotta delle classi nel teatro autobiografico di D. H. Lawrence" ["Miners and Superior Souls: Family Conflicts and Class Struggle in D. H. Lawrence's Autobiographical Drama"]. ANNALI ISTITUTO ORIENTALE NAPOLI, SEZIONE GERMANICA-ANGLISTICA, 17 (1974), 7-59.
See X3.

AA129 -----. "Sociologia e ideologia della classe operaia in TOUCH AND GO di D. H. Lawrence" ["Sociology and Ideology of the Working Class in Lawrence's TOUCH AND GO"]. ANNALI ISTITUTO ORIENTALE NAPOLI, SEZIONE GERMANICA, 15 (1972), 185-206.
See X17.

AA130 Delavenay, Émile. "D. H. Lawrence entre six femmes et entre deux cultures." EA, 22 (1969), 152-58.
See F46.

AA131 -----. "Le Phénix et ses cendres." EA, 21 (1968), 373-80.
See Z23.

AA132 -----. "Sur un exemplaire de Schopenhauer annoté par D. H. Lawrence." REVUE ANGLO-AMÉRICAINE, 13 (1935), 234-38.
See H87.

AA133 -----. "Les Trois Amants de Lady Chatterley." EA, 29 (1976), 46-63.
See U16.

AA134 Diaz de León, Martha. "El México visto por D. H. Lawrence." CUADERNOS AMERICANOS, 24, No. 2 (1965), 262-83.
See T9.

AA135 Edwards, John D. "Remarques sur la sensibilité Lawrencienne." LES LANGUES MODERNES, 62 (1968), 186-89.
See AA26.

AA136 Einseidel, W. von. "D. H. Lawrence." DIE TAT, 20 (1928), 354-59.

AA137 Elektorowicz, Leszek. "Naturalism poetycki D. H. Lawrence'a" ["The Nature Poetry of D. H. Lawrence"]. TWÓRCZOŚĆ, 31 No. 10 (1975), 72-78.

AA138   Eliot, T. S. "Le Roman anglais contemporain."
         NOUVELLE REVUE FRANÇAISE, 28 (1927), 669-75.
         See H106.

AA139   Engelborghs, Maurits. "De levende Lawrence."
         DIETSCHE WARANDE EN BELFORT, 125 (1980), 772-83.

AA140   -----. "De reputatie van D. H. Lawrence." DIETSCHE
         WARANDE EN BELFORT, 107 (1962), 726-36.

AA141   Férnandez, Diane. "D. H. Lawrence, la femme et la
         mort." LETTRES NOUVELLES (May-June 1968), pp. 150-56.
         On "The Horse Dealer's Daughter" and "The
         Princess."

AA142   Filippi, Živan. "D. H. Lawrence--Mit o ponovnom
         rodenju" ["D. H. Lawrence: The Myth of Rebirth"].
         KNJIŽEVNA SMOTRA, No. 16 (1973), pp. 41-60.
         On PS.

AA143   Fluchère, Henri. "D. H. Lawrence: Travaux d'approche."
         CAHIERS DU SUD, 18 (1931), 86-108.
         See H118.

AA144   -----. "A Propos de L'AMANT DE LADY CHATTERLEY."
         CAHIERS DU SUD, 19 (1932), 316-20.

AA145   Friedrich, Hans Eberhard. "David Herbert Lawrence."
         CHRISTICHE WELT, 47 (1933), 1083-85.

AA146   -----. "David Herbert Lawrence: Ein Dichter des
         'echten Lebens'" ["D. H. Lawrence: Poet of 'Real
         Life'"]. ECKART, 14 (1938), 384-95.

AA147   -----. "David Herbert Lawrence--Gottsucher und
         Mystizist" ["D. H. Lawrence--Seeker after God and
         Mystic"]. ZEITWENDE, 13 (1937), 678-87.

AA148   -----. "Der Dichter David Herbert Lawrence."
         DEUTSCHES ADELSBLATT, 55 (1938), 990-93.

AA149   Fujiwara, Masuko. "Egdon to Nethermere" ["Egdon
         and Nethermere"]. D. H. LAWRENCE STUDIES, 1 (1973),
         145-91.
         On Hardy and DHL.

AA150   -----. "SONS AND LOVERS ni Okeru Ai no Yukue"
         ["Locating Love in SONS AND LOVERS"]. D. H. LAW-
         RENCE STUDIES, 3 (1975), 83-108.

AA151   -----. "THE TRESPASSER ni Okeru Genjitsu to Yume"
         ["Reality and Dream in THE TRESPASSER"]. D. H.
         LAWRENCE STUDIES, 2 (1974), 99-116.

AA152   Gaya Nuño, Juan Antonio. "El lider fascista en la
         novela inglesa de nuestro tiempo." CUADERNOS
         HISPANOAMERICANOS, 72, No. 216 (1967), 632-40.
            See R7.

AA153   Gillès, Daniel. "D. H. Lawrence, ou la poésie
         immédiate." REVUE GÉNÉRALE BELGE, 100 (1964), 43-59.

AA154   Gillet, Louis. "D. H. Lawrence d'après sa correspon-
         dance." REVUE DES DEUX MONDES, 8th series, 12 (1932),
         685-98.
            See Z94.

AA155   -----. "D. H. Lawrence, mystique anglais." LES
         NOUVELLES LITTÉRAIRES, No. 465 (12 Sept. 1931),
         pp. 1, 6.
            On LCL.

AA156   Gindre, M. "Points de vue sur D. H. Lawrence." EA,
         11 (1958), 229-39.
            See H137.

AA157   Girard, Denis. "John Middleton Murry, D. H. Lawrence
         et Albert Schweitzer." EA, 12 (1959), 212-21.
            See H138.

AA158   Grassi, Leonardo. "Il problema dell'inconscio e
         l'idealismo" ["The Problem of the Unconscious and
         Idealism"]. GIORNALE CRITICO DELLA FILOSOFIA
         ITALIANA, 6 (1934), 424-51.
            On DHL's psychoanalytic essays.

AA159   Guéhenno, Jean. "Le Message de Lawrence d'après sa
         correspondance." EUROPE, 35 (1935), 103-08, 261-67.

AA160   Hashimoto, Makinori. "Hebi to Tsuki to Shochoshugi:
         D. H. Lawrence no Sozoryoku" ["Serpent, Moon, and
         Symbolism in D. H. Lawrence"]. OBERON, 15, No. 1,
         (1973), pp. 96-119.

AA161   Haya, Kenichi. "Lawrence o do yomuka" ["How to read
         Lawrence"]. EIGO SEINEN, 119 (1973), 134-35.

AA162   Henriot, Émile. "Dire ou ne pas dire." LES NOUVELLES
         LITTÉRAIRES, No. 490 (5 Mar. 1932), p. 1.
            See U28.

AA163   Hesse, Hermann. "Erinnerung an ein paar Bücher."
        NEUE RUNDSCHAU, 45, pt. 1, (1934), 454-58.
        See V177.

AA164   Ignjacević, Svetozar M. "Nasi prevodi Lorensovih
        medju ratnih romana" ["Our Translations of Lawrence's
        Novels Between the Wars"]. MOSTOVI, 11 (1980), 234-38.

AA165   Imaizumi, Haruko. "KOISURU ONNATACHI ni Okeru
        Lawrence no Ai no Kannen" ["The Idea of Love in
        D. H. Lawrence's WOMEN IN LOVE"]. DOSHISHA LITER-
        ATURE, 27 (Nov. 1973), 51-66.

AA166   -----. "MUSUKO TO KOIBITO ni Okeru Shûkyôsei"
        ["The 'Religions' in SONS AND LOVERS"]. D. H.
        LAWRENCE STUDIES, 3 (1975), 157-83.

AA167   Itô, Hidekazu. "Death-Drift karano Dasshutsu
        (Lawrence no Shoki no Shôsetsu ni Tsuite)" ["An
        Escape from Death-Drift (On D. H. Lawrence's Early
        Novels)"]. STUDIES IN LANGUAGE AND LITERATURE
        (Tokyo), No. 2 (Mar. 1968), pp. 20-50.

AA168   -----. "D. H. Lawrence to Kodoku" ["Solitude in
        D. H. Lawrence"]. STUDIES IN LANGUAGE AND LITERATURE
        (Tokyo), No. 1 (Dec. 1966), pp. 67-88.

AA169   Jaloux, Edmond. "L'AMANT DE LADY CHATTERLEY." LES
        NOUVELLES LITTÉRAIRES, No. 483 (16 Jan. 1932), p. 3.

AA170   Jarc, Milan. "D. H. Lawrence." LJUBLJANSKI ZVON,
        No. 12 (1934), pp. 693-705.

AA171   Jochems, Helmut. "Anmerkungen zu D. H. Lawrence:
        'New Mexico.'" LITERATURE IN WISSENSCHAFT UND
        UNTERRICHT, 9 (1976), 77-84.

AA172   Kabiljo-Šutić, Simha. "Filozofija vitalizma D. H.
        Lorensa i O. Hakslija--Uticaj i paralele" ["The
        Philosophy of Vitalism in D. H. Lawrence and A.
        Huxley: Influence and Parallels"]. KNJIŽEVNAK
        KRITIKA, 4, No. 3 (1973), 29-54.

AA173   -----. "Književno prijateljstvo D. H. Lorensa i O.
        Hakslija" ["The Literary Friendship of D. H. Lawrence
        and A. Huxley"]. SAVREMENIK, 37 (1973), 338-52.

AA174   Kamei, Shunsuke. "Whitman to Lawrence" ["Whitman and Lawrence"]. EIGO SEINEN, 114 (1968), 430-32.

AA175   Kamimura, Tetsuhiko. "'Kokkyôsen' to D. H. Lawrence" ["'The Border Line' and D. H. Lawrence"]. ENGLISH LITERATURE REVIEW (Kyôto), No. 10 (Feb. 1966), pp. 11-27.

AA176   -----. "Sei no Heisoku--'Shima o Aishita Otoko' Kara" ["The Blockaded Sex--from 'The Man Who Loved Islands'"]. ENGLISH LITERATURE REVIEW (Kyôto), No. 11 (Nov. 1967), pp. 44-61.

AA177   -----. "YAMAARASHI NO SHI NI OMOU Kara" ["On REFLECTIONS ON THE DEATH OF A PORCUPINE"]. ENGLISH LITERATURE REVIEW (Kyôto), No. 8 (Mar. 1965), pp. 55-70.

AA178   Kamitani, Syotaro. "On SONS AND LOVERS by D. H. Lawrence: Relativity of Human Relationships." HIROSHIMA STUDIES IN ENGLISH LANGUAGE AND LITERATURE, 21, Nos. 1-2 (1976), 30-44. [In Japanese; English abstract pp. 45-46.]

AA179   Kanters, R. "Introduction à la lecture de D. H. Lawrence." LA NEF, No. 34 (Sept. 1947), pp. 3-17.

AA180   Kayser, Rudolf. "D. H. Lawrence und sein erotisches Evangelium." NEUE RUNDSCHAU, 42, pt. 1 (1931), 569-70.
        See U36.

AA181   Kéry, László. "Felbomlás és megújulás D. H. Lawrence SZERELMES ASSZONYOK címü regényében." ["Disintegration and Renewal in D. H. Lawrence's novel WOMEN IN LOVE"]. FILOLÓGIAI KÖZLÖNY, 23 (1977), 47-64.

AA182   Kitazaki, Kaien. "A. Huxley no Shiten kara no SHIROKUJAKU Ron" ["A Study of THE WHITE PEACOCK--From A. Huxley's Viewpoint"]. D. H. LAWRENCE STUDIES, 1 (1973), 123-43.

AA183   -----. "MUSUKO TO KOIBITO ni Okeru Shûkyôteki Sokumen ni Tsuite (Paul no Motomeru 'Kami' no Imi o Megutte)"["Paul's God--A Study of Religious Aspects in SONS AND LOVERS"]. D. H. LAWRENCE STUDIES, 3 (1975), 185-98.

AA184   -----. "THE TRESPASSER ni Okeru 'Saihô' ni Tsuite"
         ["'The West' in THE TRESPASSER"]. D. H. LAWRENCE
         STUDIES, 2 (1974), 29-45.

AA185   Klakoćer, Ludvik. "D. H. Lawrence in eros" ["D. H.
         Lawrence and Eros"]. KROG (1933), pp. 134-40.

AA186   Kobayashi, Manji. "Lawrence no Shi to Hihyokatachi"
         ["Lawrence's Poetry and its Critics"]. EIGO SEINEN,
         120 (1974), 210-12.

AA187   -----. "Modernism Igo no Shijin: D. H. Lawrence"
         ["A Poet After Modernism: D. H. Lawrence"]. EIGO
         SEINEN, 122 (1976), 314-17.

AA188   Kobayashi, Toshiro. "Lawrence and Etruria." ESSAYS
         AND STUDIES IN ENGLIGH LANGUAGE AND LITERATURE (Sendai,
         Japan), 53-54 (1968), 59-78. [In Japanese.]

AA189   Koga, Masakasu. "SHIROKUJAKU Ni Okeru Shizen to
         Ningen" ["Nature and Man in THE WHITE PEACOCK"].
         D. H. LAWRENCE STUDIES, 1 (1973), 37-52.

AA190   Koljévić, Svetozar. "D. H. Lorens: ćoveki i umetnik"
         ["D. H. Lawrence: Man and Artist"]. DELO, No. 4
         (1958), pp. 654-70.

AA191   -----. "D. H. Lorens: 'Sent Mor,' 'Devica i Ciganin'"
         ["D. H. Lawrence: 'St. Mawr,' 'The Virgin and the
         Gipsy'"]. IZRAZ, 7 (1960), 106-09.

AA192   Kreemers, R. "David Herbert Lawrence, 1885-1930."
         LEUVENSE BIJDRAGEN, 27 (1935), 13-25.
             Bibliography.

AA193   Kumbatović, Filip. "O Lawrenceovih SINOVIH IN
         LJUBIMCIH" ["On Lawrence's SONS AND LOVERS"]. MODRA
         PTICA, No. 1-2 (1934-35), pp. 1-4.

AA194   Kuramochi, Saburô. "CHATTERLEY-FUJIN NO KOIBITO no
         Mori" ["Forest in LADY CHATTERLEY'S LOVER"]. EIGO
         SEINEN, 118 (1973), 642-43.
             See AA24.

AA195   -----. "Gamekeeper no Henbo: LADY CHATTERLEY'S
         LOVER no Mittsu no Han" ["The Transfiguration of the
         Gamekeeper: The Three Versions of LADY CHATTERLEY'S
         LOVER"]. EIGO SEINEN, 120 (1974), 214-15.
             See AA24.

AA196   -----. "Shosetsu wa ika ni Owaru ka? D. H. Lawrence
         no Shosetsu to 'kaishin'" ["How to end a novel? D. H.
         Lawrence's novels and 'conversion'"]. EIGO SEINEN,
         115 (1969), 224-26.
         See AA24.

AA197   Lalou, René. "D. H. Lawrence, romancier anglais."
         LES NOUVELLES LITTÉRAIRES, No. 444 (18 Apr. 1931), p. 5.
         On DHL and Aldous Huxley.

AA198   -----. "Le Message de Lawrence." REVUE DE SIÈCLE,
         1 (Apr. 1933), 82-89.

AA199   Lanoire, Maurice. "D. H. Lawrence." LA REVUE DE
         PARIS, 39, No. 4 (1932), 909-25.

AA200   Laurent, C. "E. M. Forster et D. H. Lawrence."
         LES LANGUES MODERNES, 64 (1970), 281-88.
         On SL and HOWARDS END (1910).

AA201   Lavrin, Janko. "Vzporednosti med I. Cankarjem in
         D. H. Lawrencom" ["A Comparison Between I(van) Cankar
         and D. H. Lawrence"]. ZBORNIK ZA SLAVISTIKU, 13
         (1977), 113-16.

AA202   Levý, J. "Kritické názory D. H. Lawrence" ["A
         Critical Overview of D. H. Lawrence"]. CASOPIS PRO
         MODERNI FILOLOGII, No. 30 (1947), pp. 202-17.

AA203   Linati, Carlo. "Lawrence e l'Italia." PEGASO, Apr.
         1933, pp. 385-98.

AA204   Madonna, Michèle. "Le Primitivisme dans WOMEN IN
         LOVE." LES LANGUES MODERNES, 62 (1968), 190-96.
         See AA26.

AA205   Mafud Haye, Hilda. "D. H. Lawrence, el novelista."
         NEUVA REVISTA DEL PACÍFICO, 9 (1978), 32-37.

AA206   Magny, C. E. "D. H. Lawrence, ou le mal du XXe
         siècle." ESPRIT, 9 (1941), 556-69.

AA207   Malraux, André. "D. H. Lawrence et l'érotisme.
         A propos de L'AMANT DE LADY CHATTERLEY." NOUVELLE
         REVUE FRANÇAISE, 38 (1932), 136-40.
         See U46.

AA208 Marcel, Gabriel. "In Memoriam--D. H. Lawrence."
NOUVELLE REVUE FRANÇAISE, 34 (1930), 570-72.
See F102.

AA209 -----. "Publications Lawrenciennes." L'EUROPE
NOUVELLE, 18 (1935), 799-800.

AA210 -----. "Le Testament Poétique de Lawrence."
REVUE DE SIÈCLE, 1 (Sept. 1933), 24-34.

AA211 Marnat, Marcel. "L'Envers d'un conte de fées"
["Fairy-Tales in Reverse"]. LA QUINZAINE
LITTÉRAIRE, No. 47 (1968), pp. 3-4.
See V21.

AA212 Martin, Richard. "Abgeschiedenheit und Auferstehung:
Die Entfaltung eines Motivs in D. H. Lawrence's
letzten Kurzgeschichten" ["Seclusion and Resurrection:
The Development of a Theme in D. H. Lawrence's Last
Short Stories"]. POETICA, 2 (1968), 70-78.
See V22.

AA213 Matsubayashi, Yoshihiro. "Equilibrium in Life."
HIROSHIMA STUDIES IN ENGLISH LANGUAGE AND LITERATURE,
21, Nos. 1-2 (1976), 47-59. [In Japanese; English
abstract, p. 60.]

AA214 Mauriac, François. "Eros." LES NOUVELLES LITTÉRAIRES,
No. 496 (16 Apr. 1932), p. 1.
On LCL.

AA215 Michelis, Eurialo de. "Lawrence in Versi." LETTERATURE
MODERNE, 11 (1961), 232-44.

AA216 Mikhal'skaya, N. P. "Roman D. H. Laurensa:
VLYUBLENNYE ZHENSHCHINY" ["D. H. Lawrence's Novel
WOMEN IN LOVE"]. UCHENYE ZAPISKI MOSKOVSKII
GOSUDARSTVENNYI PEDAGOGICHESKI INSTITUT IMENI
LENINA, 280 (1967), 78-95.

AA217 Milatović, Dragutin. "Srodnosti i odlike dva
konflikta: Džojsova i Lorensova verzija sukoba
generacija u romanima PORTRET UMJETNIKA U MLADOSTI
i SINOVI LJUBAVNICI" ["Conflict in Joyce's A
PORTRAIT OF THE ARTIST AS A YOUNG MAN and Lawrence's
SONS AND LOVERS"]. STVARANJE, 31 (1976), 1023-26.

AA218   Moravia, Alberto. "Il Mito Del Messico" ["The Myth of Mexico"]. IL CORRIERE DELLA SERA, 20 Nov. 1966, p. 3.
         See T18.

AA219   Mori, Haruhide. "Geijutsu no Hôkai--AARON'S ROD to KANGAROO no Shisô to Hyôgen" ["Failure of Art: Ideas and Expressions in AARON'S ROD and KANGAROO"]. ÔSAKA LITERARY REVIEW, No. 2 (July 1963), pp. 51-61.
         See AA29.

AA220   -----. "Kajaku no Yukue" ["The World of THE WHITE PEACOCK"]. KOBE MISCELLANY, 7 (Aug. 1975), 109-23.
         See AA29.

AA221   -----. "Lawrence no Gikyoku ni Kansuru Oboegaki: MRS. HOLROYD, TOUCH AND GO, DAVID" ["Notes on Lawrence's Plays: THE WIDOWING OF MRS. HOLROYD, TOUCH AND GO, and DAVID"]. PRELUDE (Ôsaka), No. 7 (Nov. 1963), pp. 26-36.
         See AA29.

AA222   -----. "Mujun to Shôsô no Hyôgen: WOMEN IN LOVE, Jinbutsu to Imêji" ["Expression of Irritation and Contradiction: Characterization and Imagery in WOMEN IN LOVE"]. PRELUDE (Ôsaka), No. 6 (Sept. 1962), pp. 26-35.
         See AA29.

AA223   -----. "THE RAINBOW no Kôzô--Imeiji no Hassô Oyobi Sakusô to Tenkai" ["The Structure of THE RAINBOW and a Study of Its Imagery"]. ÔSAKA LITERARY REVIEW, No. 1 (Apr. 1962), pp. 57-69.
         See AA29.

AA224   -----. "Shinwa to Genjitsu no Hazama--D. H. Lawrence TSUBASA ARU HEBI" ["Myth and Reality in THE PLUMED SERPENT"]. MODERN AGE (Kobe Univ.), 48 (Feb. 1974), 1-29.
         See AA29.

AA225   Müller, Erich. "Utopische und apokalyptische Elemente der englischen Gegenwart: Thomas Edward und David Herbert Lawrence" ["Utopian and Apocalyptic Elements in the England of Today: Thomas Edward Lawrence and David Herbert Lawrence"]. STIMMEN DER ZEIT, 133 (1938), 307-14.

AA226   Nardi, Piero. "Corot visto da Lawrence" ["Corot
        Through the Eyes of Lawrence"]. LA FIERA LETTERARIA,
        7 Sept. 1952, p. 6.

AA227   ─────. "Le tre redazioni dell'AMANTE DI LADY CHAT-
        TERLEY" ["The Three Versions of LADY CHATTERLEY'S
        LOVER"]. TRE VENEZIE, 21 (Apr.-June 1947), 135-42.

AA228   ─────. "Tutta una vita nei versi di D. H. Lawrence"
        ["The Life of D. H. Lawrence Through His Poems"].
        IL TEMPO, 17 June 1960, p. 3.
        Comments on the Italian translation of DHL's
        TUTTE LE POESIE (Milan: Mondadori, 1960).

AA229   Naumov, Ničifor. "David Herbert Lorens." SAVREMENIK,
        Nos. 8-9 (1958), pp. 221-35.

AA230   Nishida, Minoru. "MUSUKO TO KOIBITO ni Okeru Tankyû
        no Imi to Kôzô" ["The Meaning and Structure of Paul's
        Quest in SONS AND LOVERS"]. D. H. LAWRENCE STUDIES,
        3 (1975), 199-220.

AA231   Nishikawa, Masaharu. "Annable no Sôwa" ["On the
        Episode of Annable in THE WHITE PEACOCK"]. ENGLISH
        LITERATURE (Waseda), No. 19 (1961), pp. 210-23.

AA232   ─────. "D. H. Lawrence no Buntai" ["On the Style of
        D. H. Lawrence"]. ENLGISH LITERATURE (Waseda),
        No. 12 (Nov. 1956), pp. 54-61.

AA233   ─────. "D. H. Lawrence no Shimpishugi" ["Mysticism
        in D. H. Lawrence's Works"]. STUDIES IN ENGLISH
        LITERATURE (Tokyo), 35, No. 2 (Mar. 1959), 267-77.

AA234   Nishimura, Kôji. "Lawrence Bungaku no Konnichisei"
        ["The Contemporary Relevance of Lawrence's Works"].
        EIGO SEINEN, 120 (1974), 216-17.

AA235   ─────. "Nigenron no Yukue" ["Outcome of Dualism
        in D. H. Lawrence"]. EIGO SEINEN, 115 (1969), 624-26.

AA236   ─────. "Rananim no Yume" ["Dream of Rananim"].
        EIGO SEINEN, 116 (1970), 637-38.
        On DHL's letters.

AA237   Ocampo, Victoria. "El hombre que murió (D. H. Law-
        rence)." SUR, No. 329 (1971), pp. 33-56.
        See R16.

AA238   Okano, Keiichi. "MUSUKO TO KOIBITO no Higeki--
         Morel-Fujin ni Mirareru Kikai-Bunmei ni yoru
         Hakaisei no Shiten Yori" ["The Tragedy of SONS AND
         LOVERS--A View of Mrs. Morel's Destructiveness as
         Caused by Industrial Civilization"]. D. H.
         LAWRENCE STUDIES, 3 (1975), 31-49.

AA239   Okumura, Tôru. "Ai to Kunô no Henreki MIYO WARERA
         WA YATTE KITA!" ["Lawrence's Pilgrimage of Love and
         Agony--LOOK! WE HAVE COME THROUGH!"]. ENGLISH
         LITERARY REVIEW (Kyôto), No. 5 (Mar. 1961), pp. 12-38.

AA240   -----. "Lawrence no Leadership Novels ni Tsuite--
         AARON NO TSUE kara TSUBASA ARU HEBI made" ["On
         Lawrence's Leadership Novels--from AARON'S ROD to
         THE PLUMED SERPENT"]. REVIEW OF ENGLISH LITERATURE
         (Kyôto), No. 31 (Dec. 1973), pp. 46-62.

AA241   -----. "Lawrence Shôsetsu no Hitotsu no Imi
         MUSUKO TO KOIBITO kara KOISURU ONNA TACHI Made"
         ["A Meaning of D. H. Lawrence's Novels--from SONS
         AND LOVERS to WOMEN IN LOVE"]. REVIEW OF ENGLISH
         LITERATURE (Kyôto), No. 21 (Aug. 1967), pp. 103-17.

AA242   -----. "Michinaru Sekai o Motomete--NIJI" ["In
         Search of the Unknown World--THE RAINBOW"]. REVIEW
         OF ENGLISH LITERATURE (Kyôto), No. 17 (Mar. 1965),
         pp. 74-108.

AA243   -----. "Nikutai no Fukkatsu--CHATTERLEY-FUJIN NO
         KOIBITO" ["The Resurrection of the Body--LADY
         CHATTERLEY'S LOVER"]. REVIEW OF ENGLISH LITERATURE
         (Kyôto), No. 30 (Mar. 1973), pp. 51-63.

AA244   -----. "Paul no Higeki--MUSUKO TO KOIBITO" ["The
         Tragedy of Paul Morel--SONS AND LOVERS"]. REVIEW
         OF ENGLISH LITERATURE (Kyôto), No. 16 (Oct. 1964),
         pp. 106-40.

AA245   Onodera, Takeshi. "Forster to Lawrence" ["Forster
         and Lawrence"]. EIGO SEINEN, 119 (1973), 454-55.

AA246   Orsini, Lanfranco. "Le tre 'Lady Chatterley'"
         ["The Three 'Lady Chatterleys'"]. LE RAGIONI
         NARRATIVE, May 1960, pp. 114-36.

AA247   Perosa, Sergio. "D. H. LAWRENCE: TUTTE LE POESIE"
        ["THE COMPLETE POEMS OF D. H. LAWRENCE"]. IL VERRI,
        1 Feb. 1961, pp. 97-103.
                Review of the Italian translation of DHL's
                poetry (Milan: Mondadori, 1960).

AA248   Petrić, Vladimir. "Seksualno Jevandelje po D. H.
        Lorensu" ["The Sexual Gospel of D. H. Lawrence"].
        SAVREMENIK, No. 7 (1971), pp. 74-81.

AA249   Pirenet, Colette. "La Structure symbolique de
        WOMEN IN LOVE." EA, 22 (1969), 137-51.
                See N71.

AA250   Poulsen, Bjørn. "D. H. Lawrence som moderne profet"
        ["D. H. Lawrence as a Modern Prophet"]. DANSK UDSYN,
        38 (1958), 191-202.

AA251   Radica Bogdan. "Svet bez duha i bez ljubavi"
        ["A World Without Spirit and Love"]. NOVA EUROPA,
        No. 11 (1934), pp. 404-11.
                On LCL.

AA252   Ramos Surárez, Jorge. "El poema 'Snake,' de D. H.
        Lawrence, y la'Elegía a un moscardón azul,' de
        Dámaso Alonzo: Una influencia admitida y dos
        sensibilidades diferentes." CUADERNOS HISPANO-
        AMERICANOS, Nos. 280-82 (1973), pp. 274-83.
                See Y117.

AA253   Raya, Gino. "Lawrence prefamistra [sic?]."
        BIOLOGIA CULTURALE, 4 (1969), 126-32.

AA254   Requardt, Egon. "David Herbert Lawrence: SONS AND
        LOVERS." NS, 10 (1961), 230-35. [In German.]

AA255   -----. "D. H. Lawrence: Solipsist oder Prophet
        einer neuen Gemeinschaft?" ["D. H. Lawrence:
        Solipsist or Prophet of a New Community?"]. NS,
        12 (1963), 506-15.

AA256   Reul, Paul de. "D. H. Lawrence." REVUE DE
        L'UNIVERSITÉ DE BRUXELLES, 36 (1931), 202-30.

AA257   Rosati, S. "D. H. Lawrence Postuma." NUOVA ANTOLOGIA,
        365 (1933), 627-33.

AA258 Rossi, Patrizio. "'The Fox' e 'La Lupa': D. H. Lawrence lettore di Verga." EM, 24 (1973-74), 299-320. See V65.

AA259 ------. "Verga e l'Italia nella corrispondenza di D. H. Lawrence" ["Verga and Italy in the Correspondence of D. H. Lawrence"]. ANNALI ISTITUTO ORIENTALE NAPOLI, SEZIONE ROMANZA, 15 (1973), 25-43. See Z111.

AA260 Sandulescu, Constantin-George. "Lawrence Dramaturg." CONTEMPORANUL, 4 (Oct. 1968), 4.

AA261 Schoberth, F. W. "D. H. Lawrence in der zeitgenössischen Kritik" ["D. H. Lawrence in Contemporary Criticism"]. NS, 3 (1953), 155-62.

AA262 Schoenberner, Franz. "D. H. Lawrence." NEUE SCHWEIZER RUNDSCHAU, 24 (1931), 32-37. See F144.

AA263 Sepčić, Višnja. "Iracionalna motivacija u Lawrenceovu romanu ZALJUBLJENE ŽENE" ["Irrational Motivation in Lawrence's novel WOMEN IN LOVE"]. FORUM, Nos. 3-4 (1967), pp. 508-22.

AA264 ------. "Na raskršću realizma i simbolizma." ["At the Cross-Roads of Realism and Symbolism"]. UMJETNOST RIJEČI, No. 1 (1975), pp. 29-52. On SL.

AA265 ------. "Romansijerski eksperiment D. H. Lawrencea" ["D. H. Lawrence's Experiment as Novelist"]. KNJIŽEVNA SMOTRA, No. 17 (1974), pp. 55-65.

AA266 ------. "Struktura romana D. H. Lawrencea" ["The Structure of D. H. Lawrence's Novels"]. FILOLOGIJA (1970), pp. 183-96.

AA267 Serafini, Guglielmo. "Su David Herbert Lawrence." IL SAGGIATORE, Oct. 1932, pp. 297-304. DHL among Huxley, Joyce, and Woolf.

AA268 Shimizu, Kohya. "D. H. Lawrence ni Okeru Seishoku to Sôzô no Kairi o Megutte" ["The Discrepancy between Creation and Procreation in D. H. Lawrence"]. STUDIES IN ENGLISH LITERATURE (Tokyo), 50, No. 1 (1973), 63-77. [Engl. abstract, pp. 228-30.]

AA269   Sonoi, Eishu. "Some Notes on D. H. Lawrence's
        'Bavarian Gentians.'" STUDIES IN ENGLISH LANGUAGE
        AND LITERATURE (Fukuoka), 29 (1979), 69-81. [In
        Japanese; English Abstract, p. 209.]

AA270   Sorani, Aldo. "Incontri con D. H. Lawrence"
        ["Meetings with D. H. Lawrence"]. PEGASO, June 1932,
        pp. 702-10.
        Memoir, with comments on LCL and "The Man
        Who Died."

AA271   Soulie-Lapeyre, Paule. "Le Primitivisme dans LE
        SERPENT À PLUMES de D. H. Lawrence." LES LANGUES
        MODERNES, 71 (1977), 255-62.

AA272   Sugiyama, Yasushi. "Shinda Musuko to Uchû no Rizumu"
        ["The Son Who Died in the Rhythm of the Universe"].
        D. H. LAWRENCE STUDIES, 3 (1975), 133-56.

AA273   -----. "SHINNYUSHA ni Okeru Shi to Sei" ["Death and
        Life in THE TRESPASSER"]. D. H. LAWRENCE STUDIES,
        2 (1974), 47-64.

AA274   -----. "SHIROKUJAKU ni Okeru no Yakudô to Shi"
        ["Quickening of Life and Death in THE WHITE PEACOCK"].
        D. H. LAWRENCE STUDIES, 1 (1973), 75-94.

AA275   Temple, Frédéric J. "Au Nouveau-Mexique sur la pas
        de D. H. Lawrence." NOUVELLE REVUE FRANÇAISE, N.S.
        10 (1962), 562-67.
        See F152.

AA276   Terada, Takehiko. "D. H. Lawrence Rekishi Taiken"
        ["D. H. Lawrence: His Vision of History"]. EIGAKU,
        1, No. 4 (1957), 60-115; No. 5 (1958), 1-28.

AA277   Tetsumura, Haruo. "D. H. Lawrence no Shinpishugi
        (Tsuki no Imisuru Mono)" ["D. H. Lawrence's Mysticism:
        What the Moon Signifies"]. HIROSHIMA STUDIES IN
        ENGLISH LANGUAGE AND LITERATURE, 9, Nos. 1-2 (June
        1963), 51-65.

AA278   -----. "'The Man Who Died' ni Tsuite (Shûkyôteki
        de Arukoto to Sono Hyôgen)" ["A Study of 'The Man
        Who Died' (Religiousness as Lawrence's Quintessence)"].
        HIROSHIMA STUDIES IN ENGLISH LANGUAGE AND LITERATURE,
        14, No. 2 (Dec. 1967), 53-65.

AA279 Thiébaut, Marcel. "D. H. Lawrence." JOURNAL DES DÉBATS, 39, pt. 1 (1932), 231–34.

AA280 Torbarina, Josip. "D. H. Lawrence i njegov roman" ["D. H. Lawrence and His Novel"]. HRVATSKO KOLO (1933), pp. 168–84.

AA281 Trient, René. "Lawrence panthéiste et l'antiquité païenne." CAHIERS DU SUD, 20 (1933), 614–21. See H382.

AA282 Truchlar, Leo. "Zur Spätlyrik von D. H. Lawrence" ["About the Late Poems of D. H. Lawrence"]. NS, 18 (1969), 600–06.

AA283 Tysdahl, Bjørn J. "Kvinnesak og skjønnlitteratur: D. H. Lawrence: THE RAINBOW" ["Feminism and Fiction: D. H. Lawrence: THE RAINBOW"]. EDDA, 75 (1975), 29–36. See M80.

AA284 Vichy, Thérèse. "Symbolisme et structures dans WOMEN IN LOVE." EA, 33 (1980), 400–13. See N102.

AA285 Vuković, Vladimir. "Otkrivenje umirućeg" ["Revelation of a Dying Man"]. SAVREMENIK, No. 4 (1938), pp. 330–43. Considers APOCALYPSE among other late works.

AA286 Wahl, Jean. "Sur D. H. Lawrence." NOUVELLE REVUE FRANÇAISE, 42 (1934), 115–21. See L66.

AA287 Wellek, René. "D. H. Lawrence." ENGLISH POST (Prague), 1 (1933), 109–11. [In Czech.]

AA288 ─────. "D. H. Lawrence." LISTY PRO UMĚNÍ A KRITIKU, 1 (1933), 336–42.

AA289 Wilkin, Andrew. "Sulle traduzioni Laurenciane delle novelle di G. Verga." BIOLOGIA CULTURALE, 9 (1974), 122–27.

AA290 Yamakawa, Kozo. "'Niji' Izen-Igo: Beardsley no 'Salome' wo Megutte" ["Before and after THE RAINBOW: On Beardsley's 'Salomé'"]. EIGO SEINEN, 120 (1974), 212–13.

AA291 Yanda, Noriyuki. "On LADY CHATTERLEY'S LOVER: Uncertainty of the Opposition." ESSAYS IN FOREIGN
LANGUAGES AND LITERATURE (Hokkaido Univ.), 24 (1978),
pt. 1, 145-63. [In Japanese; English abstract, pt. 1,
p. 383].

AA292 Yoshida, Masako. "SHIROKUJAKU ni Okeru Ambivalence
no Mondai" ["An Inquiry into Ambivalence in THE WHITE
PEACOCK"]. D. H. LAWRENCE STUDIES, 1 (1973), 95-122.

AA293 -----. "Yami no Sekai e no Tabidachi--Morel-Fujin
no Shi ga Imisuru Mono" ["A Journey to 'Darkness'--
What the Death of Mrs. Morel Means"]. D. H. LAWRENCE
STUDIES, 3 (1975), 51-82.

AA294 Yoshii, Mitsuo. "Lawrence NIJI Ronkô--Buntai to
Kôsei o Chûshin to Shite" ["On Lawrence's THE RAINBOW--
Some Characteristics of Style and Structure"].
WASEDA REVIEW, 10 (July 1971), 1-13; 11 (Sept. 1972),
46-56; 12 (Sept. 1973), 97-109.

AA295 -----. "Shisô no Henreki--Lawrence AARON NO TSUE
Ron" ["Pilgrimage in Ideas--On Lawrence's AARON'S
ROD"]. WASEDA REVIEW, 14 (Sept. 1975), 30-47.

AA296 Yoshimura, Hirokazu. "MUSUKO TO KOIBITO ni Okeru
Niku to Kotoba--Sono 'Jogen' o Megutte no Ichikôsatsu"
["SONS AND LOVERS and Its 'Foreword'"]. D. H. LAWRENCE
STUDIES, 3 (1975), 3-30.

AA297 -----. "SHINNYUSHA no Wagnerteki Yôso o Megutte"
["Wagnerian Elements in THE TRESPASSER"]. D. H.
LAWRENCE STUDIES, 2 (1974), 5-28.

AA298 -----. "SHIROKUJAKU no Jinbutsu o Megutte--Cyril
Beardsall o Chûshin ni" ["Cyril Beardsall in THE
WHILE PEACOCK"]. D. H. LAWRENCE STUDIES, 1 (1973),
53-73.

APPENDIX B: STUDY GUIDES

With the possible exception of Handley's guide to SONS AND
LOVERS (AB5 below), the titles listed here offer little of
interest or value even to the beginning reader of DHL's
works. They consist chiefly of plot summaries, with inter-
spersed, elementary commentary, character sketches, questions
for study, and suggested paper topics. They are entered in
this volume to make the record of monograph- and book-length
publications on DHL more nearly complete.

AB1   Aylwin, Anthony M. NOTES ON D. H. LAWRENCE'S *THE*
      RAINBOW. London: Methuen Educational, 1977.

AB2   Bunnell, W. S. BRODIE'S NOTES ON D. H. LAWRENCE'S
      THE RAINBOW. London: Pan Educational, 1978.

AB3   Fielding, Michael L. NOTES ON D. H. LAWRENCE'S
      SONS AND LOVERS. London: Methuen Educational, 1975.

AB4   Gilbert, Sandra M. D. H. LAWRENCE'S *SONS AND LOVERS*,
      THE RAINBOW, *WOMEN IN LOVE*, *THE PLUMED SERPENT*.
      New York: Monarch Press, 1965.

AB5   Handley, Graham. NOTES ON D. H. LAWRENCE: *SONS AND*
      LOVERS. Bath: James Brodie, 1967.
            Handley's extended introduction and numerous
            textual annotations make his study guide
            marginally more useful than the other titles
            listed in this appendix.

AB6   Mackenzie, D. Kenneth M. "THE FOX." Milton Keynes,
      Engl.: Open Univ. Press, 1973.

AB7   Martin, Graham. D. H. LAWRENCE'S *THE RAINBOW*.
      Bletchley, Engl.: Open Univ. Press, 1971.

AB8   Rothkopf, Carol Zemen. *SONS AND LOVERS*: A CRITICAL
      COMMENTARY. New York: American R.D.M., 1969.

AB9   Shaw, Rita Granger. *SONS AND LOVERS*:   NOTES.
       Lincoln, Nebr.:   Cliff's Notes, 1965.

AB10   *SONS AND LOVERS*:   NOTES.   Toronto: Coles Notes, 1967.

APPENDIX C: UNVERIFIED TITLES

The publication of the following eight titles, listed in
various bibliographies of DHL studies, has not been verified.

AC1   Beutmann, Margarete. DIE BILDWELT D. H. LAWRENCES
      [THE WORLD OF IMAGES IN D. H. LAWRENCE]. Freiburg
      in Breisgau: Druck von Rudolf Goldschagg, 1940.

AC2   Kéry, László. STILUSSAJATSAGOK D. H. LAWRENCE
      REGÉNYÉBEN [THE STYLISTIC APPROPRIATENESS OF D. H.
      LAWRENCE'S FICTION]. Budapest, 1944.

AC3   Kim, D. S. AN ARCHITECT OF THE VITAL SELF: A STUDY
      OF D. H. LAWRENCE. Seoul, Korea: Hankuk Univ., 1974.

AC4   -----. D. H. LAWRENCE: ARTIST FOR HIS SAKE. Seoul,
      Korea: Hankuk Univ., 1969.

AC5   -----. D. H. LAWRENCE'S MALE LEADERSHIP IDEAS IN
      AARON'S ROD, *KANGAROO*, AND *THE PLUMED SERPENT*.
      Seoul, Korea: Hankuk Univ., 1969.

AC6   -----. A STUDY OF D. H. LAWRENCE: *LADY CHATTERLEY'S
      LOVER* AND "THE MAN WHO DIED." Seoul, Korea: Hankuk
      Univ., 1969.

AC7   Pollak, Paulina S. DIG DEEP WITHIN YOURSELF: D. H.
      LAWRENCE'S ADVICE TO A YOUNG WRITER: A DRAFT ESSAY.
      Fullerton: California State Univ., 1977.

AC8   Vallese, Tarquinio. D. H. LAWRENCE. Naples:
      Loffredo, 1940.

Indexes

AUTHOR INDEX

This index includes all authors, compilers, editors, and translators of the works entered in this volume. Also included are interviewers and interviewees, and contributors to collections and panel discussions who are named in annotations, but whose contributions are not otherwise entered and annotated in the bibliography.

Astaldi, Maria Luisa AA53
Atkinson, Curtis R5
Auden, W. H. H19, H20, Y77
Axelrod, Allen M. Z12
Ayling, Ronald X10
Aylwin, Anthony M. AB1

Baim, Joseph H21, V73, V88
Bair, Hebe Y10
Baker, Ernest A. H22
Baker, James R. Y11
Baker, Paul G. Q2, V74
Balbert, Peter H. L12, M1,
  U6
Baldanza, Frank H23, L13
Baldwin, Alice T4
Ballin, Micheal H24, T5
Bantock, G. H. H25
Barber, David S. N6, N7
Barbier, Françoise-Marie N2
Bareiss, Dieter AA54
Barez, Reva R. E4
Barnes, T. R. F11
Baron, Carl E. F124, H26,
  H27, T6, W3, Z13
Barr, Barbara Weekley F12,
  F13
Barr, William R. Q3
Barrett, Gerald R. V128
Barrière, Françoise AA110
Barry, J. M13, N8
Barry, Sandra Q4
Bartlett, Norman H28
Bartlett, Phyllis Y72, Y103
Bassoff, Bruce N9
Bates, Herbert E. V8
Bayley, John H29, H30
Beach, Joseph Warren H31
Beachcroft, Thomas O. V9
Beal, Anthony B23, G9
Beards, Richard D. E5, E6,
  L14, Z14

Beauvoir, Simone de H32, AA55
Bechot, J. AA111
Beck, Rudolf U7, AA2a, AA112
Becker, George J. G10
Becker, Henry, III V129
Bedford, Sybille F14, U8
Bedient, Calvin H33
Beebe, Maurice E7, L15
Beer, John H34, T6
Beirne, Raymond M. C7
Beker, Miroslav E33, N10,
  Z15, AA56, AA113
Bell, Clive F58
Bell, Elizabeth S. M14
Bell Michael H35
Bell, Quentin F15
Ben-Ephraim, Gavriel G11
Bennett, Arnold H36
Bennett, Joan U3
Bennett, Michael F16
Bentley, Eric H37
Bentley, Joseph H38
Bergler, Edmund V52
Bergonzi, Bernard H39, H144
Bersani, Leo H40
Bertholf, Robert J. Z74
Berthoud, Jacques M15
Bertocci, Angelo P. N11
Betsky, Seymour L16
Betsky-Zweig, Sara V75
Beutmann, Margarete AC1
Bilan, R. P. H41
Black, Michael H. H42, H43
Blackmur, R. P. Y12
Blanchard, Lydia H44, M16,
  N12, N13, U9, V150
Blanche, J. E. AA114
Bleich, David Y109
Blisset, William H45
Blöcker, Günter AA57, AA115
Bloom, Alice H46
Bloom, Harold Y125
Boadella, David G12

Authors

Nojima, Hidekatsu AA89
Nulle, Stebelton H. H278
Nuño, Juan Antonio Gaya
  See GayaNuño, Juan Antonio

Oates, Joyce Carol N70, Y5
Ober, William B. U54
Obler, Paul C. M5
O'Brien, Justin U46
Ocampo, Victoria R16, U55,
  AA237
O'Casey, Sean X10
O'Connell, Adelyn, RSCJ M60
O'Connor, Frank L48, V24
Ôhashi, Yasuichirô E29
Okada, Taiji E29
Okano, Keiichi AA238
Okumura, Tôru E29, AA239-
  AA244
Okunishi, Akira AA90
Onodera, Takeshi AA245
Oppel, Horst V156, Y116,
  AA91, AA92
Orioli, Giuseppe A58
Orliac, Jehanne d' U2, AA35
Orsini, Lanfranco AA246
Orwell, George V127
Orwell, Sonia V127
Owen, Frederick I. F126

Pachmuss, Temira H279
Padhi, Bibhu H280, V45
Page, Norman F127
Palmer, Paul R. F128
Panichas, George A. F129,
  G91, H281, H282, H290,
  Y44, Z99
Panken, Shirley L49
Park, David A. M31, N34
Parker, David U56
Parker, Gillian L22, N41,
  U25, V175

Parkes, H. B. H283
Parry, Albert E34
Parshley, H. M. H32
Partlow, Robert B. G92
Pascal, Roy L51
Paterson, John H284, Z56
Patmore, Brigit F130, F131
Patmore, Derek F132, G93
Peach, Linden H285
Pearce, Melville Chaning-.
  See Chaning-Pearce, Melville
Pearsall, Robert Brainard W7
Peckham, Morse Z57
Perkins, David Y41
Perosa, Sergio AA247
Peterson, Richard F. E35, H286
Petre, M. D. H287
Petrić, Vladimir AA248
Pettingell, Phoebe Y30
Peyre, Henri H288, AA93
Phelps, Gilbert H289
Phillips, Danna L52
Phillips, David E19
Phillips, Jill M. E36
Phillips, Stephen R. V79, V80
Pierce, David H98
Pierle, Robert C. Z58
Pinion, F. B. G95
Pinsker, Sanford H112
Pinto, Vivian de Sola B3, E37,
  G96, H290, H291, U3, Y42-
  Y44, Y80, Z59
Pirenet, Colette N71, AA249
Pittock, Malcolm Z60
Plowman, Max H272
Pocock, Douglas C. D. H74
Poesch, Jessie G25
Poirier, Richard V157, Z61
Pollak, Paulina S. F133, AC7
Pollinger, Gerald F134
Poole, Roger H. B6, G97, H293
Porter, Katherine Anne T19, U57
Potter, Stephen G98
Potts, Abbie Findlay Y45

TITLE INDEX

This index includes the titles of all books, essay collections, monographs, and pamphlets entered in this guide, as well as of all Lawrence's major publications. Article titles are omitted. In all cases of identical titles, the author's or editor's name has been placed in parentheses after the title. The entry number(s) indicates the first, or, in a few cases, each complete listing of the title with full publishing data. An essay collection, therefore, will ordinarily have but one entry number, referring the user to the collection's full entry and its annotation where cross-reference numbers for its contents are provided.

D. H. Lawrence (Draper, 1969)
G32
D. H. Lawrence (Jaensson)
G61, AA19
D. H. Lawrence (Kermode)
G65
D. H. Lawrence (Leavis) G67
D. H. Lawrence (Littlewood)
G71
D. H. Lawrence (Schorer) B5
D. H. Lawrence (Slade) G111
D. H. Lawrence (Vallese)
AC8
D. H. Lawrence (A. West)
G125
D. H. Lawrence (R. West)
F159
D. H. Lawrence (Young) G129
D. H. Lawrence: A Basic
Study of His Ideas G40
D. H. Lawrence: A
Bibliography E44
D. H. Lawrence: A Calendar
of His Works E40
D. H. Lawrence: A Check-
list E51
D. H. Lawrence: A Collec-
tion of Critical Essays
G115
D. H. Lawrence: A Collec-
tion of Criticism G48
D. H. Lawrence: A Composite
Biography F123
D. H. Lawrence: A Critical
Anthology G20
D. H. Lawrence: A Critical
Study G38
D. H. Lawrence: A Critical
Study of the Major Novels
and Other Writings G43
D. H. Lawrence: A Finding
List (Cooke) E9
D. H. Lawrence: A Finding
List (Edwards) E18

D. H. Lawrence: A First
Study G98
D. H. Lawrence: A Modern
Adventure in Thought G63
D. H. Lawrence: A Personal
Record F29
D. H. Lawrence: A Review of
the Biographies and Lit-
erary Criticism E36
D. H. Lawrence: A Selection
B6
D. H. Lawrence: A Study of
His Novels G99
D. H. Lawrence: A Study of
the Novels AA24
D. H. Lawrence: An American
Interpretation G108
D. H. Lawrence: An Annotated
Bibliography E10
D. H. Lawrence: An Appre-
ciation G2
D. H. Lawrence: An Attempt
at a Political Analysis
G13, AA3
D. H. Lawrence: An Eastern
View G86
D. H. Lawrence: An Exhibit
E35
D. H. Lawrence: An Exhibition
of First Editions E45
D. H. Lawrence: An Indiscretion
G2
D. H. Lawrence: An Unprofes-
sional Study G88
D. H. Lawrence: Apocalypse
and the Writings on Revela-
tion A76, B6
D. H. Lawrence: Artist and
Rebel G118
D. H. Lawrence: Artist for
His Sake AC4
D. H. Lawrence: Body of
Darkness G101

D. H. Lawrence: Die Charaktere in der Handlung und Spannung Seiner Kurzgeschichten V2, AA16

D. H. Lawrence: Essai sur la Formation et le Développment de sa Pensée d'après Son Oeuvre en Prose AA6

D. H. Lawrence: Et Forsøg Paa En Politisk Analyse G13, AA3

D. H. Lawrence: Ett Modernt Tankeäventyr G63, AA20

D. H. Lawrence: His First Editions E20

D. H. Lawrence: His Life and Works G80

D. H. Lawrence: History, Ideology and Fiction G54

D. H. Lawrence: Interviews and Recollections F127

D. H. Lawrence: L'Homme et La Genèse de Son Oeuvre AA7

D. H. Lawrence: Life and Works AA22

D. H. Lawrence: Novelist G68

D. H. Lawrence: Novelist, Poet, Prophet G113

D. H. Lawrence: On the Function and Strategy of Literary Irrationalism G126, AA48

D. H. Lawrence: Pilgrim of the Apocalypse G47

D. H. Lawrence: Portrait of a Genius, But . . . F1

D. H. Lawrence: Prophet of the Midlands G96

D. H. Lawrence: Reminiscences and Correspondence F20

D. H. Lawrence: St. Mawr and Other Stories B8

D. H. Lawrence: SONS AND LOVERS L4

D. H. Lawrence: SONS AND LOVERS: A Casebook L5

D. H. Lawrence: SONS AND LOVERS: Les Aspects Sociaux et Economiques, la Vision de L'Artiste L6, AA42

D. H. Lawrence: Tale as a Medium V3

D. H. Lawrence: The Critical Heritage G34

D. H. Lawrence: The Croydon Years F36

D. H. Lawrence: The Failure and the Triumph of Art G121

D. H. Lawrence: The Man and His Work F43

D. H. Lawrence: The Man Who Lived G92

D. H. Lawrence: The Novels G89

D. H. Lawrence: The Poet and the "Chatterley" Trial AA23

D. H. Lawrence: The Polarity of North and South G74

D. H. Lawrence: THE RAINBOW M7

D. H. Lawrence: THE RAINBOW and WOMEN IN LOVE M2, N1

D. H. Lawrence: "The Rocking-Horse Winner" V130

D. H. Lawrence: The World of Five Major Novels G106

D. H. Lawrence: The Writer and His Work G90

D. H. Lawrence: Zur Funktion und Funktions-Weise Von Literarischem Irrationalismus G126, AA48

D. H. Lawrence: After Thirty Years E37

SUBJECT INDEX

This index includes all historical and literary figures, literary and mythological characters, and titles named or discussed in the entries and annotations in this bibliography. Occasionally *implied* names and titles are also included (e.g., a discussion of the character Hamlet would be indexed under both HAMLET and Shakespeare, whether or not title and author are named). It also indexes literary and critical terms, kinds of criticism, and prominent themes and topics in Lawrence criticism. Finally, it includes all references to cities and nations, cultures and languages, places and institutions.

Lawrence's works are indexed, by kind and by title, under his name. All remaining historical, literary, philosophic, or other titles are indexed by title, with the author's name provided in parentheses.

Adams, Henry V181
ADELPHI (periodical) F120
Adolescence. See Children
Aesthetics G3, G75, G106,
   G121, H172, H392, H395,
   H415, L14, N32, N43, Z2,
   Z3, Z7, Z20, Z21, Z35,
   Z47, Z54, Z60, Z64, Z71,
   Z78, Z81, Z86, AA113
Africa N19. Also see
   Egypt
Alcott, Louisa May L61
Aldington, Richard F55,
   F113
ALL THINGS ARE POSSIBLE
   (Shestov) A80, B23, Z5
Allegory and parable H317,
   N51, N62, U77, V29, V112,
   V120, V129, V139, Z44
Allegret, Marc U25, U61

Allen, Walter U3
Alonzo, Dámaso Y117
Alps G17
L'AMANT DE LADY CHATTERLEY
   (film--Dir. Allegret) U25,
   U61
America: Culture and Literature A59, A65, A77, B19,
   E3, G7, G16, G17, G22, G35,
   G41, G64, G108, G117, H65,
   H80, H137, H156, H159,
   H348, H367, H380, N15, N31,
   Q9, R13, T8, T20, U37, U42,
   U58, U59, V30, V105, V157,
   V160, V181, Y9, Z19, Z43,
   Z50, Z55, Z75, Z82, Z85,
   Z86, Z97. Also see California, Illinois, New York,
   Southern Illinois, Stanford,
   Taos, Texas, Tulsa, Yale,

LADYBIRD, THE, THE FOX, THE CAPTAIN'S DOLL See V86 and V87. Also see A21.

"Last Laugh, The" See V88. Also see A24.

"Legend" See section V, iii, and "Fragment of Stained Glass, A "

"Lessford's Rabbits" See section V, iii. Also see B10, B14, B18.

"Lesson on a Tortoise, A" See section V, iii. Also see B10, B14, B18.

"Love Among the Haystacks" See V89. Also see A27, A30, B12, B27.

LOVE AMONG THE HAYSTACKS AND OTHER PIECES See section V, iii. Also see A27.

"Lovely Lady, The" See V90. Also see A28, B19, B28, V3.

LOVELY LADY, THE A28, B4, V21

"Man Who Died, The" See V91 through V106. Also see A25, B5, B11, B13, B20, B27, F113, G30, G36, G44, G61, G86, G114, G131, H52, H145, H225, V13, V20, V22, V32, Z4, AA18, AA270, AA278, AC6.

"Man Who Loved Islands, The" See V107 through V110. Also see A24, A28, V20, V22, AA176.

"Man Who Was Through with the World, The" See section V, iii. Also see A33, B20, V22.

"Mercury" See section V, iii. Also see B20.

"Miner at Home, The" See section V, iii. Also see B14.

"Miracle, The" See section V, iii, and "The Horse Dealer's Daughter "

"Mr. Noon" A31, B4, B18, F124. Also see section V, iii, and the headnotes to sections A, i, and V.

"Modern Lover, A" See V, iii. Also see A31, V23.

MODERN LOVER, A See section V, iii. Also see A31, B4.

"Monkey Nuts" See section V, iii. Also see A20.

"More Modern Love" See section V, iii, and "In Love"

"Mortal Coil, The" See section V, iii. Also see A19, B14, B18, V43.

"Mother and Daughter" See V112. Also see A28, B20.

"New Eve, The" See section V, iii, and "New Eve and Old Adam "

"New Eve and Old Adam" See section V, iii. Also see A31, B14.

"None of That" See section V, iii. Also see A24.

"Odour of Chrysanthemums" See V113 through V116. Also see A17, A37, B28, G71, H158, V19, V124, X11, X19, X22.

"Old Adam, The" See section V, iii. Also see A31, B14.

"Once" See section V, iii. Also see A27, B14.

"Tickets, Please" See
V168 through V172. Also
see A20, B19.
"Two Blue Birds" See
section V, iii. Also
see A24, B19.
"Two Marriages" See
section V, iii. Also
see A29 and "Daughters
of the Vicar, The "
"Undying Man, The" See
V173. Also see B20.
"Vicar's Garden, The"
See section V, iii, and
"Shadow in the Rose
Garden, The "
"Vin Ordinaire" See
section V, iii, and
"Thorn in the Flesh,
The "
"Virgin and the Gipsy,
The" See V174 through
V179. Also see A26,
B27, V3, V10, V29, Z4,
AA191.
--, film adaptation V174,
V175, V179
"White Stocking, The"
See section V, iii. Also
see A17, B28, V124.
"White Woman, The" See
section V, iii, and
"Witch à la Mode, The "
"Wilful Woman, The" See
section V, iii. Also
see B8, B20.
"Wintry Peacock" See
section V, iii. Also
see B20.
"Witch à la Mode, The"
See section V, iii.
Also see A31, B14.

"Woman Who Rode Away, The"
See V180 and V181. Also
see A24, B9, B13, B28,
G22, G52, G56, G64, T12,
V3, V20, V29, V30, V32,
AA18.
WOMAN WHO RODE AWAY AND
OTHER STORIES, THE See
section V, iii. Also see
A24, B4.
"You Touched Me" See V182.
Also see A20, V31.
--, dramatic adaptation.
See V182.

--, Plays. See X1 through X22.
"Altitude" See section X,
iii. Also see A45, B2, X2.
COLLIER'S FRIDAY NIGHT, A
See X9 and X10. Also see
A44, B2, G110, X1-X4, X6,
X8.
COMPLETE PLAYS OF D. H.
LAWRENCE, THE B2, X5
DAUGHTER-IN-LAW, THE See
X11 through X13. Also
see B2, X1-X4, X6, X8.
DAVID See X14 through X16.
Also see A41, B2, X1, X2,
AA221.
FIGHT FOR BARBARA, THE See
section X, iii. Also see
A43, B2, X1, X2.
"Keeping Barbara" See
section X, iii. Also See A43,
and FIGHT FOR BARBARA, THE.
MARRIED MAN, THE See section
X, iii. Also see A46, B2,
F124, X1, X2
MERRY-GO-ROUND, THE See
section X, iii. Also see
A47, B2, X1, X2.

"My Son's My Son"
(Lawrence-Greenwood)
See section X, iii.
Also see B2, X12, X13.
"Noah's Flood" See
section V, iii. Also
see B2, X2.
PLAYS OF D. H. LAWRENCE,
THE See section X, iii.
Also see A42.
TOUCH AND GO See X17
and X18. Also see
A40, B2, X1, X2, AA221
WIDOWING OF MRS. HOLROYD,
THE See X19 through
X22. Also see A39, B2,
G110, X1-X4, X6, X8,
AA221.

--, Poetry. See Y1 through
Y128.
AMORES See Y72. Also
see A49, A55.
"Bat" A54
"Bavarian Gentians" See
Y73 through Y75. Also
see A58, AA98, AA269.
BAY See section Y, iii.
Also see A52, A55.
BIRDS, BEASTS AND FLOWERS
See Y76 through Y82.
Also see A53, A54, A55,
G30, Y39.
"Cherry Robbers" See Y83.
Also see A48, F21.
COLLECTED POEMS OF D.H.
LAWRENCE, THE See
section Y, iii. Also
see A55, B3, Y72, Y76,
Y84.
COMPLETE POEMS OF D. H.
LAWRENCE, THE B3, D1,
Y10

"Corot" AA226
"Dreams Nascent" A49
"Dreams Old" A49
"Dreams Old and Nascent"
See Y84. Also see A49.
"Elegy" A50
"Figs" A54
"Fire" A59
"Fish" See Y85 and Y86.
Also see A54.
"How Beastly the Bourgeois
Is" See Y87. Also see A56.
"Hymn to Priapus" See Y88.
Also see A50.
LAST POEMS See Y89 through
Y97. Also see A58, B3,
G30, Z4.
"Last Words to Miriam" A49
"Lightning" See Y98. Also
see A48.
LOOK! WE HAVE COME THROUGH!
See Y99 through Y102.
Also see A50, A55, G30,
G63, AA239.
"Love on the Farm" A48
LOVE POEMS AND OTHERS See
Y103 through Y105. Also
see A48, A55.
"Medlars and Sorb-Apples"
A54
MORE PANSIES See section Y,
iii. Also see A58.
NETTLES See section Y,
iii. Also see A57, B3.
NEW POEMS See section Y,
iii. Also see A51, A55,
B23, Z82.
PANSIES See Y106 through
Y108. Also see A56, B3,
B23, F64, G19, G30, Y55.
"Piano" See Y109 and Y110.
Also see A51, Y42.

Shestov, Leo A80, Z5, Z109
"She-Wolf, The" (Verga)
V66
Sitwell, Edith F147
Sitwell, Osbert F147
Skepticism. See Cynicism.
Skinner, Mollie L.
F149, S2, S4-S6
Sociology and sociological
criticism F43, F47, F74,
F121, G10, G15, G22, G40,
G46, G49, G52, G56, G58,
G61, G63, G68, G72, G97,
G106, G107, G124, H13,
H15, H21, H46, H57, H74,
H77, H98, H115, H129,
H131, H134-H136, H147,
H156, H169, H183, H194,
H209, H215, H232, H271,
H274, H281, H283, H284,
H301, H335, H336, H347,
H348, H363, H369, H384,
H390, H402, H403, H412,
H414, H424, L6, L64,
L69, M1, M7, M29, M40,
M46, M48, M84, N7, N35,
N37, N60, N71, N90, P1,
Q2, R14, T6, U2, U15,
U16, U22, U26, U36, U42,
U59, V11, V25, V27, V146,
V148, V159, V161, V170,
W3, X1-X3, X8, X17, X18,
Y11, Y79, Y87, Z2, Z6, Z7,
Z51, Z57, Z77, Z119,
Z124, AA34, AA100, AA236,
AA254
Socrates H160, H411, Z119
Sons. See Family in liter-
ature, The.
SONS AND LOVERS (film--Dir.
Cardiff) L22
Sophocles L42
Southern Illinois Univ.
E45, G92

Speech in the novel. See
Language.
Spengler, Oswald G107, M13
Spenser, Edmund Z44
Spiritualism. See Theosophy.
Squire, John C. G8
Stanford Univ. F145
Steinbeck, John G42, H286
Stendhal [pseud. of Beyle,
Henri] G107, N96
Sterne, Laurence V138
Stevens, Wallace H327, V138,
Y86
Storey, David H98
STORY OF AN AFRICAN FARM, THE
(Schreiner) H178
STORY OF DOCTOR MANENTE, THE
(Grazzini) A85
Strachey, Lytton F75
Structuralism and structuralist
criticism G87, N71, N102,
V89
Structure. See Form.
Style. See Prose style.
SUMMER IN ITALY, A (O'Faolain)
Z128
Surrealism H139, H186
Suspense V2
Swinburne, Algernon C. H269,
Y88
Switzerland F8
Symbolism, imagery, and meta-
phor D1, G21, G22, G25,
G30, G32, G50, G60, G74,
G77, G80, G87, G101, G110,
G121, G126, H13, H40, H66,
H78, H88, H89, H110, H128,
H164, H181, H182, H206,
H230, H327, H329, H336,
H337, H358, H379, J3, J11,
K8, L6, L10, L20, L23,
L29, L47, L55, L59, L61,
M7, M8, M10, M14, M22,